Purchasing and Supply Chain Management

Helens College

For too long, business has focused on short-term cost advantages through low-cost country sourcing with little regard for the longer-term implications of global sustainability. *Purchasing and Supply Chain Management*, Second Edition, not only fully addresses the environmental, social and economic challenges of how companies manage purchasing and supply chains, but also delves deeper into emerging areas such as modern slavery, digital technologies and circular supply chains.

In addition to explaining the basic principles and processes of both purchasing and supply chain management, the book evaluates how to develop strategic and sustainable purchasing and supply chain management. Our key message is that purchasing and supply chain management needs to focus on value creation rather than cost cutting. This requires the development of new purchasing and supply chain models that involve circular supply structures, supply chain transparency and collaboration with new stakeholders in traditional sourcing and supply chain settings.

Aimed at students, educators and practitioners the book integrates sustainability into each chapter as a core element of purchasing and supply chain management. This second edition incorporates new examples and case studies from industry throughout, striking a balance between theoretical frameworks and guidelines for implementation in practice.

Thomas E. Johnsen is Professor of Purchasing and Supply Management at Audencia Business School, France, where he directs the M.Sc. in Supply Chain and Purchasing Management. His research revolves around sustainable supply networks and he is Associate Editor of the *Journal of Purchasing and Supply Management*.

Mickey Howard is Professor of Supply Management at the University of Exeter Business School, UK. His current research interests include inter-organizational relationships, government mechanisms and circular economy. He is a regular contributor at events such as the Academy of Management, EurOMA and IPSERA.

Joe Miemczyk is Professor of Supply Chain Management at ESCP Europe Business School based at the London, UK campus. He researches sustainable and circular supply chains in a number of sectors, publishing in a variety of supply chain and operations journals.

'Developing and improving sustainable business and supply chain practices is now obligatory for businesses, not just an option. *Purchasing and Supply Chain Management: A Sustainability Perspective*, Second Edition, builds on the ground breaking first edition by providing the most current insights from research and industry practice for sustainably managing global supply chains. Johnsen, Howard and Miemczyk provide cutting-edge insight and direction for students, practitioners and academics to successfully analyze, develop and manage purchasing and supply chain management practices that are critical for holistically improving the "triple bottom line".'

George A. Zsidisin, *Ph.D., C.P.M., CPSM,*
Professor of Supply Chain Management, Virginia Commonwealth University, USA;
Co-Editor Emeritus, Journal of Purchasing and Supply Management

'*Purchasing and Supply Chain Management* captures current developments in the field, integrating sustainability oriented analysis and resource based theory throughout. This makes the book unique as an up-to-date teaching text. I would wholeheartedly recommend it.'

Prof. Dr. Stefan Seuring,
Chair of Supply Chain Management, Faculty of Business and Economics,
University of Kassel, Germany

'This textbook provides a unique, theory-based, practical and accessible contribution on the strategic importance of purchasing and supply chain management in advancing towards corporate sustainability. It is an important addition to responsible management education.'

Dr. Anne Touboulic,
Assistant Professor in Operations Management,
Nottingham University Business School, UK

Purchasing and Supply Chain Management

A Sustainability Perspective

Second Edition

Thomas E. Johnsen, Mickey Howard and Joe Miemczyk

 Routledge
Taylor & Francis Group

LONDON AND NEW YORK

Second edition published 2019
by Routledge
2 Park Square, Milton Park, Abingdon, Oxon OX14 4RN

and by Routledge
711 Third Avenue, New York, NY 10017

Routledge is an imprint of the Taylor & Francis Group, an informa business

First edition published by Routledge 2014

British Library Cataloguing-in-Publication Data
A catalogue record for this book is available from the British Library

Library of Congress Cataloging-in-Publication Data
A catalog record has been requested for this book

ISBN: 978-1-138-06474-4 (hbk)
ISBN: 978-1-138-06476-8 (pbk)
ISBN: 978-1-315-16024-5 (ebk)

Typeset in Minion Pro
by Apex CoVantage, LLC

Visit the companion website: www.routledge.com/cw/johnsen

MIX
Paper from
responsible sources
FSC FSC™ C013985
www.fsc.org

Printed in the United Kingdom
by Henry Ling Limited

Contents

Figures

Tables

Acknowledgements

This book is written for students, academics and practitioners. As we have attempted to tackle the double hurdle of academic rigour and practical relevance it has been particularly important to us to discuss ideas with a large number of people who represent both academia and practice. Colleagues and students within the business schools where we are employed, as well as the wider academic communities we form part of, such as the International Purchasing and Supply Education and Research Association (IPSERA) and the *Journal of Purchasing and Supply Management* (JPSM) editorial team, have inspired our thinking and development of models and frameworks.

We would like to thank the following colleagues at our own academic institutions: Raffaella Cagliano, Federico Caniato, Francois Constant, Christine Harland, Toloue Miandar, Antonella Moretto, Stefano Ronchi, Steffen Boehm, Peter Hopkinson, Stefano Pascucci, Roberta De Angelis, Dan Eatherly and Adam Lumsby. We would also like to thank Anne Touboulic, Morten Moller and Wendy van der Valk for their kind reviews of the previous edition.

From companies/organizations we would like to thank: Paul Gardner (VP One-Sourcing Direct Materials, Danone), Søren Vammen (CEO, Danish Purchasing & Logistics Forum – DILF), David Dawson (Technology Executive, Rolls-Royce), Ketty Kortelainen (Head of Procurement and Supply Management, ThyssenKrupp Systems Engineering), Uffe Arlo-Theilade (CEO, Aperitas), Laura Puustjarvi (Head of Sustainability, Valmet), Stephane Pochat (Evea), Stef Kranedijk (former Chairman of Desso), Jean-Paul Jeanrenaud and Eric Dargent (WWF), Carlos Gomez and David McClintock (EcoVadis), Bart Vannieuwenhuyse and Alex Van Breedam (Trivizor).

Many of our academic colleagues have inspired our work: some are, for example, past colleagues, co-authors or research partners; there are really too many to name all of them, but we would like to mention Richard Calvi, Nathalie Fabbe-Costes, Mihalis Giannakis, Andrew Graves, Matthias Holweg, Rhona Johnsen, Dirk-Jan Kamann, Richard Lamming, Mike Lewis, Osama Meqdadi, Ole S. Mikkelsen, Katia Picaud, Jan Stentoft, Wendy Phillips, André Sobczak, Mervi Vuori, Helen Walker and George Zsidisin. Also, we thank our fellow JPSM associate editors and co-editors. Finally, we would like to thank the support team at Routledge, especially Jess Harrison and Amy Laurens. Any inaccuracies, of course, are entirely our own responsibility.

Preface to the second edition

The recent trend towards sustainability is by no means purely an academic or theoretical phenomenon. National governments and international bodies such as the European Union and World Trade Organization are debating the sustainability challenge facing the global economy and putting into place ambitious targets and action plans. Companies across all sectors and countries must adapt to a rapidly changing world in which the need for sustainable economic, environmental and social development is at the core. Many companies have made significant changes to the way they operate, fully embracing the sustainability challenge, but others still view sustainability as something that does not really concern them and might 'go away' in the next few years.

There is increasing consensus amongst researchers and practitioners that sustainable purchasing and supply cannot be viewed as a fad or transient phenomenon, because the world is rapidly running out of accessible natural resources whilst the global population keeps growing. In our view, the way companies do business has to become more sustainable. It is by no means certain that purchasing – or supply chain management – will play a central role in creating sustainable business models but many companies are developing in that direction. As companies increasingly rely on their supply chains for production of the products and services they market to their customers, purchasing and supply managers are in an important position to make these changes happen. Sustainability must avoid becoming the responsibility of a few isolated individuals within the company. Instead, it is important that sustainability becomes integrated into the fabric of the firm, as a core part of business strategy, process and function, with purchasing and supply chain management taking a leading role. This is the key purchasing and supply chain management challenge we seek to address in this book. If purchasing and supply chain managers are to embrace this challenge they have to change the way they operate. This transition requires new ways of thinking about supply structures, processes, skills and competencies.

It follows from above that sustainability is not the responsibility of a few sustainability experts, but a challenge that must be embraced company-wide. You do not have to be a climate change convert to believe in the theme of this book as sustainability, i.e. purely about natural or environmental challenges, but as tackling a range of social and economic challenges. It is for this reason that we chose the title *Purchasing and Supply Chain Management: A Sustainability Perspective*, and not 'Sustainable Purchasing and Supply Chain Management'. This book is intended as a core textbook for a normal purchasing and supply chain management course at university or business school level. The book can also be used for specialized courses in sustainable purchasing and supply chain management, but the overall aim of the book is to cover all the most important aspects of purchasing, including those aspects of supply chain that concern inter-organizational issues, e.g. sourcing and distribution, and to explain how sustainability needs to be taken into account across all of these aspects. Above all, instead of sustainability being treated as one separate lecture or chapter in a purchasing or supply chain management course, our intention is that sustainability is considered in the context of each topic.

We sincerely hope that this book will play its part in not only educating but changing the mindsets of current and future purchasing and supply chain management professionals.

Thomas E. Johnsen
Professor of Purchasing and Supply Management
Audencia Business School, France

Mickey Howard
Professor of Supply Management
University of Exeter Business School, UK

Joe Miemczyk
Professor of Supply Chain Management
ESCP Europe Business School, UK

Foreword

The role of purchasing within business has never been more recognized, nor more important. The realization is that it is a business value generator beyond simply traditional productivities and price negotiation. Whether you are at the beginning of your career, developing it or in the twilight years, the undeniable truth is that it is a very exciting place to be.

None more so when we start to look at the sustainability of our supply chains, although the notion of a chain does not capture the real picture. Our 'supply chains' are far more complicated, intricate connections of multiple ecosystems or networks, and are interdependent; some are fragile, and many are interconnected and circular, taking the waste from one network and creating value from it in another. However, most of them have uncovered risks for our businesses, and at the same time huge opportunities to make impacts on both the people and resources of our planet.

Indeed, the further we work 'upstream', the more we are learning about the items we are buying, the more we are connecting to the essence of the materials – be that packaging or the raw materials, the farmed products which are then later transformed sometimes multiple times before being used in our own factories. Many practices that we take for granted in our society are not available in many of these ecosystems, such as basic safety and protection at work, access to a respectful minimum wage, and other basic human rights that we would normally expect.

Digging a little deeper, we start to understand that an important part of the environmental impacts of farming worldwide come from these ecosystems or networks. Experience in the food industry shows that this is often due to antiquated farming practices, or poor understanding or access to training to help these communities to be the guardians of the part of the planet they cultivate.

And so we have an obligation to work differently with our suppliers, first tier, second tier, tertiary and sometimes quaternary suppliers to support them to make the changes that are necessary. Yet here, no single company can make the changes that our demands on the planet need alone. It is by the very essence of collaboration between peer companies, between competitors in a pre-competitive space, along with these communities, NGOs and with academia, that we can truly make the sustained impact that we know is needed, and in our hearts we know is the right thing to do.

In the food industry, this type of collaboration is not always intuitive, different companies, different cultures, multiple parties – a fine line to walk to ensure the project remains in that pre-competitive space. Platforms such as the Sustainable Agriculture Initiative have facilitated this type of collaboration, encouraging the adoption of a common measure and shared practices – and there are many more organizations in this space: The Livelihoods Fund for Family Farming, Cool Farm Alliance, World Business Council for Sustainable Development, to name but a few.

This book looks at the increasingly important and strategic role of purchasing within the 'supply chain' and introduces a very simple, but extremely strategic and important word – *sustainable* sourcing within a *sustainable* supply chain. Yet what does sustainable mean? Is it merely looking at the environmental and diversity impacts of what we do? Is it challenging the essence of our existing business models, which are not sustainable in the long term without significant impacts on livelihoods or the planet? In the end, it is about making collective impacts that ensure we can continue to source our materials, without depleting the resources we have, moreover to regenerate the fertility of the planet through improved practices, soil management and less dependence on chemical-based products and fertilizers. It is about learning across all of our supply networks. This book is a great place to help build your understanding and ambition for a sustainable, profitable supply network (ecosystem).

Paul Gardner
VP One-Sourcing Direct Materials
Danone

CHAPTER 1

Introduction

LEARNING OBJECTIVES

By the end of this chapter you should be able to:

- Explain the reasons why purchasing is no longer an administrative, or clerical, responsibility, but a critical and strategic priority for companies;

- Understand why purchasing is now seen as part of supply chain management and the implications of the purchasing–supply chain management relationship;

- Define purchasing and supply chain management in relation to related concepts such as sourcing and procurement;

- Evaluate the criticality of the sustainability challenge and how it affects purchasing and supply chain management;

- Argue the need for sustainability to become an integrated part of purchasing and supply chain management rather than a separate add-on consideration;

- Explain the underlying theoretical perspective and structure of the book;

- Form an overview of the structure of the book.

1.0 Introduction

Purchasing has grown tremendously as a business discipline both in practice and in academia over the past 30 years or so. Many organizations across the private and public sectors worldwide have elevated purchasing to a strategic business responsibility; the emergence of the Chief Procurement Officer (CPO) is a symbol of the rising profile of purchasing. The trend towards outsourcing of non-core activities has clearly had a positive impact on the profession as a very high proportion of value adding now stems from suppliers, and many organizations have woken up to this fact and manage purchasing accordingly.

However, the elevation of purchasing to an important, even strategic, business function is a relatively new development and in many companies purchasing remains a low priority. Purchasing is still often highly driven by achieving low prices from suppliers, regardless of whether or not the company strategy is focused on low cost. So, although purchasing in many companies has become more sophisticated there is much scope for improvement of the profession.

An increasing number of people now choose to develop a career in purchasing, but only 20–25 years ago this was by no means a normal choice of career and was often seen as a dubious one. In some ways the emergence of supply chain management has played well into the hands of the purchasing profession because purchasing is seen as a critical link in the supply chain. But, in other ways the role of purchasing in relation to supply chain management is all but clear: some people regard purchasing as an integral part of supply chain management whereas others regard it as complementary yet separate.

The recent development of sustainability as a strategic challenge for business and society has boosted the importance of both purchasing and supply chain management. A company is no more sustainable than the suppliers it sources from so creating sustainable companies means creating and managing sustainable supply chains. Top management in many companies appear to have grasped this challenge but the often short-term driven, business functions of purchasing and supply chain management are not easy to integrate with the challenge of sustainability that by definition requires a long-term perspective. However, this is the challenge taken up by this book: to try to fill the gap of how sustainability affects, and can be incorporated into, purchasing and supply chain management decisions. The book is therefore not primarily a book about sustainable purchasing and supply chain management but a book that identifies and discusses how sustainability in its various guises is relevant to 'normal' purchasing and supply chain management. To paraphrase Kraljic's (1983) message that 'purchasing must become supply management', the message of this book is: purchasing and supply chain management must become *sustainable* purchasing and supply chain management.

This chapter begins by tracing the development of purchasing from an administrative, tactical function within companies to a managerial, strategic function. The following section introduces the implications of supply chain management for purchasing, followed by a section outlining the sustainability challenge and what it means for both purchasing and supply chain management. Key concepts are defined and discussed along the way. The chapter concludes with an overview of the structure of the book.

1.1 The emergence of purchasing as an academic discipline

Compared with other business and management functions, such as marketing, finance or operations management, purchasing is relatively new and under-developed as an academic field of study. The first books and articles that considered purchasing in any detail date back to the 1960s, most notably Robinson *et al.* (1967), Webster and Wind (1972) and Sheth (1973). This early work focused on explaining organizational buying processes with a view to helping suppliers (sales and marketing people in other words) to better understand the buying process of their customers so were not really about purchasing management. In the 1970s the first proper textbooks on purchasing – or procurement – began to appear, including England (1970), Lee and Dobler (1971) and Baily and Farmer (1977). Academically, these can be seen as the foundation stones of purchasing.

However, it was not until the 1980s and early 1990s that books and articles were published that really sought to promote purchasing as an important business function and therefore as a worthwhile academic field of study. In particular, writers across Europe and North America argued that the position and status of the purchasing function within organizations should be elevated; various maturity models were developed, portraying purchasing as a reactive, passive and tactical function at one end of the spectrum to an integrative, strategic function at the other, advanced, end of the spectrum (Spekman, 1981; Reck and Long, 1988; Ellram and Carr, 1994; Gadde and Håkansson, 1993).

The lack of academic credibility of purchasing until quite recently reflected the fact that purchasing in practice used to be a clerical function focused predominantly on obtaining the lowest possible prices for goods, and administrative, mundane tasks such as record keeping. Around the same time as purchasing began to evolve as a field of study in the late 1980s and early 1990s companies had embarked on changes in industrial organization, 'farming out' or 'outsourcing' non-core competencies and activities that they used to perform in-house. This trend had major implications for purchasing because it meant that strategically important resources, or complementary competencies (Teece, 1986), had to be sourced – and purchased – from specialized suppliers.

The trend towards outsourcing continues to this day and has even accelerated; over the last decade or so outsourcing has been an integral part of globalization as companies have looked to low-cost countries for cheaper sourcing. Outsourcing reflects a deep trend; in addition to a search for low-cost sources, outsourcing is part of a wider change process of industrial reorganization in which companies focus on what they do best and connect to the rest through a network of business relationships. Technological innovation is now happening at such a rapid pace that companies can no longer do everything themselves in-house. Even if, ideally, they would prefer to control at least the most important resources and activities by keeping these in-house, they have little choice but to source these from outside companies especially as the most critical resources these days are intangible and knowledge-based.

Consider, for example, the case of Airbus: despite its history as an aircraft manufacturer Airbus has chosen to outsource the design, development, and manufacture of major aircraft sub-systems to specialized suppliers. As part of the Airbus Power8 rationalization programme, Airbus seeks to focus on its core competencies and thereby outsource major aircraft work packages to suppliers, especially those that they term 'risk sharing partners'. For example, approximately 50 per cent of aero-structure work on the Airbus A350 XWB has been outsourced. Also, production sites that were previously under Airbus ownership have been sold off, including the wing component facility at Filton near Bristol which is now operated by GKN, and other sites, including some in France, have followed. At the same time, Airbus seeks to reduce the size of its supply base so that it relies on fewer but more strategic suppliers. These include major industry players such as Rolls-Royce, General Electric and Pratt & Whitney, who assume responsibility for design and build of large aircraft sub-systems. Consequently, Airbus is not really a manufacturer anymore; Airbus relies on its network of suppliers for manufacturing and its role these days is as an aircraft systems integrator rather than a manufacturer.

Indeed, in many industries the proportion of value that stems from the supply chain is almost 80 per cent and in many companies the outsourcing ratio is over 90 per cent. Based on data from 738 UK corporations, Strassmann (2004) calculated the average outsourcing ration as 78 per cent (revenue/purchasing). For example, the outsourcing ratio at British Airways was 77 per cent, at Rolls-Royce (aerospace) it was 84 per cent and at Tesco (supermarket) and

Centrica PLC (the energy provider) it was 89 per cent. Examples of relatively low levels of outsourcing include pharmaceutical giants GlaxoSmithKline and AstraZeneca where outsourcing accounts for 'only' 45 per cent, but this is still a very significant proportion and is likely to be even higher as the outsourcing trend continues.

The consequence of the outsourcing trend is that companies become heavily dependent on the performance of their suppliers and therefore need to make sure that suppliers are effectively managed as if they were an extended part of their own company: an extended enterprise. As a central function dealing with suppliers, purchasing plays a key role in the management of supplier relationships. This role is not only a matter of cost reduction, although saving money remains a priority for any organization, but also about ensuring that the needs for a range of criteria, including, for example, quality, delivery, innovation and service, are being met by suppliers. The need to procure complex performance (Caldwell and Howard, 2011) requires not only deep collaborative relationships with suppliers, often spanning multiple decades, but also an understanding of how complex outcomes are articulated over time through a combination of contractual incentives and collaborative relationships, requiring new skills and competencies from purchasing staff.

It is against this backdrop that the elevation of purchasing from a passive low-level organizational function to a strategic function with corporate visibility and influence needs to be understood. The rise of the executive board position of the CPO is symptomatic of this trend. Companies increasingly realize the importance of improving their knowledge and competence in purchasing. They realize that they need to start filling this knowledge gap and to develop fundamentally new ways of thinking about purchasing and its potential contribution to ensure sustained competitive advantage in an increasingly competitive global business landscape.

1.2 Two developments in purchasing

Purchasing is in some ways a limited concept and rival terms have emerged, in particular, since the 1980s. In the opening chapter of this book it is important to develop an initial understanding of some of these alternative concepts and how they relate to and impact on purchasing.

The title of this book indicates that two important concepts are to be included alongside purchasing: supply chain management and sustainability. Both reflect major developments and challenges to purchasing theory as well as the purchasing profession and they affect the practice of purchasing in different ways. The following two sections explore how these are transforming purchasing.

1.2.1 Purchasing becomes supply (chain) management

Peter Kraljic's publication in the *Harvard Business Review* in 1983, 'Purchasing must become Supply Management', was a cornerstone in the rise of purchasing from a tactical to a strategic business function. His most important message, as will be further explored in Chapter 4, was that purchasing should focus more on high value and high supply risk items and that these called for 'supply management' rather than 'purchasing management'. This is a theme that has since been the subject of much debate and the purchasing profession has embraced this fundamental message to the extent that in some parts of the world, most notably North America, purchasing is now simply referred to as supply management or simply 'supply'. Indeed, the need to capture both 'purchasing' and 'supply management' is reflected in the use of the term 'purchasing and supply management' (PSM).

The rise of supply chain management since its early foundations in the 1980s is in many ways a natural extension of this development from purchasing to supply management. Adding the word 'chain' to 'supply management' may seem trivial but is, in fact, significant. The inclusion of the concept of chain hints at the multi-disciplinary genesis of supply chain management, most notably Porter's (1985) value chain (strategic management) and channel management (marketing and distribution). Whereas the focus of purchasing is clearly on supplier relationships, the focus of supply chain management is on the wider business system that includes several layers, or tiers, of suppliers, sub-suppliers, customers, distributors and so on. In some ways supply chain management has absorbed a number of business functions involved in the process of supply, including purchasing, operations, logistics and distribution management. Unfortunately, perhaps because of the relatively weak theoretical foundations of supply chain management, this has been a somewhat messy development process so that definitions and boundaries between these remain unclear.

What is without question is the fact that many organizations see their supply chain as a key driver of competitive advantage. As responsible for (or at least instrumental in) the sourcing process, purchasing is at the heart of supply chain management but supply chain management shifts the focus from direct, or 'dyadic', relationships between buyers and suppliers towards entire end-to-end supply chains. In many organizations purchasing is now an integral part of the supply chain management function, focused on the management of the part of the upstream, supplier-focused, supply chain (sourcing).

This book seeks to address a number of strategic issues in purchasing, especially sustainability. Procurement is often used to reflect a more inclusive and strategic concept than purchasing. However, purchasing remains the concept of choice by leading academic institutions, including the International Purchasing & Supply Education & Research Association (IPSERA), and the *Journal of Purchasing & Supply Management* (JPSM). The combined use of purchasing and supply management captures both tactical (purchasing) and strategic (supply management) as proposed by Kraljic (1983).

Section 1.3 discusses the varying use of the key terms in more depth but for now the important point is to note that consistently with above academic institutions this book will mostly use the term 'purchasing and supply management' to capture both non-strategic and strategic purchases.

1.2.2 The rise of sustainable sourcing and supply chain management

The second challenge to purchasing is the rapidly rising interest in sustainability. The age of the 'triple bottom line' is upon us where the assumption is that profit should no longer be at the expense of people (the social dimension) and planet (the environmental dimension). The pressure on business to deliver economic returns from greener goods is mounting and corporate social responsibility is no longer something that can be dismissed as a fad for environmental fanatics. The planet's resources are in decline and the climate is changing, placing increasing pressures on companies to reduce carbon emissions, recycle or re-use, and to develop clean technologies. Sustainable development is here to stay and only shows signs of gaining even greater momentum for the foreseeable future.

By sustainable development we usually refer to a definition provided originally by the Brundtland Commission in 1987 (named after the previous Norwegian Prime Minister who headed up this commission). Accordingly, sustainable development is defined as 'development that meets the needs of the present without compromising the ability of future generations to meet their own needs'. Sustainability therefore implies a long-term perspective which can be divided into three dimensions as shown in Figure 1.1 below.

Sustainability, in each of the three dimensions shown below, presents a risk to companies that are unprepared but also an opportunity for companies prepared to embrace the challenge. But, companies cannot tackle sustainability by themselves: implementing sustainability requires systemic change, especially radically overhauled supply models. Paradoxically, the trend towards outsourcing, particularly to low-cost countries such as China or India, has exacerbated the sustainable purchasing and supply chain management challenge. One of the negative results of global sourcing has been that companies have lost sight of what goes on within their extended supply chains and low-cost country sourcing sometimes comes at an unexpected price. Consider the problems of the BP oil spill in the Gulf of Mexico in 2010: it shows that companies cannot simply blame its suppliers when environmental disasters happen in the supply chain. Or the collapse of a garment factory in Bangladesh in April 2013 killing over 1,100 factory workers: a supplier of Western fashion companies and retailers looking for low-cost sourcing. Companies, including Apple and Nestlé, are having to completely rethink their purchasing strategies due to damaging reports of conflict minerals and modern slavery. Again, a key message of this book is that a company is no more

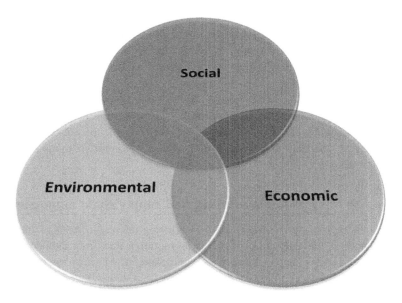

Figure 1.1　Three dimensions of sustainability

sustainable than the suppliers it sources from, putting purchasing right at the heart of sustainability implementation. New innovative purchasing strategies and methods are required not only to avoid the risks of unethical purchasing, but also to fully take advantage of the opportunities posed by sustainability.

The concept of sustainability is closely linked to several other concepts such as 'corporate social responsibility' (CSR), 'global responsibility' or simply being 'responsible'. Where some companies refer to, for example, sustainable sourcing others refer to responsible buying or CSR in the supply chain. In this book we continue to use sustainability as our main concept as this includes the three pillars or dimensions shown above and at the same time emphasizes the long-term perspective emphasized by the definition by the Brundtland Commission (1987).

In reality, is it problematic to differentiate between these terms. For example, although CSR is sometimes used very widely, i.e. to also take in environmental responsibility, it is by definition tied to social responsibility and grounded in ethics, morality and norms as guiding principles, and being socially responsible could have adverse effects on being environmentally responsible (Markman and Krause, 2016). CSR has often been criticized as a marketing tool, where companies pay lip service to pressures brought to bear by stakeholders and in reality change very little in their operational practices and rarely change suppliers due to their irresponsible activities. The idea of CSR is unevenly applied and means very different things in different contexts (Matten and Moon, 2008). Furthermore, the argument that standards and codes are private international regulations obviating the need for publicly accountable institutions challenges CSR's very legitimacy (Bartley, 2007).

We believe that companies need to move from 'do-no-harm' thinking to 'do-good' thinking (Markman and Krause, 2016). Often, companies implement a sustainable supply chain purely as a way of reducing the damage they do, typically through a compliance approach. Arguably, doing less bad is not being sustainable but purely damage limitation (Pagell and Shevchenko, 2014). In contrast, the ecologically dominant view (Montabon et al., 2016) is based on the logic that companies should not simply balance the three dimensions of sustainability, but prioritize ecology first, society second and commerce third. In other words, the environment comes before social concerns, leaving economic sustainability as a last priority. This perhaps rather idealistic thinking may not be how most companies think about sustainability at the present moment, given that they are driven by compliance, but could provide a viable way forward to avoid undesirable trade-offs.

The ecologically dominant view reflects the trend towards the idea of the circular economy that has gained momentum in the last decade. The shift in thinking towards the circular economy is reflected in the development of closed-loop supply chains that aim not only to reduce waste through product redesign and extended lifecycles, but to reuse all materials as a positive ingredient or 'nutrient' as part of the production process.

The concept of the circular economy as an exciting new business model is rapidly gaining traction in both practitioner and management research communities, offering a vision for the future of production systems as restorative and regenerative by design, where ultimately there is no waste or pollution (WEF, 2014; Blomsma and Brennan, 2017). In principle, the circular economy presents an opportunity to address impending global sustainability issues around resource scarcity and environmental degradation, offering the prospect of 'clean growth' to any organization and associated stakeholders who decide to adopt it. Yet progress to date on the actual means or methods of circular economy implementation across all major business sectors has been relatively slow. Despite recent work of institutions, such as the Ellen MacArthur Foundation (EMF, 2012; 2014) in popularizing the concept, a new British Standard in circular economy, and interest shown by leading multinational brands (e.g. Unilever, Coca-Cola, Renault), considerable work remains to identify the steps needed for a circular business transformation by all organizations across the world regardless of their size or status.

1.3 Varying use of key concepts: a discussion

Unfortunately for students of purchasing and supply chain management there is a plethora of concepts which more or less mean the same thing. Academics as well as practitioners often use these more or less indiscriminately: where some people refer to purchasing, other people refer to procurement, supply management, sourcing, acquisition or simply buying. What, then, are the differences?

1.3.1 Purchasing, procurement, supply management or sourcing?

The following statement of the purpose of purchasing is useful as a starting point: 'To purchase the right quality of material, at the right time, in the right quantity, from the right source, at the right price' (Baily and Farmer, 1977). This classic quote is a useful starting point as it highlights the different objectives, and especially as it places price as the last concern, which is often the sole issue that purchasers can think of at the expense of other priorities. For more precise definitions of key terms we can draw from the UK Chartered Institute of Procurement & Supply (CIPS), which offers the following key definitions related to purchasing:

- *Purchasing*: 'Purchasing describes all those transactional processes concerned with acquiring goods and services, including payment of invoices'.

- *Procurement*: 'Procurement describes all those processes concerned with developing and implementing strategies to manage an organization's spend portfolio in such a way as to contribute to the organization's overall goals and to maximize the value released and/or minimize the total cost of ownership. Procurement is a more comprehensive term than purchasing, which is more focused on the tactical acquisition of goods and services and the execution of plans rather than the development of strategies.'

- *Sourcing*: 'Sourcing describes all those activities within the procurement process concerned with identifying and evaluating potential suppliers, engaging with selected suppliers and selecting the best value supplier(s). The outcome of the sourcing process is usually a contract or arrangement that defines what is to be procured, on what terms and from which suppliers.'

These definitions are both accurate and comprehensive; however, we should note that the uses of these terms vary widely. One particular area of ambiguity concerns the difference between purchasing and procurement and which of these two terms is more inclusive and strategic than the other. The CIPS definitions clearly state that procurement is the more comprehensive and inclusive concept. Nevertheless, CIPS acknowledges that the two terms are often used interchangeably: 'There is little consensus on the precise definitions of terms such as "procurement" and "purchasing", and in the United States, in particular, the term "purchasing" describes what in Australia, New Zealand, Europe and Asia is more widely known as procurement ...'.

CIPS offers the following explanation for these differences: 'In Europe and Asia, the term "purchasing" is used to describe transactional processes such as raising purchase orders and reconciling invoices. However, in North America the term "purchasing" is sometimes used to describe the whole procurement process.' We would add to this that 'supply management' is a widely used term in North America and in parts of Europe, such as Finland. The use of the term 'supply management' reflects Kraljic's (1983) often-cited argument that 'Purchasing must become Supply Management', suggesting that purchasing is tactical as it concerns low-value and low-risk items, whereas supply management is strategic as it concerns high-value and high-risk items. The use of the terms is also often sector-specific, e.g. the public sector tends to use the term 'procurement' instead of 'purchasing' (Ramsay and Croom, 2008; Rozemeijer, 2008). Adding to this ambiguity, definitions, terminologies and subject boundaries have mutated over time, confusing definitions and subject boundaries (Carter and Ellram, 2003).

Table 1.1 compares some well-known textbook definitions of purchasing and procurement, showing increasingly wider – and longer – definitions that seek to capture issues to do with external resource management, strategic contribution, and supplier (relationship) management.

Interestingly, the use of these terms also varies if we compare practitioners and academics, especially when it comes to *procurement*. In an international survey of 44 senior executives and procurement practitioners and 47 academics, Callender *et al.* (2013: 681) found that 44.7 per cent of the academic respondents perceived procurement to be about 'the business management function that ensures identification, sourcing, access and management of the external resources that an organization needs or may need to fulfill its strategic objectives'. Although 29 per cent of practitioners agreed with this definition,

Table 1.1 Comparing textbook definitions of purchasing, procurement and sourcing

	Purchasing	Procurement	Sourcing
Bailey *et al.*, 1998/1968	To purchase the right quality of material, at the right time, in the right quantity, from the right source, at the right price		
Cousins *et al.* (2008)	The area of the business that manages the inputs into the organization	Some say that procurement is more strategic while purchasing is a day-to-day activity; others say exactly the reverse. We consider such wordplay specious	

Table 1.1 continued

Van Weele (2010)	The management of the company's external resources in such a way that the supply of all goods, services, capabilities and knowledge which are necessary for running, maintaining and managing the company's primary and support activities is secured at the most favourable conditions	All activities that are required in order to get the product from the supplier to its final destination	Finding, selecting, contracting and managing the best possible source of supply on a worldwide basis
Lysons and Farrington (2012)	The process undertaken by the organizational unit that, either as a function or as part of an integrated supply chain, is responsible for procuring or assisting users to procure, in the most efficient manner, required suppliers at the right time, quality, quantity and price and the management of suppliers, thereby contributing to the competitive advantage of the enterprise and the achievement of its corporate strategy	The process of obtaining goods or services by any means	The process of identifying, selecting and developing suppliers

more (31 per cent) thought that 'procurement covers a complete range of events from the identification of a need for a good or service through to its disposal or complete delivery of the services'. A stronger difference in perception was reflected in the use of *sourcing*: where 63.6 per cent of practitioners believed that sourcing refers to 'the activities involved in locating satisfactory and economical sources of supply of goods and services', 42.6 per cent of academics believed that sourcing is 'the activities involving searching markets for sources of goods and services. These activities are located at the opposite end of the supply chain from marketing'.

Although these differences might simply reflect that academics prefer more theoretical definitions, or definitions that they can link to theoretical frameworks, it is worthwhile noting that the definitions continue to vary on both sides and that:

- Procurement is sometimes seen as being more comprehensive than purchasing, including pre-purchase activities such as the make-or-buy decision. It is generally the preferred term in the public sector, which is characterized by a highly regulated process, and used widely in parts of Europe including the UK. Finally, procurement can be by non-commercial means although clearly most of the time through a commercial process.

- Sourcing is specifically related to locating or searching for suppliers. Sourcing is also the term used in the well-known supply chain management model called SCOR (supply chain operations reference model), where it effectively refers to procurement, so in supply chain management circles the term sourcing is often used instead of purchasing or procurement.

1.3.2 Supply chain management

The concept of *supply chains* – and, consequently, *supply chain management* (SCM) – was invented in the early 1980s, principally as a method of describing the much more complex concept of a business network. Supply chain management was born as a logistics concept although supply chain management is more than a new name for logistics (Cooper *et al.*, 1997). Defined as 'the management of upstream and downstream relationships with suppliers and customers to deliver superior customer value at less cost to the supply chain as a whole' (Christopher, 1998), SCM is based on the principle that supplier and customer (or simply supply) relationships are all part of a long chain of suppliers to end customers.

If supply chain management is to have meaning beyond simply a wide definition of logistics it must have a foundation in multiple functions related to the process of supply. In

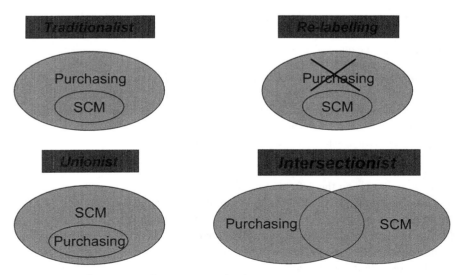

Figure 1.2 Purchasing in relation to supply chain management

Source: Larson and Halldorsson (2002).

terms of intellectual roots, Johnsen *et al.* (2008) suggest that purchasing and supply management was core to the development of supply chain management as a concept, and that a wide range of other fields, including operations management, logistics and industrial marketing, played important roles. Larson and Halldorsson (2002) suggest four different views of purchasing in relation to supply chain management: as shown in Figure 1.2, so-called 'unionists' view purchasing as part of supply chain management, whilst others believe that supply chain management has replaced purchasing.

Supply chain management focuses on multiple customer–supplier dyads, ultimately taking in original raw material extractors to final end customers (Harland, 1996). Supply chains tend to be depicted around a focal firm and its upstream and downstream relationships (Christopher, 1998; Lambert *et al.*, 1998) although there has been some debate as to whether supply chains are simple linear structures – chains – or if in reality they are more like 'supply chain networks' (or simply 'supply networks') that include interconnected supply chains (see e.g. Lamming *et al.*, 2000). The consensus seems to be that supply chains should be understood as the latter, but this is a debate we re-examine in more depth in Chapter 8.

1.3.3 Sustainable purchasing and sustainable supply chain management

Having considered various definitions of purchasing, supply chain management and related concepts, we can now turn to definitions that specifically link these to sustainability. Many definitions related to sustainable purchasing and supply chain management have been proposed but they are often partial, for example, only focusing on environmental issues. One early definition, focusing on purchasing, was by Drumwright (1994) who defined socially responsible organizational buying as attempts to take into account the public consequences of organizational buying or bring about positive social change through organizational buying behaviour. Building more obviously on the three aspects of sustainability, Walker and Brammer (2009) define sustainable procurement as: 'procurement that is consistent with the principles of sustainable development, such as ensuring a strong, healthy and just society, living within environmental limits, and promoting good governance'. In this book 'sustainable purchasing' refers to:

> the consideration of environmental, social, ethical and economic issues in the manage-
> ment of the organization's external resources in such a way that the supply of all goods,
> services, capabilities and knowledge which are necessary for running, maintaining and
> managing the organization's primary and support activities provide value not only to the
> organization but also to society and the economy.
>
> (Miemczyk *et al.*, 2012)

This definition builds on the definition of purchasing by Van Weele (2010), integrating the definition of sustainability as defined by the Brundtland Commission.

However, those definitions essentially concern purchasing and not supply chain management. Again, we can identify many different definitions where some focus on specific parts of sustainability, typically the environmental dimension, and others are more inclusive. Two definitions are interesting to note here: Carter and Rogers (2008) define 'sustainable supply chain management' as 'the strategic, transparent integration and achievement of an organization's social, systemic coordination of key inter-organizational business processes for improving the environmental and economic goals in the long-term economic performance of the individual company and its supply chains'. In a similar vein, Beamon (1999) puts particular emphasis on the need for a closed-loop supply chain by referring to 'The fully integrated, extended supply chain contains all of the elements of the traditional supply chain … but extends the one-way chain to construct a semi-closed loop that includes product and packaging recycling, re-use, and/or remanufacturing operations'.

However, it is also relevant to consider an even higher level of analysis in order to fully grasp the implications of sustainability on purchasing and supply chain management. In particular when adopting a sustainability perspective it becomes necessary to understand the supply chain as a business system that resembles a complex network of actors or stakeholders that are directly or indirectly involved in the supply process from raw material extractors to end customers/consumers.

We should note that many organizations dedicated to sustainability, such as the World Wide Fund for Nature (WWF), use the term sustainable sourcing rather than sustainable purchasing or procurement. This reflects the particular focus on sourcing, especially locational issues such as raw material sourced from rainforests and the consequent dangers to wildlife. Nevertheless, the use of the term sourcing by non-governmental organizations (NGOs) increasingly also covers issues to do with development and management of a global supply base in line with Lysons and Farrington's (2012) definition.

The following section explains the theoretical underpinning – or perspective – of this book, exploring how different levels of analysis help to understand different challenges of sustainable purchasing and supply chain management.

1.4 Underpinning theoretical framework of the book

In a recent research project we identified that a significant proportion of sustainable purchasing and supply management papers adopt stakeholder theory, institutional theory and resource-based perspectives (Johnsen *et al.*, 2017). We argued that an inter-organizational perspective, which emphasizes the need for interaction amongst stakeholders, is required. In this section we explain the theoretical foundations that underpin this book and why this matters.

The resource-based view (RBV), dating back to Wernerfeldt (1984), but later developed into a focus on core competences (Prahalad and Hamel, 1990) and dynamic capabilities (Teece *et al.*, 1997), is fundamental, because the RBV and its derivative theories provide a foundation for very important, strategic purchasing and supply chain management decisions such as whether to make or buy, or in other words, what to outsource or in-source. The RBV has identified how a company's resources can provide sources of sustained competitive advantage: as suggested by Barney (1991) resources need to be valuable, rare, inimitable and non-substitutable. RBV theory suggests that this can be the case if, for example, resources are causally ambiguous (or tacit), socially complex or history dependent. Put more simply, resources can provide sources of a long-term competitive advantage for a company if, for example, they are knowledge-based or embedded in social relationships between individual employees. So, rather than physical resources, the important resources are often, and increasingly, based on knowledge or capabilities.

Resources are inputs into the production process – they are the basic unit of analysis. The individual resources of the firm include items of capital equipment, skills of individual employees, patents, brand name, finance and so on. But, on their own, few resources are productive. Productive activity requires the co-operation and co-ordination of teams of resources. A capability is the capacity for a team of resources to perform some task or activity. While resources are the source of a firm's capabilities, capabilities are the main source of its competitive advantage.

(Grant, 1991: 118–119)

The core competence theory proposed by Prahalad and Hamel (1990) sharpened the focus on non-physical resources as the basis of competitive advantage and played an important role in popularizing the RBV, translating a complex theory into plain language.

RBV logic has often been used as the basis for the outsourcing decision, which is fundamental to purchasing as it is about what to make in-house and what to buy (from suppliers). Companies have increasingly outsourced many resources (and activities) they used to do themselves. Some companies have wisely identified which resources are strategically critical, deciding not to outsource these as this could lead to them eroding their competitive advantage. Indeed, resources that should not be outsourced are those that give the company a competitive edge, whereas those that are clearly not sources of competitive advantage can be considered 'low hanging fruit' (obvious areas of outsourcing). As explained in Chapter 5 it is exactly those areas that are neither clearly strategic nor non-strategic that cause the biggest headache for managers trying to decide what to outsource and what to keep in-house. While transaction cost economics (TCE) provides another useful theoretical perspective on outsourcing (Williamson, 1975), it is not an underpinning theory for this book.

The RBV is therefore a useful theoretical starting point for purchasing and supply chain management analysis. However, rather than the usual resource focus emphasized by RBV, this book adopts a particular resource perspective in two respects:

1 First, given the sustainability perspective, this book relies on a Natural Resource-Based View (NRBV) as first proposed by Hart (1995). This theoretical development builds on the RBV to take into account a focus on the natural environment, especially sustainable development, product stewardship and pollution prevention. Companies that develop capabilities in establishing a shared vision (a rare skill) are able to accumulate resources necessary for sustainable development; sustainable development strategies focus on new, low-impact technologies and competencies. Product stewardship requires that life-cycle assessment (LCA) be integrated in new product development processes and thereby enables a firm to minimize both economic and environmental/social costs of the product. Finally, pollution prevention can become a causally ambiguous routine that may play a critical role in a company's unique cost reductions as a source of competitive advantage. All three of these strategies require close collaboration with a range of external stakeholders; it becomes a stakeholder-oriented legitimacy-based process.

2 Second, it follows from the NRBV that it is absolutely critical how companies can access resources through supplier, and supply chain, relationships and that resources gain social legitimacy through stakeholder collaboration. Therefore, in addition to the NRBV, which highlights the importance of external collaboration, the complementary theories of institutional theory of DiMaggio and Powell (1991) and the Industrial Marketing and Purchasing (IMP) Interaction Approach (e.g. Håkansson, 1987) are important influences in this book. These theories emphasize that although it is important to protect internal strategic resources it is increasingly necessary for companies to access important resources through external relationships with other companies. In fact, relationships with other companies, including supply chain partners, can themselves be sources of competitive advantage. This realization is evident in recent developments of RBV, not only in the NRBV but also the so-called extended-RBV (Lavie, 2006). On the other hand, many sustainability initiatives are driven by institutional pressures from governments, NGOs and broader society. These rules of engagement limit what a company can do and may actually prevent differentiated strategies central to the resource-based view.

The NRBV and the IMP Interaction Approach emphasize the role of stakeholders and networks of relationships. Using these approaches enables us to better understand the bigger picture of creating sustainable purchasing and supply chain management. Traditionally, much business (or industrial) network theory (e.g. developed by IMP group) has focused on 'business actors', such as manufacturers, suppliers and distributors. These are typically also the actors considered in supply chain management analysis. However, as companies are seeking to incorporate sustainability into their purchasing and supply chain management strategies and practices new forms of actors have to be considered as integral parts of this traditional network picture: NGOs. NGOs play increasingly important roles, for example, in spearheading industry-specific initiatives that concern sourcing and procurement of ingredients or materials linked to pollution, rainforest destruction or exploitation of labour. As some companies have learned the hard way, NGOs can severely work against them, for example by exposing companies in the media. But, NGOs can also engage actively in partnerships with companies, helping companies to monitor and implement sustainability. In short, NGOs are rapidly becoming integral actors, or stakeholders, within supply, or business, networks so are essential to purchasing and supply strategy. As Roome (2001: 70) states, 'we increasingly see ourselves as part of a network society living in a network age'; 'concerns about complex environmental and social consequences of industrial activity have provoked the need for more frequent and meaningful engagement between companies and stakeholders'; 'networks have an identified role in innovation for environmental management and sustainable development'; and 'knowledge suggests that ecosystems are based on organisms connected through complex networks of energy and material flows'.

Drawing on existing classifications of network levels (Harland, 1996; Möller *et al.*, 2005; Ritter and Gemünden, 2003), we distinguish between three levels of purchasing and supply chain analysis: dyadic buyer–supplier relationships, supply chains and networks (Figure 1.3).

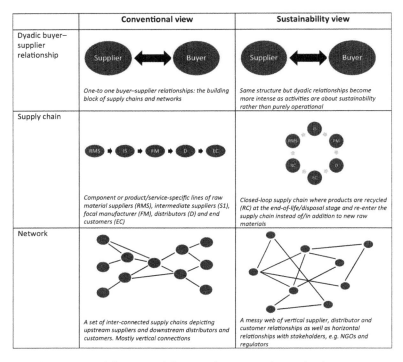

Figure 1.3 A conceptual framework for purchasing and supply chain management: a sustainability perspective – level of analysis

1.5 Book overview

As shown in Figure 1.4 the book is divided into three parts that correspond to the levels of analysis illustrated in Figure 1.3:

Part A: Purchasing and sourcing

The chapters in the first part of the book focus on dyadic buyer–supplier relationship issues: dyads are the basic building block of supply chains and networks. In order to successfully manage the whole supply chain, companies need to begin by focusing on the relationships with their immediate, direct, suppliers (or service providers). Part A therefore concerns the management of the upstream side of the company's supply chain, which is the responsibility of purchasing and sourcing management.

As the point of departure Chapter 2 begins by examining the purchasing process, that is, the steps that purchasing managers go through when buying products and/or services from suppliers. The implications of sustainability for each step are discussed. This process is situated with a wider process of sustainable supply base development and management. Chapter 3 then explains the importance and nature of purchasing strategy and explores different purchasing organizational structures, skills and competencies, and again we discuss the implications of sustainability on these. Chapter 3 concludes with a section on the

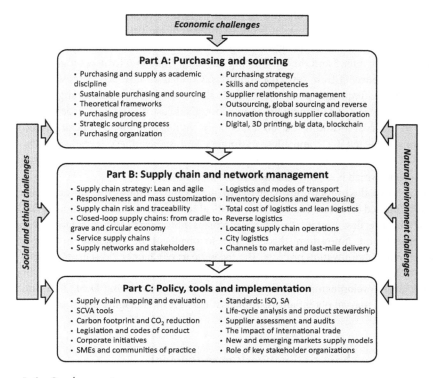

Figure 1.4 Book overview

particular challenges of purchasing within the public sector – usually called public procurement; public sector cases and examples are considered throughout the book so the main purpose of this section is to highlight some particular characteristics of public procurement.

Part A continues with Chapter 4 evaluating different sourcing strategies. In tandem with purchasing becoming more strategic, one of the key changes in sourcing strategy during the last couple of decades has been the shift from multi-sourcing strategies, whereby companies maintain a large supply base with suppliers they can play off against each other, towards parallel or single sourcing strategies whereby companies commit to a smaller number of suppliers and in turn become more dependent on the performance of these. This trend implies that the management of supplier relationships, or partnerships, becomes the cornerstone of sourcing management; this is the subject of the second half of Chapter 4. The need for supplier *relationship* assessment (as opposed to *supplier* assessment which is covered in Chapter 13) is discussed as well as the need to develop a portfolio of supplier relationships that are appropriate for different supply situations.

Chapter 5 focuses on outsourcing. The outsourcing decision is examined in terms of the 'make-or-buy' decision, that is, what should a company chose to make in-house and what is it better to buy in from suppliers. The outsourcing decision is all too often taken on a simple cost basis. Many companies have realized, especially in recent years, that there are a great many risks associated with outsourcing which therefore needs to take into account a wide range of factors other than cost. In order to mitigate these risks Chapter 5 examines some theoretical perspectives that can be used to properly inform the outsourcing decision. Closely connected to Chapter 5 and the outsourcing question, Chapter 6 focuses on global sourcing, in particular sourcing from low-cost countries. Companies now rely extensively on global sourcing but, as frequent reports in the media show, companies across a range of industries are increasingly accused of unethical and unsustainable use of suppliers, especially suppliers located in low-cost locations that do not comply with environmental, social and economic conditions expected by companies, customers and stakeholders such as NGOs in the developed world. We have witnessed a new trend away from global sourcing (re-shoring or near-shoring) which is explored at the end of Chapter 6.

Part A concludes by focusing on the role of purchasing in innovation: although purchasing is usually focused on cost reduction it has a critical role to play in value creation by facilitating innovation. The first part of Chapter 7 discusses how purchasing can facilitate product development and innovation through the involvement of suppliers in new product development and innovation projects. The second part of Chapter 7 discusses the role of new digital technology in purchasing and supply chain management and some of the latest technological developments, including Internet of Things (IoT), Big Data, 3D printing and blockchain that may all potentially disrupt existing ways of managing purchasing and supply chains.

Part B: Supply chain and network management

Part B contains four chapters dedicated to purchasing and supply issues that concern supply chains and networks. These concern the development, management and improvement of 'extra-dyadic' issues that go beyond the immediate, dyadic, supplier relationships into the extended supply chain or network. Chapter 8 opens this part by examining some fundamental supply chain definitions and models. Chapter 8 then explores different supply chain strategies, based on the notion of fit, i.e. the need to design supply chains that fit the particular context of the company in terms of the nature of products and market conditions, sometimes dichotomized as lean or agile. We explore the different ways to implement lean and/or agile supply chains. The second part of Chapter 8 explores how sustainability looks set to fundamentally change the ways in which we understand supply chain management. We discuss how the current supply chain management paradigm – the common wisdom of how supply chains should be designed and managed – means that companies face a large number of serious risks that could easily erode not only their image but also their competitive advantage. Chapter 8 explores the need to change the way in which supply chain managers perceive the nature and importance of supply chain transparency and traceability. Furthermore, we challenge the traditional conception of linear supply chains and explore the opportunities for designing a completely different system known as the closed-loop supply chain, fundamental in implementing a cradle-to-grave (or cradle-to-cradle) business philosophy.

Where Chapter 8, like the majority of supply chain management readings, focuses on product supply chains, Chapter 9 examines the relevance and nature of service supply chains. As competition for products becomes stronger, companies increasingly look to creating competitive advantage on the basis of services. Chapter 9 explores the rise of service operations and business models that move away from product-centred thinking towards models, including procurement of complex performance, servitization, product-service systems and through-life management. We explore how sustainability impacts on service supply chains, for example through re-manufacturing strategies.

Chapter 10 covers a number of key logistics management topics and shows how logistics and sustainability are inextricably linked, especially from an environmental point of view. Transport is the main issue here, as logistics management is primarily about solving the problem that products are rarely produced where they are consumed. The chapter starts by examining the role of different modes of transport and how transport planning issues can affect environmental impacts. Decisions on inventory also influence the choice of logistics strategy and so this is also dealt with, in particular related to total cost. Location decision making is a third element of logistics management, which is used to help resolve the positioning of producers and customers taking into account transport and inventory. Reverse logistics is also covered as this is an important part of sustainability in supply chains. As much of logistics today is managed by third-party providers, the chapter discusses their role in reducing costs and impacts and the final case shows how DHL, one of the largest logistics businesses, has integrated sustainability into their business strategy.

As sustainability initiatives in companies are often driven by consumer actions it is important to consider the final customer part of the supply chain. Chapter 11 deals with distribution strategies and how these impact on supply chain structures and processes. Distribution strategies tend to start with marketing channel choices and how to reach consumers. A significant recent development is that companies are heavily influenced by the opportunities of internet-based channels to customers, which in turn affects how products are delivered. This chapter assesses these different channel choices and how they influence the underlying logistics structures and processes. The chapter focuses particularly on the last delivery processes, which are often in urban areas with specific challenges related to sustainable distribution. RFID is discussed in the context of these challenges and particularly with the opportunities of improved traceability. The final case demonstrates how distribution collaboration can be used to minimize the costs and impacts this final delivery part of the supply chain.

Part C: Policy, tools and implementation

Part C is more practical in nature than Parts A and B. Part C considers how companies can implement sustainable purchasing and supply chain management: this requires a holistic understanding of purchasing and supply systems and therefore adopts a higher level of system analysis to examine the role of not only new forms of supply chains but also the need to engage with a range of network actors and stakeholders.

Chapter 12 outlines different methods for mapping and evaluating supply chains, initially those that are not exclusively designed to analyse sustainability. These include methods to analyse processes, flows, systems and knowledge within supply chains such as value stream mapping tools often used as part of lean supply chain management to identify sources of value and non-value (waste). Methods to analyse various aspects of sustainability are often closely related to lean supply chain mapping methods but adopt a long-term, often a life cycle, perspective. Chapter 12 explores the carbon footprint concept and discusses whether *lean* is *green* before Chapter 13 moves on to examining issues concerning legislation, standards and codes of conduct. The objective to implement sustainability has spurred governments and lawmakers to introduce a wide range of legislation that companies must comply with, and industry bodies and organizations have developed a myriad of standards, such as ISO14001, SA8000 and eco-labels, that provide guidelines or benchmarks for companies. In addition to guiding the reader through the jungle of standards, Chapter 13 explores the multi-stakeholder standards and guidelines on ethical supplier audits, linking to supplier assessment methods.

Chapter 14 is used to highlight recent developments in sustainability thinking related to supply chains and also some particularly promising supply chain activities that support sustainability objectives. Recent definitions of what constitutes sustainability and sustainable development are covered, with concepts such as natural capital, ecological footprint, ecosystem services and eco-efficiency. Industrial ecology (or symbiosis) is described and is shown to link to closed-loop supply chains ideas described earlier in the book. Stakeholder engagement in supply chains is also discussed here, as it is a key mechanism for businesses to understand the implications of sustainability and to help develop solutions to the issues raised. This is linked to supplier development and capacity building in developing regions. A final case on forestry is used to show how the concepts presented in the chapter are integrated into supply chain responses to sustainability imperatives. In Chapter 15 we step back from the detailed picture and adopt a helicopter perspective by drawing some high-level conclusions and reflecting on current challenges and future directions. Finally, we make some observations on the rise of sustainability and responsible management in education.

How to use this book

The structure of this book is designed so that the chapters can be read either conventionally in the order they appear, or the reader can opt to select topics of particular interest at random. Divided into three main parts, we begin with Part A: Purchasing and sourcing, Part B: Supply chain and network management, and Part C: Policy, tools and implementation. Throughout the book, we have sought to address what we perceive as the prime sustainability challenges facing purchasing and supply chain management today, combining social and ethical, economic, and natural environment challenges. Each chapter begins by highlighting which key aspects the reader is expected to understand by the end. Text boxes are integrated into the text to give further insight into specific issues and give practical examples from industry. At the end of each chapter a longer case study is used to demonstrate core themes and concepts discussed in the book.

1.6 Conclusions

This first chapter began by outlining the reasons why purchasing is no longer simply an administrative, or clerical, responsibility, but a critical and strategic priority for companies. In particular, we emphasized the importance of the trend towards outsourcing: as companies have outsourced a high proportion of production and service activities, purchasing plays a key role not only in cost reduction but also in value creation. In many companies the outsourcing ratio is around 70–80 per cent, in some cases even higher, so reducing purchase costs has a direct and significant impact on the bottom line. Furthermore, by helping to ensure that product materials, ingredients or components, as well as services, are purchased at the right quality and the right time, purchasing contributes significantly to the competitive advantage of the company. Ensuring that purchasing makes such a contribution to the company requires an understanding of purchasing as a strategic value-creating function and not simply a function whose sole aim is to save money.

Nevertheless, the concept of purchasing is still tied to the buying process for low-value and low-risk purchase items. Various alternative concepts have gained popularity and are often used to imply more strategic business functions and more comprehensive concepts than purchasing. These include procurement, which is usually the preferred terminology in the public sector but gaining popularity in the private sector too, and more recently sourcing, which is traditionally concerned with locating and searching for suppliers but which is increasingly used much more widely. The concept of purchasing is therefore being challenged by alternative concepts; one of these challengers includes supply chain management, which has a strong foundation in logistics, but is a more holistic concept that spans upstream management of supplier relationships and downstream management of distribution and customer relationships.

This book will mostly use the term purchasing and supply management to capture both non-strategic and strategic purchases. Where we simply talk about *purchasing* the reader can assume that we refer to *purchasing and supply management*, unless otherwise stated. We use *sourcing* in the traditional meaning to refer to the process of locating and searching suppliers but acknowledge that sourcing can also be used more widely, for example, in the context of global sourcing. Although we fully accept that *procurement* is widely seen as being more comprehensive than purchasing, including pre-purchase activities such as the make-or-buy decision, we make sparing use of the term procurement, instead using purchasing and supply management to capture both tactical and strategic purchases. Where we want to discuss extra-dyadic supply issues, that is, those that concern indirect suppliers (second tier, third tier, etc.) and seek to adopt an end-customer perspective, we use the concept of *supply chain management*. In other words, our use of the concept of supply chain management implies the perspective of the final end customer and therefore is used to include a long chain of sub-tier suppliers, suppliers, a focal company and distributors.

Sustainability is a rapidly emerging concept with strong implications for purchasing and supply chain management. In fact, the trend towards sustainability looks set to transform the ways in which we think about and design and manage purchasing processes and supply chains. Sustainability refers to three dimensions: the social (people), environmental (planet) and economic (profit); profit should no longer be at the expense of people and planet. The sustainability challenge is real: regardless of one's personal feelings towards climate change, the planet's resources are in decline, placing increasing pressures on companies to reduce carbon emissions, recycle or re-use, and to develop green technologies. Moreover, the current model of extensive reliance on global low-cost country sourcing is unsustainable, as demonstrated by frequent media reports into, for example, supplier labour violations.

Sustainability presents a risk to companies but also an opportunity for those companies prepared to embrace the challenge. Companies cannot tackle sustainability by themselves: they need to design and manage new sustainable supply chains and networks. Pioneering companies have developed innovative sustainable supply chain models that not only reduce the risks of getting exposed in the media for bad, non-ethical, practice but play a key part in transforming the fortunes of the company. This view of sustainability implies that sustainability needs to become an integrated part of purchasing and supply chain management rather than a separate add-on consideration or business function. That is why the title of this book is *Purchasing and Supply Chain Management: A Sustainability Perspective* and not 'Sustainable Purchasing and Supply Chain Management'. We consider this as consistent with an ecologically dominant logic rather than sustainability being treated as an add-on or damage limitation.

This chapter also introduced the underlying theoretical perspective and structure of the book. The RBV is fundamental, because the RBV and its derivative theories provide a foundation for very important, strategic, purchasing and supply chain management decisions such as whether to make or buy. However, given the sustainability perspective, we rely on an NRBV, which takes into account a focus on the natural environment, especially sustainable development, product stewardship and pollution prevention. Creating a natural resource-based competitive advantage in turn requires close collaboration with a range of external stakeholders; this book therefore explores how companies can access resources through supplier, and supply chain, relationships and how resources can gain social legitimacy through stakeholder collaboration. Therefore, in addition to the NRBV, the complementary theories of institutional theory of DiMaggio and Powell (1991) and the IMP Interaction Approach (e.g. Håkansson, 1987) are important influences in this book. These theories influence the assumption of our approach to purchasing and supply chain management that it is increasingly necessary for companies to access important resources through external relationships with other companies and that supply chain partners can themselves be sources of competitive advantage. Indeed, as companies seek to incorporate sustainability into their purchasing and supply chain management strategies and practices they need to work with and through a network of actors including NGOs, for example, in helping companies to monitor and implement sustainability in their supply chains. Where Part A of this book focuses on dyadic supplier relationships, Parts B and C shift the focus to supply chains and networks to examine the role of a wider group of stakeholders. Figures 1.3 and 1.4 illustrate the structure of the book in relation to the three levels of analysis.

References

Baily P and Farmer D (1977) *Purchasing Principles and Techniques*. London: Pitman Publishing.

Barney J (1991) Firm resources and sustained competitive advantage. *Journal of Management* 17: 99–117.

Bartley T (2007) Institutional emergence in an era of globalization: The rise of transnational private regulation of labor and environmental conditions. *American Journal of Sociology* 113(2): 297–351.

Beamon BM (1999) Designing the green supply chain. *Logistics Information Management* 12(4): 332–342.

Blomsma F and Brennan G (2017) The emergence of circular economy: A new framing around prolonging resource productivity. *Journal of Industrial Ecology* 21(3): 603–614.

Caldwell N and Howard M (eds) (2011) *Procuring Complex Performance: Studies of Innovation in Product-Service Management*. New York: Routledge.

Callender G, Nongwa T and Pardoe C (2013) An unsustainable position on terminology: A predicament facing procurement practitioners and academics. In: *Proceedings of the 22nd IPSERA Conference*, Audencia Nantes, France, 24–27 March, pp. 675–684.

Carter CR and Ellram LM (2003) Thirty-five years of The *Journal of Supply Chain Management*: Where have we been and where are we going? *Journal of Supply Chain Management* 39(2): 27–40.

Carter CR and Rogers DS (2008) A framework of sustainable supply chain management: Moving toward new theory. *International Journal of Physical Distribution and Logistics Management* 38(5): 360–387.

Christopher M (1998) *Logistics and Supply Chain Management: Strategies for Reducing Costs and Improving Services*. 2nd edn, London: FT Prentice Hall.

Cooper MC, Lambert DM and Pagh J (1997) Supply chain management: More than a new name for logistics. *The International Journal of Logistics Management* 8(1): 1–14.

Cousins PD, Lamming RC, Lawson B and Squire B (2008) *Strategic Supply Management: Theories, Concepts and Practice*. Harlow, UK: Pearson Education.

DiMaggio P and Powell WW (1991) *The New Institutionalism in Organizational Analysis*. Chicago: The University of Chicago Press.

Drumwright ME (1994) Socially responsible organizational buying: Environmental concern as a noneconomic buying criterion. *Journal of Marketing* 58(3): 1–19.

Ellram LM and Carr A (1994) Strategic purchasing: A history and review of the literature. *International Journal of Purchasing and Materials Management*, Spring: 130–138.

EMF – Ellen MacArthur Foundation (2012) *Towards the Circular Economy Volume 1: An Economic and Business Rationale for an Accelerated Transition*. Cowes, UK: Ellen MacArthur Foundation.

EMF (2014) *Towards the Circular Economy Volume 3: Accelerating the Scale Up Across Global Supply Chains*. Cowes, UK: Ellen MacArthur Foundation.

England W (1970) *Modern Procurement Management: Principles and Cases*. 5th edn, Homewood, IL: Irwin.

Gadde L-E and Håkansson H (1993) *Professional Purchasing*. London: Routledge.

Grant RM (1991) The resource-based theory of competitive advantage: Implication for strategy formulation. *California Management Review* 3(3): 114–135.

Håkansson H (ed.) (1987) *Industrial Technological Development: A Network Approach*. London: Croom Helm.

Harland CM (1996) Supply chain management: Relationships, chains and networks. *British Journal of Management* 7(special issue): 63–80.

Hart S (1995) A natural resource-based view of the firm. *Academy of Management Review* 20(4): 986–1014.

Johnsen TE, Lamming RC and Harland CM (2008) Inter-organizational relationships, chains and networks: A supply perspective. Chapter 3 in: Huxham C, Cropper S, Ebers M, *et al.* (eds) *The Oxford Handbook of Inter-Organizational Relations*. Oxford: Oxford University Press, 61–87.

Johnsen TE, Miemczyk J and Howard M (2017) A systematic literature review of sustainable purchasing and supply research: Theoretical perspectives and opportunities for IMP-based research. *Industrial Marketing Management* 61: 130–143.

Kraljic P (1983) Purchasing must become supply management. *Harvard Business Review*, Sept.–Oct.: 109–117.

Lambert D, Cooper M and Pagh J (1998) Supply chain management, implementation issues and research opportunities. *International Journal of Logistics Management* 9(2): 1–19.

Lamming RC (1993) *Beyond Partnership: Strategies for Innovation and Lean Supply*. London: Prentice-Hall, Inc.

Lamming RC, Johnsen TE, Zheng J and Harland C (2000) An initial classification of supply networks. *International Journal of Operations and Production Management* 20(6): 675–691.

Larson PD and Halldorsson A (2002) What is SCM? And where is it? *Journal of Supply Chain Management* 38(4): 36–44.

Lavie D (2006) The competitive advantage of interconnected firms: An extension of the resource-based view. *Academy of Management Review* 31(3): 638–658.

Lee L Jr and Dobler DW (1971) *Purchasing and Materials Management: Text and Cases.* 2nd edn, New York: McGraw-Hill.

Lysons K and Farrington B (2012) *Purchasing and Supply Chain Management.* 8th edn, Harlow, UK: Pearson.

Markman GD and Krause D (2016) Theory building surrounding sustainable supply chain management: Assessing what we know, exploring where to go. *Journal of Supply Chain Management* 52(2): 3–10.

Matten D and Moon J (2008) "Implicit" and "explicit" CSR: A conceptual framework for a comparative understanding of Corporate Social Responsibility. *Academy of Management Review,* 33: 404–424.

Miemczyk J, Johnsen TE and Macquet M (2012) Sustainable purchasing and supply management: A structured literature review of definitions and measures at the dyad, chain and network levels. *Supply Chain Management: An International Journal* 17(5): 478–496.

Möller K, Rajala A and Svahn S (2005) Strategic business nets – their type and management. *Journal of Business Research* 58(9): 1274–1284.

Montabon FL, Pagell M and Wu Z (2016) Making sustainability sustainable. *Journal of Supply Chain Management* 52(2): 1–34.

Pagell M and Shevchenko A (2014) Why research in sustainable supply chain management should have no future. *Journal of Supply Chain Management* 50(1): 44–55.

Porter ME (1985) *Competitive Advantage: Creating and Sustaining Superior Performance.* New York: Free Press.

Prahalad CK and Hamel G (1990) The core competencies of the corporation. *Harvard Business Review,* May–June: 71–91.

Ramsay J and Croom S (2008) The impact of evolutionary and developmental metaphors on supply chain practice: A literature critique and pilot study. *Journal of Purchasing and Supply Management* 14(3): 192–204.

Reck RF and Long BG (1988) Purchasing: A competitive weapon. *Journal of Purchasing and Materials Management* 24(Fall): 2–8.

Ritter T and Gemünden HG (2003) Interorganizational relationships and networks: An overview. *Journal of Business Research* 56: 691–697.

Robinson PJ, Faris CW and Wind Y (1967) *Industrial Buying and Creative Marketing.* Boston, MA: Allyn and Bacon.

Roome N (2001) Conceptualizing and studying the contribution of networks in environmental management and sustainable development. *Business Strategy and the Environment* 10(2): 69–76.

Rozemeijer F (2008) Purchasing myopia revisited again? *Journal of Purchasing and Supply Management* 14(3): 205–207.

Sheth JN (1973) A model of industrial buying behaviour. *Journal of Marketing* 37: 50–56.

Spekman R (1981) A strategic approach to procurement planning. *Journal of Purchasing and Materials Management,* Winter: 3–9.

Strassmann PA (2004) The economics of outsourcing. *Information Economics Journal,* June: 14–17.

Teece DJ (1986) Profiting from technological innovation: Implications for integration, collaboration, licensing and public policy. *Research Policy* 15: 285–305.

Teece D, Pisano G and Shuen A (1997) Dynamic capabilities and strategic management. *Strategic Management Journal* 18(7): 509–533.

Van Weele A (2010) *Purchasing and Supply Chain Management: Analysis, Strategy, Planning and Practice.* 5th edn, London: Thomson Learning.

Walker H and Brammer S (2009) Sustainable procurement in the United Kingdom public sector. *Supply Chain Management: An International Journal* 14(2): 128–137.

Webster FE and Wind Y (1972) A general model of organizational buying behaviour. *Journal of Marketing* 36(April): 12–19.

WEF – World Economic Forum (2014) Towards the circular economy: Accelerating the scale-up across global supply chains. WEF report: Ellen MacArthur Foundation and McKinsey & Co.

Wernerfeldt B (1984) A resource-based view of the firm. *Strategic Management Journal* 5: 171–180.

Williamson OE (1975) *Markets and Hierarchy: Analysis and Antitrust Implications.* New York: Free Press.

World Commission on Environment and Development (1987) *Our Common Future.* Oxford: Oxford University Press.

Part A
Purchasing and sourcing

CHAPTER 2

The strategic sourcing and purchasing process

LEARNING OBJECTIVES

By the end of this chapter you should be able to:

- Understand the key ingredients of the strategic sourcing process;
- Identify different types of purchase process situations;
- Evaluate the main stages of the purchasing process;
- Explain the management challenges of each stage of the purchasing process, especially from a sustainability perspective.

2.0 Introduction

This chapter is the first of five chapters that focuses on the management of dyadic buyer–supplier relationships in particular from a purchasing perspective. As Figure 2.1 shows, the purchasing process and other issues to do with purchasing including, for example, sourcing, outsourcing and supplier relationship management, predominantly concern the first level of purchasing and supply chain analysis: dyadic buyer–supplier relationships. In other words, Part A focuses on direct supplier relationships, especially how to organize the internal purchasing organization and develop a purchasing strategy in order to develop and manage these from a sustainability perspective.

Chapter 2 begins by introducing a framework for strategic and sustainable sourcing. This framework shows the main tasks involved in selecting, developing, managing and improving a high-performing and sustainable supply base. The framework includes the selection process of approved suppliers that constitute the company's long-term supply base and the continuous management and development of suppliers.

The chapter continues by focusing particularly on the purchasing process companies use when they want to buy a specific new product or service. This part begins by introducing a classic purchasing typology that

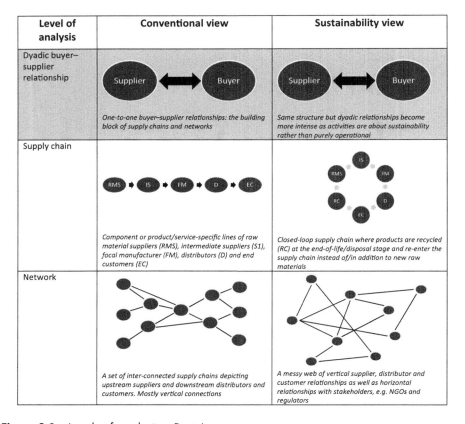

Level of analysis	Conventional view	Sustainability view
Dyadic buyer–supplier relationship	*One-to-one buyer–supplier relationships: the building block of supply chains and networks*	*Same structure but dyadic relationships become more intense as activities are about sustainability rather than purely operational*
Supply chain	*Component or product/service-specific lines of raw material suppliers (RMS), intermediate suppliers (S1), focal manufacturer (FM), distributors (D) and customers (EC)*	*Closed-loop supply chain where products are recycled (RC) at the end-of-life/disposal stage and re-enter the supply chain instead of/in addition to new raw materials*
Network	*A set of inter-connected supply chains depicting upstream suppliers and downstream distributors and customers. Mostly vertical connections*	*A messy web of vertical supplier, distributor and customer relationships as well as horizontal relationships with stakeholders, e.g. NGOs and regulators*

Figure 2.1   Levels of analysis – Part A

classifies different types of purchase and how the purchasing process differs for each type. This identifies all the potential stages involved in a purchase although usually it is part of the long-term strategic sourcing process.

2.1 A framework for strategic sourcing

The purchasing process includes a number of stages; however, it is rare that the company begins the process with no prior knowledge of the supply market. Companies want to avoid working with new suppliers with whom they have no prior experience as a new supplier always represents an element of risk. A supplier will typically attempt to make a range of promises to its customer, but without previous experience the customer – or purchaser – cannot be 100 per cent sure that the supplier will perform according to its promises. Best practice in purchasing therefore involves building up and maintaining a base of approved and preferred suppliers: in this book this is referred to as the strategic sourcing process. Purchasing will seek to select these suppliers whenever possible in order to save the cost and time associated with evaluating, verifying and contracting with new unknown suppliers. As shown in Figure 2.2 those suppliers on the company's list of approved and preferred suppliers are

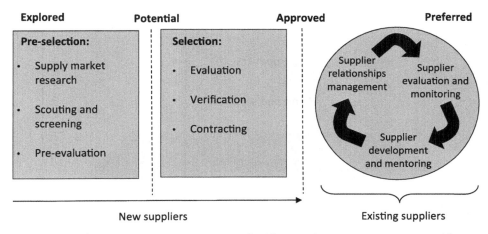

Figure 2.2   The strategic sourcing process: building and maintaining a sustainable supply base[1]

then the focus of the company's efforts to build long-term relationships through ongoing supplier evaluation, supplier relationship management and supplier development.

As illustrated in Figure 2.2, strategic sourcing is a process that begins with exploration of new suppliers as part of the pre-selection of new suppliers. This part of the process involves conducting supply market research, an ongoing process that may be done, for example, through Internet searches, trade fair attendance, industry association liaisons, or embassy consultation. The company's partners or existing suppliers can sometimes also provide useful references. The pre-selection process sometimes involves scouting for – and screening – new potential suppliers outside the company's existing supply networks. For example, when a company is in the process of developing a radically new technology, where it has little previous experience of the supply market, it is often necessary to scout for new suppliers in industries that are new to the company. This is a point we return to in Chapter 7.

The pre-selection process leads to a list of potential suppliers that need to be subjected to the more rigorous supplier selection process. Potential suppliers need to be further evaluated and all details need to verified. When everything has been checked contracts can be drawn up. Once the company has chosen suppliers through this rigorous process they in turn constitute the company's database of approved suppliers; the company will use these suppliers wherever possible to reduce the (transaction) cost and risk involved in starting all over with new unknown suppliers. Figure 2.3 illustrates a typical supplier hierarchy as used by many companies, distinguishing between the many potential new suppliers, the reduced number of approved suppliers that survive short- or medium-term evaluation, and the relatively few preferred suppliers that the company has ascertained long-term through rigorous ongoing evaluation and development present little risk: the different colours represent different perceived risk levels.

Companies increasingly seek to invest in their approved suppliers, treating them as long-term partnerships (although there is a need for differentiating different levels or types of supplier relationships). More and more companies realize that the process of selecting and

Figure 2.3 A supplier hierarchy

evaluating new unknown suppliers is so costly and risky that they prefer to rely on suppliers, whose capabilities have been demonstrated and measured over a period of time, and whom the company therefore trusts to fulfil its commitments and promises: the core of this process is supplier relationship management as will be discussed in Chapter 4. Another core part of the process of investing in relationships with approved and preferred suppliers is ongoing evaluation and monitoring of suppliers. Traditionally, this supplier relationship improvement process centres on operational performance improvements, especially cost, quality and delivery performance. However, sustainability is increasingly at the heart of this process and involves assessment of issues such as labour conditions and environmental risks at supplier premises. Many companies conduct audits as part of this process, to ascertain – to see for themselves first hand – that suppliers respect the terms and conditions specified by the company's sustainability policy. This is particularly important when companies have developed strong brands that can easily be damaged by reports of – or even just accusations of – unethical sourcing. For example, strong global leaders such as Apple, Danone and Nokia conduct regular audits of their entire supply bases and publish (negative and positive) results from their efforts in online annual reports.[2]

Monitoring the performance and compliance of suppliers is a critical part of the process of building up a strong supply base but on its own performance assessment and monitoring does little to improve supplier performance. As discussed in Chapter 4, companies need to invest in ongoing development of supplier capabilities. When dealing with, for example, suppliers in low-cost countries this is a critical process of helping suppliers to understand how to improve their processes through 'mentoring'.

The need to continue to work with existing suppliers, despite serious ethical supplier problems, is illustrated in the case of Swedish furniture giant IKEA. In May 2007, IKEA's chief executive officer (CEO), Anders Dahlvig, was interviewed by the BBC for its HARDtalk programme. He was presented with serious allegations of child labour and pollution at IKEA's suppliers in India and China. When asked why IKEA continued to source from these suppliers, he answered that IKEA's policy was to continue to monitor and help these suppliers to improve instead of simply getting rid of them. If IKEA had chosen to terminate these supplier relationships it would have meant having to subject the new suppliers to a resource-intensive – and costly – supplier selection and approval process. The IKEA case study in Chapter 6 examines these challenges in more depth.

It is in the context of this wider strategic sourcing process that the purchasing process should be understood. In other words, when a company sets out to buy something it is rare that they start from scratch with new suppliers. In most situations companies will seek to reduce purchase risk by involving preferred suppliers. As sustainability becomes an ever more important risk factor, which requires continuous supplier evaluation, development and management, working with long-term existing suppliers is more important than ever.

2.2 A purchasing process typology

The nature of the purchasing process varies significantly depending on the situation. For example, in the case of a manufacturing company requiring a completely new complex component there is likely to be a multi-phase process in place in which each phase involves a large number of people from different organizational functions and the process will be very time-consuming. In contrast, when companies buy standard office equipment simply to replenish stocks the process is much simpler. So, the nature of the process depends on what you buy.

Building on a typology developed by Robinson *et al.* (1967) it is possible to distinguish between three types of purchase situations:[3]

- A new purchase: the company requires a completely new product or service. There is no history of purchasing this so the supply market is unknown. This is therefore likely to be a long and complex purchasing process. All stages of the purchasing process will have to be managed. When companies develop an innovative new product, which requires new components, they face a new-task situation. Similarly, outsourcing projects are often a new-task situation as they are one-offs.

- A modified repurchase: the company requires a new product or service from a known supplier or may decide to approach a new supplier for an existing product or service. The process is therefore going to be less long and complex than the new-purchase situation but is nevertheless likely to require some effort.

- A straight repurchase: the company requires a known product or service from a known, approved or preferred, supplier. Therefore, there is very little uncertainty regarding the purchase because it is a repeat of previous purchases within an existing contract with the supplier. Often, this situation is managed through annual agreements and orders are typically raised through an MRP or ERP system, i.e. an e-procurement system. There is little need to activate the entire purchasing process for such purchases; instead only the final part of the process is necessary. For manufacturing companies, examples of straight repurchases could be materials and components to the manufacturing process. Other examples could be MRO items, such as office supplies.

Figure 2.4 shows that the classification proposed by Robinson *et al.* (1967) is a function of the degrees of newness, risk and uncertainty of the purchase.

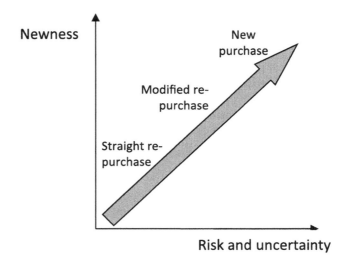

Figure 2.4 New purchase, modified purchase and straight re-purchase

Classifying purchases according to the dimensions shown in Figure 2.4 is an important starting point for understanding fundamental differences in the management of the purchasing process. The following section provides an overview of the stages involved in the purchasing process.

2.3 The purchasing process

The purchasing process involves a number of stages. In some situations each of these stages can be highly resource demanding and time-consuming but in other situations they can be more implicit. As discussed in the previous section, companies would only go through all of these when facing a new purchase situation where they have little experience with the supply market. Different depictions of the purchasing process exist; here we align ourselves with a model used by Van Weele (2010). Figure 2.5 shows six distinct stages in the purchasing process. Sometimes, the first three stages are referred to as 'source-to-contract' whilst the final three stages are referred to as 'procure-to-pay'.

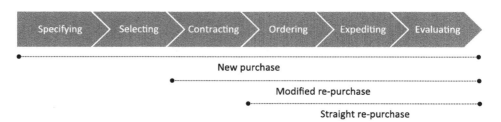

Figure 2.5 The stages of the purchasing process

Source: Adapted from Van Weele (2010).

Purchasing and supply managers play a central role in the purchasing process, but it is important to note that other functions may also be heavily involved at the different stages. For example, when companies are facing a new purchase situation involving a technical product the process is likely to be highly cross-functional. Often, specific stages within the purchasing process can in fact be led by functions other than purchasing. For example, the engineering, research and development (R&D) or design department often take the lead in the early parts of the process when a company sets out to buy technologically complex components or materials. However, ideally the purchasing department should be involved at all stages.

In the following paragraphs we explain each stage in the purchasing process in turn, identifying the role of purchasing as well as the likely involvement of other functions in the company.

2.3.1 Specifying

The specification 'specifies' the purchase needs and captures these in a document that will serve as a reference point during and at the end of the process: if at the end of the process the supplier delivers something that does not satisfy the specification it indicates a failure, as the company's needs have not been met. In particular, specifications are required to:

- Communicate to the purchasing department what to buy

- Communicate requirements to suppliers

- Establish tangible goods to be provided

- Establish intangible services to be provided

- Establish standards against which inspections, tests and quality checks are made

- Balance specification goals of different functions

Some companies differentiate between specifications and supplier requirements so that the specifications focus on the purchase item and requirements focus on wider requirements. In any case, as specifications reflect the needs of the company they should reflect the needs of both the internal customers and, ultimately, the external (end) customers. It is therefore very important to match or align the priorities detailed in the specifications with customer needs and requirements. For example, if customers prioritize high quality and innovation, the specification document should reflect those requirements instead of making automatic assumptions about, for example, low-cost requirements.

Generally, in order to avoid misunderstanding it is good practice to provide detailed specifications to suppliers. Especially when dealing with foreign suppliers there is always a risk of misunderstanding due to language problems or cultural difficulties. With the rise in global sourcing, often from low-cost countries (see Chapter 6), there is a real risk that suppliers do not fully understand specifications and buyers themselves may be unaware of such potential discrepancies in the interpretations of specifications. Use of standard specifications and commonly understood and objective terminology, help to reduce the risk of misunderstanding.

Writing a highly detailed specification may leave no scope for misunderstanding but it may also drastically reduce the number of suppliers capable of meeting the specification; there is a risk that overly detailed specifications reduce competition. Purchasers sometimes write specifications with a specific supplier or brand in mind but need to strike a balance between specifying exactly what they require and leaving room for competition between suppliers: on the one hand do not under-specify but on the other hand do not over-specify.

In some situations it can be difficult for a company to write detailed specifications because the company is not an expert in what it needs. Consider, for example, a company that needs a technologically complex component: the company knows what function the component needs to fulfil within its product or system but without being an expert in this component it can be impossible to specify all the technical details. Therefore, it makes sense to employ two different specification strategies as shown in Figure 2.6.

Detailed (or technical) specifications leave no ambiguity as to what the company requires from the supplier. All areas of uncertainty are explained in clear language and such detail that there is no scope for misunderstanding. In contrast, functional (or global) specifications provide an overall explanation in functional terms, that is, they explain what function the purchase needs to fulfil but not exactly how the supplier should go about achieving the best possible solution. Functional specifications are similar to 'black-box' specifications: the overall outlines are explained but the content is left for the supplier to decide how best to achieve it (Karlsson *et al.*, 1998). The functional specification strategy works on the assumption that the supplier has superior knowledge of its component and that therefore the supplier is best placed to decide what is the best way to meet the customer's requirements. Whereas fully detailed technical specifications leave nothing to chance but therefore also discourage supplier initiative and innovation, functional specifications encourage the supplier to innovate in its pursuit of the best solution.

The specification traditionally details the purchasing requirements in terms of technical (e.g. quality) requirements, supply chain (logistics/delivery) requirements, commercial (financial/cost) requirements, and service/maintenance requirements. However, this traditional approach does not take sustainability criteria into account and many companies still do not fully incorporate sustainability criteria into the traditional criteria, instead treating sustainability as a separate process. In fact, according to an analysis of FTSE 100 companies done by Preuss (2009), only 5 out of 44 FTSE 100 companies included corporate social responsibility (CSR) in purchase specifications, although the picture will have improved by

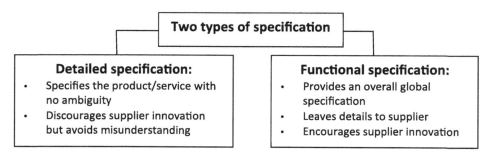

Figure 2.6 Detailed and functional specifications

now. As we argue in this book, the integration of traditional criteria with sustainability criteria is rapidly becoming a critical challenge for purchasing professionals. Table 2.1 provides an overview of a set of overall criteria and examples of sub-criteria.

Some requirements are objective and relatively easy to specify but others can be much more difficult to pin down. In general, services are much more complex to specify than products, as they are usually highly intangible (see Chapter 8). In any case, in order to avoid ambiguity and ensure that criteria are measurable and thereby comparable, requirements should be considered at an overall level and then be divided into sub-criteria as shown in Table 2.1.

Although purchasing should play an important role in developing and communicating specifications as part of the purchasing process, other organizational functions often, in reality, take charge of the process. For example, design or engineering departments in

Table 2.1 Criteria and sub-criteria for specification and supplier selection

Overall criteria	Examples of specific criteria
Technical requirements	• Technical • Quality: e.g. defect rates, TQM system, 6 sigma
Commercial requirements	• Cost • Payment terms • Liabilities • IPR • Warranty
Supply chain requirements	• Delivery terms • Lead times • Flexibility • IT systems: ERP • Supplier integration capabilities
Service requirements	• Customer service and support • Technical service • Maintenance and repairs
R&D and innovation requirements	• R&D size and budget • Patents • Staff qualifications: no. of qualified engineers, PhDs, etc.
Sustainability requirements	• Basic qualifying standards: e.g. ISO14001, SA8000 • Industry-specific codes of conduct
Sustainability requirements: environmental	• Environmental requirements • Commitment to environmental protection • Compliance with local laws • Control of emissions/pollution • Protection of biodiversity • Application of life-cycle approach: e.g. use of ISO14040–14043

Table 2.1 continued

Sustainability requirements: employment/social	• Fundamental principles and rights at work: e.g. compliance with International Bill of Human Rights • No child or slave labour • Health and safety at work • Equal opportunities/no discrimination or harassment • Minimum wage • Non-excessive working hours • Employees have written contract • Civil and political rights • Conditions of work and social protection • Human development and training in the workplace
Sustainability requirements: value/collaboration	• Willingness to disclose policies, decisions and activities: e.g. cooperation with audits/assessment • Behaviour based on honesty, ethics and integrity: e.g. anti-corruption • Promoting social responsibility in the supply chain • Respect for property rights • Values/standards compatible with those of customer • Accountability

manufacturing companies tend to manage specification of parts and materials, whereas purchasing often takes the lead for non-complex and indirect purchases (non-components). In many companies it is critical that purchasing and engineering collaborate on specifications; although engineering has the technical knowledge (which purchasers often lack) they may not consider cost or sourcing issues. As Note 2.1 shows, the introduction of 'purchasing engineers' was a key factor in the turnaround of American motorcycle company Harley-Davidson.

Note 2.1

Purchasing and engineering collaboration at Harley-Davidson

In the early 1990s Harley-Davidson's engineering division was in charge of design and testing activities, and there was little cross-functional collaboration with production and purchasing. Engineers dealt directly with suppliers and relationships with suppliers were poor. Earl Werner, vice-president of engineering, recalled, for example, that if he wanted to develop a new fuel injection system for a motorcycle, the engineering department would have to survey the supply base, identify a supplier who could best make the parts, and then confirm that the supplier had the needed technical capabilities to support the design. 'We picked suppliers whose forte was technical innovation', said Werner. 'They were low volume and didn't have a high degree of competency on the commercial side. Or they couldn't meet the scheduled requirements for manufacturing.' Supplier components came in late and production was often jeopardized.

Traditionally, purchasing had become involved in design and development once engineers had finished their designs. Therefore, there was little room for purchasing to influence supplier selection. Dividing the purchasing division into two functions – operational purchasing and development purchasing – the company enabled part of the purchasing function to focus on the long-term development of the supply base and the integration of suppliers into the product design and development process.

The term 'purchasing engineers' was developed for employees who would work side by side with engineering. 'Having engineers in purchasing is critical because they are responsible for translating the technical requirements into a voice for the supplier,' said Werner. Jayson Way, a purchasing engineer, says Harley-Davidson learned that when purchasing is not involved in the design process, the company tends to pinpoint parts that can be provided by just one source. By getting purchasing – and thereby multiple suppliers – into the design fosters early competition.

Source: Milligan and Carbone (2000)

Collaboration between engineering and purchasing can also involve value engineering (Cooper and Slagmulder, 1997). This form of analysis is often carried out for existing products with a view to reducing cost and eliminating bottlenecks caused by the use of highly specialized and difficult-to-source materials. Ideally, this should be considered before products go into production, i.e. during specification stage. Value engineering typically raises questions such as:

- Are there alternative lower cost ways to satisfy need, e.g. copper may substitute silver for use in electrical conductors, or synthetic material may substitute natural textiles/ leathers?

- Is it made on correct tooling considering volumes?

- Are limits and tolerances too tight?

- Can we use standard off-the-shelf parts, shared across our product lines?

Many companies deliberately seek to standardize their purchases, especially components, in order to generate economies of scale and thereby achieve purchasing efficiencies. For example, Swedish company IKEA makes extensive use of the same types of screws, bolts and locks, which are used when customers assemble the IKEA furniture. This not only makes customers familiar with the IKEA assembly process but also helps IKEA purchasing achieve economies of scale that are critical to its low-cost strategy. It is therefore good practice to use standard – and standardize – specifications wherever possible to reduce cost and improve quality.

2.3.2 Selecting

Once the specifications have been drawn up, the purchaser can begin the search for suppliers. In principle, the aim is initially to identify a large number of suppliers and then gradually narrow down the field until the selected supplier (or suppliers) remains. This means that the process begins with supply market research, in order to identify as many viable suppliers as possible, and then invites potential suppliers through, initially a Request For Information (RFI) and subsequently a Request For Quotation (RFQ) – also known as an RFP, or Request For Proposal.

Supply market research typically involves scouting and scanning for potential suppliers on a global basis. With the advent of the Internet much of this search can be conducted through Internet sources and processes; this has the particular advantage that it can widen up global supply markets and help to foster competition. Figure 2.7 illustrates the basic principle of narrowing down during the supplier selection process.

As explained at the beginning of this chapter and shown in Figure 2.7 companies often have an approved list of suppliers that they have purchased from in the past. As the company has previous experience of approved suppliers, trust and confidence have been built up with these suppliers as a result of past performance. Approved suppliers therefore represent lower risk for the company compared with soliciting completely new unknown suppliers. As explained at the beginning of this chapter, not all purchases need to go through all the stages of the purchasing process as this is a very time-consuming and costly process. Supply market research is typically done when companies are facing a new-task situation where there are no existing approved suppliers or where it has been decided that the time has come for a fresh look at the supply market.

Supply market research should result in a 'bidders' long list': a list of potential suppliers that seem to satisfy the basic requirements, but who require further investigation. An RFI is sometimes produced before an RFQ (or RFP) in order to gather information about the capabilities of potential suppliers. Suppliers may be contacted and visited as part of the RFI and it is often suppliers on the company's approved supplier list that are the main suppliers to be approached for the RFI. This stage should result in elimination of some of the suppliers on the bidders' long list and therefore lead to the bidders' short list. The remaining

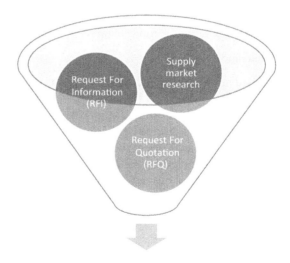

Supplier(s) selected

Figure 2.7 The supplier selection process: narrowing down the number of suppliers

suppliers on the short list are then issued with the RFQ, which contains more specific information than the RFI. The RFQ serves as the invitation to bid and typically includes details of price and, ideally, the full specifications of the product or service to be purchased. The RFQ could be used later as a legally binding document so it is important that the RFQ captures all the expectations of the purchaser in a clear and unambiguous language. An RFQ should also specify a date and time by which suppliers must submit their quote. If an RFQ is issued by a company, suppliers will most likely assume that several suppliers have been invited to bid for the contract so RFQs can be useful in promoting competition amongst suppliers. Full transparency of selection criteria can also be provided as part of the RFQ so that bidding suppliers know the basis on which bids will be evaluated and the contract will be awarded. Indeed, as companies seek to develop more open collaborative supplier relationships, it makes sense for bidding suppliers to have at least some visibility of selection criteria, although it may be appropriate not to divulge too much detail so as to retain negotiation power and discretion in the selection process.

Upon receipt of bids, the purchasing department should play a key role in evaluating the bids and in devising a process for the evaluation. For strategic purchases, such as high value and complex technological component systems, it is best practice to form a cross-functional team, including, for example, purchasing, logistics, production, engineering or quality assurance. Different functions have different priorities so it is important to ensure that these different priorities are reflected in the evaluation and selection process. Many companies have ranking systems where the selection criteria are ranked or given different weightings, and it makes sense to allow each cross-functional team member to score each supplier. When all suppliers have been evaluated the supplier with the most competitive offer will be informed that they have proceeded to the next stage where a contract is ready to be drawn up. Depending on the sourcing strategy more than one supplier can be chosen: it is only for single sourcing that a single supplier will be chosen, whereas in other situations two or more suppliers may be chosen. It is also good practice to inform unsuccessful suppliers that they have not been selected, explaining why their bid was not chosen, as it is likely that the company will want to solicit offers from those suppliers in future.

2.3.3 Contracting

Twenty years ago Sako (1992) observed that lean Japanese companies did not rely on extensive formal contracts in their management of supplier relationships. Instead, she reported that lean Japanese companies used 'contractual trust' as a first step in supplier relationship development, where contractual trust refers to the company's expectations that the exchange partner will keep its promises. It was therefore not so much the formal contract as such that mattered but the role it played in creating a foundation for further relationship development. At the time this observation led many automotive companies, seeking to learn from Japanese lean production practices, to reduce their reliance on extensive formal contracts. However, it is not a matter of either/or: contracts form an essential part of supplier relationship development even if there is a lot more to supplier relationship management than contracts, as will be discussed in Chapter 4.

Contracts are essential in order to avoid the risk of non-compliance yet the extent to which extensive formal contracts are required depends on the circumstances. For example, in the public sector the purchasing process is governed by a large number of regulations, as will be discussed later, so contracts naturally play an important role in formalizing expectations, and terms and conditions. As explained earlier, some purchasing situations are characterized by a high degree of uncertainty so it is critical to write and negotiate a contract that sets out all the customer's expectations. Consider, for example, a situation where a European company wants to buy something from a new unknown Asian supplier: due to cultural and language differences there are likely to be different perceptions of the meaning of quality and time, and understandings of property rights (who owns the legal rights to designs, technologies, etc.) may also differ; establishing expectations in a formal contract is therefore critical at this stage.

Terms and conditions are at the heart of contracts, which concern, for example, terms of payment and delivery. Although payment should perhaps ideally be upon receipt of goods or services, companies are very sensitive to payment terms as they have to manage their cash-flows and cost of capital. Therefore, most companies want to have the longest possible payment terms without impacting severely on purchase price.

In some cases payments can be made in several instalments. In construction projects, for example, the supplier will have to make significant investments a long time before completion of the project and will therefore often insist on payment up front or during the project. It is good practice in such situations to offer partial payment for partially completed work and to withhold the final payment until project completion when the quality of the work has been evaluated (Van Weele, 2010).

Purchasing should insist that the supplier guarantee the quality and delivery of the work as specified. But how can the purchaser be sure that the supplier will respect the contract and what can s/he do about it if the supplier delivers something that does not meet the performance requirements? In order to pre-empt this situation contracts should include penalty clauses, such as, say, 10 per cent reduction in the price if the performance requirements are below the expected standard. However, penalty clauses are not always sufficient as it may sometimes be necessary to refuse the work provided by the supplier, if for instance, there are serious flaws or it is delivered so late that it is no longer of value to the company. It may also be necessary to specify liabilities for non-conformance, for example, requiring suppliers to compensate direct damages. Therefore, the buyer must incorporate clauses that allow them to reject the supplier's work.

Designing contracts, and agreeing contracts with suppliers, is further complicated by the legal environment. Suppliers will typically have their own terms and conditions and may insist that these apply. It is a critical part of the negotiation process to ensure that the parties agree on whose terms and conditions apply and agree terms and conditions acceptable to both parties. Contracts are also subject to the legal requirements of the country in which the work is delivered and typically the legal rules of the supplier apply, although not always. Again, this will have to be agreed between the parties. International trade terms, such as Incoterms (see https://iccwbo.org/?s=incoterms – last accessed 22 January 2018) can sometimes be used as a compromise. The example of train buying in Denmark in Note 2.2 below shows the complexities of contracting and the need to ensure that clauses for poor quality and late delivery are fully incorporated into contracts.

Note 2.2

Buying trains: experiences from Denmark

The Danish government landed itself in much trouble when buying trains from an Italian manufacturer. The Danish national train operator, DSB, decided to buy the IC4 trains from AnsaldoBreda following a lengthy purchasing process. The trains were supposed to be state-of-the art intercity trains and were intended to replace outdated trains. However, long delays and partial deliveries turned the project into a major political issue. The trains were originally scheduled to enter service in 2003 but it was not until June 2007 that the first train entered service. In May 2008, DSB gave AnsaldoBreda an ultimatum: at least 14 trains had to be approved and ready for regular service before May 2009, or the contract would be cancelled and DSB would demand its money back. AnsaldoBreda subsequently agreed to pay DSB a compensation of DKr2billion (approximately €270million). Together with previously paid compensation fees this would mean refunding half the original contract value. DSB retained the right to cancel the contract if more than seven trains were delivered more than six months late.

In November 2010, DSB finally after a seven-year delay completed certification of multiple connected IC4 train sets. They were scheduled to enter service in January 2011 but in April 2011, DSB's director stated that further economic sanctions against AnsaldoBreda were likely to be imposed as a result of continuing problems in the quality of the trains delivered. Consequently, the trains had to be upgraded to Danish standards at DSB's own cost. Eighteen IC4 trains have now been approved for use but some are still not in daily service. In November 2011 two IC4 trains failed to stop at stop signals. This caused the authorities to ban the IC4 from running until the problems had been investigated. The controversy continues.

Contract design is sometimes regarded as so important that it constitutes a *firm capability* (Argyres and Mayer, 2007). Mouzas and Ford (2012) suggest that complex buyer–supplier interactions, information asymmetries and unforeseen contingencies increasingly lead companies to seek to explicitly state and manifest as joint consent the conditions of business relationships. This implies that contracts are manifestations of agreements that specify how a supplier's resources are acquired, used or transformed. Naturally, the challenges highlighted by Mouzas and Ford (2012) also make contracting very complex, discouraging some companies from developing detailed contracts, instead preferring so-called 'framework agreements' or 'umbrella contracts' (Mouzas and Furmston, 2008). These are less detailed agreements that place reduced emphasis on what to do if the supplier does not comply with the contract, and more emphasis on the fundamental rules and principles of the relationship, particularly the use of knowledge to create joint gains. Framework agreements are mostly relevant to knowledge-intensive relationships where there is a need for a shared mindset between the parties but can also be used more widely. Clauses in such agreements might include the categories exemplified below:

- Exclusivity: both parties have the right to obtain competitive offers

- Information: both parties will inform one another if unforeseen circumstances arise

- Notification: product damages must be communicated within two weeks

- Subcontracting: must be approved

- Assignment: must be approved

- Volume/price: to be agreed

- Invoicing: monthly basis

- Renegotiation: annual

- Force majeure: parties bear no responsibilities due to war or strikes

- Guarantee: right to refuse due to poor quality

- Liability: supplier is also liable for materials supplied by its suppliers

- Secrecy: all information is confidential

- Property rights: no transfer of property rights

- Legal venue: France

- Amendments: supplier has the right to revoke any orders in writing

- Business and product continuity

- Duration: annual

- Termination: each party has the right to terminate the agreement with two weeks' notice[4]

Performance-based contracts (PBCs) have become increasingly popular. These are a form of incomplete contract, meaning that they are less prescriptive and allow more freedom and flexibility regarding specific details of the transaction relevant to the contract (Luo, 2002). As a result, PBCs allow suppliers a certain degree of autonomy which can in turn foster innovation (Kim *et al.*, 2007; Ng and Nudurupati, 2010). PBCs are seen as being incomplete since they underline the *outcome* of the transaction rather than prescribing *how* (processes) to deliver it or which resources (inputs) to use. If performance is above the baseline it is possible to reward the supplier for the extra performance. Such examples have been reported in the healthcare sector, e.g. for quality of care and treatment outcome (Lindkvist, 1996; Lu *et al.*, 2003) but research into (and therefore knowledge of) such arrangements is scarce.

Service level agreements (SLAs) are widely used as ways of contracting when buying services. Compared with PBCs, SLAs place much more emphasis on specifying inputs and processes and not just outputs or outcomes. This is because of the difficulty of evaluating the quality of a service which is, by definition, characterized by being intangible. Note 2.3 provides an overview of this problem and the meaning of SLAs and the service issue is discussed in more detail in Chapter 9.

Note 2.3

The service specification and evaluation problem and service level agreements (SLAs)

Services are usually regarded as different from products especially because they are intangible. This creates a number of purchasing challenges.

Consider cleaning services: there is no physical product, only an invisible service being delivered. When specifying a physical product (part, component or material), purchasers can describe in detail what they require in terms of size, weight, technical performance and so on. The contract with the supplier will reflect these requirements so that when the product is delivered it is evaluated against hard physical evidence; it is possible to evaluate the quality of the product by touching it, visually analysing it and taking it apart if necessary. When buying cleaning services the same logic does not apply and the evaluation of the quality of the service is likely to be highly subjective depending on the evaluator's personal expectations and standards.

When buying services, therefore, it is useful to specify, contract and evaluate in terms of inputs, processes and outputs. So, continuing with the cleaning services examples:

- Inputs would include the resources to be used, for example, the people carrying out the service and the materials they should use.

- The process might include vacuuming, washing surfaces, polishing windows, dustings, etc.

- The output would include the expected level of cleanliness and could be tested, e.g. visually.

Service level agreements (SLAs) are often developed around this logic. Typically, they include:

- A basic contract: goal, date, period, parties

- A service definition

- Specifications:

  - Coverage and levels of service (number of working days, peak work-loads, availability, etc.)

  - Actual service: inputs and outputs

- Manpower and other resources available

- Reaction times

- Precision

- Availability, e.g. for problem solving

In recent years the fundamental difference between products and services have been questioned as there are increasingly examples of offerings that include both rather than one or the other. We discuss this issue in more depth in Chapter 9.

Source: see Axelsson and Wynstra (2002).

We might also question whether PBCs are compatible with the need to incorporate sustainability requirements into contracts. In purchasing theory this is still a very new challenge, but there is little doubt that companies need to find out how they can best include the various dimensions of sustainability in contracts as part of the purchasing process. Indeed, specifying resources and how processes should be carried out is important in order to avoid, for example, suppliers using non-sustainable natural resources, polluting production processes or exploiting labour.

Many companies have codes of conduct, for example, Preuss (2009) reported that 44 per cent of FTSE 100 companies have an ethical sourcing code. However, as will be discussed in

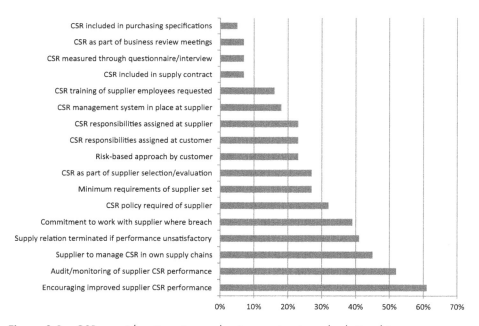

Figure 2.8 CSR considerations in purchasing contracts and relationships

Source: Adapted from Preuss (2009).

more depth in Chapter 13, it is still rare for the CSR or sustainability function to be part of the purchasing contract process: Preuss (2009) found that fewer than 10 per cent of FTSE100 companies included CSR in purchasing contracts. Figure 2.8 provides an overview of the inclusion of various aspects of CSR in purchasing contracts and supplier relationships of FTSE100 companies. Where more than 60 per cent of FTSE100 companies 'encourage' improved supplier CSR performance, fewer than 10 per cent actually included CSR in purchasing (supply) contracts.

Incorporating sustainability into purchasing contracts is complex. Companies will increasingly need to be aware of global regulations such as United nations (UN) conventions, Organisation for Economic Cooperation and Development (OECD) guidelines, international labour standards as set by the International Labour Organization (ILO) and the UN Global Compact, not least its universal declaration on human rights. We expand on issues of legislation, standards and codes of conduct in Chapter 13.

2.3.4 Ordering and expediting

Once a contract is arranged the ordering can take place. In some situations, such as a new-buy situation, the contract itself may constitute the order. In other situations, the contract provides the framework for frequent routine purchases, for example in a high-volume manufacturing operation.

Ordering increasingly takes place through electronic systems that help to automate the process and reduce transaction costs. Materials (or enterprise) resource planning systems (MRP, ERP) can automatically raise orders when the system detects a need. Whether or not the order is raised through an MRP or ERP system, the information should leave no room for ambiguity and should include, typically, an order number, a brief description of the product/service, unit price, number of units required/volume, and expected delivery time and address. Suppliers typically send an order confirmation to confirm the purchase order and its content and this can be automatically directed to the ERP. Chapter 7 discusses the use of different e-procurement methods for optimizing ordering and expediting.

Although theoretically the system should work smoothly, in practice it is often necessary for the buyer to check that the supplier has understood and delivered the order correctly. A buyer should also make sure that the supplier has not received conflicting instructions from other departments, as for example the instructions to a supplier from the company's purchasing department may differ from the instructions issued by the logistics or incoming goods department.

The role of expediting is to secure the quality and timely delivery of goods and components. In a manufacturing context, this involves monitoring the progress of manufacturing at the supplier in terms of quality, packaging, and conformity with standards and lead times. Thus the goal is to ensure that the required goods arrive at the appointed date in the agreed quality at the agreed location.

External or third-party expediters can help to keep track of the process. They can assume responsibility for inspection and notify the involved parties about progress and if any problems are detected. Expediting exists in several levels, e.g.:

- Production control: The expediter inspects to see if the production complies with the required standards.

- Quality control/assurance: The expediter checks to see if the goods (or components or materials) function as required and if they meet the required standards.

- Packaging/transport: The expediter checks that the goods are properly packaged and transported to avoid damage during delivery.

2.3.5 Evaluating

This final stage of the purchasing process concerns the evaluation after the expedition has taken place. This involves evaluation of the performance of the goods or services that have been delivered, and following up on problems. In line with the contract, penalties may have to be issued but in addition to negative action it may be at least as important to consider positive actions. Awards can be very effective in keeping suppliers motivated and in instilling a continuous improvement environment.

Best practice includes designing supplier (or vendor) rating systems, and giving scores for supplier performance. In addition, supplier audits can be conducted to scrutinize suppliers, including their processes, systems, standards, etc. Increasingly, companies need to conduct audits that specifically focus on sustainability. As shown in Figure 2.8, 52 per cent of FTSE100 companies audit or monitor their suppliers' CSR performance. This is in fact a requirement for membership of the Ethical Trading Initiative (ETI) which brings corporate, trade union and voluntary sector members together to improve employment issues that are difficult to address by individual companies.[5] As Preuss (2009) observes (see again Figure 2.8) 41 per cent of FTSE100 companies state that supplier relationships will be terminated if supplier CSR performance remains unsatisfactory, although 39 per cent modify this by indicating that they are committed to working with suppliers that are willing to improve. This reflects the standpoint of IKEA, as discussed earlier, which prefers not to terminate suppliers that do not meet IKEA's CSR requirements, instead opting to help non-complying suppliers to improve.

Walmart is another large company committed to responsible sourcing. A cornerstone of this is the continuous evaluation of suppliers to ensure that they comply with Walmart's standards and policies. These expectations are clearly communicated on Walmart's corporate website:[6]

> Through our Responsible Sourcing program, we set expectations of suppliers and the facilities they use, assess supply chain risk, monitor supply chain conditions through audits and investigations, provide training and tools for our associates and suppliers, and collaborate with others to make progress on key industry-wide issues.

Walmart relies on supplier audits to evaluate and verify social, safety and environmental compliance. The audits are planned according to the risk profile of the country in which a supplier facility is based. The level of risk is categorized into three levels based on data from the World Bank where the higher the risk, the more likely it is that the supplier is subjected to an audit. Audits are carried out through approved third-parties and result in a colour-coded facility ranking. Although Walmart seeks to help suppliers to rectify any problems, the company can also choose to terminate its business with suppliers at any point.

Walmart's approach to sustainable (or responsible) sourcing is by no means atypical. More and more companies across industries have launched similarly systematic programmes that are at the heart of their sourcing strategy and process. Increasingly, these programmes are communicated through online detailed reports that document the goals, targets and progress the company has made. It is now best practice to implement systematic responsible sourcing programmes and to document these in a transparent manner to the company's stakeholders. The end-of-chapter case study provides more details of how premium fashion company Hugo Boss manages this process and we take a closer look at supplier assessment and audits in Chapter 13.

INTEGRATING SUSTAINABILITY INTO SUPPLIER SELECTION AND EVALUATION CRITERIA AT HUGO BOSS

Hugo Boss was founded by Hugo Ferdinand Boss in the town of Metzingen in Germany in 1924 as a small clothing workshop. In the early days, the company produced a wide range of garments by hand including shirts and traditional German loden jackets. Controversially and well documented, the company also produced uniforms for the German army during the Weimar Republic and World War Two.[7] It was not until the 1950s that Hugo Boss really began to develop as a fashion company, producing its first men's suits in 1950. The Boss brand was created in 1970, which was subsequently registered in 1977. By 1985 Hugo Boss was listed on the German Stock Exchange and in later years the company began to diversify notably with production of eyewear, footwear and watches. The company also strengthened its sponsorships of 'premium' sports, such as motorsports and golf, and arts and launched its womenswear in the late 1990s.

Hugo Boss is now a global leader in the global apparel market, focusing on producing premium fashion and accessories for men, women and children. Still headquartered in Metzingen, Hugo Boss employs 13,798 employees with sales of €2.693 billion in 2016 (2016 Annual Report). Sales are truly global as collections are sold in 127 countries around the world in Hugo Boss retail stores and shops-in-shops in department stores as well as through their online store. The range includes Boss, Boss green, Boss Orange and Hugo that each caters for different customer segments.

As shown in Figure 2.9, the main production sites are located in Turkey, Germany (Metzingen), Poland and Italy. With around 4,000 employees, Izmir is the largest internal production facility, producing suits, sports jackets, trousers and shirts as well as women's outerwear. However, around 80 per cent of the production is outsourced to suppliers (or 'partners'). In Asia, China counts for 29 suppliers that are generally large operations (29,454 workers in 2017). Other significant sourcing countries include India, Vietnam, Sri Lanka, Indonesia and Bangladesh in Asia, and Turkey, Romania and Bulgaria in Eastern Europe. In Western Europe, Italy is a major sourcing country with 38 suppliers employing in total over 2,200 workers; many of these are located in Northern Italy around Lake Como.[8]

Hugo Boss prides itself on a dedication to quality, innovation and responsibility. These three priorities also shape the sustainability strategy. Hugo Boss allocates significant resources to managing the types of sustainability risks that have affected so many fashion and luxury companies in recent years. In fact, the fashion industry has been the target of much criticism over the years as well-known brands have been accused of sourcing from supplier operations that are 'sweat shops' and there have even been cases of slavery in the fashion supply chain. As one example, the company released an official statement regarding modern slavery and human trafficking (2017) prohibiting any kind of forced labour, including rejection of slavery and human trafficking, based on its Social Compliance policy derived from the Core Conventions of the ILO and the UN Universal Declaration of Human Rights.

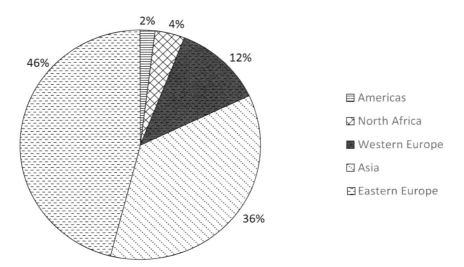

Figure 2.9 Hugo Boss global sourcing and production volumes (2016)

Source: Adapted from http://group.hugoboss.com/en/sustainability/partners/ (last accessed 26 July 2018).

Hugo Boss needs to ensure that its supplier selection process not only emphasizes operational performance, such as cost, quality and delivery, but also sustainability. This emphasis is evident in the supplier selection process from the collection of general information of suppliers through questionnaires, contracts that stipulate general purchasing terms and conditions (including social standards and restricted substances), and audits related to social issues, customs, financial status and country risk assessment. In its Sustainability Magazine (2016: 17), the company states:

> We rely on collaboration. We select our partners carefully, establish strategic partnerships and work together to achieve our goals. The basis for collaboration is the recognition of our values, our Code of Conduct and the Social Standards set out in this code. In this way, we obligate both ourselves and our suppliers to respect human rights, to protect the environment and to offer fair working conditions. To ensure adherence to these principles we conduct regular audits. We support those partners who do not meet our requirements to improve. However, where such efforts are not successful in the long term, the consequent result is to end collaboration. In order to enhance our commitment we work with the international organization Fair Labor Association and Germany's Partnership for Sustainable Textiles. Partnerships with local unions and non-governmental organizations are becoming increasingly important to us.

As a result of the company's commitment to sustainability, the following decisions have been made to ban exotic leathers, furs and angora wool, to use only sustainable down and to recycle materials, such as the use of padding made from recycled materials for all clothing lines and accessories. Table 2.2 gives an overview of key targets the company is currently working on.

CASE STUDY 2.1

Table 2.2 Hugo Boss key sustainability targets

Field of action	Goal	Date
Hugo Boss	• Implementation of concrete projects, based on priorities determined through materiality analysis • Integration of principle of sustainability within Hugo Boss Group • Implementation of group-wide and comprehensive stakeholder management strategy	Ongoing 2017 2020
Environment	• Increase environmentally friendly modes of transport (sea and rail) by 2% with simultaneous reduction in transport emissions of 4% • Implementation of sustainable store concept for construction, renovation and redesign of stores in all regions • Reduction of CO_2 emissions by 40% (base year 2016)	2018 2020 2025
Employees	• Continuous optimization of global employee retention • Expansion of employee survey to 80% of employees to improve employee satisfaction • Revision of global strategy on occupational health and safety with the goal of establishing a uniform, company-wide standard	2020 2020 2020
Partners	• Increase in transparency of social and environmental performance factors for the supply chain • Procurement of more than 90% of materials from suppliers who achieve a result of 'satisfactory' or better on social audits • All strategic suppliers must achieve GSCP level 1: They must be compliant with the law and make employees aware of environmental issues	Ongoing 2020 2020
Products	• Complete ban of farmed fur, including raccoon, fox and rex rabbit fur, in all collections starting in 2016 • Publication of binding commitment on use of sustainable cotton • Publication of binding commitment on use of sustainable leather • Market launch of an innovative, sustainable Hugo Boss product line	Ongoing 2017 2018 2018
Society	• Promotion of education at HUGO BOSS sites and along supply chain with goal of educating potential employees and strengthening society • Promotion of equal opportunities and support for disadvantaged children	Ongoing Ongoing

Source: Adapted from Hugo Boss Sustainability Magazine 2016. Available at: http://group.hugoboss.com/files/user_upload/Nachhaltigkeit/Nachhaltigkeitsbericht/Sustainability_Magazine_2016.pdf (last accessed 22 January 2018).

Hugo Boss is determined to tackle sustainability risks in its supply chain and a cornerstone in this endavour is to ensure a rigorous supplier selection process followed up by continuous supplier assessment and development that incorporate a wide range of sustainability standards.

CASE STUDY 2.1

2.4 Conclusion

This chapter introduced a framework for strategic sourcing which conceptualizes the purchasing process as part of the process of selecting, developing, managing and improving a high-performing and sustainable supply base. The framework highlights the importance of building up and maintaining a group of approved suppliers that constitute the company's long-term supply base. The chapter also explained a classic typology that identifies different purchase process situations: we distinguished between new purchases, modified re-purchases and straight repurchases. Generally, where new purchases require a full purchasing process, modified repurchases and, in particular, straight repurchases do not normally necessitate the first parts of the purchasing process, i.e. specifying, supplier selection and, in the case of straight repurchases, contracting. Increasingly, companies will manage the purchasing process as part of the wider sourcing process.

Chapter 2 evaluated the main stages of the purchasing process, including specification, supplier selection, contracting, ordering, expediting and evaluating. We described each stage and explored the implications of sustainability on each of these. For example, ways to incorporate sustainability criteria into the specification and supplier selection process were identified, and the need for contracts and supplier evaluation to include sustainability was discussed. However, few companies incorporate sustainability criteria into traditional specification and supplier selection criteria, instead treating sustainability as a separate process. What is more, it is still only a minority of companies that appear to incorporate sustainability and CSR issues into purchasing contracts. Although many companies 'encourage' improved supplier CSR performance, few actually include CSR in purchasing and supply contracts. This chapter provides guidelines for companies to begin this process.

Chapter 4 returns to sourcing issues by discussing different sourcing strategies and supplier relationship management. Before that we continue the book by examining purchasing strategy and organizational issues.

Notes

1 Figure 2.2 is inspired by a model used by Nokia Siemens Networks.
2 See the hyperlinks below for examples of sourcing reports focusing on sustainable (or responsible) sourcing: http://www.apple.com/supplierresponsibility/reports.html; http://www.danone.com/en/publications/; https://www.unilever.com/Images/slp-unilever-responsible-sourcing-policy-2014_tcm244-409819_en.pdf (all last accessed 22 October 2013).
3 Robinson *et al.* (1967) used a slightly different terminology: 'new-task situation', 'modified rebuy' and 'straight rebuy'. We use purchasing instead of buying as it is a more modern term better reflecting current practice.
4 This example is adapted from Mouzas and Furmston (2008: 44) and concerns a retail environment.
5 For ETI see http://www.ethicaltrade.org/ (last accessed 22 October 2013).
6 https://corporate.walmart.com/responsible-sourcing (last accessed 23 January 2018).
7 https://group.hugoboss.com/en/group/about-hugo-boss/history/ (last accessed 22 January 2018).
8 http://group.hugoboss.com/en/sustainability/partners/ (last accessed 22 January 2018). This website also links to a supplier disclosure list (2017) with business names and addresses.

References

Argyres N and Mayer KJ (2007) Contract design as a firm capability: An integration of learning and transaction cost perspectives. *Academy of Management Review* 32(4): 1060–1077.

Axelsson B and Wynstra JYF (2002) *Buying Business Services*. Chichester: Wiley.

Cooper R and Slagmulder R (1997) *Target Costing and Value Engineering*. New York: Productivity Press.

Karlsson C, Nellore R and Söderquist K (1998) Black box engineering: Redefining the role of product specifications. *Journal of Product Innovation Management* 15: 534–549.

Kim S, Cohen MA and Netessine S (2007) Performance contracting in after-sales service supply chains. *Management Science* 53(12): 1843–1858.

Lindkvist L (1996) Performance based compensation in health care – a Swedish experience. *Inquiry – Excellus Health Plan* 43(1): 34–53.

Lu M, Ma CA and Yuan L (2003) Risk selection and matching in performance-based contracting. *Health Economics* 12(5): 339–354.

Luo Y (2002) Contract, cooperation, and performance in international joint ventures. *Strategic Management Journal* 23(10): 903–919.

Milligan B and Carbone J (2000) Harley-Davidson win by getting suppliers on board. *Purchasing* 129(5): 52.

Mouzas S and Ford D (2012) Contracts as a facilitator of resource evolution. *Journal of Business Research* 65(9): 1251–1253.

Mouzas S and Furmston M (2008) From contract to umbrella agreement. *The Cambridge Law Journal* 67(1): 37–50.

Ng ICL and Nudurupati SS (2010) Outcome-based service contracts in the defence industry – mitigating the challenges. *Journal of Service Management* 21(5): 656–674.

Preuss L (2009) Ethical sourcing codes of large UK-based corporations: Prevalence, content, limitations. *Journal of Business Ethics* 88(4): 735–747.

Robinson PJ, Faris CW and Wind Y (1967) *Industrial Buying and Creative Marketing*. Boston: Allyn and Bacon.

Sako M (1992) *Prices, Quality and Trust: Inter-firm Relations in Britain and Japan*. Cambridge, UK: Cambridge University Press.

Tate WI, Ellram LM and Kirchoff JF (2010) Corporate social responsibility reports: A thematic analysis related to supply chain management. *Journal of Supply Chain Management* 46(19): 19–44.

Van Weele A (2010) *Purchasing and Supply Chain Management: Analysis, Strategy, Planning and Practice*. 5th edn, Harlow, UK: Thomson Learning.

CHAPTER 3

Purchasing strategy and organization

LEARNING OBJECTIVES

By the end of this chapter you should be able to:

- Understand the concepts of purchasing strategy and strategic purchasing;

- Analyse the stage of purchasing maturity within a company;

- Discuss the state of purchasing following the economic crisis that began in 2008;

- Identify different types or categories of purchase, including commodities and the sustainability challenges linked to buying of commodities;

- Analyse different organizational structures of the purchasing function and how these might need to be adapted to better address sustainability requirements;

- Identify skills and competence requirements for the development of the purchasing function including those that relate to sustainability;

- Evaluate the particular characteristics of public sector purchasing (public procurement), the complexities of public procurement and how it can be used as a lever for sustainable development.

3.0 Introduction

Research shows that purchasing and supply management can have a profound impact on a firm's financial performance (Ellram and Liu, 2002; Singhal and Hendricks, 2002). So, perhaps not surprisingly, more and more companies have realized that purchasing needs to be managed as a strategic function but what does that mean and how can you tell if purchasing is strategic within a given company? Does 'strategic' imply that the purchasing function is not only about ensuring the lowest possible costs of purchased inputs but also about other priorities? Can we measure how 'strategic' a purchasing function is and in what ways a focus on sustainability can be considered as part of this question? These are key questions examined in this chapter which begins with a discussion of the meaning and significance of strategic purchasing and how it relates to purchasing strategy. The concept of purchasing maturity is introduced as a way of evaluating how advanced (or strategic) purchasing is within a given company. The role of purchasing in the organization is also explored in the context of the global financial (and later economic) crisis that began in 2008.

Chapter 3 continues by identifying differences between different types of purchase, including those that relate to direct and indirect purchases. A brief discussion of category management is included with a focus on commodities that are known to provide sustainability challenges. Examples of commodities with significant sustainability challenges are provided including discussions of recent progress in these areas.

One key feature of a strategic purchasing function is how it is organized and the skills and competencies required of purchasing employees. Generally, there is a need for a wider set of skills of purchasing people so Chapter 3 examines the nature of these skills, how they can be developed and measured, and how they relate to overall corporate competency requirements. The challenge of incorporating sustainability skills into traditional purchasing organizations and the need for development of new purchasing skills and competencies is explored. The chapter finishes with an overview of the special challenges related to public sector procurement.

3.1 Purchasing strategy and strategic purchasing

Fundamentally, the term strategic purchasing suggests that purchasing is managed in a strategic way within a company. More specifically, it implies that purchasing contributes to, and aligns with, the overall corporate and business strategies of the company. In other words, when purchasing is strategic it reflects the priorities and goals of the company as a whole. These should be a result of the external environment, especially customer demand and stakeholder expectations, as well as internal resources and capabilities which provide the company with the ability to innovate. Figure 3.1 shows the logic of these fundamental drivers of strategy development and the logic of alignment of strategies at different levels within the

Figure 3.1 Strategic alignment of organizational objectives

company. The concept of strategic alignment is that strategies of different functions within a company, such as purchasing, logistics, marketing and operations, should be mutually supportive and aim for the same, or at least mutually consistent, objectives. All too often this is not the case in many companies where instead purchasing seems to have its own objectives independent of what the company seeks to achieve overall at corporate level.

Typically, in many companies the purchasing function aims for cost reduction as the overriding goal and this priority is evident in the performance measures against which the purchasing department and its employees are evaluated. In many ways the narrow focus on cost reduction is a historical feature of how the purchasing function is perceived: purchasing is seen as a function whose main performance objective is to reduce the costs of inputs purchased, thereby ignoring the potential for value creation through the purchasing function. Put differently, purchasing is seen purely as a function that can reduce the level of expenditure (often simply called 'spend'), and the potential for improving revenue through, for example, sourcing better quality or more sustainable materials is ignored.

The important point is that a focus on cost reduction, where cost is the dominant priority, can be strategic but only if the company identifies low cost as a strategic differentiator – a source of competitive advantage. Therefore, for companies competing on low cost, such as discount retailers (Lidl or Aldi), it would make strategic sense if purchasing emphasized low cost above everything else. For such companies it would therefore be strategic if sourcing strategy decisions, such as supplier selection criteria and the use of global sourcing, prioritized low cost. Furthermore, performance metrics such as Key Performance Indicators (also known as KPIs) used internally for evaluating purchasing staff performance and externally for evaluating supplier performance, should likewise be aligned with and therefore prioritize low cost. However, for companies competing on, for example, superior quality, innovation, sustainability, or perhaps a combination of those competitive priorities, it would not be strategic for purchasing to prioritize low cost at the expense of other priorities. Yet, low cost is sometimes disproportionately prioritized in companies whose corporate and business strategies are not about low cost differentiation. Consider for example the focus on cost reduction at the expense of (perceived) quality at Mercedes-Benz in the late 1990s which severely damaged the company's hard-earned reputation for superior quality and reliability. Unfortunately, such misalignment is all too common even in large companies and it means that purchasing does not contribute effectively to creating a sustainable competitive advantage for the company. Instead, decisions taken by purchasing may undermine what should be a clear strategic business profile.

In sum, the existence, and nature, of a company's purchasing strategy is a key ingredient of strategic purchasing so formulating a purchasing strategy is an essential step in making purchasing strategic. Purchasing maturity models, discussed in the following section, are used to identify the level of maturity or sophistication of purchasing within a company and to show the characteristics of different stages of maturity and to indicate ways to improve.

3.2 Purchasing maturity

When purchasing plays a strategic role within a company it reflects a high degree of purchasing maturity. Mature purchasing functions are visible and recognized at corporate levels and often exert real influence on strategic decisions within the company. But purchasing maturity is also characterized by a range of other factors and purchasing maturity models have evolved over the last 25 years or so to help to evaluate the stage of purchasing maturity within companies.

There have been many models of purchasing management maturity proposed in the past. The model of operations management sophistication developed by Hayes and Wheelwright (1984) clearly inspired the original purchasing maturity model proposed by Reck and Long (1988), which identified four stages: passive, independent, supportive and integrative. Table 3.1 shows the original Reck and Long (1988) model.

Table 3.1 Reck and Long's (1988) model of purchasing maturity

	Passive ➔	Independent ➔	Supportive ➔	Integrative
Nature of long-term planning	None	Commodity or procedural	Supportive of strategy	Integral part of strategy
Impetus for change	Management demands	Competitive parity	Competitive strategy	Integrative management
Career advancement	Limited	Possible	Probable	Unlimited
Evaluation based on	Complaints	Cost reduction and supplier performance	Competitive objectives	Strategic contribution
Organizational visibility	Low	Limited	Variable	High
Computer system focus	Repetitive tasks	Techniques and efficiency	Specific decision request	Needs of decision makers
Sources of new ideas	Trial and error	Current Purchasing Practices	Competitive strategy	Inter-functional informational exchange
Basis of resource availability	Limited	Arbitrary/affordable	Objectives	Strategic requirements
Basis of supplier evaluation	Price and easy availability	Least total cost	Competitive objectives	Strategic contributions
Attitude towards suppliers	Adversarial	Variable	Company resource	Mutual interdependence
Professional development focus	Deemed unnecessary	Current new practices	Elements of strategy	Cross-functional understanding
Overall characterization	Clerical function	Functional efficiency	Strategic facilitator	Strategic contributor

Source: Adapted from Reck and Long (1988).

Reck and Long's (1988) model identified a set of characteristics of four stages of maturity, including for example the focus in terms of short-term/long-term perspective, visibility and influence within the company, supplier relationships and supplier evaluation bases, information and communication, and purchasing skills. However, although the model is still used to determine purchasing maturity it is inevitably somewhat outdated as it was developed at a time when purchasing was only beginning to emerge as a serious discipline, several years before supply chain management came onto the scene. More modern maturity models have since been developed; these are generally based on the same logic as the original Reck and Long (1988) model, but include more features that characterize modern advanced purchasing functions.

Developed on the basis of a synthesis of existing maturity models, from the original to the latest models, we suggest a purchasing maturity model as illustrated in Table 3.2. Unlike the Reck and Long model, this model includes supply chain management features as they relate to purchasing and integrates sustainability maturity indicators. The model can be used as a starting point for diagnosing the level of purchasing maturity or sophistication in any company. Ticking each appropriate box provides an overall profile or score and the least mature areas are likely candidates for improvement towards a more mature purchasing function.

Maturity models can indicate the current state and potential areas of improvement. However, they are not designed to provide a detailed roadmap for improvement even if they provide inspiration for improvement. Maturity models do suggest that the process of making changes in purchasing is an incremental one, requiring gradual changes in structures, processes, people and inter- and intra-organizational relationships; jumping steps can be problematic (Reck and Long 1988).

Table 3.2 A purchasing and supply management (PSM) maturity model

	Clerical ➔	Developing ➔	Supportive ➔	Strategic contributor
PSM strategy	None	Emerging, informal	Formal strategy supportive of corporate strategy	PSM integral part of corporate strategy
Global sourcing	None or ad hoc international sourcing, only as needed	International (including LCC) sourcing developing	Global sourcing strategies integrated across worldwide locations	Global sourcing strategy integrated across worldwide locations and functional groups
Organizational visibility and influence	Low, viewed as a cost saving service function	Gaining (indirect) visibility	Direct visibility at senior level, but still limited real influence	Direct influence at senior strategic (board) level, CPO position
Data, communication and organization	Low level of spend information, basic ICT, decentralized organization	Improving information, change towards ICT, centralized organization	Cross-functional and ICT-enabled, hybrid organization	Full spend information, ICT-enabled, centre-led organization

Table 3.2 continued

	Clerical →	Developing →	Supportive →	Strategic contributor
KPIs	Price savings	Small set of easy-to-measure KPIs	A range of KPIs aligned with PSM strategy	A range of KPIs aligned with PSM strategy, including soft behavioural factors
Skills training and development	Minimal, low level, tactical	Current popular best practice	Cross-functional	Cross-functional, leadership, change management
Basis of supplier selection and evaluation	Price and availability	Change towards TCO, but ultimately cost-driven	Multiple weighted criteria	Multiple weighted criteria aligned with PSM strategy
Supplier involvement in NPD	None, suppliers approached during prototyping	Attempts at early involvement, i.e. during early design and development planning	Close early involvement of key suppliers, some even during concept development	Close early involvement of key suppliers, including between NPD projects
Supplier development	None	External accreditation, reactive problem solving	Systematic vertical supplier development, e.g. supplier assistance, training, one-way approach	Systematic development extending beyond direct suppliers, horizontal supplier collaboration, two-way mutual improvement approach
Supplier relationships	Mostly adversarial	Emerging partnerships	High proportion of partnerships, SRM	A portfolio of appropriate varied relationships, SRM
Sustainability Strategy	No consideration	Partial and emerging	Integrated sustainability and PSM strategy.	Integrated sustainability and PSM strategy.
Sustainability implementation	None or limited	Some initiatives to avoid negative exposure	Ethical supply chain evaluation, e.g. CO_2 supply chain measurement, company audits. Mostly direct suppliers focused.	Ethical supply chain evaluation, e.g. CO_2 measurement and audits but also supplier development. NGO involvement. Extends to indirect suppliers
Sustainability reporting	None	Ad hoc mention of, e.g. sustainability policy or code of conduct	Some disclosure including online reports. Still elements of 'green washing'	Fully transparent reporting including online reports and video clips from supplier factories. Honest self-assessment
Overall score				

Source: © Johnsen *et al.* (2013).

3.3 The role of purchasing in the organization

As purchasing functions mature they rise within the ranks of the organization. Where purchasing in many companies used to have limited visibility and influence in organizations, being placed at a low level within the organizational hierarchy, purchasing has climbed to the top of the table within many organizations that understand the need for a mature high-performance purchasing function.

The title of Chief Purchasing Officer (CPO) – also sometimes called Chief Procurement Officer – signifies a rise in the status and influence of senior purchasing directors. CPOs may have various formal job titles, such as 'General Manager' or 'Purchasing Director', although these titles seem to be decreasing and the 'Vice-President' (of Purchasing, Procurement or Sourcing) title has been found to be increasingly popular at least in North America (Johnson and Leenders, 2011). If a company, therefore, has a Vice-President of Purchasing, or a similar position, it indicates that purchasing is seen as an important contributor to overall corporate performance within the company. Nevertheless, not all companies have CPO positions and a CPO position does not always mean that purchasing necessarily exerts a great deal of influence at a strategic level in reality.

In general, purchasing's visibility and influence depend on a number of factors such as purchasing's share in the end-product's cost price and the extent to which the company is dependent on its supply chain. Put simply, where purchased inputs represent high cost and risk for a company, thus potentially having a strong impact on the bottom line, purchasing is more likely to be viewed as important by senior management. Therefore, purchasing is more likely to have a presence at senior management level.

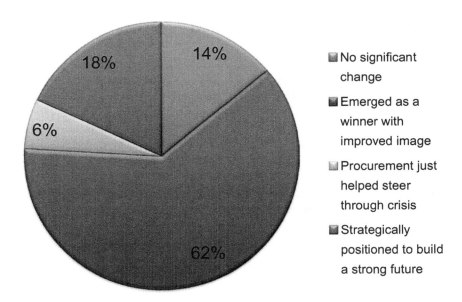

Figure 3.2 Position of procurement after managing the crisis

Sources: Capgemini Consulting (2010); Chief Procurement Officer Survey (2010: 14).

The global economic recession of the late 2000s was widely seen as pushing purchasing to the forefront of many companies. Companies realized that in order to save costs, they needed to focus on their purchasing. Interestingly, various surveys showed that purchasing employees felt that the recession presented an opportunity for purchasing to gain visibility within organizations. For example, a survey by Capgemini Consulting in 2010 (see Figure 3.2) reported that of over 150 CPOs and senior supply chain leaders from around the world, 62 per cent believed that the procurement function has emerged from the global economic downturn as a winner, with a better profile within their organizations. Another sign of the raised profile of the procurement function was the fact that nearly 70 per cent said that the purchasing function reported directly into the boardroom and 25 per cent said that procurement now reported directly to the Chief Executive Officer (CEO). A 2016 survey by the Chartered Institute for Procurement and Supply (CIPS) supports this picture, finding that 71 per cent of procurement professionals stated that procurement is very much valued within their organization, with 66 per cent believing that perceptions of procurement had improved over the last year.

3.4 Managing different purchase categories

Companies buy a vast array of very different things. For a manufacturing company many of these are materials in various forms that enter the production, or value creation, process and are transformed into products. These are known as direct materials and include raw or semi-manufactured materials/ingredients and components. In addition, companies buy various indirect materials that do not enter the production/value creation process but enable this to function, such as maintenance, repair and operating materials (known as MRO items: office equipment, spare parts and so on). Closely related to MRO items is capital equipment (known as CAPEX: factories, office buildings and so on) that similarly enables the company to function.

As direct materials enter the production process for a company's products that are to be marketed to its customers they can be viewed as particularly important. If the company buys components of poor quality or with dangerous ingredients the effect on sales and company image are likely to be immediate and significant. However, indirect materials also play a vital part in purchasing and, notably in the case of CAPEX, represent major company investments. In fact, CAPEX items, being major investment goods, are often not controlled by purchasing and supply management but instead by finance departments. Where direct materials are part of the company's value creation process, indirect materials actually lose value over time so represent a different management challenge. Although purchasing has not traditionally been involved in CAPEX buying this has changed in many companies so that purchasing can influence or control the process.

For non-manufacturing companies and organizations purchasing relates particularly to indirect materials. For service organizations, such as financial services/banks or hotels and restaurants, the customer perception of the physical premises plays a key part in customer perceptions of quality and value. 'Pure' service organizations, such as management consultancies, effectively buy no direct materials whereas, for example, a restaurant relies on both direct and indirect materials (represented respectively by, e.g. food ingredients and furniture). Another example is retail companies where a very large proportion of purchase items is finished products, bought from manufacturers (branded or own label) and sold on to consumers in unchanged form. Retailers likewise, however, also rely greatly on the purchasing of CAPEX: shop buildings, warehouses, technical/computer systems, etc.

Regardless of whether companies are defined as manufacturers or service providers, they need to buy a range of services in order to function. In fact, more and more companies have outsourced services as these are viewed as non-core activities (see Chapter 5). This trend implies that service purchasing is becoming increasingly important yet in many companies services such as employee travel are not within the remit of purchasing, being managed by finance or administration. As service purchasing is associated with many specific challenges this is often a source of poorly managed expenditure (and thus an opportunity for saving).

The different purchase items briefly outlined above each come with specific knowledge, skills and management challenges. They represent totally different levels of cost, value and risk and when companies look to organizing their purchasing department, division into different categories is a logical first step. Nevertheless, purchasing category management, and category sourcing, is actually a relatively new practice, spurred on by the outsourcing trend of a host of widely different business functions, and is set to become increasingly important especially for large companies with a wide portfolio of very different purchase items.

Trautmann *et al.* (2009) define a category as encompassing a group of similar items that are required for specific business activities of the firm. They suggest that different categories require different information processing capacities and different organizational designs. Clearly, buying raw materials from commodity markets is entirely different from buying high-tech components, which is again completely different from buying CAPEX and logistics services.

From a sustainability perspective, food commodities, such as coffee beans, soya or palm oil, are often sourced from developing countries and although they are traditionally highly price-focused they are also the very cases that require supply market monitoring and engagement with local communities (see Note 3.1). Similarly, sourcing of wood (timber) for paper and pulp or furniture poses particular challenges. However, this is not limited to sourcing from developing countries: fish is an example of a diminishing natural resource where buyers need to be highly focused on the sustainability of fish stocks. To put the challenge into perspective the World Wide Fund for Nature (WWF) estimates that:[1]

- 75 per cent of global fisheries are fished at or beyond capacity – ever-growing consumption will accelerate this.

- Aquaculture has grown nearly 10 per cent per year over the past 30 years and now represents more than half of the seafood consumed.

- Cotton is the largest money-making non-food crop produced in the world.

- The annual turnover of timber and other wood products from forests is valued at more than US$200 billion.

- The annual rate of natural forest loss is about 13 million hectares.

- Bio-fuel production could increase by 50 per cent the amount of land under agriculture or 'monoculture' forest plantations by 2050.

Note 3.1

Buying commodities: responsible soya sourcing campaign by WWF and RTRS

The soya (or soy in US English) bean provides three main products: soya oil (for human consumption and bio-fuel), soya beans for human consumption and soya meal for animal feed. A large proportion of soya bean crops is grown for oil production, and high-protein defatted and 'toasted' soya meal is extensively used as livestock feed. Of the world's soya bean crop, 80–85 per cent is processed into soya bean meal and vegetable oil and soya beans are the second-most valuable agricultural export in the United States behind corn. A smaller percentage of soya beans is used for human consumption; in Asia the bean and products made from it are a popular part of the diet, for example, the Chinese tofu and Japanese miso, and vegetarians substitute meat for soya for its protein content.

However, there are several negative implications of soya production. The threats include:

- forest clearing;

- loss of biodiversity, pollution;

- disregard for community and indigenous rights, and displacement of small-holder subsistence crops;

- it is capital-intensive and large-scale.

As a result of these threats, public pressure in the UK began to grow on UK supermarkets to improve their soya sourcing policies. Liz Callegari, Campaigns Manager at WWF-UK explained:

> We called up the seven big supermarkets a few months in advance to tell them we were launching a campaign and we'd like to meet with them – to get them up to date on the issues, and to listen to their concerns. ... When a business hears they're going to be the target of a campaign, they're usually keen to meet. (WWF, 2012: 18)

The campaign focused on Brazil's Cerrado: a large expanse of savannah and woodland, which is home to 5 per cent of all life on earth, and locks up large amounts of carbon. Worryingly, in the last few decades, half the Cerrado has been lost to agriculture – and soya production is one of the main causes. The majority of UK soya sourcing is from South America and with increasing demand for soya the pressure on vital ecosystems like the Cerrado is critical. The 'Save the Cerrado' campaign brought the issue to public attention. Producing a short film about the Cerrado (see: http://vimeo.com/23203701 – last accessed 22 October 2013) and its wildlife, as well as a report, an organized press trip to the Cerrado and a business webinar ensured the supermarkets' attention.

WWF aims to reduce the negative social and environmental impacts of soya production by supporting the Round Table on Responsible Soya (RTRS: http://www.responsiblesoy.org/ – last accessed 22 October 2013), a certification scheme that ensures soya production meets strict criteria designed to benefit people and nature. RTRS guidelines for responsible soya production include requirements that farmers respect the rights of local communities, treat workers fairly, and do not expand on native forest or other land that is valuable for conservation. Shortly before the first RTRS certified soya entered the marketplace in June 2011, campaigners, at WWF's urging, sent nearly 30,000 emails to the UK's seven leading supermarkets, asking them to commit to using 100 per cent RTRS soya by 2015.

The UK supermarket Waitrose was first to commit to WWF's campaign and the RTRS targets. Other supermarkets soon followed. Others have made encouraging time-bound commitments to sourcing responsible soya – and WWF expect RTRS will play a major role in these commitments which has forced the supermarkets to examine their soya supply chains. WWF-UK constantly reports on progress by publishing updates on its website. 'It's vital these commitments lead to concrete action', says Liz Callegari. 'We'll be watching and following up, and offering guidance and support when needed to make sure they do.' (WWF, 2012: 19)

Only one year after the introduction of RTRS-certified soya, in May 2012, nearly 150,000 hectares of soya plantations have been certified. A leader in the sustainable sourcing of soya, Waitrose says: 'Producers aren't going to pursue RTRS certification until they know people want to buy it', says Quentin Clark, responsible for sustainable sourcing at Waitrose. 'One hundred per cent RTRS soya by 2015 is a challenging commitment, but we and our customers need to be confident that Waitrose is part of the solution, not the problem. By aligning ourselves with WWF on this issue, we know we are.' (WWF, 2012: 19)

Source: WWF (2012)

The issue of commodity buying and sustainability is a topic we return to in Part C of this book. Overall, category management is a very different yet complementary way of managing different purchase items from the portfolio management approach, which will be discussed in Chapter 4. Identification of different product- or service-based categories is often required before any other classification takes place but we would advise that the two ways are considered in tandem.

3.5 Purchasing organizational design

The organizational design of the purchasing department sets the structure and therefore the framework for purchasing strategy and the processes that take place within the department. Organizational design therefore plays an important part in implementing purchasing strategy and decisions. As discussed in the previous section, if purchasing has a position at senior management level within the company it is directly visible at that level and can influence corporate decision making.

There are many ways of designing organizations, including individual functions such as purchasing. Fundamentally, as suggested by contingency theory, organizational design should be appropriate to the particular contingency, or context, of the company. In his *Images of Organization* (1986) Morgan suggested that organizations adapt to the environmental context and as these differ for different companies there is no one best way of organizing. Seeking the most appropriate fit between the circumstances and the company is critical – it is a case of 'horses for courses' (Bowen *et al.*, 2001).

Historically, many large companies used to be structured into multi-layered hierarchies with clear functional departments, such as Production (or Operations), Marketing, Finance, Human Resources (or Personnel) and so on. In fact, traditionally Purchasing would not constitute a separate department but would fit underneath another department, typically Production or Finance. Hierarchical structures imply a high degree of centralization and strong departmental boundaries with clearly defined responsibilities and decision-making processes. But, where organizational designs with fixed, or sometimes rigid, structures used to be seen as appropriate for stable slow-changing environments, much more fluid and dynamic organizational designs are now required for companies to keep up with the constant market and industry changes and increasingly disruptive innovations that can make companies obsolete overnight (Christensen, 1997). Consequently, many companies have made major changes in purchasing (and supply chain) frameworks and the trend is away from simple structures towards more complex hybrid ones.

Developing sustainable purchasing further adds to the need for complex hybrid organizational structures. In many companies the corporate social responsibility (CSR) or sustainability function exists as a separate department disconnected from purchasing (or supply chain management). In fact, both departments may work on similar issues but the structural separation makes it hard to fully integrate sustainability and purchasing. Some companies have developed innovative organizational forms to cope with this challenge and we explore examples of interesting solutions at the end of this section.

3.5.1 Centralization or decentralization?

The fundamental question for organizational design of purchasing is whether to opt for a high degree of centralization or to pursue decentralization. This is a particularly important question for large companies that operate on an international level and that are therefore likely to have multiple business units such as manufacturing plants and subsidiaries worldwide. Where centralization is about global coordination, integration and synergy across dispersed organizational units, decentralization implies flexibility and adaptability to local conditions. Figure 3.3 and 3.4 opposite illustrate how centralized and decentralized purchasing organizational structures might look.

Decentralized purchasing has many advantages. When purchasing decisions are delegated to individual business units it is possible for these to take advantage of local knowledge of supply market conditions and adapt to these. For example, it can be much easier for a local factory to source local material from local suppliers, taking advantage of local opportunities. Financially, sourcing locally may reduce transaction costs and, from a sustainability perspective, local sourcing can reduce environmental impacts. Organizations that have a large portfolio of different purchase categories are often reluctant to be dictated to by central purchasing

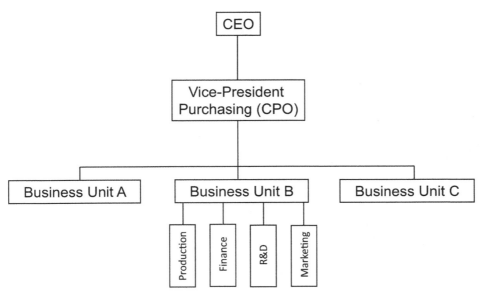

Figure 3.3 Centralized purchasing organization structure

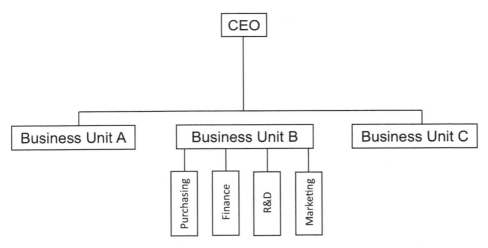

Figure 3.4 Decentralized purchasing organization structure

management as they believe that they can obtain better deals themselves as they have superior local supply market knowledge. This is often the case in public sector organizations that are naturally decentralized. For example, the UK National Health Service (NHS) consists of a great number of sub-organizations across the UK, including, for example, hospitals, which are managed by local trusts, doctors' surgeries and specialist clinics and centres. Traditionally, many purchasing decisions have been left to the local units and recent initiatives to impose a central purchasing catalogue have met with much resistance (although this has also resulted in substantial savings – see Note 7.1). However, a decentralized organization can easily result in a spirit of competition for resources between units instead of collaboration and synergy.

Achieving synergy across multiple business units is key to centralizing the purchasing organization. Purchasing synergy can be defined as the increase in performance (efficiencies and effectiveness) resulting from the joining of forces, information, knowledge, and/or the sharing of functional resources of two or more purchasing units (Rozemeijer, 2000). Bundling expenditures and suppliers can result in better deals through increased economies of scale and scope (Englyst *et al.*, 2008).

Building on Goold and Campbell (2000) and Rozemeijer (2000) we identify the following forms of synergy that can be achieved through centralization of purchasing:

1 *Pooled negotiation power*: gaining leverage over suppliers by joint buying, reducing the cost and/or improving the quality of the goods purchased. In other words, economies of scale (lower unit costs) can be achieved by increasing market power through volume bundling and standardization of categories (Trautmann *et al.*, 2009). Raw materials, components and MRO items are often pooled to benefit from synergies. Companies can obtain lower prices by combining orders to a common supplier so as to take advantage of quantity discounts (Arnold, 1997; Tella and Virolainen, 2005). Pooling can also include cooperation with competitors or other companies. In the public sector so-called collaborative procurement initiatives (or collaborative procurement hubs) have become popular ways to pool the purchasing power of for example hospitals that belong to the same overall national healthcare service (Bakker *et al.*, 2008). Similarly, the concept of consortium purchasing or purchasing consortia is often used by industrial companies.

2 *Shared resources*: benefits from economies of scale and elimination of duplicated efforts by pooling corporate purchasing employees, purchasing information and communication systems, corporate management group (overheads), and/or office space and other facilities.

3 *Shared knowledge*: perhaps even more important than shared resources are the benefits associated with the sharing of intangible resources, that is, knowledge and competencies. Examples of knowledge to be shared include purchasing strategies and policies, purchasing tools, techniques and best practices, purchasing skills and competencies, supplier or supply market knowledge. Also, so-called 'economies of process', i.e. establishment of a common way of working, can create a globally consistent line of conduct to suppliers, benchmarking procedures and results, and joint training and development (Faes *et al.*, 2000). From a sustainability perspective such benefits are of particular importance as, for example, sharing of sustainability policies, contracts and codes of conduct needs to be across organizations in order to have serious impact. Furthermore, shared and standardized product specifications are very important drivers of economies of scale, especially in capital-intensive industries such as the automotive industry. Companies can also reduce administration and transaction costs, for example, as negotiations are handled by one central unit instead of many decentralized units (Essig, 2000).

4 *Coordinated strategies and policies*: benefits from aligning strategies of two or more businesses, e.g. reduced internal competition for the same resources. As explained above, alignment of strategies and policies is of particular importance to implementing

sustainable purchasing as companies are under pressure to ensure a corporate coherent (Rozemeijer *et al.*, 2003) approach to managing their supplier relationships.

5 *Vertical integration*: benefits from the ability to reduce inventory costs, improve market access and increase capacity utilization through improved supply chain management.

6 Combined new business creation: benefits that stem from the creation of new businesses by combining know-how from different units, by extracting activities from different units to put into a new unit, and by internal joint ventures or alliances between units.

Many organizations have achieved significant savings and value creation through consolidation of fragmented purchases. As discussed in Chapter 2, it makes sense to standardize product components and parts as much as possible, avoiding unnecessary use of different parts where the same parts can be used instead, allowing purchasing to obtain economies of scale. Note 3.2 exemplifies an initiative to consolidate purchasing through joint purchasing, implementation of collaborative procurement hubs, lead forces and e-procurement.

Note 3.2

Procurement consolidation by the UK police

The UK police buy a great variety of things including for example: forensic services, aircraft, uniforms, medical services, stationery, catering, IT systems, dog food, insignia and salvage services. At the beginning of the new millennium the UK police realized that as each of the 55 regional forces had its own procurement unit there were 55 different procurement units each with different finance and purchase ordering systems and reporting structures. As a result the police found that procurement was reduced to an administration activity, information about spend was lacking and maverick buying was widespread. Moreover, procurement had little leverage over suppliers and limited scope for economies of scale. As an example, there were no standard specifications for police uniforms so 48 styles of uniforms on 11 different types of cloth purchased around the country. Even with some different regional needs (for example to cater for different climates in the north and south) this was not sustainable.

Realizing that there was much room for improvement, the police force created a national strategy for procurement, creating centres of excellence and lead forces that would show other regional forces the best ways forward. Collaborative procurement was also initiated and by 2012, 13 police forces in the UK were using a National Police Procurement Hub: an e-procurement platform that provides a portal to a range of approved goods and services online from over 900 suppliers. The Hub is expected to save the police service £69m over a six-year period by supporting collaboration across multiple forces and reducing the cost of purchases through their joint buying power and managing suppliers better. Lee Tribe, director of procurement for the Metropolitan Police, said:

The benefits for our suppliers in automating the ordering process will enable them to avoid re-keying Met orders into their sales systems and speed up the end to end process. Users within Met have access to a greater variety of products and services and faster delivery times.

Sources: Hastings and Harland (2003)

The potential benefits of a centralized purchasing organization that stem from improved synergies are significant. However, in reality synergies are difficult to achieve. For example, it took PepsiCo's Corporate Purchasing Group more than a year to agree to jointly purchase toilet paper for their restaurants Taco Bell, Pizza Hut and KFC, and to save several hundred thousand dollars per year (Collins and Montgomery, 1998). Often, the theoretical benefits are difficult to implement in practice, not least because of internal resistance to comply with centrally determined decisions. US pharmaceutical and healthcare company Wyeth (now part of Pfizer) explored the option of group purchasing in 2007 but ultimately rejected the idea. As the senior director for strategic sourcing, Paul Bestford pointed out: 'There is a huge complexity in aligning non-production specifications internally, let alone with other companies' (Martindale, 2008). Furthermore, centralizing decision making means taking away decisions from local purchasing teams or individual buyers who used to enjoy a free hand, for example, when it comes to supplier selection or contract negotiation. As Joseph Raudabaugh, President of AT Kearney Procurement Solution, says:

The real challenge if I'm a category manager is that I'm not sure I want to go and convince my internal stakeholders that we're switching and now they have to work with a third party. They either lack the self-confidence or the stature to effect it in their organization or they don't want to go to the effort.

(Martindale, 2008)

The UK NHS has shifted towards a purchasing structure that relies greatly on regional collaborative procurement hubs. Ray Searles, director of procurement at the UK-based North West Collaborative Procurement Hub, which represents 52 NHS trusts, including hospitals and ambulance services, describes how individual members even compete to 'beat the hub' in their own dealings with suppliers: 'The benefits in terms of time and in taking to the market a much bigger spend are obvious, but that doesn't stop people pushing against it when they feel their authority is threatened' (Martindale, 2008).

Due to the many problems of centralized purchasing, several organizations have moved towards decentralization or a mixture of the two extremes: hybrid organizations that combine the best of both worlds: centre-led purchasing in which corporate purchasing sets strategies and policies centrally but leaves operational day-to-day decisions to the local level. Typically, centre-led purchasing is organized around the following:

- A central organization handling all purchases with a single upward reporting structure

- A mixture of centralized and decentralized organization with responsibilities split by function or category

- A decentralized organization with a centralized coordinating function, e.g. a network of 'lead buyers' reporting to different geographic regions or business units, yet managing categories on behalf of the company as a whole

We explained earlier that the right choice of purchasing organization structure depends on the circumstances: it is a question of horses for courses (Bowen *et al.*, 2001). Often, the choice of purchasing organizational structure depends on two factors (Rozemeijer *et al.*, 2003): purchasing maturity and corporate coherence (see Figure 3.5). Indeed, as purchasing functions mature the trend is for companies to move away from pure centralized or decentralized models towards hybrid or, ultimately, a centre-led model that combines the best of both worlds. In cases of low purchasing maturity and low corporate coherence, decentralized purchasing is most likely to be found as central coordination efforts are difficult to achieve. At the opposite end of the scale, where purchasing maturity and corporate coherence are high, a centre-led structure is appropriate. Federal (or local-led) purchasing is often found in mature purchasing functions but clearly reflects low corporate coherence. In this situation corporate purchasing staff support autonomous decentralized purchasing units in their voluntary efforts to exploit potential synergies (Rozemeijer *et al.*, 2003). In situations of medium purchasing maturity and corporate coherence, hybrid structures can be found that combine centralization and decentralization and use voluntary purchasing coordination.

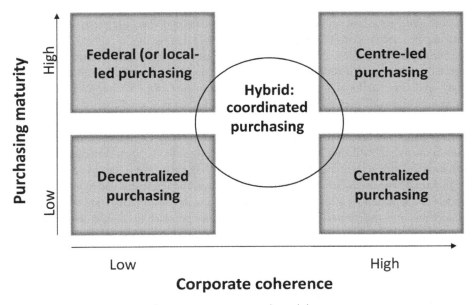

Figure 3.5 Corporate purchasing organizational models

Source: Adapted from Rozemeijer *et al.* (2003).

Table 3.3 Team usage changes 2003–2011

Team usage	2011	2003
Cross-functional teams	4.08	3.93
Commodity teams	3.60	3.57
Purchasing councils	3.00	2.83
Teams with suppliers	2.95	2.87
Co-location of purchasing personnel with user	2.69	2.64
Supplier councils (primarily key suppliers)	2.33	2.11
Teams with external customers	2.02	1.96
Consortium buying (pooling with other firms)	1.79	1.83
Teams with suppliers and external customers	1.79	1.65

Source: Adapted from Johnson and Leenders (2011).

One way to implement hybrid and centre-led purchasing structures is to use commodity teams (e.g. Trent, 2004). A commodity team is a centrally coordinated team that develops and implements company-wide strategies for a given commodity. In this context, the term commodity is not restricted to low-value or low-risk items, but merely indicates a basic standard, market or material homogeneity to enable pooling and negotiation across business units (Englyst *et al.*, 2008). Commodity teams are a coordination or pooling structure within a larger firm, typically multinational and consisting of a number of individual business units. They usually join purchasing professionals on a temporary project basis, for example, to establish and pursue cost-reduction strategies, to evaluate and select suppliers, and to support sourcing for selected items (Guinipero and Vogt, 1997).

Commodity teams provide a way to combine centralized and decentralized purchasing especially in large multinational/multidivisional companies. However, hybrid organizations imply split organizational responsibilities and companies often encounter problems, for example, to do with personal development and advancement opportunities. Commodity teamwork is time-consuming and removes buyers from what they will perceive as their primary responsibilities. To avoid problems of commodity-team commitment and motivation, goals, rewards and KPIs should be incorporated into commodity-team participation, aligned with each individual team member's career objectives (Englyst *et al.*, 2008).

The trend towards the use of various forms of coordination teams and hybrid centre-led models is supported by a longitudinal study by Johnson *et al.* (2014), showing a greater reliance on cross-functional teams, commodity teams, purchasing councils, and teams with suppliers (see Table 3.3). They note that team usage scores have increased over time, although with strong differences across sectors, placing more emphasis on effective team management.

In summary, there are a number of advantages and disadvantages of pure centralized and decentralized purchasing structures and these move companies towards hybrid and centre-led models as they mature and seek corporate coherence. Both of these factors, as discussed, are important from a sustainability perspective, not least to enable the implementation of globally consistent sustainability strategies and policies. Figure 3.6 summarizes the main

Less bureaucratic purchasing
procedures

Direct responsibility for profit centres

Fit with local requirements, local
suppliers

Local buyer motivation

Increased responsiveness to local
conditions

Reduced bargaining power due to
lack of economies of scale

Inconsistent strategies, policies and
codes of conduct across business
units

Limited synergy and knowledge
sharing

Duplication of efforts – waste

Figure 3.6 Advantages and disadvantages of decentralized purchasing

advantages and disadvantages of decentralized configurations. Generally, the opposite can be assumed for centralized purchasing.

3.5.2 Integrating purchasing and sustainability functions

The question of how to organize the purchasing function is now further complicated by the need to integrate purchasing decisions with the sustainability agenda. On the one hand, integrating the purchasing and sustainability functions is merely a matter of devising structures and processes for cross-functional collaboration. As discussed in Chapter 2 (see Note 2.1 – Harley-Davidson), purchasing needs to collaborate with research and development (R&D), or engineering, in order to ensure that new product development projects take sourcing issues into account. Similarly, a focus on supply chain management emphasizes collaboration between functions involved in the process of supply, not least the purchasing and the logistics departments. On the other hand, sustainability is not a traditional business function and may be regarded within companies as a bit of a stand-alone function with goals that do not, at least initially, seem compatible with a profit-seeking company. Indeed, the goals of a sustainability function, or department, may even be seen as conflicting by purchasing people who are usually under pressure to reduce cost and whose performance is often measured on cost savings.

The premise of this book is that sustainability is as much an opportunity as it is a risk to purchasing but it may require radical changes in the mindsets of purchasing staff to realize how they can embrace the sustainability challenge. Some companies have put in place 'sustainable purchasing directors' (or 'sourcing directors') to lead this development. For example, Danone has a 'Sustainable Sourcing Director' (see the Danone case study at the end of Chapter 4) and as the case study at the end of this chapter shows, Starbucks' position on 'Ethical Sourcing' has played a strong part in its turnaround strategy that began in 2008. The implications for new skills and competencies to address these challenges are discussed in the following section.

3.6 Purchasing skills and competencies

As purchasing has become more important in companies it is not surprising that the requirements for the skills and competencies of people working in purchasing have increased. We saw earlier in this chapter how maturity models show a progression of skills and competencies as purchasing functions become increasingly mature and sophisticated: for example, integrative and strategic purchasing functions require purchasing managers and directors to be able to collaborate with a range of other organizational functions, to provide clear leadership, and to act as change managers driving organization-wide changes in their efforts to implement change projects. Such projects require redefinition and reallocation of existing roles, training and development, recruitment, and, sometimes of course, firing of people who are not able or willing to change. As noted by the past Chartered Institute of Procurement and Supply (CIPS) CEO Simon Sperryn: 'No other profession has this breadth and depth ... it's crying out for talented people'.

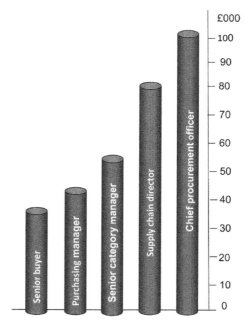

Figure 3.7 Procurement and supply salaries

Source: Adapted from the CIPS/Hays 2016 Survey.

The 'talent gap' appears to be very much alive. In a survey of 218 CPOs around the world conducted by Ardent Partners in 2011, 76 per cent of CPOs felt the skills of their purchasing staff either 'need improvement' (65 per cent) or display a 'significant gap' (11 per cent) (Supply Management, 2011b). According to the survey, CPOs rated a range of skills as below average: managing supplier performance, managing supplier risk, supply market knowledge, leveraging of technology to drive business value, cash management and business consulting skills.

Clearly, purchasing and supply managers will increasingly need to develop their skills and competencies on an ongoing basis. However, this is recognized by many companies that are willing to offer good salaries for top purchasing and supply people.

Figure 3.7 shows results from the CIPS/Hayes Salary Survey 2016. This annual survey, based on over 4,000 professionals globally, reflects very competitive and generally rising salary levels for procurement and supply management professionals. On average, salaries increased from £41,661 in 2015 to £44,226 in 2016 and this rise was almost twice as high compared with the national UK average. CIPS/Hays reported the highest salary increases at Contracts Officer, Supply Chain Executive, Procurement Analyst and Category Officer levels. Procurement Directors experienced average salary increases from around £89,000 in 2015 to around £95,000 in 2016. Overall, the salary trends are therefore on an upward trend reflecting a continued 'talent gap' as companies struggle to recruit people with the right skills and qualifications.

Developing and maintaining a wide skill set of 'soft' and 'hard' skills is also identified by Guinipero *et al.* (2006) as important for future purchasing and supply managers. Their research suggests that the following skills are likely to be important in future:

- Team building: leadership, decision making, influencing, compromising

- Strategic planning skills: project scoping, goal setting and execution

- Communication skills: presentation, public speaking, listening and writing

- Technical skills: web-enabled research and sourcing analysis

- Broader financial skills: cost accounting and making the business case

Current research shows that these skills remain as top priorities. In fact, the latest, including the CIPS/Hays survey discussed above, identify 'communication/soft skills' as the most important followed by 'negotiation', 'supplier relationship management', 'influencing' and 'sourcing'. These vary according to sector with 'negotiation' being relatively more important in the private sector and 'influencing' being more important in the not for profit sector.[2]

3.6.1 The challenge of integrating purchasing and sustainability skills and competencies

The need for purchasing people to acquire a wide range of skills and competencies has certainly not decreased with the need to embrace sustainability. Where purchasing people have traditionally had good commercial skills, sustainability presents new challenges and new mindsets. In particular, purchasing needs to interact with or even integrate with CSR functions. This is a difficult challenge as these two functions involve people who traditionally are likely to have belonged to two different worlds. Leadership, team building and communication skills are therefore critical to managing this new challenge. Furthermore, purchasing and supply management people will need to acquire new skills in learning about a host of environmental and social standards (see Chapter 13) as well as skills related to conducting ethical supplier audits.

This is also emerging in recent research (Schulze *et al.*, 2018), which suggests that beyond functional-oriented competence new competencies are required to deal with the sustainability challenges facing purchasing and supply management professionals. In particular, these include cognition-oriented competencies (e.g. systems thinking, and social-oriented competencies – cross-functional networking and stakeholder communication skills) and meta-oriented competencies (e.g. commitment to change and self-reflection).

As these skills are new to many purchasing and supply management professionals it is important to keep up with the development of these: to recruit new people with the right combination of skills and to reskill. There will be a need for companies to attract and recruit people with new skill sets and new perspectives. In-company training may be one option for companies to develop new skills, to develop understanding of the implications of sustainability on purchasing and supply management. Perhaps the most difficult challenge will be the changing of mindsets of traditional purchasing and supply employees who may perceive sustainability as a fad or something to which they simply have to pay lip service.

An increasing number of education and training providers, including universities, business schools, professional bodies, non-governmental organizations (NGOs) and management consultancies, offer courses on many aspects of purchasing and supply chain management and courses addressing the specific skills that are needed for managing sustainability are beginning to emerge. In fact, this is one of the key trends in education and training and indeed one to which the authors of this book aim to contribute.

3.6.2 Frameworks for evaluating purchasing skills and competencies

Educational bodies, including universities, business schools, professional bodies/institutes, management consultancies and training organizations, naturally have their own approaches to and frameworks for identifying sets of skills and competencies. Frameworks can be

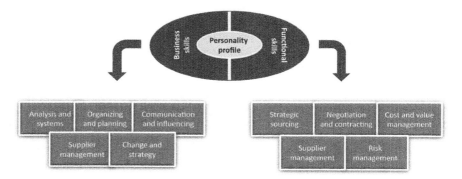

Figure 3.8 DILF's skills and competence assessment framework (Compass)

Source: The Danish Purchasing and Logistics Forum (DILF).

designed and used to identify gaps within organizations and areas of development. There are too many to show here but one is useful as a good example: the Danish Purchasing and Logistics Forum (DILF) uses a skills and competence assessment framework called Compass containing 100 detailed competencies grouped into ten clusters around two broad groups: Business Skills and Functional Skills. Functional skills include a range of 'harder' analytical skills, for example, supply market research, category strategic analysis, cost modelling, and price modelling, in addition to negotiation skills, contracting skills, etc. Business skills include 'softer' skills such as conceptual thinking, problem solving, developing procedures and policies, listening and communicating, presenting, team building, leading and recruiting, delegating, mentoring, coaching and so on. Interestingly, the DILF framework includes a set of risk management skills many of which relate directly to sustainable purchasing and supply management:

- Risk assessment

- Value at risk analysis

- Corporate social responsibility

- Ethical sourcing

- Supplier risk assessment

- Compliance management

- Policy implementation

- Regulatory compliance

- Inventory management

- Financial and commodity hedging

3.7 The special case of public procurement

Purchasing in the public sector, usually known as public procurement, is often treated as a special case. Throughout this book we use public sector examples but it is useful here to identify some of the particular characteristics and challenges of public procurement, especially those that concern sustainability. In fact, public procurement represents approximately 15 per cent of gross domestic product (GDP) in Organisation for Economic Cooperation and Development (OECD) countries and typically 25–30 per cent of GDP in developing countries (Roos, 2012) making government the single largest customer within many countries. Due to such high levels of spend, governments have realized that they can use their economic influence to drive changes towards growth, innovation and sustainability. Therefore, governments increasingly seek to deliver policy objectives through public procurement initiatives, for example, by investing in large-scale projects to create economic growth during the economic crisis. However, public procurement is a very complex process influenced by extensive regulation and political interests amongst stakeholders, as exemplified by Note 3.3.

Note 3.3

Public procurement troubles in the UK

In July 2011 the UK government announced that it would award the £3bn Thameslink contract to a consortium led by German manufacturer Siemens instead of Canadian train manufacturer Bombardier. Bombardier Transportation employed approximately 6,000 people in the UK but had already announced possible layoffs. Failing to win the contract for the Thameslink was seen as a major blow to the company's factory in Derby. The company blamed the government's decision to award the Thameslink contract to Siemens for laying off 446 permanent staff and 983 temporary workers.

The contract was part of a £6bn upgrade of the Bedford to Brighton Thameslink route. This would extend the service from 50 to 150 stations and almost double peak-time capacity on its central London section. Bombardier Transportation was the last remaining train manufacturer in the UK so awarding the contract to a non-UK manufacturer was highly unpopular, especially at a time when the government had proclaimed that manufacturing would carry the country out of recession.

The decision was greeted with anger by unions and politicians. Transport minister Theresa Villiers argued that the Siemens bid represented the best value for money for taxpayers and would benefit Thameslink passengers with modern, greener and more reliable trains. She also suggested that the contract would create up to 2,000 jobs in the UK by supporting train suppliers and contractors. Nevertheless this was a controversial decision: 'Philip Hammond, the Transport Secretary, and I recently wrote to the Prime Minister to highlight the issue of public procurement and how we should manage the process in the public sector to sustain a competitive supply base that meets the UK's strategic needs within EU procurement rules', said Vincent Cable, the UK Business Secretary. He went on to state that the government 'recognize that there is a need to examine the wider issue of whether the UK is making best use of the application of the EU procurement rules ... We can't reopen that whole [tender] process,' he said. 'What we can do is make sure that, in the future, public procurement operates not in a protectionist way – that's what we don't want – but in a way that value for money is assessed so that it helps British industry and British suppliers'.

Transport Secretary Philip Hammond pushed the responsibility on to the previous government stating that:

> It has fallen to us to announce the result of that competition but actually we had no ability to influence the outcome of that decision. The simple fact of the matter is, under the criteria that the previous Government set out in the contract, Siemens were the winner of that competition and under European procurement law we had no choice but to announce them as the preferred bidder.

Reactions from labour unions were predictably strong: Len McCluskey, general secretary of the Unite union, called for swift action to save Britain's last train manufacturer. 'The dire consequences of the Government's misguided decision to exclude Bombardier from the contract to build carriages for the Thameslink project is now becoming a reality', he said. 'It's a tragedy because these redundancies would have been needless if the Government really cared about British manufacturing and British skills.' Tye Nosakhere, GMB trade union regional officer, echoed this saying that 'This decision is the ultimate in stupidity. The Prime Minister has to call in this decision and start again. Losing 1,400 manufacturing jobs is a body blow for both Derby and the UK economy.'

Darren Barber, an electrician and union rep at Bombardier, said the disappointment among the workers on the site today was palpable. The 42-year-old father of three said: 'We could not believe we've been left in the wilderness. It's a massive blow.'

Sources: *The Times* 5 July 2011; *The Guardian* 3 July 2011

As a provider of services to the public, public sector bodies are service providers rather than manufacturers but they buy a wide range of goods, works and services from suppliers. One characteristic of public procurement is the preference for national suppliers as this means support of domestic companies and therefore the national economy. However, if all countries were to follow the same path there would be little scope for open competition amongst international suppliers and the users of public services (i.e. taxpayers) would be worse off, as comparative advantages would be ignored; this would consequently be inconsistent with government objectives of providing best value for money. Various international, regional and national legislation has been put in place to avoid protectionist behaviour by individual nations and to prescribe fair public procurement procedures. As a fundamental principle, public procurement decisions should not be influenced by national considerations but, as Note 3.3 illustrates, there are often national pressures to circumvent this principle.

3.7.1 European public procurement regulation

The regulations for public procurement within the European Union (EU), as developed by the European Commission (EC), govern EU member states. Many non-EU states are also affected by EC rules, for instance, where the same rules apply under trade agreements with the EC (e.g. Norway and Iceland under the Economic Area Agreement (EAA)) or where states are expected to follow at least the basic principles of EC procurement law under trade agreements. The EC's regime has also influenced the design of other regimes, such as the World Trade Organization's (WTO) Agreement on Government Procurement (GPA). Therefore, it is worth taking a closer look at EC public procurement regulations as an example of a public procurement regulatory regime (Arrowsmith, 2009).

EU member states have signed up to EU procurement law as laid down in the European directives of public procurement. The directives were introduced in the 1970s but have since undergone several revisions. Consistent with the EU principle of free movement of goods and people, the European directives work on the basis of non-discrimination due to nationality, equality, transparency and proportionality; contracts should not be awarded due to the nationality of the supplier. The European directives prescribe the procedures, with which companies must comply, making public procurement a rather complex and slow process.

The most important specific provisions of the EC Treaty for public procurement are Article 28 on free movement of goods and Article 49 on freedom to provide services. Only in exceptional circumstances can these provisions be circumvented, usually in cases of public security, such as defence procurement from national suppliers to ensure a national defence capability. Discriminatory procurement can be justified on the basis of environmental protection and improvement of working conditions although this remains a grey area. However, purely economic interests can never be used to justify restrictions on trade, and supporting jobs or employment in uncompetitive industries or developing infant industries also cannot be used as a justification (Arrowsmith, 2009: 256).

The EC directives on public procurement regulate the procedures for awarding major contracts and provide the means to enforce these. These procedures are based on the principle of transparency. The Public Sector Directive applies to all entities including state/government departments, local and regional authorities/municipal authorities and federal state governments, associations formed by public bodies and those bodies governed by public law. The first procurement directives focused on 'works' and 'supply' contracts. These have since been extended to encompass other situations. Two directives from 2004 are of particular importance:

1 Directive 2004/18/EC (Public Sector Directive): regulates most major contracts awarded by public bodies, replacing three previous directives (Works Directive 93/37), supply contracts (Supply Directive 93/36) and services contracts (Services Directive 92/50)

2 Directive 2004/17/EC (Utilities Directive): regulates procurement in four areas: water, energy, transport and postal services.

Table 3.4 Thresholds triggering EU-wide rules (2018–2020)

Public contracts directive (2014/24/EU)	Thresholds (excl. VAT)
Public works contracts	€5,548,000
Supply and service contracts and design contests (central government authorities)	€144,000
Supply and service contracts and design contests (sub-central contracting authorities)	€221,000
Works contracts (Utilities Directive 2014/25/EU)	€5,548,000
Supply and service contracts and design contests (Utilities Directive 2014/25/EU)	€443,000
Works contracts (Defence and Security Directive 2009/81/EC)	€5,548,000
Supply and service contracts (Defence and Security Directive 2009/81/EC)	€443,000
Concession contracts (Concessions Directive 2014/23/EU)	€5,548,000

Sources: https://europa.eu/youreurope/business/public-tenders/rules-procedures/index_en.htm; https://www.ojeu.eu/thresholds.aspx.

The directives apply only to contracts above certain financial thresholds revised every two years (see Table 3.4 for key thresholds).

Thresholds

In principle, the relevant value for determining the threshold is the value of each contract. The EC directives prohibit buyers from dividing contracts in order to bring the value of contracts below the threshold.

The so-called 'light touch' regime for social and other specific services raises the thresholds, for example, to €750,000 in the case of public works contracts. Further exclusions are, for example, contracts governed by different procedural rules connected with joint projects with non-member states, those by international bodies (e.g., the United Nations (UN) or World Bank (WB)) and defence contracts.

3.7.2 Public procurement award procedures

Public sector authorities must use one of five types of award procedures. As a general rule the first two of these, open and restricted, should be used; the others require special circumstances (Article 28). In brief, these are:

Open procedure

This is a formal tendering (bidding) procedure that requires: clear specifications as the basis for submission of bids; advertisement of the contract in the EU's Official Journal; allowing all interested firms to bid; and evaluation of bids without entering into significant negotiations. The directive specifies minimum time limits for the key phases to ensure suppliers have sufficient time to respond (at least 35 days to tender from the date of dispatch of the contract notice).

Restricted procedure

This is also a formal tendering procedure that again must be advertised in the EU's *Official Journal*. The main difference from the open procedure is that the public procurement authority can select a limited number to bid from those who express interest. The authority may invite a pre-stated number of firms to bid, although this should be at least five, and it should indicate which evaluation criteria will be used. Authorities must allow at least 37 days for firms to respond and 40 days to bid, although an accelerated version of the procedure (10 and 15 days respectively) is available for cases of urgency.

Competitive dialogue

The competitive dialogue procedure was introduced in 2004 to provide more flexibility in awarding complex contracts, especially for major infrastructure projects. It applies to situations where the procurement body is unable to define the technical, financial or legal aspects of the project, typically because the body does not have the required know-how. The competitive dialogue procedure requires: advertisement of the contract in the *Official Journal*; selection of a limited number of suppliers to participate (minimum three); a dialogue phase to determine proposed solutions; and a final tender stage.

Negotiated procedure with a contract notice

This is a relatively less structured competitive procedure, requiring advertisement of the contract in the EU's *Official Journal* and selected participating suppliers but procurement bodies may proceed to select the supplier simply through negotiations. The same award criteria as other procedures must be used, but the directives do not otherwise regulate the process for choosing the best offer. This can only be used in special cases including those where specifications cannot be drawn up with sufficient precision in order to enter formal tendering under the open or restricted procedures, where works are purely for research, experiment or development purposes, or in exceptional cases where overall pricing is not possible, e.g. because of the nature of the works or risks of performance. Examples of this procedure could be the restoration of historical buildings where limited experts are available.

Negotiated procedure without a notice

This variation of the negotiated procedure allows the authority simply to negotiate with a selected supplier to choose the best offer, without advertisement or competition. It is appropriate (see Article 31), for example, where the contracting authority did not receive any bids or the bids were unsuitable; for the purchase of a prototype; or where only one supplier is available for technical or artistic reasons or for reasons connected with exclusive rights (e.g. intellectual property rights). Other cases include extreme urgency due to unforeseeable circumstances, extra work being awarded to an existing contracting partner, or design content, e.g. to design a public building with an unusual architecture.

3.7.3 Framework agreements

The principle of open competition is core to EC public procurement regulation but recent regulation allows for long-term framework agreements, in recognition of the benefits of long-term partnerships that are widely used by private sector companies. Article 1(5) Directive 2004/18/EC defines a framework agreement as 'an agreement between one or more contracting authorities and one or more economic operators, the purpose of which is to establish the terms governing contracts to be awarded during a given period, in particular, with regard to price and, where appropriate, the quantity envisaged'. Framework agreements allow the central negotiation of a contract, while permitting devolved users to manage their spending (Caldwell *et al.*, 2005). Framework agreements are appropriate for repeat purchases, in particular when it is difficult to estimate the timing or quantity of requirements.

Framework agreements involve advertising the requirement and obtaining tenders, selecting a limited number of suppliers (or even a single supplier), and then placing orders on a periodic basis. This avoids the need for a wholly new tendering procedure for every new order. They do not constitute a special type of award procedure, but a variation of the directives' normal procedures.

3.7.4 Rules on specifications and contract award criteria

Article 23(8) prohibits buyers from referring to goods of a specific make or source, or to a particular process, or to trademarks, patents, types, origin or means of production, where this has the effect of favouring or eliminating certain firms or products. Public procurement bodies must define specifications in one of two ways (or a mixture of the two):

1 By reference to specified European or international standards (e.g. ISO), or if necessary national-level standards. The reference must be accompanied by the words 'or equivalent' and functional equivalents must be accepted.

2 By using performance or functional requirements: when standards do exist authorities can choose either these or performance or functional requirements. When standards do not exist, authorities must use performance or functional specifications.

Contracts must be awarded on either lowest price basis or the most economically advantageous (Article 53). The latter allows consideration of non-price as well as price criteria. In any case the permitted criteria must be linked to the subject matter of the contract. This means, in particular, that authorities cannot take account of social or environmental considerations unconnected with contract performance. The authority must disclose in the advertisement or contract documents the criteria to be used and their relative weighting.

3.7.5 Using public procurement as a lever for sustainable development

This section, 'The special case of public procurement', began by stating that EU member states increasingly use procurement to promote their own policy goals. This remains a controversial issue under the EC procurement regime but an international study of public procurement, documenting procurement changes across 13 countries, found that public procurement is moving towards a policy role enabling alignment of procurement policy with government policy, effectively engaging procurement as a lever of social reform (Harland *et al.*, 2004).

As illustrated in Figure 3.9, sustainable public procurement sits at the interface between sustainable development and public procurement and is a growing trend globally. A survey comparing sustainable procurement practices across 20 countries, found that buying from local suppliers, especially small and medium enterprises (SMEs), in ways that protect worker welfare was relatively common in all countries (Brammer and Walker, 2011). Analysis of country differences showed European practices focused on environmental aspects and US organizations focused on buying from minority-owned suppliers. Interestingly, they found UK practices to be more focused on buying from small local companies, with relatively little focus on environmental aspects (Walker and Brammer, 2009).

The focus on buying from small and local suppliers, not least in the UK, is at odds with public procurement regulation and could be seen to distort competition. Even more controversial is the way in which governments have been using public procurement to 'kick start' the economy following the economic recession that began in 2008. Aligning procurement strategy with government strategy is clearly a strategic positioning of procurement, progressing procurement from a transaction and cost-focused function to a strategic

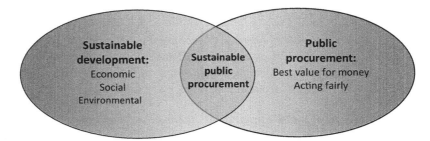

Figure 3.9 Sustainable public procurement at the crossroads of sustainable development and public procurement

Source: Adapted from Roos (2012).

contributor (see Figures 3.1 and 3.2) but careful attention must be paid to ensure public procurement regulations are respected.

Public procurement legislation has been continuously adapted worldwide to keep up with best practices and innovation. This is particularly the case in developing countries: recent publications of the OECD-DAC Task Force on Procurement demonstrate progress in strengthening national procurement systems by following a structured approach to procurement reform and capacity development.[3] The EU is increasingly focused on integration of environmental and social criteria into public procurement processes and has set ambitious targets for its member states. The EC public procurement strategy outlines six priorities:

1 To ensure the wider uptake of innovative, green and social procurement

2 To professionalize public buyers

3 To increase access to procurement markets

4 To improve transparency, integrity and data

5 To boost the digital transformation of procurement

6 To cooperate to procure together

In addition to the focus on sustainability, the latest EC public procurement strategy therefore also focuses on innovation in order to support public procurement of innovation. This is part of an ambition to dispense with the bureaucracy and risk avoidance culture that have traditionally hampered public procurement. The move towards public procurement of innovation addresses both the need for innovation in the process and outcomes of innovation. This implies, for example, that public buyers are encouraged to become involved in the research and development of products or services that do not yet exist and to facilitate the success of start-up companies.[4]

Australia, US and Japan use similar frameworks and initiatives are spreading to other major emerging economies such as Mexico, Argentina, Brazil and some developing countries (Roos, 2012). Note 3.4 lists some international initiatives promoting sustainable public procurement.

Note 3.4

Some international initiatives promoting sustainable public procurement

European Commission: Buying Green and Buying Social initiatives. http://ec.europa.eu/environment (last accessed 22 October 2013).

ICLEI: Non-profit association of over 1200 local government organizations from 70 countries supporting SPP http://www.procuraplus.org (last accessed 22 October 2013).

International Green Purchasing Network (IGPN): Based in Tokyo, platform for networking and collaboration for international organizations, local authorities and NGOs active in procurement. http://www.igpn.org (last accessed 22 October 2013).

North American Green Purchasing Initiative (NAPGI): Engages manufacturers, purchasers and stakeholders; develops tools and conducts research. http://www.cec.org (last accessed 22 October 2013).

UNEP: Capacity Building for Sustainable Public Procurement in Developing Countries. http://www.unep.fr/scp/procurement/ (last accessed 22 October 2013).

Source: Roos (2012)

CASE STUDY 3.1

STARBUCKS

Starbucks is a company that thrives on the strength of its brand and the quality of its coffee is clearly also a very important factor in its success story. It is only quite recently however that Starbucks has focused so strongly on communicating its commitment to global responsibility and ethical sourcing. Visit a Starbucks café and you are increasingly likely to experience an interior that tells the story of how the company sources its coffee beans, tea and cocoa and how it works with local communities. This is rapidly becoming a key part of the Starbucks appeal to customers.

Starbucks was founded in Seattle in 1971 by three coffee-loving academics as a coffee bean roaster and retailer. In 1982 Howard Schultz (Starbucks' current chairman, president and CEO) joined the company. In 1983 Schultz travelled to Italy where he became so captivated with Italian coffee bars and the whole romance of the coffee experience that he wanted to bring the Italian coffeehouse tradition back to the United States. Starbucks subsequently started setting up its first cafés. Since these early beginnings Starbucks has grown to become a major global player with more than 28,000 stores in 76 countries, making it the premier roaster and retailer of specialty coffee in the world.[5] The expansion kicked off in the 1990s when the company went public: in 1992 there were 165 cafes and by 1997 this had grown to 1,400 across North America and the Pacific Rim. During this period the company opened up at least one shop per day.

However, despite the growth and its current success, Starbucks fell on hard times. In 2008 the company announced a net loss of US$6.7 million, for the quarter ending June 2008. In fact, net revenue had grown 9 per cent during the same period but clearly many stores were under-performing. Starbucks announced it would close down 600 stores in the US, nearly all its stores in Australia and shed approximately 1,000 non-store jobs (James, 2008). The global economic crisis hit sales, as customers could no longer afford to buy expensive coffee, but there were other reasons for the swift decline. The rapid international expansion had meant poor service in some cafés, café design was disparaged and, even worse, the quality of the coffee and the espresso machines were criticized. The manual La Marzocco machines had been replaced by automatic machines which reduced customer perceptions of quality and interaction with baristas. The coffee was expensive but the quality did not live up to customer expectations. Indeed, a report in the New York Times in September 2006 claimed that Starbucks lattes and frappuccinos were very high in calories: a frappuccino with whipped cream contained 650 calories – equivalent to a McDonald's coffee plus 29 packets of sugar and 11 creamers. The same year Starbucks was accused by the government of Ethiopia of blocking trademark protections for the names of the country's top coffees; Ethiopia fought hard for this acknowledgement to allow its poverty-stricken farmers a chance to make more money.

Schultz, who had stepped down as CEO in 2000, rejoined in 2008 in response to the problems. Since then the company has gradually regained its strong position but it required tough decisions. From February 2008 to January 2009, Starbucks terminated an estimated 18,400 US jobs and closed 977 stores worldwide (Allison, 2009). Schultz also instigated a number of modifications, including change of espresso machines and brewing equipment, training of baristas and a customer loyalty programme. However, seriously embracing global responsibility was another key factor in the turnaround. Starbucks already had a partnership with Conservation International (CI) but wanted to take this much further.[6]

Purchasing was one of the challenges facing the company in 2008. The prices of coffee and milk had increased rapidly: between October 2006 and June 2010 the price more than doubled. What is more, the company had to respond to the negative media reports, some of which focused on inadequate global responsibility. Starbucks now partners with leading NGOs, including CI and Fairtrade. Through these partnerships Starbucks has now transformed the way it manages its global supply base.

The company is committed to minimizing its environmental footprint and to helping farmers run their businesses in an environmentally mindful way. Starbucks states that it strives 'to cultivate lasting relationships with the people who grow our products and create our manufactured goods as we work together to produce high-quality, ethically sourced products' (Starbucks website). The following summarizes its current commitments in core sourcing areas:

Coffee

Starbucks is committed to buying coffee that is responsibly grown and ethically traded. The company has established farmer support centres, farmer loan and forest conservation programmes. Starbucks defines 'ethically sourced' as coffee that is third-party verified or certified, through Fairtrade or C.A.F.E. Practices (C.A.F.E. stands for Coffee and Farmer Equity and is a set of environmental, social and economic guidelines developed jointly by Starbucks and CI) or other externally verified or certified programmes. Starbucks has offered Fairtrade coffee since 2000 and is one of the largest purchasers of Fairtrade certified coffee in the world. By 2017, at 99 percent, Starbucks had almost achieved its goals of ethically sourcing 100 per cent of its coffee through C.A.F.E. practices by 2020. Starbucks pursue a green coffee pricing model that aims to pay the prices premium quality commands, while fostering price stability and mutually beneficial relationships with suppliers.

Tea

The Starbucks approach to tea sourcing is similar to its responsible coffee sourcing so supports farmers and their communities throughout the tea supply chain. The company has been working with the Ethical Tea Partnership (ETP) since 2005 collaborating with others in the tea industry. Again, third-party independent audits are conducted based on the social and environmental criteria outlined in the ETP Global Standard. Other initiatives include the CHAI (Community Health and Advancement Initiative) project with MercyCorps supporting 200 farming communities in India and Guatemala.[7]

Store merchandise

Starbucks' commitment to ethical sourcing also stretches to the merchandise, furniture and other items found in their stores. Suppliers need to comply with tough standards and Starbucks offer suppliers assistance when corrections need to be made. Since starting the programme in 2006, Starbucks has conducted over 500 factory assessments. In 2012 the company assessed 128 factories and found that 36 failed their zero-tolerance standards. The company says that even though their approach is to work with suppliers to correct the issues, there are times when they halt business due to the nature of the issues and until adequate resolution takes place; the company discontinued sourcing from 15 supplier factories.

Forest conservation

As a final example, Starbucks work with CI and farmers in three unique coffee-producing communities to identify and test effective strategies for improving the sustainability of coffee production processes, the conservation and restoration of natural habitat, and opportunities to facilitate farmer access to forest carbon markets or other forms of assistance. For example, in Chiapas in Mexico Starbucks engaged more than 200 farmers in 23 communities and helped them protect ten species of plants in nearly 500,000 hectares in three protected area reserves. Capturing the carbon value of this investment in tree plantings has helped farmers receive additional income in the form of payments for carbon credits.

2012 tax controversy

In October 2012, Starbucks faced criticism after a Reuters investigation found that the company reportedly paid just £8.6m in corporation tax in the UK over 14 years, despite generating over £3bn in sales. No tax was apparently paid on £1.3bn of sales in the three years prior to 2012. Starbucks' chief financial officer appeared before the UK Public Accounts Committee in November and made a number of concessions. In 2015 the company paid a significant amount of UK tax (reportedly £8.1 million) on its profits for the first time. There is no suggestion Starbucks has broken any laws but does it fit with the global responsibility profile?

Sources: Starbucks 2016 Global Social Impact Performance. Available at: https://globalassets.starbucks.com/assets/9265e80751db48398b88bdf09821cc56.pdf (downloaded 21 February 2018); Allison (2009); BBC News (2007); Reuters (2012)

3.8 Conclusion

This chapter has evaluated a wide range of issues concerning purchasing strategy and organization. We began by defining strategic purchasing in terms of alignment between corporate objectives and purchasing objectives. This means that the competitive priorities that drive purchasing decisions should support or even drive corporate strategy. Purchasing maturity models were introduced as analytical models to identify the stage of purchasing maturity within a company. Overall, surveys show that purchasing has become more strategic in companies and the title of Chief Purchasing (or Procurement) Officer – CPO – is an indicator of the increasingly strategic role of senior purchasing professionals within companies. Indeed, the economic crisis that began in 2008 has increased the profile and visibility of purchasing as senior executives have realized the amount of cost and risk controlled by the purchasing function, and therefore the significance of purchasing in transforming corporate performance.

Different types or categories of purchase were briefly outlined; it is important to note that different types of purchase represent different management challenges. We focused on those that are seen as commodities and explored some of the sustainability challenges linked to the buying of commodities. Using the example of soya sourcing we illustrated how multiple stakeholders, including WWF and leading UK retailers, have joined forces to tackle sustainability challenges such as deforestation and pollution: this type of collaborative action amongst traditional supply chain actors and other stakeholders is a theme we focus on later in the book.

Chapter 3 also examined different ways of organizing the purchasing function. The traditional trade-offs between centralized and decentralized models were discussed, including ways to combine these two extremes into hybrid models. Centre-led (rather than centralized) purchasing organizations may be ideally suited to addressing the needs for synergy and corporate coherence while avoiding the traditional drawbacks of centralized structures; centre-led structures are also important to ensure coherent sustainability policies and requirements. Purchasing professionals, the people who make up organizations, are increasingly presented with a wider portfolio of challenges, which in turn require different skills and competencies. In addition to functional, or hard, skills such as negotiation and spend analysis, current and future professionals need strong management and leadership skills. The sustainability challenge means that purchasing professionals need to learn a host of new skills, such as how to do risk assessments and ethical supplier audits but also how to collaborate with CSR specialists within and outside the company.

Chapter 3 devoted a final section to discussing the particular characteristics of public sector purchasing, usually called public procurement, and the complexities of public procurement, in particular its regulatory nature. We outlined the most important public procurement regulations, focusing on EC directives, and discussed the background for these and when and how they need to be considered in the purchasing/procurement process. We concluded this section by exploring how public procurement is increasingly used as a lever for policy changes, in particular changes in sustainable development but also innovation: the public sector is striving to change procurement from a transaction and cost-focused function to a strategic contributor playing a key role in sustainable economic development.

Notes

1 http://wwf.panda.org/what_we_do/ (last accessed 22 October 2013).
2 See also the recent EU funded project Purchasing Education and Research for European Competences Transfer (PERFECT): http://www.perfect.lfo.tu-dortmund.de/ (last accessed 13 July 2018).
3 The Organisation for Economic Co-operation and Development (OECD) Development Assistance Committee. See http://www.oecd.org/dac/ (last accessed 22 October 2013).
4 See EC 'Consultation document on guidance on public procurement of innovation' (2017).
5 See https://news.starbucks.com/facts (last accessed 13 July 2018).
6 See https://www.conservation.org/partners/pages/starbucks.aspx (last accessed 13 July 2018).
7 See http://www.mercycorps.org/articles/starbucks-change-brewing (last accessed 13 July 2018).

References

Aberdeen Group (2009) The CPO's Agenda 2009: Smart strategies for tough times.

Allison M (2009) Starbucks struggles with reducing environmental impacts. *The Seattle Times*, 14 May (last accessed 22 October 2013).

Arnold U (1997) Purchasing consortia as a strategic weapon for highly decentralised multi-divisional companies. In: *6th international IPSERA conference proceedings*, T3/7-1-T3/7-12, Naples.

Arrowsmith S (2009) EC regime of public procurement. In: Thai K (ed.) *International Handbook of Public Procurement*. Boca Raton, FL: CRC Press, Auerbach Publications Taylor & Francis Group, pp. 251–284.

Bakker E, Walker H, Schotanus F and Harland C (2008) Choosing an organizational form: The case of collaborative procurement initiatives. *International Journal of Procurement Management* 1(3): 297–317.

Bowen FE, Cousins PD, Lamming RC and Faruk AC (2001) Horses for courses: Explaining the gap between the theory and practice of green supply. *Greener Management International* 35(Autumn): 41–60.

Brammer SJ and Walker HL (2011) Sustainable procurement in the public sector: An international comparative study. *International Journal of Operations and Production Management* 31: 452–476.

Caldwell N, Walker H, Harland C, Knight L, Zheng J and Wakeley T (2005) Promoting competitive markets: The role of public procurement. *Journal of Purchasing and Supply Management* 11(5–6): 242–251.

Capgemini Consulting (2010) Chief procurement officer survey.

Christensen CM (1997) *The Innovator's Dilemma: When New Technologies Cause Great Firms to Fail*. Boston, MA: Harvard Business School Press.

Collins DJ and Montgomery CA (1998) Creating corporate advantage. *Harvard Business Review*, May–June: 71–83.

Ellram LM and Liu B (2002) The financial impact of supply management. *Supply Chain Management Review* 6(6): 30–37.

Englyst L, Jørgensen F, Johansen J and Mikkelsen OS (2008) Commodity team motivation and performance. *Journal of Purchasing and Supply Management* 14(1): 15–27.

Essig M (2000) Purchasing consortia as symbiotic relationships: Developing the concept of consortium sourcing. *European Journal of Purchasing and Supply Management* 6: 13–22.

Faes W, Matthyssens P and Vandenbempt K (2000) The pursuit of global purchasing synergy. *Industrial Marketing Management* 29(6): 539–553.

Goold M and Campbell A (2000) Taking stock of synergy: A framework for assessing linkages between businesses. *Long Range Planning* 33(1): 72–96.

Guinipero LC, Handfield RB and Eltantawy R (2006) Supply managements evolution: Key skill sets for the supply manager of the future. *International Journal of Operations and Production Management* 26(7): 822–844.

Guinipero LC and Vogt JF (1997) Empowering the purchasing function: Moving to team decisions. *International Journal of Purchasing and Materials Management* 33(1): 8–15.

Harland CM, Knight LA, Caldwell ND and Telgen J (2004) Government reform and public procurement – executive report of the first workshop. *International Research Study on Public Procurement*, University of Bath, UK.

Hastings C and Harland C (2003) *Radical reform of strategic purchasing and supply in complex confederal networks – the case of the police service*. CRiSPS Seminar, 29 January, University of Bath, UK.

Hayes RH and Wheelwright SC (1984) *Restoring Our Competitive Edge: Competing Through Manufacturing*. New York: John Wiley.

James A (2008) Rollergirls bump up against Starbucks. The Seattle Post-Intelligencer 24 May. Retrieved 2 July 2008.

Johnson F and Leenders MR (2011) Supply Organizational Roles and Responsibilities 2011. CAPS Research.

Johnson PF, Shafiq A, Awaysheh A and Leenders MR (2014) Large supply organizations in North America: A twenty-four year perspective on roles and responsibilities 1987–2011. *Journal of Purchasing and Supply Management*, June 20(2): 130–141.

Martindale N (2008) Collective action. Supply Business. Available at: www.supplybusiness.com/previous-articles/spring-2008/features/collective-action/ (last accessed 3 November 2013).

Morgan G (1986) *Images of Organization*. Newbury Park, CA: Sage Publications.

Reck RF and Long BG (1988) Purchasing: A competitive weapon. *Journal of Purchasing and Materials Management* 24(3): 2–8.

Roos R (2012) United Nations Procurement Capacity Building Centre and United Nations Environment Programme: Sustainable public procurement. Briefing note.

Rozemeijer FA (2000) How to manage corporate purchasing synergy in a decentralised company: Towards design rules for managing and organising purchasing synergy in decentralised companies. *European Journal of Purchasing and Supply Management* 6: 5–12.

Rozemeijer FA, van Weele A and Weggeman M (2003) Creating corporate advantage through purchasing: Toward a contingency model. *Journal of Supply Chain Management* 39(4): 4–13.

Schulze H, Bals L and Johnsen TE (2018) Individual competences for sustainable purchasing and supply management (SPSM): A literature and practice perspective. Manuscript in review.

Singhal VR and Hendricks KB (2002) How supply chain glitches torpedo shareholder value. *Supply Chain Management Review* 6(1): 18–24.

Starbucks (2012) Global Responsibility Report—Goals and Progress. Available at: www.starbucks.com/assets/d0ce9fa1502e4aa6a9b827bf5185feee.pdf (last accessed 22 October 2013).

Supply Management (2011a) Greater Rewards for Strategic Roles. 7 June.

Supply Management (2011b) Survey Uncovers Major Procurement Gap. 28 July.

Tella E and Virolainen V (2005) Motives behind purchasing consortia. *International Journal of Production Economics* Vols 93–94: 161–168.

Trautmann G, Bals L and Hartmann E (2009) Global sourcing in integrated network structures: The case of hybrid purchasing organizations. *Journal of International Management* 15(2): 194–208.

Trent RJ (2004) The use of organisational design features in purchasing and supply management. *Journal of Supply Chain Management* 40(3): 4–18.

Walker HL and Brammer SJ (2009) Sustainable procurement in the United Kingdom public sector. *Supply Chain Management: An International Journal* 14(2): 128–137.

WWF (2012) Better production for a living planet. Available at https://www.worldwildlife.org/publications/better-production-for-a-living-planet (last accessed 13 July 2018).

CHAPTER 4

Sourcing strategy and supplier relationship management

LEARNING OBJECTIVES

By the end of this chapter you should be able to:

- Define and evaluate the advantages and disadvantages of a range of sourcing strategies including single and multi-sourcing as well as hybrid sourcing strategies including parallel, network and triadic sourcing;

- Evaluate the nature and appropriateness of partnership sourcing;

- Illustrate and apply sourcing and supplier relationship portfolio models;

- Explain the meaning and increased importance of supplier relationship management and understand critical relationship constructs including trust, commitment and power;

- Explain the main stages of supplier relationship management implementation.

4.0 Introduction

This chapter concerns two important issues in purchasing and supply management: sourcing strategy and supplier relationship management (SRM). Sourcing strategy is often used to imply different things. Leaving the major question of where to source from (local or global sourcing) to Chapter 5, this chapter begins by examining three aspects of sourcing strategy. First, the structural decision concerning how many suppliers should be used for the purchase of the same, or very similar, items. We evaluate the strategies known as single-sourcing, multi-sourcing and various forms of hybrid sourcing. Second, we examine sourcing decisions that concern the purchase of items that represent different categories and therefore different purchasing and supply management challenges. Purchase categories typically concern different types of product (or service) but in addition to category segmentation it is necessary to consider how items differ in terms of cost (or value) and supply market risk and complexity. Third, we evaluate the question of the type of supplier relationship that is appropriate for different supply situations, in particular, the relevance of partnership sourcing compared with more arm's-length adversarial sourcing strategies.

Different sourcing situations call for different supplier relationships and this chapter places particular emphasis on different trends in supplier relationship models. In short, the general trend in recent years has been to rely on fewer but more strategic suppliers; attention is directed towards those suppliers that represent the highest level of risk and value. In general, therefore, we can identify a long-term trend towards more collaborative and strategic supplier partnerships. Nevertheless, recent years have seen many companies shy away from too much dependency on single suppliers as this represents a high risk for companies.

Where companies have an SRM function, suppliers are likely to have their own customer relationship management (CRM), or similar, function in place to manage their customer relationships. This mirror organizational function suggests that both the customer, or purchaser, and the supplier seek to manage what is effectively the same relationship, merely seen from different sides of the relationship. Understanding the interactive nature of customer–supplier relationships is a useful point of departure so after a brief overview of the history of the evolution of customer–supplier relationship models, this chapter examines a model developed in the 1980s, which encapsulated the complex nature of buyer–supplier relationships: the Interaction Model. This mindset is important as it emphasizes that suppliers need to be treated as active participants that can – and should – be sources of value to buying companies. We discuss how to assess and develop buyer–supplier relationships and conclude the chapter by presenting a route map for supplier relationship management development.

4.1 Sourcing strategy

The concept of sourcing strategy encompasses several dimensions. In addition to the major complex issue to do with geographical location, i.e. local or global sourcing, which is separately examined in Chapter 5, one important aspect of sourcing strategy concerns the structural decision of how many suppliers should be used for the purchase of the same, or very similar, items. Another important aspect of sourcing strategy is the need to develop an approach which is appropriate for the particular nature of the purchase item. This decision is about different purchase categories and different purchase situations; it is about finding the appropriate response to different situations that represent fundamentally different challenges.

4.1.1 Structural sourcing options

At the two extremes, purchasing and supply managers would normally distinguish between a multi-sourcing (or 'multiple') strategy and a single- (or sole) sourcing strategy.

Multi-sourcing is the use of several suppliers for buying the same or very similar products or services. For example, a company can choose to source office stationery from three or four suppliers. These suppliers would offer practically the same products and even if the buyer might choose to buy different types of stationery from the different suppliers, they have the option of switching supplier if necessary. Therefore, the company avoids dependency on any single supplier and spreads the risk as much as possible. Companies can 'play off' suppliers against each other, especially if they are made aware of the presence of the other suppliers. Traditionally, using several suppliers is regarded as good practice because the buyer avoids a high degree of dependency, or 'lock-in', always maintaining alternative supply options. However, multi-sourcing is a strategy that seeks to create and capitalize on an adversarial atmosphere within buyer–supplier relationships; this strategy still has its place but is becoming increasingly outdated as companies require more collaborative supplier relationships.

One of the observations of the superior performing Japanese automotive industry in the 1990s (e.g. Womack *et al.*, 1990; Nishiguchi, 1994) was that unlike their Western counterparts, the Japanese manufacturers did not multi-source from suppliers – they single-sourced. Instead of focusing on getting the best deal from suppliers by emphasizing competition amongst these, lean Japanese manufacturers used extensive single-sourcing strategies.

Defined as the fulfilment of all corporate requirements for a particular product by one selected supplier (Treleven and Schweikhart, 1988), single sourcing was pursued by lean Japanese automotive manufacturers, especially Toyota, who deliberately adopted a long-term perspective towards operational and supply chain performance improvement. Choosing to accept and manage the risks associated with dependency, Japanese manufacturers chose to increase purchase volumes from a fewer number of suppliers and, perhaps more importantly, to commit to and invest in those suppliers, for example, through supplier development programmes. This strategy enabled the single-source suppliers to benefit from economies of scale and helped the Japanese manufacturers to obtain not only lower prices but lower underlying supply chain costs. In other words, where multi-sourcing allows the buyer to reduce the contribution margins of suppliers, single sourcing reduces cost but not necessarily margins. Moreover, keeping a smaller total number of direct suppliers significantly reduces the costs of negotiation with, and managing, a large supply base and therefore transaction costs.

Nevertheless, on further inspection of the Japanese method the reality appeared to be more complex. Research by Richardson (1993) showed that in the 1990s Toyota only single-sourced 28 per cent of their vehicle components. Richardson described how the Japanese did not single-source so much as they used a strategy which he termed 'parallel sourcing' defined as:

> two or more suppliers with similar capabilities are concurrently sole-source suppliers for very similar components. While using a sole source for a component, the assembler establishes parallel sources to provide performance comparisons and competitive bidders for the next model cycle.

> (Richardson, 1993: 342)

Parallel sourcing, as defined by Richardson (1993), therefore provides a way to maintain competition between suppliers that have similar capabilities and deliver the same type of components. Parallel sourcing is a strategy where the buyer seeks to keep its options open, exploring other sources, and thereby putting pressure on the single-source supplier.

Hines (1995) identified another hybrid sourcing strategy which he called network sourcing. At its core, network sourcing involves using multiple suppliers for groups of similar components and distributing volumes to the best performing supplier. Arguing that network sourcing combines the benefits of single and multiple sourcing by enabling both cooperation and competition, Hines (1996: 8) suggests that network sourcing involves:

- Tiered supply structure with a heavy reliance on small firms for lower tiers.

- Small number of direct (first-tier) suppliers with individual parts sourced from one supplier but within a competitive dual-sourcing environment.

- High degrees of asset specificity among suppliers and mutual risk sharing.

- Supplier involvement in product development and process improvement.

- Close, long-term relations between network members, involving a high level of trust, openness and profit sharing.

- Supplier assessment systems including supplier self-certification.

- Supplier coordination by the customer company across tiers.

- Supplier development activities at several tiers.

Hines' (1995, 1996) network sourcing strategy focuses not only on the dyadic level between the buyer and the direct suppliers but also considers indirect suppliers and how these collaborate amongst themselves. More recently, a new hybrid sourcing strategy has been proposed by Dubois and Fredriksson (2008): triadic sourcing. Again, this strategy seeks to capture the best of both worlds of cooperation and competition but 'the distinctive feature of triadic sourcing is that the buyer actively creates interdependencies between two suppliers' (2008: 170). In other words, where the operations of the two competing suppliers in more traditional sourcing models, apart from creating a sense of competition for the customer's business, are largely decoupled (Wu and Choi, 2005), triadic sourcing specifically seeks to encourage collaboration amongst the three parties. Based on observations from practices at Volvo Cars, Dubois and Fredriksson (2008) describe how triadic sourcing offers opportunities for creating interdependencies between the suppliers. Volvo deliberately makes two suppliers (seat suppliers Lear and JCI) jointly responsible for developing technically interdependent components. Furthermore, Volvo would allow one supplier to produce what the other has developed and vice versa.

Figure 4.1 illustrates the different structural sourcing strategies and their main characteristics. Single and multi-sourcing are simple to illustrate. Parallel sourcing is similar to dual-sourcing although whereas the latter is simply about having two suppliers delivering the same product or service, the dual supplier in parallel sourcing is kept as a backup rather than an ongoing second supplier. The concept of network sourcing shifts the focus from dyadic to supply chain or network: at the dyadic level network sourcing relies extensively on parallel or dual sourcing and this structure is continued, or cascaded, beyond the dyad into sub-tier suppliers. In addition, suppliers are brought together by the focal firm to share knowledge and transfer best practice. Triadic sourcing again focuses on direct suppliers and

	Multi-sourcing	Parallel sourcing	Single sourcing	Network sourcing	Triadic sourcing
Illustration	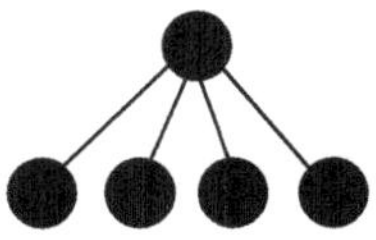	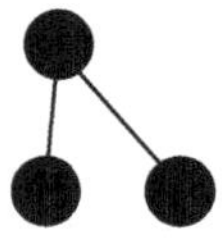		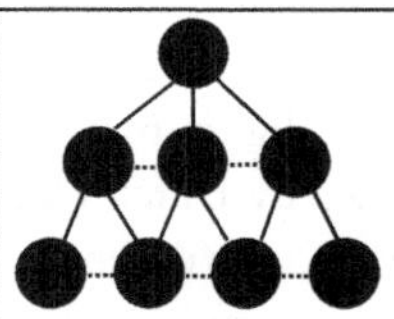	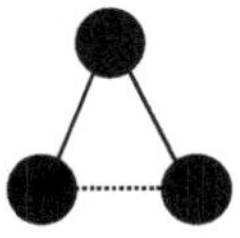
Characteristics	• Competition between suppliers • Spreading risk • Reducing dependency	• Focal firm–supplier collaboration and supplier–supplier competition • Accepting some dependency and risk but backup supplier at hand	• Collaboration between focal firm and supplier • Accepting high degree of dependency • Supplier partnerships	• Focal firm–supplier collaboration • Supplier–supplier collaboration and competition • Delegated tiered supply structure • Parallel/dual sourcing to spread risk	• Collaboration between focal firm and supplier • Competition and facilitated collaboration between suppliers • Reducing dependency

Figure 4.1 Sourcing strategies compared

does not consider indirect, or sub-tier, suppliers. Like network sourcing, the recent concept of triadic sourcing allows for collaboration between the two dual suppliers but in triadic sourcing this collaboration is taken a step further through focal-firm initiated interdependencies between the three parties. For example, where in network sourcing there is some sharing of knowledge between suppliers, in triadic sourcing the two suppliers may jointly develop components for (and with) the focal firm and thereby create operational interdependency.

4.1.2 Towards single sourcing – and back to multi-sourcing?

A number of empirical studies, most notably part of the International Motor Vehicle Program (IMVP) founded at the Massachusetts Institute of Technology in 1979, documented how lean Japanese companies out-performed their Western counterparts in terms of cost, quality, delivery and innovation advantages. Single and parallel sourcing were seen as an essential explanatory factor in the 'Japanese advantage' (Nishiguchi, 1994); as buyer–supplier collaboration for continuous product development and process improvement was at the heart of this lean supply model (Lamming, 1993), the model was soon labelled as 'partnership sourcing' (Macbeth and Ferguson, 1994) even though the emphasis was on both collaboration and competition. Since the 1990s companies in Europe and North America have learned from the Japanese lesson and have begun to emulate their practices to the extent that, for example in the UK, this was described as a 'Japanization of British industry' (Oliver and Wilkinson, 1992). Moving from multi-sourcing towards extensive use of single sourcing and tiered supply networks was part and parcel of this trend.

During the last 10 years or so the Japanese lean supply model has come under scrutiny. Supply chain experts have suggested that some industrial contexts require agile rather than lean practices (e.g. Christopher, 2000). Consequently, question marks over the heavy reliance on single sourcing have been raised as it restricts the ability of companies to cope with radical and unforeseen changes in the environment.

An example illustrates the risk of single sourcing (Chopra and Sodhi, 2004): when in 2000 lightning hit a power line in Albuquerque (New Mexico), causing a fire at a local plant owned by Dutch electronics giant Philips, two competing Scandinavian mobile phone companies with different sourcing strategies had to take immediate action. Finnish Nokia, which pursued a multi-sourcing strategy, switched its chip orders to other suppliers. Swedish LM Ericsson, which pursued a single-sourcing strategy, was locked-in to the one struggling supplier and had no other sources of microchip supply. Ericsson was forced to stop production with very heavy losses (approximately US$400million). The lesson: in times of stability, where changes are merely small and incremental, single sourcing is a good strategy but in turbulent conditions single sourcing leaves companies at risk.

The global financial crisis, which hit the world in 2008, created such turbulence and uncertainty that companies that had relied on extensive single sourcing found their supply chains unable to cope with the new conditions. With many suppliers struggling to survive, companies faced the problem that their single-source suppliers were unable to supply them on time or even faced bankruptcy. Purchasing and supply managers are therefore becoming much more cautious before entering into single-sourcing agreements. Partnerships with strategic suppliers are still essential but it is no longer an either-or choice: a portfolio of different sourcing strategies and different types of supplier relationships is required more than ever before.

4.1.3 A sourcing portfolio approach

The most widely applied purchasing portfolio model is the model developed by Kraljic (1983) that specified that purchasing and supply management decisions be taken according to the levels of first, supply market complexity and second, importance of the purchase.

1 The first dimension is a key factor in purchasing and supply management: it is a measure of the external supply market conditions. As supply markets are becoming increasingly complex, for example, as a result of extensive use of global sourcing, this dimension is as critical as ever.

2 The second measure is another key factor in purchasing and supply management: it is a measure of the internal relative importance of the purchase item. Items purchased in high volumes increase the importance of the item.

Later adaptations of the Kraljic model have modified the two dimensions into 'supply risk' and 'profit impact' (e.g. Gelderman and Van Weele, 2005), the latter often in practice translated into 'value'. Purchase items should be ranked, e.g. as low and high, or using 1–10 scores on each dimension and then be plotted across the four boxes. Appropriate measures should be identified for the two dimensions. As shown in Figure 4.2 these might be cost and impact on profitability (for the vertical axis) and number of suppliers (low number representing high supply risk) and product novelty or complexity (for the horizontal axis). In

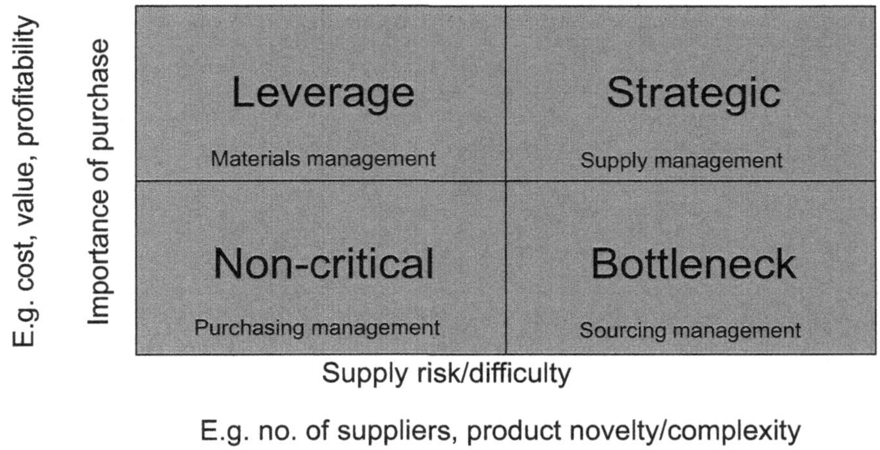

Figure 4.2 The Kraljic portfolio model
Source: Adapted from Kraljic (1983).

addition to emphasizing the need for differentiated strategies for each box, Kraljic (1983) also made the point that whereas companies tend to focus on the non-critical items they should dedicate much more time to the other items which are more challenging, especially strategic items, hence the title of Kraljic's article: 'Purchasing must become supply management'.

The four boxes, i.e. purchase situations, require four different strategies, as indicated by each box. Kraljic (1983) suggested that non-critical items were the responsibility of purchasing, bottleneck items needed a focus on sourcing, leverage items required materials management, and strategic items supply management. In his vision, therefore, supply management was a strategic activity; the concept of supply management is used to this day in North America to reflect a strategic function where the combined concept of 'purchasing and supply management', as used in this book, is often used in Europe to encapsulate both tactical and strategic activities. Non-critical items are relatively simple to manage but purchasing managers should be careful not to waste time and money on transactional activities as transaction costs, such as searching for suppliers and negotiating with these, could easily be higher than actual item costs; the focus therefore should be on efficiency. Bottleneck items represent low purchase importance but high supply chain risk. This is a tricky situation because although the item is of low importance it is still likely to create significant problems if it cannot be sourced. The challenge here is therefore to explore alternative sources or to create safety stocks. Finally, leverage items allow for the company to exploit its bargaining power and as these are high cost/value items this is an important task. Whereas Kraljic (1983) basically prescribes diversification for bottleneck items the advice is for full exploitation of power for leverage items. Non-critical and strategic items could be characterized by different buyer–supplier power balances, but again, the buying company should seek a position of power and exploit it where possible. Table 4.1 characterizes each of the four supply situations and typical strategies for managing these.

Table 4.1 Characteristics and appropriate strategies for the four Kraljic categories

	Non-critical	Leverage	Bottleneck	Strategic
Main sourcing focus	Can be multi-sourcing, but focus on efficient processing, reduction of admin cost/time (transaction costs)	Price/cost control Logistics Dual-source LCC sourcing	Secure delivery Reduce dependency and risk: re-source globally Explore alternative designs	Manage TCO Single or parallel source
Make versus buy	Always buy Outsource purchasing	Buy (or make if cost competitive)	Explore options for in-sourcing	Consider in-sourcing (based on strategic core competence analysis)
Number of suppliers	Many but possibly few global service providers	Many approved suppliers (to guarantee competition), few active suppliers	Very few suppliers by definition. Constant search for new suppliers	Few suppliers by nature. Need to look out for new suppliers
Supplier relationships	Medium to long, e.g. framework agreement with full-service providers	Competitive bidding short- (or medium-) term contracts	Long term, nurture relationship	Nurture and develop strategic partnership: trust, commitment, openness
Price/cost negotiation	Product price is insignificant compared to TCO E-procurement Pool requirements to achieve bargaining power	Constant price reduction pressure. Exploit bargaining power, aggressive negotiation E-auctions	Price is not an issue	Open book policy; TCO reduction with risk sharing
Supplier assessment and development policy	Supplier assessment	Supplier assessment Negotiated investment to obtain full benefit	Market/supplier monitoring Limited investment in supplier development	Supplier relationship assessment Co-development and experience sharing with suppliers. Invest in supplier development
Early supplier involvement in NPD	No, suppliers can be involved late in NPD	Limited	Purchasing involvement in NPD to avoid bottleneck situation	Yes, as black- or grey-box suppliers
Substitution policy and risk management	No investment Standardization of parts or commodities	Screen the market Cost, productivity and value analysis	Explore product/supplier substitutes: value analysis Safety stocks, volume insurance (at premium if necessary) Contingency planning	Monitor alternatives: value analysis Risk management

Required information	Good market overview, Short-term demand forecast, economic order quantity, inventory levels	Good market data, short- to medium-term demand planning, accurate vendor data, price/ transport rate	Medium-term supply/ demand forecasts, very good market data, inventory costs	Long term supply/ demand information, sharing of strategic information, e.g. technology roadmaps

Source: Adapted from EFQM (2006).

The Kraljic (1983) model focuses on two variables and so it is perhaps not surprising that the model has been criticized for being over-simplistic (Dubois and Pedersen, 2002). There are also practical implementation problems, such as identifying exactly where to differentiate between categories, category movers, i.e. conditions change over time; it does not take into account that several items representing different boxes may be supplied by the same supplier and that having very different strategies to deal with this supplier is not optimal. Finally, the model focuses on given 'items' and not supplier relationships so it is important to note that it says nothing about how relationships with suppliers might differ even if the different boxes clearly require different types of supplier relationships and that it is strategic items that call for supplier partnerships.

Nevertheless, the model is extensively used by companies around the world to this day and part of its appeal is no doubt its simplicity in application. Some companies encounter the inherent simplicity of the model by having several sophisticated measures of its dimension. Also, by combining different models, for example, conducting an initial screening for levels of risk and value, followed by analysis of, say, supplier attractiveness (as suggested by Olsen and Ellram, 1997) may help to avoid being over-simplistic and ignoring important features of the supply situation. This may be an ideal practical method of portfolio model application; however, attempts to over-complicate portfolio analysis arguably imply that they lose their appeal of inherent simplicity (Gelderman and Van Weele, 2005).

However, is the Kraljic (1983) model compatible with a focus on sustainability and if not can it be modified? Pagell *et al.* (2010) evaluated the Kraljic model in light of the need to create sustainable supply chains, suggesting that:

- The horizontal dimension 'Importance of purchase' is purely focused on economic importance. From a sustainability perspective the importance of purchasing an item should also include an assessment of importance in terms of its impact on the 'Triple Bottom Line' (TBL): economic, environmental and social impact.

- The vertical dimension is still a question of supply risk but a TBL focus implies that these are not only economic but also environmental and social. If, for example, a supplier does not comply with the company's standards for labour conditions it indicates a high supply risk. Interestingly, although the supply chain risk literature has grown significantly over the last few years (e.g. Christopher and Lee, 2004; Manuj and Mentzer, 2008; Tummala and Schoenherr, 2011), undoubtedly in response to frequent supply chain disruptions, environmental and social risks tend not to be

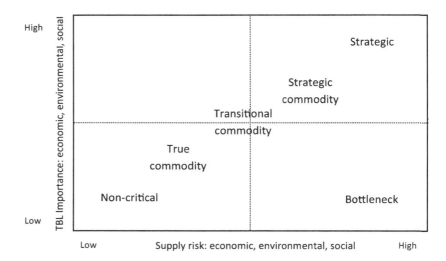

Figure 4.3 Revised Kraljic model: a sustainability perspective

Source: Adapted from Pagell *et al.* (2010).

considered at all or feature at the bottom of the list of priorities. Chapter 7 discusses supply chain risk in more detail.

Figure 4.3 shows the revised Krajlic model where both dimensions focus on sustainability. Non-critical, bottleneck and strategic remain as in the original model but the assessment of what places items into those categories should depend on the levels of risk and impact from a TBL perspective. The leverage category is divided into three sub-categories:

1 True commodities: basically the same as the original leverage items, although the item has a high impact only on one element of the TBL. Thus, item cost (or price) is still critical although social or environmental issues should also be considered.

2 Transitional commodities: items with temporarily high supply risk, for example, due to lack of compliance with (or lack of information required to assure) the buyer's sustainability requirements. Once corrected through supplier assessment and development these can revert to the true commodity sub-category.

3 Strategic commodities: critical commodities that transcend simple market economics. Strategic commodities have non-economic attributes that could be leveraged into a long-term competitive advantage.

In addressing the same question, Krause *et al.* (2009: 21) proposed the following for each of the four categories:

1 Strategic items: these items require close supplier partnerships, for example to ensure collaborative product and process development. These efforts should include

sustainability. In particular, buying organizations should consider collaborating and cross-fertilizing their know-how with suppliers of strategic items in order to minimize the environmental and social impacts of new products. Supplier partners should be encouraged to adopt sustainability as one of their own competitive priorities.

2 Leverage items: packaging suppliers are typical leverage suppliers. Sustainability should be enforced in such supplier relationships, for example, greater emphasis on the use of recyclables and material reduction. Again, these suppliers should place the same requirements on their own suppliers.

3 Bottleneck items: given the high level of supply risk the buyer is likely to be in a position of low power and therefore will find it difficult to influence suppliers; pushing suppliers for sustainability will thus be more problematic. Krause *et al.* (2009) suggest that in this situation, buyers could instead try to develop or promote industry-wide standards and norms that are conducive to sustainability. One example would be of hospitals pooling their power to certify responsible waste management service companies' processes and equipment. Krause *et al.* (2009) argue that Kraljic's focus on cost and risk minimization contradicts the idea of sustainability for bottleneck items.

4 Non-critical items: buying companies should use their power to enforce compliance with sustainability criteria. There is likely to be a good choice of suppliers offering items so if any of these do not comply with the buying company's sustainability requirements they should not be retained.

Comparing the suggestions for each category by Krause *et al.* (2009) with the revised model and suggestions by Pagell *et al.* (2010), one sees much consistency even if Pagell and his colleagues suggest that leverage items in the traditional sense become rarer and need to be divided into three sub-categories. Overall, the message is clear: fundamentally, Kraljic's (1983) model and the categories still apply from a sustainability perspective but the two dimensions of the model need to take into account not only economic but also social and environmental issues. What is more, a focus on sustainable sourcing strategies further emphasizes the need to shift the focus from items or commodities to the suppliers that supply these. The remaining part of this chapter therefore focuses on the role of relationships from a traditional and a sustainability perspective.

4.2 Foundational models of customer–supplier relationships

Models of customer–supplier relationships (or 'buyer–supplier relationships') have come a long way since the first models emerged in the 1970s. Summarizing the main thinking behind some of these early developments is a useful starting point for understanding current thinking in SRM. In fact, in order to track down the earliest models of customer–supplier relationships it is necessary to look outside purchasing and supply management to business-to-business marketing, or as it was known then, organizational buying behaviour. It is only relatively recently that a purchasing and supply management perspective on supplier relationships has emerged.

4.2.1 Early models of customer–supplier relationships

The organizational buying behaviour theories proposed by Webster and Wind (1972) and Sheth (1973) are sometimes referred to as important starting points for purchasing theory. However, they did not really seek to explain buying behaviour from a buyer perspective but were designed to provide suppliers, or in fact sellers, with a better understanding of the customers' buying organization and processes so that sales people could better target the right decision makers within the customer organization. The idea that the buying organization might actively seek out suppliers, never mind manage these, was not considered. Instead, buyers were simply seen as passive recipients, almost victims, of sales and marketing activity.

In the 1970s two theories emerged that provided grounding for later models of customer–supplier relationships: inter-organizational theory advanced by, among others, Van de Ven (1976) and new institutional economics (Williamson, 1975). Van de Ven's inter-organizational theory focused on relationships between individual organizations and the environment and relationships between groups of organizations. Williamson's theory is also discussed in Chapter 5, focusing on his analysis of alternative forms of vertical organization, i.e. the make-or-buy decision. The main focus in Williamson's models was transactions between companies rather than long-term relationships, although in his model relationships build up over time, principally as companies engage in repeat buying and selling transactions.

In the late 1970s and early 1980s a group of researchers known as the Industrial Marketing and Purchasing (IMP) group changed the focus from discrete one-off exchanges or transactions to long-term relationship evolution and processes of institutionalization and adaptation (Ford, 1980). Their model is examined in more depth in the following section.

4.2.2 The interaction model

Figure 4.4 is a contemporary version of the original model where the main parts of the model are identical to the original but where parts have been simplified and examples are consistent with current practice. The model distinguishes between short-term exchanges and long-term exchanges within relationships that institutionalize and adapt to each other (Håkansson, 1982). Short-term exchanges (episodes) can involve product or service, information, financial and/or social exchange. Long-term adaptations happen, for example, when the two parties develop strategically in the same direction (strategic alignment) or when engaging in long-term sharing of risk and reward sharing arrangements. Adaptations are often highly specific to the counterpart and of little use in other relationships. Institutionalization implies that processes over time become systematized and routinized and in the long run such adaptations and institutionalization may blur the boundary between the two parties as they reflect and resemble each other in many ways. All relationships require investment, not least supplier relationships, and efforts to evaluate and develop supplier capabilities can be seen as part of long-term adaptation and routinization processes. So, a relationship evolves over time as the two parties interact with each other; the exchanges are not discrete and independent but part of a long-term process of relationship creation.

Exchanges take place between two participants or actors; the model differentiates two levels of actors: organization and individual. Clearly, this is a major simplification when considering the number of intra-organizational authorities and stakeholders that characterize

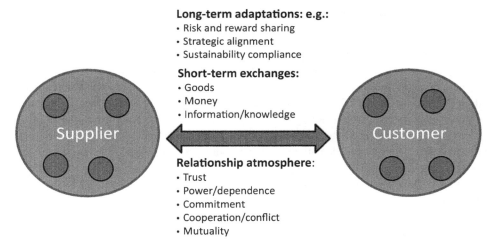

Figure 4.4 The interaction model

Source: Adapted from Håkansson (1982).

complex organizations. But the separation helps one to understand how individuals and sometimes internal departments and functions may have their own aims and experiences, which may affect their behaviour and performance, and in turn pull the relationship in different directions. Although it is possible to describe an overall company-to-company relationship, in reality, relationships are also between the individual employees and departments within the companies.

The interaction model further incorporates a relationship 'atmosphere'. In the original model the atmosphere was described in terms of the power–dependence relationship between the parties, the level of conflict and/or cooperation, overall closeness or distance and mutual expectations (Håkansson, 1982: 20). In the adaptation of the model shown in Figure 4.4 trust is added as it is now widely considered a critical aspect of relationship atmosphere. The original model included a relationship environment consisting of market structure, dynamism, internationalization, position in the manufacturing channel and the social system. These are valid to this day although the terminology for these may be different. The interaction model is useful for describing and understanding key features of dyadic buyer–supplier relationships (i.e. between two actors) on the basis that these form the basic building blocks of supply chains and networks.

Although the model does not specifically focus on sustainability the variables of the model could certainly include aspects of sustainability. In particular, when a company requires a supplier to comply with its sustainability requirements it is a form of adaptation and there is clearly a need for institutionalization of sustainability practices within buyer–supplier relationships. Besides, if a company wishes to monitor and implement sustainability practices within a supplier's business it requires the right sort of atmosphere: the company needs to be in a position of power and the two parties need to be willing to share information, which is potentially controversial, so trust and commitment are important. Imposing sustainability on a supplier could, of course, also create friction and conflict, and thereby a very different atmosphere.

4.3 Understanding supplier partnerships

Changes in purchasing and supply management practices during the last couple of decades have altered the way that organizations manage supplier relationships. Originally inspired by Japanese practices, Western organizations have transformed their supplier relationships, moving on from the old assumption that transactional short-term supplier relationships are desirable, given minimal dependency and consequently limited risk. Instead, the focus is now on developing and managing close long-term relationships, which therefore shifts the focus away from how to manage individual transactions and one-off exchanges towards understanding long-term adaptations and institutionalization. Supplier relationships are increasingly seen as conduits to supplier capabilities that are essential not only in the company's cost reduction efforts but also in its efforts to continuously improve its products and processes and to come up with innovations. Such a view transforms the way that supplier relationships are understood and necessitates a long-term perspective.

Long-term supplier relationships were labelled 'partnerships' in the 1990s (Macbeth and Ferguson, 1994; Carlisle and Parker 1989). Inspired by Japanese automotive practices (Womack *et al.*, 1990) supplier partnerships became a popular concept across the world, and are generally regarded as a core ingredient of a *lean* supply chain, although the term 'partnership' has been criticized for its misleading notion of cosy and non-competitive relationships (Lamming, 1993).

The trend towards supplier partnerships continues to this day. Whether viewed in terms of companies in integrated supply chains, 'extended' or 'connected' enterprises, long-term collaborative relationships are essential ingredients. Many companies say that they now operate partnership relations with some – or even all – of their suppliers. The trend towards partnership suppliers certainly indicates a growing interpretation of supplier relationships as relying on soft values, such as trust, commitment and mutuality. Purchasing and supply managers understand that it is no longer simply a matter of writing up a formal contract – although contracting is clearly an important part of partnership development. We should note here that although the term 'partnership' can imply a formal legal arrangement (like a strategic alliance or joint venture) this is not the way partnerships are discussed here.

In any case, it is not so much what a company says that matters but what it actually does and how it goes about it. Unfortunately, the 'partnership' metaphor is sometimes used very loosely to the extent that it ceases to be meaningful. Therefore, a better understanding of the definitions of partnerships is required. There are many definitions but the following provides a useful starting point: 'an ongoing relationship between two firms that involves a commitment over an extended time period, and a mutual sharing of information and the risks and rewards of the relationship' (Ellram and Hendrick, 1995: 41–42).

In brief, definitions of buyer–supplier partnerships share a number of important ingredients:

- Shared goals: various terms may be used for this, including strategic alignment. A partnership requires that the two parties seek to develop in the same direction.

- Mutual benefit: sometimes expressed as risk and reward sharing. Mutuality concerns the extent to which a company is prepared to relinquish its own goals for the sake of a relationship. Mutuality implies that there are common goals and interests that bind firms in a shared purpose.

- Long-term commitment: the parties stick to the relationship even through difficult times. Commitment implies a lasting intention to build and maintain a long-term relationship.

- Trust and open sharing of information: trust is often regarded as an essential ingredient of successful partnerships but is difficult to define.

4.3.1 Understanding trust

Partnerships are based on the existence of several important relationship characteristics, one of which is trust. Without trust one cannot share sensitive information and knowledge. In many ways trust is an underlying and very fragile concept. Trust takes a very long time to develop, usually through demonstrating to the partner that one is trustworthy. Trusting suppliers therefore means that suppliers demonstrate over a period of time that they can deliver according to the specified performance objectives. Also, trust implies not acting opportunistically, for example, taking advantage of knowledge or over-charging the customer. In other words, trust safeguards against opportunistic behaviour – like an informal contract. Without doubt, the quickest way to destroy trust is to act opportunistically, as anyone who has been on the receiving end of opportunistic behaviour will realize. Linking trust to safeguarding against opportunistic behaviour means that trust is a way to reduce and manage risk (Thorelli, 1986; Cousins, 2002).

Sako (1992) distinguishes between three types of trust:

Contractual trust: the trust that the other party will adhere to the explicit and implicit points of the contract as agreed;

Competence trust: the trust that the other party has the ability, or competence, to be able to produce what the contract requires;

Goodwill trust: the trust that the other party will perform tasks in excess of the agreed terms and conditions.

As shown in Figure 4.5, she further suggests that the latter two become more important as the relationship develops over time; initially as a new relationship is explored it is based around compliance with the contract. As the relationships develop the supplier will need to prove that it has the competencies to fulfil its promises, for example, in relation to delivery on time and quality standards. As the relationships mature, and become a partnership, it is the willingness to help each other out of difficulties that counts.

Trust can be a difficult concept to apply in a business context where contracts may seem more important. Nevertheless, trust is an important ingredient in successful partnerships and a key factor in preventing opportunistic behaviour by the party. Where formal contracts provide a legal mechanism for companies to fall back on, trust is an informal and social mechanism. In essence, using a trusted supplier is typically expressed in terms of using a 'safe pair of hands'. As such, trust is equivalent to confidence (Cousins and Stanwix, 2001).

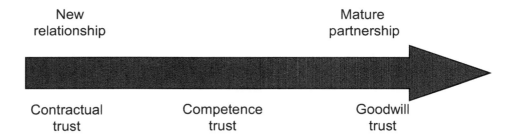

Figure 4.5 Progression of trust over time

Source: Adapted from Sako (1992).

4.3.2 Understanding power

The Kraljic model shows that multiple strategies need to be applied when managing different supply situations. Where strategic items require long-term supplier relationships that build on openness and trust, leverage items call for use of bargaining power to achieve the desired objectives. Buyers need to try to maximize their power position over suppliers, for example by limiting dependence on single sources, but aggressive exploitation of power in the wrong situation can backfire.

Consider the news reports about UK retailer Tesco in 2014 when *The Independent* newspaper and other media reported procurement practices that could best be described as bullying suppliers to lower their prices.[1] Under pressure to cut costs, Tesco buyers were reportedly treating suppliers with little respect, exploiting their position to demand discounts based on empty promises and delaying payments to deliberately boost Tesco profits. As one supplier said:

> For years we have been bullied and browbeaten by Tesco's buyers, who demand a lowball price for our goods then keep screwing us for more as the contract goes on. … Now compare that with Aldi. Don't get me wrong, Aldi drives a very hard bargain, but once you've agreed a deal for a year, it sticks for a year. They don't come back demanding new bonuses, discounts and every other trick.[2]

Such buying behaviour clearly does not lead to good relationships but is all about seeking short-term gains at the expense of long-term profitability. What is more, re-building supplier trust afterwards, as Tesco has since tried to do, is very difficult. As the Tesco example shows, power and trust can be seen as opposites, as the exploitation of power is detrimental to trust.

But, power comes in different guises and is not necessarily about exploitation. So, what do we mean by power? Someone is powerful when they have an 'ability to persuade another person to do something that he/she would not otherwise have done' (Dahl, 1961). However, it is useful to distinguish between coercive power and non-coercive power. Coercive power can be described as 'the expectation on the part of P that he will be punished by O if he fails to conform to the influence attempt' (French and Raven, 1959). Non-coercive power is about more subtle ways of using power, for example through being able to offer (and potentially withhold) rewards for good performance or by having expertise or legitimacy to perform certain tasks, such as helping suppliers to improve.

Using power to coerce suppliers to reduce cost against their will can certainly be seen as inconsistent with trying to foster strategic supplier relationships. On the one hand, such use of power does not sit well with attempts to develop a sustainable supply chain and could even make suppliers resist sustainability requirements (Reuter *et al.*, 2010). On the other hand, as explained in relation to Figure 4.3, it may be necessary to enforce sustainability compliance in suppliers (Touboulic *et al.*, 2014). However, it is advisable to use non-coercive power to motivate rather than coerce suppliers, for example, by offering rewards for sustainability performance (Meqdadi *et al.*, 2017).

4.4 A portfolio of supplier relationships

Whereas the Kraljic (1983) portfolio model provides a way for companies to devise different ways of managing purchasing and supply management according to purchase items, a related issue is to analyse the portfolio of supplier relationships. Clearly, supplier relationships vary greatly and it is very important not to think of all supplier relationships as partnerships. Only a relatively small proportion of a company's suppliers are usually considered as partnerships, regardless of the label being used to describe these. Companies need to match the desired performance outcome with the appropriate relationship type. Although partnerships are becoming increasingly important, not all relationships will necessarily be long term or strategic – such as when buying low-value, repeatable commodity items.

It is tempting to consider supplier relationships simply in terms of two extremes: short-term adversarial relationships and long-term partnerships. However, as discussed in this chapter, a range of other relationship dimensions means that relationships vary according to many different dimensions, so any attempt to describe relationships along simple dichotomies would be over-simplistic. Since the early 1980s some companies have therefore implemented relationship portfolio strategies; like Kraljic, they include two dimensions but they focus on relationships instead of items and they may help purchasing and supply managers to avoid falling into the trap of developing the wrong type of relationship in the wrong circumstances, for example, to 'over-partner' where not feasible. Relationship portfolios describe multiple relationships along, typically, two dimensions, enabling differentiated relationship management strategies in terms of balancing relationship investment relative to relationship intensity or criticality. Figure 4.6 shows a relationship portfolio model designed around two dimensions: level of confidence and level of dependence.

The horizontal axis is essentially about the level of trust in the supplier, because as discussed earlier trust is equivalent to confidence. Confident signifies a high level of trust, whereas unconfident signifies a low level of trust. The vertical axis is about dependency and therefore also about power. At the top of the model there is a further dimension: one-sided dependency and mutual dependency. If a relationship is one-sided it means that one party is dependent on the other but not the other way around, so, as suggested in the top left-hand box, this could lead to opportunistic behaviour and therefore a risky situation. If, as suggested by the top right-hand corner, the high level of certainty were combined with mutual dependency this would be an appropriate situation to develop strategic supplier relationships. Interestingly, the boxes end up quite similar to Kraljic but as a Kraljic analysis would reveal very little about the state of supplier relationships, this model is a useful supplement to a Kraljic portfolio analysis, as it provides further insight into relationship conditions.

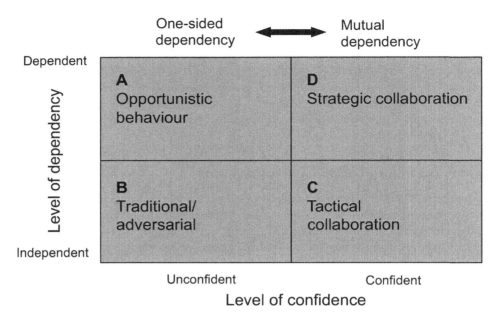

Figure 4.6 A relationship portfolio model

Source: Adapted from Cousins (2002).

4.5 Supplier relationship assessment and development

Supplier relationship assessment is closely related to traditional supplier assessment methods (see Chapter 13). Supplier assessment essentially involves the buying company measuring the performance of suppliers. In comparison with traditional applications of supplier assessment, there is now increasing attention on the communication of the results to suppliers, and on providing incentives for suppliers to improve (Modi and Mabert, 2007; Prahinski and Benton, 2004). In fact, some suppliers now also issue evaluation surveys to their customers, identifying areas in which the customer should improve; it is sometimes due to the customer's own internal processes that the supplier is unable to meet customer expectations. Companies should realize that a supplier's inability to meet its performance expectations might lie within its own company. For example, the expectations, specifications and performance criteria may not be well communicated and understood by the supplier.[3]

In addition to the two parties measuring one another's performance it is also possible to conceive of an alternative approach to performance measurement, which focuses neither on supplier nor on customer performance, but on *relationship* performance: the health of the relationship (Lamming *et al.*, 1996; Johnsen *et al.*, 2008). This approach considers the supplier relationship as a separate unit of analysis from either the customer or the supplier firm, as shown in Figure 4.7.

The argument for relationship assessment instead of supplier assessment is that if companies wish to develop long-term partnerships with some of their suppliers, it makes

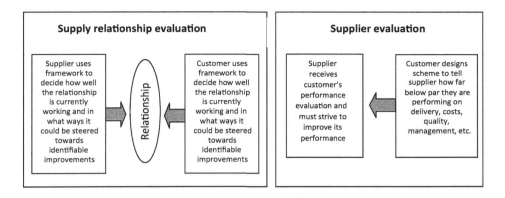

Figure 4.7 Supplier assessment and supplier relationship assessment

Source: Johnsen *et al.* (2008).

sense to analyse not only how their supplier performs (a one-way approach to performance assessment) but how the relationship with the supplier performs. At least in the context of strategic partnerships this focus makes good sense.

The idea of relationship assessment can be traced to the 1990s. Lamming *et al.* (1996) presented the Relationship Assessment Process (RAP) on the basic argument that supplier (or vendor) assessment exercises often turn into blaming exercises (Figure 4.7 shows the basic logic of this argument), and thus fail to address any root causes of supplier problems (Lamming *et al.*, 1996; Johnsen *et al.*, 2008). Based on this argument, Table 4.2 provides a framework to assess relationship maturity (stages of relationship health or performance) measured through a set of relationship characteristics (Johnsen and Ford, 2008). The purpose of this framework is to map a supplier relationship to see how advanced or mature it is across the different characteristics. Three relationship maturity stages are identified and descriptions of each are provided:

1 Exploration refers to the research and test phase in relational exchange. In the exploratory stage customers and suppliers begin to engage in discussion and negotiation. Customers may test a supplier's potential through small orders and negotiation of terms or product specifications. There may be little mutuality and cooperation at the exploratory stage, but the level of inconsistency may be high as each company is dealing with unknown issues and raising questions.

2 In the developing stage interaction and learning between a customer and supplier grows in terms of intensity and develops through increasing mutuality and growth in commitment. The expansion stage is characterized by continuous improvement in the benefits obtained by the parties, contributing to their increasing interdependence. Customers increase their purchases from suppliers and consider longer-term contracts. Cooperation and trust in the counterpart increases and power becomes increasingly shared.

3 If a relationship reaches the mature stage the parties can benefit from stability mutual dedication, more balanced power and established domains of expertise. However, one must also be aware of inertia or lack of initiative during the stable stage. Routines and institutionalization may mean that the relationship is taken for granted and does not reach its full potential. As stable relationships build on trust, commitment and relationship-specific investments the switching costs at this advanced stage are high.

Table 4.2 A framework for evaluating relationship maturity

	Maturity stage		
	Exploratory and tactical ➜	Developing ➜	Stable and strategic
Mutuality	— Goals differ for each party: no strategic alignment — Win-lose strategy	— Current goals aligned to achieve profitability for both parties — Partial strategic alignment	— Goals for future developed in tandem — Strategic alignment — Win-win: shared risks and rewards
Exclusivity	— Limited adaptation of each party — Limited relative commitment to relationship	— Concessions made by each party for mutual benefit — Security sought through commitment to relationship	— Long-term investment, adaptation and commitment over and above that of other relationships
Co-operation	— Initial ideas for cooperation explored — Cooperation depends on performance evidence — Limited information sharing: knowledge is power	— Joint projects and plans established to achieve improved capabilities for each party — Parties becoming more open with each other, but still guarded	— Long-term projects for enhancement and achievement of capability development, e.g. supplier development programme — Transparency: high level of information sharing
Conflict	— Conflicts arise through lack of knowledge of other party's systems, processes and responsibilities: destructive conflicts — One-way conflict resolution/ blaming	— Disagreements arise over integration of roles, responsibilities and targets — Partial moves towards joint problem solving	— Experience of conflict and its resolution enhance debate and depth of understanding: constructive conflicts — Joint problem solving
Intensity	— No commitment to regular interaction between individuals and teams — Single interface — Low-level operational involvement	— Regular pattern of interaction established with clearly defined roles and routines — More functions involved in relationship — Middle-management involvement	— Friendships and close professional ties underpin long-term interaction and patterns of behaviour/ responses — Multi-interface and corporate (director) involvement

Interpersonal inconsistency	— Different approaches to relationship within each party, e.g. across functions — Different approaches to relationship over time, creating inconsistent communication	— Common approaches to relationship begin to be defined — Communication patterns become established	— Both parties work to shared principles and patterns for communication — Behaviour and communication consistent over time and across functions
Power/ Dependence	— One-sided relationship — Stronger party controls strategic and tactical decisions, e.g. ordering process, quality and prices — Weaker party concerned with proving capability/ attractiveness	— Domains of expertise becoming defined and separate — Interdependent relationship strategy developing	— Commonly understood and firmly established distribution of power and expertise in different areas — Interdependent relationship strategy established
Trust	— Ensuring contractual compliance — Controlling performance through tight measures	— Focus on competence-based trust in defined areas for each party	— Focus on goodwill trust: helping each other out when necessary — Equal commitment to long-term health and growth of relationship

Source: Adapted from Johnsen *et al.* (2010).

4.6 A route map for supplier relationship management

So far, we have mostly discussed a range of conceptual issues concerning supplier relationships. We began the chapter by outlining different sourcing strategies and exploring supplier portfolio thinking. We established the idea of understanding supplier relationship development and management as a process of interaction and we considered relationship factors, such as trust and power, that are critical to understanding what makes relationships successful. We also evaluated the need for supplier assessment and development and how these practices might contribute to improving supplier performance.

In this section, we outline how a company can implement a supplier relationship management (SRM) programme, taking into account the ways of thinking about supplier relationships that we have established in this chapter. Figure 4.8 builds on the simple framework we introduced in Chapter 2 to illustrate a supplier hierarchy. Beginning with the bottom of the pyramid, we can identify potential suppliers as those that have not gone through the company's approval process, the approved suppliers that have gone through this process but are still relatively unknown quantities, the preferred suppliers with which the company has accrued significant experience and trust, and finally the relatively small number of strategic partners. The arrows in Figure 4.8 indicate how key relationship characteristics and strategies change as the level of supplier importance increases. Any SRM programme needs to focus on the most important suppliers, whether these are labelled preferred or strategic suppliers, and make sure that the strategies and methods to manage these suppliers are significantly different to how suppliers lower down in the hierarchy are managed.

Having linked the supplier hierarchy framework with the relationship concepts discussed in this chapter, we can progress to examining the process of developing an SRM programme. Figure 4.9 shows the main stages in a typical systematic SRM development process. The model consists of six implementation stages and shows a set of factors that can enable the process.

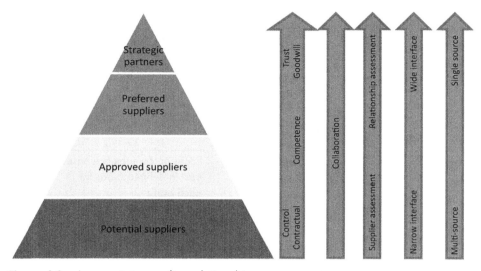

Figure 4.8 Appropriate supplier relationship management

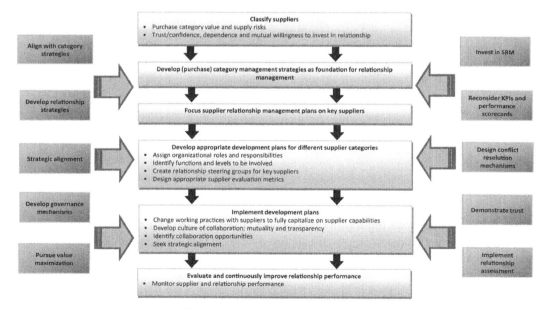

Figure 4.9 A supplier relationship management route map

The process begins by classifying suppliers in order to identify which suppliers are really 'key' based on analysis of, e.g. purchase category value with supplier, supply risks, trust and confidence levels, and dependence and mutual willingness to invest in the relationship. There is a need to align the SRM implementation with (purchase) category management strategies to create a foundation for appropriate relationship management strategies. Different purchase categories present different risks and opportunities (see Chapter 3) that need to be considered before developing SRM strategies. Supplier relationship management plans need to focus on key suppliers: although SRM programmes can focus on several different supplier categories it is important that the main focus is on the most important, strategic, suppliers as they are the ones with the most value creation potential. Appropriate development plans for different supplier categories are then required. As part of this stage, companies need to:

- Assign organizational roles and responsibilities e.g. 'supplier relationship managers', who act as relationship 'owners'. There is a need to identify other key stakeholders to involve such as functions or departments and levels (e.g. top management).

- Develop governance mechanisms including formal mechanisms such as framework agreement and/or contracts and informal mechanisms such as trust. Best practice here includes the formation of relationship steering groups for key suppliers.

- Design appropriate supplier evaluation metrics, reconsidering existing KPIs to ensure that these are strategically aligned with company and category/supplier relationship strategies.

Following the planning stage, the implementation stage should involve activities that seek to:

- Change working practices with suppliers to fully capitalize on supplier capabilities;

- Develop a culture of collaboration: change from 'need-to-know' to information transparency; listen to supplier views and suggestions;

- Identify collaboration opportunities such as joint improvement and innovation;

- Seek strategic alignment: share strategic plans and work towards common goals.

Finally, there is a need to continuously monitor supplier and, where relevant, relationship performance. This process should take into account the various metrics discussed earlier in this chapter, ensuring alignment with strategic objectives.

4.7 Supplier relationship management: hard work

Despite all the recommendations from theory as well as the popular press, supplier relationships are often in practice far from perfect. A survey reported in *CPO Agenda* (Hughes and Weiss, 2007) showed that only 8 per cent of sourcing and procurement executives were 'extremely satisfied' by the value they realized through their key supplier relationships, and just under a third were 'fairly satisfied'. The conclusion of a subsequent survey of more than 300 companies in North America, Europe and Asia-Pacific was that the value potential of supplier relationships was not captured:

Companies generally treat their most important suppliers in ways that are only margin-ally or intermittently different from the way they treat their arms-length commodity vendors. They may sporadically work with key suppliers to develop new technology or jointly analyze opportunities to improve supply chain efficiency, but they have not insti-tutionalized new ways of working with these suppliers as partners rather than vendors.

(Hughes and Weiss, 2007: 19)

Figure 4.10 shows the range of perceived barriers to suppliers delivering more value for their customers. Unsurprisingly, it is particularly suppliers that feel frustrated but customers recognize the problem areas themselves. In any case, it is notable that there is a general consensus that customer companies do not capture sufficient value from their supplier relationships because of a short-term focus, lack of transparency, lack of commitment and respect for supplier expertise, and too rigid bidding processes and one-sided contracts. Also, where customer companies apparently see little reason for suppliers to have access outside procurement (purchasing), suppliers tend to believe that this would be beneficial. Finally, this survey shows that a lack of internal alignment is a frequent problem; lack of internal collaboration can often prevent a company from being an effective external partner. For example, one department might have a very close relationship with the equivalent department at the supplier but another department might have an entirely different relationship. Such interdepartmental or interpersonal inconsistency is not unusual in buyer–supplier relationships as illustrated in the interaction model (Figure 4.4 – Håkansson, 1982).

The reality is that in many companies the potential value from supplier relationship management is not realized. This concerns not only potential cost savings but also joint innovation opportunities with suppliers that remain untapped. Many companies are also unwilling to use the label supplier relationship management (SRM) and prefer such terms as

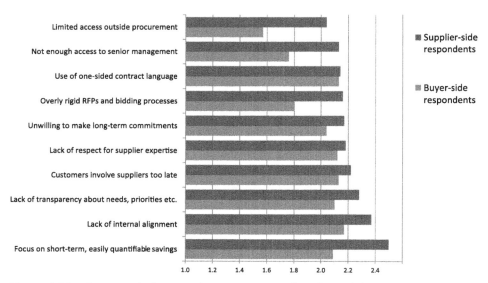

Figure 4.10 Customer behaviour that prevents suppliers from delivering more value

Source: Hughes and Weiss (2007).

supplier management, *key supplier management* or *vendor management*. This is misguided because it gives a false perception of control and sends the wrong signal internally and to suppliers. The reason for this unwillingness to embrace the term 'relationship' is often that companies, not least purchasing and supply chain management professionals, are uncomfortable with the idea of developing relationships with suppliers. This is often due to a fundamental misunderstanding about relationship management and a belief that it is unhealthy to have relationships with suppliers because this implies getting too close to suppliers and thereby losing power and authority. Rather than viewing suppliers as passive it is far better to view suppliers as competent sources of capabilities and innovation that demand honesty, trust and respect.

DANONE[4]

Danone is among the global leaders in the food and beverage sector, committed to creating and sharing sustainable value for all. With global sales totalling €24.7 billion and a workforce amounting to 99,187 employees worldwide (2017), Danone relies on four main Businesses: Essential Dairy and Plant-Based products; Waters; Early Life Nutrition; and Advanced Medical Nutrition. 'Essential Dairy and Plant-Based' products, which include famous brands like Activia, Oikos and Danette, accounted for 52 per cent of global sales in 2017. Danone is the global market leader in fresh dairy products, the global market leader in plant-based food and beverage as well as the leader in Europe in medical nutrition.

Danone's signature, 'One Planet. One Health', expresses a vision of social, societal and environmental responsibility that the company has upheld for many years. Since 2006, the definition of Danone's mission of 'bringing health through food to as many people as possible', centred the Company's strategy on three categories of challenges:

- Ensuring consumers' safety and fostering healthier eating and drinking habits: relates to challenges relating to product safety and quality, and to efforts to promote a healthy lifestyle and nutritional education;

- Communicating and engaging with stakeholders: relates to challenges relating to employee development and involvement, relationships with suppliers and development of communities, consideration of the regions where the company operates including concern for the environment and local economic development;

- Contributing to protecting the planet: relates to environmental challenges, including preservation of natural resources, fighting pollution, preventing loss of agricultural land, limitation of the impact of the agri-business on the environment across the life cycle of raw materials, production, packaging, transport, sales, consumption and end of life/disposal.

Reflecting its 'One Planet. One Health' vision, Danone is now working on product re-design and production, reducing the number of ingredients where possible, and proposing new organic and non-genetically modified (GMO) product lines. Other commitments include promoting sustainable agriculture, conserving water, reducing waste, reducing its carbon footprint, promoting animal welfare

CASE STUDY 4.1

and investing in the community. These initiatives reflect Danone's ambitions around product stewardship and circular economy.

Sustainable sourcing and supplier development

Danone's name for purchasing is Cycles and Procurement. With the Cycles, Danone protects and secures its key resources (milk, water and plastic) and takes a strategic approach to procurement to support the business and social agenda of Danone. In terms of value, milk represents the main raw material purchased by Danone. Danone sources milk, directly and indirectly, from over 140,000 milk producers in around 30 different countries. A very high proportion of these are small producers located mainly in emerging countries of Africa and Latin America that own fewer than ten cows (so-called 'subsistence farms') or 'family farms' with less than 300 cows. Often, milk is collected from collection centres to which these small producers deliver their production daily. For dairy and beverage products, fruit is another critically important raw material. Other food raw materials include fruit-based preparations and sugar, and packaging materials, such as plastics and cardboard. Given the nature of these raw materials, supply markets can be volatile.

For milk sourcing, Danone typically enters into agreements with local producers or cooperatives through its operating subsidiaries. Liquid milk prices are set locally, over contractual periods that vary from one country to another. The company aims to ensure a sustainable long-term supply, to minimize risks by optimizing the use of all milk components using new technologies, and to pool the needs among the various businesses, especially across the 'Essential Dairy and Plant-Based', and 'Early Life Nutrition' businesses.

Cost volatility of raw materials is controlled through a range of measures. In addition to the reduction of production waste and the use of lighter packaging and more effective use of milk sub-components, there is a focus on pooling purchasing requirements across subsidiaries. The purchasing policy known as 'Market Risk Management' defines the rules for securing the physical supply and price setting with suppliers. Monitoring of exposures and policy implementation are managed at raw materials category level by the central purchasing team. Buyers typically negotiate forward purchase agreements with suppliers, as full hedging against price volatility is not available in the current financial markets.

In addition to the operational priorities, Danone's purchasing is dedicated to ensuring that the sustainability criteria of the group are respected by all suppliers who are informed of the standards and requirements of Danone from the outset. Sustainability criteria are increasingly incorporated into specifications, supplier selection processes, contracts and ongoing evaluations of supplier performance.

In the case of packaging, purchases are managed through global and regional purchasing programmes. In this category, the goal is to reduce the environmental impacts by, for example, developing new 100 per cent recyclable materials, increasing the share of recycled PET from 10 per cent to 25 per cent in several countries and ultimately producing bottles made from second-generation, 100 per cent bioplastics.

In the milk supply chain, Danone has been working on traceability since the 1990s, based on its FaRMS (Farmer Relationship Management Software) programme that assesses the farming practices that can affect food safety and milk quality as well as environmental impacts and conditions for workers. Through the FaRMS initiative, Danone evaluates the performance of farmers on food safety and traceability as well as a wider range of economic, social and environmental criteria. In 2017 this covered approximately 90 per cent of milk producers that Danone works with directly. The FaRMS tool is gradually being reorganized into different, more specialized and dedicated tools on topics such as animal welfare, greenhouse gas emissions, water consumption and a range of social issues.

The RESPECT programme for tier-one suppliers

Danone has developed a programme called RESPECT which aims to ensure that suppliers comply with Danone's fundamental social principles that reflects the fundamental rights of ILO conventions and focus on:

1. Child labour

2. Forced labour

3. Non-discrimination

4. Freedom of association and right to collective bargaining

5. Health and safety at work

6. Working Hours

7. Pay

RESPECT applies to first-tier suppliers across all of Danone's purchasing categories except raw milk, i.e. transformed raw materials (fruit preparations, powdered milk, etc.), packaging, production machinery and transport and other services. Subcontractors, i.e. suppliers that manufacture finished products on behalf of Danone, are also covered by the RESPECT programme. However, Danone uses very little subcontracting, as the majority of its finished products are produced at its own production sites.

The RESPECT programme is based on the process of:

- Contractualization of Danone's sustainability principles;

- Self-assessment by the suppliers of their CSR performance through a questionnaire, completed by Sedex intelligence;

- External social audits for 'at risk suppliers';

- Set-up of corrective action plans to remedy the noncompliance identified through the audits.

The figure that follows illustrates the process:

CASE STUDY 4.1

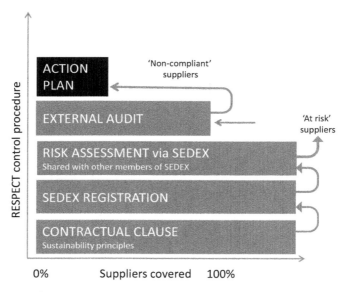

Figure 4.11 The RESPECT process
Source: Danone (2012: 46).

The RESPECT programme in turn is managed through the SEDEX (the Supplier Ethical Data Exchange – a not-for-profit membership organization dedicated to improving responsible and ethical business practices in global supply chains). The RESPECT programme focuses on:

- Integrating Danone's sustainability principles into supplier contracts and terms and conditions;

- Sharing information through supplier self-assessment concerning their CSR performance, using the SEDEX platform shared by consumer goods industry players;

- Auditing CSR performance using the SMETA (Sedex Members Ethical Trade Audit) benchmark for at-risk suppliers: see www.sedexglobal.com/ethical-audits/smeta – last accessed 22 October 2013).

By the end of 2017, 4,082 first-tier supplier sites had been registered on the SEDEX platform. Through the AIM Progress consortium for responsible sourcing, Danone can access audits commissioned by its peers on common suppliers, thus reducing the burden of multiple audits. In 2017, 195 SMETA audits were conducted on Danone first-tier suppliers, commissioned either by Danone or by peers. The audits are carried out by independent audit companies and evaluate supplier compliance against the four pillars of the SMETA protocol – Labour Rights, Health and Safety, Environment Management and Business Ethics – that are encompassed in Danone's sustainability principles.

When non-compliance is identified through the audits, the procurement teams verify that the suppliers implement the corrective action plans defined by the auditors. Most cases concerned health and safety issues, working hours or compensation. In July 2017, Danone introduced an indicator to monitor the timely launch of SMETA audits (after the suppliers have been identified as at risk) and the timely closure of the non-compliance: 65 per cent of Danone's suppliers complied with Danone's standards; this rate was 100 per cent for central procurement.

The aim is to close all non-compliances and improve suppliers' sustainability performance; in some cases, there is no alternative but to terminate relationships with suppliers who do not collaborate.

In 2017, Danone launched a process to upgrade RESPECT and evolve towards a due diligence approach, reinforcing the first-tier suppliers approach, covering also its upstream supply chain and focusing in particular on human rights. This process is inspired by the UN Guiding Principles on Business and Human Rights (UNGP) and contributes to the development of a vigilance plan, as required by the 2017 French Corporate Duty of Vigilance Law.

In order to reinforce first-tier supplier assessment, Danone developed a new approach at the end of 2017 to segment its suppliers according to three levels of priority. Danone will determine these levels proactively, using geographical, sector-specific trade data. Audits will be mandatory for all high-priority suppliers. Appropriate assessment measures will also be taken for medium-priority suppliers.

Upstream risk mapping and traceability

In 2017, Danone mapped major potential risks for the 20 most exposed categories of procurements. Risks were analysed according to a grid based on ISO 26000, GRI G4 and SA 8000 standards, integrating potential impacts of purchased products in the areas of social and human rights, local communities, consumers, fairtrade practices and the environment. Combined with stakeholder expectations, this risk analysis determined the priority categories of product and service procurements on which Danone will focus its attention in the coming years. By 2017, risks identified included workers employed through labour agencies or service providers, palm oil, cocoa, cane sugar and fruit. The potential risks brought to light are mainly situated in farms and plantations, located upstream in the supply networks. Supported by independent experts, Danone has initiated traceability actions on these priority categories. In agriculture, the progress as of early 2018 is:

- Palm oil: at the beginning of 2018, Danone achieved 100 per cent traceability back to mills and 68 per cent back to plantations.

- Fruit: Danone has determined the priority supply chains based on its materiality matrix specific to fruit procurement. Danone has asked first-tier suppliers to map their own sources of supply back to farms and to identify major potential risks. More than 65 per cent of volumes have been traced back to farms.

- Cocoa and cane sugar: for each category, Danone has developed a traceability and risk assessment procedure starting in 2018. As part of the traceability work done with first-tier suppliers in respect of fruit, in 2016, Danone chose to assess suppliers at production locations in certain priority geographic areas. An audit programme was carried out in 2016 and 2017 on a representative sample of farms covering seven main categories of fruit representing 75 per cent of total volumes purchased. These audits were conducted by independent third parties based on the Sustainable Agriculture Initiative (SAI) FSA 2.0 tool. The results served to define a reference base and an improvement plan for environmental focuses. Starting in 2018, Danone will be launching field investigations in the area of human rights with local stakeholders.

Tackling forced labour

In 2016, Danone joined the Consumer Goods Forum's (CGF) collective initiative to eradicate forced labour from global supply chains. CGF members commit to eradicate forced labor drivers from their own operations and global supply chains, based on the three following principles: every worker should have freedom of movement; no worker should pay for a job; and no worker should be indebted or coerced to work.

For several years now, Danone has cooperated with specialized stakeholders to strengthen action to combat the various forms of forced labor in supply chains. For example, to fight informal employment in recycled plastic procurement, Danone has developed cooperatives of waste-pickers with support from local partners, enabling these workers to leave the informal economy and gain access to paid employment, recognized by public authorities, and complemented by social benefits.

Driving change through industry collaboration

Although auditing and evaluating supplier compliance with Danone's policies is key to Danone's approach to sustainable supply chain development, the company does not see evaluation of compliance as an end in itself; Danone also supports suppliers when non-compliance is identified, engaging with independent organizations in driving sustainability improvement. Through the AIM-PROGRESS group Danone collaborates with other food manufacturers, many of which are competitors, including Nestlé, Kraft, Unilever, Diageo, Mars, PepsiCo and Cadbury. The AIM-PROGRESS group develops common standards on CSR around four pillars – Health and Safety, Labour Standards, Environmental Management and Business Ethics – with the purpose of mutualizing information and results of audits concerning common suppliers. Members have agreed to share experiences, ideas and solutions while respecting confidentiality; the idea is that common standards imposed on suppliers by several major food industry members will have greater impact.

4.8 Conclusion

Fostering and managing collaborative supplier relationships, where extensive information and knowledge are openly shared, is at the heart of successful purchasing and supply chain management. The conventional wisdom is that companies should avoid becoming overly dependent on suppliers, as these will otherwise take advantage of the situation and over-charge buyers. In the old days, purchasers were advised to always source from several suppliers – to multi-source – and not to engage in long-term relationships with suppliers, thereby avoiding any form of dependence and minimizing risk exposure.

However, as companies outsource more and more they become increasingly dependent on suppliers. This is especially so when companies outsource even what they used to consider as strategic activities or items. In these situations it no longer makes sense to manage suppliers on an arm's-length relationship basis. The idea of 'partnership suppliers' or 'partnership

CASE STUDY 4.1

sourcing' focuses on close collaborative long-term supplier relationships often based on single sourcing. This chapter has explored in which circumstances such sourcing models are appropriate, which are those that represent high value and risk but also those in which the right relationship conditions are in place. Various hybrid models that combine the benefits of single sourcing and multi-sourcing while avoiding the limitations of both extremes have been discussed; in general these provide better alternatives to the high-risk single-sourcing strategy.

Supplier relationships are multi-faceted and involve not only collaboration but also potential conflict. Trust is an important feature of relationships but the role of power and dependence should not be underestimated. Using power is often seen as a negative but is fundamental in order to gain influence over suppliers. In the context of sustainability, using power is important to enforce supplier compliance but companies are advised to use non-coercive power to avoid ruining collaborative relationships.

We explored various models of relationship assessment and development. As part of this, we proposed a supplier relationship development route map that sets out a systematic process for implementing supplier relationship management. A key message of this chapter is that companies need to develop and invest in relationships with a range of different suppliers that are all unique yet they may share common features. It is through supplier relationships that companies access capabilities that allow them to continuously develop and offer new products and services to their customers. Supplier relationship management is therefore critical, but not as a set of tools or a piece of software but as a systematic process and a way of thinking about relationships.

Notes

1 http://www.independent.co.uk/news/business/analysis-and-features/tesco-crisis-they-say-every-little-helps-but-supermarket-s-demands-are-never-little-9752106.html (last accessed 11 May 2017).

2 See also http://4pillars.org/tesco-procurement-practices-exposed-and-its-not-pretty/; https://www.theguardian.com/business/2016/jan/26/tesco-ordered-change-deal-suppliers (both last accessed 11 May 2017).

3 Ways to overcome a pure one-way perspective on supplier assessment is discussed further in the section above: 'Towards single sourcing – and back to multi-sourcing?'

4 This case is based on the Danone 2017 Registration Document, and http://iar2017.danone.com/performance-in-2017/human-rights-and-responsible-procurement/ (last accessed 22 March 2018), and a keynote presentation by Danone VP Sourcing and Supplier Development, Paul Gardner, Audencia Nantes School of Management, 26 March 2013.

References

Bensaou M (1999) Portfolios of buyer–supplier relationships. *Sloan Management Review,* Summer: 35–44.

Carlisle J and Parker R (1989) *Beyond Negotiation: Redeeming Customer–Supplier Relationships.* Chichester, UK: Wiley.

Chopra S and Sodhi MS (2004) Managing risk to avoid supply-chain breakdown. *MIT Sloan Management Review* 46(1): 53–62.

Christopher M and Lee H (2004) Mitigating supply chain risk through improved confidence. *International Journal of Physical Distribution and Logistics Management* 34(5): 388–396.

Christopher MG (2000) The agile supply chain – competing in volatile markets. *Industrial Marketing Management* 29: 37–44.

Ciliberti F, Pontrandolfo P and Scozzi B (2008) Investigating corporate social responsibility in supply chains: A SME perspective. *Journal of Cleaner Production* 16: 1579–1588.

Cousins PD (2002) A conceptual model for managing long-term inter-organizational relationships. *European Journal of Purchasing and Supply Management* 8(2): 71–82.

Cousins PD and Stanwix E (2001) It's only a matter of confidence!: A comparison of relationship management between Japanese- and UK non-Japanese-owned vehicle manufacturers. *International Journal of Operations and Production Management* 21(9): 1160–1180.

Dahl RA (1961) *Who Governs? Democracy and Power in an American City.* New Haven, CT: Yale University Press.

Dubois A and Fredriksson P (2008) Cooperating and competing in supply networks: Making sense of a triadic sourcing strategy. *Journal of Purchasing and Supply Management* 14: 170–179.

Dubois A and Pedersen A-C (2002) Why relationships do not fit into purchasing portfolio models – a comparison between the portfolio and industrial network approaches. *European Journal of Purchasing and Supply Management* 8: 35–42.

Ellram LM and Hendrick TE (1995) Partnering characteristics: A dyadic perspective. *Journal of Business Logistics* 16(1): 41–64.

European Foundation for Quality Management (EFQM) (2006) *The EFQM framework for managing external resources*, ISBN 90-5236-610-1.

Financial Times (2010) Backlash greets BP's internal report, 9 September. Available at: https://ftalphaville.ft.com/2010/09/09/338391/backlash-greets-bp%E2%80%99s-internal-report/ (downloaded 29 January 2013).

Ford ID (1980) The development of buyer–seller relationships in industrial markets. *European Journal of Marketing* 14(3): 72–84.

French JRP, Jr. and Raven B (1959) The bases of social power. In: Cartwright D (ed.) Studies of Social Power. Ann Arbor, MI: University of Michigan, Institute for Social Research, pp. 150–167.

Gelderman CJ and Van Weele AJ (2005) Purchasing portfolio models: A critique and update. *The Journal of Supply Chain Management* 41(3): 19–28.

Håkansson H (ed.) (1982) *International Marketing and Purchasing of Industrial Goods: An Interaction Approach.* Chichester: Wiley.

Henke J (2012) The never-ending journey. CPO Agenda, Summer: 16–21.

Hines P (1995) Network sourcing: A hybrid approach. *International Journal of Purchasing and Materials Management* 31(2): 17–24.

Hines P (1996) Network sourcing: A discussion of causality within the buyer–supplier relationship. *European Journal of Purchasing and Supply Management* 2(1): 7–20.

Hughes J and Weiss J (2007) Getting closer to key suppliers. CPO Agenda, Spring: 19–25.

Johnsen RE and Ford D (2008) Exploring the concept of asymmetry: A typology for analysing customer–supplier relationships. *Industrial Marketing Management* 37(4): 471–483.

Johnsen TE, Johnsen RE and Lamming RC (2008) Supply relationship evaluation: The relationship assessment process (RAP) and beyond. *European Management Journal* 26: 274–287.

Johnsen TE, Johnsen R and Lee C-J (2010) Towards a managerial model for supplier relationship evaluation. In: *Proceedings of the 26th International Marketing and Purchasing Conference*, 2–4 September, Corvinus University of Budapest, Hungary.

Kaplan RS and Norton DP (1992) The balanced scorecard – measures that drive performance. *Harvard Business Review* 70(1): 71–80.

Kraljic P (1983) Purchasing must become supply management. Harvard Business Review, Sept.–Oct.: 109–117.

Krause DR, Vachon S and Klassen RD (2009) Special topic forum on sustainable supply chain management: Introduction and reflections on the role of purchasing management. *Journal of Supply Chain Management* 45(4): 18–25.

Lamming RC (1993) *Beyond Partnership: Strategies for Innovation and Lean Supply*. Hemel Hempstead, UK: Prentice Hall.

Lamming RC and Hampson JP (1996) The environment as a supply chain management issue. *British Journal of Management* 7(special issue): 45–62.

Lamming RC, Caldwell ND, Phillips WE and Harrison D (2005) Sharing sensitive information in supply relationships: The flaws in one-way open-book negotiation and the need for transparency. *European Management Journal* 23(5): 554–563.

Lamming RC, Cousins PD and Notman DM (1996) Beyond vendor assessment: Relationship assessment programme. *European Journal of Purchasing and Supply Management* 2(4): 173–181.

Macbeth D and Ferguson N (1994) *Partnership Sourcing: An Integrated Supply Chain Management Approach*. London: Financial Times/Pitman Publishing.

Manuj I and Mentzer J (2008) Global supply chain risk management. *Journal of Business Logistics* 29(1): 133–155.

Meqdadi O, Johnsen TE and Johnsen R (2017) The role of power and trust in spreading sustainability initiatives across supply networks: A case study of the bio-chemical industry. *Industrial Marketing Management* 62: 61–76.

Min H and Galle WP (2001) Green purchasing practices of US firms. *International Journal of Operations and Production Management* 21(9): 1222–1238.

Modi SB and Mabert VA (2007) Supplier development: Improving supplier performance through knowledge transfer. *Journal of Operations Management* 25(1): 42–64.

Nishiguchi T (1994) *Strategic Industrial Sourcing*. Oxford and New York: Oxford University Press.

Oliver N and Wilkinson B (1992) *The Japanization of British Industry*. 2nd edn, Oxford: Blackwell.

Olsen RF and Ellram LM (1997) A portfolio approach to supplier relationships. *Industrial Marketing Management* 26(2): 101–113.

Pagell M, Wu Z and Wasserman ME (2010) Thinking differently about purchasing portfolios: An assessment of sustainable sourcing. *Journal of Supply Chain Management* 36(1): 57–73.

Prahinski C and Benton WC (2004) Supplier evaluations: Communication strategies to improve supplier performance. *Journal of Operations Management* 22(1): 39–62.

Pressey AD, Winklhofer HM and Tzokas NX (2009) Purchasing practices in small- to medium-sized enterprises: An examination of strategic purchasing adoption, supplier evaluation and supplier capabilities. *Journal of Purchasing and Supply Management* 15: 214–226.

Rao P (2002) Greening the supply chain: A new initiative in South East Asia. *International Journal of Operations and Production Management* 22(6): 632–655.

Rao P and Holt D (2005) Do green supply chains lead to competitiveness and economic performance? *International Journal of Operations and Production Management* 25(9): 898–916.

Reuter C, Foerstl K, Hartmann E and Blome C (2010) Sustainable global supplier management: The role of dynamic capabilities in achieving competitive advantage. *Journal of Supply Chain Management* 46(2): 45–63.

Richardson J (1993) Parallel sourcing and supplier performance in the Japanese automobile industry. *Strategic Management Journal* 14: 339–350.

Sako M (1992) *Prices, Quality and Trust: Inter-firm Relations in Britain and Japan*. Cambridge, UK: Cambridge University Press.

Sako M (2004) Supplier development at Honda, Nissan and Toyota: Comparative case studies of organizational capability enhancement. *Industrial and Corporate Change* 13(2): 281–308.

Seuring S and Müller M (2008) From a literature review to a conceptual framework for sustainable supply chain management. *Journal of Cleaner Production* 16: 1688–1710.

Sheth JN (1973) A model of industrial buying behaviour. *Journal of Marketing* 37: 50–56.

Thorelli HB (1986) Networks: Between markets and hierarchies. *Strategic Management Journal* 7: 37–51.

Touboulic A, Chicksand D and Walker HL (2014) Managing imbalanced triadic buyer–supplier–supplier relationships for sustainability: A power perspective. *Decision Sciences* 45(4): 577–619.

Treleven M and Schweikhart SB (1988) A risk/benefit analysis of sourcing strategies: Single vs. multiple sourcing. *Journal of Operations Management* 7(4): 93–114.

Tummala R and Schoenherr T (2011) Assessing and managing risks using the Supply Chain Risk Management Process (SCRMP). *Supply Chain Management: An International Journal* 16(6): 474–483.

Vachon S (2007) Green supply chain practices and the selection of environmental technologies. *International Journal of Production Research* 45(18–19): 4357–4379.

Vachon S and Klassen R (2006) Extending green practices across the supply chain – the impact of upstream and downstream integration. *International Journal of Operations and Production Management* 26(7): 795–821.

Van de Ven AH (1976) On the nature, formation, and maintenance of relations among organizations. *Academy of Management Review* 1(October): 24–36.

Venkatraman N and Ramanujam V (1986) Measurement of business performance in strategy research: A comparison of approaches. *The Academy of Management Review* 11(4): 801–814.

Webster FE and Wind Y (1972) A general model of organizational buying behaviour. *Journal of Marketing* 36(April): 12–19.

Williamson OE (1975) *Markets and Hierarchy: Analysis and Antitrust Implications*. New York: Free Press.

Womack JP, Jones DT and Roos D (1990) *The Machine That Changed the World*. New York: MacMillan International.

Wu Z and Choi TY (2005) Supplier–supplier relationships in the buyer–supplier triad: Building theories from eight case studies. *Journal of Operations Management* 24: 27–52.

CHAPTER 5

Outsourcing

LEARNING OBJECTIVES

By the end of this chapter you should be able to:

- Define key concepts related to outsourcing;
- Compare transaction cost, resource-based and network-based perspectives on the outsourcing decision;
- Apply a framework for analysing 'make, buy or ally' decisions;
- Evaluate the connections between outsourcing and sustainability.

5.0 Overview

Outsourcing refers to the practice of contracting out activities or functions to specialized suppliers. It concerns both manufacturing and services and can relate to either domestic or international sourcing markets. In other words, outsourcing is not restricted to moving activities or functions to lower cost or 'best low cost' locations, although in recent years outsourcing has been closely tied to this trend. The outsourcing decision is naturally followed by a sourcing decision, that is, once a company has decided not (or no longer) to perform a component manufacture or service operation in-house, the next immediate challenge is to find a supplier or service provider that can perform this function on its behalf. New terminology has emerged that begins to question the idea of outsourcing such as local supply or 'localism', hinting at the difficulties of monitoring expansion overseas and the competitive advantage of sourcing goods and services from markets nearer to home.

The chapter begins by examining outsourcing decision models by evaluating the so-called 'make-or-buy' decision. In order to understand these we evaluate and compare some well-known theoretical perspectives including transaction cost economics, the resource-based view (and natural resource-based view) and the interaction approach. The final part of this chapter explores the future challenges for outsourcing in terms of the implications for introducing more sustainable approaches.

5.1 Outsourcing: 'make-or-buy' analysis

Outsourcing, or 'outside resource using' to use traditional terminology, means contracting out functions or activities outside of the organization. Whereas outsourcing of mundane peripheral activities, such as cleaning, catering and security, used to be the focus of outsourcing projects, outsourcing increasingly concerns more strategic activities, such as manufacturing, design and logistics (McIvor, 2009). This means that whereas in the past outsourcing decisions were relatively easy because they did not touch on the company's strategic activities, outsourcing decisions have become much more complex as companies now fear that by outsourcing a strategic activity they risk losing control of critical strategic assets that constitute sources of competitive advantage.

Many companies used to approach the outsourcing decision from a simple cost-saving perspective: a supplier has offered to take responsibility for an activity cheaper than we can do it ourselves, so why hesitate? Approaching outsourcing from such a simplistic and short-term perspective is one of the reasons why so many outsourcing projects fail (Cox, 2005). Instead, companies need to make a strategic evaluation of what it should make in-house and what should be bought in: the make-or-buy decision. This is a more complex question because it concerns the definition and identity of the company: what are we and what do we do?

The outsourcing decision therefore needs to be approached from a strategic perspective where the key question is: is this core or non-core to our business? In fact, as companies have already outsourced peripheral activities the real question is: how close to the core is this? An underlying theme of a strategic approach to outsourcing is that the boundary between the company and its environment is no longer clear cut. Companies can no longer be experts at everything so are increasingly dependent on specialized knowledge and technologies controlled by suppliers to the extent that we now talk about the borderless organization. Outsourcing stresses the importance of strategic thinking in considering how external resources can reinforce a firm's position in competitive terms. It also emphasizes the potential risks of outsourcing vital public services (e.g. health, welfare, waste management) to private profit-seeking corporations (see Note 5.1).

Arnold's (2000) outsourcing model emphasizes four elements of outsourcing: the outsourcing subject or firm, outsourcing object, i.e. the process, product or service which might be outsourced; partner or supplier; and the outsourcing design or 'degree of manufacturing penetration' in terms of core/non-core activities which the supplier may provide (Figure 5.1). Based on a core competence approach (Prahalad and Hamel, 1990) this model provides a useful starting point for identifying what should and should not be outsourced: the closer to a company's core (competence) an outsourcing object gets the higher the risk. Peripheral activities are 'low hanging fruit' that can be outsourced with minimal risk, distinct activities can possibly be outsourced but at higher risk, and core activities (i.e. very close to the company's core) are unlikely to be feasible for outsourcing. As this model indicates, the challenge lies within the close-to-core activities and it is here that many outsourcing discussions have focused in recent years.

Figure 5.1 suggests that it is not simply a question of make or buy, but that in-between options exist. Some authors have argued that it is a matter of 'make, buy or ally' (e.g. Jacobides

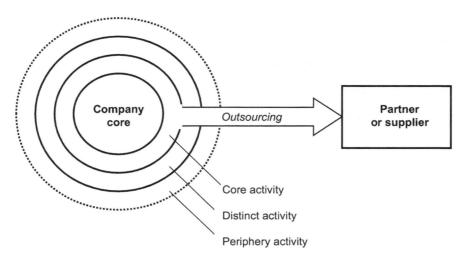

Figure 5.1 Outsourcing model

Source: Adapted from Arnold (2000).

and Billinger, 2006). 'Ally' implies an alliance-based collaborative approach where suppliers (or outsourcing service providers) make a significant investment in the core operations of the outsourcing company and effectively become an extension of the company, but where the outsourcing provider technically retains its independence from the focal firm. Firms adopting an alliance approach may do so because on the one hand they are unable to produce the required goods or services themselves, for example because they lack the internal technological know-how, but on the other hand they need more control than a traditional transactional purchasing arrangement allows. An example of the alliance-based approach is pharmaceutical manufacturing firms in China forming partnering agreements with patent-holding firms to produce drugs under licence.

5.2 Theoretical perspectives informing the outsourcing decision

To consider the make-or-buy decision from a more theoretical perspective it is necessary to explore three important theories: transaction cost economics (TCE), the resource-based view (RBV) and the interaction approach developed by the Industrial Marketing and Purchasing (IMP) group. Management research examines outsourcing from a theoretical perspective to explain the internal and external dynamics of the firm and to understand what is happening in areas such as core skills, capabilities and more transient elements such as knowledge. Although TCE and RBV are often presented as conflicting approaches supported by theorists with widely differing views, there are points at which they intersect such as the pursuit of long-term competitive advantage (e.g. Arnold, 2000), even if the means by which this is achieved is not the same. The three theories are now briefly examined in the following sections and then compared in order to identify differences and similarities.

Note 5.1

Outsourcing public services in the UK

Outsourcing is often associated with the practice of handing over public services to be managed by private corporations. The National Audit Office estimates that the UK government spends £187bn on buying in goods and services every year. Although the reason cited by government is almost always to do with cost saving and capacity constraints, the trend towards ever greater outsourcing is putting vital public services (e.g. health, highways, prisons, waste management) in the hands of potentially unstable profit-seeking conglomerates while still leaving the public sector with the asset risk related to maintaining core infrastructure. Companies such as Serco and G4S are some of the biggest outsourcing firms in the UK who manage hundreds of diverse contracts for national and local government agencies. They are constantly searching for opportunities to find growth and secure additional profit, which means capturing new contracts and winning renewals in a competitive market. Specialist contracting companies Biffa and Veolia are market leaders in domestic waste collection and are also under pressure to generate financial leverage and boost shareholder returns from contracts with the public sector. Biffa recently had to write down roughly £1bn of debt to restructure its high level of borrowing. As one of Britain's biggest waste management firms delivering a service once performed by local council workers, it is drawing up plans for a stock market flotation less than three years after financial problems prompted a takeover by its lenders. The move comes as Biffa, which employs more than 6,000 people and operates 2,500 waste collection trucks, some of which powered by bio-fuel from waste cooking oil, seeks to take advantage of the growing demand for recycling services in the UK.

5.2.1 Transaction cost economics

Transaction cost economics (TCE) is one of the most established economic theories, which underpins not only the concept of outsourcing but also purchasing and supply (chain) management. Although not without its critics (e.g. Ghoshal and Moran, 1996), TCE provides a theory for how production transformation is organized. TCE's chief exponent Oliver Williamson (1975; 2005; 2008) puts forward a theory of determining the most economical governance structure for a firm, polarized as to whether the firm decides to be vertically integrated and produce goods in-house or buys from the market. Focusing on transactions (not relationships) as the unit of analysis, Williamson's model of TCE concentrates on minimization of transaction costs as the principal driver of make-or-buy decisions and places much importance on the role of contracts. Williamson's work on transaction costs and how to approach the boundary of the firm is central to the division between the provision and commissioning of goods and services: in other words, the decision over whether a firm will make or buy. To grasp the basic tenets of TCE it is important to understand the following concepts: transaction cost, asset specificity and opportunism.

- *Transaction cost* is the cost incurred in making any economic exchange, for instance when buying or selling goods and services, gathering market information such as price, invoicing and payment, writing a contract, and the whole process of negotiation between buyers and suppliers.

- *Asset specificity* is defined as the extent to which the investments made to support a particular transaction have a higher value to that transaction than they would have if they were redeployed for any other purpose. Such assets are specialized and unique to a specific task, for example the production of a certain component may require investment in specialized equipment, e.g. steel tools designed for complex plastic mouldings, or the delivery of a service that requires a particular set of professional skills, e.g. legal advice offered during an industrial dispute. If a supplier makes customized components for a customer there is a high degree of asset specificity as they are specific to that customer.

- *Opportunism* means self-interest seeking on the part of an organization involving some kind of guile or deliberate deceit, including deliberately withholding or distorting business information, doing less work than agreed, or failing to fulfil formal/informal obligations. It occurs in trading activities where rules are lacking and where the opportunist actor has the power to influence an outcome by the attitude which he/she chooses to take. An example of opportunism is a property maintenance company gradually reducing what it perceives to be 'non-essential' time spent by its ground staff on tending to communal flower beds and tree husbandry. Another example might be a supplier selling its products to a customer despite having promised exclusivity of those products to another customer. Some authors suggest that organizations in business behave in a similar manner to animals in the natural world whereby all are driven to compete for their survival and ultimately to further their own self-interest (Cousins 2002). This makes the chances of opportunism highly likely between organizations, all of whom may be competing in the same market environment and over the same, often dwindling, pool of natural resources.

TCE makes a number of behavioural assumptions. Firstly, actors are assumed to behave rationally but as they have neither total information nor perfect information-processing capacities and they have to make decisions within increasingly tight time-frames, they behave according to 'bounded rationality' (Simon, 1991). Secondly, business actors are assumed to be profit-driven and the assumption is that if a good opportunity arises they will generally grasp it; opportunism is assumed as standard behaviour and the way to control it is through control and audit. This is opposite to theories such as interaction theory (Håkansson, 1982), where a much greater emphasis is placed on the role of trust and where opportunism is seen as damaging to the development of trust. TCE places much less emphasis on trust and instead argues that significant 'hold-up risks' (for example a supplier playing off two customers against each other) are likely when asset specificity is high, risk of opportunism is high and there is incomplete contracting. Transactions with highly uncertain outcomes, that occur more frequently and that require higher levels of transaction-specific investments, should be performed within the firm, and therefore not outsourced, because the company cannot safeguard itself against opportunistic behaviour (Guldbrandsen *et al.*, 2009).

Assets that are specific to a transaction are more likely to be internalized within the firm than non-transaction specific assets. Thus, if a supplier delivers parts which are specific to a product then the manufacturer is more likely to seek hierarchical control to reduce opportunism.

A particular problem that can occur is opportunistic re-contracting, where either buyer or supplier can act opportunistically when contracts are renewed, for example by increasing prices or decreasing service levels. Nevertheless, Williamson cautions against vertical integration:

> Because added bureaucratic costs accrue upon taking a transaction out of the market and organizing it internally, internal organization is usefully thought of as the organization form of last resort: try markets, try hybrids and have recourse to the firm only when all else fails.

(Williamson, 2008: 9)

When applying TCE during outsourcing decisions, the focus is on ensuring safeguards through control mechanisms rather than relying on trust. TCE has attracted growing criticism over the years because of ignoring the role of capabilities in economic organization, and neglecting issues such as long-term relationships, especially trust and other social elements in buyer–supplier relationships. In the words of Granovetter (1985), Williamson demonstrates an under-socialized view of markets, while holding an over-socialized view of organizations. Furthermore, TCE is concerned with (transaction) cost minimization and so places little emphasis on value creation. A seminal paper by Ghoshal and Moran (1996) even claims TCE to be 'bad for practice' because it fails to recognize the difference between organizations structuring efficient transactions and the marketplace, in other words: the organization cannot simply be viewed as a substitute for the market. Organizations possess unique advantages for governing certain kinds of economic activities which should not be overlooked solely on the basis of transaction cost.

5.2.2 The resource-based view

The resource-based view (RBV) of strategic management was proposed in the 1980s and emphasizes the importance of a firm's idiosyncratic attributes to competitive position (Wernerfelt, 1984; Barney, 1991; Teece *et al.*, 1997). RBV focuses on the unique resources and capabilities controlled by the firm as sources of sustainable competitive advantage; the term sustainable (or *sustained*) in this context implies a long-term focus rather than a focus on environmental or social issues.

The central logic of the RBV approach is that a firm's success is determined by the resources it owns and controls. RBV theory has developed in several different directions, the most influential to practitioners being that of core competencies by Prahalad and Hamel (1990) which has clear consequences for the outsourcing question (see Figure 5.1). Identifying core competencies enables the firm to understand its core strengths, thereby affecting decisions over activities it seeks to outsource. The underlying focus of RBV is to identify and build sustainable competitive advantage at the level of the firm so from an outsourcing perspective the lesson is to nurture and retain core competences internally, leaving those that are 'non-core' to be developed and supplied by external companies (Quinn, 1999).

One difficult question is: what qualifies as core competencies? Prahalad and Hamel (1994) argue that core competencies must provide customer value, competitor differentiation (i.e. it must be unique) and form the basis for entry into new product markets (extendibility). This is taken directly from RBV theory which proposes that the basis for firm-level competitive advantage lies in the application of a bundle of valuable resources (Wernerfelt, 1984) that meet four different criteria: Valuable, Rare, Inimitable and Non-substitutable or 'VRIN' (Barney, 1991; Peteraf, 1993). Physical or tangible resources might meet these VRIN conditions, but intangible or 'invisible' (Itami and Roehl, 1987) knowledge-intensive resources, such as capabilities and competencies are more likely than physical resources to satisfy the VRIN criteria.

Even if the RBV clearly has some very useful implications for outsourcing decisions, particularly in the form of core competence theory, it has been criticized on a number of dimensions. Various observers (e.g. Porter, 1991; Priem and Butler, 2001) have argued that RBV is tautological: the theory identifies criteria that resources must satisfy in order to qualify as sources of sustainable competitive advantage, but provides little guidance on how to *develop* resources that meet these requirements. Most importantly, although RBV provides the foundations for resource accumulation and exploitation, the theory assumes that unique (whether tangible and/or intangible) resources have to exist and be preserved within the boundary of the firm so it underplays the importance of accessing complementary resources/ competences outside the company, for example from suppliers. What becomes clear is that firms cannot expect to 'purchase' sustained competitive advantage on open markets. Rather such advantages must be found in the rare, imperfectly imitable, and non-substitutable resources already controlled by a firm (Barney, 1991).

As identified by Ramsay (2001) this assumption is also evident in the core competence theory: 'The embedded skills that give rise to the next generation of competitive products cannot be "rented in" by outsourcing and OEM-supply relationships' (Prahalad and Hamel, 1990). In addition to a strong internal focus, RBV is a static theory which can sometimes be interpreted as a 'stick to your knitting' approach. In other words, RBV (and core competence) can lead to an assumption that companies should focus on past strengths and therefore not focus sufficiently on developing new strengths. As the pace of innovation across industries is increasing, a competitive advantage could be nullified or even transformed into a weakness, i.e. core competences risk becoming core rigidities (Leonard-Barton, 1992). There are three more recent theoretical developments in RBV which seek to address such criticisms and are discussed further here: dynamic capabilities, extended resource-based view, and natural resourced-based view.

The theory of *dynamic capabilities* extends classic RBV to the realm of evolving capabilities (Teece *et al.*, 1997; Winter, 2003). The important point is not so much whether we talk about capabilities or competences, but that these are dynamic: viewed as future strengths. Dynamic capabilities are defined as the ability to integrate, build and reconfigure internal and external processes and competences to address a rapidly changing environment, where the ability to maintain and adapt these capabilities is the basis of competitive advantage (Teece *et al.*, 1997). The dynamic capabilities theory therefore addresses the danger that RBV and core competence theory might encourage firms to rest on past laurels, accentuating instead the need for firms to change and innovate. The dynamic capabilities theory focuses on the unique, idiosyncratic and path dependent nature of resources and capabilities: incremental evolution, in other words. However, while moderately changing markets tend to rely on existing knowledge and linear execution, higher velocity markets may require disruptive innovation (Eisenhardt and Martin, 2000). Moreover, dynamic capability theory is still predominantly internally focused and provides only a partial account of competitive advantage in interconnected or networks of firms, where unique and difficult to replicate capabilities are those that concern how companies access capabilities through relationships with other companies (Lavie, 2006). These limitations of both RBV and dynamic capability theory have resulted in several complementary theories, suggesting that value lies in the resource configurations and socio-technical interfaces *between* firms, rather than the nature of the capabilities which reside *within* the firm.

The *extended resource-based view* (ERBV) presents the most recent interpretation of classic RBV, conceived where the structure and function of a relationship relates to the specificity of resources to be transferred. ERBV emerges as a response to the development of competitive advantage in situations where resources and capabilities are held beyond the boundary of the firm (e.g. Mathews, 2003; Arya and Lin, 2007). The ERBV focuses on the assumption that strategic resources beyond the boundaries of the firm can be accessed especially given the existence of certain types of inter-firm relationship. Extended resource-based advantage in this context means that the difficulty to replicate stems from the composition of strong collaborative relationships, including those within supply chains and networks.

The ERBV is closely related to the relational view proposed by Dyer and Singh (1998) as part of the growing literature on the importance of trust in, and relation building between, firms in order to develop competitive – and collaborative – strategic advantage. The relational view argues that relations with outside parties, including suppliers, are essential to developing a sustainable competitive advantage and that it is the relations that constitute the unique and difficult-to-imitate resources. The focus shifts to *relational competence* (Cox, 1996). Therefore, the nature of the relationship may matter more than the nature of resources (Lavie, 2006). ERBV, therefore, gives structure to the idea of ongoing collaboration between organizations across the wider supply network which stimulates resource accumulation and development based on complex interactions and inter-organizational relationships.

The question remains over whether knowledge flowing across the boundary of the firm, e.g. through outsourcing relationships, can be held as proprietary knowledge, or whether knowledge diffusion makes advantage hard to maintain (Lewis *et al.*, 2010). The concept of flowing and diffuse strategic knowledge, and intellectual property, presents a dilemma for firms, as on the one hand they need to source critical resources and technologies from outside the company but on the other hand they need to protect these from competitors. TCE advocates formal safeguards, such as control mechanisms and contracts, whereas, e.g. the relational view (Dyer and Singh, 1998) emphasizes informal safeguards such as trust and commitment. Arguably, informal mechanisms are much more difficult to imitate because they are socially complex and idiosyncratic to the exchange relationship so have greater potential to deliver superior performance, owing to: 1) lower contracting costs; 2) lower monitoring costs; 3) lower adaptation costs; 4) lower re-contracting costs; and 5) superior incentives for value-creation initiatives (Dyer and Singh, 1998: 671).

The *natural resource-based view* (NRBV) was introduced in Chapter 1, so will not be repeated in depth here. NRBV is still in its infancy, but we should note this recent development of the RBV as it attempts to build on the RBV to take into account a focus on the natural environment. Hart (1995) argues that sustainable development, product stewardship and pollution prevention constitute potential sources of sustainable competitive advantage.

All three of these strategies require close collaboration with a range of external stakeholders thus sharing the focus on external resources with the ERBV and the relational view. The NRBV takes this analysis one step further as it suggests that resources gain social legitimacy through stakeholder collaboration. The NRBV therefore relies not only on models of strategic alliances, but on more complex stakeholder or network models. For this reason we turn to the final theory that informs the outsourcing decisions and places much importance on collaborative relationships and the embeddedness of these within complex business networks: the interaction approach.

Note 5.2

Resources, competitive advantage and sustainability

The debate around unique, bounded resources and their contribution to competitive advantage is particularly relevant to environmental sustainability. For instance, should the tacit and explicit knowledge of good practice in areas such as low carbon procurement, circular economy and corporate social responsibility be viewed as a source of sustainable competitive advantage (SCA) available only to a few world-class organizations? Or should such core knowledge be shared with other firms and their suppliers as part of a wider concern over slowing the rate of harmful activities and depletion of non-renewable natural resources which affects the whole planet? Such arguments begin to question the assumptions of classic economic theory around bounded resources as a source of competitive advantage focused at firm or organization level, and gives support to emergent ideas over the extended resource-based view and the benefits of knowledge accumulated from more synergistic or shared supply chain interactions.

The *interaction approach* developed by the Industrial Marketing and Purchasing (IMP) group shares many views with the ERBV and relational view, but predates both by around 20 years (e.g. Håkansson, 1987). The interaction approach is not a theory of the firm as such and focuses far less on how to achieve a sustainable competitive advantage, but it is relevant here because it is an established buyer–supplier relationship and network theory and it has frequently been relied on by authors in purchasing and supply management including those analysing the outsourcing question (e.g. Dubois, 1998). The interaction approach emphasizes that although it is important to protect internal strategic resources it is increasingly necessary for companies to access important resources through external relationships with other companies; like the relational view (Dyer and Singh, 1998) the interaction approach suggests that relationships with other companies, including suppliers, can themselves be sources of competitive advantage. Yet managing the outsourcing relationship requires considerable resources after the decision has been made, where buyer–supplier integration takes time to evolve and is contingent on strategic priorities (Kaipia and Turkulainen, 2017).

However, the view within this school of thought takes the focus on inter-organizational relationships further by challenging the view of boundaries between companies as being separate (Gadde and Håkansson, 2010). Companies are intrinsically interconnected through resource ties, activity links and actors' bonds. So, instead of focusing on where the boundary should be between two firms (as in a typical make-or-buy decision) the firm should understand its multiple boundaries with a range of firms within the wider supply network and its position within this network. The outsourcing decision – moving an activity from inside the firm to another firm within the network – has implications not only on these two actors but on the total pattern of activities: there are network-wide implications that need to be understood (Gadde and Hulthén, 2009). From this perspective, the question of insourcing becomes equally important to the question of outsourcing, where 'make-or-buy' analysis becomes supply network analysis.

There are obvious complementarities between the IMP interaction approach and the NRBV as both emphasize the role of stakeholders and networks of relationships. The interaction approach has the potential to shed light on the process of implementing sustainability within supply networks yet so far only sporadic attempts at applying an interaction approach to sustainable purchasing and supply management (e.g. Crespin-Mazet and Dontenwill, 2012) have been undertaken.

5.3 Synthesis of the theoretical approaches to outsourcing

The discussion of theoretical perspectives that inform the outsourcing decision shows that different theories have different units of analysis and are based on different assumptions. Consequently the recommendations regarding outsourcing differ. The purpose of this section is to try to bring together these differing implications and recommendations for the outsourcing decision, thereby moving from a theoretical to a more practical focus.

The main conclusion from TCE is this: the outsourcing decision should be viewed as a strategic make-or-buy decision. Transactions with highly uncertain outcomes, that occur more frequently and that require higher levels of transaction-specific investments, should not be outsourced, because the company cannot safeguard itself against opportunistic behaviour. Companies should focus on minimization of transactions costs as the principal driver of make-or-buy decisions. TCE points to the importance of developing hybrid approaches, but formal safeguard mechanisms are essential to protect the outsourcing company against opportunism.

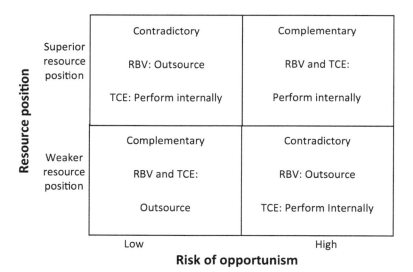

Figure 5.2 RBV and TCE prescriptions in outsourcing decisions

Source: Adapted from McIvor (2009).

The main conclusion from traditional RBV theory with obvious implications for outsourcing seems clear: develop and protect strategic resources/core competences and do not outsource these. In addition, resources and competences sourced externally do not provide sources of sustainable competitive advantage. Recent spin-offs from the RBV, such as the ERBV and the relational view, state that companies can source critical resources and competences from strategic partners and that their ability to access these – relational capability – in fact can constitute a source of sustainable competitive advantage. Figure 5.2 captures the two key dimensions from TCE and RBV in a matrix: the resource position and the risk of opportunism. According to this model, TCE and RBV give conflicting recommendations in situations of superior resource position/low risk of opportunism and weaker resource position/high risk of opportunism and it is only in the opposite situations that the two actually agree.

Arnold (2000) provides an alternative framework for reconciling the TCE and RBV recommendations for outsourcing. Figure 5.3 shows a framework developed on the basis of his original framework, which in turn draws from Quinn (1999). The framework here is simplified yet incorporates the RBV VRIN criteria more explicitly and highlights the importance of safeguard mechanisms. Arnold's model presents the make-or-buy question as more of a continuum which includes a mid-phase termed 'ally/partner' as a possible third option. This suggests that a hybrid approach exists between that of adopting either a pure institutional hierarchy (make) or market-based approach (buy). However, although forming an alliance agreement to work with partners such as suppliers may seem a sensible option, this approach to sharing workload may open the firm up to certain risks such as the loss of intellectual property if the relationship deteriorates.

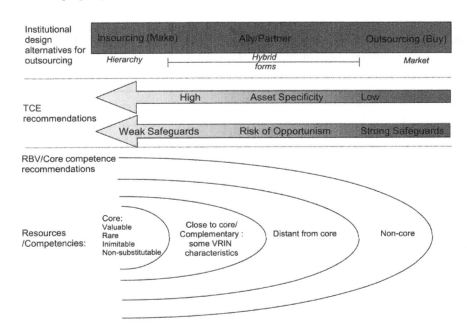

Figure 5.3 Combined TCE and RBV outsourcing model

Source: Adapted from Arnold (2000).

Both NRBV and the interaction approach put emphasis on understanding individual companies as parts of complex business networks. Instead of making make-or-buy decisions in isolation, companies should understand the network-wide implications of outsourcing decisions. There is therefore a much wider acceptance that critical competences are not so much core as *distributed* across business/supply networks (Grandstrand *et al.*, 1997). Like the relational view, the interaction approach puts more emphasis on relational competences and the role of informal rather than formal safeguards, including trust, commitment and mutual dependency.

Understanding whether a firm makes, buys or opts for some form of hybrid alliance approach, such as developing a (formal or informal) strategic partnership with a supplier, is a complex decision, where much depends on the level of in-house capability and strategic criticality of the component, product or service in question. Particularly in industries dependent on technological development involving longer lead times, such as the aerospace and pharmaceutical sectors, decisions over inward investment, partnerships and tactical sourcing from the supply chain are critical in the planning of new products. In the aerospace industry today, a considerable proportion of investment by firms such as the engine maker Rolls-Royce is spent on tackling how to reduce the weight of components (e.g. use of composites, alloys) as a means of reducing fuel consumption during flight. The development of lighter engines using lightweight components is a source of sustainable competitive advantage to Rolls-Royce and one which depends on understanding how to engage with the supply chain and wider market environment.

The analysis matrix in Figure 5.4 gives an example of not only how the firm decides to 'make or buy' based on a sliding scale of firm capability over business criticality, but where the control and protection of key knowledge and skills fit into the overall picture of outsourcing and supply strategy. As Figure 5.4 shows, Rolls-Royce considers not only the make/do or buy options, but also options for controlling through licensing agreements and protecting through strategic supplier partnerships. Rolls-Royce clearly seeks to make only very little in-house, and accesses everything else through a variety of external sourcing mechanisms.

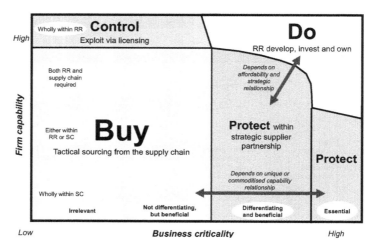

Figure 5.4 Business analysis matrix

Source: Adapted from Rolls-Royce.

OUTSOURCING HOSPITAL CLEANING IN THE UK NATIONAL HEALTH SERVICE

The decision to outsource cleaning contracts was first taken in the 1980s as a means to reduce UK hospital operating costs. Today about 40 per cent of hospitals use the private sector to provide cleaning services, particularly in busy areas such as wards, yet there is evidence that the practice has led to a drop in standards and a rise in infections (Lethbridge, 2012). To underline the seriousness of the issue, in 2008 at the Royal College of Nursing conference it was overwhelmingly voted for a motion proposing an end to the practice of contracting out cleaning to private firms. In response, the government has made cleaning one of its highest priorities to tackle common infections such as MRSA and Clostridium difficile. Yet despite such concerns, the Department of Health claims ensuring hospitals are clean and safe is not as straightforward as simply bringing all cleaning back in-house to be performed by NHS staff.

This case briefly describes the build-up of events which lead to this difficult decision over the outsourcing of cleaning, and some of the key background information that describes the complexity which surrounds the UK National Health Service (NHS).

The NHS was launched in 1948, born out of a long-held ideal that good healthcare should be available to everyone, regardless of wealth. Apart from charges for prescriptions, optical services and dental services, the NHS today remains free at point of use for all UK residents, which currently stands at more than 64 million people. For the financial year 2015/16, the overall NHS budget was around £116 billion, with NHS England managing £101 billion of this. The structure of healthcare is now devolved in the UK, with England, Northern Ireland, Scotland and Wales each having their own systems of public healthcare funded by and accountable to separate governments and parliaments, together with smaller private sector and voluntary provision. Each of the four autonomous regions in the UK now has different policies and priorities, resulting in a variety of differences existing between these systems. Yet the challenges of providing a modern and well-equipped health service capable of meeting the demands of a growing population with a high proportion of elderly people expecting to live well into their 80s and 90s is taking its toll on NHS hospital capacity and resource planning. Despite this, in a 2014 report ranking developed-country healthcare systems, the UK was ranked the best healthcare system in the world overall and in the following categories: quality of care (i.e. effective, safe, coordinated, patient-oriented), access to care, efficiency, equity and overall palliative care. On the other hand, in 2005–2009 cancer survival rates lagged ten years behind the rest of Europe and, according to the OECD, the UK still has a poor record of preventing ill health where some hospitals remain so short-staffed and underequipped that people are dying needlessly because of lack of investment.

This verdict of an organization struggling to cope from the Organisation for Economic Co-operation and Development (OECD) will make embarrassing reading for the UK government, particularly as the so-called 'cash-strapped NHS' (Independent.com) heads for another winter crisis caused by falling temperatures, rising levels of illness in the elderly and hospital facilities increasingly unable to meet demand. Medical staff are frequently too rushed to improve levels of care that have in many areas fallen below countries such as Turkey and Poland. Almost 75,000 more doctors and nurses are needed to match standards in similar countries, the OECD said in its annual study comparing the quality of healthcare across 34 countries. While access to care is 'generally good', the quality of care in the UK is 'poor to mediocre' across several key health areas as the NHS struggles to get even the basics right such as ward hygiene and cleanliness. Furthermore, the report cites a fundamental lack of investment in hospitals over the last six years and short-term cost cutting as the prime culprits (see Figure 5.5).

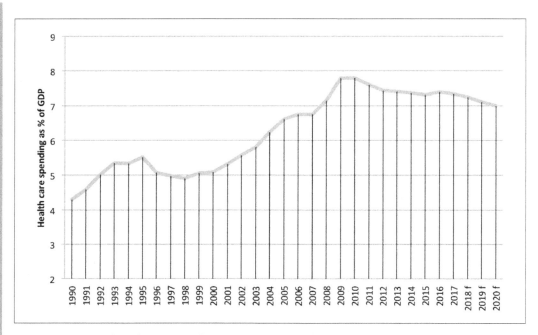

Figure 5.5 NHS healthcare spending as percentage of GDP

So, what is to be done over the decision to outsource cleaning services in NHS hospitals? Brought in originally as a means of cutting maintenance costs, the long-term impact has actually increased infection levels on wards, with the effect of raising costs in overall patient care. Yet to reverse the practice of outsourcing and give back cleaning responsibility to nurses now would significantly affect hospital spending, and take many medically trained nurses away from frontline patient care, a duty which is increasingly being entrusted to them as opposed to doctors and consultants. For hospitals to take control of daily in-house cleaning operations would require a major culture shift in an organization that has become used to looking to the outside world for a whole spectrum of medical, technical and maintenance-related services. With around one-fifth of all clinical services being outsourced today by the NHS (CHPI, 2015) such a shift would go against current trends, requiring in-house training and an expansion of ancillary nursing staff, meaning the introduction of further cost commitments into an already struggling UK public health sector. There are around 53,000 contracts now between the NHS and the private sector, where the safety and quality of healthcare is dependent on how these contracts are managed. Hospitals need to recognize that contracting for healthcare can be highly problematic, particularly where 'asymmetry of information makes it impossible for a commissioner of services to know whether a provider is delivering according to the terms of the contract, or is cutting corners or reducing quality in order to gain extra revenue' (CHPI, 2015: 4).

Outsourcing therefore is a challenging activity for the health sector. When executed correctly, it provides organizations with the flexibility to manage their service requirements according to demand over time, and within a defined cost framework. Providing that proper measures can be applied to monitor the quality of essential outsourced services such as hospital cleaning and maintenance, the trend for outsourcing in the NHS is likely set to continue.

CASE STUDY 5.1

5.4 Conclusion

The outsourcing decision is highly complex, requiring analysis of a range of issues related to internal and external resource and capability positions, transaction costs (that are often difficult to quantify) and business risks. The outsourcing, make-or-buy or 'make, buy or ally' decision has significant implications for almost all functions in the company because of the changes working with outside organizations bring to the firm. In simple terms, outsourcing involves asking a series of questions starting with the strategic importance of the activity or function in question, but it also requires assessment of how the relationship with the outsourcing provider (or supplier) is going to be managed and the investment required to develop the relationship and control any business risks. The closer to the core competences of the company, the greater the risks, but the boundaries between the company and its supply network are becoming increasingly blurred as competencies become distributed across multiple supply network actors each with their own specialized competencies. Indeed, managing a network of outsourcing relationships is becoming a core competence in itself.

References

Arnold U (2000) New dimensions of outsourcing: A combination of transaction cost economics and the core competence concept. *European Journal of Purchasing & Supply Management* 6(1): 23–29.

Arya B and Lin Z (2007) Understanding collaboration outcomes from an extended resource-based view perspective: The roles of organizational characteristics, partner attributes, and network structures. *Journal of Management* 33(50): 697–723.

Barney JB (1991) Firm resources and sustained competitive advantage. *Journal of Management* 17(1): 99–120.

Barney JB (1999) How a firm's capabilities affect boundary decisions. *Sloan Management Review* 40: 137–145.

CHPI (2015) The contracting NHS – can the NHS handle the outsourcing of clinical services? *Centre for Health and the Public Interest*. Available at: www.chpi.org.uk/wp-content/uploads/2015/04/CHPI-ContractingNHS-Mar-final.pdf (last accessed 21 April 2016).

Cousins PD (2002) A conceptual model for managing long-term inter-organizational relationships. *European Journal of Purchasing and Supply Management* 8(2): 71–82.

Cox A (1996) Relational competence and strategic procurement management. *European Journal of Purchasing and Supply Management* 2(1): 57–70.

Cox A (2005) Why outsourcing doesn't fly. *CPO Agenda*: 20–29.

Crespin-Mazet F and Dontenwill E (2012) Sustainable procurement: Building legitimacy in the supply network. *Journal of Purchasing and Supply Management* 18(4): 207–217.

Dierickx I and Cool K (1989) Asset stock accumulation and sustainability of competitive advantage. *Management Science* 35(12): 1504–1511.

Dubois A (1998) *Organising Industrial Activities Across Firm Boundaries.* London: Routledge.

Dyer JH and Singh H (1998) The relational view: Cooperative strategy and sources of interorganizational competitive advantage. *Academy of Management Review* 23(4): 660–679.

Eisenhardt K and Martin J (2000) Dynamic capabilities: What are they? *Strategic Management Journal* 21: 1105–1121.

Gadde L-E and Håkansson H (2010) *Supply Network Strategies.* Chichester: John Wiley & Sons.

Gadde L-E and Hulthén K (2009) Improving logistics outsourcing through increasing buyer–provider interaction. *Industrial Marketing Management* 38(6): 633–640.

Ghoshal S and Moran P (1996) Bad for practice: A critique of the transaction cost theory. *Academy of Management Review* 21: 13–47.

Granovetter MS (1985) Economics action and social structure: the problem of embeddedness. *American Journal of Sociology* 91(3): 481–510.

Granstrand O, Patel P and Pavitt K (1997) Multi-technology corporations: Why they have 'distributed' rather than 'distinctive core' competencies. *California Management Review* 39(4) Summer: 1–19.

Gulbrandsen B, Sandvik K and Haugland SA (2009) Antecedents of vertical integration: Transaction cost economics and resource-based explanations. *Journal of Purchasing and Supply Management* 15(2): 89–102.

Håkansson H (ed.) IMP Group (1982) *International Marketing and Purchasing of Industrial Goods: An Interaction Approach*. Chichester: Wiley.

Håkansson H (ed.) (1987) *Industrial Technological Development: A Network Approach*. London: Croom Helm.

Hart SL (1995) A natural-resource-based view of the firm. *Academy of Management Review* 20(4): 986–1014.

Independent (2014) Autumn statement: Chancellor George Osborne to pledge 2bn boost for cash-strapped NHS. Available at: https://www.independent.co.uk/news/uk/politics/autumn-statement-chancellor-george-osborne-to-pledge-2bn-boost-for-cash-strapped-nhs-9893409.html (last accessed 21 April 2016).

Itami H and Roehl T (1987) *Mobilizing Invisible Assets*. Cambridge, MA: Harvard University Press.

Jacobides M and Billinger S (2006) Designing the boundaries of the firm: From 'make, buy, and ally' to the dynamic benefits of vertical architecture. *Organizational Science* 17(2): 249–261.

Kaipia R and Turkulainen V (2017) Managing integration in outsourcing relationship: The influence of cost and quality priorities. *Industrial Marketing Management* 61: 114–129.

Lavie D (2006) The competitive advantage of interconnected firms: an extension of the resource-based view. *Academy of Management Review* 31(3): 638–658.

Leonard-Barton D (1992) Core capabilities and core rigidities. *Strategic Management Journal*, Summer special issue: 111–126.

Lethbridge J (2012) *Empty Promises: The Impact of Outsourcing on NHS Services*. Technical Report. London: UNISON.

Lewis M, Brandon-Jones A, Slack N and Howard M (2010) Competing through operations and supply: The role of classic and extended resource-based advantage. *International Journal of Operations & Production Management* 30(10): 1032–1058.

Mathews J (2003) Strategizing by firms in the presence of markets for resources. *Industrial and Corporate Change* 12(6): 1157–1193.

McIvor R (2008) What is the right outsourcing strategy for your process? *European Management Review* 26(1): 24–34.

McIvor R (2009) How the transaction cost and resource-based theories of the firm inform outsourcing evaluation. *Journal of Operations Management* 27: 45–63.

OECD (2015) *Focus on Health Spending: OECD Health Statistics 2015*. Available at: www.oecd.org/health/health-systems/Focus-Health-Spending-2015.pdf (last accessed 21 April 2016).

Peteraf MA (1993) The cornerstones of competitive advantage: A resource-based view. *Strategic Management Journal* 14(3): 179–191.

Porter ME (1991) Towards a dynamic theory of strategy. *Strategic Management Journal* 12(special issue): 95–117.

Prahalad CK and Hamel G (1990) The core competence of the corporation. *Harvard Business Review* 68(3): 79–91.

Prahalad CK and Hamel G (1994) *Competing for the Future*. Boston, MA: Harvard Business School Press.

Priem RL and Butler JE (2001) Is the resource-based theory a useful perspective for strategic management research? *Academy of Management Review* 26(1): 22–40.

Quinn J (1999) Strategic outsourcing: Leveraging knowledge capabilities. *Sloan Management Review* 40(4): 9–21.

Ramsay J (2001) The resource based perspective, rents, and purchasing's contribution to sustainable competitive advantage. *Journal of Supply Chain Management* 37: 38–47.

Simon HA (1991) Bounded rationality and organizational learning. *Organization Science* 2(1): 125–134.

Teece D, Pisano G and Shuen A (1997) Dynamic capabilities and strategic management. *Strategic Management Journal* 18(7): 509–533.

Wernerfelt B (1984) The resource-based view of the firm. *Strategic Management Journal* 5(2): 171–180.

Williamson OE (1975) *Markets and Hierarchy: Analysis and Antitrust Implications*. New York: Free Press.

Williamson OE (2005) Transaction cost economics and business administration. *Scandinavian Journal of Management* 21(1): 19–40.

Williamson OE (2008) Outsourcing: Transaction cost economics and supply chain management. *Journal of Supply Chain Management* 44(2): 5–16.

Winter SG (2003) Understanding dynamic capabilities. *Strategic Management Journal* 24: 991–999.

CHAPTER 6

Global sourcing

LEARNING OBJECTIVES

By the end of this chapter you should be able to:

- Define key concepts related to global sourcing;
- Distinguish between international and global sourcing;
- Evaluate the drivers of global sourcing and the limitations of a pure cost focus;
- Explain the trend towards re-shoring and near-shoring;
- Analyse the sustainability challenges in the context of global sourcing.

6.0 Overview

Global sourcing is the practice of contracting out activities or functions to specialized suppliers around the world. The most basic meaning of the term sourcing is 'product searching' and is often associated with the prefix 'global', 'international' or 'strategic'. Whereas Chapter 5 examined outsourcing decision models by evaluating the so-called 'make-or-buy' decision, here we focus on the particular challenges of sourcing to, and from, global supply markets, especially low cost-countries (LCCs) such as China, which over the past 30 years have emerged as major supply markets due to significant cost advantages. In short, because of the effects of globalization, global sourcing has become synonymous with standard practice for many companies, whether seeking to source auto parts, computer components, fashion clothing or relocate call centre services offshore.

A number of consequences have emerged as a result of these low-cost-driven, global supply networks, not just concerning risk and resilience issues of products and services supplied over long distances, but of the challenges associated with supply chain transparency and supplier accountability, particularly in demonstrating a firm's commitment to corporate social responsibility (Walker *et al.*, 2008; Lund-Thomsen and Lindgreen, 2014). One area of major concern for many consumers today is the working conditions of employees in supplier organizations based in developing countries: an aspect of operational practice, where global brands such as Mattel and Apple have been criticized (Brammer *et al.*, 2011). In fact, some companies are beginning to reverse their earlier global sourcing decisions, resulting in practices such as 're-shoring' or the moving production of goods and services back towards local sources of supply (Gray *et al.*, 2013; Tate,

2014). These recent changes in sourcing practice hint at the difficulties of monitoring expansion overseas and the competitive advantage of sourcing from markets nearer to home (Steinle and Schiele, 2008).

Best cost country sourcing (BCCS) is now a term often used instead of low-cost country sourcing, as a means of going beyond evaluating benefit based primarily on labour costs. BCCS seeks to adopt a total cost of ownership approach by including factors such as inflationary pressures on wages in emerging markets, shifting currency values, regulatory compliance, logistics costs, and an increasing focus on greener, more sustainable and socially responsible supply chains (Dutzler *et al.*, 2011). The final part of this chapter explores the future for sustainable global sourcing given the challenges highlighted above.

6.1 International and global sourcing

There is no doubt that a major driver of the increase in outsourcing in recent years has been the opportunity to drastically reduce costs due to low labour costs in developing and industrializing countries such as China and India. In fact, the concept of low-cost country sourcing is often used to reflect this particular form of global sourcing, although global sourcing should not be purely a question of accessing low-cost labour. A report by the Boston Consulting Group (BCG, 2007) listed a range of advantages of sourcing from China, including robust product and process innovation, sophisticated and diversified supply bases, a low-cost, highly skilled labour pool that can support production and R&D, low-cost plants and equipment, national and local government incentives, a vast and growing domestic market, and in certain sectors, e.g. plastics, printing and electronics, highly developed clusters. However, the report also noted that companies sourcing from China are encountering increasingly tough challenges. A later BCG report (2010) showed that many companies are rethinking LCC sourcing strategies due to growing labour costs, currency fluctuations, volatile commodity prices, quality concerns, labour shortage and double-digit wage inflation, and growing protectionism.

Best cost country sourcing – or BCCS – is described as the 'next generation' approach to global sourcing, where leading consumer goods and retail companies rank their overseas sourcing initiatives according to their level of maturity: novice, progressing and best in class (Dutzler *et al.*, 2011). Although cost reductions of between 15 and 30 per cent in sectors such as textiles and apparel, housewares, injection-moulded plastics and electronics still remains a prime reason for global sourcing for Western European companies, recent pay rises and rising inflation in China and India mean companies must revisit their sourcing strategies and re-evaluate the possibility of alternative destinations (e.g. Vietnam, Cambodia, countries in Africa), locating manufacturing closer to the market (e.g. Eastern Europe in the case of European companies) and the need to create a greener, more sustainable strategy by reducing 'merchandizing miles'. IKEA, for example, plans to double its sourcing volume in India and increase its coverage of retail stores in the country.

This section now explores the rationale for global sourcing in more detail, and then clarifies the meaning of global sourcing compared with international sourcing. A model of different stages of international and global sourcing is presented, where global sourcing is the penultimate stage. However, as is subsequently discussed, there are signs of growing localism, or 're-shoring' which may indicate that the global sourcing trend has peaked.

6.1.1 Why global sourcing?

The traditional motive for global sourcing, especially when it relates to LCCs, would appear to be all about cost, but access to suppliers offering quality components and technology as well as a way to access a new market for sales and marketing purposes, circumventing trade barriers in the process, are also part of the equation (Guinipero and Monczka 1990; Alguire *et al.*, 1994; Quintens *et al.*, 2006). Indeed, companies may have little choice but to source from the region in which they wish to expand as local content rules, e.g. in China, often require firms to purchase specified quantities of components from suppliers in the country where the firm opens a manufacturing plant (Munson and Rosenblatt, 1997; Nassimbeni and Sartor, 2007).

Note 6.1

Volkswagen's global sourcing strategy

Europe's largest automaker Volkswagen AG acknowledges that its production plants in western Germany make little profit. The Wolfsburg plant in Lower Saxony, VW's headquarters, is a sprawling 13-square-kilometre site employing 48,000 people. Here it takes around 40 hours to build the popular Golf model, with its closest competitor the Renault Megane requiring only 17. With new car enterprises emerging all over China, and China set to overtake Japan as the second largest market after America, the prospect of sourcing cheaper products from the East poses both opportunities and serious threats for VW chiefs over maintaining levels of employment in their home production plants as well as promoting sound corporate social responsibility values in their partner organizations across China. Volkswagen was the first foreign carmaker to invest in China with the joint venture called Shanghai Volkswagen Automotive Company in 1984. With German brands – particularly German automotive brands – highly popular and trusted in China, VW has done well in the region because they know the territory in terms of market trends and regional production capability. They can also compete directly with Chinese competitors and present a better, more reliable image to local customers. However, VW's strategy may backfire in the long term, with foreign automakers only allowed to manufacture cars domestically in China through joint ventures with local partners. The requirement to transfer technology and know-how through forced joint ventures are fundamentally at odds with the commitments China made when it joined the World Trade Organization.

Source: Hawranek (2006); Akan (2017)

Research by Nassimbeni (2006) showed the importance of access to low-cost resources, but also pointed out the significance of access to scarce and distinctive resources. One example here is that rare metal ores and minerals, which are used to produce, e.g. mobile phones, computers and cars, are almost exclusively available from Chinese mines that account for 97 per cent of rare ore and mineral production worldwide. In fact, many companies are increasingly dependent on such rare materials that are also vital ingredients in green technologies (Energy Outlook, 2012). Therefore, although access to less expensive resources

Table 6.1 Global sourcing drivers, facilitators and barriers

	Drivers	Facilitators	Barriers
Product	Cost advantages (materials and components) Better delivery performance Higher-quality products Unique or differential products Obtain better technology	Product type Supplier certification Top management support Nationality of parent company	Limited production volume Different product standards Regular design changes Insufficient product modifications Delivery delays
Firm/management	Assure organizational flexibility Global attitude, orientation and experience Centralization of decision making Integration of worldwide activities	Knowledge on foreign businesses, exchange rates and global opportunities Planning for global purchasing Operational philosophy (lot sizes, number of suppliers, etc.)	Parallel trade Lack of resources needed for global purchasing (staff, time, money, etc.) Cost of travel and communication
Network	Take advantage of existing logistics systems Diversification of supplier base	Long-term relationship prospects Buying alliances	JIT sourcing requirements Finding qualified suppliers Foreign supplier image
Industry/competition	Competitive positioning Protect proprietary technology Gain a foothold in new markets Market size	Type of industry Technological orientation of industry	Diverse business practices Limited industry information Agents'/brokers' fees Intensity of foreign competition
Environment	Cost advantages (labour) Satisfy countertrade requirements Guard against currency fluctuations Stimulating foreign government policies Advantageous legal and economic environment	Development of trade zones Better foreign transport and communication Capable intermediaries Cultural similarities	Import quotas Country of origin image Adverse political environment Adverse economic environment Customs regulations Different time zones Lack of government assistance Language/cultural differences

Source: Quintens et al., 2006.

remains an important driver of global sourcing, it is increasingly considered a source of long-term sustainable competitive advantage (Nassimbeni, 2006).

Table 6.1 is taken from Quintens *et al.* (2006), who conducted a major review of existing global sourcing research. The table provides an overview of global sourcing drivers (or motives), facilitators and barriers.

6.1.2 International and global sourcing: what is the difference?

Often global sourcing is used in the same vein as international sourcing or purchasing, but what are the differences? The important difference is not so much whether we talk about purchasing or sourcing, but the distinction between international and global matters. In short, global sourcing suggests a more advanced stage and tends to imply an integration and coordination of sourcing strategies on a worldwide scale. A useful definition is provided by Trent and Monczka (2003), describing global sourcing as the worldwide integration of engineering, operations, logistics, procurement, and even marketing within the upstream portion of a firm's supply chain. Where international sourcing implies buying from a foreign supplier on an *ad hoc* basis, global sourcing infers a much more strategically consistent approach (Bozarth *et al.*, 1998).

Capturing the benefits of globalization requires a global sourcing strategy which involves the integration of engineering, operations and purchasing functions across the global supply network. But, although adopting a global business strategy is seen as critical by companies that wish to expand on a worldwide basis, most firms do not have a well-developed approach to global sourcing in place, with many improvement opportunities left unrealized (Trent and Monczka, 2005). In reality, many companies operate at best an international sourcing strategy as they do not present a coordinated, standardized global image.

6.1.3 The global sourcing process: a stages model

The development of a global sourcing strategy does not happen overnight but tends to evolve over a number of stages, beginning with domestic purchasing and progressing to international purchasing before becoming global. Trent and Monczka's (2005) model (Figure 6.1) suggests a linear progression of increasing excellence in sourcing capability that finishes with the development of a global sourcing strategy integrated across worldwide locations and functional groups.

The distinction between international and global sourcing is therefore one of sourcing strategies: global sourcing is not so much dependent on the number of worldwide sourcing location; it is the integration and consistency of sourcing strategies across worldwide locations and functional groups. In other words, global sourcing implies a systematic extension of purchasing policy worldwide and a strategic orientation of purchasing activities (Arnold 1999). Quintens *et al.* (2006) have identified four dimensions of global purchasing (or sourcing) strategy:

1 Purchasing process configuration

2 Standardization of global purchasing process

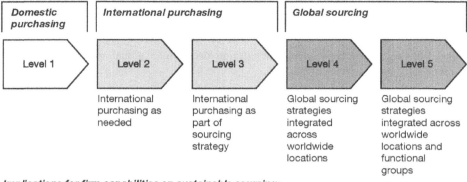

Figure 6.1 Progression towards global sourcing

Source: Adapted from Trent and Monczka (2005).

3 Standardization of product-related characteristics

4 Standardization of personnel-related characteristics

Global sourcing strategy decisions therefore concern, in particular, issues of standardization and relate to questions of organizational structure and processes. These decisions are closely tied to the drive for purchasing synergies that were discussed in earlier chapters, for example, using standardized material and component specifications across global locations enables high volumes, improved quality through reduced variety, and even customization. For capital-intensive industries, such as the automotive industry, product architectures increasingly rely on shared platforms and standardized modular components and it is critical that suppliers worldwide play their part in and comply with these standards.

There are both economies of scale and process (establishment of a common way of working) that are essential in creating a globally consistent line of conduct to suppliers, benchmarking procedures and results, and joint training and development (Faes *et al.*, 2000). A global rather than international sourcing strategy is therefore also critical in order to implement sustainability within the supply network; global sourcing implies a shared sustainability strategy and policies, and shared and consistent contracts and codes of conduct across worldwide locations.

Is global sourcing sustainable? Global sourcing and the lure of low-cost manufacture from overseas suppliers became a trend in the 1990s by Western firms taking advantage of reduced barriers to trade and costs of transportation. Particularly in high-volume, relatively simple goods such as plastic toys, watches and calculators, the risks involved in setting up the supply chain seemed low in return for such potentially high profits. But it was not until corporations started to outsource more complex components that they began to appreciate the implications of the term 'hidden costs' to their business. Even relatively minor quality issues in electronic equipment, such as wiring harnesses critical to the core function of the motor car, meant prestige brands with strong track records in engineering reliability were forced into sudden and unintended product recalls. Firms caught out by over-stretching their supply chains had to confront the issue that sticking with local suppliers might have been financially more viable in the long run when considering the costs of quality assurance and the resultant impact on product reliability, or brand image from corporate social responsibility (CSR) problems. Global sourcing requires substantial transaction costs, including for example the increased costs of supplier selection, contracting, monitoring and auditing. In their drive for lower costs, companies have often underestimated these hidden costs, focusing instead on the much more obvious lower piece prices. Cost advantages tend to disappear in the total acquisition/landed costs (Steinle and Schiele, 2008; BCG, 2007).

The argument for reverting to local sourcing, however, is not only based around issues of quality, brand and total cost. Going local or 'localism' is a term used in conjunction with the protection of more vulnerable cultures or communities (e.g. O'Riordan, 2001), particularly those containing small businesses in developing regions that are threatened by global economic forces. Volatile movements in the price of commodities is one consequence of the global economy we all live in and yet it is often those upstream, at the end of the supply chain, who are most affected (see Note 6.2 – Fairtrade coffee). Introducing the idea of equity or fairness into purchasing's spectrum of business concerns may seem an odd approach when compared with more traditional portfolio management models, but the rapid uptake of the Fairtrade movement over the past decade with its strong popular appeal to globally aware consumers, demonstrates the power of pledging support to developing regions around the world. Coffee, clothing and jewellery are now all sold via Fairtrade, one of the first and best known independent consumer organizations, which guarantees workers in developing countries get a better deal from international trade.

Note 6.2

Fairtrade coffee – telling the local smallholders' story

Coffee is mostly grown by 25–30 million smallholder farms in around 80 countries in the tropical regions of the world. Each smallholder farms between 0.1 and 5.0 hectares of coffee, with most directly depending on the crop as their primary source of income. Between the producer and consumer there is a long chain of traders, exporters, manufacturers, wholesalers and retailers, each demanding a mark-up on the original price based on kilogram of coffee bean. Located at the end of the supply chain, smallholders are vulnerable to the effects of market fluctuation where oversupply causes prices to drop, which in turn can force them out of business as their small volume does not allow bargaining power and their margins are kept very low.

Fairtrade was launched in 1994 as an independent consumer guarantee for products that enables farmers and workers in developing countries to get a better deal from international trade. Fairtrade describes itself as a 'grassroots consumer choice movement that empowers consumers to take responsibility for the role they play when they buy products from developing countries'. When shoppers buy a product such as coffee, bananas, wine or clothing carrying the Fairtrade mark they are the most important link in the supply chain to the producers: an act of solidarity ensures that producers receive extra income through the guaranteed price and additional premium to improve their businesses and develop their local communities. Despite representing an innovative and radical movement in the support of family-owned farms in the developing world, Fairtrade and the principles it supports is not without its critics. Some argue that the fixed-price element does not encourage improvements in productivity or quality of the coffee. Others suggest that the rise of 'green' marques such as the Rainforest Alliance is confusing to the consumer and clouds the core message of Fairtrade, which in essence is about the responsibilities of global sourcing.

Source: www.fairtrade.org.uk (last accessed 3 November 2013)

6.2 Going local: a trend towards re-shoring?

The worldwide economic crisis that began in 2008 has further highlighted the need for companies in industrialized countries to question the benefits of global sourcing. The crisis unearthed a wide range of risks that companies expose themselves to when sourcing from offshore locations. In particular, many observers are beginning to question if the benefits in terms of total cost of ownership actually justify the increased risks. Subsequently, some companies have moved back production activities to their home country, i.e. 're-shored' or 'back-shored', and more companies look set to follow (Tate, 2014; Tate *et al.*, 2014). Politically speaking, the bringing back of manufacturing jobs in terms of 'onshoring' or 'near-shoring' is, of course, seen as attractive and important to boost struggling manufacturing sectors in the US as well as parts of Europe (Brandon-Jones *et al.*, 2017). According to a report by the Boston Consulting Group (BCG, 2010), many companies are rethinking LCC sourcing strategies due to growing overseas labour costs, currency fluctuations, volatile commodity prices and quality concerns. This report highlights:

- A possible trend towards 'near-shore' countries
- Increasing focus on TCO/landed costs
- Labour shortage and double-digit wage inflation
- Growing protectionism

The attraction of drastically lower wages was a significant factor in the offshoring of banking call centre services from Western countries such as the UK and US to Asia (see Note 6.3), enabled by improvements in fibre optic cables and broadband technology, which transferred traditionally localized information-based services to virtually anywhere in the English-speaking world. Although investment in information and communication technology to improve communications between customers and suppliers is one important aspect, of potentially greater significance in terms of long-term resource allocation is the investment in time required to form effective working relationships with other management teams. As can be seen in the example of the UK banking sector's initial decision to offshore its customer service call centres in Note 6.3, the cost benefits can sometimes be outweighed in the long term over difficulties in transferring core skill sets outside of the focal firm.

Note 6.3

UK banking's decision to offshore (and re-shore) customer call centres

The UK banking sector's decision to offshore its customer service call centres began in the 1990s driven by the opportunity to cut operational costs by exploiting drastically lower wages overseas in regions such as India and China. Once a small but significant component of the UK economy with many customer call centres based in Scotland, such services along with software and back-office IT support now represent 6 per cent of the Indian economy with annual revenues of £49 billion. Yet the offshoring trend in the UK and US has become a controversial issue, not just over growing unemployment, but also service quality issues along with concerns for the welfare of overseas employees who often work long hours for very low pay. Multinational companies may need to think again about offshoring to cheaper locations on the basis that they may not be that much cheaper. In India wages are rising fast, but innovations in productivity mean overall benefit is keeping pace. In China manufacturing wages have risen 69 per cent between 2005 and 2010, and if they continue to rise at this rate China's cost advantage over the West could eventually disappear. Santander is the first bank to decide to relocate – or re-shore – all of its call centres back to the UK following customer complaints of the services provided from overseas.

The perceived difference in cost used to be so significant that shifting manufacturing to a low-cost country location was imperative if cost was high on the agenda. Low labour costs, cheap commodities and favourable exchange rates ensured that the decision to outsource to global suppliers was seen as fairly straightforward, although decisions have often been taken on relatively simple price calculations rather than total cost of ownership (TCO), analysis which often drastically reduces the real cost savings.

Suppliers in historically low-cost countries such as China have been able to offer 'perceived' prices of between 25 to 40 per cent lower than those available onshore: the typical threshold or tipping point for moving off shore (Ferreira and Prokopets, 2009). However, companies have typically tended to underestimate the global sourcing challenge including the hidden costs (e.g. TCO). As Hamid Mughal, executive vice-president of manufacturing engineering and technology at Rolls-Royce recently said:

Some of the decisions made in the past few decades by companies to outsource based on unit costs did not take full account of the total costs of putting bases elsewhere, such as inflexibility, lack of responsiveness from very distant plants, and leakage of intellectual property. These are very tangible burdens on companies and, in a hurry to outsource, people forgot that.

(Cooper, 2012)

Companies frequently report on quality problems, longer and more complex supply networks, and loss of intellectual capital as a result of the decision to offshore. Moreover, rooting up suppliers from an established supply base, sometimes within an important industrial cluster, to new suppliers in a distant low-cost location also means that companies may risk losing their ability to innovative in collaboration with their key suppliers (Steinle and Schiele, 2008) and to customize products and services according to customer needs. Offshoring requires shipping container-size minimum orders and months-long order cycle times, thereby reducing supply chain flexibility and responsiveness (Ferreira and Prokopets, 2009). With inflexible supply chains, companies are no longer able to effectively tailor products and services to unique customer and channel needs.

More and more companies now realize that the cost advantages are beginning to erode. Labour costs are rapidly rising each year as are commodity and transportation costs, e.g. for ocean freight. Furthermore, many foreign currencies are gaining in value compared to the Western currencies such as the US dollar, the euro and the UK pound. In a recent survey of 39 US and European companies, 59 per cent were already changing their manufacturing/ supply strategy, with 26 per cent having already relocated manufacturing and sourcing and 33 per cent being more selective in making offshoring decisions. A further 30 per cent, shown in Figure 6.2, were contemplating a change. This is a relatively small survey, but the media increasingly report similar stories. For example, Auto Styling Truckman in the UK saw import costs for vehicle accessories increase by 6 per cent in 2012 and expected further increases. Sourcing hard tops for pick-up trucks from Thailand, they faced increasing costs

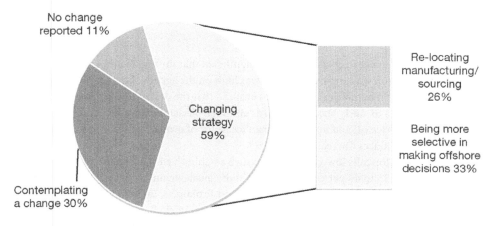

Figure 6.2 Manufacturers reporting changes in manufacturing supply strategy

Source: Ferreira and Prokopets (2009).

due to the Thai government having introduced a national minimum wage of 300 baht ($10/£6) a day from January 2013. Mike Wheeler, Managing Director, said:

> When we started importing from Thailand in 2003, wages were about $3 a day and they are now $10. It is frightening that workers can live on that little, of course, but it shows the upwards trend. [If] shipping costs continue to go up at the same time as labour costs, it may well become more competitive to manufacture in Britain.
>
> (Cooper, 2012)

Although more and more companies are contemplating re-shoring from low-cost country suppliers to domestic or nearby suppliers, one serious obstacle is that in many cases the skills and competence gap has decreased or even reversed. Asian suppliers used to represent low quality but in recent years Asian suppliers have developed tremendously so that these days they are often able to offer superior quality. Manufacturing skills in the US and Europe have declined in recent years partly as a result of these jobs being offshored and many observers believe that it is going to be a hard task to re-create these skills. Daliah Simble, head of sourcing and production for Roland Mouret, the French fashion house, expressed the dilemma:

> I cut my teeth in UK manufacturing in the mid-1990s but I globalised when everyone else did. Over the past five years, however, there has been a swing and I have spent that time rebuilding my UK manufacturing address book. Most factories we are working with are rammed to capacity, but the issue is that the skills are not here anymore.
>
> (Cooper, 2012)

One thing seems certain: companies will continue to move their supply chains away from low-cost countries if they do not continue to offer significant cost advantages. Moving activities home may be one option, but another option is simply to look for alternative, BCCS or 'best cost' locations, especially if labour costs still constitute a significant proportion of the cost basis. For example, China is slowly losing work to countries such as Bangladesh, Vietnam and Cambodia for cheaper, labour-intensive goods like casual clothes, toys and simple electronics that do not necessarily require literate workers and can tolerate relatively unreliable transportation systems and electrical grids. Li & Fung, a Hong Kong company that handles sourcing and apparel manufacturing for companies like Walmart and Liz Claiborne, reported in 2010 that its production in Bangladesh jumped 20 per cent last year, while China, its biggest supplier, slid 5 per cent.

Importantly, the supply chain risks associated with sustainability have also caused companies to reconsider their LCC strategies towards BCCS. Activities such as supplier audits and supplier development should now be included in total cost calculations, making LCC sourcing even more questionable. However, from a sustainability perspective, the case is not so clear-cut: re-shoring (or near-shoring) may reduce one kind of sustainability problem, but also implies removing jobs from developing countries. Global sourcing has been instrumental in the economic boom of developing countries as well as Western countries, so simply stopping this trend may not be the right answer. It is clear therefore that companies engage in global sourcing for a variety of reasons, not only to achieve lower costs or economies of scale, and that given the increasing challenge over issues such as CSR, future considerations will involve greater sharing of knowledge and information, and how to implement best practice (Trautmann *et al.*, 2009). The case study on IKEA now illustrates some of the challenges of global sourcing, examining the initial rationale for moving away from domestic suppliers in Sweden, towards LCC – and now BCCS – sources. It discusses the sustainability challenges IKEA has encountered, and how it has tried to deal with them.

GLOBAL SOURCING AT IKEA – BALANCING LOW-COST STRATEGY AND SUSTAINABLE SOURCING

The Swedish home furnishing giant IKEA was founded by Ingvar Kamprad in the region of Småland in Sweden in 1943. The first IKEA store was opened in Älmhult, Sweden in 1958. The first store outside Sweden was established in Norway in 1963 and the first store outside Scandinavia was established in Switzerland in 1973. The business idea that has driven the firm throughout the years has been to offer affordable home furnishings at prices that make it possible for as many people as possible to afford them and to grow through duplication of a global market offering.

IKEA's ground-breaking idea of involving customers in the value-adding process by flat-packing pieces of furniture that are then assembled by customers, has been a key characteristic of IKEA's business model. In fact, a key component in the low-cost strategy at IKEA has been to own only a small proportion of the means of production. In addition, IKEA has developed a wide product range based around highly standardized components, including screws, bolts, nuts and locks. The high volumes of such componentry coupled with the assembly are critical factors in IKEA's low-cost strategy and its successful growth over several decades.

In 2017, IKEA's annual turnover reached €38.3billion and the number of IKEA stores worldwide, including those run by franchisees, was 403 spread across 49 countries. The number of IKEA 'co-workers' have reached 194,000 (2017): 'co-workers' include employees working for all the different IKEA companies with different owners. IKEA products are all principally the same in IKEA stores around the world: same design and same Swedish names that ensure customers come away from shopping trips with a Swedish experience that even extends to the iconic meatballs served in the IKEA restaurants. Products that are sold across IKEA stores, including well-known products like the BILLY bookcase, the PAX wardrobe and the SULTAN bed, are to a large extent sourced from a global supply network.

The initial development of a supply network outside the Nordic countries and later in Eastern Europe was the result of a ban on supplying IKEA by the Swedish furniture trade organization. IKEA founder Ingvar Kamprad famously said:

It was our first contacts with the Poles. We knew that [Poland] had a big furniture industry. But back then, focus was on quantity rather than quality. […] I often wonder if IKEA would exist today without all those difficulties. The reason we turned to Denmark and to Poland, and abroad at all, was the enormous blockade that we faced.

The conflict between IKEA and the Swedish furniture industry was because of the persistent search for cost reductions by IKEA, which the Swedish industry was not ready to adopt at the time. However, the establishment of supplier relationships in Poland and in other parts of Eastern Europe enabled IKEA to develop and sustain its position as a low-cost alternative in the market for home furnishing. The establishment of Poland as a sourcing market was the beginning of an expansion of sourcing markets

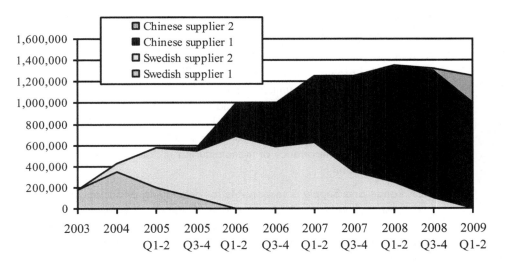

Figure 6.3 PAX sourcing development 2003–2009

Source: Hultman *et al.* (2012).

that has continued ever since. The development of supply chains in low-cost countries outside the immediate sales markets in the mid-1960s, when IKEA sold primarily to the domestic and Nordic markets, initially took place in other parts of Eastern Europe (e.g. Czechoslovakia, Romania and Hungary), and later in more distant locations (e.g. China, Indonesia and Malaysia). By 2009 around two-thirds of its products were sourced from European countries, where the largest single supply market is China with a 20 per cent share of the supply and the second largest is Poland with 18 per cent (Hultman *et al.*, 2009).

Since the 1960s IKEA gradually internationalized its supply network. One major driver of this trend has, of course, been the continuous search for low cost but also to secure capacity as the business has expanded rapidly to become truly global. Coordination with suppliers is channelled through a large number of trading offices situated around the world. Considering the global nature of IKEA's operations, we take a closer look at its governance and structure.

Corporate governance and structure

In 2016 IKEA initiated changes in its governance structure. Inter IKEA Holding B.V. (located in the Netherlands) is the new holding company for all IKEA-related businesses. Globally, a large number of companies operate under the IKEA trademarks. Inter IKEA Group and INGKA Group have the same founder, and a common history and heritage, but have operated under different owners and management since the 1980s. Within Inter IKEA Group there are the following important organizational units:

1 IKEA Franchising: All IKEA franchisees are independent of Inter IKEA Group although a large group of franchisees are owned and operated by INGKA Group. Inter IKEA Systems B.V. is responsible for franchising systems, methods and proven solutions to franchisees for the sale of IKEA products under the IKEA trademarks. Inter IKEA Systems ensures successful development

of franchises in existing and new markets. IKEA franchisees are responsible for developing and managing their local business.

2   IKEA Industry manufactures wood-based furniture for IKEA customers and secures production capacities for growth. The largest producer of wooden furniture in the world, IKEA Industry consists of 40 production units in ten countries: China, France, Hungary, Lithuania, Poland, Portugal, Russia, Slovakia, Sweden and the USA. IKEA Industry employees around 19,000 co-workers and together with external IKEA suppliers represents the IKEA production capacity. IKEA Industry produces furniture in solid wood and lightweight or board-based wood. Due to the importance of manufacturing in Poland, Inter IKEA Group has a separate Polish industry unit.

3   IKEA Range and Supply is responsible for developing and supplying the global IKEA range and consists of two units: IKEA of Sweden AB (product range) and IKEA Supply AG (supply). IKEA Supply AG owns the goods in the distribution centres and is responsible for cross-border flows and replenishment of goods throughout the IKEA network of retailers and wholesalers. This unit counts circa 6,800 co-workers in total. IKEA Supply AG represent the IKEA supply chain operation including purchasing and logistics.

A closer look at IKEA Range and Supply

IKEA Range and Supply works with the value chain end to end from supplier to customer. From the needs and wants of the many people, through product development and the sourcing of raw materials, to a product's end of life. Together with other units, IKEA Range and Supply is responsible for communicating the IKEA home furnishing offer.

IKEA of Sweden AB is responsible for developing and managing the product range and is based in the county of Småland in southern Sweden. With almost 10,000 products in total, IKEA's product range is very large. What is more, IKEA introduces around 2,000 new products each year. IKEA product development is based on the concept of 'democratic design' which seeks to develop better products at lower costs. When developing new products, IKEA designers focus on form, functionality, quality, sustainability and, of course, low price. Working on innovations in materials and process technology to reduce dependency on raw materials, IKEA is increasingly dedicated to sustainability.

IKEA of Sweden AB (product range) is structured into ten business areas:

1   Livingroom and Workspace

2   Bedroom and Bathroom

3   Kitchen and Dining

4   Children's IKEA

5   Lighting and Home Smart

6   Textiles

CASE STUDY 6.1

7   Cooking, Eating and Decoration

8   Outdoor, Storage, Organization and IKEA Family

9   Free Range

10 IKEA Food

IKEA Supply AG's particular focus is on efficient production and logistics. The aim is to be lean and economical with resources, finding more efficient ways to manufacture products and striving to make more from less. IKEA co-locates supply networks and production and also production facilities and sales markets as well as strategically planning the locations of distribution units. More than 60 per cent of products are shipped directly from suppliers to the IKEA stores.

Organizational units include:

- IKEA Components

- Regional Supply teams

- Purchasing Development

- Logistic Development

- Sales and Supply Planning

- Transport

- Purchasing Operations

- Quality Support Centres

- IKEA Communications AB

- Product Development Centre (China)

IKEA purchasing operations and business development teams are located in 24 offices, within nine purchasing operations areas: South Europe, South East Europe, North Europe, North East Europe, Central Europe, Americas, South Asia, South East Asia and East Asia. Likewise, logistics operations have a global presence which spans Global Distribution Network Design, Global Goods Flow and Capacity Planning, Global and Regional Transport Purchasing and Operations, Regional Supply Teams in Europe, Asia Pacific and North America, Regional Quality Support Centres and Customs Service Centres.

Where in the past IKEA had a larger supply base and a more aggressive approach to supplier management, fewer and long-term supplier relationships now appear to be the norm. In the mid-1990s IKEA had more than 2,000 suppliers, but in 2010 decided to reduce its supply base to around 1,200 suppliers, despite increasing sales volumes, as part of a consolidation strategy to build secure capacity for continued growth. These days IKEA prides itself that the average supplier relationship lasts for 11 years. In 2017 IKEA had 978 home furnishing supplier relationships spread across 50 countries.

CASE STUDY 6.1

Growing commitment to a sustainable supply chain

Sustainable business practices increase resource efficiency in everything IKEA does. Using fewer resources and raw materials means a lower environmental impact but also lower costs. For example, it has officially done away with wooden pallets in its goods flow. Instead, it uses paper pallets and loading ledges. This solution is not only more sustainable, but it improves filling rate and significantly reduces handling material costs.

IKEA has built a reputation for supplying flat-pack domestic furniture which is cheap, yet at the same time stylish and sturdy, supported by a network of suppliers located across the world. While interested in the principles of sustainable living for several decades and mindful of the public scrutiny from non-governmental organizations (NGOs), by 2000 IKEA launched a sustainability code of conduct named 'IWAY' to complement its approach to global supply chain management.

'IWAY' is short for IKEA's WAY on Purchasing Home Furnishing Products. The corporation understands that while some of its suppliers are located in countries where the environmental and social issues have been a high priority for many years, it also works with many suppliers where the agenda is only just emerging. IKEA recognizes that negative publicity over environmental or social conditions of its suppliers could damage the IKEA brand considerably. IWAY defines a code of conduct of supplier responsibilities in approved areas such as legal requirements, working conditions, wages and working hours, child labour, environmental improvements, emissions, discharge and noise, discrimination, harassment, fire prevention, wood procurement and forestry management. To implement the code of conduct, IKEA has established a set of procedures for suppliers worldwide where all potential partners are informed about its sustainability requirements. On-site audits by IKEA auditors are conducted after a supplier has been selected and before the first delivery. Using the principles established by IWAY, a typical audit takes around two days and involves interviews of randomly selected employees and management representatives, as well as observations of factory working conditions and checks of employment contracts, levels of pay and factory conditions.

IKEA's strategy of engaging in long-term relationships with suppliers means that in the event of non-compliance with the IWAY code of conduct, it does not break off relations with a supplier that shows willingness to improve. IKEA requires suppliers to prepare an action plan for all failed items and specify in writing how the areas of non-compliance will be rectified. For example, issues over waste water treatment might involve a change in the supplier's attitude, an alteration to existing procedure and possibly investment in the plant's infrastructure. IKEA requires corrective action to be carried out within a period of 24 months, where suppliers continue to be audited on a regular basis with the same team of internal auditors working with the supplier for periods of up to five years. Once a supplier is IWAY-approved, the IKEA purchasing team follow up with regular contact to ensure that the code of conduct remains a high priority.

IKEA's reputation amongst suppliers as a 'tough customer' ultimately benefits successful suppliers who have achieved IWAY and are provided with a strong reference when applying for work with new customers. IKEA constitutes an important customer for many of its suppliers who strive to fulfil the requirements both in terms of product specification as well as the sustainable code of conduct. Given IKEA's size and reputation, suppliers cannot afford to give IWAY low priority as this might cause a termination of their relationship with the global furniture firm, which in turn would be very damaging to their business.

Monitoring the levels of sustainability at sub-tier suppliers across IKEA's global supply chain is a major undertaking. As a result of the complexity of the supply chain, ensuring the compliance of many thousands of sub-tier suppliers around the world represents a major challenge for the enterprise as a whole, particularly given the fact that IKEA does not at present audit sub-tier suppliers over compliance issues. This may need to change if IKEA's latest initiative on the circular economy takes off (Edie, 2017). IKEA now considers that furniture recycling is not just part of corporate responsibility at IKEA, but also makes commercial sense. Looking at the whole life of products in terms of reuse and repair may deliver further benefit to the company, instead of just following the traditional, linear route for disposal of old furniture via landfill or incineration. Using the 'Furniture Reuse Network', UK customers wishing to replace large items such as sofas can have their old one collected from home for free and assessed by IKEA for possible refurbishment and redistribution or, if in very poor condition, dismantling into its constituent parts. This puts increasing emphasis on suppliers complying with requirements such as standardizing material usage across IKEA's global furniture supply network, and explains why the Swedish furniture giant thinks its global sourcing approach, when connected with the circular economy, will deliver commercial benefits in future.

6.4 Conclusion

The adoption of a global sourcing strategy has been a long-term trend where Western firms for decades have taken advantage of significantly lower costs in developing regions of the world through low-cost country sourcing. However, in addition to ever diminishing cost advantages from LCC sourcing strategies, companies are increasingly realizing the importance of best cost country sourcing (or BCC) – where leading companies rank their overseas sourcing initiatives according to a range of factors which includes managing the ethical supply risks that come with the territory. Companies have to invest in the monitoring of supplier compliance in areas such as workforce rights, protection of natural habitats and emission of toxic substances, particularly at sub-tier supplier level, which is more difficult to police and susceptible to 'public outings' as the result of investigation by NGOs. These policing activities all represent costs that are difficult to calculate and easy to underestimate. So, there are signs of a rethink of LCC sourcing strategies: not only is the difference in labour costs between East and West diminishing, resulting in some sectors such as banking services beginning to re-shore, but there is an increased awareness of the total costs of conducting business worldwide, a factor which is persuading some managers to reconsider their global sourcing strategy altogether, particularly those that rely on an LCC strategy. Continuing concern over the world economy is a major factor in growing protectionism of home markets and the susceptibility of foreign firms to increases in barriers to trade. While many corporations have announced their intentions towards becoming more sustainable and have begun to take the first steps in reviewing their global sourcing strategy, few have translated this into a coherent, end-to-end supply chain policy that includes long-term prospects for both local sources of production as well as safeguarding the regions around the world in which they operate.

References

Akan E (2017) How China made Volkswagen the world's biggest carmaker. *The Epoch Times*. Available at: http://www.theepochtimes.com (last accessed 5 May 2017).

Alguire MS, Frear CR and Metcalf LE (1994) An examination of the determinants of global sourcing strategy. *Journal of Business and Industrial Marketing* 9(2): 62–74.

Arnold U (1999) Organization of global sourcing: Ways towards an optimal degree of centralization. *European Journal of Purchasing and Supply Management* 5(3/4): 167–174.

Arnold U (2000) New dimensions of outsourcing: A combination of transaction cost economics and the core competence concept. *European Journal of Purchasing & Supply Management* 6(1): 23–29.

Boston Consulting Group (BCG) (2007) Sourcing from China: Lessons from the leaders. 27 July.

Boston Consulting Group (BCG) (2010) Global sourcing in the post downturn era. October.

Bozarth C, Handfield R and Das A (1998) Stages of global sourcing strategy evolution: An exploratory study. *Journal of Operations Management* 16(2–3): 241–255.

Brammer S, Hoejmose S and Millington A (2011) Managing sustainable global supply chains: A systematic review of the body of knowledge. London and Ontario: Network for Business Sustainability. Public report.

Brandon-Jones E, Dutordoir M, Neto JQF and Squire B (2017) The impact of reshoring decisions on shareholder wealth. *Journal of Operations Management* 49: 31–36.

Cooper K (2012) Made in Britain: It's not a dream. *The Sunday Times*, 11 November.

Dutzler H, Philips D, Mansson A and Parthasarathy S (2011) Best cost country sourcing: A next generation approach. *Strategy&* (formerly Booz & company). Available at: www.strategyand.pwc.com/media/file (last accessed May 2017).

Edie (2017) Why IKEA sees circular economy as a business opportunity. Available at: http://exhibition.edie.net/show-news (last accessed May 2017).

Energy Outlook (2012) Online report by Sia Partners. Available at: energy.sia-partners.com/2054 (last accessed 23 October 2013).

Faes W, Matthyssens P, Vandenbempt K (2000) The pursuit of global purchasing synergy. *Industrial Marketing Management* 29(6): 539–553.

Ferreira J and Prokopets L (2009) Does offshoring still make sense? *Supply Chain Management Review* 13(1).

Gray JV, Skowronski K, Esenduran G and Johnny Rungtusanatham M (2013) The reshoring phenomenon: What supply chain academics ought to know and should do. *Journal of Supply Chain Management* 49(2): 27–33.

Guinipero LC and Monczka RM (1990) Organizational approaches to managing international sourcing. *International Journal of Physical Distribution & Logistics Management* 20(4): 3–12.

Hawranek D (2006) Vexing problems plague Volkswagen. *Der Speigel*. 13 February.

Hultman J, Hertz S, Johnsen R and Johnsen T (2009) Global supply chain development – a case study on supply chain internationalization. In *Proceedings of the 25th IMP Conference*, September. Marseille, France.

Hultman J, Johnsen R, Johnsen T and Hertz S (2012) An interaction approach to global sourcing: A case study of IKEA. *Journal of Purchasing & Supply Management* 18(1): 9–21.

Lund-Thomsen P and Lindgreen A (2014) Corporate social responsibility in global value chains: Where are we now and where are we going? *Journal of Business Ethics* 123(1): 11–22.

Munson CL and Rosenblatt MJ (1997) The impact of local content rules on global sourcing decisions. *Production and Operations Management* 6(3): 277–90.

Nassimbeni G (2006) International sourcing: Empirical evidence from a sample of Italian firms. *International Journal of Production Economics* 103(2): 694–706.

Nassimbeni G and Sartor M (2007) Sourcing in China: A typology. *International Journal of Production Economics* 107(2): 333–349.

O'Riorda T (ed.) (2001) *Globalism, Localism and Identity: Fresh Perspectives on the Transition to Sustainability*. London: Earthscan Publications Ltd.

Quintens L, Pauwels P and Matthyssens P (2006) Global purchasing: State of the art and research directions. *Journal of Purchasing & Supply Management* 12(4): 170–181.

Steinle C and Schiele H (2008) Limits to global sourcing? Strategic consequences of dependency on international suppliers: Cluster theory, resource-based view and case studies. *Journal of Purchasing & Supply Management* 14(1): 3–14.

Tate WL (2014) Offshoring and reshoring: US insights and research challenges. *Journal of Purchasing & Supply Management* 20(1): 66–68.

Tate WL, Ellram LM, Schoenherr T and Petersen KJ (2014) Global competitive conditions driving the manufacturing location decision. *Business Horizons* 57(3): 381–390.

Trautmann G, Bals L and Hartmann E (2009) Global sourcing in integrated network structures: The case of hybrid purchasing organizations. *Journal of International Management* 15(2): 194–208.

Trent RJ and Monczka RM (2003) Understanding integrated global sourcing. *International Journal of Physical Distribution & Logistics Management* 33(7): 607–629.

Trent RJ and Monczka RM (2005) Achieving excellence in global sourcing. *MIT Sloan Management Review*, Fall: 25–32.

Walker H, Di Sisto L and McBain D (2008) Drivers and barriers to environmental supply chain management practices: Lessons from the public and private sectors. *Journal of Purchasing & Supply Management* 14(1): 69–85.

CHAPTER 7

Innovation and technology

LEARNING OBJECTIVES

By the end of this chapter you should be able to:

- Identify the rationale for early supplier involvement (ESI) and early purchasing involvement (EPI) in new product development (NPD);

- Identify success factors and best practices of ESI and EPI;

- Apply an NPD process framework of ESI and a model to evaluate the extent of ESI in companies;

- Discuss the concepts of design for environment and design for sustainability;

- Explain purchasing's role in discontinuous innovation and the challenges of this form of innovation;

- Discuss the role of e-procurement and digital supply chains, and the rise of new technological innovations such as 'big data' and Internet of Things (IoT);

- Evaluate disruptive technologies such as 3D printing or additive manufacturing in terms of their potential impact on purchasing and supply;

- Evaluate the role of technology as an enabler of sustainability.

7.0 Introduction

Purchasing and supply chain managers need to understand and engage with innovation, especially because innovation offers ways to change what and how technologies are sourced and how products and services are produced and delivered to customers. Therefore, innovation affects purchasing and supply chain managers both in terms of product and process innovation. Purchasing's role in product innovation is to facilitate the successful development of new products and services. Its role in process innovation is to develop new ways of managing supply chain and network processes, including interfaces with suppliers. Where purchasing's contribution to companies is traditionally viewed as cost savings, innovation offers the potential for purchasing to contribute to value creation.

As companies rely extensively on external suppliers for production activities and service provision, they need to source new and innovative components and technologies from suppliers. In the past companies sought to internalize resources and activities that were closely tied to innovation but as technologies are becoming increasingly complex it is virtually impossible for companies to make and also develop new product and service offerings completely by themselves. Innovative companies often choose to focus on a small set of core competencies and access complementary competencies through various forms of business networks such as innovation networks (Powell *et al.*, 1996) and supply networks (Lamming *et al.*, 2000).

The need to source specialized technologies and capabilities is particularly important when companies seek to develop new environmentally friendly products. Companies need to involve their suppliers in environmental improvement projects in order to benefit from supplier expertise in areas such as new green technologies and green packaging solutions.

Various organizational functions interact with suppliers as part of new product development (NPD) projects. Traditionally, engineering and research and development (R&D) departments have taken lead roles in liaising with suppliers for technological developments but purchasing can perform a critical go-between function and facilitate early supplier involvement (ESI) processes (Wynstra *et al.*, 2000; Lakemond *et al.*, 2001). The role of purchasing in facilitating NPD has long been recognized (e.g. Farmer, 1981) if not widely implemented in all industries. The concept of early purchasing involvement (EPI) (Schiele, 2010) emphasizes the fact that if suppliers need to be involved at an early stage in NPD projects so does purchasing.

ESI and EPI concern the early involvement in NPD of, respectively, suppliers and purchasing. However, innovation is more than NPD and is usually, but not always, associated with a high degree of newness, for example, in product/technology, process or market. In recent years many industries have faced discontinuous innovations that involve a technological paradigm shift and in doing so are often competence-destroying (Olleros, 1986; Veryzer, 1998). For example, Dyson's dual cyclone vacuum cleaner applied a different technology to the normal paradigm (the bag system) and launched the world's first bag-less vacuum cleaner. Thereby it disrupted the existing business model in the industry even if a new vacuum cleaner might not at first glance to most people seem like an innovation. This is particularly important from a sustainability perspective because the development of green products or processes, for example, requires a fundamental rethinking of products and processes to eliminate environmental impacts at the source; companies need to expand their experience base and competencies by drawing on outside expertise (Mollenkopf *et al.*, 2010). The challenge explored in this chapter is what this means for purchasing and its role in securing ESI.

This chapter also considers process innovation by discussing how information communication technology (ICT) is used to improve the purchasing and supply process. We begin by discussing the impact of early electronic data interchange (EDI) systems in terms of improving basic transaction efficiency through speed and standardized communication between firms. We then move on to the role of electronic procurement and how by incorporating the Internet it connects the whole enterprise (Straub *et al.*, 2004). Specific tools such as collaborative hubs and electronic auctions from the 2000s onwards revolutionized the way buyers and suppliers work together. Improvements in online technology often meant that agreement over product specifications could be made without people actually having to meet, which if not treated with care could introduce new challenges into purchasing, production and delivery.

An era dominated by the digital supply chain has now emerged, with the number of fixed and portable computing devices (e.g. smartphones, tablets, laptops, PCs) used for both work and leisure purposes rising exponentially in the past decade (Cecchinel *et al.*, 2014). Individual devices increasingly contain communicating sensors which, when linked together, create a computing intelligence that is called the Internet of Things (IoT). This refers to a mesh of devices all producing considerable amounts of information or 'big data' about user lifestyle choices and purchasing preferences. The application of the Internet in the business environment means that it has become an important strategic element in supply chain management (Lancioni *et al.*, 2003). There are also rising expectations around the digital operational capabilities required of suppliers, meaning they have, for example, the ability to engage in real-time communication between supply chain members, create interlocking databases and have 24-hour shipment tracking. Widespread digital application in diverse areas such as social media, reverse logistics and 'smart cities' means that the use of digital technologies has become an essential element in the purchasing and supply chain professional's toolkit.

This chapter also discusses the disruptive nature of promising new technologies such as additive manufacturing and 3D printing with the capability to produce complex 3D components with flexible machines using digitally controlled laser technology. Such devices are often small and portable, and in theory eliminate the need for traditional tiers of suppliers performing sub-assembly operations in the manufacturing process. In some specialist sectors requiring product customization, such as surgical implants, 3D printing presents a radically different mode of production which looks set to change the role and structure of medical supply chains forever. In other sectors, such as automotive, where high volumes of identical components are required, it is less likely that 3D printing will alter traditional, centralized modes of production (Holweg, 2015), but there are still appropriate applications even within traditional high-volume industries. The chapter concludes with how digital technology has become an enabler for sustainable supply chains, using the example of business-to-business online collaborative sharing sites (i.e. hubs or portals) for supply chain environmental, social and safety compliance and auditing.

7.1 Early supplier involvement (ESI) in new product development (NPD)

In innovation circles the buzzword of the last 15 years or so has been 'open innovation' (Chesbrough, 2003). This implies that instead of developing and protecting technologies and competencies internally, companies choose to connect to these through their business networks. Companies increasingly consider suppliers as critical sources of innovation and try to involve and integrate suppliers of key components or technology into design and development processes. However, not only do suppliers need to be closely involved in NPD projects, but they also need to be involved *early*. The concept of ESI emphasizes the importance of involving suppliers early in the NPD process in order to fully capitalize on suppliers' specialized capabilities, which is an important step in ensuring design-for-manufacture.

7.1.1 Early supplier involvement: why 'early'?

As a rule of thumb many companies estimate that as much as 80 per cent of total product cost is committed or 'locked-in' during the concept and design stages (Handfield *et al.*, 1999). This means that it is in fact much more important to strive to reduce product costs during the NPD process than to reduce costs once a product is in production. Furthermore, it is during the early stages of the NPD process that significant changes can be made to product designs and specifications, so effective cost minimization requires early intervention in the NPD process. Figure 7.1 helps to understand the reasons for this:

The NPD process illustrated in Figure 7.1 is typical of high-volume manufacturing industries. The first stage, 'idea generation', or 'ideation', is about searching for an idea for a new product so involves creative thinking and exploration of potential ideas and concepts. There is no commitment to solutions at this stage. The following stages gradually involve commitment to particular solutions as these are evaluated from different perspectives, e.g.:

- Marketing: is the market sufficient?

- Finance: is it financially viable?

- Engineering: can it be developed?

- Operations/production: can it be produced?

- Purchasing/sourcing: who needs to be involved from the supply chain?

As the design and development process progresses, the company commits to particular solutions and it becomes both difficult and expensive to make changes, for example, to a different design or use of different materials. The product and process engineering stage requires investment in prototypes and tooling and this is traditionally the stage when companies release product specifications and start to consider who is going to produce the various components. However, as the company has already made significant commitments and investments at this stage it is very difficult and costly to change anything that has already passed the earlier stages of approval.

ESI means involving suppliers of key components (parts or ingredients) as early as possible, i.e. during concept development or early product planning (e.g. as part of feasibility studies). Involving suppliers at this stage enables design for manufacture and helps to prevent,

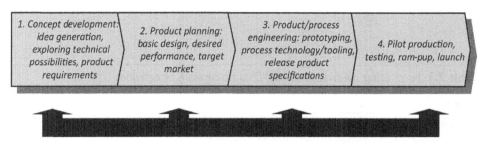

Figure 7.1 The new product development process and supplier involvement

reduce or introduce earlier, costly design changes: it is a 'first time right' method. Design for manufacture means that the design (and development) process is carried out with a specific view to putting the product into production. This is by no means a certainty in many companies where the early stages of the NPD process are the domain of creative people, such as the marketing department, who may have a great feel for what might succeed in the marketplace but do not have the same appreciation of who will end up producing and supplying the product. As Note 2.1 (in Chapter 2) illustrated with an example of purchasing and engineering collaboration at Harley-Davidson, it is also by no means certain that the technical people in a company will be concerned about the production of products and its parts being developed; in fact, they might even fight against involvement of suppliers at this stage as they may see supplier involvement as a threat.

7.1.2 Purchasing's role in early supplier involvement

We should note that supplier involvement is not the same as purchasing involvement. Purchasing plays an important role in facilitating the development of new products because purchasing can act as a facilitator between new product development (NPD) projects and the technologies and capabilities of suppliers (Burt and Soukup, 1985). Through its boundary-spanning role, purchasing can naturally provide useful insights into the cost, availability, quality and reliability of supplied components.

However, managing ESI is not solely the prerogative of purchasing and as the Harley-Davidson case shows traditional purchasing professionals such as buyers or purchasing managers are rarely seen as natural internal partners in NPD projects. As discussed in Chapter 2, purchasing should have significant input into the product design and development process, in particular in order to avoid the situation where product specifications are purely technical and do not reflect the supply situation. As explained by Wynstra *et al.* (2000), it is critical that purchasing be involved in both individual NPD projects, where for example they can assist in providing input on early product design, and ongoing discussions with suppliers about, for example, potential future technologies. Table 7.1 provides a framework for managing purchasing involvement in NPD, focused around a set of activities categorized into four groups. We return to the distinction between NPD project-specific activities and ongoing activities later in the chapter.

Table 7.1 Purchasing involvement in NPD: a framework of activities

Areas	Activity
Development management	Determining which technologies to keep/develop in-house and which ones to outsource to suppliers
	Formulating policies for the involvement of suppliers
	Formulating policies for purchasing related activities of internal departments
	Communicating policies and procedures internally and externally
Supplier interface management	Monitoring supplier markets for technological developments
	Pre-selecting suppliers for product development collaboration
	Motivating suppliers to build up/maintain specific knowledge or develop certain products
	Exploiting the technological capabilities of suppliers
	Evaluating suppliers' development performance
Project management	*Planning:*
	Determining specific develop-or-buy solutions
	Selecting suppliers for involvement in the development project
	Determining the extent ('workload') of supplier involvement
	Determining the moment of supplier involvement
	Execution:
	Coordinating development activities between suppliers and manufacturer
	Coordinating development activities between different first tier suppliers
	Coordinating development activities between first tier suppliers and second tier suppliers Ordering and chasing prototypes
Product management	*Extending activities:*
	Providing information on new products and technologies being developed or already available in supplier markets
	Suggesting alternative suppliers, products and technologies that can result in a higher quality of the final product
	Restrictive activities:
	Evaluating product designs in terms of part availability, manufacturability, lead-time, quality, and costs
	Promoting standardisation and simplification of designs and parts

Source: Wynstra *et al.* (2000).

7.1.3 Does early supplier involvement work in practice: some evidence

Returning to the general topic of early supplier involvement (ESI), it is important to ask whether or not ESI actually works in practice. For this we can turn to studies of the Japanese automotive industry that resulted in (some) Japanese manufacturing philosophies and methods being labelled as lean. The studies of the Japanese automotive industry of the 1980s by Clark and Fujimoto (1991) and Clark (1989) provided evidence that collaboration with suppliers for product development reduced time to market by four to five months and saved vehicle manufacturers around 800,000 engineering hours per car development project. Later results by American researchers (Ragatz et al., 1997), which focused on several different industries, were also positive: they found that the most successful cases of supplier involvement resulted in median improvement of 40 per cent for product quality, 25 per cent for development cycle time and 15 per cent in product costs.

However, a few early studies were less convincing. Hartley (1994) found that there were hardly any or no effects of supplier involvement in NPD on product costs, quality or development lead time. Nevertheless, Birou and Fawcett (1994) found that the results of supplier involvement across several industries were in fact *negative*, both in terms of development time and product performance. Although the vast majority of later studies have shown positive effects, these early studies indicate that it is not easy to make ESI successful. Indeed, any project involving multiple partners is more difficult to control and the experience of how to manage ESI, which the Japanese automotive manufacturer had in abundance in the 1980s and beyond, is certainly a critical success factor and a key factor in explaining the Japanese advantage (Nishiguchi, 1994).

Overall, research evidence points to conflicting early results, but if ESI is well managed the consensus now is that by collaborating with suppliers as part of NPD processes, companies can improve NPD performance, for example, by getting products to market faster, at lower cost and better quality (e.g., Petersen et al., 2005; Van Echtelt et al., 2008). However, positive results should not be taken for granted; indeed first attempts to implement ESI processes may not bear fruit. The following section examines success factors in managing ESI.

7.1.4 Early supplier involvement success factors

Extensive research has been done on ESI, including what makes ESI successful. According to Johnsen (2009), success factors of ESI can be grouped into three categories as shown in Figure 7.2: 1) supplier selection; 2) supplier relationship development and adaptation; and 3) internal customer capabilities. The specific factors within these categories have been identified in a great number of research studies as contributing to improving NPD performance in terms of achieving a shorter time to market, improved product quality, and reduced development and product costs.

Successful ESI requires selection of the right suppliers at the right time. Suppliers of high value and complex parts that represent high risk (Kraljic, 1983; Wynstra and ten Pierick, 2000) should be involved early and either assume a black box or grey box responsibility

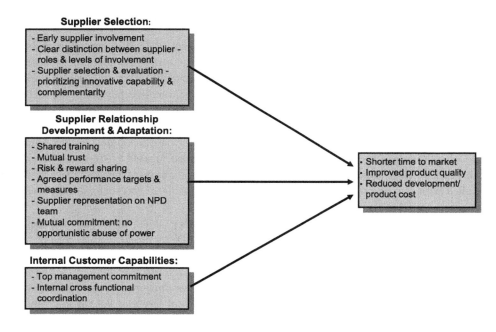

Figure 7.2 Supplier involvement success factors

Source: Johnsen (2009).

(Le Dain *et al.*, 2010). These strategically important suppliers should not only be selected and evaluated on the basis of cost, quality and delivery factors, but also, and more importantly, on their innovative capabilities and complementarity with the company (Hartley *et al.*, 1997; Petersen *et al.*, 2005). Le Dain *et al.* (2010) have proposed a model for identifying and classifying different levels of supplier involvement. Based on Wynstra *et al.* (2000), their model specifies two dimensions: a) the degree of development risk, which depends on, e.g. the number of sub-components used in the building block, links between the individual component and other components, and whether it is on the 'critical path'; and b) the appropriate degree of supplier autonomy or responsibility, which depends on, e.g. the nature of the supplier's technologies and capabilities vis-à-vis the company's own and supplier availability and interest in working with the company. Different forms of specifications should be provided to suppliers, ranging from entirely customer-driven (white box) to supplier-driven (black box); the grey box situation requires joint development of specifications. Strategic co-design and development requires close cooperation and extensive exchange of information but a significant amount of responsibility is delegated to the supplier who is viewed as the real expert. In critical co-design and development, specifications need to be jointly developed by the two parties requiring extensive collaboration. White-box collaboration resembles classic sub-contracting or coordinated development depending on the degree of development risk; the customer should provide detailed technical specifications

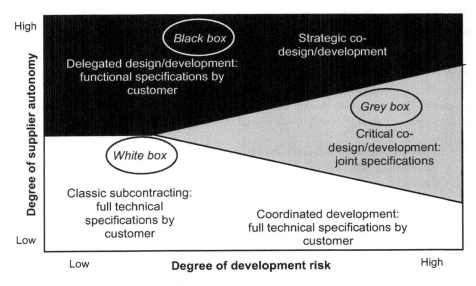

High — Degree of supplier autonomy — Low

Black box

Strategic co-design/development

Delegated design/development: functional specifications by customer

Grey box

Critical co-design/development: joint specifications

White box

Classic subcontracting: full technical specifications by customer

Coordinated development: full technical specifications by customer

Low — Degree of development risk — High

Figure 7.3 Forms of supplier collaboration and specifications

Source: Adapted from Le Dain *et al.* (2010).

to the supplier, leaving as little space as possible for misunderstanding of buyer needs and requirements. This situation involves less intensive collaboration and communication and suppliers can be involved at a later stage in the NPD process.

Successful ESI also requires ongoing supplier relationship development and adaptation. For example, the company should provide shared training (Ragatz *et al.*, 1997) and seek to foster mutual trust and commitment (e.g. Song and Benedetto, 2008). Moreover, it is important to have clear arrangements for the sharing of risks and rewards (Ragatz *et al.*, 1997) and agreed performance targets and measures (Petersen *et al.*, 2005; Van Echtelt *et al.*, 2008). Supplier representation on the customer's NPD team, for example, by inviting key suppliers to share a physical space within the company's premises, can help to create the right form of relationship atmosphere (Petersen *et al.*, 2003). An atmosphere of buyer–supplier collaboration is necessary to foster successful ESI projects.

Finally, the internal capabilities of the company need to be adapted to fully benefit from ESI. Top management within the company needs to support and be committed to ESI (Ragatz *et al.*, 1997) and cross-functional coordination between different internal functions, such as purchasing, R&D, logistics, production and marketing, is critical (Takeishi, 2001). In particular, departments that are traditionally responsible for technological development (i.e. R&D) need to accept suppliers taking responsibility for activities traditionally handled internally. The same applies to purchasing's role in NPD which can be viewed by R&D as a threat. The management of good external relationships begins by ensuring that the right internal relationships are in place.

7.1.5 Supplier involvement in sustainable new product development and innovation

So far this chapter has focused on the development of (early) supplier involvement in NPD in general. We should emphasize at this point that the need for this practice is in no way diminished when the focus is on development of new green, or environmentally friendly, products. The concept of 'design-for-manufacture' (DfM) is mirrored in the concept of 'design-for-environment' (DfE), or eco-design, which focuses on:

- Design for environmental manufacturing, including raw material extraction, processing and manufacturing using non-toxic materials and processes. This includes the minimization of waste and hazardous by-products, air pollution and energy expenditure.

- Design for environmental packaging, ensuring that materials used in packaging are environmentally friendly, materials and also pallets used for transportation are reusable and recyclable, and unnecessary paper and packaging products are eliminated.

- Design for disposal or reuse, involving reuse or refurbishing of a product when it reaches its end of life. This relates to the concepts of closed-loop supply chains and product stewardship that will be discussed in depth in Chapter 14.

Research on supplier involvement in the development of green products and DfE is still in its infancy but it seems from this emerging body of knowledge that the same factors that enable ESI processes for 'normal' NPD projects also apply for green product development. However, some additional challenges are likely to concern the credibility of the company that requires suppliers to engage in environmental practices, for example if the buying company lacks (or is perceived to lack) environmental commitment and concrete practices (Gattiker *et al.*, 2008). In a case study of Body Shop International (BSI), Wycherley (1999) found that suppliers were sceptical towards the (perceived) creeping cost increases of implementing environmental improvements and the negotiations with suppliers for the distribution of benefits between suppliers and BSI were difficult due to supplier mistrust of BSI.

Design for sustainability, or 'D4S' (Crul and Diehl, 2006), is an eco-design concept that expands the focus to include not only the environmental dimension of sustainability but also the social and economic dimensions. The concept of D4S is being promoted by the United Nations Environment Programme (UNEP) to encourage companies to develop long-term innovation strategies that will alleviate the negative environmental, social and economic impacts within the supply chain and throughout the product life cycle. Akin to the cradle-to-cradle concept (Stahel and Reday-Mulvey, 1976) discussed in Chapter 8, D4S requires radical product innovations and potentially also innovations in product-service systems, which challenge current consumption and production patterns by completely re-thinking products in light of consumer needs. These product system innovations are designed to create win-win solutions for businesses, local communities, supply chains, the environment and consumers (Clark *et al.*, 2009).

For example, an innovation to satisfy the need for cycling in busy cities could be that cities develop a network of rentable bicycles instead of a model where people have to buy their own bicycle. This enables more people to use bicycles for transportation, including those with limited incomes, e.g. in developing countries, and puts the onus for maintenance and eventual disposal onto a supplier or city council, thereby reducing the problem of disposal of bicycles.

The above example implies that environmental and sustainable innovations often involve development of new processes rather than new products, or a combination of the two. The second part of this chapter focuses specifically on process innovations; at this point we will simply point out that supplier involvement also relates to environmental process innovations. In a study of how automotive companies collaborated with their suppliers to develop a new greener paint process, Geffen and Rothenberg (2000) found that suppliers played a critical role not only in improving the performance of paint shop operations, but also in initiating ideas for achieving reductions in environmental effects from the use of solvents and chemicals. Therefore, as companies develop and innovate their products and processes to eliminate environmental impacts, they need to capitalize fully on the expertise that exists within the supply base.

7.1.6 A model of early supplier involvement

Figure 7.4 is based around the same four-stage NPD process model as used earlier in the chapter. While the number and names of the stages may vary in different industries and companies, it provides a useful generic NPD process stage-model. The model is not meant as an inclusive NPD model but focuses specifically on issues that concern supplier involvement at different stages of the NPD process. It shows a number of activities that companies should consider doing at each of the four stages of each individual NPD project. In addition, it lists some activities that companies should do as part of their ongoing development activity independently of, or in between, individual NPD projects.

As part of each NPD project, the first stage requires a basic develop-internally or source-from-supplier's decision. This must be a strategic decision that takes into account the company's own core competencies (see also Chapter 5). This stage also necessitates classification of different levels of supplier responsibility roles and levels of involvement. The framework provided in Figure 7.3 is a useful starting point for this exercise. At this early stage only the most important strategic suppliers should be mobilized. Figure 7.4 lists a number of activities that should be done with these suppliers, including obtaining their commitment to the project, formulating risk and reward sharing agreements, communicating policies, specifications and performance requirements and so on. It may also be necessary to encourage these suppliers to mobilize their own strategic suppliers and other important partners. As these suppliers will be experts in their field they only need functional specifications, i.e. they should decide themselves how best to develop the part provided that it meets the global and functional specifications.

The second stage, basic design, involves mobilizing further important suppliers that were not involved right from the beginning but are deemed important to involve at this stage. Similar activities should be performed with these suppliers. Once the project reaches the third stage, detail engineering, it is time to mobilize the more tactical suppliers; these are typically white-box suppliers who may be consulted for design suggestions but require detailed technical specifications so that there is no uncertainty as to what the buyer wants from the supplier. The final stage is the pilot product and product launch stage; here the final (tactical white-box suppliers) need to get involved and all suppliers need to be monitored on an ongoing basis to ensure that they are prepared for the launch.

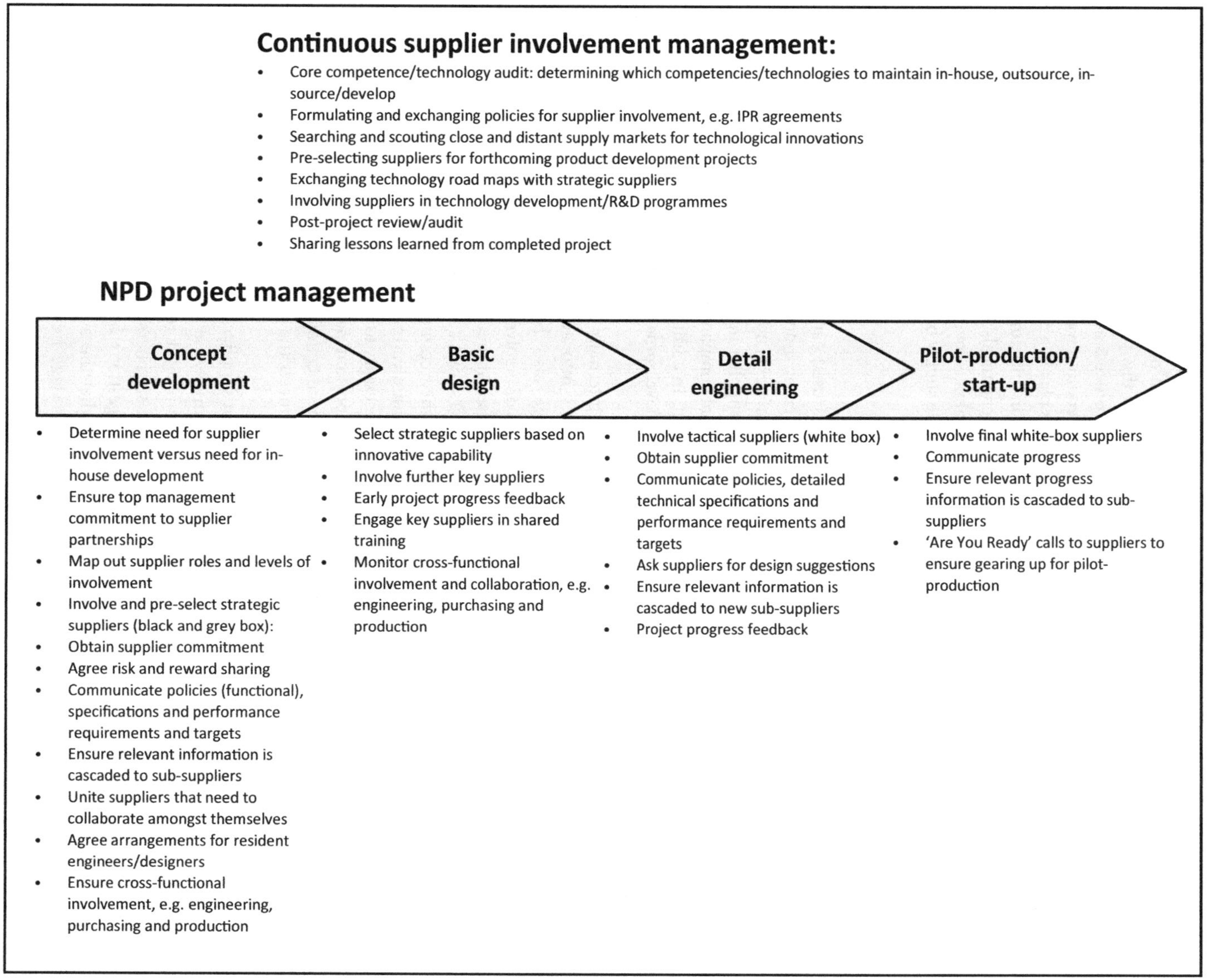

Continuous supplier involvement management:

- Core competence/technology audit: determining which competencies/technologies to maintain in-house, outsource, in-source/develop
- Formulating and exchanging policies for supplier involvement, e.g. IPR agreements
- Searching and scouting close and distant supply markets for technological innovations
- Pre-selecting suppliers for forthcoming product development projects
- Exchanging technology road maps with strategic suppliers
- Involving suppliers in technology development/R&D programmes
- Post-project review/audit
- Sharing lessons learned from completed project

NPD project management

Concept development	Basic design	Detail engineering	Pilot-production/ start-up
• Determine need for supplier involvement versus need for in-house development • Ensure top management commitment to supplier partnerships • Map out supplier roles and levels of involvement • Involve and pre-select strategic suppliers (black and grey box): • Obtain supplier commitment • Agree risk and reward sharing • Communicate policies (functional), specifications and performance requirements and targets • Ensure relevant information is cascaded to sub-suppliers • Unite suppliers that need to collaborate amongst themselves • Agree arrangements for resident engineers/designers • Ensure cross-functional involvement, e.g. engineering, purchasing and production	• Select strategic suppliers based on innovative capability • Involve further key suppliers • Early project progress feedback • Engage key suppliers in shared training • Monitor cross-functional involvement and collaboration, e.g. engineering, purchasing and production	• Involve tactical suppliers (white box) • Obtain supplier commitment • Communicate policies, detailed technical specifications and performance requirements and targets • Ask suppliers for design suggestions • Ensure relevant information is cascaded to new sub-suppliers • Project progress feedback	• Involve final white-box suppliers • Communicate progress • Ensure relevant progress information is cascaded to sub-suppliers • 'Are You Ready' calls to suppliers to ensure gearing up for pilot-production

Figure 7.4 A process-based framework for supplier involvement

The separation of activities into 'project' and 'continuous' management in this model is similar to Wynstra *et al.*'s (2000) framework shown in Table 7.1. The point is that not all activities should be focused on individual NPD projects; suppliers may be involved, for example, in R&D or technology programme's involvement that span several NPD projects. Furthermore, long-term technology strategies (sometimes called technology roadmaps) are important to share and align with strategic suppliers in order to ensure that the company and its strategic suppliers develop in the same direction and follow the same, or at least compatible, technological trajectory.

Appendix 7.1 is built around the principles of the process model presented in Figure 7.4 and provides a simple framework to enable companies to assess their current level of supplier involvement. Managers should tick the appropriate boxes, ideally in consultation with colleagues to get cross-functional input, and calculate their overall score. While the framework does not offer guidance for implementation per se, it helps to identify areas of weakness and thus improvement.

7.2 The challenging case of discontinuous innovation: sourcing new suppliers

ESI is widely recognized by practitioners and researchers of the field as being a best practice for improving NPD performance. However, where ESI is appropriate for incremental NPD projects, discontinuous innovation requires a different approach. In other words, when companies are dealing with NPD projects that require completely new technologies, traditional ESI is no longer the right course of action (Primo and Amundson, 2002).

Although this is still a new field, and there is some disagreement as to the appropriateness of ESI in situations of discontinuous innovation, research shows that when companies are faced with innovations, which break with existing technological paradigms (Martin, 1984), new ways of sourcing ideas and knowledge from suppliers are required. Figure 7.5 provides a simple illustration of the concept of discontinuous innovation: as a technology in an industry grows over time it follows an s-curve as it develops from an early embryonic position to maturity and eventually declines; towards the end of this life cycle a new technology appears from under the radar of the established industry players and ends up partially or completely replacing the existing technology. Consider, for example, the fate of analogue camera technology, the various types of technologies for saving electronic files (floppy disks, zip-drives, CD-ROMs) or paper-based books and newspapers that are rapidly being replaced with electronic and online alternatives.

Discontinuous innovations are often associated with completely new (to the world) technologies but, in fact, often happen when an existing technology from an entirely different industry is introduced into, and adapted to, an industry where it transforms the existing industry. The incumbents are often reluctant to embrace the innovation as it threatens their business model but face the risk of getting left behind as new players take over control of the industry.

The relevance of this to ESI is that this form of innovation calls for a different way of collaborating with suppliers. Figure 7.6 builds on a seminal typology of innovation by Abernathy and Clark (1985), extended by recent work on discontinuous innovation by Phillips *et al.* (2006), to identify appropriate supplier collaboration across the four quadrants:

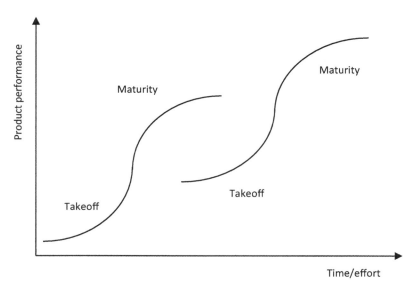

Figure 7.5 Discontinuous innovations: s-curve

Source: Adapted from Foster (1986).

1 Regular innovation: exploit existing technological capabilities and supplier relationships for continuous improvement. For example, BMW developing its 6-generation 3-series (F30), which was launched in 2012, to replace the seven-year-old previous generation 3-series (E90).

2 Revolutionary innovation: existing technological capabilities need to be overturned through existing supplier relationships. For example, a company implementing a state-of-the-art e-procurement system with existing suppliers used to paper-based processes.

3 Niche creation: creating new markets using existing technological capabilities (market innovation) through new similar suppliers. For example, entering a new geographical market and establishing a new but similar supply chain with local suppliers (e.g. in China).

4 Architectural/discontinuous innovation: requires destruction of both existing technological capabilities and markets.

Discontinuous innovation implies that existing technological capabilities and markets become obsolete and are therefore discontinued over time as they are replaced by new technological and market capabilities. The problem for companies that excel at collaboration with long-term existing suppliers (ESI) is that such partnerships have limited innovative potential (Bessant *et al.*, 2005): if you always only source ideas, knowledge and technologies from the same old partners this risks reinforcing the old ways of doing things. Therefore, innovating companies faced with discontinuous innovation should embrace Chesbrough's (2003) concept of open innovation and seek to explore new potential supplier relationships,

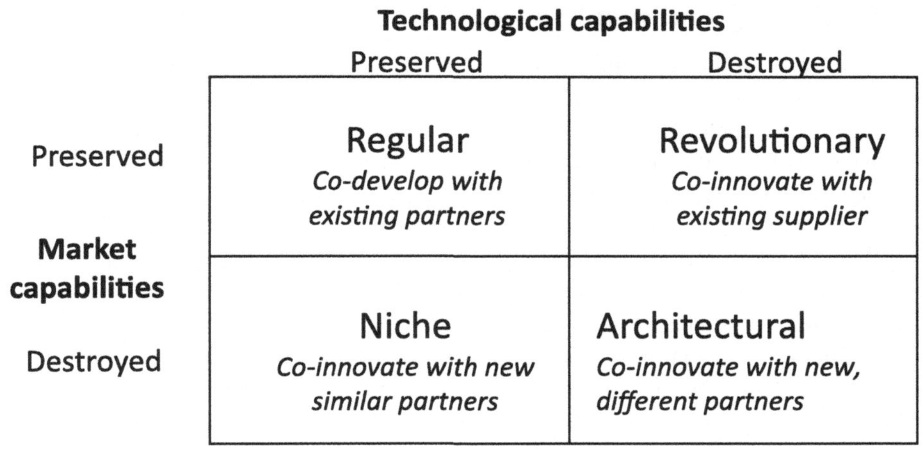

Technological capabilities

	Preserved	Destroyed
Preserved	**Regular** *Co-develop with existing partners*	**Revolutionary** *Co-innovate with existing supplier*
Destroyed	**Niche** *Co-innovate with new similar partners*	**Architectural** *Co-innovate with new, different partners*

(left axis label: **Market capabilities**)

Figure 7.6 Typology of innovations and supplier relationships

Sources: Adapted from Abernathy and Clark (1985); Phillips *et al.* (2006).

or 'flirt with new partners' (Lamming and Phillips, 2005), from outside the company's usual perceived supply chain boundary. These could potentially provide critical sources of discontinuous innovation but are outside the company's usual search and selection environment.

Considering its supplier-facing responsibility, purchasing and supply management should be involved in innovation projects although innovation is traditionally managed by R&D (Mikkelsen and Johnsen, 2018). Two organizational options are debated: either a special sourcing department needs to be created alongside the existing sourcing department whose specific task is to search, and scout, for potential new innovative technologies. Or, each sourcing staff needs to have the dual task of searching existing and new potential supply markets, although there are question marks over the abilities of the same staff performing both of these quite different tasks. Companies are experimenting with such different solutions: BMW has divided its 'advanced sourcing' department into two: one dedicated to supporting the NPD process and another dedicated to the scanning of supply market for innovations. Similarly, L'Oréal has an innovation management function within its purchasing department which is dedicated to identifying new products from new and unfamiliar suppliers (Maury, 2012). In any case, it is important that purchasing and supply management becomes a sparring partner of R&D, facilitating access to existing or new suppliers.

Although the challenges of discontinuous innovation for purchasing and supply management are only beginning to be addressed by researchers as well as by practitioners, it is worth reflecting on the relevance of this to sustainability. There is little doubt that creating sustainable business models requires discontinuous innovations. Consider the scale of innovation required, for example, in developing electric, or hydrogen, cars and that these types of innovation are likely to make the old technological paradigm of combustion engines obsolete; or a shift from fossil-based energy sources to sustainable energy sources. Implementing new sustainable business models therefore forces companies to engage with the challenges of managing discontinuous innovation.

7.3 Purchasing and supply process innovation and technology

The next part of this chapter shifts the focus from product to process innovation by discussing how information-related technologies are used to improve or sometimes radically disrupt the purchasing and supply process. We begin by evaluating the early use of electronic data interchange (EDI), exploring forms of electronic procurement, including e-hubs and e-auctions, and more recent digital supply chain developments involving 'big data' and the 'Internet of Things'. The impact of additive manufacturing or 3D printing techniques are discussed, as well as the rise of social media where we reflect on the opportunities these developments present to purchasing and supply in the future, particularly in terms of how they may affect supply chain performance, structure and sustainability.

Given the significant number of different terminologies used to describe new or emerging technologies, it is important not to get confused. For example, terms such as digital and digitalization are often used interchangeably with electronic and e-business, depending on the context of their application across the organization and supply chain (Swaminathan and Tayur, 2003). Some terms and phrases have also fallen out of fashion, such as the prefix 'electronic' to denote Internet-enabled technology in connection to a specific administrative function. In the first section, we explore the early developments of information technology in relation to purchasing and supply, exploring each process innovation as far as possible in the chronological order of its introduction.

7.3.1 The emergence of electronic data interchange

The introduction of information technology in purchasing and logistics began with the emergence of electronic data interchange (EDI) in the 1960s. Described as the beginnings of the 'computerization of business' (Straub *et al.*, 2004), EDI was used by road and rail transport firms who realized the benefit of document standardization and replacing previous paper-based processes with electronic communication (Threlkel and Kavan, 1999). As an early example of an inter-organizational system, EDI used bespoke computer hardware and common IT infrastructure (e.g. telephone networks), to send coded information such as goods delivery schedules, dispatch notes and confirmation of goods received. EDI originated from firms wishing to automate the exchange of data with suppliers as a secure link offering a rapid and reliable means of communication (Swatman and Swatman, 1992).

The integration of EDI across the supply chain faced a number of difficulties, including high costs of entry, proliferation of electronic protocols and coercive pressures on suppliers from powerful customers. Firms using EDI often found themselves tied into a technology that replicated the hierarchical nature of traditional, adversarial customer–supplier relationships (Sako 1992). For instance, the Ford Motor Company in the 1980s developed its EDI network 'Fordnet' in the manner of a competitive weapon, to gain advantage over competitors by locking in suppliers through investment in customized IT systems (Webster, 1995).

The emergence of systems such as web-EDI in the late 1990s, using eXtensible Markup Language (XML) and personal computers (PCs), offered a low-cost solution for all suppliers seeking connection to their business partners via the Internet. E-commerce offered online development using 'virtual spaces' in which manufacturers and suppliers could collaborate on joint design and development. Hence potential benefits were not only reductions in transaction costs through minimizing delay and uncertainty, but also sharing of ideas in new product (or service) development. The explosion in worldwide connectivity has led to a proliferation of electronic-based collaboration, resulting in profound implications for buyer–supplier relationships.

Internet-based communication between a buyer and its suppliers has meant the introduction of a web-EDI system into the supply chain, bringing a number of largely process-based benefits. Although today a somewhat old-fashioned term, as all computers are assumed to be web-enabled, web-EDI eliminates manual processes including paperwork such as the supplier (or vendor) pick-up sheet, advanced shipping notice, and stock movement report. Daily shipment instructions can be entered only once into the system and then accessed remotely by suppliers. This solution allows the firm to provide information to suppliers and logistics partners, conducting dialogue within minutes instead of days regarding key aspects such as component scheduling. The primary objectives are typically the creation of a reliable electronic audit trail, elimination of waste and duplicated effort, such as paperwork, faxes and phone calls, reductions in product delivery lead time, and an increase in inventory turnover. Such systems also improve supply chain visibility where any product or service quality problems are visible to supply chain partners.

7.3.2 E-procurement

E-procurement can be defined as 'using Internet technology in the purchasing process' (De Boer *et al.*, 2002: 26). The rise of e-procurement coincided with the spread of Internet-enabled desktop computers from the early 1990s onwards. Their use meant not only better information processing internally, but also allowed access to inter-organizational collaborative platforms linked to other parts of the supply chain. Purchasing therefore was now able to more easily connect with functions such as material planning, logistics and product development using

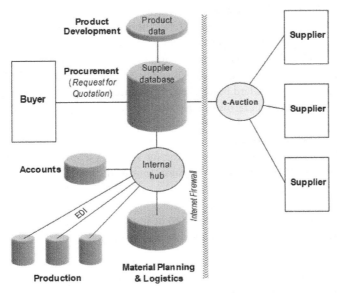

Figure 7.7   Example of an industry e-procurement system with Internet auction

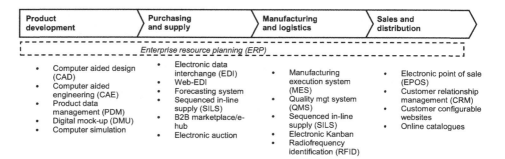

Figure 7.8 Common applications of purchasing and supply IT

online tools such as catalogues, e-auctions, request for quotations, invoicing and collaborative engineering (Figure 7.7).

A common perspective of the burgeoning range of information and communication technologies (ICT) is one that corresponds with four core processes – including purchasing and supply – across the organization (see Figure 7.8). This includes both terrestrial and web-enabled ICT applications that connect to the enterprise by means of an enterprise resource planning (ERP) system 'backbone' with electronic linkages to external sites such as sales outlets and suppliers.

7.3.3 E-hubs and catalogues

The term 'e-hub' covers portal, trade exchange, Internet-driven electronic marketplace, and cyber-purchasing systems (Kaplan and Sawhney 2000, Skjøtt-Larsen *et al.*, 2003). E-hubs can be defined as 'web-based systems that link multiple businesses together for the purposes of trading or collaboration' (Daniel *et al.*, 2003: 39). The purpose of e-hubs is to expand choice available to buyers, give suppliers access to new customers, and reduce transaction costs, by aggregating a large number of buyers and suppliers and automating transactions (Bakos, 1998). E-hubs provide a marketplace, or collaborative platform, where operators earn revenue by extracting fees for the transactions. Business-to-business trade through e-hubs is increasingly becoming a standard purchasing, or procurement, practice.

E-hubs can be classified in terms of what they exchange, e.g. products and services, and how they exchange it, for example, either straight repurchases for approved suppliers or spot sourcing and commodity trading. For the latter, the buyer's goal is to fulfil an immediate need at the lowest cost, such as commodity trading for steel by NewView (formerly named the 'e-Steel' hub). In terms of ownership structure, we can distinguish between the following (using automotive examples):

- *A private trade exchange* is owned and operated by a single firm (e.g. 'SupplyPower' owned and operated by General Motors);

- *A third-party exchange* is operated by a group of non-competing firms or one that is not considered a trading partner (e.g. 'SupplyOn' operated by Bosch, Continental, Ina, SiemensVDO, SAP and ZF Friedrichshafen);

- *A consortium exchange* is where the ownership is shared between competing firms (e.g. 'Covisint' owned by Ford, General Motors, DaimlerChrysler, Renault-Nissan and Peugeot Citroen – until sold in January 2004).

Electronic catalogues (e-catalogues) provide a common method of storing information that refers to lists of parts or finished products for sale by a firm, accessible digitally via the web. Many firms offer product information digitally, packaged as an electronic parts catalogue (EPC). The advantage of electronic catalogues means a faster and cheaper method of storage and retrieval of product data by the customer, buyer or supplier. Items listed in a catalogue can be direct items associated with production or indirect items, such as office furniture and computer equipment. By agreeing to use catalogues from a limited number of selected suppliers, firms can secure preferential pricing arrangements and control their total annual spending. An advantage of using an approved firm's product catalogue is that they reduce the tendency for 'maverick spending' (off-contract) particularly on indirect items, such as stationery, where staff choose a one-off purchase from an external source without consent from the purchasing department, ending up paying a higher price without the benefit of any discount. Note 7.1 summarizes the use of e-catalogues by the English National Health Service (NHS).

Note 7.1

NHS-Cat

The English National Health Service (NHS) relies on a very wide range of purchased products and services. As a publicly funded healthcare system the NHS provides healthcare to UK citizens (and legal immigrants) with most services free at the point of use. Largely funded through taxation, the NHS traditionally offered its healthcare services through primary care trusts although as part of NHS reforms these were changed to clinical commissioning groups in March 2013.

Fragmented spend is a long-term problem for the NHS. Traditionally, general practitioners (doctors), dentists, opticians, hospitals and so on would largely manage their purchasing individually although the national body, the NHS Purchasing and Supply Agency (Pasa), would create framework agreements, coordinate major purchase categories, and develop purchasing strategies and policies. In 2006 NHS Logistics and parts of Pasa were outsourced to DHL in a ten-year deal (now operating as NHS Supply Chain).

One of the changes designed to achieve £1 billion in savings by 2016 was the introduction of an e-catalogue in 2007: NHS-Cat. NHS Supply Chain supply over 620,000 healthcare products and employ over 2,400 people across eight sites. Medical products such as orthopaedics, dental consumables, operating theatre products, audiology products, drapes and gowns as well as non-medical products, such as food, stationery, clothing and office furniture can be purchased online using a shopping basket facility. The NHS-Cat enables online ordering, gives better choice and controls maverick buying.

7.3.4 E-auctions and electronic reverse auctions

Although auctions existed prior to the Internet in sectors such as antiques, art and bulk flower selling, their spread in the business world is largely due to the accessibility of web-enabled computer technology. E-auctions allow buyers to consider multiple bids in a defined period of time by suppliers in the market worldwide. A typical scenario of an electronic auction first involves a decision by the purchasing department over whether the product, component or service required (or for sale) is suitable for auction. This decision also revolves around the need for an open market or more selective system of bidding from suppliers, and whether the identity of the firms needs to be protected, i.e. sealed bidding. Types of e-auctions include:

- English auctions: sellers offer a (minimum) starting price that gradually increases until no one is willing to pay more for the item;

- Dutch auctions: sellers start with a high price and the price gradually decreases until a buyer is found;

- Reverse auctions: buyers post the item and the price they are willing to pay whilst suppliers compete for the business.

Electronic reverse auctions (ERAs) are the most relevant for purchasing. It is perhaps tempting to think that ERAs are mostly relevant for low-value purchases; however, Wagner and Schwab (2004) found that provided that the product or service can be specified properly, higher-value purchases can equally be purchased through ERAs and will in fact result in higher savings. In addition, they state (2004: 22) that 'all that counts is competition': competition among suppliers participating should be as strong as possible in order for ERAs to be successful.

There is a question mark over whether or not ERAs are unsuitable for long-term buyer–supplier relationships and if they encourage opportunistic behaviour. Furthermore, even though an upfront saving can be made by achieving a lower price, there is a risk that long-term costs increase. Critics also argue that suppliers experience more disadvantages than advantages from the use of ERAs and tend to dislike ERAs. However, Cäniels and van Raaij (2009) found that some suppliers were actually positive about ERAs and that suppliers from developing economies appeared to perceive ERAs as an opportunity rather than a threat, as ERAs could help to open up established and closed buyer–supplier relationships creating a level playing field for suppliers across countries. In comparison, large Western companies competing on quality and innovation capabilities seemed more likely to refrain from taking part in ERAs.

7.4 Digital supply chains, 'big data' and the Internet of Things (IoT)

From the 2010s onwards there has been an exponential rise in the number of fixed and portable computing devices (e.g. smartphones, tablets, laptops, PCs) used for both work and leisure purposes. Each device contains communicating sensors which link to computing intelligence, creating what is called the Internet of Things (IoT) or the Industrial Internet. The

IoT is defined as many interconnected physical objects, creating a mesh of devices all producing information about user lifestyle choice and purchasing preferences (Cecchinel *et al.*, 2014). The sensors in these devices in our surrounding environment (e.g. cars, buildings) continuously collect data on our choices as customers which can be invaluable as predictors of future buying trends and for online marketing firms to conduct targeted campaigns on specific consumer groups or individuals. Such is the connective power of the current digital era that terms such as 'smart cities' are now being used to describe the reach and application of digital technology (Li *et al.*, 2016).

The idea of smart cities is based on the integration of urban infrastructures with information and communication technologies (ICT) to enable the development of new operations models. Digitized infrastructures offer opportunities for public and private organizations to design and deliver more customer-centric products or services relating to remote grocery delivery, shared transportation, and access to use of household items (e.g. washing machines) on a pay-per-use basis via online booking and payment systems. The use of IoT data in a domestic setting can also be used by companies to understand patterns of consumption and enable reverse supply chain management. For example, increasing online visibility by the user over all aspects of their purchase, such as experience, consumption, interaction and depletion, can help service providers predict when to take back used products for reuse, repair or recycling of valuable components and materials (e.g. electrical items, cardboard, metals), as well as optimizing replenishment levels to match demand (Parry *et al.*, 2016).

The application of the Internet in today's business environment means that it has become an important strategic element in supply chain management. The Internet has in many ways positively affected the ways firm operations are managed, where it has encouraged the move away from single firm competition in favour of competitive supply chain networks. As companies are becoming more aware of their competition, this is driving up the levels of adaptation and cooperation necessary in the supply chain, so that electronic commerce takes on an increasingly critical role. The expectations around digital operational capability required of most suppliers today means the ability to engage in real-time communication between supply chain members, interlocking databases and 24-hour shipment tracking. The Internet and digital know-how therefore have become essential elements in the purchasing and supply chain manager's personal toolkit.

One of the most recent developments affecting the digital supply chain is the introduction of digital currency or 'cryptocurrency'. One of the best-known currencies is bitcoin (see Note 7.2). Digital currency was created for people to conduct business without the costs or bureaucracy of the banking system. During the purchase, the transaction is recorded in a digital record or ledger called the blockchain which is located across users' computers. Bitcoins are registered to bitcoin addresses and accessed by their owners via their own private passkey. People who put their computer to work verifying blockchain transactions are rewarded with new bitcoins in a process known as bitcoin mining. Despite the lack of centralized banking control, many governments are experimenting with blockchain technology to store information, such as land registry records, while supermarkets are looking at blockchain to help track food through the supply chain, from farmyard to the consumer, as a means of ensuring 100 per cent traceability and avoiding meat processing scandals of the past (e.g. horsemeat in UK burgers).

Note 7.2

What is bitcoin and where did it come from?

The cryptocurrency bitcoin was created by an unknown individual or group in 2009. The philosophy behind the payment system's conception is that it is borderless and completely decentralized, i.e. owned or controlled by no one individual, bank or government. In many ways it is a utopian project where users interact with one another and all transactions are recorded and stored forever on a large, secure online public ledger. Like the various currencies which followed it, bitcoin was seen as an alternative to the traditional economy which at the time in 2009 was going through a financial crisis. Although there are many legitimate uses for cryptocurrency, such as investors and people who don't trust their own country's currency, there are also alleged links with criminal activity and the Dark Web. Criminals can use cryptocurrency to buy drugs, weapons or Internet hacking tools. North Korea, for example, has been stockpiling bitcoins to try to circumvent international sanctions. Although such currencies aren't anonymous, their air of exclusivity and borderless, password-protected accounts can make it difficult for the authorities to trace and claim any tax payments which may be due.

7.5 Social media and cloud computing

Most people these days are active users of social media and use social media to connect with friends and colleagues, and to exchange information, pictures and so on. Marketing professionals now consider social media as a core ingredient of their communication with customers but how does this affect purchasing? In fact, very little research has been done on the use of social media in purchasing but there is no doubt that social media has a number of interesting applications for purchasing professionals.

A survey by Rozemeijer *et al.* (2011) on the use of social media by purchasing professionals found that over 90 per cent used LinkedIn while over 40 per cent used Facebook and Twitter and over three-quarters of the respondents expected their use of social media to significantly increase over the next two years. Many considered social media to improve:

- Purchasing and supply management performance;
- Collaboration with suppliers;
- Quality of sourcing decisions.

Social media can be used to collect information on suppliers but gaining access to experts in the field, advancing of professional careers and sharing of best practices, news and so on are also common motivators. Clearly social media play an increasing role in consumer buying behaviour but are also likely to become more important in professional purchasing and supply management.

A related area is cloud computing; most people are now familiar with Dropbox and Google Cloud that are increasingly used to store and share data. In purchasing, and supply chain management in particular as discussed in the following chapter, sharing up-to-date information amongst multiple actors is critical. Using cloud computing to share information is an opportunity, although concerns about security remain. Nevertheless, major companies have implemented cloud computing because of the potential benefits involved. Cloud computing implies the sharing of resources via computer-based information networks which achieve economies of scale and coherence between distributed users. The 'cloud' means not only sharing by multiple users often across multiple time zones, but also the capability to dynamically re-allocate according to local need. For example, a web server can be redirected to serve the North American market after the European operation has closed for the night. This approach maximizes the use of computing power and can reduce environmental impact in areas such as energy usage from air conditioning and cost of maintaining multiple computer housing facilities.

7.6 3D printing and additive manufacturing

Since the dawn of industrial revolution and the emergence of the factory system over 200 years ago, manufacturing has been portrayed as typically centralized, machine-based production operations with firms seeking economies-of-scale cost optimization (Srai *et al.*, 2016). The rise of globalization over the past 30 years has seen the spread of international manufacturing sites serving regional and global markets where centralization is still characterized by long and unresponsive supply chains. The emergence of new technologies and approaches to production, however, is starting to challenge previously accepted notions of the supply chain as a basic building block in the manufacturing process. Distributed manufacturing (DM), for example, is a new approach in which breakthroughs in production and infrastructure technologies have enabled smaller and micro-scale manufacture much closer to the end user (Srai *et al.*, 2016). These new forms of manufacturing are enabled by technologies such as sensors and process analytics providing enhanced production control as well as ICT, enabling closer customer involvement in the process, from product conception right through to final delivery. At the heart of this distributed, small-scale production approach is additive manufacturing and 3D printing technology. In the following paragraphs we will refer to this using the term '3D printing'.

3D printing refers to an industrial laser which melts powdered resin or plastic material into any desired shape as determined by a digital programme and robotically controlled arm to which it is connected. It is claimed that 3D printer units are poised to transform the industrial economy with their extreme flexibility not only allowing for easy customization of goods but also eliminating assembly and inventory requirements, and enabling production close to the point of purchase so reducing transport and inventory costs (d'Aveni, 2015). In addition, 3D printing offers the potential to manufacture product components, such as replacement parts, close to local markets at dealerships or retailers instead of returning these to large centralized factories. The concept of additive manufacturing is not entirely new as early versions of the technology were used several decades ago for pre-production prototyping and rapid tooling. What makes the latest range of printers exciting is their portable size which enables flexibility of location and ability to create durable and safe products for sale to customers in low to moderate quantities. Applications have been demonstrated across many different sectors, from aerospace and medical to biotechnology and food production.

Some observers have suggested that the day will come when, at the push of a button at a local printer, any part can be made, rendering global supply chains obsolete. Others argue that 3D printing only works best where customization is important (e.g. Holweg, 2015), e.g. when printing bespoke hearing aids, dental implants or customized images in chocolate for a child's birthday cake. Where customization is unimportant, for instance in long production runs involving identical automotive or home appliance components, then 3D printing is not yet competitive but this may change in future. Yet, Adidas has already developed a new sports shoe where the mid-soles will be mass-produced using 3D printing. However, 3D printing involves significant before- and after-processing, including setting up, removal of parts, cleaning and polishing, all of which incur significant labour costs.

While at one level 3D printing represents the ultimate 'lean supply chain', producing parts exactly when and where they are needed (Holweg, 2015), on another level the limitations around large-scale production capability suggests a more practical application is in sectors where relatively small numbers of customizable products are required. In sum, 3D printing has undoubtedly great potential but is unlikely to replace traditional large-scale manufacturing in the immediate future.

7.7 Technology as an enabler of sustainable supply chains

Technology also offers new ways to tackle supply chain risks related to sustainability and for companies to ensure compliance and transparency across their supply chains. Given the enormity of the challenge for single companies to tackle these supply chain risks on their own, more and more companies choose to collaborate with other companies, including their competitors, to jointly manage these challenges. An increasing number of hubs or platform providers are emerging to facilitate the process of supplier monitoring and developmental efforts. The advantage of these platforms is that they provide a way to address supply chain sustainability risks at multiple company or industry level. They are typically run by non-profit consortiums, aimed at establishing standard processes for the sharing of business information between firms (i.e. B2B). Examples include computer and consumer electronics, electronic components, semiconductor manufacturing, telecommunications and logistics companies, all working to create industry-wide, open e-business process standards. These standards create a common e-business language which helps to connect supply chain partners around the world.

Information sharing hubs are often operated by service providers such as 'Achilles', 'Sedex' and 'Ecovadis', and have an increasing role in developing sustainable supply chains, used extensively for sharing sustainability risk data in supply chains for compliance purposes (Note 7.3). The most mature hubs go beyond collecting data through online questionnaires aligned with global standards, typically the Global Reporting Initiative (GRI). For example, these might offer system training and support, audit and embedded system features, such as warnings of incomplete or expired data, and access to third-party data for verification purposes. More recently established hubs, such as 'Aperitas', typically target smaller companies with relatively simple-to-use offerings.

Note 7.3

Hub technology for supply chain compliance and auditing

RosettaNet, Sedex and Ecovadis are all examples of application of technology used to promote supply chain sharing of key information. Such information is needed by customers and manufacturers for compliance purposes when seeking to prove a product conforms to legislation, such as the use of harmful substances. Sedex: the Supplier Ethics Data Exchange seeks to 'empower sustainable and ethical supply chains' by encouraging responsible supply chain practice. As a non-profit organization, its core product is a secure, online database which allows members to voluntarily store, share and report on information on four key areas: labour standards, health and safety, the environment and business ethics. Similarly, the EcoVadis hub aims at 'improving environmental and social practices of companies by leveraging the influence of global supply chains'. EcoVadis claims to operate the first collaborative platform enabling companies to monitor the sustainability performance of suppliers using a system of ratings and easy-to-use monitoring tools. Although the portal operators claim it allows companies to manage risks and drive eco-innovations in their global supply chains, a drawback of all such third-party hubs/portals is the option by unscrupulous suppliers simply not to use them and avoid detection over possible material use, environmental or human rights infringements.

CASE STUDY 7.1

DEVELOPING THE AIRBUS A380 SUPERJUMBO[1]

The A380 superjumbo was not only the biggest airliner ever built but also a major challenge for Airbus to develop. When Airbus set out to develop the A380 it knew it had to transform its aircraft development process. The high level of investment coupled with the technological scale and complexity of the venture made it imperative for Airbus to seek supplier involvement in the development of the A380. Seeking to share the vast development costs, Airbus created what it called 'risk sharing partnerships' with more than 30 major suppliers including Alenia, Eurocopter, Fokker and Saab, covering $3.1 billion or 25 per cent of the total estimated non-recurring costs (Morris, 2001; AT Kearney, 2003). Table 7.2 provides an overview of major component suppliers on the A380 and the estimated value per ship-set. The five largest contributors by value are Rolls-Royce, Safran, United Technologies, General Electric (GE) and Goodrich.

Challenges in managing early supplier involvement in the A380 programme

The A380 programme represented a mentality shift within Airbus towards supplier involvement. In contrast with previous programmes, Airbus approached major suppliers asking for their solutions to design problems rather than asking suppliers to 'build to print'. Suppliers were involved earlier and more extensively in the A380 programme than on previous aircraft programmes. Airbus decided that the moment of involvement should depend on issues such as component importance, risk and technological uncertainty: where new materials had to be developed, e.g. for wing development, suppliers became involved as concepts were frozen. Less critical suppliers were involved later during product planning, following concept development. In some component groups, such as landing gear, Airbus involved at least two suppliers to work in parallel within Airbus premises on separate technical solutions for the same problem. These suppliers gained what Airbus called 'early plateau': a physical shared space for suppliers within Airbus. At a later stage Airbus would select the supplier offering the best solution, enabling the company to capitalize on ESI, while avoiding the problem of early supplier lock-in. Actually, some supplier involvement even commenced prior to the A380 programme. Market research for a 'Megaliner' was conducted as early as 1991 and a joint feasibility study of a Very Large Commercial Transport (VLCT) aircraft was commenced by Boeing and several companies in the Airbus consortium in January 1993 (originally aiming to form a partnership to exploit what was then seen as a limited market).

The trend in Airbus is towards even earlier involvement of key suppliers. The A350 programme, which has followed in the footsteps of the A380, has seen suppliers of landing gear and fuel systems being involved on average one milestone, or one and a half years, earlier. This is partly because suppliers were already contracted onto the A350 programme before it was re-conceptualized from scratch, but there is little doubt that the experiences from the A380 programme resulted in a realization across Airbus that key system suppliers need to be involved no later than at concept development, and ideally in the R&D process preceding individual programmes.

Airbus provided two main types of work package to suppliers: 'build-to-print' and 'design and build'. 'Build-to-print' packages referred to traditional arms-length relationships where the supplier was issued with a set of drawings and specifications and a contract to produce a product to drawings. Airbus held regular consultation meetings and design reviews to encompass supplier capabilities and invite suggestions. 'Design and build' was used extensively across several component groups, involving partial supplier authority to design, develop and manufacture components or assemblies in partnership with Airbus. Benefiting from early involvement in the programme, 'Design and build' suppliers aligned and integrated design and development methods with Airbus. Where build-to-print resembled a white-box strategy, design and build indicated a black-box strategy, although 'design and build' packages often resembled more collaborative grey-box relationships.

The shift towards increased supplier involvement has been coupled with a strategy of supply base rationalization. Small suppliers have been either replaced by larger ones able to take on more work or lost their direct contact with Airbus being relegated to 'sub-tier' status. This has created administrative cost savings for Airbus, having to deal with fewer suppliers, and increased operational efficiency by enabling task partitioning and employing a more 'modular' process. Airbus clearly pursues a systems integration strategy, reducing and tiering the supply chain, and allocating major sub-systems integration roles to major first-tier suppliers. The Power8 programme seeks among other cost reduction initiatives to consolidate the supply base, giving more responsibility to risk sharing partners.

Airbus counteracted the potential problem of dependency on suppliers with a parallel sourcing strategy across major high-value components. Parallel suppliers cooperated with Airbus while simultaneously competing on price and performance. This strategy was evident in the engines provided by both General Electric (GE) and Rolls-Royce. The operational choice was left to the airline company buying/leasing the aircraft. For example, Emirates has opted for a GE engine, while Malaysia Airlines has selected Rolls-Royce. Similar sourcing strategies existed for brakes and tyres driven by airlines in order to avoid dependency on any one major supplier. More than one supplier for these components was therefore approved and certified by Airbus to allow airlines to negotiate deals directly with suppliers for the duration of the aircraft.

Table 7.2 Major suppliers on Airbus A380

Company	Components supplied	Estimated ship-set value per A380 (US$ millions)
Rolls-Royce	Trent 900 engine	18
Safran	Nacelles, braking controls, nose landing gear, communications and data systems: 10% share of GP7200 engine	15
United Technologies	Auxiliary Power Unit, air conditioning system, GP7200 engine (JV with GE)	10
General Electric	GP7200 engine (JV with Pratt & Whitney)	9
Goodrich	Landing gear, flight control systems, evacuation systems, cargo loading, aerostructures, engine components	8
Finmeccanica	4% share of airframe production, air conditioning, humidification, insulation systems	5
Alcoa	Aluminium, fasteners, fuselage sections, fuselage stringers and skins, support structures, fittings	3.5
Thales	Cockpit control and displays, in-flight entertainment, radio altimeter	3.5
MTU	22.5% share of GP7200 engine	3.2
Honeywell	Flight management system, SATCOM, navigation systems, wheels and brakes	2.5
Smiths Group	Actuation, landing gear systems, fabrications	1.5
Rockwell Collins	Avionics and navigation equipment, communications infrastructure	0.5

Source: Adapted from Babka, 2006.

Case conclusions

Using ESI to develop the A380 was a real challenge. Airbus avoided involving too many suppliers early in the A380 programme by varying the timing of involvement according to levels of component complexity and risk. Airbus wisely engaged key suppliers in risk sharing agreements reducing its

CASE STUDY 7.1

investments by making suppliers responsible for high value-added activities in design, manufacture and assembly. Did the increasing involvement of suppliers in developing the A380 hinder or enhance performance? The A380 programme suffered several setbacks, including a launch delay by approximately two years and escalating programme costs. The original $10.7 billion development budget is said to have over-run by several billion dollars; estimates suggest $16 billion (Matlack, 2006) or even $18 billion (Wallace, 2007). On two key measures of NPD performance the A380 has therefore under-performed, although it may take over a decade to judge if the ultimate measure of success – financial break-even – has been realized. It is tempting to suggest that supplier involvement in developing the A380 has not paid off and that Airbus would have been better off not involving suppliers. Supplier involvement can lead to a myriad of problems including loss of control over the development process and internal resistance. However, Airbus simply could not have developed the A380 on their own so whether or not supplier involvement were to be adopted was not the question: it was a question of how best to implement. The A380 programme acted as a demonstrator for future aircraft development programmes, so lessons on how to make the most of supplier involvement are already under way.

7.8 Conclusion

This chapter has discussed a range of issues in purchasing that concerns innovation and technology. The first part of the chapter focused on the role of purchasing in enabling product innovation through early involvement of key suppliers in new product development (NPD) projects – early supplier involvement or ESI. There is extensive research evidence to suggest that by collaborating with suppliers as part of NPD processes, companies can improve NPD performance, for example, by getting products to market faster, at lower cost and better quality. However, it takes time and skill to manage ESI and reap the rewards and this chapter has described some of the key success factors and frameworks in managing ESI.

Chapter 7 also explored the challenge of discontinuous and disruptive innovations and how this potentially changes the role of purchasing and suppliers: where NPD projects usually call for collaboration with existing suppliers, discontinuous innovations require sourcing of new technologies and capabilities so new suppliers from outside the existing supply chain may become necessary. This is a new area of research where new practices are still emerging. Discontinuous innovation, however, is particularly important from a sustainability perspective because green products or processes require a fundamental rethinking of products and processes to eliminate environmental impacts at the source. The chapter therefore explored developments in concepts such as design for environment, eco-design and the most recent version, design for sustainability, which requires system-wide innovations to address environmental, social and economic aspects of sustainability.

The second part of the chapter focused on purchasing and supply process innovation by discussing how technology is used to improve the purchasing process. We evaluated the use of electronic data interchange, and more recent forms of e-procurement including hubs, catalogues and auctions, and the potential spread of social media in purchasing. In fact, the latter has great potential but is still a widely unknown area. One underlying theme and frequent criticism of e-procurement methods such as auctions is that they largely encourage competition at the expense of collaboration. In other words, where much recent purchasing theory focuses on the benefits of partnering with key suppliers, and reducing costs through long-term collaboration, methods such as auctions may also reduce costs but at what long-term expense? We argued here that although there is a risk of achieving short-term savings at the expense of long-term cost increases, combining collaboration with competition can be a powerful strategy. Indeed, the concept of 'coopetition' captures this double-sided effect where the effectiveness of coordination mechanisms on knowledge sharing in intra-organizational networks consists of both collaborative and competitive ties (Tsai, 2002). In fact, from a social sustainability perspective e-procurement methods may help to allow suppliers from developing countries to bid for work as otherwise they may find it difficult to break into established buyer–supplier relationships.

The rise of digital supply chains, driven by big data analytics and IoT interconnectivity, has significant implications for purchasing and supply management. The mesh of devices in today's business and leisure environment are all producing information about user lifestyle choices and purchasing preferences (Cecchinel *et al.*, 2014). This is helping to predict future buying trends and online marketing firms to conduct targeted campaigns on specific consumer groups or individuals. Such is the connective power of the current era that terms such as 'smart cities' are now being used to describe the impact of digital technology on business practice and societal well-being (Li *et al.*, 2016). The rise of technologies such as additive manufacturing and 3D printing now have the capability to produce complex 3D components using small, flexible machines with digitally controlled lasers. Their portability in theory means eliminating the need for traditional tiers of suppliers and fixed or unresponsive supply chains. In practice, however, while in some specialist sectors that require high product customization this is true, in other high-volume sectors, the traditional centralized production models are unlikely to change in the near future (Holweg, 2015). In terms of information sharing benefits, Internet technology has become an enabler for sustainable supply chains with the increased use of business-to-business online collaborative sharing sites (i.e. hubs or portals) for supply chain environmental, social and safety compliance and auditing.

Note

1   This case study is based on research reported in Johnsen and Lewis (2009).

References

Abernathy WJ and Clark KB (1985) Innovation: Mapping the winds of creative destruction. *Research Policy* 13: 3–22.

Babka S (2006) *EADS: The A380 Debate*, Morgan Stanley Research Europe, September.

Bakos J (1998) The emerging role of electronic marketplaces on the internet. *Communications of the ACM* 41(8): 35–42.

Bessant JR, Lamming RC, Noke H and Phillips WE (2005) Managing innovation beyond the steady state. *Technovation* 25(12): 1366–1376.

Birou LM and Fawcett SE (1994) Supplier involvement in integrated product development: A comparison of US and European practices. *International Journal of Physical Distribution and Logistics Management* 24(5): 4–14.

Bowersox D and Closs D (1996) *Logistical Management: The Integrated Supply Chain Approach*. New York: McGraw-Hill.

Burt DN and Soukup WR (1985) Purchasing's role in new product development. *Harvard Business Review* 63(3): 90–97.

Cäniels MCJ and van Raaij EM (2009) Do all suppliers dislike electronic reverse auctions? *Journal of Purchasing and Supply Management* 15(1): 12–23.

Cecchinel C, Jimenez M, Mosser S and Riveill M (2014) An architecture to support the collection of big data in the internet of things. In: *Services, IEEE World Congress*: 442–449.

Chesbrough HW (2003) The era of open innovation. *Sloan Management Review* 44(3): 35–41.

Clark KB (1989) Project scope and project performance: The effects of parts strategy and supplier involvement on product development. *Management Science* 35(10): 1247–1263.

Clark KB and Fujimoto T (1991) *NPD Performance: Strategy, Organization, and Management in the World Auto Industry*. Cambridge, MA: Harvard Business School Press.

Clark G, Kosoris J, Hong LN and Crul M (2009) Design for sustainability: Current trends in sustainable product design and development. *Sustainability* 1: 409–424.

Crul M and Diehl J (2006) *Design for Sustainability: A Practical Approach for Developing Economies*. Paris, France: UNEP & TU Delft.

Daniel E, White A, Harrison A and Ward J (2003) The future of e-hubs: Findings of an international Delphi study. Information Systems Research Centre, Cranfield Centre for Logistics & Supply Chain Management.

d'Aveni R (2015) The 3-D printing revolution. *Harvard Business Review* 93(5): 40–48.

De Boer L, Harink J and Heijboer G (2002) A conceptual model for assessing the impact of electronic procurement. *European Journal of Purchasing & Supply Management* 8: 25–33.

Farmer D (1981) The role of procurement in new product development. *International Journal of Physical Distribution and Materials Management* 11(2/3): 46–54.

Foster R (1986) *Innovation: The Attacker's Advantage*. New York: Summit Books.

Gattiker TF, Tate W and Carter CR (2008) *Supply Management's Strategic Role in Environmental Practices*. Tempe, AZ: CAPS Research.

Geffen CA and Rothenberg S (2000) Suppliers and environmental innovation: The automotive paint process. *International Journal of Operations and Production Management* 20(2): 166–186.

Handfield RB, Ragatz GL, Petersen KJ and Monczka RM (1999) Involving suppliers in new product development. *California Management Review* 42(1): 59–82.

Hartley JL (1994) Understanding supplier involvement in their customer's product development, doctoral thesis, Department of Quantitative Analysis and Operations Management, University of Cincinnati.

Hartley JL, Zirger BJ and Kamath RR (1997) Managing the buyer–supplier interface for on-time performance in product development, *Journal of Operations Management* 15: 57–70.

Helper S and MacDuffie JP (2003) B2B and modes of exchange: Evolutionary and transformative effects. In: Kogut B (ed.) *The Global Internet Economy*. Cambridge, MA: MIT Press.

Holweg M (2015) The limits of 3-D printing. *Harvard Business Review*. Online forum at: https://hbr.org (last accessed 23 July 2018).

Howard M, Vidgen R and Powell P (2006) Automotive e-hubs: Exploring motivations and barriers to collaboration and interaction. *Journal of Strategic Information Systems* 15(1): 51–75.

Johnsen TE (2009) Supplier involvement in product development and innovation – taking stock and looking to the future. *Journal of Purchasing & Supply Management* 15: 187–197.

Johnsen TE and Lewis M (2009) Supplier involvement in the development of the A380 Super Jumbo. In: *Proceedings of the 17th Annual IPSERA Conference*, Wiesbaden, Germany, April.

Kaplan S and Sawhney M (2000) E-hubs: The new B2B marketplaces. *Harvard Business Review*, May–June: 97–103.

Kraljic P (1983) Purchasing must become supply management. *Harvard Business Review*, Sept.–Oct.: 109–117.

Lakemond NF, van Echtelt F and Wynstra F (2001) A configuration typology for involving purchasing specialists in product development. *Journal of Supply Chain Management* 37(4): 11–20.

Lamming RC, Johnsen TE, Zheng J and Harland CM (2000) An initial classification of supply networks. *International Journal of Operations and Production Management* 20(6): 675–691.

Lamming RC and Phillips WE (2005) Flirting with new partners. *CPO Agenda*, Summer: 23–26.

Lancioni RA, Smith MF and Schau HJ (2003) Strategic Internet application trends in supply chain management. *Industrial Marketing Management* 32(3): 211–217.

Le Dain MA, Calvi R and Cheriti S (2010) Developing an approach for design-or-buy-design decision-making. *Journal of Purchasing and Supply Management* 16(2): 77–87.

Li F, Nucciarelli A, Roden S and Graham G (2016) How smart cities transform operations models: A new research agenda for operations management in the digital economy. *Production Planning & Control* 27(6): 514–528.

Martin MJC (1984) *Managing Technological Innovation and Entrepreneurship*. Reston, VA: Reston Publishing Company, Inc.

Matlack C (2006) Airbus' behemoth hits turbulence. *Business Week*, 14 June.

Maury M (2012) Responsable innovation: Pour capter les avantages compétitifs. *La Lettre des Achats* 208: 31–33.

Mikkelsen OS and Johnsen TE (2018) Purchasing involvement in technologically uncertain new product development: Challenges and implications. *Journal of Purchasing & Supply Management*, forthcoming.

Mollenkopf D, Stolze H, Tate WL, et al. (2010) Green, lean, and global supply chains. *International Journal of Physical Distribution and Logistics Management* 40(1/2): 14–41.

Nishiguchi T (1994) *Strategic Industrial Sourcing*. Oxford and New York: Oxford University Press.

Olleros FJ (1986) Emerging industries and the burnout of pioneers. *Journal of Product Innovation Management* 3(1): 15–18.

Parry GC, Brax SA, Maull RS and Ng IC (2016) Operationalising IoT for reverse supply: The development of use-visibility measures. *Supply Chain Management: An International Journal* 21(2): 228–244.

Petersen K, Handfield, R and Ragatz G (2003) A model of supplier integration into new product development. *Journal of Product Innovation Management* 20(4): 284–299.

Petersen KJ, Handfield RB and Ragatz GL (2005) Supplier integration into new product development: Coordinating product, process and supply chain design. *Journal of Operations Management* 23(3–4): 371–388.

Phillips WE, Lamming RC, Bessant JR and Noke H (2006) Discontinuous innovation and supply relationships: Strategic dalliances. *R&D Management* 36(4): 451–461.

Powell WW, Koput KW and Smith-Doerr L (1996) Inter-organizational collaboration and the locus of innovation: Networks of learning in biotechnology. *Administrative Science Quarterly* 41(1): 116–145.

Primo MAM and Amundson SD (2002) An exploratory study of the effects of supplier relationships on new product development outcomes. *Journal of Operations Management* 20(1): 33–52.

Ragatz GL, Handfield RB and Scannell TV (1997) Success factors for integrating suppliers into product development. *Journal of Product Innovation Management* 14(3): 190–202.

Rozemeijer F, Quintens L and Konstantin K (2011) *Social Media Use by Purchasing Professionals*, Final Report, Maastricht University.

Sako M (1992) *Prices, Quality and Trust. Inter-Firm Relations in Britain and Japan*. Cambridge, UK: Cambridge University Press.

Schiele H (2010) Early supplier integration: The dual role of purchasing in new product development. *R&D Management* 40(2): 138–153.

Skjøtt-Larsen T, Kotzab H and Grieger M (2003) Electronic marketplaces and supply chain relationships. *Industrial Marketing Management* 32: 199–210.

Song M and Benedetto AD (2008) Supplier's involvement and success of radical new product development in new ventures. *Journal of Operations Management* 26(1): 1–22.

Srai JS, Kumar M, Graham G, Phillips W, Tooze J, Ford S, ... and Ravi B (2016) Distributed manufacturing: Scope, challenges and opportunities. *International Journal of Production Research* 54(23): 6917–6935.

Stahel WR and Reday-Mulvey G (1976) The potential for substituting manpower for energy. Report to the Commission of the European Communities, Brussels.

Straub D, Rai A and Klein R (2004) Measuring firm performance at the network level: A nomology of the business impact of digital supply networks. *Journal of Management Information Systems* 21(1): 83–114.

Swaminathan JM and Tayur SR (2003) Models for supply chains in e-business. *Management Science* 49(10): 1387–1406.

Swatman PM and Swatman PA (1992) EDI system integration: A definition and literature survey. *Information Society* 8: 169–205.

Takeishi A (2001) Bridging inter- and intra-firm boundaries: Management of supplier involvement in automobile product development. *Strategic Management Journal* 22: 403–433.

Threlkel M and Kavan B (1999) From traditional EDI to Internet-based EDI: Managerial considerations. *Journal of Information Technology* 14: 347–360.

Tsai W (2002) Social structure of 'Coopetition' within a multiunit organization: coordination, competition, and intra-organizational knowledge sharing. *Organizational Science* 13(2): 179–190.

Van Echtelt FEA, Wynstra F, Van Weele AJ and Duyesters G (2008) Managing supplier involvement in NPD: A multiple-case study. *Journal of Product Innovation Management* 25: 180–201.

Veryzer JRW (1998) Discontinuous innovation and the new product development process. *Journal of Product Innovation Management* (15): 304–321.

Wagner SM and Schwab AP (2004) Setting the stage for successful electronic reverse auctions. *Journal of Purchasing & Supply Management* 10(1): 11–26.

Wallace J (2007) Airbus all in on need for jumbo – but Boeing still doubtful, Seattle PI, 24 October. Available at: http://www.seattlepi.com/business/336611_airbus24.html (last accessed 26 October 2013).

Webster J (1995) Networks of collaboration or conflict? Electronic data interchange and power in the supply chain. *Journal of Strategic Information Systems* 4(1): 31–42.

Wycherley I (1999) Greening supply chains: The case of the Body Shop International, *Business Strategy and the Environment* 8(2): 120–127.

Wynstra F and ten Pierick E (2000) Managing supplier involvement in new product development: A portfolio approach. *European Journal of Purchasing and Supply Management* 6: 49–57.

Wynstra JYF, Van Weele AJ and Axelsson B (2000) Purchasing involvement in product development: A framework. *European Journal of Purchasing and Supply Management* 5(3–4): 129–141.

Useful websites

Ecovadis www.ecovadis.com (last accessed 26 October 2013)
Sedex www.sedexglobal.com (last accessed 26 October 2013)
RosettaNet www.rosettanet.org (last accessed 26 October 2013)
MySourcingTeam www.mysourcingteam.com (last accessed 26 October 2013)
GlobalSCM www.globalscm.net (last accessed 26 October 2013)
eSourcingWiki www.esourcingwiki.com (last accessed 26 October 2013)

Appendix 7.1 Supplier involvement in new product development: An audit instrument

	Yes	Don't know/ neutral	No
We formally analyse the need for supplier involvement across part/component groups			
We use a strategic framework for this analysis, assessing issues such as technological risks and supplier capabilities relative to our capabilities			
We are confident that the framework we use for this analysis is appropriate for our business			
We explicitly identify different supplier roles and their different levels of involvement in projects, e.g. black, grey and white box			
We communicate and agree these roles and expectations to the suppliers and our own internal departments			
We involve strategic suppliers in the concept development stage or at least early design stage			
We issue functional or global specifications to strategic/ black box suppliers and ask them for solutions to problems			
We select and evaluate strategic suppliers based on their innovative capabilities			
We obtain full motivation and commitment by strategic suppliers			
We mutually agree risk and benefit sharing arrangements with suppliers			
We clearly communicate our policies, specifications and performance requirements to suppliers			
We listen to the strategic suppliers' feedback and suggestions regarding above			
We have shared training with key supplier personnel			
We do our best to ensure that relevant information reaches sub-suppliers			
We take part in uniting suppliers that need to collaborate amongst themselves			

PURCHASING AND SOURCING

	Yes	Don't know/ neutral	No
We have arrangements for resident engineers/designers with strategic suppliers			
We ensure that strategic suppliers agree with performance targets			
We adopt a root cause analysis approach to problem solving instead of blaming suppliers when things go wrong			
Our top management is committed to and supports our supplier partnerships			
Several internal functions are involved in supplier partnerships and these all collaborate to ensure their success			
We have conducted a core competence and/or a technology audit to decide which competencies/ technologies to maintain in-house, which to outsource, which to in-source/develop internally			
We have formulated and exchanged our policies for supplier involvement, e.g. IPR agreements			
We continuously search supply markets for new technological innovations			
We pre-select suppliers for forthcoming product development projects			
We exchange technology road maps with strategic suppliers			
We involve suppliers in technology development/R&D programmes			
Result:	Leading-edge ESI practices	ESI practices need investigation	Lack of ESI holding back organization

Part B
Supply chain and network management

CHAPTER 8

Supply chain strategy

LEARNING OBJECTIVES

By the end of this chapter you should be able to:

- Define supply chain management;

- Discuss the development of supply chain strategy over time from mass production and mass customization, towards more sustainable approaches such as the circular economy;

- Apply lean, agile and hybrid supply chain strategies to business practice;

- Discuss the issues around supply chain traceability and transparency;

- Understand the impact on supply chains in terms of risk and disintermediation;

- Analyse the developments from conventional to closed-loop supply chains;

- Discuss the broader economic implications of sustainability and the circular economy for supply chain strategy.

8.0 Introduction

Supply chain strategy is the collaborative response to market demand by all firms in the supply chain working together to coordinate the delivery of products and services to the end customer. The strategy adopted by the focal firm is usually driven by the type of product, patterns of demand, customer requirements, and any associated risks which may delay delivery by the supply chain. There are many strategies to choose from, however, including lean, agile, 'leagile' and mass customization, as well as an array of enabling digital technologies. This chapter starts by clarifying the concept of supply chain (and supply network) management. We include some background on early production, strategies such as mass production and mass customization, which have helped shape current thinking. We explore how supply chains are affected by issues such as transparency, risk and disintermediation. The chapter concludes with a discussion around closed-loop supply chains and the real-life case of a carpet manufacturer who has embarked on a 'cradle-to-cradle' programme involving both customers and supplier.

8.1 Supply chains and networks

The use of the term 'supply chain' has become common across the business and management community. It is used to describe almost any setting where production requires a staged sequence of processes involving suppliers producing parts or components and building sub-assemblies, delivering them to a focal organization, an assembler or integrator, who then distributes the product to sales outlets. Figure 8.1 provides an illustration of a conventional supply chain comprising a simple flow of raw materials from extraction, through manufacture and customer delivery to 'disposal'.

Basic definitions of supply chain management were provided in Chapter 1. Here it is important to note that the linear or 'stream' aspect of supply chains is an important and well-established aspect of management thinking today: it is derived from the idea of a value stream where goods and services flow towards the customer without impediment (Rother and Shook, 1988; Hines and Rich, 1997; Hines *et al.*, 2000).[1] There are many definitions of Supply Chain Management or 'SCM'. One definition focuses on the process integration: 'The integration of business processes from end user through original suppliers that provides products, services and information that add value for customers' (Cooper *et al.*, 1997).

Another definition focuses on the importance of connecting supply chain actors through relationships: 'the management of upstream and downstream relationships with suppliers and customers to deliver superior customer value at less cost to the supply chain as a whole' (Christopher, 2005).

More comprehensively, supply chain management can be defined as:

The management of a network of relationships within a firm and between interdependent organizations and business units consisting of material suppliers, purchasing, production facilities, logistics, marketing, and related systems that facilitate the forward and reverse flow of materials, services, finances and information from the original producer to final customer with the benefits of adding value, maximizing profitability through efficiencies, and achieving customer satisfaction.

(Stock and Boyer, 2009)

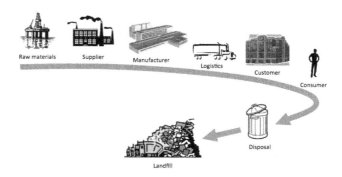

Figure 8.1 Conventional supply chain

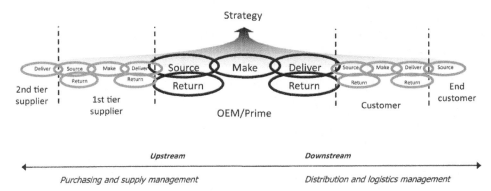

Figure 8.2 Supply chain management core processes

The common denominator here is the focus on satisfaction of end customers by maximizing customer value whilst minimizing cost. Building on these definitions and the supply chain operations reference (SCOR) model developed by the Supply Chain Council, we can depict supply chain management as in Figure 8.2.

Figure 8.2 identifies the core processes in supply chain management as source, make, deliver and return. Integrating these core processes within and across organizations, it is possible to break down barriers or silos that otherwise prevent a smooth flow of supply to end customers. In theory, supply chain management covers all the actors involved in the production of a product and/or service from ultimate raw material extractors to end customers. All the supply chain actors are interlinked and therefore dependent on each other to satisfy end customers. In practice, few companies have the required visibility over their entire supply chain and many companies focus their supply chain management on the internal supply chain or, at best, their immediate supply chain, i.e. with direct first-tier suppliers (Fawcett and Magnan, 2002). The concept of supply chain management as 'end-to-end' is therefore rarely practised.

The concept of supply chain management has been criticized on a number of points, three of which are highlighted here. Firstly, the metaphor of a chain, although useful for emphasizing the importance of interdependent supply relationships, suggests that supply structures are simple linear structures where in reality supply structures are much more complex. This has led some authors and companies to use the alternative concept of 'supply chain networks' or simply 'supply networks' (Lamming *et al.*, 2000), although 'supply network' in practice tends to refer to only the upstream network of suppliers. As companies rely on global networks of suppliers, the concept of supply chains is an over-simplification of what is, in reality, a highly complex supply system.

Second, supply chain management assumes that all the actors in the supply chain are willing to partner with each other and work towards common objectives. As argued by Cox (1999), this is certainly not always the case and, ultimately, companies are driven by the need to make profit for their own company and not all supply chain actors are willing to collaborate. Supply chain management assumes that the best way for actors in a supply chain is to strive towards common goals; although in some cases this may be an accurate assumption, it only works where supply chain actors are highly interdependent and where the focal company exerts a significant amount of influence and power over other supply chain actors (Harland *et al.*, 2001).

Third, the traditional linear supply chain design, which ends with products being disposed of in landfill sites, is being replaced by closed-loop, or circular, supply chains. Dumping in landfills represents one of the ultimate symbols of a wasteful society, meaning whatever has been discarded has either not been designed for disassembly or reuse by the manufacturer, or the systems needed to enable recycling are not in place. Closed-loop supply chains are designed to tackle this problem by finding novel ways to return the waste, which results from disposed products, back into raw material supply chains. We return to this important theme later in the chapter.

The limitations of traditional supply chain management concepts are therefore exacerbated when adopting a sustainability perspective, underscoring the need for a network or stakeholder perspective (Figure 8.3). As explained in Chapter 1, the theories influencing this book – the natural resource-based view of strategy (NRBV) and the Industrial Marketing and Purchasing (IMP) interaction approach – emphasize the role of stakeholders and networks of

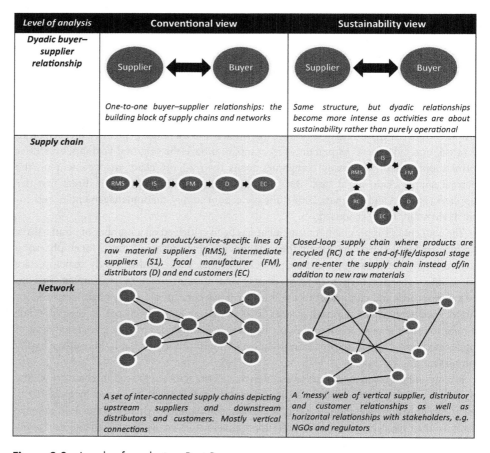

Figure 8.3 Levels of analysis – Part B

relationships. As companies seek to incorporate sustainability into their supply chains they need to consider not only their indirect suppliers, who may be located thousands of kilometres away, but also other stakeholders such as non-governmental organizations (NGOs) that play an increasingly critical role in, e.g. monitoring and auditing suppliers in developing countries.

Figure 8.3 presents the shift in focus from a level of analysis focused on dyadic buyer–supplier relationships, where purchasing is the central issue, to supply chain and network management. This chapter now outlines and discusses some of the most important concepts of traditional supply chain management and strategy that companies can pursue. In order to put this into context, the next section provides a brief overview of how industrial organization has changed over time. We return to the non-linear and complex aspects of supply chains and networks at the end of the chapter and in more depth later in the book.

8.2 Background: mass production and mass customization

Since the beginning of the Western Industrial Revolution in the mid-eighteenth century, the focus for development of production was on improving the manufacturing process in terms of cost, performance and product quality. Very little thought was given to the social welfare of the workers, product disposal (or 'end-of-life'), or what impact disposal would have on the surrounding environment. The overriding factors driving industrial production at the time were economic growth and profit. Widespread industrial implementation of closed-loop or reverse supply chains designed for product recycling did not emerge until the last quarter of the twentieth century, resulting in a prolonged period where economy of scale was considered the overriding factor in firm competitive advantage. This section reviews the major eras of production to understand how thinking around strategy has evolved from a purely operational focus towards sustainable supply chain management.

The origins of production as a scientific management activity began with the Industrial Revolution (1750–1850) which started in the United Kingdom and spread to Western Europe, North America and Japan. Improvements in agriculture, manufacturing, mining and technology heralded an unprecedented period of entrepreneurship and economic growth over the next two centuries, which saw the world's average per-capita income increase tenfold. Towards the end of the 1700s, a transition began to occur in the UK's previously manual labour- and draught animal-based economy. The shift towards machine-based manufacturing started with the mechanization of the textile industries, development of more refined iron making and increased use of coal to fuel steam-powered engines. While elements of what was later to be termed 'mass production' emerged during the 1800s such as the division of labour, interchangeable parts and mechanization (Duguay et al., 1997), the dominant paradigm at the time was craft production. Craft production centres on the skills of the individual who, in a pre-industrialized world, engages in a process of one-off manufacturing and hand-fitting of pieces together without the aid of machine tools (e.g. pottery, cabinet making).

Mass production is probably the most well-known production paradigm in operations and supply management. Traditionally associated with the dominance of the US automobile industry, it was pioneered by Henry Ford's first moving assembly line for his 'Model T' vehicle built in Dearborn, Michigan in the United States in 1913. The early effects of mass production were felt throughout the 1800s driven by successive developments in mechanization and interchangeable parts (Duguay et al., 1997). For example, the Springfield Armoury (1777–1968) was the centre for the manufacture of US military firearms and became the site of a number of technological innovations of global importance, including tooling to enable interchangeable parts and hourly wages. The introduction of lathes and other machine tools of enabled high precision and the mass reproduction of identical parts.

Mass production is not only concerned with the process itself but also the organization of production to make work easier to manage. This interest in organization led to the concept of 'Scientific Management' by F. W. Taylor (1865–1915), involving painstaking studies of everyday manual tasks such as assembly, drilling and shovelling in order to find the most efficient or 'one best way' of execution. The principles of scientific management or 'Taylorism' led to a fragmentation of tasks on the shop floor and an increasing divide between workers and the management controlling them. Workers became almost as interchangeable as the parts used in their products, with the resultant continual hiring and firing of workers becoming a criticism of the narrow efficiency focus of Taylor's technique. The main characteristics of mass producer firms are their concern for reducing costs by increasing volume of production, i.e. economies of scale, and an adversarial relationship with suppliers who are 'considered opportunists and are kept at arm's length and are pitted against each other to obtain the best deal' (Duguay et al., 1997: 1185). Mass production reached its peak in the 1960s in the US. The emergence of foreign competition threatened US homeland markets, followed by the oil shock in the early 1970s which forced Western manufacturers to reconsider their predictions over growth.

The term 'mass customization' was coined by Stan Davis in his visionary book *Future Perfect* in 1987 which suggested that there are no truly mass markets any more, and that each customer represents their own unique requirements who deserves exactly what he/she wants at a price they want to pay. The concept of progressing from mass markets, through segments and niches, to mass customized markets was further developed by Pines (1992) who put forward the idea that companies must recognize this new frontier in production where not only is every customer effectively their own market, but customers may want different offerings at different times under different circumstances. Mass customization is defined as the production of tailored or customized goods and services to meet individual consumers' requirements at near mass production cost. It is enabled by technologies such as computer-aided design and manufacturing (CADCAM), flexible manufacturing systems (FMS), the Internet and modularization. The concept of mass customization assumes a totally flexible production system every customer can, in theory, have what they want. The goal for firms of becoming more customer-centric became a useful refocus and competitive differentiator, particularly against traditional mass producers who still compete on price.

Despite the evolution of production from craft, through mass production, to mass customization, it is not correct to say that production is 'returning to its roots', e.g. reviving craft-based manufacture (Figure 8.4). The vision of offering customers *exactly* what they want has never completely materialized because the trade-offs between production cost, volume and variety have never been fully resolved despite advances in technology and process innovation. Considerable efforts have been made by manufacturers, however, to create a wider range of customer choice available at minimal cost. For example, the developments in modularization and platform-sharing in the 1990s led by Volkswagen, who adopted a system of sharing major structural body components where the same running gear (i.e. suspension, floor pressing and engine/powertrain) could be used interchangeably in different vehicle models. Using reconfigurable product architecture in this way enabled manufacturers to offer wider product choice, while saving on new vehicle development costs (Salvador *et al.*, 2002). Yet as car-buying customers have become more sophisticated and understand the technologies used in new models, they have also become wary of premium vehicles sold with parts identical to standard vehicles. Considerable effort is expended today by vehicle manufacturers towards protecting their brand values and differentiating their products, often by integrating higher levels of service before and after the vehicle sale. An important supply strategy largely pioneered by the car industry and which represents a major departure from the mass production era is the concept of building to order (BTO), described in Section 8.4 as part of responsive supply chain strategy.

It is interesting to speculate what type of approach to production and supply chain strategy will evolve next. Will the focus continue to shift away from volume and economies of scale, towards a more responsive, customer-orientated approach incorporating environmental and ethical issues? Figure 8.3 indicates the latest thinking to include more information-rich, digitalization of our supply chains, such as Industry 4.0 (Bentley, 2017; Holmström *et al.*, 2016) and the rise of the circular economy (see Section 8.8). We envision that a new era will emerge altogether that focuses on the broader needs of society and reflects the theme of 'sustainable consumption' rather than our production-driven past, where concerns over product use and life cycle often ceased after departure from the factory. With many of the world's major corporations setting out their sustainable visions for the future, attention is already shifting to concerns over the practical means of supply chain implementation and the extent to which customers and suppliers become motivated and engage with sustainability as an integral element of supply chain strategy.

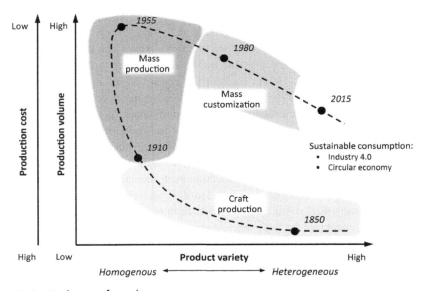

Figure 8.4 Evolution of production

205

8.3 Lean and agile supply chain strategy

Lean is about doing more with less. The term is generally used in the context of lean manufacturing as part of a 'zero inventory' or just-in-time (JIT) approach to managing the supply chain (see Note 8.1). The use of lean as a supply chain strategy has become legendary in the history of continuous improvement (Womack and Jones, 2003, 2005; Hines *et al.*, 2004). Lean was popularized in 1990 by Womack, Jones and Roos in the best-selling book *The Machine that Changed the World* which revealed the staggering 2-to-1 difference in productivity between Japanese and Western automotive manufacturers. Womack and Jones present lean as a practical, step-by-step approach derived from the Toyota Production System, which can be applied in almost any organization context and across the total enterprise or supply chain (Womack and Jones, 1994, 1996, 2003).

The goal of lean is to eliminate all sources of waste or 'muda' in the workplace, a philosophy that emerged from Toyota's resource-starved production halls in Japan after World War II (Monden, 1983; Ohno, 1988; Shingo, 1988). Central to lean thinking is the JIT method of delivery which is used to minimize the accumulation of component stocks (also termed inventory) in the supply chain. Although originally devised to improve manufacturing performance by focusing on material flow, pull and defining value according to the customer, lean has more recently been applied to eliminate process-related waste such as unnecessary paperwork, movement of equipment and people, and handwritten authorization signatures in the services sector such as insurance, banking and health (Swank, 2003). Challenged by rival improvement techniques such as business process re-engineering (BPR) and total quality management (TQM), the longevity of lean as a business management tool is attributed to the core principles of value creation, standardization and putting people at the centre of the operation (Hines *et al.*, 2004). Lean philosophy on production demands that freed-up human resources as the result of process improvement exercises are not considered for redundancy or as an opportunity to reduce costs, but must be redeployed to other, more value-adding areas of the business (Womack and Jones, 2003).

A strong following has emerged among practitioners to adopt lean as a supply chain–wide approach which continuously improves the end-to-end customer order fulfilment process (Shapiro *et al.*, 1992; Hines, 1994). Traditionally conceived as a means of production management which controlled the movement of components on the shop floor, it is now applied across multiple firms coordinated as a supply chain. Lean strategies make the distinction between real demand that is 'pulled' from the end customer according to their product requirements, in contrast to forecast-based demand 'pushed' by production which often creates unwanted inventory and serves only to keep the production line running (Monden, 1983). As a reaction against production push mentality the elimination of waste has now become a mantra which can be applied to all firms seeking ways to create changes to the effectiveness and efficiency of their business. Lean is perceived both as a supply chain strategy and a practical tool for daily incremental improvement, applied by shop floor and office staff to ensure any idea for improvement, no matter how small, is considered in terms of potential benefit to the business. As an improvement tool, the principles of lean thinking are used to describe the movement of goods and exchange of information, which are systematically recorded as part of a collaborative team-based exercise often involving key suppliers, before steps are proposed for a more streamlined future state using less stock, effort and resources (Rother and Shook, 1988).

Note 8.1

Component suppliers deliver just-in-sequence to Volvo Cars, Sweden

Just-in-time delivery is an important element in lean production. In Torslanda, Sweden, the Volvo Car Corporation assembles the XC90 premium family utility vehicle at its final assembly hall just outside the city of Gothenburg. Volvo has assembled its key component suppliers or 'first tier suppliers' within close proximity of its manufacturing facilities to enable quick delivery of critical vehicle parts such as braking systems, cockpit module, carpets and glazing to the final assembly line. Volvo runs 2 or 3 production shifts a day and requires a delivery of parts and sub-assemblies from each supplier per shift. If any delivery is late causing the production line to be halted then the supplier responsible potentially faces a heavy fine, but this is usually a very rare event. Because of the high percentage of passenger vehicles built to specific customer requirements, production schedules at Volvo are incredibly detailed and require a high proportion of suppliers to deliver components not only exactly when needed, but in a specific sequence to match the individual specifications of each vehicle as it passes through the final assembly hall. This has given rise to use of the term 'just-in-sequence' delivery in production management circles.

A lean supply chain requires more collaborative supplier relationships, however, than are traditionally found in many industries. The term 'lean supply partnership' (Lamming, 1993) has entered into the language of supply chain management as part of a shift towards collaborative relationships involving procurement and logistics efficiency and effectiveness (Sako, 1992; Harrison, 1993; Hines, 1994). The rise of the concept of lean supply partnerships implies that the process improvement benefits once exclusively enjoyed by original equipment manufacturers (OEMs), i.e. automotive manufacturers such as Ford and General Motors are now extended across the supply chain in return for closer, long-term commitment from the supply base. Driven by mutual benefits and trust-based relationships, the idea of partnerships is an opportunity for all firms in the supply chain to contribute and gain from process improvements. Influenced by the uniquely Japanese approach *keiretsu*, a form of industrial organization similar in principle to the 'extended family', the idea of lean partnerships took off in the West when industry leaders realized the potential of closer buyer–supplier collaboration. Lean supply partnerships offered opportunities for performance improvement not only in terms of supply chain–wide cost reductions through JIT inventory management initiatives, but also reduced new product cycle times gained as a result of closer supplier involvement during new product development programmes.

As one of the most popular management improvement paradigms since the 1980s, lean, however, is not without its critics. Derived from the production-orientated language of the automotive and aerospace industries, concerns over applicability and effectiveness arise when faced with more customer-facing, service-orientated operations where standardization of supplier–customer exchanges may be impractical and inappropriate (James-Moore and Gibbons, 1997). Cultural differences between East and West working patterns and behaviours have also been suggested as a possible source of social friction in some of the early sites or 'transplants' where firms such as Toyota, Honda and Nissan set up manufacturing plants outside Japan using hybrid lean production systems, such as in the US and UK (Wickens, 1987). Japanese workers generally tend to have greater respect for authority within the organizational hierarchy and adhere more readily to workplace rules and procedures, leading to suggestions of 'Tayloristic' style management practices by some Western observers (e.g. Forza, 1996). Further, as the implementation of lean production creates strategic resources which may in fact aid competitive advantage, the continued focus on incremental improvement over time may 'curtail the firm's ability to achieve long-term flexibility' (Lewis, 2000: 959). Nevertheless, since its rise in popularity in the 1980s, lean remains a powerful concept in supply chain strategy particularly where improvement within and between firms is needed and demands closer buyer–supplier participation.

An important question here is: is lean green? Over the past decade or so a connection has been made between lean thinking and sustainability, i.e. 'lean and green', by scholars making the link between the efficiency paradigm of doing more with less, and minimizing the use of resources and output of industrial emissions to protect the natural environment (e.g. King and Lenoz, 2001; Simpson and Power 2005; Mollenkopf *et al.*, 2010). While there is evidence for the lean and green concept at a theoretical level, there remains considerable potential for industry to adopt lean and eliminate waste in order to resolve complex operational issues involving sustainability such as the implementation of a low carbon procurement strategy (see Chapter 12). A further issue is that lean supply chains may no longer be sufficient, or indeed appropriate, in industries facing increasingly turbulent and volatile markets, particularly when facing fluctuating commodity and raw material prices.

The agile supply chain is responsive to the changing needs of the market over time, requiring a high level of manoeuvrability as product life cycles shorten and global economic and competitive forces create uncertainty (Christopher, 2000). Agile supply strategy reflects the interest in time-based competition where responding quickly to specific customer demands is seen as a source of competitive advantage. A considerable distinction is drawn between lean and agile philosophies in management literature, although the 'agile camp' claims that leanness may be an element of agility in certain circumstances! Professor Christopher is a leading exponent of agile supply chain strategy who draws from Webster's dictionary to make the distinction clear: 'it defines lean as "containing little fat", whereas agile is defined as "nimble"' (Christopher, 2000: 38). A key characteristic of an agile organization or supply chain is flexibility, whose origins as a business concept lie in flexible manufacturing systems (Kidd, 1994; Gunasekaran, 1999). Such systems use state-of-the-art machine technology (e.g. multi-headed, five-axis, computer numerically controlled machines) capable of delivering high levels of product variety to meet customer requirements. There is also likely to be a high level of usage of information technology to feed back customer requirements to production, making the supply chain more capable of responding to real customer demand rather than forecast-based information. Agile supply chains, therefore, must be market sensitive: able to cope with responding to individual customer requirements in short lead times, as well as coping with the peaks and troughs of demand over time (Christopher and Towill, 2000).

A problem in many supply chains is the restricted visibility of real, customer-based demand. The nature of supply chains today, i.e. extended over large distances, means there are often multiple points at which inventory is stored, meaning supply chain managers have to rely on forecast-driven rather than customer-driven information. The exact position where real demand reaches into the supply chain is called the decoupling point, and represents the meeting of market pull and production push. The issue here is how far real demand in the form of customer orders is made visible to the supply chain, where order information is often distorted and delayed by actions of a third party or an inadequate information system. The decoupling point dictates where inventory should be held, which acts as a buffer between the part of the supply chain directly geared towards satisfying customer orders, and the part based on production planning. This is also the point in the supply chain where real customer orders enter the process and are assigned to individual products or basic sub-assemblies of the product. According to Christopher (2000: 41), 'the aim of the agile supply chain should be to carry inventory in as generic a form as possible, that is, standard semi-finished products awaiting final assembly'. He argues that the agile supply chain should hold inventory in a generic form (that is, standard, semi-finished products) awaiting final assembly until the final customer requirements and destination of the order is known. This is known as postponement, or delayed configuration, and is an important supply chain tactic.

The decision over where the customer order enters the production process has implications for sustainability in terms of waste. Supply chains which are capable of building product to customer order, rather than simply keeping production running and piling up inventory in the hope that someone will want to buy the product, will face fewer problems in terms of how to deal with excess stock and wasted resources. Building the perfect agile supply chain has considerable cost implications, however, and while it may seem preferable to adopt a demand-driven approach, there are considerable costs involved and a trade-off may have to be reached in terms of how far upstream customer orders can penetrate. Understanding where production meets customer demand in the supply chain means placing inventory 'strategically' so that it assists the order fulfilment process rather than clogging up the process flow. There are also other methods, such as modularization, which can help to alleviate the effects of product variety in production.

An emerging train of thought regarding strategy is that supply chains cannot be thought of as lean or agile in isolation, but instead evolve as a blended or hybrid approach, named by Naylor et al. (1999) as 'leagile'. In the early stages of entering a new market the lean paradigm enables the product to penetrate the market achieved through low-cost production. As the market matures, demand for higher levels of variety grows and the agile paradigm begins to replace it. 'Leagile' strategy or 'customized "leagile" strategy' means the supply chain is agile enough to respond to what is actually selling, with product availability and short delivery lead times supported by information transparency as the critical market winners (Christopher and Towill, 2000: 212). Returning to the respective typical characteristics of supply chain strategy, lean requires the fat to be eliminated, whereas agile must be nimble because lost sales are gone forever. Although important differences exist between the two approaches (e.g. lean supply chains tend to adopt level scheduling whereas agile supply chains require additional capacity to cope with volatility), there is increasing pressure on firms for lean supply chains to become agile as markets mature and become more customized. Companies such as Dell computers and Zara, the high street fashion retailer, are both good examples of 'leagile' hybrid supply chain strategy (Note 8.2). While not as well known as either lean or agile, 'leagile' strategy combines elements of both approaches with the concepts of decoupling and the 'information-enriched' supply chain (Mason-Jones et al., 2000).

> **Note 8.2**
>
> **Zara: high street fashion meets 'Leagile' supply chain strategy**
>
> Zara is a highly successful Spanish high street retail company selling fashionable clothes to an international market. It is a good example of a hybrid supply chain strategy in a fiercely competitive environment, combining an agile supply chain which includes many lean characteristics i.e. leagile. It has developed an effective quick response system which starts with cross-functional teams such as fashion, commercial and retail specialists all working together at Zara's design department in the company headquarters in La Coruña, Spain. The team's understanding of fashion is guided by regular updates of Electronic Point of Sale data from the company's stores all around the world. Zara's manufacturing systems are similar to other firms, combining the late configuration ideas of Benetton with the cost efficiency of Toyota. Only economies-of-scale operations such as dying, cutting, labelling and packaging are conducted in-house, with the more labour intensive finishing stages completed by networks of around 300 small sub-contractors who specialise in one type of garment or process. While the supply chain is designed to be flexible to cope with sudden market changes, production at Zara is kept at a level slightly below sales to keep stock moving through the warehouses to the retail outlets.
>
> Source: Ferdows *et al.*, 2003; Christopher, 2000

8.3.1 Matching the supply chain with the product and the market

Understanding the link between supply chain strategy and product type is crucial to realizing optimum performance. A common mistake is where the supply chain evolves over time to include many different varieties of product line to suit as many different types of customer demand as possible. This results in the supply chain becoming bloated with inventory, sluggish, unable to respond efficiently or effectively to demand, and often clogged with high levels of unwanted finished stock. An important article by Fisher in 1997 on the subject asks: 'what is the right supply chain for your product?' This seemingly simple question was the result of over ten years of field research by the US professor who realized that despite the improvements in technology and management thinking in the past decade, the performance of supply chains had never been worse, with – in some cases – costs rising to unprecedented levels because of adversarial buyer–supplier relationships and poor practices such as overreliance on price promotions leading to heavy discounting.

Fisher established that waste in the affected industries was running into billions of dollars, and yet in many supply chains there was too much of some types of product and not enough of others because of inability to predict demand. He devised a simple framework which started by defining whether the product was functional (i.e. predictable demand, long product life cycle, low variety) or innovative (i.e. unpredictable demand, short product life cycle, high variety).

The second important parameter determines the operating conditions of the supply chain: either physically efficient or market-responsive supply chains. Physically efficient processes are defined as 'supply predictable demand efficiently at the lowest possible cost' and

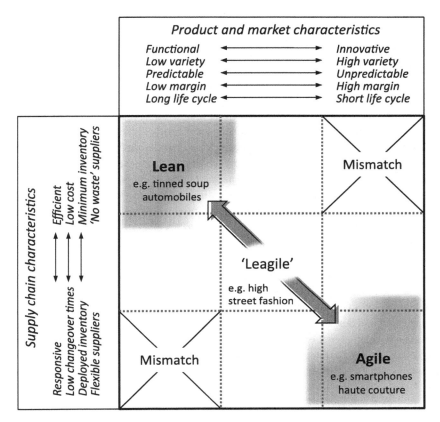

Figure 8.5 Lean and agile supply chain strategy

market-responsive processes are defined as to 'respond quickly to unpredictable demand in order to minimize stock-outs, forced markdowns and obsolete inventory' (Fisher 1997: 108). By understanding their supply chain in terms of operating environment and market conditions, and matching this with the type of product, managers were better able to devise the ideal supply chain strategy and avoid the possibility of 'mismatch', e.g. functional products delivered by unnecessarily responsive supply chains.

Figure 8.5 develops the ideas of Fisher with the concepts of lean and agile supply chain strategy. It builds on the connection between product and market, and supply chains, by including closely defined characteristics. Lean and agile are positioned diagonally in the matrix, which offers the opportunity to blend particular aspects of both strategies and opt for a leagile approach, i.e. positioned in the middle. While initially most managers are likely to adopt either a lean or agile approach, they should definitely avoid the areas of mismatch marked by an 'X' in the opposite corners of the model in Figure 8.5.

Lean supply chain strategy is characterized by functional, relatively low variety, long life-cycle products with predictable but low-profit-margin-type market demand. Lean supply chains are devised around the principle of efficiency and low cost, based on minimum inventory and with suppliers striving towards the goal of 'no waste'. Typical examples of products which are suitable for lean supply chains include tinned soup and family motor cars, although some types of specialist sports vehicles in the premium market segment, such as Aston Martin or Lamborghini, will adopt a more customer-centric and responsive 'leagile' or even agile supply chain approach.

Agile supply chain strategy is characterized by innovative, high variety and shorter life-cycle products with unpredictable but high-margin market demand. Agile supply chains are designed to be customer responsive, with manufacturers and their suppliers capable of offering the flexibility for low production changeover times. Inventory is often held close to the market in order to respond swiftly to specific customer demands. Examples include niche fashion such as 'haute couture' where specialist garments are made or adapted to suit an individual's requirements. Smartphones are another good example, with new models such as the Apple iPhone being updated every year encouraging high levels of turnover and product obsolescence. Although the physical hand units may appear identical at the point of purchase, each customer has the ability to quickly customize to his or her own preferences by buying aftermarket cases and via built-in or downloadable software applications, offering very high levels of product customization. The concept of agility has also been linked with the mitigation of risk in the supply chain (see 'responsiveness and building to order') where supply chain agility is defined as the capability of the firm, both internally and in conjunction with suppliers and customers, to adapt and respond to market changes as well as to potential disruptions (Braunscheidal and Suresh, 2009).

A model developed by Lee (2002) also expands on Fisher's model and the debate on lean and agile supply chain strategies, suggesting a wider range of factors be taken into account when analysing uncertainty. Lee suggests that it is not only demand uncertainty but also

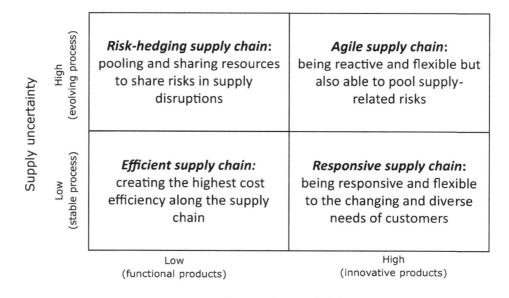

Figure 8.6 Lee's supply chain strategy matrix (adapted)

supply uncertainty that creates supply chain challenges. In addition to Fisher's distinction between functional and innovative products, Lee's model distinguishes between low supply uncertainty (stable process) and high supply uncertainty (evolving process). Stable supply processes are characterized by, for example, mature and highly automated manufacturing processes and an established supply base with secure long-term supplier relationships. In comparison, evolving supply processes are immature with fewer and less reliable suppliers and technology is still emerging. Lee's matrix in Figure 8.6 suggests four different strategies for managing the different supply and demand uncertainties. Where efficient supply chains are appropriate for low levels of demand and supply uncertainty, and agile supply chains are required for high demand and supply uncertainty, Lee's framework introduces the concepts of risk-hedging supply chains for situations of low demand uncertainty coupled with high process uncertainty and responsive supply chains for situations of high demand uncertainty but low supply process uncertainty.

Resembling a lean supply chain strategy, the efficient supply chain should seek to create high cost efficiency along the supply chain. Risk-hedging supply chains focus on managing supply chain process risks through hedging strategies by pooling inventory or other capacity-related resources with other companies or development of new supplier relationships. Responsive supply chains focus on being responsive to changing and diverse customer demands. This can be done through build-to-order (BTO) strategies and mass customization strategies. Agile supply chains are both risk-hedging supply and responsive to customer demands: agile supply chains should be truly reactive and flexible hedging the risks of supply shortages or disruptions and be responsive to changing customer demands. In the following section, we explore in more detail the nature of supply chain responsiveness and BTO strategies.

8.4 Responsiveness and building to order

A significant landmark in strategic thinking is the conceptual shift beyond firm-level competitiveness towards supply chain responsiveness, where supply chains as a whole compete globally and cope with high degrees of volatility (Handfield and Bechtel, 2002; Ferdows et al., 2004). Responsiveness is about reacting to customer requirements, not just in terms of matching the customer's product or service specifications, but fulfilling the order in the shortest lead time possible (Holweg and Pil, 2001). As competition increased in the 1990s, with customers becoming more demanding, and developments in information technology helping to improve forecasting and logistics, responsiveness, and the ability to build-to-order (BTO) has become a new differentiator in supply chain competitive advantage.

One of the first sectors where the importance of supply chain responsiveness emerged was the grocery or fast-moving consumer goods (FMCG) sector, with the launch of the Efficient Customer Response (ECR) movement in 1994. ECR was a joint trade and industry body working towards making groceries and FMCG more responsive to consumer demand and promoting the removal of unnecessary costs such as excess stock from the supply chain. Characterized by the emergence of collaborative management along the supply chain, it argued that consumers can be served better, faster and at less cost by firms working together with their trading partners rather than resorting to traditional adversarial tactics. ECR distinguished between the customer, often seen as the most powerful stakeholder (e.g.

supermarkets), and the end consumers or 'online shoppers' who expect better choice, service convenience, quality, freshness and safety from their store.

Advances in information technology (IT) have resulted in an increase in processing power and reduction in the size of computers, allowing electronic point of sale (EPOS) units with barcode scanning technology to be used as standard in all store check-out stations today. This means staff can instantly record the sale of goods in real time, and alert the back office to replenish shelves to avoid any stock-out of popular items. Developments in the more effective use of information, particularly sharing with logistics operations, has led to companies such as Tesco consolidating several stages of their delivery process and introducing facilities such as the cross-docking warehouse to speed up the transfer of goods from in-bound trucks to out-bound delivery to the stores. In the past, non-standardized operational practices and the rigid separation of the traditional roles of supplier and retailer threatened to block the supply chain unnecessarily, and failed to exploit the synergies from new IT and planning tools. ECR and similar concepts such as Collaborative Planning, Forecasting and Replenishment (CPFR) has enabled firms to create competitive advantage by demonstrating their ability to work with trading partners and add value through superior service (Danese, 2007).

Associated with supply chain responsiveness is the concept of delivery precision: the ability to build a product according to customer specifications and deliver within a short order lead time. The ability to introduce precision into production operations and supply chain management is known as build-to-order or 'BTO' (Holweg and Pil, 2001; Gunasekaran and Ngai, 2005) and has its roots in automobile production strategy. In the early days of Henry Ford, vehicle manufacture was about maintaining a high volume of production, where the factory was responsible for pushing out as many products as possible usually with strong market demand. While experiments in production mechanization and interchangeable parts were state of the art during this time, the practice of delivery and supply of the finished product was very basic and based on make-to-stock (MTS). A product supplied from stock means the customer has no choice in its configuration: it is not 'factory fresh' and may have been built many months ago. Today, if the preferred specification is not available within a few days, this means customers haggle with the salesperson for a discount, thereby reducing the firm's opportunity to make a profit. Despite the introduction of initiatives such as lean, and fuelled by constant product segmentation and niche marketing, the production-centric approach employed by many Western carmakers has resulted in huge stockpiles of unsold

Make-to-stock (MTS) Traditional 'push' approach	Locate-to-order (LTO)	Build-to-order (BTO) 'Customer pull'
• Forecast driven • Optimized production planning • High stock levels • Customer buys cars from stock • Discounts	• Based on the traditional approach, but with an open pipeline of orders	• Customer order driven • High material flexibility needed • Low stock levels • Customer orders car according to specification • Better profit margin

Figure 8.7 From make-to-stock to build-to-order

vehicle inventory worth billions of dollars, a phenomenon that has persisted into the twenty-first century (Holweg and Pil, 2005). Today, many vehicle manufacturers are rethinking their business strategy in order to reduce stocks by reconnecting with the customer. This means not only considering distribution and supply as playing a central role in the organization, but also how BTO fits strategically with production operations, finance and marketing.

Implementing a BTO strategy across the enterprise does not, however, happen overnight. All volume vehicle manufacturers in the West since the early 1900s have until recently been operating a system where production takes priority and is generally considered the primary constraint because of the sunk costs and complexity of the process involved. Hence, material resource planning (MRP) systems are geared towards optimizing the highest flow of products through the system, often regardless of the proportion of 'real' customer orders. Conventional practice also involves the vehicle manufacturer sending every dealership a monthly quota of new vehicles to sell, based on past sales, meaning the dealer is forced to sell products that do not always match current market requirements. Car buying customers are becoming increasingly dissatisfied with the traditional ways of negotiation and compromise during the car sales process, and instead are demanding that new products be delivered according to a customized specification, pre-agreed price, and exact delivery date (see Figure 8.7). A paradigmatic shift from MTS to BTO can take decades, however, with the manufacturer starting with company initiatives that focus on one aspect at a time, e.g. inventory, product variety, customer focus, etc., which gradually begins to affect the whole supply chain's performance (Miemczyk and Howard, 2008). As part of the transition towards BTO, a mid-phase is often adopted, called locate to order (LTO). Here, improvements to the information system shared between tier-one suppliers and the manufacturer means a 'pipeline' of forthcoming vehicle orders can be viewed and amended (e.g. alterations to product mix, prioritize specific customer orders) to enable operational and supply chain planning.

Understanding product variety and the impact on production costs is an important factor in supply chain strategy (Berry and Cooper, 1999; Salvador et al., 2002). Before vehicle manufacturers fully understood the impact it had on their business, it was assumed that the more choice offered to customers in terms of vehicle specification, the better. For example, this meant some automakers offering four different shades of green and ten different types of radio in their vehicle catalogues! Yet the implications upstream in the supply chain, not just in terms of line-side inventory, but also the cost of stock held further upstream by suppliers, was crippling the business. Some customers simply became bewildered by the complexity of vehicle options on offer. As manufacturers such as Toyota began to sell standard equipped vehicles with higher levels of specification than Western equivalents at comparable prices, Western firms began to realize the importance of product standardization (one of the core principles of lean) and the cost benefit it could bring to the supply chain. Rather than arbitrarily reduce choice to the customer, vehicle manufacturers in the 1990s began to make informed decisions over what model configurations and options sold best. This sparked a wave of innovative design and new technology to overcome the cost of complexity to production through techniques such as universal body pressings (i.e. to suit both left- and right-hand drive), common 'plug and play' electronics, modularization and the late configuration of colour-coordinated components such as body trim to minimize disruption in the manufacturing process. Controlling product variety and the resultant impact of complexity in production is an important enabler for manufacturers and their suppliers seeking to develop BTO as an integral element in their supply chain strategy.

Note 8.3

Responsiveness and the 3DayCar programme

The 3DayCar programme (1999-2002) was launched by the University of Bath, Cardiff University, and the International Car Distribution Programme to investigate the feasibility of building new vehicles to customer order in the UK. Six research streams: marketing, finance, system, organization, environment and technology worked with 25 industrial sponsors representing dealers, vehicle manufacturers, suppliers, logistics, trade associations, credit & finance, government and IT management consultancies. 3DayCar was a vision of a system in which every customer receives a car produced exactly to specification and delivery date. For some this means getting the car as quickly as possible i.e. in 3 days. Research during the programme revealed that it took on average 40 days to fulfil an order, but only 1.5 days are spent actually building the vehicle, the majority of time is wasted on inefficient processes such as order scheduling, production sequencing and vehicle distribution. In terms of benefit for the automotive industry, the capability to build-to-order in short lead times offers a considerable prize: the elimination of excess vehicle stock (Figure 8.7) and retail discounting which erode profitability. The predecessor to the 3DayCar was the study by the International Motor Vehicle Programme at the Massachusetts Institute of Technology into automotive productivity.

Source: (Womack et al., 1990).

8.5 Supply chain risk

Supply chain risk is an established field of study in purchasing and supply chain management (e.g. Chopra and Sodhi, 2004; Christopher and Lee, 2004; Spekman and Davis, 2004; Harland et al., 2003). While individual firms have been aware of the need for risk management and contingency planning throughout the twentieth century, the firm-level view offers limited application for global supply chains (Manuj and Mentzer, 2008). Managing risk or 'vulnerability' (Svensson, 2000) in supply chains is an increasingly important topic because of a number of industry trends: high dependence on outsourcing by firms, market globalization, reliance on suppliers for specialized capabilities, and the increased use of information technology to coordinate and control the extended supply chain (Narasimhan and Talluri, 2009). The adoption of a lean supply strategy has also had its part to play in this trend as Western organizations have outsourced much of their manufacturing activity to suppliers in low-cost countries. The assessment of risk therefore is of fundamental importance in this unpredictable era of the global economy, where design of the supply chain must take into account the uncertainty of demand. Zsidisin and Ritchie (2008), for example, argue that demand uncertainty can cut two ways: there is the risk that unexpected demand will not be met on time, and the reverse problem, the risk that demand is overestimated and excessive inventory costs are incurred. There are also other more general risks involved, such as unreliable vendors, delayed shipments, and natural disasters. In examining what is an important aspect of management research, Kleindorfer and Saad (2005) argue that there are really only two broad categories of risk affecting supply chain design and management:

1 Risk arising from the problems of coordinating supply and demand, e.g. inventory control issues and stock-out situations;

2 Risks arising from disruption and delay to normal supply chain activities, e.g. natural disasters, civil unrest and the emergence of ethical issues in the workforce. This section concerns mostly the second category.

It might be tempting to think that the analysis of supply chain risk is all about the negative consequences and impact on organizations. But it is worth remembering that without taking some degree of risk, the firm will not benefit from the possibility of positive consequences. The key is to understand the types of risks that may be involved, their impact, the probability of occurrence, and to be able to distinguish their significance to the business overall. Risk can result from internal issues within the firm, e.g. labour strikes, as well as the external environment, although the majority of the literature on risk in supply chains covers the increasing exposure of firms to global phenomena and world events. There are a number of classifications, frameworks and models which incorporate risk as their focus (e.g. Harland *et al.*, 2003; Chopra and Sodhi, 2004), providing a breakdown of the categories and drivers of risk. While some offer ideas for 'risk mitigation', e.g. adding capacity and inventory, redundant suppliers, increasing responsiveness and flexibility, it is also accepted that the purchasing and supply professional cannot predict every possible future scenario in terms of supply chain disruption. They can, however, prepare contingency plans for the most likely events, such as considering a multiple sourcing strategy for critical, bottleneck components from suppliers located in remote, geographically exposed or socio-economically unstable areas.

On 10 March 2011 a powerful force 9.0 earthquake hit north-eastern Japan triggering a tsunami with 10-metre-high waves that devastated large areas of the coastal region, causing considerable loss of life, the obliteration of whole towns, and a nuclear reactor crisis lasting several months following an explosion at the Fukushima nuclear power plant. While shocking in intensity, the tragic events of that day were compounded by the long-term impact on Japan's already fragile economy with disruption to much of its automotive and computer component manufacturing industry. Not only was Japan left without an adequate supply of parts to maintain production at its own factories, but overseas customers also were suddenly facing a shortfall in supply of vital components such as silicon chips, metal alloy die-cast motor casings, engine radiators and moulded thermoplastic interior trim coverings for passenger vehicles. The tsunami that hit Japan revealed the vulnerability that is often inherent in modern, extended supply lines driven by JIT delivery. If possible, manufacturers will source parts from multiple locations to spread the risk, but in the case of Japan, as a major exporter of high-quality components this is not always possible, leading to major brands such as Apple and Toyota becoming hamstrung as retailer shelves and distribution warehouses rapidly become empty after such large-scale disruption.

In order to build resilience into their operations and systems, companies must become more aware of how the whole supply chain operates *before* the unexpected happens. Supply chain resilience has become a common expression in risk analysis circles particularly following the aftermath of events such as a tsunami, hurricane, factory fire or act of terrorism. The trend of chasing cheap labour rates across the world by major multinational firms means it is now common for supply chains to extend anywhere between 6,000 to 12,000 miles and involve lengthy sea crossings by container ship taking several weeks or more. Scenario planning and the use of risk tools and matrices (see Table 8.1) involve trying to identify potential risks or places where the supply chain is most vulnerable, and taking steps before the problem occurs. With the arrival of 'peak oil' (i.e. supply of oil from all known major sources reaching maximum yield), and rising costs of land and sea transportation, there is a growing argument for relocating manufacturing back to the US and Western Europe. However, for firms considering such a move, there will have to be clear business benefits and a supporting case from risk analysis before such a high cost proposal can be implemented. And despite the obvious advantages in the reduction of harmful emissions from fossil fuels used during transportation, an impact assessment on the communities losing out economically would also have to be conducted and contingencies put in place to manage the exit strategy.

Table 8.1 illustrates the types of mitigation strategies available to firms deciding to take action after conducting a supply chain risk assessment. Increasing the level of inventory is

Table 8.1 Risk assessment: category, driver and mitigation strategy

Category	Driver of risk	Mitigation strategy
Disruption	• Natural disaster, e.g. earthquake, flood • Act of terrorism, civil unrest or war • Labour disputes and strike action • Supplier insolvency	– Increase inventory – Have redundant suppliers – Review sourcing strategy, i.e. single, dual, multiple, etc.
Delay	• Inflexibility of supplier • High capacity utilization at source • Poor quality • Excessive handling during transportation • Customs clearance required at border control	– Add capacity – Increase inventory – Increase responsiveness and flexibility
IT systems	• Internal IT failure and systems shutdown • Systems integration with supply partners • External threat from www of hackers and viruses • Reliability and security of e-commerce	– Conduct a supply chain–wide IT audit – Switch off IT legacy systems – Conduct an information security audit – Implement full firewall protection
Forecasting and communication	• Inaccurate forecasts due to long order-to-delivery lead times, seasonality, variety • Information distortion due to lack of visibility in the supply chain or promotions/incentives • Different metrics and performance measures used by supply chain partners	– Increase responsiveness – Aggregate or 'pool' customer demand
Intellectual property (IP)	• Vertical integration means IP may become out of date • IP spread across market through global outsourcing	– Decide on core competencies of the firm – Reconsider 'make or buy' decisions based on future design and innovation requirements

Legal and economics	• Fluctuation in monetary exchange rates • Long-term versus short-term contracts • Financial strength of customer base	– *Operate in a range of countries to spread the effect of exchange rate fluctuation* – *Build up a customer base in source country* – *Match product type (e.g. commodity, leverage, etc.) with appropriate type of relationship*
Procurement	• Raw material of key component procured from a single source • Capacity utilization of supply base • Cost of capacity	– *Add capacity and increase inventory* – *Increase flexibility* – *Have redundant suppliers*
Inventory	• Degree of product obsolescence • Cost of holding inventory • Uncertainty of supply and demand	– *Increase responsiveness* – *Aggregate demand* – *Increase supplier capability in inventory management*
Ethical and social conduct	• Operational competence of suppliers not adequately monitored or controlled • Employment conditions in source country do not match expectations of buyer and customers • Adherence to local customs and traditions preventing change in working practices	– *Commit to corporate responsibility* – *Buyer to introduce standards of ethical business conduct to supplier early on* – *Seek agreement from supplier during contract negotiations on standard measures* – *Joint investment in continuous training*

Source: Adapted from Chopra and Sodhi (2004).

often the simplest and most effective way of 'buying time' in the event of a disruption to the supply chain. Also, decentralizing inventory of predictable, lower value products has the effect of spreading the risk across several production locations. However, in the case of more complex products it may not be possible from a cost perspective to hold more stock, so other options must be considered:

- Having more redundancy in terms of suppliers, e.g. through dual or multi-sourcing is an effective means of mitigating the risk of disruption. Redundancy here therefore means having a 'spare' or a backup supply source in case problems occur, e.g. breakdown or stoppage. The approach tends to favour more redundant supply for high volume products, and less for low volume.

- Increasing capacity of production is a longer-term approach, requiring more investment in the supply base. Predictable demand should focus on low-cost, decentralized capacity. More unpredictable demand suggests building centralized capacity.

- Pooling or aggregating (i.e. bringing together – also termed 'consolidating') demand is a useful strategy when market unpredictability grows. Pooling demand helps the supplier to utilize economies of scale where possible, and over time to apply smoothing techniques to balance production.

- Increasing supply chain responsiveness as a result of delay in the system means implementing strategies such as ECR and BTO, discussed earlier in the chapter. Responsiveness requires greater coordination between supplier and prime manufacturer, as well as investment in the integration of IT systems such as EPOS across the business. Increasing flexibility means reducing the time it takes for suppliers to switch supplying one type of product to another in accordance with customer demand. This is particularly important in low-volume, unpredictable items.

A growing risk for the extended supply chain which is not captured in traditional supply chain management risk analysis literature is the rise of ethical and social conduct issues, particularly around the lower tier suppliers in low-cost countries. This aspect is included in Table 8.1 because not only do the consequences of unethical practices such as child labour, uncontrolled hours and poor safety perpetuate the misery of millions of people around the world, but ultimately the exposure of unscrupulous or imprudent multinational corporation behaviour leads to an impact on the supply chain through media exposure similar to the effects of disruption and delay (see Note 8.4). This type of risk is often not included in supply chain frameworks but companies today realize they have to invest in greater levels of reputational risk monitoring.

Note 8.4

Learning from Nike

Negative publicity means risk to the corporation by driving down sales which results in lost revenue. During the 1990s sportswear manufacturer Nike was criticized for contracting with suppliers in China, Vietnam, Indonesia and Mexico, with activist groups claiming violations of minimum wage and overtime laws. Nike claims that this practice has now stopped, but has attracted much critical media coverage over poor working conditions and exploitation of cheap overseas labour. A BBC documentary in 2001 revealed the use of child labour and poor working conditions in a Cambodian factory manufacturing Nike products. Most shocking was the coverage of girls working seven days a week often sixteen hours a day. Campaigns were launched by Colleges and Universities, including involvement from several anti-sweatshop groups to highlight worker conditions overseas. Nike accepts that it must learn from past experience and has begun to implement changes in the way it deals with the supply chain. In 2004 Nike bought the Starter brand which was a departure from its usual corporate strategy. Selling in stores such as Walmart, Starter shoes are considered a value or entry level product for consumers on tight budgets, but most noticeable is their connection to manufacturers in Latin America and Asia. By showing interest in the value industry, Nike wanted to demonstrate that it was committed to maintaining labour compliance with all of its products and markets. Nike also developed a corporate responsibility department, furthering their involvement in ethically and socially responsible supply chain strategy. Yet auditing overseas factories' labour compliance remains a big challenge for the corporation seeking to simultaneously standardize and monitor working practices across six or more manufacturing regions.

8.6 Supply chain traceability: the sustainability challenge

Successful supply chains rely on transparency of supply and demand information. Technology, such as radio frequency identification (RFID), helps supply chain actors to track stock as it moves in and out of warehouses. Tracking and tracing of items within the supply chain is therefore integral to supply chain management, but sustainability requires a different form and level of traceability. Consider the horse meat scandal that hit the media in early 2013. DNA tests carried out by the Food Safety Authority of Ireland (FSAI) revealed that one range of Tesco burgers contained up to 29 per cent horse meat (Leach, 2013). Other retailers, including Aldi and IKEA, found horse meat in some of their products that were labelled and sold as beef. The retailers were quick to withdraw the products from their shelves, promising to trace the root of the problem. In the immediate aftermath of investigations the retailers traced the horse meat to suppliers in the UK, Ireland and France and these in turn traced the sources of the horse meat to suppliers in Eastern Europe where it may or may not have been sold as horse meat. Traders in Cyprus and the Netherlands were also reported to have been involved (Arumugam, 2013). In any case, the horse meat scandal shows that many food retailers do not have visibility over their food supply chains; they are apparently unable to trace the ingredients of what goes into some of their products.

The horse meat scandal is by no means a stand-alone case. In recent years there have been numerous examples of products that have been found to contain the wrong or downright dangerous ingredients, including high levels of lead-based paint in Mattel toys (in some cases 180 times the legal limit), palm oil in Nestlé's KitKat chocolate bar (palm oil being linked to deforestation and thereby destruction of natural habitats for animals such as gorillas), sunscreen products found to contain nano-ingredients despite labelling as 'non-nano', which, according to Friends of the Earth in 2012, in a worst-case scenario could lead to skin cancer. In 2017, Walmart trialled the use of blockchain technology to monitor its pork and mango sourcing in response to problems with contaminated pork from Chain. Working in collaboration with IBM and Tsinghua University, Walmart's goal is to use this emerging technology to trace farm products from farm to table.

The paradox is that although supply chain technologies have evolved to an extent where companies should be able to keep track of moving goods throughout their supply chains, the complexity of global supply networks means that companies in reality often do not have anywhere near perfect visibility so that, consequently, they lose sight of such critical issues as what their products actually contain. Certainly, when problems are discovered information will be shared by consumers, journalists or NGOs and will spread rapidly and globally through a range of media including the Internet and social media. Nestlé learned this the hard way when Greenpeace exposed its use of palm oil in its KitKat chocolate bar, creating a satirical KitKat promotional video on YouTube.

Companies show very different levels of commitment to provide supply chain transparency. Some undertake meticulous analysis of their sources of supply, stretching back five or six tiers of supply or more, but others hardly know their first-tier suppliers (New and Brown, 2011). The use of 'middlemen' or agents tends to make supply chains more complex and therefore more opaque. In fact, supply chains often become less transparent as product complexity increases: a large number of ingredients or components mean a wide supply base, both direct first-tier and sub-tier suppliers.

Chapter 2 explained some of the ways that companies evaluate their suppliers and Chapter 13 returns to these issues, focusing on specific methods that companies can use, for example in conducting supplier audits. The fundamental questions are about how and what data to collect, how it is verified and how to enable the data to be stored and handled (New and Brown, 2011). A strategy of delegation (Johnsen, 2011) places the responsibility on first-tier suppliers to manage second-tier suppliers and so forth but a more interventionist strategy, where companies personally engage in, and take responsibility for, analysis beyond the first tier, may be required to ensure compliance within the extended supply network. Naturally, the latter strategy requires much more time and effort and risks upsetting supplier relationships, as intervention may be seen by suppliers as potentially interfering in their business.

In any case, existing ERP systems are unlikely to capture the required data. Instead companies need to carry out supplier audits but must be careful that suppliers are not subjected to separate audits by separate departments, e.g. it is not uncommon for firms to separate supplier environmental and ethical auditing from traditional operations and supply chain requirements (New and Brown, 2011), leaving suppliers with contradictory demands from the buying organization. Chapter 3 discussed the organizational challenges of integrating sustainability (or CSR) and purchasing organizations and highlighted the need for companies not only to structurally integrate these functions but also to develop new skills and competencies so that, for example, purchasing personnel are equipped with knowledge about how to evaluate supplier sustainability risk profiles and performance.

The use of product labels has traditionally given consumers a minimal amount of information such as the country of origin. In the fashion industry, for example, labels usually show not only product materials (e.g. cotton or polyester), but also country of manufacture and assembly. Yet as the production process is generally highly outsourced, some companies now choose to label their garments in more creative ways such as 'designed in', and labels are increasingly used to provide information about environmental and ethical certifications. Showing barcodes (or numbered product codes) on labels provides a further way to allow not only companies to trace their products through the supply chain, but also consumers to trace the product they have bought. Using mobile phone applications (or 'apps'), consumers can scan a code to learn more about products or services.

California winemaker, the Blankiet Estate, labels its bottles with a code – BubbleTag™ – that when entered on the company's website (www.blankiet.com/authentication), authenticates the wine. New Zealand–based Icebreaker became famous for its 'BAA Code' which enabled consumers to trace their merino wool garments to specific sheep farms although the company stopped this system when the company grew and its supply chain became too complex to continue this system. The trend towards traceability continues with companies such as eco-fashion brand Rapanui (https://rapanuiclothing.com/traceability-clothing/) creating a business model based on supply chain traceability or what they call 'from seed to shop'. Such business model innovations, which are based on providing supply chain tracking and transparency for consumers, aim not only to mitigate supply chain risks but also to create a competitive edge in the marketplace.

8.7 Intermediation and disintermediation strategy

An intermediary is someone who acts as a link between groups of people, sometimes termed a middleman. In the context of supply chain strategy, intermediation means the link or facilitator between goods manufacturers and customers, requiring a range of knowledge and skills in marketing, operations and distribution. Free trade and globalized markets have raised the profile of intermediation strategy as goods made in one part of the world can be shipped and delivered to a customer in another, provided the location is served by a network of local offices and warehouses controlled by the intermediary organization which accepts a percentage of the revenue for their services, usually between 5 and 25 per cent (McFarlan and Young, 2002). Original equipment manufacturers (OEMs) typically in the auto and aerospace sectors can be considered as the focal firm, who not only profit from product sales but also the lucrative aftermarket in 'OE' parts and components for servicing and fleet repair. As component suppliers seek to increase their margins, usually because of overly harsh contractual pricing agreements, this may tempt them to bypass the OEM and sell parts directly to the customer: a strategy defined as 'disintermediation', with major consequences for the buyer–supplier relationship (Rossetti and Choi, 2005, 2008).

Disintermediation can occur in almost any industry, including capital goods (e.g. aircraft, trucks, passenger vehicles), retail (e.g. books, home computers), or the tourism sector (e.g. hotels, airline flight bookings). Disintermediation often occurs with the emergence of new technology, e.g. the Internet which enables new entrants such as Dell, EasyJet or Amazon to design online customer information systems and bypass one or more stages of the supply chain, e.g. the retailer's store or travel agent (Chircu and Kauffman, 2000; Evans and Wurster, 1997). Today, the rise of what is termed peer-to-peer marketing or the 'sharing economy' means that it is not just disruptive technology which is challenging traditional ways of offering services, but new business models, for example informal tourist accommodation provided by the likes of Airbnb (Cusumano, 2015).

The Hong Kong trading company 'Li & Fung' had expanded to sales of US$2billion by the year 2000 and had come a long way from its roots in matching Chinese manufacturers with Western buyers (McFarlan and Young, 2002). However, there was real concern from the company's managing director over the effect of the Internet and a third party putting together all the information on buyers and factories online: 'Would the internet disintermediate us? Would we get Amazoned?' After some business research the company realized that although the Internet was indeed a facilitator for the supply chain, it was no substitute for the network of relationships built up over decades by the 5,000 Li & Fung employees with local manufacturers spread across six continents. The key was to have old economy know-how, but be open to new economy ideas. Li & Fung decided to launch Li&Fung.com in 2000, despite concerns over cannibalization of the core business and uncertainty over the market's response to an Internet portal. Today it operates a hybrid system, maintaining Internet-based communications with its largest customers including Avon, Coca-Cola and Disney, with the sophistication of the connection varying with the nature of communications infrastructure available in any specific region. While some firms send digital photos of their product samples to head office (what is sometimes termed a 'thick connection'), others prefer to do business the more traditional way: if not face to face, then by email, Skype or telephone.

A prime example of sector-wide disintermediation, or the bypassing and cutting out of once powerful middle players, is the case of the US aerospace industry's parts supply. Rossetti and Choi (2005) describe the strategic blunder of major OEMs in the 1990s such as Airbus, General Electric and Honeywell where, despite implementing strategic sourcing over the past decade, the supply chain was literally coming apart with suppliers selling their components directly to the buyer's customers. Referring to the phenomenon as 'supply chain disintermediation' (2005: 46), Rossetti and Choi argue that the core tenets of strategic sourcing – long-term relationships and co-prosperity – had been misapplied, with supplier relationships marked by gamesmanship and deception. At the root of the supplier's motives to bypass its former paymasters was the increasing tendency of the OEMs to offer false promises of long-term contracts simply to gain the lowest component prices and, once the contract was in place, to force suppliers to absorb risks such as holding inventory and cash flow management. As OEM buyers began to rationalize the supply base as part of consolidation to the point where competition disappeared, the resultant effect was unintentionally to create fewer, more powerful suppliers who were able to use their stronger bargaining position in the industry to negotiate more favourable terms. In summing up their observations in terms of the preventative steps against future supply chain disintermediation, Rossetti and Choi recommend:

- Understanding the supply market and supplier's reactions to strategic initiatives;

- Using spend consolidation to increase supplier efficiency and guard against bankruptcy;

- Incorporating broader supply chain metrics that better reflect corporate goals;

- Using long-term agreements to reduce transaction costs and promote co-prosperity based on trust.

Disintermediation can be deployed as a strategy by firms over time to gain control of a project, sector or market. This is particularly the case in restricted markets where there are only a few large suppliers offering specialist services, such as the Western defence sector. The award of a government defence contract, for example, offers the opportunity of significant revenue and long-term security to OEMs who increasingly offer facility and programme management services as well as platform (i.e. warship, tank, fighter plane) fabrication and engineering. As Western governments such as in the UK seek to reduce their commitment in terms of the fixed costs of managing design, construction, maintenance and support, private multinational firms have stepped in to gain control of almost all stages and stakeholders in the defence commissioning process. These private OEMs therefore have much control over what is meant to be a public sector service, i.e. national security. A study of the supply dynamics over time focusing on the management of a government warship design and build contract highlights the disintermediation strategies deployed by powerful suppliers to secure their future in the sector. As a result of extensive outsourcing in the UK by government, one OEM has gained such a level of responsibility that it now assumes the role and influence over major projects formerly adopted by the ministry of defence (Howard *et al.*, 2016).

8.8 Closed-loop supply strategy and the circular economy

The decision to adopt a closed-loop supply strategy has significant implications for the firm in terms of sustainable supply management. It shows that the organization has begun to consider the issues of environmental management and product life cycle in terms of the business vision, and can distinguish traditional supply chains from closed-loop supply chains (Guide and Van Wassenhove, 2003). Yet introducing a closed-loop or 'reverse logistics' supply chain into the business is not simple, particularly as product recycling is rarely considered as a value creating system (Guide and Van Wassenhove, 2003). Closed-loop supply chains require considerable investment in time and resources, initially in understanding the configurations of information flow and parts distribution that serve the product while in use, and then in developing a collection system which takes back or 'harvests' the product at its end of life, while integrating the cooperation of customers, suppliers and not-for-profit organizations (Kumar and Malegeant, 2006).

The process of product disassembly and remanufacturing can be particularly tricky as the condition of used products may vary greatly, can be distributed across the world and, even if retrievable, may have to be discarded if damaged beyond repair. A combination of increasingly stringent government legislation (e.g. European law on vehicle scrapping and disassembly) and manufacturer-led initiatives means most industry sectors today have active recycling schemes in operation, e.g. photocopiers, computers, electronics (Spengler and Schröter, 2003). A criticism of some recycling schemes is that they have been retro-introduced at some considerable time after the original plans to design, manufacture and distribute the product, hence have never been fully integrated into the supply chain. The circular economy, however, offers a radically different approach as:

> an industrial economy that is producing no waste and pollution, by design or intention, and in which material flows are of two types, biological nutrients, designed to re-enter the biosphere safely, and technical nutrients, which are designed to circulate at high quality in the production system without entering the biosphere as well as being restorative and regenerative by design.
>
> (EMF and McKinsey & Co., 2012)

The circular economy is now the topic of considerable debate in corporations, universities and parliaments across Europe and beyond (see, for example, Aminoff and Kettunen, 2016; Antikainen and Valkokari, 2016; De Angelis *et al.*, 2018). Given rising concerns around resource scarcity and pollution, high hopes are being pinned on the circular economy as a strategy which enables firms to transition from the take–make–waste linear production model, towards alternative modes of production that allow goods to be designed and produced from the outset with reuse, repair and refurbishment in mind (Figure 8.8). The concept of 'circular business advantage' is used where firms exploit the circular economy concept to create a regenerative production system that achieves limitless growth whilst producing no waste. Such an idea may seem far-fetched, but with the recent launch of the EU's Circular Economy Package and the 2017 release of British Standard 8001 Framework for Implementing Circular Economy Principles, it may soon become standard practice. Introducing greater circularity into all supply chains is important because the typical nation's resource usage is inefficient and wasteful, with only around 15 per cent of Europe's plastics currently being recycled, and China consuming more aluminium, steel and cement than the whole of the OECD[2] put together. This imminent crisis in natural resources and the knock-on effect of waste on polluting the land, air and oceans requires a more radical approach towards resource effectiveness than recycling. Adopting a circular approach potentially offers a solution, but with the degree of out-of-the-box thinking, investment and new regulation required, it represents a major challenge to business and society.

Closed-loop supply chains are challenging in their design and operation, and also have important implications for supply chain strategy (Savaskan *et al.*, 2004). They include traditional forward supply chain activities, but also the additional activities of the reverse supply chain such as the returns process, movements of goods, product testing and sorting, and remarketing (Guide *et al.*, 2003). Although described in detail in Chapter 10, it is worth pointing out here that despite reverse logistics systems being practised since the 1920s (e.g. in the automotive sector), there lacks today the strategic-level thinking required to integrate the concept of the closed-loop supply chain into mainstream business activity. Closed-loop or reverse systems are typically treated as a silo, isolated from the core business, where common activities are yet to be established and not fully understood in different contexts because of variations in complexity and perceptions in managerial importance. Industry and academia have a tendency to focus on the operational and tactical, e.g. how to create a remanufacturing programme, rather than to tackle the broader, more strategic issues of business profitability and the underlying motivations for why the firm has adopted such a scheme in the first place. In the now contentious words of Guide and van Wassenhove (2003: 86): 'no rational company will invest in environmental measures to save the earth. That's not what companies are for, and legislation is not going to change that.'

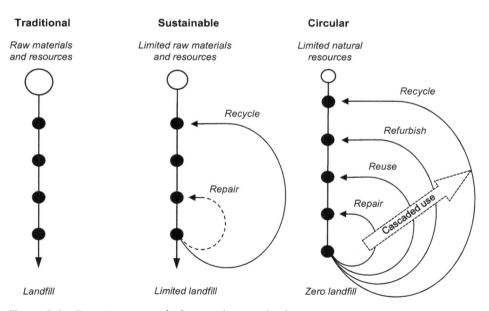

Figure 8.8 Transition towards the circular supply chain

Source: Adapted from De Angelis *et al.* (2018).

Before examining the case of a carpet manufacturer who adopted a closed-loop supply chain strategy, it is helpful to discuss the work of Pagell and Wu (2009) in the context of sustainable supply chain strategy. In their study of ten exemplar firms seeking to build more sustainable supply chains, they suggest that conventional best practice in supply chain management can be used as a foundation for sustainability. This means that traditional aspects of supply chain management, e.g. proactive stance and commitment, business redefinition, supplier certification, life-cycle thinking and closed-loop logistics, can be combined and integrated with newer behaviours such as greater commitment to employees, supply chain integration, sustainable values to help in recruitment and adding new suppliers to spur sustainable innovation. Pagell and Wu's research also suggests that reconceptualizing the supply chain to include sustainability requires not only 'changing the cognition of managers' but the realization of more intrinsic and long-term benefits, e.g. supplier commitment, employee motivation, customer loyalty, etc., which are derived from the development of sustainable business values and the adoption of closed-loop supply chain strategy.

CASE STUDY 8.1

DESSO CARPETS AND CRADLE-TO-CRADLE® CHALLENGE

This case examines the carpet manufacturer Desso, based in the Netherlands, after its decision to adopt Cradle-to-Cradle® principles and the subsequent reframing of the firm's understanding of supply chain management. Although the company had been involved in stand-alone sustainability initiatives such as wind-powered energy generation before the management buy-out in 2007, no one in the organization had dared consider incorporating concepts as bold as Cradle-to-Cradle® into the heart of the enterprise.

Cradle-to-Cradle® is a play on the phrase 'cradle to grave' which, in contrast to traditional linear manufacturing models, promotes the use of non-toxic manufacturing systems where products are designed for disassembly using pure materials which can be safely recycled.[3] The concept of Cradle-to-Cradle® or 'C2C®' as it is often abbreviated, was popularized by Braungart and McDonough in their book *Cradle to Cradle: Remaking the way we make things.* Published in 2002 and updated in 2009, their book is now considered a sustainability classic. Phrases such as 'cradle to grave' allude to a more traditional, linear manufacturing model dating from the Industrial Revolution, sometimes called a 'take, make, waste' system. While this system has played a role in improving quality of life, it has generated many unintended and undesirable global consequences such as the production of vast amounts of waste and pollution, the depletion of natural resources and loss of biodiversity. C2C® in contrast promotes non-toxic manufacturing systems where products and materials are designed from the outset to enhance quality of life and ensure safe recycling once product life has expired. C2C® takes its design inspiration for products and processes from nature. The model aims to mimic the planet's natural cyclical nutrient flows, its use of solar energy, and its creation of diversity and abundance. In nature, for example, there is no such thing as waste. Materials are continuously recycled to nourish new organisms.

Convincing an organization of the need to change represents a challenge, but asking customers and suppliers to change a lifetime of ingrained habits means change at all levels of the enterprise, from strategic vision to daily operations, which doesn't happen overnight. Add to this the challenge for Desso of balancing economic survival in the worst worldwide recession for over 50 years on one hand, with introducing its aspirations for the long-term well-being of people and planet on the other. As the process of C2C® implementation has started to gather momentum at the firm, the management team at Desso – led by Stef Kranendijk (ex-Procter & Gamble) – is beginning to understand the extent of the complexity involved in changing the organization and supply chain. This includes aspects such as material sourcing, information sharing with suppliers and a deep commitment to go further than current legislation requires.

Since the restructuring of the company and announcement of the adoption of C2C®, Desso has steadily increased annual profits in terms of EBIT from 1 per cent in 2007 to 9.2 per cent in 2011.[4] Traditionally in carpets there is not much money to be made: 'if you make 10 per cent you're doing great!' Stef Kranendijk believes and proves that C2C® is not only good for the environment, but also drives personal health, innovation and business acumen which leads to higher profits. His ambitious design objectives for the company are to have every product supported by the C2C® vision by 2020: 'From the moment we started to publicise C2C, from February 2008 … and we have been communicating our ideas a lot over the years to end users, architects, CEOs … people react very positively to it'. At the beginning his new management team had to decide which product category from the existing portfolio to start with. They chose carpet tiles: a popular product with commercial customers particularly in busy office environments, but composed of around 120 ingredients some of which are toxic though acceptable to the industry and comply with current regulations (such as REACH and CE labelling), and contain elements that are not allowed by Cradle-to-Cradle® criteria. A major component of the typical carpet tile is the natural material bitumen used as backing. This is the thick residue left after petrochemicals have been removed in the separation process from crude oil. Bitumen contains sometimes unknown and thus difficult-to-control ingredients, adding to the issue of end-of-life treatment which often leads to the dumping of used carpet tiles in landfill sites.

After Stef Kranendijk became acquainted with Michael Braungart and C2C®, introducing the concept to the site at Desso's production facilities at Waalwijk was not simple. 'The people in R&D and Manufacturing got worried and said "What is going on?!"' Desso's carpet tile production line was one of the first to start rethinking its product and production process, and required considerable collaboration with architects, non-governmental organizations (NGOs) and suppliers such as Dow Chemical to decide how best to replace the bitumen used in the backing material. 'We have developed together with EPEA[5] and Dow Chemical [the new carpet tile backing] we call EcoBase™ where the polyolefin based layer can be fully and safely recycled at a high level'. The EcoBase™ backing is specifically designed for disassembly and recycling in Desso's own production plant. Carpet tiles with DESSO EcoBase® have achieved Cradle-to-Cradle® Silver Certification reaching a level where up to 97 per cent of the materials are positively defined.[6]

A particular challenge for Desso is the 'take-back' initiative, which the company has offered since 2008. Under this system the company offers to retrieve used carpet tiles from buildings undergoing refurbishment (also termed 'urban mining') and then recycles them at the plant in Waalwijk. Desso's take-back and recycling process is called ReFinity® which separates the post-consumer carpet into its main components, either for recycling into new carpet yarn, or for downcycling into road building materials and for use as secondary fuel in the cement industry.

Encouraging contractors such as the independent carpet fitter to collaborate is one difficult issue, but determining the material used in the tiles which may have been manufactured by a competitor is

CASE STUDY 8.1

another. Much of the material is over ten years old and may have a high bitumen content which is the heavy part or stabilizer of the tile and is non-recyclable, traditionally burnt in incinerators or simply landfilled. While Desso is currently exploring the use of incinerated material for use in cement, its objective for carpet tile recycling is to separate the yarn and other fibres from all the other materials for use again, where the tile is typically built up of different layers, e.g. polyester, polypropylene and polyamide. Desso has developed a process of separation which involves shredding and fluffing old carpet. A special colour dye removal process has been developed by a supplier where 'other methods have been tried such as directly extruding the fibre, but this leaves the colour in which is no good for light coloured carpet'. Desso's innovative manufacturing and recycling methods mean the white yarn can continuously be re-used, albeit with a certain loss of material with each cycle of the tile at a rate of around 11 per cent. Innovation on the scale envisaged by Desso through the implementation of C2C® requires significant investment in time, resources and technologies. To develop the yarn recycling process alone, for example, has taken the company two years. In the words of the sustainability director: 'It takes guts ... it's about challenging the framework and thinking outside the box'.

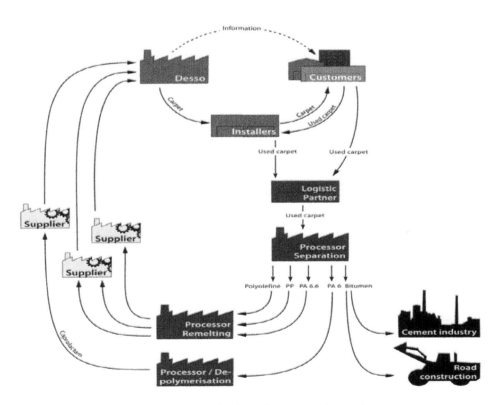

Figure 8.9 Desso's closed-loop supply chain for carpet tile production

Source: Desso (2012).

Adopting a more circular, Cradle-to-Cradle® approach by Desso is complex because it means rethinking traditional supply chain thinking, where once periphery issues of product end-of-life and disposal become central to the solution. C2C® requires more than an adjustment to supply chain management because rather than outsourcing responsibility to suppliers, under C2C® the prime manufacturer plays a leading role in persuading partners to be receptive to legislation and cooperate through sharing information, process improvement, product design and materials research. Inter-company relationships become forged by C2C®, recasting traditional notions of 'upstream–downstream' and supply chain hierarchy. The concept of the circular economy is significant today because it introduces 'new rules of the game' over pricing and incentive structures which requires support from all stakeholders, including NGOs and government. While C2C® is similar in its closed-loop approach to reverse logistics and design for disassembly, it redefines thinking around the way recycled materials are treated in terms of upcycle or downcycle, and presents the idea of emulating nature's cycles as the basis for a new industrial model of production and consumption. C2C® reframes our understanding of supply chain strategy, because instead of a linear approach leading to landfill, it adopts the language of circular, closed-loop supply systems and repeat material use.

8.9 Conclusion

Supply chain strategy is important today because world markets are at great risk of disruption with many industries facing turbulent and volatile operating conditions particularly from fluctuating commodity and raw material prices. As many regions around the world are increasingly disrupted by abnormal weather, terrorism, sole commodity ownership (e.g. China) and price volatility (e.g. grain, oil, gas), the traditional practice of supply chains designed exclusively around single narrow strategies may be coming to an end. Supply chain designs should no longer be based on assumptions of a stable operating environment, but need to incorporate flexibility and resilience in order to counter the effects of constant disturbance (Christopher and Holweg, 2011). Furthermore, the basic principle of controlling an end-to-end process to create a seamless flow of goods must be questioned, where assumptions over long-term stability no longer hold true. Managing supply chains in an age of constant turbulence may mean embracing volatility as an opportunity rather than viewing it as a risk and by trying to understand its true nature and impact. This means reducing the supply chain's exposure to risk by combining different approaches, such as dual sourcing, asset sharing, postponement, flexible labour and additive manufacturing (Holmström et al., 2016).

This chapter has also discussed the implications of sustainability for supply chain strategy and starts by defining common terms such as supply chain and supply network. It applies lean, agile and hybrid supply chain approaches to industry practice by considering the importance of product and market characteristics. The evolution from mass production to mass customization emphasizes the production-centric nature of past approaches, and raises the prospect of a more customer-orientated and responsive approach in future based on more sustainable consumption using circular models of material supply. New models incorporating environmental and ethical issues in their approach must also embrace the ideas of traceability and transparency. Supply chain strategy today must not only mitigate for the possible impact of risks through tsunami, flooding or labour exploitation, but also understand the effects of disintermediation through new technology or supplier activity. In shifting from conventional supply chains towards closed-loop supply chain strategy there are considerable challenges in reframing our engagement with customers, suppliers, NGOs and government, particularly in terms of product redesign, supplier relationships, and the whole end-to-end business implementation side of how to introduce the circular economy.

Notes

1 The concept of value stream management is covered in Chapter 12 where practical value stream mapping methods are presented.
2 Organisation for Economic Co-operation and Development. The mission of the OECD is to promote policies that will improve the economic and social well-being of people around the world. See: www.oecd.org.
3 Cradle-to-Cradle® is the registered trademark of McDonough Braungart Design Chemistry (MBDC). The concept was first used by Stahel and Reday-Mulvey in 1976. See also: Stahel and Reday-Mulvey (1981).
4 These figures refer to the normalized EBIT of the original carpet business. The 'normalization' is defined internally by management.
5 Environmental Protection Encouragement Agency (EPEA) GmbH founded by Professor Dr Michael Braungart who works with clients worldwide to apply the Cradle-to-Cradle® methodology to the design of new processes, products and services.
6 Positively defined means all ingredients have been assessed as either Green (optimal) or Yellow (tolerable) according to the Cradle-to-Cradle® assessment criteria. As described in the Cradle-to-Cradle® Certification Program Version 2.1.1, prepared by MBDC, September 2008, and updated January 2010.

References

Aminoff A and Kettunen O (2016) Sustainable supply chain management in a circular economy. In: Setchi R, Howlett R, Liu Y and Theobald P (eds) *Sustainable Design and Manufacturing*. Springer, pp. 61–72.

Antikainen M and Valkokari K (2016) A Framework for sustainable circular business model innovation. *Technology Innovation Management Review* 6: 5–12.

Arumugam N (2013) The Romanian horse cart ban that's (probably) behind Europe's horse meat scandal, *Forbes Magazine*, 14 February. Available at: http://www.forbes.com (last accessed February 2014).

Bentley C (2017) The manufacturing industry 4.0 UK readiness report. Available at: www.themanufacturer.com.

Berry W and Cooper M (1999) Manufacturing flexibility: Methods for measuring the impact of product variety on performance. *Journal of Operations Management* 17(2): 163–179.

Braunscheidal M and Suresh N (2009) The organizational antecedents of a firm's supply chain agility for risk mitigation and response. *Journal of Operations Management* 27: 119–140.

Chircu A and Kauffman R (2000) Reintermediation strategies in business-to-business electronic commerce. *International Journal of Electronic Commerce* 4(4): 7–42.

Christopher M (2000) The agile supply chain: Competing in volatile markets. *Industrial Marketing Management* 29: 37–44.

Christopher M (2005) *Logistics and Supply Chain Management: Creating Value Adding Networks.* Harlow, UK: Pearson Education.

Christopher M and Towill D (2000) Supply chain migration from lean and functional to agile and customized. *Supply Chain Management: An International Journal* 5(4): 206–213.

Christopher M and Holweg M (2011) 'Supply chain 2.0': Managing supply chains in the era of turbulence. *International Journal of Physical Distribution & Logistics Management* 41(1): 63–82.

Christopher M and Lee H (2004) Mitigating supply chain risk through improved confidence. *International Journal of Physical Distribution & Logistics Management* 34(5): 388–396.

Chopra S and Sodhi M (2004) Managing risk to avoid supply-chain breakdown. *MIT Sloan Management Review* 46(1).

Cooper MC, Lambert DM and Pagh J (1997) Supply chain management: More than a new name for logistics. *The International Journal of Logistics Management* 8(1): 1–14.

Cox A (1999) Power, value and supply chain management. *Supply Chain Management: An International Journal* 4(4): 167–175.

Cusumano MA (2015) How traditional firms must compete in the sharing economy. *Communications of the ACM* 58(1): 32–34.

Danese P (2007) Designing CPFR collaborations: Insights from seven case studies. *International Journal of Operations & Production Management* 27(2): 181–204.

Davis S (1987) *Future Perfect.* Reading, MA: Addison-Wesley.

De Angelis R, Howard M and Miemczyk J (2018) Supply chain management and the circular economy: Towards the circular supply chain. *Production Planning & Control.* Forthcoming.

Duguay C, Landry S and Pasin F (1997) From mass production to flexible/agile production. *International Journal of Operations & Production Management* 17(12): 1183–1195.

EC (European Commission) (2015) *Circular Economy Package: Questions and Answers.* Available at: http://europa.eu/rapid/press-release_MEMO-15-6204_en.htm (last accessed December 2015).

EMF (Ellen MacArthur Foundation) and McKinsey & Co. (2012) *Towards the Circular Economy: Economic and Business Rationale for an Accelerated Transition.* Available at: http://www.ellenmacarthurfoundation.org/business/reports (last accessed May 2017).

EMF and McKinsey & Co. (2013) *Towards the Circular Economy: Opportunities for the Consumer Goods Sector.* Available at: http://www.ellenmacarthurfoundation.org/business/reports (last accessed May 2017).

Evans P and Wurster T (1997) Strategy and the new economics of information. *Harvard Business Review*, Sept.–Oct: 71–82.

Fawcett SE and Magnan GM (2002) The rhetoric and reality of supply chain integration. *International Journal of Physical Distribution & Logistics Management* 32(5): 339.

Ferdows K, Lewis M and Machuca J (2003) Zara – case study. *Supply Chain Forum: An International Journal* 4(2): 62–67.

Ferdows, K, Lewis M and Machuca J (2004) Rapid-fire fulfilment. *Harvard Business Review*, November.

Fisher M (1997) What is the right supply chain for your product? *Harvard Business Review* March–April.

Ford D and Håkansson H (2002) How should companies interact in business networks? *Journal of Business Research* 55: 133–139.

Forza C. (1996) Work organization in lean production and traditional plants: What are the differences? *International Journal of Operations & Production Management* 16(2): 42–62.

Friends of the Earth (2012) *Nano-ingredients in Sunscreen: The Need for Regulation.* Available at: http://nano.foe.org (last accessed February 2014).

Gadde L-E and Håkansson H (2001) *Supply Network Strategy*. Chichester, UK: John Wiley & Sons.

Guide V and Van Wassenhove L (2003) Closed loop supply chains: Practice and potential. Editorial to the special issue. *Interfaces* 33(6): 86–93.

Guide V, Harrison T and Van Wassenhove L (2003) The challenge of closed loop supply chains. *Interfaces* 33(6): 3–6.

Gunasekaran A (1999) Design and implementation of agile manufacturing systems – editorial. *International Journal of Production Economics* 62: 1–6.

Gunasekaran A and Ngai E (2005) Build-to-order supply chain management: A literature review and framework for development. *Journal of Operations Management* 23: 423–451.

Hakansson H (1987) *Industrial Technological Development: A Network Approach*. London: Croom Helm.

Handfield R and Bechtel C (2002) The role of trust and relationship structure in improving supply chain responsiveness. *Industrial Marketing Management* 31: 367–382.

Harland C, Brenchley R and Walker H (2003) Risk in supply networks. *Journal of Purchasing & Supply Management* 9(2): 51–61.

Harland C, Lamming R and Cousins P (1999) Developing the concept of supply strategy. *International Journal of Operations & Production Management* 19(7): 650–673.

Harland CM, Zheng J, Lamming RC, Johnsen TE (2001) A taxonomy of supply networks. *Journal of Supply Chain Management* 37(4): 21–27.

Harrison A (1993) *Just-In-Time Manufacturing in Perspective*. London: Prentice Hall.

Hines P (1994) *Creating World Class Suppliers*. London: Pitman.

Hines P and Rich N (1997) The seven value stream mapping tools. *International Journal of Operations & Production Management* 17(1): 46–64.

Hines P, Holweg M and Rich N (2004) Learning to evolve: A review of contemporary lean thinking. *International Journal of Operations & Production Management* 24(10): 994–1011.

Hines P, Lamming R, Jones D, Cousins P and Rich N (2000) *Value Stream Management: Strategy & Excellence in the Supply Chain*. UK: FT Prentice Hall.

Holmström J, Holweg M, Khajavi SH and Partanen J (2016) The direct digital manufacturing (r) evolution: Definition of a research agenda. *Operations Management Research* 9(1–2): 1–10.

Holweg M and Pil F (2001) Successful build-to-order strategies – start with the customer. *Sloan Management Review*, Fall: 74–83.

Holweg M and Pil F (2005) *The Second Century: Reconnecting Customers and Value Chain through Build-to-Order. Moving Beyond Mass and Lean in the Auto Industry*. Cambridge, MA: MIT Press.

Howard M, Jeanrenaud S and Correia F (2012) Desso and the cradle-to-cradle challenge: Rethinking carpet as a closed loop supply system. *European Case Clearing House* 612-031-1.

Howard M, Wu Z, Jia F, Caldwell N and König C (2016) Performance based contracting in the UK defence industry: Exploring triadic dynamics between government, OEMs and suppliers. *Industrial Marketing Management* 59: 63–75.

James-Moore S and Gibbons A (1997) Is lean manufacture universally relevant? An investigative methodology. *International Journal of Operations & Production Management* 17(9): 899–911.

Johnsen TE (2011) Supply network delegation and intervention strategies during supplier involvement in product development. *International Journal of Operations & Production Management* 31(6): 286–708.

Kidd P (1994) *Agile Manufacturing – Forging new Frontiers*. Wokingham, UK: Addison Wesley.

King A and Lenoz M (2001) Lean and green? An empirical examination of the relationship between lean production and environmental performance. *Production & Operations Management* 10(3): 455–471.

Kleindorfer P and Saad G (2005) Managing disruption risks in supply chains. *Production & Operations Management* 14: 53–68.

Kumar S and Malegeant P (2006) Strategic alliance in a closed-loop supply chain: A case of manufacturer and eco-non-profit organization. *Technovation* 26: 1127–1135.

Lamming R (1993) *Beyond Partnership – Strategies for Innovation and Lean Supply*. London: Prentice-Hall.

Lamming RC, Johnsen TE, Zheng J and Harland CM (2000) An initial classification of supply networks. *International Journal of Operations & Production Management* 20(6): 675–691.

Leach A (2013) Supply chain reactions. *Supply Management* 18(2): 14–15.

Lee HL (2002). Aligning supply chain strategies with product uncertainties. *California Management Review* 44(3): 105–119.

Lewis M (2000) Lean production and sustainable competitive advantage. *International Journal of Operations & Production Management* 20(8): 959–978.

Manuj I and Mentzer J (2008) Global supply chain risk management. *Journal of Business Logistics* 29(1): 133–155.

Mason-Jones R, Naylor B and Towill B (2000) Engineering the leagile supply chain. *International Journal of Agile Management Systems* 2(1): 54–61.

McDonough W and Braungart M (2009) *Cradle-to-Cradle*: *Remaking the Way We Make Things*. London: Random House.

McFarlan F and Young F (2002) Li & Fung: Internet issues. *Harvard Business School Case Study* 9-301-009. December.

Miemczyk J and Howard M (2008) Managing global auto operations: Supply strategies for build-to-order. *Supply Chain Management – An International Journal* 13(1): 3–8.

Mollenkopf D, Stolve H, Tate W and Ueltschy M (2010) Green, lean, and global supply chains. *International Journal of Physical Distribution & Logistics Management* 40(1/2): 14–41.

Monden Y (1983) *Toyota Production System – A Practical Approach to Production Management*. Atlanta, GA: Industrial Engineering and Management Press.

Narasimhan R and Talluri S (2009) Perspectives on risk management in supply chains. *Journal of Operations Management* 27: 114–118.

Naylor J, Naim M and Berry D (1999) Leagility: Interfacing the lean and agile manufacturing paradigm in the total supply chain. *International Journal of Production Economics* 62: 107–18.

New SJ (2010) The transparent supply chain. *Harvard Business Review* 28(10): 76–82.

New SJ and Brown D (2011) The four challenges of supply chain transparency. *European Business Review*, July–August: 4–6.

Ohno T (1988) *The Toyota Production System: Beyond Large-scale Production*. Portland, OR: Productivity Press.

Pagell M and Wu Z (2009) Building a more complete theory of sustainable supply chain management using case studies of 10 exemplars. *Journal of Supply Chain Management* 45(2): 37–56.

Pines J (1992) *Mass Customization: The New Frontier in Business Competition*. Boston, MA: Harvard Business Review Press.

Rossetti C and Choi T (2005) On the dark side of strategic sourcing: Experiences from the aerospace industry. *The Academy of Management Executive* 19(1): 46–60.

Rossetti C and Choi T (2008) Supply management under high goal incongruence: An empirical examination of disintermediation in the aerospace supply chain. *Decision Sciences* (39)3: 507–540.

Rother M and Shook J (1988) *Learning to See: Value Stream Mapping to Create Value and Eliminate Muda*. Cambridge, MA: The Lean Enterprise Institute.

Sako M (1992) *Prices, Quality and Trust*. Cambridge, UK: Cambridge University Press.

Salvador F, Forza C and Rungtusanatham M (2002) Modularity, product variety, production volume, and component sourcing: Theorizing beyond generic prescriptions. *Journal of Operations Management* 20(5): 549–575.

Savaskan R, Bhattacharya S and Van Wassenhove L (2004) Closed loop supply chain models with product remanufacturing. *Management Science* 50(2): 239–252.

Shapiro B, Rangan K and Sviokla J (1992) Staple yourself to an order. *Harvard Business Review*, July–August: 162–171.

Shingo S (1988) *Non-stock Production: The Shingo System for Continuous Improvement*. Cambridge, MA: Productivity Press.

Simpson D and Power D (2005) Using the supply relationship to develop lean and green suppliers. *Supply Chain Management: An International Journal* 10(1): 60–68.

Spekman R and Davis E (2004) Risky business: Expanding the discussion on risk and the extended enterprise. *International Journal of Physical Distribution & Logistics Management* 34(5): 414–433.

Spengler T and Schröter M (2003) Strategic management of spare parts in closed-loop supply chains – a systems dynamics approach. *Interfaces* 33(6): 7–17.

Stahel WR and Reday-Mulvey G (1976) The potential for substituting manpower for energy. *Report to the Commission of the European Communities*, Brussels.

Stahel WR and Reday-Mulvey G (1981) *Jobs for Tomorrow: The Potential for Substituting Manpower for Energy*. New York: Vantage Press.

Stock J and Boyer S (2009) Developing a consensus definition of supply chain management: A qualitative study. *International Journal of Physical Distribution & Logistics Management* 39: 690–711.

Svensson G (2000) A conceptual framework in the analysis of vulnerability in supply chains. *International Journal of Physical Distribution & Logistics Management* 30(9): 731–749.

Swank H (2003) The lean service machine. *Harvard Business Review*, October: 123–129.

Wickens P (1987) *The Road to Nissan: Flexibility, Quality & Teamwork*. London: Macmillan Press.

Womack JP and Jones DT (1994) From lean production to the lean enterprise. *Harvard Business Review* 72(2): 93–103.

Womack JP and Jones DT (1996) Beyond Toyota: How to root out waste and pursue perfection. *Harvard Business Review*, Sept.–Oct.: 140–144.

Womack JP and Jones DT (2003) *Lean Thinking: Banish Waste and Create Wealth in Your Corporation*. 2nd edn, New York: Free Press, Simon & Schuster.

Womack JP and Jones DT (2005) Lean consumption. *Harvard Business Review*, March: 1–11.

Womack JP, Jones DT and Roos D (1990) *The Machine That Changed the World*. New York: Rawson Associates.

Zsidisin GA and Ritchie B (eds) (2008) *Supply Chain Risk: A Handbook of Assessment, Management, and Performance* (Vol. 124). Springer Science & Business Media.

CHAPTER 9

Service-based supply chains

LEARNING OBJECTIVES

By the end of this chapter you should be able to:

- Define what is meant by service operations, servitization and service-dominant logic;

- Discuss the role of purchasing and supply in service-based business models;

- Understand the significance of operating models such as 'power by the hour' and 'contracting for availability';

- Discuss the implications for buyer–supplier collaboration in outcome-based models involving complex performance;

- Analyse a supply chain in relation to potential for remanufacturing and product recovery;

- Discuss the connection between service-based business models and sustainability.

9.0 Introduction

This chapter introduces the concept of services to the supply chain as an important source of adding value and as a distinct yet complementary approach to production operations. It is sometimes easy to mistake the supply chain as merely an efficient mechanism for the delivery of goods and indeed many people readily associate fast-moving consumer goods with the term 'supply chain'. The reality today, however, is that many organizations particularly in the West derive most of their revenue from complex bundles of services delivered downstream from production. This is not to say that products are no longer important (they are). We argue that products and services must be understood as an integrated package that has major implications when it comes to dealing with issues of extended life cycle, designing product recovery systems, emergent new operating models and how organizations such as manufacturers will increasingly engage with suppliers and customers in future in order to become more sustainable.

9.1 The rise of service operations

Although the concept of service alongside the use of goods has existed since the earliest recorded society, it is only in the last 30 years that the orientation and importance of services in their own right, not just in relation to the product, has begun to be seriously examined (e.g. Potts, 1988; Quinn *et al.*, 1990; Oliva and Kallenberg, 2003; Araujo and Spring, 2006). Products and production have tended to dominate thinking in business management not only because their strong physical characteristics have often defined the nature of the enterprise, but also because the majority of a supply chain's resources are committed to product design, manufacture and delivery. In his seminal paper on the rise of service management, Johnson (1994) describes the origins of production and operations as based on a 300-year evolution of factory and pre-factory, craft development, where the core operation in the organization typically accounts for around 70 per cent of manpower and 80 per cent of the company's total assets. It is perhaps no surprise then that management research has traditionally focused on the role played by manufacturing with only limited attention devoted to services and service operations management. Today, services are recognized as the fastest growing source of economic revenue around the world. This means not just in terms of the value represented by support services in the aftermarket, or the potential for new markets using Internet-driven smart technology, but the recognition that all industrial sectors are fundamentally affected by services and the quality of their service operations (Roth and Menor, 2003; Corrêa *et al.*, 2007).

A legacy of the dominance of production-orientated thinking is the tendency by scholars to emphasize the *differences* between products and services (e.g. intangibility, heterogeneity, perishability) from either a manufacturing or marketing perspective, instead of highlighting areas of intersection and similarity (Silvestro *et al.*, 1992; Van Looy *et al.*, 1998). Such a polarized view makes little sense today given the inexorable slide in the West towards a post-industrial society, where service-based sectors including finance, healthcare, IT telecoms and tourism represent the majority of a developed country's total economic output. Hence current thinking in management literature asks how businesses can integrate products and services to deliver value via 'service-driven supply chains' (Youngdahl and Loomba, 2000). Such business models that incorporate services into the core operation are increasingly being applied in the UK and US, where service industries now account for between 80 to 90 per cent of the total labour force employed (IfM-IBM, 2007). While the role of the product remains significant, the importance of value-added services such as extended warranties, customer support and product upgrades are increasingly recognized as key to expanding the firm's capability to compete beyond traditional measures of manufacturing competitiveness such as cost, quality, flexibility and delivery (Youngdahl and Loomba, 2000). Service-based supply chains, therefore, acknowledge the value of activity at all stages of the product life cycle, particularly those delivered downstream of production operations, and now involve combinations of in-service support including reverse-loop logistics activities such as product recovery.

Note 9.1

London 2012 Olympics and buying services

The London 2012 Olympics was the first sustainable games with core procurement principles supported by a range of policy documents including a *Sustainable Sourcing* Code and a *Diversity and Inclusion Charter*. Comprising 17 days of competition and involving 205 nations, 10,500 athletes, 70,000 volunteers and 8 million tickets issued, the London games organising committee had to get their event planning right first time given the immovable deadline and intense media interest. In terms of buying the necessary goods (e.g. buildings) and services (e.g. catering, media, security), interestingly over 60% of the suppliers were comprised of SMEs. All suppliers of the games were reminded of the need to observe the key themes of the games: **climate change, waste, biodiversity, inclusion** and **healthy living**. However, while the games were ultimately heralded as a great success, the challenges of buying services for such a large-scale event were demonstrated by the 'G4S fiasco': the British security group who failed to provide enough guards at the London Olympics, costing it around £50 million. G4S Chief Executive Nick Buckles was forced to apologize in a televised session in Westminster for blunders over recruitment which forced the British government to deploy extra troops to guard the London Olympics at the last minute.

Considerable textbook space in the past has been devoted to trying to define the precise attributes of products and services. The result has been an impression where both are easily distinguishable and therefore largely delivered and consumed apart from one another. As research into service operations has developed it is now regarded that there are very few examples of 'pure' goods and services, with almost all business models representing a combination or blended approach. Even a live concert, sporting event or counselling session involves combining elements of both (Note 9.1). Traditional definitions incorporate concepts around intangibility, heterogeneity, inseparability and perishability: the 'IHIP' model, which some authors argue only distinguishes products and services from a manufacturing perspective (Vargo and Lusch, 2004). Goedkoop *et al.* (1999) define a product as a tangible commodity manufactured to be sold and, put simply, as something capable of falling on your toe! Confusingly, a service is sometimes defined by what it is not, i.e. a product (Schemmer, 1995), and the term 'service' can be used to describe the level of performance, as in delivering good service. For the purposes of this chapter services refer to a commercial offering which include elements such as maintenance, repair, support, upgrade, warranty and insurance (Baines *et al.*, 2009).

Despite calls for greater integration between products and services during the production and delivery process, it is important to acknowledge the growing body of literature dedicated to the study of services in their own right and the emerging field of service operations management (Oliva and Kellenburg, 2003; Johnson and Clark, 2005; Araujo and Spring, 2006, 2009; Jacob and Ulaga, 2008; Baines *et al.*, 2009). Although not possible to review all aspects of services in this chapter, a helpful starting point in understanding some of the basic service characteristics and how they affect the supply chain is the service operations view of

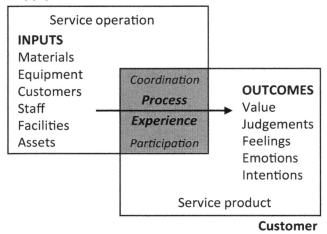

Figure 9.1 Managing the service operation

Source: Adapted from Johnson and Clark (2005).

the transformation model (Figure 9.1). The traditional view of operations management involves the transformation model as consisting of inputs, i.e. raw materials, which are transformed via production into outputs, i.e. finished products. The manufacturing process involves fabrication of components and assembly of parts, and means there is often a considerable *separation* or length of time between manufacturing and the customer actually receiving the goods: an aspect which distinguishes it from service operations which usually requires a high degree of real-time interaction between the customer and supplier.

While the service operations version of the model includes inputs such as materials, technology and equipment, it also includes customers who undergo their own process experience as part of the transformation, where outcomes involve a 'service product' incorporating a complex combination of value, emotions, judgements and future intentions (Figure 9.1). Presenting the service operation as a simultaneous experience in this way suggests that, unlike more traditional views of manufacturing 'the customer's experience is an intrinsic part of the operations process' (Johnson and Clark, 2005: 10). The idea of process experience and simultaneity in relation to service operations presents a considerable opportunity and challenge to supply chains in understanding what really represents value in terms of the buyer–supplier relationship: a reoccurring theme in this book. One good example where the service operation is critical to the customer experience is the running of a ski resort (see Note 9.2).

Services pose the idea that unique impressions are formed of the enterprise by both internal and external customers, all of whom are involved with operational and supply chain processes and despite their importance to the performance outcome, cannot be wholly captured or controlled by traditional product-based measures. Figure 9.1 therefore shows a simple representation of managing services and service operations with the process experience of the customer, in conjunction with staff and equipment, forming the central element to the

Note 9.2
Service supply chains and technology in ski resorts

We usually associate supply chain management with manufacturers that source physical materials into finished products and deliver these to customers. However, supply chains also need to be managed in 'pure' service operations such as the tourism industry. In the case of ski resorts the various actors involved have to make sure operations are managed in order to satisfy (and thrill) customers, and good supply chain management is all part of this.

Ski resort operators, such as hotels and restaurants, clearly have to source a range of materials that will be transformed into finished outputs. For example, they need to source meat and vegetables for food. As nature loving customers increasingly expect sustainable offerings, more and more hotels strive to source local produce as part of their efforts to offer a sustainable and regional culinary experience. Likewise, many hotels work hard to reduce their energy consumption and rely on renewal energy such as solar or hydro power. Many resorts are either car free, allowing only electric buses and taxis, such as Swiss high-end resort Zermatt, that is well-known for its strong sustainability profile (see: https://www.zermatt.ch/en/sustainability).

One critical service supply chain issue concerns the management of capacity. Where product supply chains need to manage capacity to keep lead times short with minimum inventory, service supply chains manage capacity in order to reduce the time customers spend queuing. One particular capacity constraint for ski resorts is lift capacity: "mile hungry" skiers do not want to waste their time in lift queues but spend as much time as possible on the slopes. Old-fashioned lift systems still hamper some resorts that have struggled to invest in new efficient lift systems, but modern resorts have invested in gondolas or chair lifts with capacities of up to 4000 or even 5000 passengers per hour. These transform the customer experience as they greatly reduce the time spent in lift queues.

RFID technology is now widely used to reduce lift queuing. Ski passes contain an RFID tag so that skiers no longer have to take out their card and show it (in the cold...), but can leave the ski pass in their pocket for it to be registered by an RFID card reader as they pass through the lift barrier. RFID technology can also enhance the customer experience by tracking ski or snowboard metrics (e.g. total miles or max speed) and sharing this on social media. North American resort Vail implemented an RFID system in the 2008-2009 season, connecting visitors through a platform called EpicMix, which gives information on snow conditions, live webcams, trail maps, and link experiences via iPhone or Android apps. RFID technology also reduces ski pass fraud and can even help with mountain safety as skier movements through the lift systems are tracked.

Naturally, ski resorts cannot offer their services without snow and with global warming affecting snow falls, snow cannons have become widespread in recent years. This has raised environmental concerns regarding water supplies and energy consumption to operate snow cannons. Usually, water is sourced from reservoirs, streams or lakes but heavy-treated sewage water is also used in some resorts. With high energy consumption from snow making machines, one option is to install wind turbines to produce the required electricity. Skiing has become big business, but face many future challenges that will make service operations and supply chain management ever more important.

delivery of a desired outcome. Understanding the subtle challenges of service operations, as a distinct departure from production operations, means managers now need to consider how to manage the response from multiple customers in terms of their experiences in real time, coordinating different parts of the organization, encouraging innovation, and managing short-term and long-term tasks simultaneously (Johnson, 1994; Johnson and Clark, 2005). Such challenges make a marked change to traditional production-centric concepts such as quality (e.g. physical dimensions, part conformance) and delivery lead time (e.g. logistics and information efficiency), introducing new questions over how to measure and maximize value for the duration of the customer relationship.

A wide range of terminology has grown around the rise in services and service operations literature including terms such as 'servitization' (Vandermerwe and Rada, 1988; Voss, 2008), 'integrated solutions' (Davies *et al.*, 2006), 'service-dominant logic' (Vargo and Lusch, 2004), 'service science' and 'service innovation' (IfM-IBM, 2007). The increasing influence of supply chain management has played a considerable role in driving the language of services into everyday purchasing and supply business usage (e.g. Lindberg and Nordin, 2008), particularly the involvement of outsourcing decisions requiring managers to consider exactly what type of outcomes are desired and who in the supply chain is responsible for their delivery. Vandermerwe and Rada (1988) were the first to publish their work on what they termed the 'servitization of business' where corporations add value to their corporate offerings through services. 'Corporations [are] increasingly offering fuller market packages or bundles of customer-focused combinations of goods, services, support, self-service and knowledge. But services are beginning to dominate' (Vandermerwe and Rada, 1988: 314). They argue that there are three reasons why manufacturing firms should servitize: to lock out competitors, to lock in customers, and to increase the levels of product differentiation. Yet the concept of bundling has proved problematic for some manufacturers used to their production-centric rather than market-centric models which emphasize high volume and repeatability. Creating a 'bundle' is the term used by several leading twentieth-century strategists to describe the coordination or grouping together of resources, products, services and knowledge in order to sell it in the most attractive way to the customer (Penrose, 1959; Porter, 1985). An example of bundling is where a smartphone is sold with the capability built in to offer a range of functionality such as faster broadband, video streaming, remote billing, the latest games and handset support applications, but the customer must pay extra to activate their specific choice of configuration. The limitation of the bundling approach is where the customer no longer wishes to receive all of the attributes offered as part of the standard package, and competitor firms are able to offer different product-service combinations to meet the specific needs of the market. Such differentiation is often achieved by offering various levels of service and designed around a standard core product.

There is some debate, however, over whether servitization genuinely represents new thinking or such a concept has existed alongside the product as a longstanding extension of the delivery process. Voss (2008) argues that servitization and the bundling of goods and services has been with us for some time, with a number of industry sectors already having well established involvement in managing their installed base by incorporating servicing into their core product offering, e.g. elevators, mainframe computers, commercial laundry services. IBM has learnt to care about services because it realized in the 1980s that its primary source of growth was coming not from selling hardware due to personal computers quickly becoming commoditized, but focusing on customer-orientated services (Cusumano, 2008) reaching around 50 per cent of total revenue in 2004. IBM's growth depends on the ability to provide what it calls business performance transformation services to its clients. This means not just installing complex computers into the core of their client's business network, but providing a wide range of business-to-business information support and optimization services such as strategic outsourcing, business performance transformation and customer call centres (Figure 9.2). However they are described or defined, one thing is certain: services have become an essential component to twenty-first-century business practice and will continue to play an increasingly important role across the supply chain in driving performance.

The increasing focus on services integration (Oliva and Kallenberg, 2003) and the blurring between products and services means a new take on competitive strategy, based on the provision of total service or 'integrated solutions' (Davies *et al.*, 2006; Brax and Jonsson, 2009) where preventative maintenance and other support packages are central to the delivery process and included by multinationals such as IBM, Hewlett-Packard and General Electric. Companies ranging from capital products to janitorial supplies have begun to view the concept of adding services, creating value packages for their new products and providing '24/7' servicing as not only a significant revenue generator, but also an advantage to getting closer to customers and delaying the margin-eroding characteristic of product commoditization (Oliva and Kallenberg, 2003; Corrêa *et al.*, 2007).

Taken from a customer perspective, why would a customer buy a servitized product? The answer is not always straightforward. In the 1970s, televisions were rented because they were

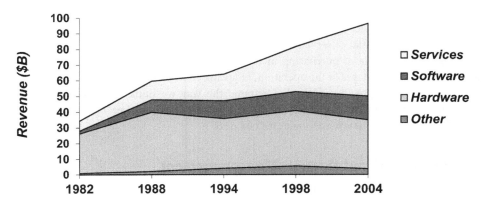

Figure 9.2 Business services enabled by advances in IT drive economic growth at IBM
Source: IBM (2007).

unreliable and rental agreements included servicing which mitigated risk for the user against breakdown (Voss, 2008). A more recent example is the UK's Ministry of Defence whose initiative to develop through-life capability which focused on considering ways of delivering value at all stages of defence equipment's life cycle (not just cost considerations at the initial purchase stage) as part of a prolonged programme to reduce spending across the air, sea and land forces. This meant outsourcing from the public domain work long associated with the military and now being offered to private firms on the basis of competitive tendering.

Given the general trend of manufacturing moving eastwards, gravitating towards low-cost countries, the debate in the West over services is about the choices open to public and private organizations in how they manage their installed base of equipment or facilities, e.g. generators, trucks, ships, hospitals. This may mean focusing less on new build capital projects and more on leveraging the revenue potential for supporting assets already in use as part of downstream supply chain operations. The high proportion of existing products or equipment in comparison to new sales in the market, known as the 'installed base', makes economic sense for manufacturers to focus on service support packages for the customer (Neely, 2008). Lindberg and Nordin (2008) argue that a new complexity is emerging in procurement, driven by the rise in service-dominant business logic and the associated issues around service intangibility. This means a higher proximity to relational issues between customer and supplier at all stages of the life cycle, and not simply a case of suppliers meeting the basic contractual obligations at the product's installation. Today, there is a shift towards attempts to evaluate quality of service by suppliers achieving predefined service level agreements or 'SLAs'. The SLA approach involves considering overall performance levels delivered over time often by several organizations, where performance is expressed as an outcome of the whole operation, e.g. reliability expressed in hours/days of uptime, flexibility in terms of choice available to the customer, sustainability in terms of reductions in carbon footprint or landfill. SLAs are more effective than traditional short-term target setting, because they can be used to bind supply chain partners together as a means of motivating firms to adopt a sense of collective action towards achieving a desired end result for the enterprise.

The recognition of services as a major source of added customer value and revenue means more than just managing customer relationships after a product has been sold. The rise of service operations has prompted a shift in operations and supply chain literature, where emergent product-service thinking now incorporates the dynamics of adapting to structural change, and the potential of services to add value but also risk to the firm, raising serious questions over the role of purchasing in the process. In looking beyond manufacturing, purchasing affects all stages of the operation, requiring concepts such as product life cycle to engage with new business models that reframe the way we think about supply chains. Examples of such models include: through-life management, power by the hour and contracting for availability, which are examined next.

9.2 Purchasing and through-life management

Purchasing has undergone a considerable evolution over the past 30 years particularly in areas such as the commissioning of new equipment (e.g. ships, planes) and construction of complex facilities (e.g. schools, highways, hospitals). Its traditional role, chiefly one of searching the market for the cheapest bid, meant suppliers and contractors were assessed on the basis of price as part of reaching a contractual agreement, with little concern over the longer-term implications for servicing, generally termed maintenance, repair and overhaul (MRO). Key partners including prime contractors and 'commissioners' (often central government) viewed the success of a project in terms of the platform or facility being built within budget and according to schedule, with concern for downstream support often treated separately and seen as a periphery issue, not a priority.

Possibly as a result of longer-than-expected life spans of twentieth-century equipment and facilities, or difficulties in using short-term measures to predict support requirements that spanned several decades or more, the use of contracts alone to retain product maintenance and upgrade services from the supply base has been problematic in the past. The reasons for failure vary considerably, for instance: poor systems of project or programme control, over-distinction between product and service elements in the contract, unforeseen union intervention, lack of consistency in government policy and poor levels of stakeholder collaboration. Generally speaking, however, there is a greater emphasis today on the need of a more central role for procurement (Stremersch *et al.*, 2001; Lindberg and Nordin, 2008). As complex product-service systems such as warships, highways and hospitals progress through their life cycle, it is often public procurement that holds operational responsibility and has to make escalating payments to private contractors (who work strictly to the letter of the contract) in order to maintain ageing yet essential national infrastructure. Such arbitrary contractual working practices have now largely ceased thanks to numerous improvement programmes and public–private initiatives emphasizing the need for closer, more joined-up industrial collaboration (NAO, 2003, 2007). Yet a period in the UK from the 1970s to 1980s will remain notorious for its typically confrontational and litigious industrial relationships (e.g. automotive, railways, shipyards and coal production), fuelled by restrictive union practices and the widespread use of 'cost plus' contracts where rigid agreements between the public procurer and private contractor often meant firms could claim additional payments for any construction or maintenance work considered to be outside the terms of the original agreement (Sanderson, 2009).

As the role of purchasing and supply has become more prominent in the organization, the value of including a procurement professional in preliminary talks with suppliers before production commences is now recognized as standard practice. It means increasing the chance of reduced costs further down the line by considering life-cycle issues such as service support, disassembly and product recycling *upfront* at the same time as initial platform or facility design. By using the purchasing function to build stronger buyer–supplier relationships at the beginning of a construction programme, and as part of the process of drawing up of working agreements and incentives (e.g. encouraging suppliers to reduce costs, keep to schedule and continuously innovate), a significant benefit is often shorter and more flexible contracts. Contracts designed with clear incentives enable suppliers to continue working in the event of a problem and, providing appropriate measures are in place to do so, actively seek a solution as part of the customer–supplier team rather than simply stopping work and waiting to consult with a legal representative over contractual responsibilities. Such cohesive buyer–supplier relationships are not easily achieved, and require considerable nurturing, involvement of purchasing from 'day one' of project planning and leadership skills from the prime organization (Brady and Davies, 2011). There is always the temptation in large projects involving service support programmes to create distance between firms in an attempt to control them, to outsource responsibility, and ultimately put any blame on the lower and less powerful tiers of the supply chain. The ultimate test of any buyer–supplier relationship, therefore, is when an issue arises between the partners that behaviours do not dissolve into confrontational-type firm territorialism, but the goals of the project or programme are put first and resolution achieved through joint problem solving, creativity and innovation.

It is only relatively recently, from the 1990s on, that thinking around product life cycle and through-life management has begun to change the sometimes negative early perceptions of service support as an ancillary activity or even a 'necessary evil' which could be mitigated through the product's disposal and purchase of new equipment. With the rising cost of build programmes making regular new product acquisitions prohibitive, many organizations view the prospect of capturing supplementary services or 'going downstream' (Quinn *et al.*, 1990; Anderson and Narus, 1995; Wise and Baumgartner, 1999) and offering 'full service contracts' as one solution to cutting costs and boosting revenue (Stremersch *et al.*, 2001). In order to capitalize on the opportunities offered downstream of the initial design, build or construction phase, supplier firms must first consider the generic processes associated with the facility or platform lifecycle. To take the defence industry as an example, Figure 9.3 shows the CADMID (concept, assessment, demonstration, manufacture, in-service support and disposal) model as a standardized view of all the major phases military equipment undergoes during its life. It illustrates both the traditional role of purchasing as concerned primarily only with design and build, and the shift towards end-to-end procurement or 'supply management' that recognizes the importance of considering all stages of the product life cycle. By integrating the requirements of in-service support through planned expenditure, product upgrades, use of logistics data and supplier involvement, the advantage of the through-life management approach is that it includes the 10- to 50-year life-cycle issues at the same time as the initial project or programme design, enabling long-term planning to be built around projected risk, shared benefit and overall performance requirements. Such an approach means contracts can be proactively developed to reflect the precise needs of the programme and can also incentivize desired supply chain behaviours from the outset.

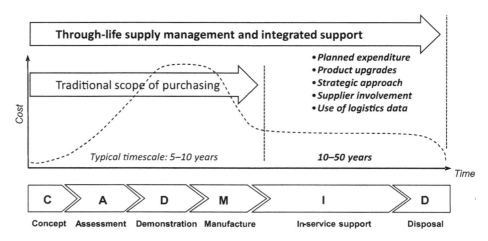

Figure 9.3 Purchasing and the CADMID cycle

Sources: Adapted from MoD (2005); Johnsen *et al.* (2009).

One of the most significant changes in the UK defence industry is the shift towards a policy of 'smart acquisition' and, more specifically, through-life management (TLM). TLM is broadly derived from product life-cycle management literature and defined in public procurement circles as 'an integrated approach to all … acquisition processes, planning and costing activities across the whole system and whole life of a project' (NAO, 2003). The concept has become a driving force in defence procurement policy (MoD, 2005), for example where defence contracts attempt to link all phases of the product-service life cycle, from conceptualization and design, to manufacture, support and disposal of products. This requires a new approach towards supply strategy and reveals some important trends where, in the past, the primary focus for industry contractors was to win contracts based on upstream design and manufacturing-based activity because this was where the firm perceived the quickest payback for minimum risk to be.

The concept of TLM fundamentally alters the relationship between the UK Ministry of Defence (MoD) and its strategic suppliers. A UK government white paper titled 'Defence Industrial Strategy' published in 2005 emphasized the need for through-life capability management based on open product architectures, allowing long-term upgrading and support, reflecting the shift away from successive generations of platform-orientated defence programmes. This new approach requires 'leaps of capability with major new procurements', towards 'a capability-based approach … a new paradigm centred on support, sustainability and the incremental enhancement of existing capabilities from technology insertions' (MoD, 2005: 17). An extreme example of the extended use of platforms is the B52 bomber used by the US Air Force, originally designed in 1949, but planned to continue to see active service until 2050 by which time it will be a 100-year-old airframe design! This implies that although innovation in the defence industry is considered critical, it will mainly happen through the continuous upgrading of existing technology platforms rather than the development of new stand-alone platform designs. Because of the increasing need to keep product platforms in service for as many decades as possible (the new generation of the UK's aircraft carriers are expected to be used for 50 years), technology insertion – or capability insertion – will be the concept used in the continuous upgrading of platforms with new technologies, such as IT software. In defence terms, the concept of TLM is captured in the CADMID life-cycle model (Figure 9.3) which reflects the anticipation that industrial relationships should change to enable the new focus through long-term, strategic and assured relationships. Through-life *capability* management, therefore, suggests a shift from a contractor's responsibility ending after they have built to the blueprint, towards proactive and participatory relationships involving the MoD 'buying capability' in terms of a supplier's total skill and knowledge, rather than the one-off purchase of a piece of equipment.

The procurement strategy of the UK's Ministry of Defence is to change its stance towards risk and benefit sharing with suppliers. This shift towards strategic alignment emphasizes a new focus on collaboration in relationships between the MoD and key suppliers. The view is that alignment will require industry visibility of the MoD's future plans for resource allocation and the MoD will need visibility of the industry business model: there will be much need for shared processes and partnering, especially as major suppliers gain responsibility for in-service support. There is also a perceived need for a total cost of ownership approach to costing as suppliers are required to guarantee 'end-to-end service provision'. Traditionally, however, there have been disincentives for suppliers to pay for repairs. Consequently, as suppliers take on more responsibility they seek new arrangements for sharing of gains, costs as well as risks: suppliers are dissatisfied with fixed price arrangements. The MoD recognizes that planning needs to be around whole-life costing and capability rather than a simple upfront purchase cost. MoD reports suggest use of incentivization of gain sharing to encourage industry and MoD to improve performance.

Some UK defence suppliers are worried that contractors will find savings to the detriment of aspects such as air safety (Haddon-Cave, 2009) and suppliers are not incentivized to over-maintain military aircraft as has traditionally been the case by armed forces MRO personnel (see Note 9.3). Nevertheless, general policy is to keep markets open, not just rely on one prime contractor. The defence IT and communications market, for example, remains open to all commercial Internet providers at present. This shift in supply chain strategy means a fundamental change in the relationship between the MoD and industry. In simple terms it means shifting from singular, static, formal and one-dimensional relationships, towards multiple, non-linear, dynamic, partnered and multidimensional relationships. Similar dimensions around purchasing and supply have inspired research into the phenomenon coined 'procuring complex performance', described next.

Note 9.3

Nimrod MRA4 aircraft disaster and the outsourcing of maintenance services

On September 2nd 2006, a Royal Air Force Nimrod surveillance aircraft was on a routine mission over Helmand Province in Southern Afghanistan in support of NATO and Afghani ground forces when it suffered a catastrophic mid-air fire leading to the total loss of the aircraft and death of all 14 crew members on board. In the subsequent investigations after the crash, the technical cause of the accident was found to be the escape of fuel after air-to-air refuelling, ignited by exposed elements of faulty electrical equipment. However an independent review titled 'The Loss of Nimrod XV230: A Failure of Leadership, Culture and Priorities' found the causes of the crash to be not just in terms of the aircraft's design flaws, which had failed to be spotted in a number of previous incidents, but a 'general malaise' that had affected the performance of checks carried out by the Integrated Project Team and two private firms acting as maintenance contractor and independent safety advisor. Senior judge Charles Haddon-Cave QC summed up the enquiry by saying that it was organisational causes which played a major part in the loss of the 40 year old Nimrod XV230. Significant structural changes took place in the MoD during the years when a crucial Nimrod Safety Case was being prepared, between 2001 and 2004. During this time the MoD was being downsized and shifting from functional to project orientated lines, internal organizations were amalgamated into larger more general purpose management structures, and the practice of outsourcing in-service support to industry was increasing.

Source: Haddon-Cave (2009).

9.2.1 Procuring complex performance

Procuring complex performance, or 'PCP', examines the multiple and often conflicting challenges of managing total supply chain operations during all phases of a major project or programme including design, build, service support and disposal (Caldwell and Howard, 2011; Lewis and Roehrich, 2009). As an emerging area in business-to-business research based on industry sectors such as building and construction, defence, transportation and healthcare, PCP seeks to combine theory in the areas of complexity, purchasing and supply, markets and innovation management. PCP poses that the traditional combination of hierarchy, linear project management and high levels of contractual control has increasing difficulty adapting to the dynamics of customer requirements today. This is particularly the case in mega-projects (van Marrewijk *et al.*, 2008) involving capital intensive public–private collaborations where there is an increased risk of oligopolistic market conditions (i.e. limited choice of supplier/ manufacturer) and the effects of political interference via government control.

Complex performance means a combination of delivering high value product or platform infrastructure, with long-term (often multi-decade) requirements for in-service support. The complexity element stems from the need for a significant number of operational and supply decisions, such as through-life asset management, product upgrade strategy, cost and risk modelling, new forms of contractual control and adoption of new business models that emerge over the duration of the life cycle. The addition of a procurement perspective highlights the need for a more coordinated and upfront approach to buying, made necessary by the task being so composed of sub-elements that it cannot be achieved by the sequential or additive achievement of individual transactions: an approach widely applied in the past to production-specific scenarios. The diminished importance of the individual transaction in managing complex performance and the rise of more embedded knowledge in supply relationships create a need for buyer–supplier agreements that focus on outcomes rather than tightly specified inputs or products across organizational boundaries. Put simply, the buying or commissioning of complex performance means going beyond managing the buyer– supplier interface, and involves a mindset shift from production-orientated delivery models towards the coordination of long-term assured services (Howard and Caldwell, 2014).

The procuring complex performance approach goes beyond traditional project management techniques such as Gantt chart methodologies that have a tendency to force predefined, sequential steps that conclude at completion of the facility or platform installation. PCP draws on the work known as Complex Product-Systems (CoPS) (Hobday, 1998; Davies and Hobday, 2005; Davies *et al.*, 2006). CoPS involve engineering-intensive products or systems supplied in single or small batches, usually tailored to meet the precise requirements of each customer. The creation of CoPS often involves extreme production and innovation complexity. Industries that supply CoPS are usually restricted markets with a few large suppliers facing a few large customers in each country. However, PCP differs from CoPS in four aspects:

- the focus on procurement and supply;
- customer value is delivered as an integrated product-service (not a product system) where a significant proportion of value is delivered as support services located up and downstream from manufacture/construction;

- the process of co-creation of value between partners involves a greater emphasis on the interplay between inter-firm relationships and contractual governance;
- CoPS are concerned first and foremost with technological progress, while PCP is focused on the sum of performance outcome and economic efficiency.

Where CoPS can be viewed as 'a subset of projects concerned with the development, manufacture and delivery of complex capital goods' (Davies and Hobday, 2005: 22), PCP speaks to the whole-life issues of complex projects, concerned as much with the performance capability to supply sustainable support and maintenance over extended periods, as the initial phases of design and build. There is more similarity between PCP and CoPS in the need for strong coordinating roles for the purpose of linking various stages of the project together (Davies and Hobday, 2005), leading Hobday (1998) to see project management and systems integration as the core capability for successful CoPS involving temporary structures consisting of many firms.

The extended, multi-decade timeframes typical of the PCP approach maximizes the opportunities for political interference and the waxing and waning of government policy drivers. See, for example, the concern with politically inspired interference in mega-projects (van Marrewijk *et al.*, 2008). Further, PCP suggests that the static world of matrix-based procurement models such as Kraljic (1983) are less suitable for such dynamic and political environments, and require further consideration around the co-creation of value between multiple stakeholders and management of extended, typically 40- to 50-year, life cycles. Such challenges involving the considerable timescales around service support, remanufacturing and end-of-life disposal can only be tackled if they are considered upfront at the beginning of

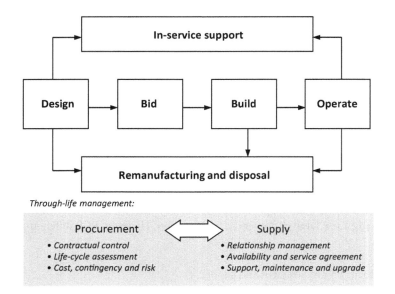

Figure 9.4 Managing procurement and supply across the extended life cycle

Source: Adapted from Caldwell and Howard (2011).

the programme or project before the design phase commences (Figure 9.4). This suggests, therefore, that all stakeholders including customers, buyers, suppliers and NGOs must come to an agreement at the beginning of working together to ensure the optimum outcome throughout the programme's total lifespan.

Figure 9.4 presents a vision for integrating the management of procurement and supply which draws from the PCP approach. Rather than show service support, remanufacturing and product disposal at the end of the process, it shows them as parallel streams of expertise considered upfront at the beginning of a project or programme, which run alongside the more traditional phases of design, bid, build and operate. The procurement and supply functions are included as separate yet coordinated groups of tasks, focusing initially during the start-up phase on contractual design and control, life-cycle assessment, cost, contingency and risk, moving increasingly towards longer-term issues such as service agreements, product maintenance, repair and upgrade (Figure 9.4; Caldwell and Howard, 2011).

PCP and other new performance-based operating models are similar in some respects to *outcome-based* supply chain thinking proposed by Melnyk *et al.* (2010). The governance literature has already reached a degree of agreement that a contract cannot, even in simpler contractual arrangements, hope to cover all eventualities and circumstances (Dyer and Singh, 1998; Poppo and Zenger, 2002). Given the necessity of a contract, therefore, under PCP it is likely that there will be a combination of relational and contractual approaches, varying in proportion over time but dominated by relational approaches. There is also a growing need to understand how the customer looks beyond output as a consequence of the purchasing decision, to buying an outcome that includes predefined performance measures (Davies and Brady, 2000; Melnyk *et al.*, 2010). The putting in place of organizational routines and learning processes (Davies and Brady, 2000) explains how suppliers of complex product systems build capabilities based on past performance to develop new lines of business or 'repeatable solutions'. There is a parallel here between solutions and the outcome-based approach where 'supply chains ... deliver one or more outcomes' (Melnyk *et al.*, 2010: 34). For example, selected outcomes will include measures scaled in proportion to their importance relative to the project such as cost, responsiveness, security, sustainability, resilience and innovation, as opposed to traditional delivery mechanisms based around task-orientated piecework. Once a blend of outcomes has been selected at the start of the project or programme, it influences critical characteristics in the design and build phase, and continues as a major focus into downstream support and disposal, delivered by the whole supply chain.

9.3 New operating models and the servitized supply chain

Of all the terms to emerge from recent business research, 'servitization' and the 'servitized supply chain' are probably the most well known by practitioners as a means to improving the manufacturing and industrial sectors performance (Baines *et al.*, 2009; Neely, 2008). The basic premise of the servitized supply chain is: 'in order to survive in developed economies manufacturing firms have to move up the value chain, innovating and creating ever more sophisticated products and services, so they do not have to compete on the basis of cost' (Neely, 2008: 103). With firms in the West having to cut costs by an average of 30 per cent in order to compete with goods manufactured in China, the importance of finding ways to differentiate in the global economy is paramount to their survival. Hence minimizing cost and maximizing revenue throughout the product life cycle is a top priority for firms across European and US industrial sectors. The renewed interest in modes of working such as 'pay-on-production' (Kuka robots), 'Power by the Hour' (Rolls-Royce) and 'pay per print' (Xerox), reflects the shift in emphasis away from product sales, to offering alternative forms of goods and services delivered in ways where customers can choose the method that suits them best. Such operating models demonstrate the need for a greater understanding of life-cycle considerations and the meaning of value to the customer, and have led to a shift in the way many firms contract for products and services. Two of the best known operating models are reviewed below:

9.3.1 Power by the Hour (PbtH)

This is a term originally coined in the 1960s to describe a support service provided for engines in the UK business jet aircraft sector. PbtH meant that for a fixed sum per flying hour, a complete engine and accessory replacement service was provided by the manufacturer, allowing the operator to forecast costs with great accuracy, and relieving the purchaser of the need to purchase stocks of engines and accessories. Rolls-Royce Plc reinvented the programme in the 1980s where the key feature of the model is that it undertakes to provide the operator with a fixed engine maintenance cost over an extended period of time. The benefits of the approach mean operators being assured of a smooth cost projection over a fixed period and avoiding unexpected costs associated with breakdowns; hence PbtH has become a popular option for many airlines. Although the 'term power by the hour' is commonly used across the industry, PbtH is owned and protected by Rolls-Royce, although other aircraft engine manufacturers such as General Electric and Pratt & Whitney offer similar packages. Unlike extended warranties purchased by consumers for a fixed payment to cover repairs on products like cars or white goods appliances, complex systems such as the engine, flight control and navigation modules found in aerospace and defence require more sophisticated relationships between buyers and suppliers. In these industries, it is very hard to guarantee product or component availability due to significant uncertainties in product reliability and usage, as well as inherent product complexity, resulting in large risks to both the customer and service provider. Service support in these industries was until relatively recently conducted using fixed-price or cost-plus contracts. Today, manufacturers are recognizing the value of offering product-service packages which offer an assured level of service for an all-inclusive, fixed price as part of PbtH and are now actively designing their systems with in-built support requirements for easier maintenance and repair.

9.3.2 Contracting for availability (CFA)

This was conceived by the UK Defence Equipment & Support (DE&S), a public organization under the control of the Ministry of Defence, in response to rising costs of supporting the UK's fleet of aircraft, tanks, surface warships and submarines. It is based on recent defence industrial strategy (MoD, 2005) where the responsibility for providing platform support services such as engineering, stores, training, IT systems and equipment upgrade is devolved from the military to selected suppliers. CFA was first conceived for small vessels such as minesweepers and coastal patrol ships, using a transformational staircase model to illustrate to contractors the shift in supply chain practice from 'traditional support', through 'spares inclusive' to 'contracting for availability' and ultimately 'contracting for capability': the ultimate level of service delivery. Although this new style of partnering with industry still requires a full legal contract, considerable emphasis is put on partnering principles such as mutual benefits, openness and trust, exchange of information, innovation, 'no surprises' and value for money. Above all, the working relationship between the MoD and industry is to emphasize a *no blame* policy, focusing on key performance indicators such as service level, measurement of performance linked to payment and continuous improvement.

The benefits of outsourcing logistical and repair activities to private contractors adopting CFA principles has been a fixed monthly rate of charter hire for each vessel, a fixed rate of maintenance charges, and a transfer of the majority of risk to the supplier in return for a pre-agreed fee: all of these have resulted in a lower overhead cost per ship. Further, the availability improvement in terms of warships ready to go to sea has increased also. Yet sceptics of these new agreements point out that while this approach may work for purpose-built vessels, supporting the maintenance requirements of older ships suffering from obsolescence issues means difficulties over predictability stemming from equipment unreliability. In other words, CFA support schemes seem to work well on new vessels, but are more problematic on older platforms when the original manufacturer may no longer exist and current suppliers are reluctant to accept the high levels of risk associated with service contracts involving legacy hardware, such as Nimrod aircraft (see Note 9.3).

Power by the hour and contracting for availability are good examples of new operating models that deploy the servitized supply chain approach. They consider all elements of the product life cycle in terms of its potential value, where supply chain collaboration is dependent as much on relationship management and incentives as on contractual obligation. Taking an upfront and outcome-based view of the programme that includes the uncertainties of long-

Note 9.4

The Rolls-Royce Engines TotalCare® package

The TotalCare® package was introduced in 2005 by Rolls-Royce who assumed responsibility for the long-term support of Olympus and Tyne gas turbines engines used in the Royal Navy's older warships in the UK. The £137 million contract is based on similar packages developed for the defence and civil aerospace business, and covers the turbines until they are decommissioned in 2016. A similar scheme is provided for the French, Belgium and Royal Netherland navies. Under the previous arrangements, the Royal Navy was responsible for all aspects of engine maintenance and repair, with requirements passed to Rolls-Royce through rigid, individual contracts. Now Rolls-Royce is responsible for all engine maintenance, overhaul and inventory management, basically ensuring power is available to keep the ships at sea for the duration of the contract with target cost-based prices for engine availability related to the number of running hours. An agreed fee is paid monthly to Rolls-Royce by the Ministry of Defence.

Source: Rolls-Royce (2006)

term use helps to ensure accommodation for future performance needs (e.g. IT software upgrades), which even if specifics are not yet known, can still be included as part of the plan for the overall package. Many variations on the PbtH and availability theme that shift from product-based delivery towards assured services have now emerged over the past ten years, and include a practice which seeks to cover legacy scenarios such as the TotalCare® solution for supporting older ships' turbines (Note 9.4).

9.4 Product-service systems (PSS)

The term product-service systems, or 'PSS', has evolved in the literature to describe integrated bundles of customer-focused products, services and knowledge-based activity which increase the value of a core offering (Manzini *et al.*, 2001; Mont, 2002; Aurich *et al.*, 2006). Interest in PSS has steadily increased as industrial firms seek new ways to compete and create value by shifting from production-dominant to service-dominant business models. PSS was initially perceived as part of the expansion of downstream activity such as maintenance, repair and overhaul, by leveraging value in areas such as customer support services and product upgrade (e.g. Potts, 1988; Quinn *et al.*, 1990). As interest in PSS research grew, new areas and perspectives were adopted, not only product and service-based, but themes such as complexity, project management and innovation began to emerge. Related to PSS is the work of Davies and Hobday (2005), who adopt the perspective of complex product systems, seeking to improve understanding of the characteristics and dynamics of innovation in the high-technology, high-value capital goods sector. A distinctive feature of PSS is the recognition that the 'physical product core' is surrounded by a non-physical service shell, often represented

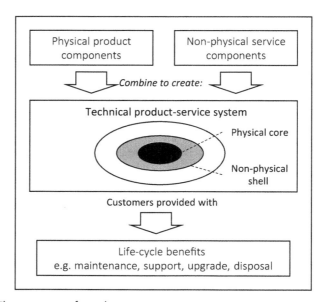

Figure 9.5   The structure of product-service systems

Source: Adapted from Aurich *et al.* (2006).

as concentric rings in schematic diagrams of PSS (Figure 9.5) which help to identify precisely where value is added in the delivery process and how these activities enable life-cycle-orientated benefits to the customer (Aurich *et al.*, 2006).

An important development in the rise of PSS thinking is the recognition that the distinction between product and service is unhelpful to business. What really counts is the 'nature of producer-user interactions and the institutional structure of production rather than on any essentialist feature of products and services' (Araujo and Spring, 2006: 797). While services are playing a more important role in manufacturing firms, considerably more by way of complexity remains to be discovered through exploring the novel combinations of customer–supplier interaction, contractual arrangements and infrastructure which articulate the requirement for high-performance outcomes (e.g. Caldwell and Howard, 2011; Lewis and Roehrich, 2009).

A dominant theme which has emerged over the past decade or so is the role of PSS in sustainable consumption, where PSS are divided into services providing value into the product life cycle. In this sense, PSS can be defined as a business innovation strategy offering a marketable mix of products and services jointly capable of fulfilling the client's needs, with the facility to offer higher added value and a smaller environmental impact as desired (Manzini *et al.*, 2001; Mont, 2002). The life-cycle design of technical product-service systems – introducing modularization, ease of maintenance, retrofitting and refurbishment considerations – means more sustainable production and consumption, offering economic, ecological and social benefits through improved product differentiation, consideration for the environment and focus on knowledge and skills from staff (Aurich *et al.*, 2006).

Sweitzer and Aurich (2010: 158) define industrial product service systems as 'customer life cycle-orientated combinations of products and services realized in an extended value creation network'. In the capital goods industry PSS are typically made up of a complex physical core which is enhanced during its life cycle by a range of mainly non-physical, complementary services which deliver value whilst in use (see Figure 9.5). The authors argue that where traditionally manufacturers have focused on the design, realization and distribution of products, increasingly their customers are expected to be provided with high-quality integrated services which are tailored to individual needs. To support this change, manufacturers have realized the merits of becoming service providers, not only keeping up existing product functionalities, but providing additional ones as well as a continuous stream of service options along the whole of the product life cycle. Manufacturers now have adopted life-cycle-orientated PSS that focus on customer solutions, and enabling the closer integration between product and service planning, design and operations. A particular challenge to continuous improvement of PSS life-cycle management is the process of standardized process description which requires all partners in the extended value network having a common understanding of the necessary design, production and servicing processes. Typically the processes furthest away from the manufacturer are the most difficult to control and yet it is the cooperation and information shared by the customer and contractors, towards the end of the life cycle, which are the most crucial to boost high rates of return in older products, which may be repairable or capable of disassembly for re-use and remanufacture. Improving the process for new generations of PSS requires the feedback information and return of product which, because of its low perceived economic value, is often the most difficult in terms of incentivizing the supply chain to deliver or retain.

9.5 Remanufacturing

It might seem odd to put 'remanufacturing' in a chapter about service-based supply chains. The process of product recovery is a key element of downstream sustainable supply chain activity, but one of the last and most difficult to control as it is often conducted many years after production. Remanufacturing is the disassembly and recovery of modules, sub-assemblies and (eventually) components from used machines or equipment including automobiles, trucks, computers and planes. It involves the repair, reconditioning, replacement and reassembly of worn-out components. Any parts which are judged to be sufficiently worn to affect the overall performance or expected life of the whole product are replaced. Where possible, the removed component is either reconditioned or broken down into its constituent material class for recycling. In essence, remanufacturing is a complex form of a product recovery process which differs from other recovery processes in its completeness: a remanufactured machine should match the same customer expectation as a new machine. Other forms of product recovery that can be distinguished from remanufacturing include reuse, repair, refurbishment and recycling (see Note 9.5).

There are a number of definitions for remanufacturing, one of the first being a published report by Lund (1984) who describes remanufacturing as:

> an industrial process in which worn-out products are restored to like-new condition. Through a series of industrial processes in a factory environment, a discarded product is completely disassembled. Useable parts are cleaned, refurbished, and put into inventory. Then the product is reassembled from the old parts (and where necessary new parts) to produce a unit fully equivalent and sometimes superior in performance and expected lifetime to the original new product.

The range of products capable of being remanufactured is very wide and includes: aerospace, air conditioning units, carpet tiles, compressors, defence equipment, excavation equipment, industrial food processing equipment, machine tools, office furniture, pumps and starter motors. There are three types of remanufacturing activities, each with different challenges:

- *Remanufacturing without identity loss* – with this method, a machine is rebuilt on a used product base, receiving all of the enhancements, expected life and warranty of a new machine. The physical structure, i.e. the chassis or frame, is inspected for soundness, with the whole product refurbished and critical modules overhauled, upgraded or replaced. This involves customized remanufacturing of complex and often one-off items such as machine tools, airplanes, computer mainframes, large medical equipment and other capital goods.

- *Remanufacturing by recoating of worn parts* – many engine parts and components are large and expensive and after a period of use become worn. An example is the cylinder engine bores in an engine block. Instead of disposing of them, remanufacturing has resulted in re-use of the parts by coating them with a special hardening plasma. Remanufacturing by recoating of parts is also very popular in the aircraft, geothermal pipes and automotive engine sector.

- *Repetitive remanufacturing without identity loss* – this method involves the additional challenge of scheduling the sequence of dependent sub-assembly processes and identifying the location of parts in the inventory buffers. There is a fine distinction here between repetitive remanufacturing without loss of identity and product overhaul. However, the critical difference is that remanufacturing is a complete process, where the final output has a like-new appearance and is covered by a warranty.

Note 9.5

Product recovery and the '5Rs'

There is more to the subject of product recovery as an important element in sustainable supply chain development than simply introducing terms such as recycling and remanufacture. As we can see from the definitions above, the term remanufacturing is applied only in specific conditions. However it can be easy to confuse remanufacturing with other methods of product recovery, hence a brief summary of the '5Rs' is provided here:

- *Reuse* – items that are used by a second customer without prior repair operations or as originally designed;

- *Repair* – the process of bringing worn or damaged components back to a functional condition;

- *Refurbish/recondition* – the process of restoring components to a functional state as per their original specification using methods such as resurfacing & repainting;

- *Remanufacture* – part of an industrial process where worn-out products are restored to a like-new condition;

- *Recycle* – the process of taking a component material and processing it to make the same material, or a useful degraded material.

As the importance of remanufacturing has grown, offering opportunities to turn used products into new ones, so too has the awareness of challenges such as choosing the appropriate reverse channel structure for product collection (Savaskan *et al.*, 2004), the varying condition of used components and means of collection, and imbalances in return and demand rates as part of production control (Guide, 2000). Technically speaking, a remanufactured product can be sold in new product markets, that is, there is no distinction between a remanufactured and a manufactured product. Yet few firms can match the established networks which demand high-volume, commodity-type replacement products such as Canon, Hewlett-Packard or Xerox's ink toner cartridges, for example, who boast a saving of 40–65 per cent in manufacturing costs through the re-use of parts and materials. Whilst similar programmes have achieved varying rates of success in sectors such as FMCG packaging, automotive components and carpet tiles, achieving optimal returns appears to favour shorter life-cycle products with relatively low complexity and disassembly implications in order to keep costs of reprocessing to a minimum. Some authors suggest that 'assumptions around centralized control' of reverse-loop supply chains in remanufacturing operations needs to be 'relaxed' (Savaskan *et al.*, 2004) in order to engage better with outlying stakeholders in the process, such as suppliers and customers, and encourage their participation in returning used goods and being agreeable to adopt new charging models and buying habits (i.e. accepting used goods for new). In short, the practice of remanufacturing increasingly needs to be viewed as core to sustainable supply chain planning, not as something at the periphery or 'end-of-pipeline' (Jayaraman *et al.*, 1999).

ISLABIKES, UK

Islabikes was founded in 2006 in the UK, when former professional cyclist Isla Rowntree decided to change the future of children's bikes forever. Islabikes sells premium children's bikes, and was started by Isla after her sister and other friends said they couldn't find decent bikes for their kids. When Isla looked into it she was appalled at what was available: prevailing bikes were too heavy, with too much material in terms of steel and aluminium, and much stronger than was required. In the 1980s, the mountain bike craze encouraged manufacturers to make kids' bikes even bigger, with oversized tubes, 'suspension forks' and triple chain sets: they were just a mass of steel. A child's power-to-weight ratio is actually very high, but the prevailing bikes were not ergonomically designed. The cranks were too long and standard handlebar fittings meant kids couldn't reach the brakes. So, while they passed safety standards, they were actually dangerous as kids couldn't stop the bike. Isla didn't want kids to have a poor first experience of cycling, and so with Islabikes she had a vision of giving all children a better experience. This has extended not only to designing bikes which are properly scaled for children to ride, but also towards considering what happens when the child grows out of their existing bike and needs a bigger one. Hence the Imagine Project was born.

Islabikes employs around 35 people, is based in Bromfield, Ludlow, and has an annual turnover of around £6million. While their headquarters are in the UK, manufacturing of the bikes is done in Vietnam and then shipped to Ludlow. Islabikes does the final assembly, including 'PDI' or pre-delivery inspection at its site, with the bikes then sold direct to customers, who place orders (and their preferences, accessories, etc.) by email, online or phone. In this way, Islabikes can cut out the retailer and third-party distributor, and go direct to the customer. The worldwide cycle industry has a complex supply chain structure. Taking the international brand Specialized as an example, its headquarters are in Morgan Hill, California, where the design, marketing, financing and human resource functions are based. But the actual manufacturing is carried out by third parties in Asia (Taiwan, Vietnam) who make bikes for other brands. These in turn get components made in another tier of specialist third-party suppliers (e.g. saddles, brakes, etc.). The bikes are built and finished to Specialized's specifications and then shipped to another set of third-party distributors, one in each country with the contract to supply Specialized bikes. These distributors have agreements with a specific bike dealer in every town who complete the final assembly.

Islabikes' business model means it has complete control of the PDI and hence the quality of the product as well as the safety of the set-up, and thus the child's experience of cycling. The employees have a rigorous training regime to learn the basic PDI routines with many months of practice and supervision.

CASE STUDY 9.1

Depending on the individual, it can quite feasibly take a few years to be 'signed off' on all models. Although not strictly necessary, the company supplements its rigorous internal training with an externally assessed Cytech accreditation which is nationally recognized across the UK. This allows the technician a broader understanding of bicycles beyond the models they work on every day. Isla is very influenced by lean manufacturing principles and ensures that her whole operation is about customer pull, and elimination of all wastes including wasted labour (e.g. wasting time looking for the correct tools for doing the PDI), where the work stations are bespoke designs with everything that the workers need. The stations are also on wheels so they can be moved around when the inventory builds up in the Ludlow warehouse.

The significance of the Imagine Project is that it rethinks the way bicycles will be made and supplied in the future. Its proposition is 'to manufacture and supply children's bikes for rent to the UK market'. Isla believes that the future supply chain will be based on renting the same product multiple times rather than selling it once. The products will be made in small factories close to the market. Ownership will be a thing of the past, and factories will retain ownership. Bicycles therefore will be rented to the user. When they are finished with (either because the owner no longer requires a bike, or has grown out of it) they will be returned to the factory, refurbished and rented to another rider. This will prevent precious raw materials from going into landfill.

Isla argues that 'we will have to make bikes that last for much longer than they do now so that we can rent them for as long as possible'. The bicycles will be designed so that when they finally reach the end of their lives all raw materials can be separated and reused. This is known as a 'closed-loop' or circular supply chain. The aim is that nothing will go into landfill. Indeed, it's anticipated that raw materials will become so precious that business and government will begin mining our landfill sites later this century to recover what was thrown away in the last. Islabikes have always been designed and made with longevity in mind and are renowned as lightweight yet robust and serviceable bikes for children, which can withstand the rigours of use by successive young riders. Unfortunately, as with any bicycle, due to the natural fatigue of the materials they are made from they will eventually reach the end of their useful life. When this happens there is at present no established mechanism to recover and reuse all of the precious materials which are used in their manufacture. In future, therefore, the plan is to transition from the traditional linear 'take, make, dispose' supply of bicycles to an innovative, sustainable circular product and full-service-based approach.

9.6 Conclusion

This chapter defines what is meant by services and service operations, emphasizing the growing importance of terms such as servitization and the concept of the service-based supply chain. Services offer considerable scope to expand firm revenues particularly in the context of an installed base of existing equipment, but also introduce additional complexity in terms of managing multiple customer and supplier interaction simultaneously as part of a professional service offering. Purchasing and supply management has an extremely important role to play in service-based business models, identifying upfront during programme planning the type of support requirements needed, and selecting the best suppliers to deliver defined performance outcomes and continuous innovation as part of long-term maintenance and product upgrade. Perhaps the most difficult task is re-engaging with customers and suppliers at the product, platform or facility's end of life to instigate a product recovery programme which meets all legislative requirements and rewards stakeholders for their participation. This means shifting current business models based on ownership, towards leasing and services by the manufacturer for the purpose of extending use and increasing the product life cycle. Improving downstream supply chain operations through increased collaboration and information sharing, and developing economic models which actively encourage remanufacturing activity as a standard component of after-sales customer service are expected to drive the future agenda on service innovation in supply chains.

References

Anderson JC and Narus JA (1995) Capturing the value of supplementary services. *Harvard Business Review* 73(1): 75–83.

Araujo L and Spring M (2006) Services, products, and the institutional structure of production. *Industrial Marketing Management* 35(7): 797–805.

Araujo L and Spring M (2009) Service, services and products: Rethinking operations strategy. *International Journal of Operations & Production Management* 29(5): 444–467.

Armistead C and Clark G (1991) A framework for formulating after-sales support strategy. *International Journal of Operations & Production Management* 11(3): 111–124.

Aurich J, Fuchs C and Wagenknecht (2006) Lifecycle orientated design of technical product-service systems. *Journal of Cleaner Production* 14(17): 1480–1494.

Baines TS, Lightfoot HW, Benedettini O and Kay JM (2009) The servitization of manufacturing: A review of literature and reflection on future challenges. *Journal of Manufacturing Technology Management* 20(5): 547–567.

Brady T and Davies A (2011) Learning to deliver a mega-project: The case of Heathrow Terminal 5. In: Caldwell N and Howard M (eds) *Procuring Complex Performance: Studies of Innovation in Product-service Management*. New York: Taylor & Francis Group.

Brax SA and Jonsson K (2009) Developing integrated solution offerings for remote diagnostics: A comparative case study of two manufacturers. *International Journal of Operations & Production Management* 29(5): 539–560.

Caldwell N and Howard M (2011) *Procuring Complex Performance: Studies of Innovation in Product-service Management*. New York: Taylor & Francis Group.

Caldwell N and Howard M (2014) Contracting for complex performance in markets of few buyers and sellers: The case of military procurement. In: Howard M and Caldwell N (eds) Special Issue in Procuring and Management Complex Performance. *International Journal of Operations & Production Management* 34(2): 270–294.

Corrêa H, Ellram L, Scavarda A and Cooper M (2007) An operations management view of the services and goods offering mix. *International Journal of Operations & Production Management* 27(5): 444–463.

Cusumano AM (2008) The changing software business: Moving from products to services. IEEE Computer Society. *Computer*, January: 20–27.

Davies A and Brady T (2000) Organisational capabilities and learning in complex product systems: Towards repeatable solutions. *Research Policy* 29(7–8): 931–953.

Davies A and Hobday M (2005) *The Business of Projects: Managing Innovation in Complex Projects and Systems*. Cambridge, UK: Cambridge University Press.

Davies A, Brady T and Hobday M (2006) Charting a path towards integrated solutions. *MIT Sloan Management Review* 47(3): 39–48.

Dyer J and Singh H (1998) The relational view: Cooperative strategy and sources of interorganizational competitive advantage. *Academy of Management Review* 23(4): 660–679.

Ellram LM, Tate W and Billington C (2008) Offshore outsourcing of professional services: A transaction cost economics perspective. *Journal of Operations Management* 26(2): 148–163.

Goedkoop M, van Halen C, Te Riele H and Rommens P (1999) *Product Service Systems: Ecological and Economic Basics.* The Hague: VROM.

Guide V (2000) Production planning and control for remanufacturing: Industry practice and research needs. *Journal of Operations Management* 18: 467–483.

Haddon-Cave C (2009) *The Nimrod Review – The Loss of RAF Nimrod XV230: A Failure of Culture and Priorities. Report HC1025.* London Stationery Office, Crown Copyright.

Hobday M (1998) Product complexity, innovation and industrial organisation. *Research Policy* 26(6): 689–710.

Howard M and Caldwell N (2014) Editorial to the special issue in procuring and managing complex performance. *International Journal of Operations & Production Management* 34(2).

Howard M and Miemczyk J (2011) Supply management in naval defence. In: Caldwell N and Howard M (eds) *Procuring Complex Performance: Studies of Innovation in Product-service Management.* New York: Taylor & Francis Group.

IfM-IBM (2007) Succeeding through service innovation: Developing a service perspective on economic growth and prosperity. A discussion paper with recommendations for education, business and policy, by University of Cambridge Institute for Manufacturing (IfM) and International Business Machine (IBM).

Jacob F and Ulaga W (2008) The transition from product to service in business markets: An agenda for academic enquiry. *Industrial Marketing Management* 37: 247–253.

Jayaraman V, Guide V and Srivastava R (1999) A closed-loop logistics model for remanufacturing. *Journal of the Operational Research Society* 50: 497–508.

Johnsen T, Howard M and Miemczyk J (2009) UK defence change and the impact on supply relationships. *Supply Chain Management: An International Journal* 14(4): 270–279.

Johnson R (1994) Operations: From factory to service management. *International Journal of Service Industry Management* 5(1): 49–63.

Johnson R and Clark G (2005) *Service Operations Management – Improving Service Delivery.* 2nd edn, Harlow, UK: FT Prentice Hall.

Kraljic P (1983) Purchasing must become supply management. *Harvard Business Review* 61(5): 107–117.

Lewis M and Roehrich J (2009) Contracts, relationships and integration: Towards a model of the procurement of complex performance. *International Journal of Procurement Management* 2(2): 125–142.

Lindberg N and Nordin F (2008) From products to services and back again: Towards a new service procurement logic. *Industrial Marketing Management* 37: 292–300.

Lund R (1984) Remanufacturing. *Technology Review* 87(2): 19–29.

Manzini E, Vezzoli C and Clark G (2001) Product-service systems: Using an existing concept as a new approach to sustainability. *Journal of Design Research* 1(2).

Melnyk S, Davis E, Spekman R and Sandor J (2010) Outcome-driven supply chains. *MIT Sloan Management Review*, Winter(special issue): 33–38.

MoD – Ministry of Defence (2005) *Defence Industrial Strategy.* Defence White Paper. Ref: Cm 6697. London Stationery Office, House of Commons.

Mont O (2002) Clarifying the concept of product-service system. *Journal of Cleaner Production* 10: 237–245.

NAO – National Audit Office (2003) *Through-Life Management.* Report by the Comptroller and Auditor General. London Stationery Office, House of Commons.

NAO – National Audit Office (2007) *Transforming Logistics Support for Fast Jets*. Report by the Comptroller and Auditor General. HC 825 session. London Stationery Office, House of Commons.

Neely A (2008) Exploring the financial consequences of the servitization of manufacturing. *Operations Management Research* 1(2): 103–118.

Oliva R and Kallenberg R (2003) Managing the transition from products to services. *International Journal of Service Industry Management* 14(2): 160–172.

Penrose E (1959) *The Theory of the Growth of the Firm*. Oxford, UK: Oxford University Press.

Poppo L and Zenger T (2002) Do formal contracts and relational governance function as substitutes or complements? *Strategic Management Journal* 23(8): 707–725.

Porter M (1985) *Competitive Advantage: Creating & Sustaining Superior Performance*. New York: Free Press.

Potts G (1988) Exploit your products service life cycle. *Harvard Business Review*, Sept.–Oct.: 32–36.

Quinn J, Doorley T and Paquette P (1990) Beyond products: Service-based strategy. *Harvard Business Review*, March–April: 58–67.

Rolls-Royce (2006) Service package shifts focus from support to availability. *Indepth Rolls-Royce* 10: 22–23.

Roth A and Menor L (2003) Insights into service operations management: A research agenda. *Production and Operations Management* 12(2): 145–164.

Sanderson J (2009) Buyer–supplier partnering in UK defence procurement: Looking beyond the policy rhetoric. *Public administration* 87(2): 327–350.

Savaskan R, Bhattacharya S and Van Wassenhove L (2004) Closed loop supply chain models with product remanufacturing. *Management Science* 50(2): 239–252.

Schemmer RW (1995) *Service Operations Management*. Englewood Cliffs, NJ: Prentice-Hall.

Schweitzer E and Aurich JC (2010) Continuous improvement of industrial product-service systems. *CIRP Journal of Manufacturing Science and Technology* 3: 158–164.

Silvestro R, Fitzgerald L, Johnston R and Voss C (1992) Towards a classification of service processes. *International Journal of Service Industry Management* 3(3): 62–75.

Stremersch S, Wuyts S and Frambach R (2001) The purchasing of full-service contracts. *Industrial Marketing Management* 30: 1–12.

van der Valk W (2008) Service procurement in manufacturing companies: Results of three embedded case studies. *Industrial Marketing Management* 37(1): 301–315.

van Looy B, Gemmel P and Van Dierdonck (1998) *Services Management: An Integrated Approach*. Harlow, UK: FT Prentice Hall.

van Marrewijk A, Clegg SR, Pitsis TS and Veenswijk M (2008) Managing public–private megaprojects. *International Journal of Project Management* 26: 591–600.

Vandermerwe S and Rada J (1988) Servitization of business: Adding value by adding services. *European Management Journal* 6(4): 314–324.

Vargo S and Lusch R (2004) The four service marketing myths: Remnants of a goods-based manufacturing model. *Journal of Service Research* 6(4): 324–335.

Vargo S, Maglio P and Akaka M (2008) On value and value co-creation: A service systems and service logic perspective. *European Management Journal* 26(3): 145–152.

Voss C (2008) Thoughts on servitization. Presentation at the *1st International Euroma Service Operations Management Forum*. University of Exeter, UK.

Wise R and Baumgartner P (1999) Go downstream – the new profit imperative in manufacturing. *Harvard Business Review* 77(5): 133–141.

Youngdahl W and Loomba A (2000) Service-driven global supply chains. *International Journal of Service Industry Management* 11(4): 329–347.

CHAPTER 10

Logistics decisions in the supply network

LEARNING OBJECTIVES

By the end of this chapter you should be able to:

- Understand the role of logistics in overall supply chain processes and performance;
- Balance transport and inventory in total costs of logistics;
- Show strengths and weaknesses of different location decision models;
- Understand the pros and cons of third-party logistics service provision;
- Analyse the role of each of the logistics elements in sustainability.

10.0 Introduction

Logistics management primarily concerns the coordination and control of the flow of materials in a supply chain from the movement of raw materials through to delivery to end customers. Logistics decisions involve the disposition of inventory or stocks and the means to transport this inventory from one stage in the supply chain to another, either in the downstream or upstream positions (Christopher, 1992). Often the definition of logistics management follows high-level definitions of supply chain management in general, but for the purpose of this chapter we will concentrate on the flow of goods and decisions relating to transport and inventory. From a sustainability point of view, logistics is where some of the most significant environmental impacts have their origins, explicitly stemming from transportation. Hence the role of transport in the sustainability debate will receive particular attention. Nevertheless, the goods (inventory/stock) themselves also have sustainability consequences, for example when they become waste and require disposal. Therefore subjects such as reverse logistics will also be covered in this chapter. While there are direct logistics processes such as transport and product disposal, which have impacts on society, many of the generic decisions in logistics management will lead to specific social and environmental outcomes. For this reason many of the recent discussions in logistics management are also included in the scope of the chapter.

To highlight the trends in the logistics sector that relate to sustainability the following list shows that there are both opportunities to improve and challenges to overcome in the next decade (Piecyk and McKinnon, 2010; WEF 2016):

- Further relocation of production capacity to other countries

- Increase in primary consolidation of inbound loads to manufacturing plants and/or distribution centres

- Significant growth in online retailing

- Reverse logistics is likely to gain in importance with more products re-entering the supply chains for recycling, refurbishment and resale

- More frequent 'out-of-hours' operation, especially increase in proportion of night-time deliveries

- Growth in the use of advanced IT systems for transport planning and management (telematics, computerized vehicle routing and scheduling, etc.), including new supply chain analytics, logistics control towers and artificial intelligence (AI)

- Autonomous trucks and drones for delivery

- Increase in logistical collaboration initiatives between companies, sharing transport and warehouse assets to increase efficiency along the lines of circular economy principles

- Greater use of online freight exchanges and load-matching services as well as supply chain orchestration by logistics and supply chain specialists

- Fuel prices and availability of drivers identified as major threats to the road freight industry.

Therefore it is clear that logistics management, especially recent trends, is affected by sustainability issues.

This chapter first covers issues relating to transportation in logistics systems. As many of the sustainability implications of transport relate to the mode used, this first section is mainly focused on road- and water-based modes of transport, and finishes with a comparison of the main modal types. Inventory is also a significant decision element in logistics management. Some of the key inventory models are covered in this second section. The chapter then ties these two elements and relates them to total cost and sustainability. A third important element in logistics management is decisions over location, e.g. for warehouses. Reverse logistics is also treated in this chapter, having strong links to sustainability through recent environmental regulation and innovations in closed-loop supply chains mentioned earlier in the book. The issue of managing third-party logistics (3PL) providers is also covered because one of the current challenges in logistics today is that much of a company's carbon emissions are produced by their contracted transport providers. Finally, the chapter finishes with a case study looking at a logistics strategy as developed by DHL.

10.1 Transport decisions in supply chains: modes of transport

Logistics management primarily concerns the transport and storage of inventory to meet customer needs. Regarding the sustainability of supply chains, transport has key impacts on the environment, meaning that any decision on transport will have a corresponding impact on the environment. Due to this issue, transport has become a preoccupation for governmental agencies, and has led to the development of many rules and regulations constraining transport operations by limiting technological choices and controlling physical logistics processes. In recent years there has been progress in decoupling economic growth from transport impacts, as seen in Figure 10.1, with increases in GDP per capita, while freight transport by road has stayed steady at around 17,000 billion tonne-kilometres each year since 2010 in the EU 28 countries, and overall transport-related GHG emissions have reduced. However, despite this progress carbon footprint and GHG emissions are not the only concern. Recent announcements by the French and British governments to phase out diesel technologies, and various commitments by vehicle manufacturers to significantly increase the share of electric vehicles shows that transport environmental impacts are still very much on the agenda.

One of the key decisions that is taken in transport planning that can impact the environment is on the mode of transport used to move goods through the supply chain. This can have major effects on the costs involved, but also the service levels received by customers. Typically the fastest or most flexible modes of transport give the highest service levels but also the highest costs. Therefore it is imperative to make the right choices regarding the mode, which balances customer needs on price and delivery requirements. Therefore this section of the chapter focuses mainly on modes of transport.

10.1.1 Making modal choice decisions

The basic decisions in transportation planning concern the balancing of costs and service levels. At this first level there is a trade-off between minimizing the costs of transportation and the level of service provided, which is often translated as speed and reliability of service.

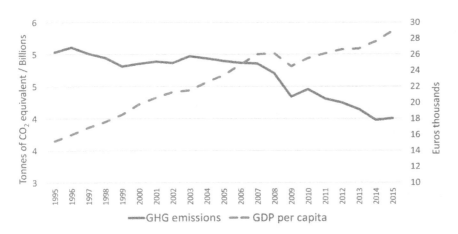

Figure 10.1   Decoupling growth from transport in Europe

Source: Figure created based on Eurostat data, 2017.

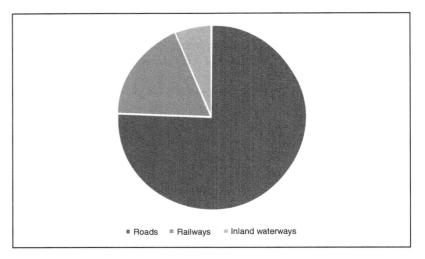

Figure 10.2 The proportion of land transport modes used in Europe

Source: Eurostat (2017).

The key reason for this trade-off is the availability of transportation capacity, most often in the form of trucks, trailers or containers. The more capacity is available along with greater investment in transport resources, the greater the chance of frequent and rapid transport. Not only is this choice based on capacity availability but also the actual cost of transportation. This varies significantly from the mode and technology being used.

Decisions on the appropriate method of transport will not only depend on cost, however. There are other performance measures which are increasingly taken into account for transportation, including flexibility, reliability, as well as the more common cost and speed measures. Hence, depending on the strategic objectives of the supply chain overall, the choice of transport will vary according to a combination of performance objectives.

In general, as seen in the figure transport particularly in Europe is dominated by road transport, making up nearly 50 per cent of all freight transport. The majority of this chapter section, therefore, focuses on this mode.

10.1.2 Road transport

This mode is based on the road network and is hence dependent on the available infrastructure in the country. Road transporters or motor carriers offer the ease of point-to-point access with flexibility and while perhaps not the most cost-efficient form of transport, this mode offers many advantages that shippers prefer. The scope of road transport depends on various geographic factors but in general these services range from local, regional through to continental deliveries. Regarding the issue of capacity mentioned before, there are two types of road transport offers, truck load (TL) or less than truck load (LTL). Therefore contracts for transport typically distinguish between these two types.

While the majority of carriers are generalized, i.e. 40-tonne flatbed articulated lorries, some are clearly specialized for particular materials. There are many strict regulations governing both the design of trucks and their use, and handling of the materials themselves, especially in the case of hazardous materials such as flammable fuels and solvents.

A key element of road transport decisions is the calculation of costs for a given service level. At a basic level the costs can be thought of as related to the human resources (drivers), the physical assets (vehicles), running materials (fuel, etc.) and the time. When summed, these costs are often represented as costs per package, cost per distance or the ratio of these such as the tonne kilometre (tkm, as used in the Eurostat figures on freight transport, see Figure 10.1). Typically the cost of transport is divided into the fixed costs such as depreciation of the vehicle and insurance, and variable costs such as the driver wages and fuel. The understanding of these costs is vital to how environmental considerations are incorporated into transport cost decisions. Examples of this include the vehicle taxing regime. In Europe this normally includes a scale according to the emissions of the vehicle in order to incentivize the investment in low-emission vehicles. Perhaps the most significant of these regimes is the tax on fuel, which is a major revenue generator for governments, but also provides an incentive to reduce fuel use by efficiency measures in order to reduce costs. Therefore we can see that sustainability imperatives are highly integrated into all road transport decisions, from the investment in vehicles, through to the efficient operation of road transport.

10.1.3 Reducing road transport impacts

While variable costs tend to be directly related to reducing impacts from fuel use, other costs can increase when attempting to reduce environmental effects. When considering how to reduce emissions, for instance, we can see that improved technology – hybrid engines for example – may increase investment costs, while operational optimization such as improved routing and capacity utilization may reduce both costs and impacts.

Technology is an important area that holds significant opportunities to reduce emissions from engines in particular. The principal development in road transport technology regarding emissions has been on the improvement of engine efficiency and exhaust treatment. The regulations in Europe on emissions have been steadily tightened over the last 20 years, focusing on a suite of specific polluting chemicals. Each revision in the standard implies a cost in terms of engine development and a general increase in the acquisition cost of vehicles even though there are also improvements in fuel efficiency. One of the barriers to reducing transport impacts is that these costs for new engine technology are not always affordable especially for small logistics companies operating on low margins. In this case the time to renew a fleet of vehicles with the latest technologies can equate to many years based on the long replacement and investment cycles of these companies.

Another option for reducing impacts of road transport is to modify routing and timing of transport. Research suggests that, environmentally speaking, it is better to make deliveries during non-peak times when congestion is low. Some researchers have suggested that improvements of around 3 per cent in CO_2 can be made by rescheduling deliveries to the early morning for short journeys or during the night for long journeys (Palmer and Piecyk, 2010). The same authors warn that when there is a free flow of traffic and trucks can reach speeds of 75km/hr the benefits can be lost as fuel consumption increases with speed. A further issue with this type of rescheduling is noise, where local populations are clearly more sensitive to noise at night or early morning.

A key principle in transport planning is optimizing capacity use to gain economies of scale. Research indicates that using bigger-capacity trailers, for example, has a large potential in reducing CO_2 emissions by reducing the total number of trucks on the road for a given quantity of freight moved, although the relationship is not straightforward. Holter *et al.* (2010) show that using double-deck trailers which increases fuel use per truck (from 29 to 32 l/100km, for example), but the capacity increase of around 50 per cent, reduces fuel use and emissions per unit of capacity theoretically by 15 per cent. In reality the use of large double-deck trailers is less flexible in terms of routes due to bridge heights and other constraints, so modelling of single- versus double-deck trailers has led to potential improvements of only around 3 per cent in carbon emissions. Forward planning is another key to optimizing transport, especially in terms of routing, scheduling and planning efficient loads. However, short planning cycles required by the just in time (JIT) type of operations means there are fewer opportunities to gain economies of scale to reduce transport costs and therefore emissions (Halldórsson and Kovács, 2010). In addition to these pressures on planning, the level of uncertainty can also have a big impact on efficiencies. Recent research has shown that higher levels of demand and supply uncertainty can lead to significantly increased environmental impacts from unplanned transport, emergency shipments and so on (Sanchez-Rodrigues *et al.*, 2010).

Note 10.1

Autonomous vehicles or 'self-driving trucks'

The drive for autonomous vehicles in the freight sector is linked to a number of different trends. Congestion continues to grow in many urban locations, yet at the same time there are fewer people wanting to join the trucking profession. It can be a stressful job and often monotonous and therefore safety is a paramount concern for all road users. Alongside this there are advances in intelligent technologies allowing drivers to use their time differently to just concentrating on the road. Many new entrants in the field including Google (Alphabet) and Tesla are proposing new solutions to the trucking industry to capitalize on these advances. At the same time the economics of using trucks is driven not just by the variable costs of drivers but also the total cost of ownership, and there are opportunities to reduce this further through automation. The current incumbents such as Daimler and Volvo are actively working on self-driving trucks which in theory at least could lead to safer roads and more eco-friendly driving. For example, in 2016 six convoys of semi-automated 'smart' trucks arrived in Rotterdam's harbour in an experiment that could revolutionize future road transport on Europe's roads. More than a dozen self-driving trucks made by six of Europe's largest manufacturers arrived in the port in so-called 'truck platoons' which act almost like trains but on the road rather than railway tracks. While this is just the beginning, technologies are rapidly becoming more mature and are likely to have a significant impact on the sustainability of road freight transportation.

Source: https://www.theguardian.com/technology/2016/apr/07/convoy-self-driving-trucks-completes-first-european-cross-border-trip (last accessed 17 July 2018)

10.1.4 Sea and inland water transport

The majority of global trade is transported by sea. The reason for this is that it is well suited to high volumes regarding unit cost. However, it is not suitable for time-sensitive shipments due to long lead times and also the many possibilities of delay (due to inclement weather and so on). Containerization has transformed this mode of transport since the 1970s when the standard container unit was devised – the ISO container. The volume of global transport of containers is closely linked to export trade flows across the world and has seen a steady increase since the opening of global markets through trade agreements, although there was a drop in exports in 2015–2016 (see Figure 10.3).

There are some key characteristics of this industry, particularly the use of the liner conferences, that impacts the capacity and pricing of sea-based transport services. Rather like OPEC, the conferences represent the main companies and help determine prices of transport. In the conferences' view this practice reduces price volatility (to help planning) and helps the industry itself plan ahead on their huge investments in seagoing vessels. However, this practice is also negative as the US and European governments view conferences as a price fixing cartel potentially subject to anti-trust or anti-competitiveness litigation through the World Trade Organization. The principal stakeholders in the industry are the shipping lines themselves (such as Maersk), shipping agents focusing on the commercial port activities and freight-forwarders who coordinate the point-to-point collection and delivery of the products.

Overall this mode of transport is seen as one that leads to the least emissions for carbon. However, this is subject to considerable variability. As Leonardi and Browne (2010) show, the least efficient container ship shows transport CO_2 efficiency values of about 100 grams CO_2e/tkm, whereas the most efficient vessel observed has reached a value of 19 grams CO_2e/tkm. Also, different routes, origins and destinations, and different logistics organizations, show great variability. For example, the use of a hub is shown to reduce emissions (–23 per cent emissions per kg of product) and the use of charter vessels for direct trips instead of a container vessel on a shipping line improves the efficiency by about 28 per cent. Such figures

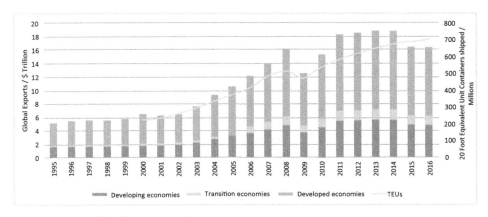

Figure 10.3 Global exports and container transport volumes

Sources: OECD, World Bank (2017).

are difficult to understand unless compared or put into context. For example, the seagoing transport impact for a chest of drawers sourced in Brazil and bought in Europe can be about the equivalent of the consumer trip by car to the furniture shop to buy it (Leonardi and Browne, 2010).

While water is seen as the most environmentally friendly form of transport, there are impacts that need to be considered. Perhaps the most publicized is the risk of accident and the resultant pollution. At the time of writing two major accidents are in the international news. The first is the Costa Concordia accident in Italy, and while this is not a 'supply chain' incident, it highlights the dangers of fuel leakage of capsized vessels especially in naturally sensitive areas. The second is the Erica disaster where oil from this stricken oil tanker damaged hundreds of kilometres of Brittany coast in France. The cost of clean-up was estimated at US$100million, with sea birds being flown to Exeter, UK for treatment. Although this occurred on 12 December 1999, the legal process was only reaching resolution in 2012. Other types of impact include the dumping of ballast water containing 'alien species', leading to the imbalancing of biodiversity in certain regions.

Although seagoing freight dominates the world's trade flows in terms of volume, inland waterways also provide savings in cost but provide good access to urban areas. Both rivers and canals can provide useful modes of transit for freight, with canals being purposefully designed for this activity. Many of the world's rivers and canals reach directly into the centre of towns and cities and therefore provide an alternative to trucks accessing town centre distribution points and retail outlets.

Note 10.2

Monoprix, France

A successful example of using inland waterways is Monoprix in France. Monoprix is a retail chain serving most of France and is based in Paris. The company sells a range of products from clothes to food. Much of the product sold by Monoprix is brought into France from outside of Europe, 78 per cent of which uses sea containers, most are shipped to Le Havre in the north west of France. The port at Le Havre is located at the mouth of the Seine river which also passes through Paris. A number of years ago Monoprix decided to shift the majority of the supplies brought into Le Havre from the autoroute to rail and river on their way to the Paris warehouse in Seine-et-Marne. Around 81 per cent is transported by train and river barges. Now Monoprix counts 35 per cent of freight inbound to Paris on the Seine river route. Clearly the inland water route saves costs but has also been estimated to save 231 tonnes of CO_2 emissions. In addition, Monoprix estimate to have kept 12,000 trucks from entering Paris and serving its 94 retail outlets. The solution was again to use rail from the warehouse to a hub (3,700m^2) in central Paris and then use 26 trucks running on natural gas (the biggest private fleet in France) to service each of the retail outlets.

Source: https://entreprise.monoprix.fr/monoprix-sengage/respecter-lenvironnement/modes-de-transports-responsables (last accessed 21 September 2018)

10.1.5 Other transport modes

Road- and water-based modes of transport account for the majority of logistics movements today. While rail and air freight – as well as pipeline-based transport – play a very important role in logistics flows, they tend to fill specific needs. In particular, air freight is clearly a mode of choice when speed is paramount but also the relative value of the products is high enough to justify the costs, which is why a company like Zara will use significant air freight transport. Rail has often been cited as a preferred alternative to road transport particularly in Europe, but the structural inflexibilities still limit the use so far. As a general summary there are several trade-offs when considering different modes of transport (Table 10.1). In addition to the traditional trade-offs, the environmental consequences are receiving more consideration. For example, companies are beginning to take into consideration the carbon emissions relating to each mode.

In summary, the key decision variable relating to transport and sustainability is that of modal choice. While there are clear trade-offs between these different options, companies are beginning to move towards modes with less impact where possible. One of the other issues which can also have a big impact from an environmental point of view is transport planning. Forward planning activities are vital to achieving economies of scale, and yet the trend is towards shorter and shorter planning cycles in order to minimize inventory costs, discussed next. A further complication to this is the level of demand uncertainty. Where uncertainty is high the level of unscheduled transport can significantly increase with a commensurate impact on vehicle emissions.

10.2 Inventory decisions in the supply chains

Alongside decisions on transportation in logistics it is also vital to take into account the issues of inventory. In one sense transport and inventory decisions are inextricably linked where requirements for reduced quantities of stock can lead to an increase in the frequency of delivery and often an increase in transport costs. The following section is not intended to provide an exhaustive treatment of inventory decisions in the supply chain, but instead to

Table 10.1 Trade-offs in modal choices (1 best – 5 worst)

	Rail	Road	Water	Air	Pipeline
Cost	3	4	1	5	2
Speed	3	2	4	1	5
Flexibility	2	1	4	3	5
Volume/weight limits	3	4	1	5	2
Accessibility	2	1	4	3	5
CO_2 emissions	3	4	1	5	2

give a brief overview of the issues and how decisions on inventory might affect sustainability objectives.

The question of why companies keep stocks of products has many answers. The following list shows some of the reasons why inventories are important (Christopher, 1998).

- Insurance against uncertainty of demand and inaccurate forecast
- Counteracts lack of flexibility in production such as large batch sizes
- Take short-term opportunities in the market
- Anticipate future demands to ensure availability
- Reduce overall costs, bulk price, through larger batch or order quantities
- Increase in value, e.g. wine
- Fills processing pipeline to ensure capacity is being utilized

The decisions on inventory holding also have a number of dimensions that need to be taken into account. These dimensions all relate to the cost of ordering and holding stock. A first consideration is the actual acquisition of goods. Here a significant factor can be if the price varies with the amount ordered from a supplier (order quantity discounts); however, if a total cost view is not taken this can elevate overall costs. Where forecasts can be relied upon the company can order only what is needed; however, as is more often the case when demand is uncertain extra stocks may be required alongside more frequent restocking which may help keep stocks in line with the real need from the market. Storage space is another consideration where greater stock levels may be desirable, but lack of physical space may hinder large inventories. Each time products are ordered from suppliers there are costs related to the purchasing price but also the ordering activity. These costs relate to setting up the purchase order, communicating with the supplier, transport of the goods and receiving and checking the goods. These costs are borne each time an order takes place and more frequent orders will increase these costs. There is also the storage costs which can increase linearly with the amount stored and even exponentially when considering the management (sorting, locating, picking) of more stock holding units.

There are a large number of models used for deciding on ordering timing and quantity. The following summarizes three of the most popular models. The first is fixed level ordering. This is when the inventory drops to a specific level; an order is triggered according to the rate of stock use and the lead time of delivery from a supplier. As shown in the following diagram the reorder point is defined as the level of stock that is reached that corresponds to how much stock will be consumed in the time it takes to order and deliver from a supplier minus any safety stock. Clearly there is an assumption that the order lead time does not vary and that the consumption does not change significantly, leading to a stock-out situation. The actual quantity ordered will be that which minimizes the ordering (frequency) and holding costs, i.e. all the costs mentioned in the previous paragraph. If there is constant change in the supplier lead time and the amount of demand, the situation will need to be monitored on a regular basis and may lead to additional expedition costs from the supplier.

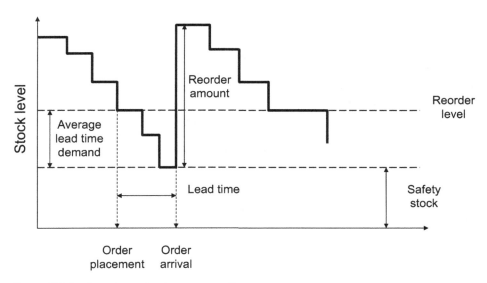

Figure 10.4 Reorder point inventory policy

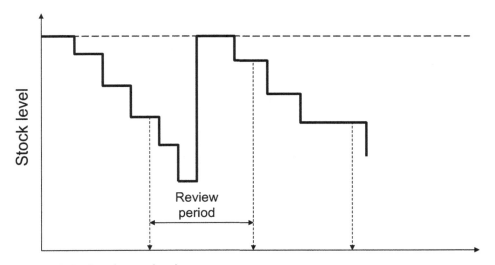

Figure 10.5 Fixed period ordering

One of the most common methods where demand is not stable and the value of stock is relatively low is the fixed period ordering approach. In this sense orders are set on a regular basis, weekly for example, and the amount ordered will vary, accounting for the quantity left in stock. As shown above it is clear that the review period needs to correspond with the stock usage rate. The negative aspect of this method is that it is easy to over order what is required and hence the stock holding costs will not be optimum, and so the relevance is only to low-value items such as office supplies.

A third important, and more sophisticated, approach to inventory ordering is based on total cost. As mentioned already, effective logistics decisions should take into account the full costs of transportation, including unforeseen expediting, and stock holding, including obsolescence costs and the hidden costs of defects. One approach to this is known as the economic order quantity model. This model balances the costs involved in ordering from suppliers including the transportation element, compared with the stock holding costs. Hence, for a given demand over a period the decision can be made to order once for the total amount required for the year, minimizing order costs (only one order event) or to order a part of the period's demand on a frequent basis, raising the order costs, but reducing the inventory costs. There are key assumptions behind this model. The main assumption is that demand is even during the period. In the following equation, the optimization of the order size is subject to a square root law, in that over the order period the demand steadily decreases so that in half the order period, half the inventory has been consumed. Clearly this may not be the case and so the optimal order quantity may be insufficient (too much demand) or overestimated (too much stock holding cost).

$$EOQ = \sqrt{\frac{2AS}{i}}$$

A = Annual usage

S = Ordering cost/set-up cost

i = inventory carrying cost

One of the impacts of minimizing the inventory costs is that the order lot sizes reduce and thus the potential utilization of trucks is reduced as fewer truck loads are needed. Combined with rising fuel cost, the minimization of inventory can therefore increase transport costs and impacts. Companies today try to avoid these trade-off situations and some approaches are discussed in the next chapter.

10.3 Balancing total cost, lean and sustainable logistics

Current trends in logistics mean that total costs and high levels of customer service are the principal drivers of logistics decisions. This does not mean that most companies adopt these approaches to the full, but there is a growing recognition of the need to look beyond quantity discounts and unit prices, and internal measures of order fulfilment. Looking at total costs is not easy, especially where there are many uncertainties both on the supply and demand sides. Models such as the economic order quantity can be criticized in their basic form because they do not sufficiently take into account these uncertainties, often assuming demand is stable and predictable. Although more sophisticated versions of this model exist, there is still a gap between the theory and the actual use of these models in practice (Schniederjans and Cao, 2001). In parallel, lean approaches have developed to minimize some of these risks, particularly related to inventory holding (obsolescence and so on) as well as the costs of stock. This has led to the so-called just in time (JIT) logistics methods whereby the order sizes are minimized as much as possible taking into account the resulting inefficiencies in transportation due to low capacity utilization of trucks in particular. These types of logistics processes are typical in the automotive industry where the value of products and demand variability is high.

There is now an increasing amount of research that has looked at the relationship between inventory models such as economic order quantity and sustainability (Bouchery *et al.*, 2012). There are ways to incorporate the environment – often in terms of carbon emissions – specifically into models that balance inventory and transport costs, by including the 'externalities' into the cost part of the model or by adding new variables such as carbon emissions (Bonney and Jaber, 2011). However, without placing a realistic value on the environment (carbon cost, for example) it is difficult to compare different scenarios and make decisions on them. Therefore, for the moment these types of studies remain theoretical, giving additional information rather than proposing realistic total cost solutions. Despite this, some companies are considering whether the optimum total cost is worth foregoing in order to minimize the transport cost element and hold extra stocks to cope with demand uncertainties. For example, Saunier Duval in France, a manufacturer and distributor of heating systems, have recently relaxed some of their JIT delivery policies across Europe to do just this. Again, to date there has been little research examining the impact of JIT logistics systems on the environment, and that which exists shows conflicting results (Yang *et al.*, 2011).

10.4 Location decision making

One of the key decision variables in logistics planning in addition to transport and inventory is the location of sites in a supply chain. It is clear that transportation costs are directly related to the location of factories, warehouses and retailers and ultimately final customers, so one of the options in logistics strategy is to change locations to balance the requirements of costs and service levels (ReVelle and Eiselt, 2005). As mentioned in the next chapter, companies like Amazon are using location advantage to provide new service levels (next-day delivery) putting e-commerce retailers in direct competition with traditional sales channels. It is not only the end of the supply chain where location decisions are critical, however; these decisions occur throughout, from raw material choices (cement works next to sources of lime) to co-location of suppliers to car manufacturers in supplier parks to reduce logistics costs and improve responsiveness (Howard *et al.*, 2006). Yet, making decisions on location is not straightforward as there are many variables and constraints to take into account. This section provides a brief overview of the main approaches and how sustainability indicators can be included in these decision models.

At a basic level the choice of locations for a warehouse or factory can be based on the relationship between fixed and variable cost, and the overall volume of demand likely for the location. This is known as breakeven analysis and allows the decision on which sites to choose based on each site's specific cost structure and how efficiently the site can process orders. From a sustainability standpoint the fixed costs can include environmental licences to operate and variable costs can be impacted by social charges for personnel, therefore making some sites less favourable because of these additional costs. This has led to the 'pollution haven hypothesis' where companies choose sites because of the lowest cost including environmental costs, which are often in regions and countries with low regulation levels (Smarzynska and Wei, 2001). However, the academic evidence for this is rather weak (Millimet and List, 2004).

A second popular location decision model uses multi-criteria decision making as the core component. This approach improves on breakeven analysis by expanding the comparison from only looking at costs to including other decision variables such as skills and community-based factors. While there are many rigorous methods for this type of analysis, such as analytical hierarchy processes, or AHP for short (Alberto, 2000), many companies tend to use a simple weighted factor approach. Selecting factors and allocating importance weights to them is typically done by a cross-functional group of managers who have a stake in the site selection decision – logistics, production, sales and human resources (Korpela and Lehmusvaara, 1999). Once weights are decided the group then compares scores across a number of preselected/pre-existing locations. While it is possible to add criteria related to environmental laws or social conditions, there is no significant research that has reviewed these practices.

The two previous examples of decision making models for location assume that locations are already known and that managers just need to select between them. In logistics networks this is not always possible, especially when setting up a new structure to service multiple customers from multiple suppliers. Thus the centre of gravity method allows a comparison of geographic locations based on optimizing the costs of transport from suppliers to customers through a centralized warehouse location (de la Fuente and Lozano, 1998). As the goal is to minimize transport costs overall, given differing demand levels, one might assume that environmental impacts from emissions are also reduced by the selected location. Again, there is very little research that has tested this approach to examine costs and emissions, but of the few studies one at least has shown that there is not necessarily a direct link, where the cost optimum might not be the environmental optimum (Harris *et al.*, 2011). Further, these models are very sensitive to vehicle utilization levels, which is often very difficult to model realistically due to aforementioned problems of short planning cycles and uncertainties. Recent reviews of network design modelling research has shown that sustainability metrics are being included more and more and methods are being proposed to better integrate sustainability into location decision making (Eskandarpour *et al.*, 2015).

10.5 Reverse logistics

As the name suggests, reverse logistics is the process of bringing products back from the distribution channel or final customers in order to recuperate value or to meet regulatory demands. Today's huge growth in Internet-based shopping means that more and more companies have to deal with this additional cost to serve their customer, which can be more than double the cost of delivering products in the first place.[1] These additional movements of products can also significantly increase their carbon footprint. Reverse logistics has the same characteristics as forward logistics flow except in the opposite direction: 'the role of logistics in product returns, source reduction, recycling, materials substitution, reuse of materials, waste disposal, and refurbishing, repair and remanufacturing' (Stock, 1992). Despite the additional costs, reverse logistics provides a number of opportunities to improve profits ranging from building customer loyalty, developing secondary channels and having fewer markdowns in retailers by repositioning stocks. In parallel to these profit opportunities reverse logistics also gives rise to cost reduction possibilities (Carter and Ellram, 1998). One obvious area of cost reduction is in raw material purchasing whereby materials recovered and recycled from end customers can return to the manufacturing process, thereby avoiding buying virgin materials.

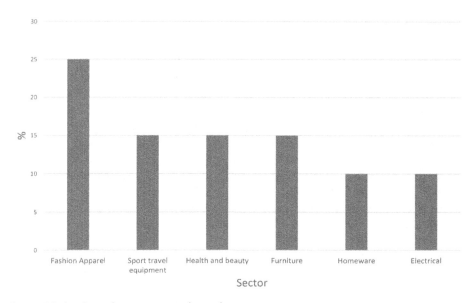

Figure 10.6 Sample return rates by industry

Source: *Financial Times.*[2]

Industries vary considerably according to the rate of return, with some industries that are well established in providing reverse logistics services (magazine publishing) and others relatively immature in this field (mail order computers). The following figure indicates the return rates in a selection of industries.

There are a number of types of returns which can be subject to reverse logistics processes and these are characterized primarily by the reason for returning the product. Customer returns are those which relate to customers not wanting to keep the product they have bought because it does not fit their requirements. A good example of this is online retailing of clothing whereby the customer is not sure whether the garment will fit prior to receiving the product, hence catalogue and online retailers have put in place well-established returns processes to bring back unsuitable products at no cost to the customers. Companies such as La Redoute in France have done this for many years as they are using public postal service distributions systems. Marketing returns are another type of return which was developed because products are in the 'wrong' place at the 'wrong' time. For example, where products have reached obsolescence or have simply gone out of fashion, they need to be returned to the manufacturer or relocated in a different distribution channel more suitable for the product. An example of this is end-of-line clothing which is returned to be resold at a discount in a factory outlet store. A further type of return is asset returns, where assets belonging to the company have to be repositioned or redeployed. A clear example of this is the return of packaging materials such as pallets or stillages, which are designed to circulate several times through a supply chain. It is very important in logistics to have packaging that can be returned as this saves cost instead of buying new packaging, and can be specifically designed to protect certain kinds of product. A common risk here is that without the right packaging, products may not be delivered effectively; hence keeping track and returning these assets is vital to the continued forward flow of products. The use of returnable packaging has also been incentivized by European packaging regulation limiting the use of disposable packaging.

Another common type of return is that related to faulty products, normally known as recalls. This is an especially important process for safety-critical products such as food or vehicles where any defects need to be rectified before accidents or harmful effects can happen. In the car industry, it is normal for vehicles to be returned to dealerships for replacement of faulty parts, but as cars pass from one owner to another it can become difficult to track the owners of specific vehicles from a production batch, thus causing a problem of acquisition. In some cases the products need to be returned, analysed and destroyed as in the case of ricin in the baby food industry in 2004.[3] A final type of return is known as environmental returns and these are placed typically to avoid the disposal of products in landfills, often as a response to legislation. In Europe there has been a specific focus on legislating the return of end-of-life vehicles (ELVs) and electrical and electronic equipment (WEEE) with the implementation of a number of directives.

Although reverse logistics shares many of the same characteristics and objectives as forward logistics, there are some specific challenges that have to be addressed. The first challenge is product acquisition. As the product itself is often held by the end consumer (for example, in the case of mobile phones), it is difficult for the reverse logistics organization to locate the product, especially if the sellers of the product have been out of touch with the end customer. The product is often sold through retail outlets, but once sold the number of potential locations of the product increases significantly bringing additional problems of logistics. Another difficulty with acquisition is if products have been passed on to other customers, for example in the second-hand product market, such as the used car market. Here the information on location of the product is even more difficult to obtain.

A second difficulty in reverse logistics is the assessment of product quality. It is clear that in order to obtain value from the returned product the potential 'value' has to be assessed. Where products require high amounts of work to render the product saleable again, the potential value is reduced. Thus a reverse logistics process requires a stage whereby quality is evaluated. Often this process also includes a sorting stage where the products are allocated to categories of quality depending on the work needed to bring the product to saleable quality, and if the quality is too low, to decide to recycle or to simply dispose of the product if allowed by law.

The third main difference compared with forward logistics is the actions that can take place after the return of the product. As shown in Figure 10.7, returned products can take a variety of routes. The first possibility is the repair of the product and this is the most common approach for recalls in the automotive industry, for example. If the product is beyond basic reparation, the next stage would be to recondition the product, ready for resale into secondary markets which might accept lower quality. This approach is relatively common for old laptops, where some components are replaced and the software is upgraded but the quality of the product means the price is much lower than as new. The third option is complete remanufacturing, where the product is completely disassembled and processed and

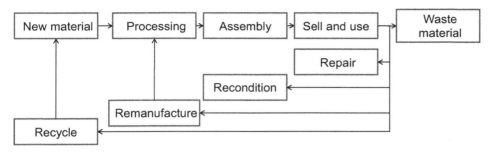

Figure 10.7 The various routes for returned products

reassembled as new, to levels of quality expected for new products (described in Chapter 7). The final possibility where the product is beyond remanufacturing for technical or economic reasons, is recycling of the materials to be used as new raw material.

The following example shows that in reality all the routes above can be used for products depending on the structure of the product, the variability of quality of returned products and the nature of the market. This example of Xerox is well documented and is in place for many years even though regulation for end-of-life product recovery is relatively recent. While steel makes up nearly 50 per cent of the product (the chassis or frame), there are a number of other materials which are significantly more difficult to reuse or recycle. Here nearly 40 per cent of the product is plastic (ABS or PVC) which is far more difficult to recycle due to the lack of established recycling markets. While the Xerox approach to reverse logistics is not only driven by an environmental imperative to reduce waste (although they achieved 92 per cent reuse/recycling in 2011), the process taken achieves good results meeting those required by new regulations in Europe.

What makes the Xerox reverse logistics system work both environmentally and economically is the business model in the industry. In most cases photocopiers are leased from Xerox or their local operating companies. The customer of the photocopier does not own the machine itself and rather pays on the service level given. In recent years Xerox has moved toward a pay per print model with customers so that only the use of the product is charged directly. In particular, ensuring that the machine is available for use is the main concern for Xerox who is then responsible for maintaining the product (see product-service systems in Chapter 9). As the machine becomes older and less reliable, the cost of maintenance increases and it is at this point that Xerox 'retires' the machine and replaces it for the customer. This is the trigger point for the reverse logistics process. Xerox uses a third-party logistics provider to return the product from the operating company (who is in charge of maintenance and replacement) to the 'asset recovery centre' (ARC) in the UK for European customers. The logistics provider carries out some basic quality tests on the product to decide whether it should be remanufactured or recycled. At the ARC the Xerox runs its own remanufacturing process including disassembly, storage of base (standard copier) units, then reassembly and customer configuration, according to end-customer demand. If the product is not viable for remanufacturing the product is passed to an on-site recycling company who disassembles but also removes all the parts based on material type, to then be sold into specific material

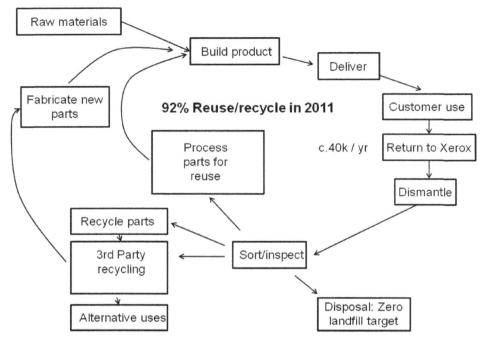

Figure 10.8 Xerox's reverse logistics process

Source: Adapted from King *et al.* (2006).

markets. Xerox also recycles ABS plastic on-site (avoiding the transport costs), by granulating and cleaning the plastic to be used as a new recycled 'raw' material for the plastic covers of the photocopier machine. This is an example of closed-loop reverse logistics (see Chapter 9). The following diagram gives an overview of the main steps in the Xerox reverse logistics process.

10.6 Logistics service providers

It is worth mentioning here that while logistics is a core element of supply chain management and is the basis for global trade, many companies outsource their logistics processes to specialist service providers. There are many reasons for this but in short companies often have neither the global reach nor the specific competencies to manage the physical flow of goods from suppliers to end customers (Langley *et al.*, 2003). For this reason a huge industry has grown out of the provision of logistics services. The development started with the use of local transport contractors who are able to reach a local population of customers and has now developed into a multibillion dollar sector with large logistics firms such as DHL (see case study at the end of this chapter), UPS and TNT.

The key reasons for using third-party logistics providers has remained largely constant over the years with cost reduction being the main driver, mainly due to the reduced need for capital investment in transport assets and warehousing. Service level is the second most important reason with expectations on speed and reliability being essential. Flexibility is also seen as an important element, probably enabling better service levels, but also from a strategic perspective. Other drivers include change management imperatives and the need to focus on core competences such as manufacturing or managing the customer interface (Van Laarhoven *et al.*, 2000).

Part of this argument is the opportunity for economies of scale, whereby the capacity of the provider is shared across a number of customers, through consolidation, and so the unit costs fall (Wu and Dunn, 1995). As the diagram shows, it is often the case that there are numerous opportunities to share capacity, especially in the case of 'less-than-truck-load' services. In the example here, one logistics provider shows what percentage of supplier locations are shared by end customer locations (in this case vehicle manufacturing sites). In this case 11 per cent of the suppliers are shared by the three automotive plants, so in one collection the provider could in theory collect three times the quantity. By taking this approach, the logistics provider can collect supplies from single suppliers with multiple customers, thereby increasing the amount collected each time and reducing the chance of underutilization of the trailer capacity. This is particularly important in the automotive industry where delivery quantities are low in order to minimize inventory costs driven by lean initiatives. An example of consolidation of logistics flows on the distribution and delivery side is given in the next chapter.

Managers raise numerous concerns about contracting to third-party logistics providers especially during the pre-contract phase of negotiations. Issues such as trust and adequate levels of knowledge are often cited as difficulties, but also the risks of overdependence and loss of control. During third-party logistics contracts many of these negative perceptions decline although lack of service quality and problems of IT integration often remain in place (Van Laarhoven *et al.*, 2000). There are many criteria that can be used to help select logistics service providers. While many of these criteria are common with other supplier selection indicators (as discussed in Chapter 2), there are some that could be considered specific to logistics, especially measures of reliability and speed, but also compatibility of planning systems (Razzaque and Sheng, 1998). Today companies are coming to realize that many of their environmental impacts are rooted in the supply chain, and especially the transportation links between customer and suppliers. Therefore sustainability has arisen as an additional criterion for choosing logistics service providers (Wolf and Seuring, 2010). Although criteria related to sustainability are used in logistics provider selection (Kudla and Klaas-Wissing, 2012), it seems more for information purposes than really to 'deselect' lower performing providers. In fact the evidence shows that problems persist in that shippers make inconsistent demands and that real cooperation on improving environmental performance with logistics providers is still a challenge (Wolf and Seuring, 2010).

Logistics service providers have started to take on broader roles in supply chain management beyond managing transport and warehousing operations. This increased strategic involvement has led to terms such as 'fourth-party logistics providers' (4PLs) or even supply chain orchestrators (See TriVizor case study in the next chapter). Table 10.2 presents recent classifications of LSPs showing that a number of factors influence whether they will take on more complex tasks in the supply chain for their clients. From this the factors of competence, uncertainty, customization and complexity all play a role in whether LSPs will take on more complex and strategic activities in the supply chain.

Table 10.2 The development and scope of logistics service providers

Dimensions	Roles and services	References
Scope of outsourced activities	Transport Transport and warehousing Transport, warehousing and additional services Transport, warehousing and additional services, and value-add activities 4PL	Fabbe-Costes *et al.*, 2008; Halldórsson and Skjøtt-Larsen, 2004
Competence (and asset specificity) and degree of integration	Market exchange Customized solutions Joint logistics solutions (In-house solutions)	Halldórsson and Skjøtt-Larsen, 2004
Based on levels of buyer uncertainty and providers experience	Translating Re-engineering Fine-tuning Developing	Selviaridis et al., 2013
Complexity of distribution collaboration and intensity of collaboration	Transactional 3PL Relational 3PL Problem-solving 4PL Collaboration specialist	Hingley et al., 2011

Source: Adapted from Michon and Miemczyk (2017).

CASE STUDY 10.1

DHL'S SUSTAINABLE LOGISTICS STRATEGY

In their 2016 CSR report Dr Frank Appel, DPDHL CEO, made some bold statements:

We want to support the global community in achieving the United Nations' two-degree climate target. After achieving our own climate protection target well ahead of schedule in 2016, we have now articulated a new, ambitious vision for the future. By the year 2050 we want to be the first logistics company to make emissions-neutral transport a reality.

He goes on to state:

First, we plan to improve our carbon efficiency by 50% over the 2007 baseline. Second, we want 70% of deliveries to be made with clean, green solutions such as electric vehicles. Third, we want over 50% of our sales to incorporate Green Solutions. And fourth, we want 80% of our employees to participate in sustainability training measures and get actively involved in environmental and climate protection projects.

The group offers standardized products as well as innovative and tailored solutions – from dialogue marketing to industrial supply chains. It is organized into four operating divisions, each of which operates under the control of its own divisional headquarters:

- The MAIL and e-commerce division is the only provider of universal postal services in Germany. It delivers mail and parcels throughout Germany and internationally, and proposes press distribution services and electronic services as well.

- The EXPRESS division offers courier and express services to business and private customers.

- The GLOBAL FORWARDING, FREIGHT division handles the carriage of goods by rail, road, air and sea.

- The SUPPLY CHAIN division is the global market leader in contract logistics, providing warehousing, managed transport and value-added services at every link in the supply chain for customers in a variety of industries.

In 1997, Deutsche Post started to expand to the global level, in order to respond to customers' growing demands of a single service provider for all of their domestic and international shipping activities. By 1998 they offered a European express service, and then expanded its strategy worldwide through acquisitions. Deutsche Post World Net completed the purchase of DHL in 2002 and of Airborne Express in 2003 and integrated it into DHL, which is now known as DHL Express.

For Deutsche Post DHL – and by expansion any company in the logistics industry – there are a large number of sustainability-related influencing factors. They can be grouped into the following four generic categories. The transport industry worldwide is one of the top four contributors to greenhouse gases at 14 per cent[4] and Deutsche Post DHL, with a global presence through a both owned and subcontracted fleet (trucks, vans, planes) contributes significantly to that number. According to a recent logistics and transportation survey conducted by Transport Intelligence, 73 per cent of respondents who award logistics contracts include sections on environmental compliance in the contract. Only 46 per cent, though, actually make provision for the extra costs involved. In 2008, two-thirds of Deutsche Post DHL's top customers had concrete reduction targets and expect Deutsche Post DHL to contribute to achieving their targets. Major competitors such as TNT and key industry players like Lufthansa had equally announced corporate climate initiatives. Finally, rising fuel costs are both a threat and an opportunity: it is an opportunity for those who move fast and efficiently as fuel-efficient operations can be the source of a sustainable competitive cost advantage while those companies that move too slowly or make sub-optimal choices will be hit with a double cost disadvantage: first because the operating costs grow faster than those of best-in-class competitors, and second because legislation is increasingly penalizing fuel-inefficient products and services.

Environmental legislation has been implemented globally – including emerging markets such as China and India – and is becoming increasingly demanding on all stakeholders in the logistics industry. Cost increase from legislation alone could increase cost to €1.3 billion by 2020, reducing EBIT margin by 1 percentage point. Furthermore, cities around the world are attempting to reduce emissions and optimize traffic flows in the city centres. As these initiatives are quite diverse, the impact to DP DHL will vary case-by-case; however, very often low-emission vehicles get preferential treatment. At the same time legislation – typically through taxation and subsidization – is lifting the economic barriers that are holding back the introduction to sustainable practices.

As a low-carbon economy will inevitably become reality over the next two decades, carbon-friendly technological innovation is booming. Secondly, the topic of carbon is very high on the agenda of all economic actors – governments, companies and citizens, which fuels a mechanism that erodes the traditional cost – and risk barriers associated to the introduction of new technology. That in turn accelerates the general market acceptance of such technology. This means there is considerable technological advancement and new technology is able to compete with traditional technology relatively fast. In brief, the forces at work are diverse and impact directly on the basic business fundamentals of DP DHL – and any logistics company.

In 2001 DHL set up a Corporate-level Policy and Environment team, part of the newly formed Corporate Public Policy and Environment department, in recognition of the growing importance of environmental issues. The team's initial task is to set the group's strategy on the environment, and to work with existing divisional teams to implement it. The responsibilities of the corporate team are broadened to include wider sustainability issues, and the development of the group's global partnerships with the United Nations and other organizations. In 2002, DHL developed 'Green Tonnage', DHL's first 'green' product. DHL research showed that 70 per cent of their customers in Sweden take the environment into consideration when buying transportation services, and that many are willing to pay a premium for an environmentally friendly option. DHL Sweden introduces *Grøna Ton* ('Green Tonnage'), DHL's first 'green' value-added transport service, to meet this demand. With *Grøna Ton*, transport volumes equivalent to their purchased *Grøna Ton* volumes are transported somewhere in the DHL network using renewable fuels. This results in low-emission transportation for which the customer receives the carbon reduction credit. In 2005, DHL Parcel Germany piloted its *Grünes Paket* ('Green Parcel'), a carbon-neutral parcel shipping service. With this service, all CO_2 emissions relating to the transportation and handling of each Green Parcel are calculated and offset through climate-protection projects. The Green Parcel is a forerunner for the *GOGREEN* parcel, launched in 2006.

DHL started working on the reduction of CO_2 emissions by following Kyoto recommendations. The key levers of the climate protection programme are the optimization of the air and ground fleets, improved energy efficiency in buildings and plants, the development of innovative technologies, motivating employees and the involvement of subcontractors.

'Correctly measuring and managing our CO_2 efficiency at the relevant level is extremely important. We are working intensively on this' (Lawrence A. Rosen, CFO, Deutsche Post DHL). One of the important milestones in developing their GOGREEN strategy (see Table 10.3) is identifying where the impacts actually come from; in this case DP DHL adopted the Kyoto approach. Scope 1 emissions include direct CO_2 emissions from one's own operations (as classified by the Greenhouse Gas Protocol). Scope 2 emissions are CO_2 emissions corresponding to the electricity, district heating and cooling purchased. Scope 3 emissions are CO_2 emissions from subcontracted transport. Through this analysis DP DHL found that they account for 0.1 per cent of global man-made emissions, which is certainly a call for action.

According to DHL, subcontracted transportation is responsible for about 80 per cent of the group's carbon footprint. In particular, in the area of road freight, transparency and subcontractor engagement is very difficult to achieve due to the high number of subcontractors and limited industry standards. One project involving more than 100 road subcontractors gave a good understanding about the level of information they would be able to get from the market, which DHL could use to improve the carbon efficiency throughout the external road transport chain. In addition, DHL has stated they were committed to helping to improve carbon standards and data sources in the logistics industry in general to increase the level of comparability and the engagement of subcontractors.

Capacity utilization is another important lever to improve CO_2 efficiency. Ideally, trucks should be fully loaded at all times. In reality, an average of 30 per cent of vehicle mileage is running empty, especially on the outward or return leg of local journeys. In 2008, DHL Freight Euronet in Germany determined that the relocation of empty trailers was responsible for nearly 10 per cent of the total empty kilometres. In 2009, an initiative was started to reduce these empty kilometres and the resulting CO_2 emissions. DHL defined clear responsibilities to increase backloads, trained dispatchers to optimize capacity utilization and installed a real-time information tool to monitor vehicle availability. As a result, there were 7,000 fewer empty runs and the CO_2 efficiency improved from 100 to 70g CO_2 per revenue tonne kilometre.

For the last decade, different factors have led companies to invest in a green supply chain. But if this result is not encouraging, a study[5] conducted in 2008 showed that 78 per cent of the respondents considered that going green was important to their companies' overall strategy. They also consider that improving customer relations, being part of a larger corporate responsibility agenda, and a decreased fuel bill were the most important drivers for transport and logistics greening.

Table 10.3 shows the recent development of carbon emissions at DP DHL. As mentioned before, this is one of the largest industrial footprints of any industrial company. The two rows show the internal operations emissions Scope 1 and 2 over which DP DHL have direct control and the external emissions of contractors Scope 3 over which they have limited control, and which is significantly higher. This is because DP DHL outsources a large proportion of their activities, namely transportation. Hence to have a significant impact on their emissions overall there is a need to work closely with their transport contractors to find ways of reducing the carbon footprint. While the figures look quite stable, a useful measure is to compare these emissions with output or productivity. Hence the next table (Table 10.4) shows an index, on which their emissions targets are based.

DP DHL also developed a carbon efficiency index showing the relationship between economic measures and emissions. The original target of 30 per cent increase in carbon efficiency was reached in 2016. Interestingly each business unit measures efficiency differently due to the different types of activity (see note below table) with more transport-based activity using tkm or volume measures and supply chain using more asset-based efficiency metrics such as warehouse space. While this could be criticized in that it hides the true impacts, it can be helpful for the business to set targets based on better utilization which then also reflects cost advantage which will increase motivation to improve.

While DP DHL still has a long way to go to achieve those targets of carbon neutrality, the first step is to measure how the business is improving on the chosen metrics. From there the company can decide what innovations and technologies to invest in to achieve their longer-term goals, whether it is electric vehicles, autonomous vehicles or intelligent planning systems. In reality, of course, it is a combination of these that will help create more sustainable logistics solutions.

Table 10.3 Total carbon emissions for DP DHL

Total CO_2 emissions (million tonnes CO_2)	2007	2013	2014	2015	2016
Scopes 1 and 2 emissions	6.60	5.62	5.66	6.05	6.05
Scope 3 emissions	26.70	22.69	23.36	20.97	20.87

CASE STUDY 10.1

Table 10.4 Carbon efficiency index for DP DHL

	2007	2008	2009	2010	2011	2012	2013	2014	2015	2016
Group	0	3	9	15	18	20	22	26	29	30
						(1,278,297)	(2,195,062)	(3,660,516)	(4,583,553)	(4,446,547)
Post – E-commerce – Parcel	0	16	17	18	27	26	25	28	31	31
						(77,391)	(85,745)	(104,601)	(101,387)	(99,451)
Express	0	9	23	28	30	32	35	36	37	37
						(57,026)	(124,557)	(195,503)	(382,079)	(417,072)
Global forwarding	0	0	2	9	10	11	15	20	21	23
						(945,212)	(1,898,075)	(3,240,606)	(4,088,872)	(3,922,186)
Supply chain	0	-3	-4	11	20	26	23	27	32	30
						(198,668)	(86,685)	(119,806)	(11,215)	(7,838)

Index based on 2007 figures: Post = CO_2/litre (volume); Express = CO_2/tkm; Forwarding = CO_2/tkm or TEU; Supply chain = CO_2/warehouse space or transport revenue. Numbers in brackets are actual CO_2 emissions for customer shipments, in tonnes, CO_2 equivalent from 2015, verified by SGS.

10.7 Conclusion

This chapter has shown that logistics management and sustainability are inextricably linked, particularly on the transport planning side of logistics decisions. Transport provides the physical link in supply chains, and although is not always the most significant cost, it is often the biggest contributor to impacts on the environment. Transport costs increase with distance travelled, so are often correlated to impacts such as vehicle emissions. This means that reducing CO_2 can also reduce costs. Today there are many new technology opportunities to provide more sustainable transportation ranging from intelligent planning systems to electric vehicles. However, investments will often bring many additional costs to companies, who in this 'tight margin' industry can rarely afford to renew technologies as fast as desired by society. The real challenge is to be able to make decisions which are based on total costs, when many of the social costs are not sufficiently taken into account effectively by current systems. There are ways to optimize transport and reduce environmental impacts by increasing capacity utilization, and encouraging flexibility in delivery schedules (less frequent, during low-traffic periods). The question is whether these attempts to optimize transport flows is sufficient to address the burgeoning problems of pollution on public health and the stresses on limited fuel resources. If this is really the case, then not only will new technologies become imperative, but logistics managers may need to rethink their models for delivering products by completely redesigning the networks themselves and not just 'tinkering' with the processes.

Notes

1   https://www.ft.com/content/52d26de8-c0e6-11e5-846f-79b0e3d20eaf (last accessed 23 July 2018).
2   Ibid.
3   http://www.washingtonpost.com/wp-dyn/articles/A21755-2004Jul28.html (last accessed 25 October 2013).
4   Stern, The Economics of Climate Change, 2007.
5   Green Transportation and Logistics (2008): www.eft.com/green2008 (last accessed 23 January 2014).

References

Alberto P (2000) The logistics of industrial location decisions: An application of the analytic hierarchy process methodology. *International Journal of Logistics* 3(3): 273–289.

Bonney M and Jaber MY (2011) Environmentally responsible inventory models: Non-classical models for a non-classical era. *International Journal of Production Economics* 133(1): 43–53.

Bouchery Y, Ghaffari A, Jemai Z and Dallery Y (2012) Including sustainability criteria into inventory models. *European Journal of Operational Research* 222(2): 229–240.

Carter CR and Ellram LM (1998) Reverse logistics: A review of the literature and framework for future investigation. *Journal of Business Logistics* 19(1): 85–102.

Christopher M (ed.) (1992) *Logistics: The Strategic Issues*. London: Chapman & Hall.

Christopher M (1998) *Logistics and Supply Chain Management. Strategies for Reducing Costs and Improving Services*. 2nd edn, London: FT Prentice Hall.

de la Fuente D and Lozano J (1998) Determining warehouse number and location in Spain by cluster analysis. *International Journal of Physical Distribution & Logistics Management* 28(1): 68–79.

Eskandarpour M, Dejax P, Miemczyk J and Péton O (2015) Sustainable supply chain network design: An optimization-oriented review. *Omega* 54: 11–32.

Fabbe-Costes N, Jahre M and Roussat C (2008) Supply chain integration: The role of logistics service providers. *International Journal of Productivity and Performance Management* 58(1): 71–91.

Halldórsson Á and Kovács G (2010) The sustainable agenda and energy efficiency: Logistics solutions and supply chains in times of climate change. *International Journal of Physical Distribution & Logistics Management* 40(1/2): 5–13.

Halldórsson Á and Skjøtt-Larsen T (2004) Developing logistics competencies through third party logistics relationships. *International Journal of Operations & Production Management* 24(2): 192–206.

Harris I, Naim M, Palmer A, Potter A and Mumford C (2011) Assessing the impact of cost optimization based on infrastructure modelling on CO_2 emissions. *International Journal of Production Economics* 131(1): 313–321.

Hingley M, Lindgreen A, Grant DB and Kane C (2011) Using fourth-party logistics management to improve horizontal collaboration among grocery retailers. *Supply Chain Management: An International Journal* 16(5): 316–327.

Holter A, Liimatainen H, McKinnon A and Edwards J (2010) Double-deck trailers: A cost-benefit model estimating environmental and financial savings. *15th Annual Logistics Research Network Conference*. Leeds.

Howard M, Miemczyk J and Graves A (2006) Automotive supplier parks: An imperative for build-to-order? *Journal of Purchasing and Supply Management* 12(2): 91–104.

King A, Miemczyk J and Bufton D (2006) Photocopier remanufacturing at Xerox UK. A description of the process and consideration of future policy issues. In: Brissaud D, Tichkiewitch S and Zwolinski P (eds) *Innovation in Life Cycle Engineering and Sustainable Development*. Netherlands: Springer, pp. 173–186.

Korpela J and Lehmusvaara A (1999) A customer oriented approach to warehouse network evaluation and design. *International Journal of Production Economics* 59(1): 135–146.

KPMG (2017) *Future Proof Reverse Logistics Report*.

Kudla NL and Klaas-Wissing T (2012) Sustainability in shipper-logistics service provider relationships: A tentative taxonomy based on agency theory and stimulus–response analysis. *Journal of Purchasing and Supply Management* 18(4): 218–231.

Lambert DM and Stock JR (1993) *Strategic Logistics Management*. 3rd edn, Boston: McGraw Hill.

Langley CJ, Allen GR and Colombo MJ (2003) Third-party logistics: Results and findings of the 2003 eighth annual study. Georgia Institute of Technology, FedEX Supply Chain Services, and Cap Gemini Ernst & Young.

Leonardi J and Browne M (2010) A method for assessing the carbon footprint of maritime freight transport: European case study and results. *International Journal of Logistics: Research and Applications* 13(5): 349–358.

Michon V and Miemczyk J (2017) Horizontal logistics collaboration. *International Journal of Logistics Management*, in review.

Miemczyk J and Holweg M (2004) Building cars to customer order – what does it mean for inbound logistics operations? *Journal of Business Logistics* 25(2): 171–197.

Millimet DL and List JA (2004) The case of the missing pollution haven hypothesis. *Journal of Regulatory Economics* 26(3): 239–262.

Palmer A and Piecyk M (2010) Time, cost and CO_2 effects of rescheduling freight deliveries. *Proceedings of the logistics research network annual conference*. University of Leeds, Leeds.

Piecyk MI and McKinnon AC (2010) Forecasting the carbon footprint of road freight transport in 2020. *International Journal of Production Economics* 128(1): 31–42.

Razzaque MA and Sheng CC (1998) Outsourcing of logistics functions: A literature survey. *International Journal of Physical Distribution & Logistics Management* 28(2): 89–107.

ReVelle CS and Eiselt HA (2005) Location analysis: A synthesis and survey. *European Journal of Operational Research* 165(1): 1–19.

Sanchez-Rodrigues V, Potter A and Naim MM (2010) The impact of logistics uncertainty on sustainable transport operations. *International Journal of Physical Distribution & Logistics Management* 40(1/2): 61–83.

Schniederjans MJ and Cao Q (2001) An alternative analysis of inventory costs of JIT and EOQ purchasing. *International Journal of Physical Distribution & Logistics Management* 31(2): 109–123.

Selviaridis K, Spring M and Araujo L (2013) Provider involvement in business service definition: A typology. *Industrial Marketing Management* 42(8): 1398–1410.

Smarzynska BK and Wei S-J (2001) Pollution havens and foreign direct investment: Dirty secret or popular myth? *National Bureau of Economic Research Working Paper No 8465.*

Stock GN, Preis NL and Kasarda JD (1999) Logistics, strategy and structure: A conceptual framework. *International Journal of Physical Distribution and Logistics Management* 29(4): 224–239.

Stock J (1992) Reverse Logistics: White Paper. Oak Brook: Council of Logistics Management.

Van Laarhoven P, Berglund M and Peters M (2000) Third-party logistics in Europe – five years later. *International Journal of Physical Distribution & Logistics Management* 30(5): 425–442.

WEF (2016) Digital Transformation of Industries White Paper: Logistics Industry. World Economic Forum in collaboration with Accenture.

Wolf C and Seuring S (2010) Environmental impacts as buying criteria for third party logistical services. *International Journal of Physical Distribution & Logistics Management* 40(1/2): 84–102.

Wu H-J and Dunn SC (1995) Environmentally responsible logistics systems. *International Journal of Physical Distribution & Logistics Management* 25(2): 20–38.

Yang MGM, Hong P and Modi SB (2011) Impact of lean manufacturing and environmental management on business performance: an empirical study of manufacturing firms. *International Journal of Production Economics* 129(2): 251–261.

CHAPTER 11

Distribution systems

LEARNING OBJECTIVES

By the end of this chapter you should be able to:

- Describe the main channels to market and their implications;
- Understand the main physical distribution structures;
- Identify the key challenges of customer order fulfilment;
- Understand the specific difficulties of final delivery to customers especially in urban environments.

11.0 Introduction

This chapter links to Chapter 8 on supply chain strategies because these strategies determine how a distribution system will be structured. Specifically, this chapter focuses on the physical structures and processes which enable delivery of products to final customers. In recent years there has been a revolution in distribution systems across the globe. This is primarily driven by the rise of Internet-based retailing either through completely new businesses such as Amazon or the adaptation of existing sales channels with companies such as Carrefour and Tesco offering products directly for sale through the Internet.

The chapter is structured in the following way: the first part looks at the factors that determine the main channels to market from manufacturers to retailer and ultimately to final customers. This part adopts a marketing perspective in the sense this is one of the key interfaces between the marketing function and the supply chain. The second part examines the different structures that can be put in place to physically distribute products to end customers, with a focus on how cost and service levels can be managed through different distribution designs. Order fulfilment processes are covered in the following section, as this is the core process in distribution systems. The next section is related to how the final delivery portion is executed, often known as the last mile, and is related to a recent sub-discipline of city logistics. RFID (radio frequency identification) is discussed, as this is one of the key technological developments that can transform physical distribution processes of the future. The chapter ends with a case study on distribution collaboration to address cost and environmental impacts.

11.1 Channels to market

There are a number of channels to market that firms choose according to their overall strategy objectives. What the channel aims to achieve relates to how well the channel choice allows availability of the product, the impact this has on the ability to sell (i.e. if special knowledge is required), taking into account commercial constraints such as order quantities, service levels and costs. Furthermore, the ability to obtain information feedback – for example, on demand – may also be very important.

Note 11.1

Amazon's new ways to reach consumers

While Amazon has received plenty of press coverage over its trialling of drones as a means to deliver to customers, this is only one of their many innovations to distribute better. One of the key investment areas is artificial intelligence (AI, and use of big data) to provide much better predictions of what customers will buy and where these consumers are located. This is even to the extent that Amazon are willing to place certain items on trucks without an order, 'betting' that there will be a customer on the truck's route who needs the product in the next few hours. The combination of autonomous vehicles, whether drones or road-based vehicles, AI, big data and connected devices are being heralded to bring a new generation of distribution systems, spearheaded by the likes of Amazon. Yet these developments are accelerating faster than the pace of regulation, and the question of societal impacts is far from answered.

Source: https://www.smartdatacollective.com/amazon-wants-predictive-analytics-offer-anticipatory-shipping/ (last accessed 18 July 2018).

The primary functions of marketing channels according to Coughlan *et al.* (2006) are as follows: carrying inventory, demand generation, physical distribution, after-sale service and extending credit to customers. Clearly holding inventory in a distribution channel is key to meeting end-customer demand as without stocks somewhere in the channel, time becomes a major constraint to meeting customer demand. Creating demand from end-customer needs (today using electronic point of sale – EPOS – type data) is another important function, leading to issues of how quickly good quality demand information is transmitted to other channel members to help their own planning activities (stocks and resource allocations). The physical distribution part of the channel relates to the movement of goods which is important to meeting lead time expectations of customers but also can introduce significant cost into the process. Further, as products are not always 100 per cent reliable or if customers require training in the use of the product, certain channel types can be essential for repairing or taking back products or for providing information to customers. A final important financial role is the provision of credit to customers both as an incentive to buy but also to reach the greatest range of customers in terms of customer segments.

In addition to these general aims and functions of distribution channels there may also be specific characteristics or factors that need to be taken into account to understand and help select the structure of channels of distribution. Where the market of potential customers is very large, such as for fast moving consumer goods, it may be necessary to have many steps in the chain to reach customers, i.e. a complex network of retailers, local and regional warehouses such as in the supermarket sector. Conversely this chain could be relatively simple if there are few customers (a direct delivery approach). The products themselves may also provide specific constraints on the type of channel used. High-value items may allow more costly direct delivery as the margins are higher, although this is not necessarily the case. For example, high-value but technically complex products, such as cars, may require a highly specialized retail base to explain technical details such as safety features. Time-sensitive products with 'sell by' dates require fast and short channels. Or consider products which require specific handling such as hazardous chemicals that will also need specialized channels. Figure 11.1 provides a combined list of channel choice factors based on a number of research findings (Webster, 1976; Mallen, 1996). In sum, the choice of channel and its design will depend on the combination of these factors, raising many possible trade-offs relating to costs and service level. The fact that certain channel factors are required can introduce inefficiencies on the physical delivery side (fast, frequent movements), raising transport costs and subsequently environmental impacts.

Product factors	*Customer factors*
Unit value	Frequency of purchase
Product characteristics	Purchasing effort
Replacement rate	Rapidity of consumption
Gross margin	Significance of purchase
Adjustment	Waiting time
Rate of technological change (including	Searching Time
fashion changes)	Significance of each individual purchase to the
Technical complexity	consumer
Product complexity	Consumer need for service (before, during
Product life-cycle stage	or after sale)
Volatility of demand	Frequency of purchase
Brand positioning on quality	Rapidity of consumption
Perishability	Extent of usage (number and variety of
	consumers and variety)
Market factors	*Company factors*
Target focus on mass market	Range of products
Rate of technological change	Order size
Intensity of competition	Market share
Geographic concentration of market	Desire of control
	Retailer investments
	Number of support programmes
	Promotion budget
	Size of the firm

Figure 11.1 Channel choice factors

11.1.1 Main channel structures

This next section describes the main channel structures that can be put in place, particularly from a trading perspective (the physical structures for logistics elements will be discussed in the next subsection). The aim of these structures is to organize the link between production and the final customer, often a retailer – although direct links bypassing the retailer are becoming more and more common. Figure 11.2 outlines the main possible configurations within distribution channels.

11.1.2 Indirect channels

Manufacturer control over the channel has become less prevalent in recent years, where the ownership of the main components including DCs remains with the company. Relatively few companies are able to retain this structure in an efficient and effective manner, with exceptions such as the brewing industry where the handling and control of the product is very specific (dedicated containers, chilling and handling requirements). As large multi-site retail stores grew with the emergence of companies such as Tesco and Carrefour, retailer-controlled distribution from manufacturers has become more common. In this case the retailer designs the route of delivery from the suppliers of products including the management of distribution centres. Recently the transport and distribution centre management has been outsourced to logistics specialists although the overall control still rests with the retailer.

Wholesalers have remained in place in channel structures which serve multiple, smaller, often independent retailers. The main advantage here is that the wholesaler can obtain a price

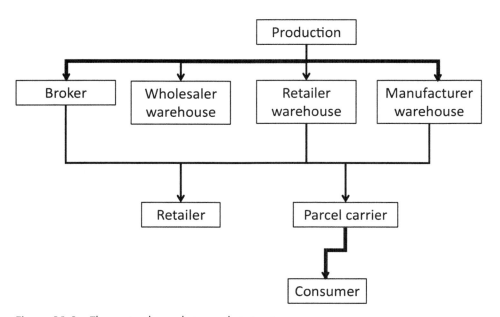

Figure 11.2 The main channels to market structures

reduction by making large order quantities. In many cases the wholesalers own the physical distribution part, including warehouses and transport capacity, which is often dedicated to specific types of products. Again, this is prevalent in food retailing with companies such as Brakes providing this type of service to smaller caterers, restaurants and so on.

Note 11.2: Reducing food miles – a flawed concept

For a number of years retailers focused on the food miles indicator to show improved sustainability of the food distribution process. However, recent studies are beginning to show that this approach is overly simplistic and simply reducing the distance travelled by food does not necessarily equate to better environmental and social implications. For example, the assumption that growing vegetables locally to avoid inter-continental transport is not necessarily less carbon-intensive when local greenhouses are used to grow food compared with growing outside but overseas. Instead, companies are starting to look at the carbon footprint of the whole process of growing, delivering and selling our food – for example, one company (G's Fresh) decided to move salad onion production to Senegal, with the crop freighted by ship rather than being grown and flown from Mexico and Egypt. This reduced greenhouse gas emission by nearly 8,000 kg CO_2 per tonne of produce – a reduction of over 90%.

Source: https://www.bangor.ac.uk/reo/news/what-happened-to-food-miles-20806
(last accessed 18 July 2018).

Third-party distribution companies have started to create specific channel structures. Often these types of service providers specialize in a particular market segment or product (such as glass or garments) that require specific assets for handling the product. A less used channel structure is one that uses brokers as an intermediary, and may only be a trading channel with no influence on the actual physical distribution structure, and while this may seem similar to the wholesaler structure the company only maintains a marketing/trading function.

11.1.3 Direct to customer channels

The last main channel structure is one which bypasses physical retailers entirely and has developed significantly due to the ubiquitous use of the Internet. This so-called business-to-consumer (B2C) channel has been in place for many years through the organization of mail order companies such as the French fashion retailer La Redoute. Typically the 'virtual' retailer has regional warehouses served by their manufacturers, which then use parcel delivery companies to make the final delivery. The main form of direct to consumer sales today is through Internet shopping websites such as Amazon (See Note 11.1). Again, Internet retailers typically have regional distribution centres in place which use aggregated demand from all end consumers to plan inventory levels. The delivery is then undertaken by third-party logistics specialists usually of next-day parcel delivery type. There are a number of advantages to this type of distribution channel. In particular, Internet-based companies can offer a large range and have high product availability performance as well as being very reactive on pricing and promotional activities according to changing demand. On the downside, customers have a completely different experience, they have to wait for delivery and have additional transportation costs. Although home delivery can be cheaper than a personal shopping trip, few customers take this into account when planning purchases (see section below on last mile delivery). Also if something goes wrong (quality problem or wrong product delivered), reverse-logistics costs can also be high compared to a traditional retailer.

The larger traditional retailers have realized that they cannot ignore the rise of the Internet-based selling model and this has led to retailers with multi-channel structures, notably physical shops and Internet sales. This became a particular conundrum for the sale of groceries from supermarkets which are difficult to handle (frozen goods) and time-sensitive (fresh products). Tesco was one of the pioneers in this field and started off having Internet demand fed from regional distribution centres and using small trucks to deliver direct to customers. However, Tesco experienced difficulties in managing this structure as the distribution centres (DCs) required multiple processes feeding outlets and individuals. This model later progressed to one where the fulfilment process was managed by the supermarkets themselves where customer orders are prepared and then collected by customers from the retail site without having to enter the shop. This model prevails today with the likes of Tesco in the UK, and Carrefour and Leclerc in France.

11.1.4 Key distribution channel issues

While the main physical distribution issues are dealt with in Section 11.2, there are also a number of other issues in marketing channels which need to be managed and can affect the overall performance and these include product ownership, risk sharing and organization of ordering and payment (Coughlan *et al.*, 2006). The first issue is managing the ownership of the products passing through the channel, with the main distinction being when the manufacturer relinquishes control of the product. Inventory management models, such as consignment stock or vendor-managed inventory, mean that the producers retain control of the product to the point of use, even at the customer's site. This is typically used in the business-to-business channel between suppliers and assemblers of products. Clearly more changes in possession and ownership in the channel mean more instances of profit margins being added and therefore higher end prices. Other processes include promotional activities where the manufacturer may promote products directly at the retailer using merchandizing displays (e.g. those used by Gillette). Manufacturers may also be directly involved in the financing process to stimulate sales as is the case in the automobile industry. Here the manufacturers have their own finance divisions that the retailer can use to offer credit to consumers, making use of the large manufacturers' superior credit opportunities.

Channel partners may also be involved in sharing the risks in the channel. Often, manufacturers want retailers to hold sufficient stocks to meet all expected sales in order to minimize lost sales. On the other hand, retailers seek to minimize the risk of over-stocks and therefore loss of profitability due to discounting to move inventory. This contradiction has led to a number of risk-sharing approaches that can be employed to attempt to optimize risks at a supply chain level and balance the risks between the manufacturer and the retailer. Contracts that include a buy-back clause are common in some sectors, originating in the book distribution channel. In this case the manufacturer offers to buy back any unsold products at a percentage of the wholesale price. In effect, this means the risk is shared and retailers hold more stock than they would do normally. However, the downside to this approach is that the distribution channel is governed by retailers' orders only (affected by choices of under- and over-stocks), and thus introduces significant demand distortion compared to the actual demand. In addition, efficient reverse logistics processes need to be put in place as described in the previous chapter, which can add significant costs. Another risk-sharing approach is revenue-sharing contracts where the manufacturer sells the product to the retailer at a low wholesale price but share a proportion of the end sales profit with the retailer. This has a similar effect as a buyback clause in distorting demand, can be expensive to put in place and clearly relies on a trusting relationship between the retailer and manufacturer. Quantity flexibility contracts are a more common approach today whereby manufacturers and retailers jointly seek to reduce the risks due to demand distortion. In this case the retailer can modify order sizes once more is known about the demand in order to have more accurate inventory holding. In this case the manufacturer holds some of the risks (excess inventory) but avoids buy-back and return costs. These types of arrangements are now common in fashion retailers, but do require good quality demand information relying on EPOS information.

11.1.5 Managing demand and cash in channels

The final set of essential issues involved in the distribution channel relate to the order process and payment process. Consider Dell, who has both an online retailer channel and a traditional physical retailer channel (recently introduced) but the two processes are entirely different. In the physical channel Dell sells through supermarket retailers, for example, receiving orders based on expected demand from the market. In turn Dell manufactures these 'stock' computers according to the aggregate demand from all such outlets; therefore orders arrive in a batch at different times from different retailers. However, payment is based on these large orders and improves visibility to Dell on expected revenue as contracts include minimum order quantities. From the customer perspective the order, payment and delivery processes are instantaneous; there may be an opportunity for a discount, but the choice of products can be restricted. In comparison, for the online channel, Dell receives 'real' end-consumer orders on a constant basis and only assembles the product once the order has been received, therefore avoiding demand distortion from order batching and unrealistic retailer forecasts. However, Dell has less payment visibility and risks losing customers who are unwilling to wait for direct shipments from the assembly site that can take more than a week. So, the order fulfilment processes are completely different with many advantages for the direct sales channel, but also risks.

In fact demand distortion is a generic supply chain challenge that occurs in any sector and at any level of the supply chain. To cope with demand distortion, it is essential to understand and communicate final customer demand throughout the supply chain. This phenomenon is also known as the bullwhip effect where demand signals get amplified from retailers through wholesalers to manufacturers of products (Lee *et al.*, 1997). In this case the demand at a factory can be extremely variable when the final demand at the end customer is quite stable. This introduces extra costs and risks of shortages for the final consumer. Therefore as a general rule, shorter distribution channels, and especially direct channels, can reduce the amount of demand distortion.

Due to its importance to distribution systems, the order fulfilment process will be discussed in more depth later in this chapter (Section 11.3).

11.2 Physical distribution structures

The main physical supply chain structures are reviewed in this part of the chapter. The key drivers of supply network structures (from a physical distribution perspective) are cost and service levels. As outlined in the previous chapter, logistics costs are primarily related to the cost of holding inventory and the cost of transporting products. From this perspective the total costs (sum of inventory and transport costs) should always, where practicable, be taken into account in designing physical distribution structures. A principal issue here is service level, in this case having product availability or high speed of delivery. Availability is dependent partly on the positioning of stock in the network (again related to distribution channel choices and can be thought of vertically – how close in the chain to the customer, and horizontally – across the range of customer locations) and the actual range (assortment in marketing terms) and quantity of stocks held in the network.

11.2.1 P:D ratio and lead time gap

One of the distribution network design factors is customer expectations on delivery times compared with production and delivery lead times. This partly depends on the level of customization versus standardization as mentioned in Chapter 8, but also the physical ability of the supply chain to deliver what the customer wants in a reasonable time-frame. This comparison of the customer expectation on delivery time and the capability of the supply chain is known as the lead time gap or the production lead time: demand lead time (P:D) ratio (Mather, 1988).

Where products are standard, customers are typically unwilling to wait for delivery as many alternative sources are likely. Conversely if products are more customized or exclusive

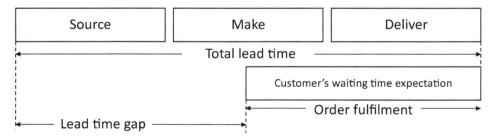

Figure 11.3 The P:D ratio and lead time gap

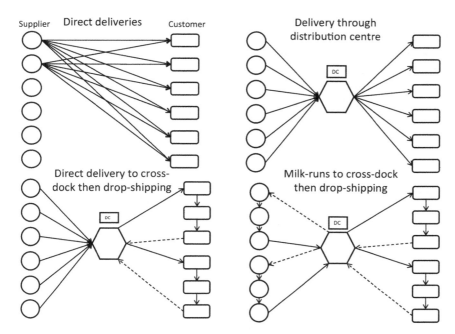

Figure 11.4 Typical distribution network structures

with limited supply sources, customers are more likely to accept or even expect a delivery delay. The challenge today, however, is that many products have a very long lead time, but short delivery expectation, such as fashion items sourced from South East Asia that typically have a lead time of six months. These products need to be stored close to the customer but require a very fast replenishment process. This is where a fast and flexible distribution system is essential.

The main distinctions in the design of the physical distribution network relate to stock holding (to meet expected service levels) and transport costs. In general, stocks of finished goods can be held either by the manufacturer or at any point between the manufacturer and retailer. Where there are intermediaries such as wholesalers (as defined in Section 11.1), stocks may be held in between to obtain certain advantages in performance. However, once transportation costs are added to the equation, there are a number of other options available to compensate for the rising transport costs that we see today. These include multiple pick-up and drop-shipping approaches, as well as consolidation and cross-docking operations. These elements are particularly focused on reducing the costs of transport where reduced order quantities, more frequent deliveries and lower finished goods stocks are concerned, and have become more common to help match supply with demand. These options are discussed next and summarized in Figure 11.4.

11.2.2 Manufacturer direct shipments

In this case manufacturers hold their finished goods stock at the factory, or in a finished goods warehouse waiting for end-customer orders. Once an order arrives the product is then shipped directly to the customer. This approach is the most cost-effective in terms of inventory holding because the manufacturer is able to aggregate all the demand from retailers or end consumers. This is particularly useful if products have high value, with a low but unpredictable demand. If these products were stocked close to the customer the risks of having the wrong products in the wrong place increase. On the downside the transportation costs are relatively high, especially where parcel carriers are used to deliver products directly to end users. The problem is exacerbated when there are multiple suppliers of related items, for example a PC and monitor from different manufacturers. The risk is that these will be delivered separately and could create customer dissatisfaction.

11.2.3 Direct shipment to a cross-dock, direct shipment to customer

In this case, where there is more than one manufacturer, shipments are grouped together at a distribution centre (or cross-dock operation). This is also known as a merge in transit operation. In some cases collections can be made from multiple manufacturers in order to reduce the transportation costs if only small quantities are collected. This is a practice that has been particularly driven by just in time (JIT) scheduling systems and has led to the term 'milk-run' or 'milk-round' collection to denote multiple suppliers delivering to a distribution centre on the same truck, often several times per day. One of the difficulties with this method is that coordination and information processing costs are high because the goal of the cross-dock is to avoid stock holding and only to transfer goods from the inbound to the outbound. Therefore, the collection from manufacturers has to be synchronized with the outbound transport from the cross-dock facility. This structure is sensitive to disruptions and increased

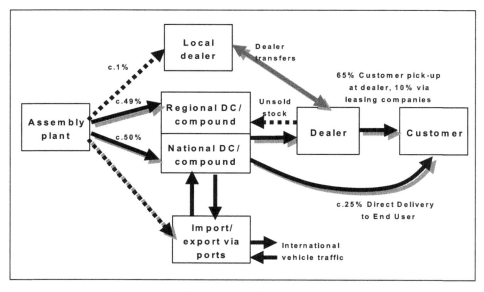

Figure 11.5 Distribution network structure in the automotive industry

Source: Holweg and Miemczyk (2002).

likelihood of stock-out situations, so the risks need to be minimized. Cross-docking approaches are typically used in the automotive sector to manage deliveries into vehicle assembly plants which hold very little stock.

11.2.4 Multiple pick-ups through a consolidation centre with multiple drop delivery

This last option minimizes the transport costs while being able to collect small quantities from suppliers and deliver small quantities to retailers or end consumers. Instead of a cross-dock this more traditional distribution centre is able to hold stock to buffer the differences in supply and demand. It is clear that the coordination costs and requirements for integrated information systems are high in this case. Consequently, mainly integrated distribution systems such as those used and importantly controlled by the big supermarkets use this type of organization. This is particularly useful where the demand is variable, so planning of deliveries is challenging, and where products have a high value or are perishable, such as fresh foods. Hence for the distribution of yoghurt, which can comprise a very wide variety (pot size, flavour, yoghurt type) this approach is key to minimizing obsolescence at both retailers and at distribution centres. The case at the end of the chapter highlights this approach, but specifically where suppliers work together through logistics service providers to offer a dedicated, efficient and responsive distribution system to their common customers.

In summary, the choices over direct delivery, routing through a cross-dock (merge in transit), through a distribution centre or use of milk-run collections or multi-drop delivery depends on a number of decision factors. These physical distribution factors are based primarily on the value of the product (and related inventory costs including obsolescence) and the nature of demand. Volatile, unpredictable demand for these products will necessitate fast replenishment systems either at retailers or distribution centres generally resulting in smaller collection and delivery batch sizes. At the same time the shift towards increasing numbers of consumers buying over the Internet implies that final destinations have increased exponentially, requiring even greater levels of distribution flexibility. Hence, the continued trend in product proliferation and Internet-based shopping means that it is likely that the use of these more flexible, responsive and rapid distribution systems will continue in the future and being deployed by Amazon, for example. The challenge ahead is to design systems that can maintain this level of reactivity, at a reasonable cost financially and to the environment.

There have been a number of studies investigating the energy efficiency implications of a variety of different distribution options. For example, in the wine industry, ironically it is the direct collection of wine from cellars and vineyards by end consumers (the most enjoyable way of buying) that provides the most impact, whereas traditional sales through supermarkets (less enjoyable) have the lowest impacts (Cholette and Venkat, 2009). The overall conclusion from many of these studies is that it is the consumer's trip to collect the product that uses the most energy and therefore the most carbon emissions (Browne *et al.*, 2008; Rizet *et al.*, 2010). Interestingly, this notion may be in conflict with the current trend in local sourcing of food products where customers pick up products from a farm shop, thereby increasing the total number of 'food miles'. Therefore, this chapter dedicates a section to the concept of last mile delivery to discuss some of the options for dealing with this final part of the distribution chain.

11.3 Order fulfilment cycle

The key process related to distribution systems is order fulfilment (Croxton, 2003), also known as the order management cycle (Shapiro *et al.*, 2001). Although this process is often viewed as a single entity, in reality it can comprise many 'sub-processes', as many as 10–20 in large organizations, especially where manufacturing planning is also required as part of fulfilment (see Table 11.1 – manufacturing planning (items in italics) may or may not be part of the fulfilment process). Therefore, before products even get into the distribution systems there are many sub-processes through which orders pass in order to be manufactured, creating time delays. Assuming the product is already manufactured, i.e. held in stock at a manufacturer or some other part of the distribution structure, there is still a series of steps that are needed. These include the order-generation and entry process, which if done manually can create significant delays. The processing of the order and handling of necessary documentation can also take significant time, which is why many companies have now invested in information systems to handle this part of the process, such as ERP systems. However, many small companies do not have these types of integrated technologies and therefore require manual input of information into spreadsheets before they are shared with the next step in the fulfilment process. Once the order is generated and scheduled the next step is to physically fill the order by retrieving and preparing the stock of the inventory location and scheduling it on the right delivery route. This might include final tests of functionality and packaging of the product, all of which introduce further delays in the process.

The order fulfilment process is seen as key – but often ignored – to the success of e-commerce today (Ricker and Kalakota, 1999). As this channel essentially replaces the instant gratification of the physical retailer, passing orders as quickly as possible is vital (Lee, 2002). Fulfilment is seen as an essential part of 'eService Quality' measures (Zeithaml *et al.*, 2002). Although this is not the only measure of quality of Internet-based shopping experiences – others include information availability and content, ease of use or usability, privacy/security, graphic style – if fulfilment goes wrong the impact on quality perceptions can be drastic. Wolfinbarger and Gilly (2002) identify fulfilment reliability as the most important predictor of customer satisfaction. This highlights that it is not only speed which is important, but also the ability to deliver to the promised date. Furthermore, not only technological advances improve the customer experience, but organizational resources enable faster cycle times through generating new, even risky, ideas and embedding learning into the process, requiring hard-won competitively valuable capabilities (Hult *et al.*, 2002).

In summary, the main point is that more often than not it is the processing of orders that creates the most delays in many distribution systems (Shapiro *et al.*, 2001). While it is important to consider the impact of speeding up the physical logistics part of the process, it is likely this will increase costs and environmental impacts to some degree (as mentioned in the next section). It makes more sense to look at information and order processing first, to optimize this to the greatest degree possible, and then tackle the transportation part of the process. In this way it is likely that the customer will be satisfied more quickly and the related trade-off with environmental performance can be avoided or at least minimized. However, this is not an easy task because it is essential that the different functional units be integrated in terms of information and aligned in terms of objectives. Here, organizational culture and internal political forces can be the biggest barrier to customer satisfaction.

Table 11.1 Main sub-processes of the order fulfilment process

Sub-processes	Inputs	Outputs
Order entry system	Orders, committed orders, bills of materials, and inventory status	Committed orders
Master production scheduling	Committed orders, bills of materials, capacity planning and material plan	Monthly build plan, and order committed dates
Weekly production scheduling	Monthly build plan, bills of materials, capacity plan, and material plan	Weekly build plan
Daily production scheduling	Weekly build plan, bills of materials, capacity plan, and material plan	Daily build plan
Capacity planning	Shop floor configuration, and job contents	Capacity plan
Material requirement planning	Monthly, weekly, and daily build plans; and inventory status	Materials plan
Supply chain management	Materials requirement plan and supplier information	Purchase orders
Shop floor control	Daily work order	Job dispatching and resource allocation
Order filling	Product type and location	Product in distribution preparation area
Packaging and shipping	Product and accessories, pallet requirements	Product package ready for logistics
Distribution plan	Product, order dates and customer locations, vehicle and route availability	Delivered products
Returns and claims	Customer claim	Product replaced or client compensated
Post-sales service	Request for repair, upgrade, maintenance, disposal	Service delivered

11.4 Last mile and city logistics

This section deals with the final delivery portion to the end customer or as in most cases to a final retail location. This is often known as last mile logistics and can be one of the most costly parts of the distribution chain in terms of transport, but also the one where the customer directly experiences the impact of service level, especially if things go wrong (Fernie *et al.*, 2010). Related to this is the fact that the majority of 'last mile' operations occur in the urban environment. As urban infrastructure continues to be under pressure from the multitude of users, and is also where populations are most sensitive to damaging effects of pollution and noise and so on, the management of distribution systems takes on a clear social dimension.

From this, a strand of logistics has developed, known as city logistics, which is marked by many successful and failed examples of how a balance can be achieved between competitive priorities and social externalities.

11.4.1 Last mile logistics

The last mile delivery service is, as the term suggests, delivering to the final consumer of the product, the last portion of the chain from manufacturer through the distribution system to the point of use. In most cases when discussing last mile logistics, the concern is reaching private individuals in their homes. In reality, this part of the chain is simply the last leg of the journey which could equally be a business such as a factory or a retailer. According to Kuehne and Nagel (Goodman, 2005), last mile delivery is 'the time-sensitive delivery of parts to the ultimate end user in a way that's time-specific as opposed to, you get there when you get there on the route or when the parcel delivers. It's a custom time delivery.' The physical delivery of products to customers depends greatly on the channel to market chosen by the company. A key challenge today is the rise of Internet retailing requiring direct delivery to customers' homes through companies such as Amazon. A recent development is for retailers to join this channel by offering a home shopping service. Here customers either receive their groceries from a distribution centre (DC) or from a local store, and they are then delivered to the home or customers collect the complete order from the store themselves. The efficiency (and therefore cost) of each of these options is variable. A typical home delivery from a DC might include 14–18 deliveries per route (usually during a single driver's shift of eight hours). As stores are more dispersed compared with DCs this can be higher (16–20) in the same time-frame, thus more efficient. Compare this with the B2B office supplies service from companies such as Staples or OfficeDepot and the route can have up to 40 deliveries for a similar value of orders, and therefore be even more efficient (Boyer et al., 2005). This greater efficiency is driven by the fact that businesses tend to be closer to each other (on industrial estates) and their delivery windows are more predictable and wider (usually 9am–5pm). There are specific difficulties with this delivery mode, however. Picking errors can increase because the process often relies on single-item picking operations (instead of batch picking in a typical DC). Damage can also increase due to more handling in general of single items and also the issue that fresh goods may not be of the best quality. Furthermore, companies like Tesco have needed to adapt small vans to carry frozen, chilled and standard products.

One of the key sustainability issues related to last mile delivery is the comparison between tradition retail delivery and online retailing involving direct delivery to customers' homes. While there are significant difficulties in comparing the two (Edwards et al., 2011), there do seem to be advantages to direct home delivery from a carbon reduction point of view. However, when it goes wrong – the driver misses a delivery window or the goods need to be returned – the impacts can be significantly greater (as shown in Table 11.2). As anyone who frequently shops online knows, home delivery is often far from ideal. As drivers have a limited timescale they will usually leave products in a nominated location, leave with a neighbour or require a designated delivery slot. These tactics to reduce cost may have unintended consequences (such as theft or anti-social delivery times) and will be dependent on cultural and legal situations.

The trade-off between speed and cost is one of the key issues related to last mile delivery and is a key issue in the trend for increasing responsiveness of distribution systems. As

Table 11.2 Comparison of home delivery options

Shopping activity type	gCO$_2$	Factor
Bus travel during busy period (5 or more items bought)	78	0.43
Standard home delivery drop	**181**	**1.00**
30% first-time delivery failure rate	235	1.30
Trip chain by bus (shopping 25% of distance)	316	1.75
Average shopping trip by bus	1,265	6.99
Average shopping trip by car	**4,274**	**23.61**
Home delivery drop with consumer return via retailer	4,509	24.91
Failed delivery, consumer collection via local warehouse	**5,188**	**28.66**

Source: Based on Edwards and McKinnon (2009).

already mentioned, one of the impacts of not holding stock at retailers is the need for direct deliveries that do not exceed the customers' willingness to wait. Research in the automotive sector is useful for illustrating this issue and the potential effects this can have. In the 3DayCar programme – a UK ESPRC[1] research project comprising universities and companies – researchers examined the impact of faster and more frequent deliveries to the final destination, in this case customer pick-up at a car dealership. The economics of car transporters (vehicles

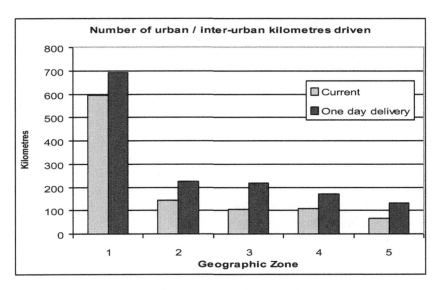

Figure 11.6 Increased fuel use from more rapid vehicle delivery

Source: Holweg and Miemczyk (2002).

that carry up to 12 cars at a time) mean that a delivery is only justified when the transporter has a full load. A large dealership might sell 10 or 12 cars per week, justifying one delivery per week. However, if faster delivery were required – for example, everyday delivery so customers do not wait – a transporter would need to visit multiple dealers (4–5 dealers) each day dropping 2–3 cars each time. This extends the overall distance travelled, on the so-called dispersion leg of the journey (Holweg and Miemczyk, 2003). Researchers examined the overall logistics network of a car carrier and modelled the costs and impacts of a one-day delivery lead time (delivering every day), finding that vehicle kilometres driven and therefore costs and carbon emissions could rise by 30 per cent, as shown in Figure 11.6 (Holweg and Miemczyk, 2002).

11.4.2 City logistics

The majority of direct delivery challenges, whether from supermarkets or other online retailers, stem from the need to deliver into dense urban areas. This presents a multiplicity of sustainability-related problems from road pollution, noise pollution, congestion and so on (O'Connor, 2010). Thus a particular strand of logistics management has developed known as 'city logistics'.

Note 11.3

City logistics in London

Being the largest city in Europe, London has been at the forefront of urban logistics innovations for many years, with the London mayor Sadiq Khan's manifesto commitments including improving air quality, ensuring safety and tackling congestion.

London is a net importer of goods, where road is the main mode of transport with around 130 million tonnes delivered in 2012 (water – 8.7, rail 6.7 and air 1.6 million tonnes each). Heavy goods vehicles movements have been stable over the years, but light goods vehicles with nearly 4 billion vehicle Kms in 2012 (Allen *et al.*, 2014) are increasing rapidly. This is partly from growing home delivery services with light goods transport likely to increase by 20 per cent in the next 10 years or so.[2]

One example to reduce the impact of urban freight transport is the consolidation centre opened in Edmonton in 2014 serving the council boroughs of Camden, Enfield, Islington and Waltham. These boroughs comprise libraries, schools, care homes, offices and commercial premises. Using a common procurement platform and consolidation centre has saved procurement costs through a reduced supply base and shorter distances. At the same time vehicle trips are reduced by 46 per cent, distance transported reduced by 45 per cent (with a 41 per cent CO_2 reduction), improved vehicle utilization rates (about 70 per cent) and numerous other benefits.

Other initiatives in London include timed deliveries to reduce congestion. Transport for London has set itself a target of re-timing 500 sites and 4,000 deliveries (currently reaching 144 sites); this also means engaging with over 200 stakeholders to find the right solutions. Working with these stakeholders, companies such as McDonalds, Waitrose, Savers and DHL have saved costs, CO_2 impacts and time by shifting to earlier deliveries – avoiding the 7am–11am peak.[3]

To overcome the issue of missed home deliveries there are now more 'click and collect' options, creating a network across London where consumers can pick up their online orders without generating more traffic. Service providers include Amazon Locker, Parcelly, CollectPlus and HubBox offering an alternative delivery option to retailers.

Urban freight distribution strategies are difficult to implement as they typically involve higher costs and delays. There are three main urban distribution strategies. The first strategy is to rationalize deliveries so that fewer trucks enter the city centre to deliver to retailers, with the intention of minimizing congestion. What normally happens is that deliveries are restricted to certain times of the day, avoiding the daytime for example. Night-time deliveries are also an option or delivery times that avoid peak traffic periods. This means that deliveries are concentrated to certain times of the day which creates its own peaks in freight movements which in turn creates inconveniences and makes finding efficiencies more difficult. Added to this there are difficulties in matching deliveries and pick-up times so that return journeys are often empty. There has been a move to attempt to consolidate deliveries across multiple retailers in the same area but then finding common delivery windows is even more of a challenge. Also retailers may have widely different products, so the handling issues become significant, especially when synergies are sought between completely different sectors such as retail and waste collection.

The second strategy to enable consolidation is the use of shared freight facilities. These can take the form of urban freight distribution centres located out of town (acting as a hub for the town centre) or for local freight stations placed in a specific district from which consumers can pick up their products. Urban consolidation centres are often located closer to the town centre to create consolidation services and other value-added activities for the local demand. Often these facilities require public funding initially and as this often disappears many such centres across Europe have closed down (see Note 11.3). This is not only a European phenomenon, for example with Tenjin within the city of Fukuoka in Japan, where authorities found that at least 61 per cent of delivery trucks covered the same routes and so found solutions to consolidate them (Brown *et al.*, 2009).

A third urban logistics strategy is adapting the modes used (Nemoto *et al.*, 2006). Normally this means using smaller vehicles for the delivery providing a smaller footprint to reduce congestion, better manoeuvrability and higher load efficiency. On the downside, more vehicle movements are required for the same demand volume with significantly increased costs. Even bicycle delivery systems have been put in place in some cities as a less capital-intensive, lower-cost solution. Mixed modes have also been used, for example, the failed cargo-tram system in Amsterdam or the more successful distribution of books through the metro system in Seoul, South Korea.

The key problem with these three distribution system solutions is that the costs of delivering a unit is bound to increase. This is due to the increased handling costs, greater coordination costs and reduced vehicle efficiency. While consolidation does provide a partial solution, the overall cost is often too high to justify by private companies, and retailers are often unwilling to pay a premium for this type of service. The main challenge is that the environmental externalities (costs of congestions, damage to health, and impact of accidents) are not included in the costs of delivery; instead they are borne by the community, local authorities and national health institutions. For this to really work either these externalities need to be transferred to the delivery cost through taxes or fiscal measures (such as the London congestion charge), or local authorities need to be compensated through national policy to subsidize these schemes and in the current economic climate this seems not to be a priority.

11.5 RFID use in distribution

Another recent development aimed at creating efficiencies in distribution systems is the use of RFID (radio frequency identification) technologies. An RFID tag is a chip with a radio antenna, that can store data related to manufacturing date, delivery destination and shelf-life information, and be attached to products or packaging. The information on the chip is collected by a reader, which is connected to an information system such as a warehouse management system. Cost has been the main barrier to RFID adoption so far, and so the complete replacement of barcode systems is still a future aspiration (see Table 11.3 comparing RFID and barcodes). They have only been used where they can be justified, usually in JIT

Table 11.3 Comparison of barcodes and RFID

RFID	Barcode
Does not need a 'line-of-sight'. So location/ orientation of the reader does not matter if within range	Requires line-of-sight
Many tags read simultaneously	Only one read at a time
Durable: resistant to heat, dirt and solvents and hence are not physically damaged easily	Easily damaged
RFID tags can be self-powered (active tags). Can also collect information and store it locally	Only a static label
RFID tags can be written multiple times, making them reusable	Not reusable
Expensive (relative to barcodes)	Less expensive
Liquids and metals near or around the tags cause read problems	Can be used on or around water and metal with no performance loss
RFID tags must be added to during production process	Can be printed before production or directly on the items

Source: Adapted from Delen *et al.* (2007).

delivery systems or for valuable assets such as reusable containers, and within internal company operations, such as inside warehouses where they can be reused easily. However, the difficulty is in using RFID for tracking items in open supply chains where tags cannot be recovered from the end consumer.

In recent years, cost effectiveness has improved to the point that companies such as Walmart include RFID tags at the item level, for example on clothing products such as jeans.[4] This is particularly useful for products with many stock keeping units (SKUs) (e.g. when there are multiple styles and sizes), which are difficult to track leading to stock inaccuracies and so on. Walmart is working with its main suppliers to ensure the tags are attached to clothing from the moment of manufacture, and helping suppliers incorporate RFID data into their own warehousing and inventory management systems, so that the investment pays off for both parties. At the retailers the tags give Walmart information about the location of products throughout the store from goods-in inventory to checking the items are in the right shelf area. Due to personal data protection the tags are not used for point of sale information and therefore RFID information is not related to customer details, even though the tags are left on the items for customers to remove at home.

There is a growing field of research on RFID ranging from technical development to impacts from an organizational and managerial perspective (Dutta and Whang, 2007), much of which has focused on the value and benefits of RFID technologies. The main benefit has been posited as the improvement in visibility at the supply chain level (Delen et al., 2007). Others have argued that the benefits of RFID come in three main forms: labour cost savings (efficiency and accuracy of auditing inventory levels), reduction in shrinkage (discouraging theft, preventing crime and improving recovery of products) and improved visibility (avoiding sales loss due to inaccurate replenishment) (Dutta et al., 2007). There are also challenges related to the use of RFID mainly concerning the management of the data received. These can be summarized into problems of missing reads (false negatives), multiple reads (false positives) and the overall challenges of managing datasets which are orders of magnitude greater than those generated by barcode-based systems (Delen et al., 2007).

There is little research to date on the impact of RFID technology on sustainability (Dukovska-Popovska et al., 2010). Yet there are some opportunities to improve environmental performance through the use of this type of technology by improving efficiencies overall (Dao et al., 2011). For example, RFID can be used to provide better tracking of products through closed-loop supply chains (Visich et al., 2007). Companies have also claimed that the improved inventory visibility has reduced truck journeys (Bose and Yan, 2011), with Walmart claiming a saving of 3.2 per cent in journeys (Karakasa et al., 2007). Another key problem that can be addressed by RFID is that of traceability, especially in sectors such as food where safety and traceability are inextricably linked (Kelepouris et al., 2007), as shown in the recent equine DNA in beef scandal (see also Chapter 8). This technology can also be used to detect when food products may have changed temperature, leading to bacterial development risks, for example, salmonella risks in frozen chicken (Huang et al., 2006). Furthermore, there has been some controversy over the use of RFID to help distribution and retail workers. Tesco has used RFID chips to track warehouse worker movements and help them manage information, but the ethical implications of tracking people (including during their break time) has been raised by many observers as contravening of basic worker rights.[5]

SUPPLY CHAIN ORCHESTRATION BY TRI-VIZOR

In Europe there is a growing phenomenon of product manufacturers in the FMCG sector working together to save costs in their physical distribution channels. The pressure to reduce logistics costs, deliver more responsively and to do so while reducing carbon footprint has led to a number of recent collaborations in Europe. This goes beyond the traditional consolidation and groupage described earlier in this chapter and requires that shippers synchronize their deliveries with their competitors so that they can coordinate deliveries into retailers, in order to reduce empty truck space. More often than not this requires shared planning and warehouse operations. The trend has been driven by less and less capacity in the transport sector, alongside looming driver shortage, despite often very low load utilization in trucks. While overall volume in the FMCG sector in Europe has remained stable the number of shipments has increased with smaller and smaller order sizes to reduce inventory costs. Alongside this, the average speed of delivery in Europe has reduced from around 65km/hour in the 1990s to 55km/hour now, making more responsive logistics even more challenging.

Tri-Vizor is a small company based in Belgium set up by two entrepreneurs, Alex Van Breedam and Bart Vannieuwenhuyse. Both are experienced and visionary supply chain experts who realized that logistics capacity could not grow in an unlimited way. Clustering and pooling capacity on the one hand and consolidating and bundling of flows on the other hand would be necessary to cope with the future capacity shortages. Both entrepreneurs had been working for the Flanders Institute for Logistics, experimenting with logistics collaborations and communities and realized very soon that there was a need for a neutral and impartial orchestrator to let two or more companies work together. Consequently, in 2008 they founded the first commercial, but neutral, orchestrator. The basic idea behind their business is to provide a logistics coordination service between horizontally collaborating shipping companies to allow them to utilize their mutually spare transport/order capacity. Their concept appears to fit seamlessly into a physical Internet concept where, like the web-based Internet, common data sharing platforms allow complete connectivity. Ultimately Tri-Vizor can be seen as a neutral supply chain orchestrator able to synchronize capacity and flows both across and between supply chains to reduce costs, maximize asset utilization and minimize environmental impacts. Another way of looking at their business model is to think of car-sharing schemes but for trucks. So the ambition of Tri-Vizor is to set up collaboration in logistics among peer companies in a structural way rather than dealing with ad hoc co-loadings based on a casual match.

One of the first and most successful examples of how Tri-Vizor has done this is the collaboration set up by them for the distribution consolidation of Nestlé and PepsiCo and operated by STEF, a logistics service provider. In this example Nestlé and PepsiCo – through STEF – share transport and warehouse capacity, while still competing with each other, to provide very frequent deliveries of chilled products to supermarket chains in Belgium and Luxembourg. Working with competitors to share logistics is not a natural behaviour for these types of shippers and there are also significant legal barriers to overcome as well. Both companies have to demonstrate that they do not fall victim of EU anti-trust legislation, proving that they are not operating a closed, cartel-type arrangement fixing pricing of goods and services. This is partly where Tri-Vizor adds value as a neutral broker or logistics trustee. This project was strongly supported by BABM (Belgilux Association of Branded Products Manufacturers). This is where the challenge in horizontal logistics really occurs. It is vital that demand and stock information are made visible; however, the competitors cannot be seen as sharing this information. Hence

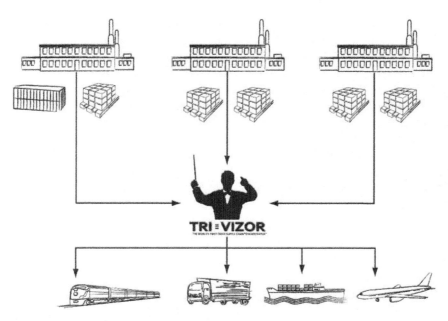

Figure 11.7 Depiction of Tri-Vizor's role as orchestrator

Source: Tri-Vizor.

Tri-Vizor guarantees the 'Chinese Walls' between the shippers involved while generating the gains and benefits of the consolidation. It is essential that Tri-Vizor holds a high level of trust with the cooperating partners. Another key challenge is sharing the benefits in an equitable way. Again Tri-Vizor has to assure that the benefits (gain sharing) of combining loads and orders provide benefits to all sides in the partnership, which is not easy when the partners do not have full information on who is gaining the most from load sharing. In the initial phase STEF handled 220 SKUs and 21,000 tonnes of volume combined, operating from its temperature-controlled warehouse in Saintes (Brussels), and delivered to 112 customers with 20 per cent common ship-to addresses. Impressively these shared customers made up more than 90 per cent of the total delivery volume, providing huge transport and logistics synergies. The collaboration was started in 2012 and was even extended in 2017 after a joint effort of the community to better synchronize the deliveries to the common customers.

Another couple of notable examples coordinated by Tri-Vizor are also based in Belgium. Within the framework of NexTrust (an EU Horizon 2020 project on building sustainable logistics through collaborative networks across the entire supply chain), Tri-Vizor coordinated the set-up of the first Multi-Retailer Multi-Supplier Platform (MSMRP) for cookies. These kinds of products are often delivered in small quantities which impacts on cost and efficiency and hence carbon footprint for both the manufacturers and retailers. The companies involved in a first pilot included the retailers Delhaize, Colruyt, RPCG and Okay, the cookie suppliers Vondemolen, Poppies, Vermeiren Princeps and Desobry, with Kuhne and Nagel as logistics provider. This has become a true orchestration effort between the four retailers on one hand and the main four cookie producers on the other hand. The objective is to reduce the truck movement to and from the consolidation platform as much as possible to full trucks. The fill rate of the trucks improved from 48 per cent previously to almost 91 per cent with the MSMRP. This pilot and additional calculation revealed that gains could be realized on inventory as well as on transport and that a redistribution of the gains by the orchestrator would be required to encourage all parties to participate on the platform. As always in these horizontal collaborations the improved capacity utilization results in both improved costs and a reduced carbon footprint are reached simultaneously. A double-digit gain in both domains – cost efficiency and environmental benefits – appears to be a realistic goal. In cases where after bundling volumes a modal shift towards alternative transport modes, like water or rail, is feasible, a real breakthrough in carbon footprint could be realized (reduction of up to 30 per cent).

11.6 Conclusion

The main developments in distribution systems in recent years have stemmed from the need to respond to widespread use of Internet channels to reach customers. While Internet-only retailers have enjoyed huge growth in the consumer goods industry, the more traditional retailers have also adapted their channels and structures in reaction to this changing competitive landscape. As a result there have been significant shifts in the physical distribution structures put in place to connect manufacturers with consumers. Alongside greater needs for speed and responsiveness, transport and warehouse networks have been adapted to provide greater levels of customer service without compromising on cost. Technological advances such as RFID are also beginning to influence the practices in distribution systems, allowing greater levels of automation and performance enhancement in a number of areas.

Many initiatives have been put in place to provide solutions to delivering products to customers in a sustainable way. This is partially driven by the fact that distribution systems provide the link to the final customer, who is becoming more sensitive to sustainability issues. There are also burgeoning environmental costs such as increasing fuel price and taxing of the road infrastructure in urban areas. Thus distribution organization is now particularly challenging when there is a shift in customers' buying behaviour, where retailers have to find new delivery solutions with a reasonable cost which do not contradict environmental and social imperatives.

Notes

1   Engineering and Physical Sciences Research Council – a UK-based research funding body.
2   https://www.london.gov.uk/moderngov/documents/s52363/Appendix%201%20-%20Light%20 Commercial%20Traffic%20views%20and%20information.pdf (last accessed 18 July 2018).
3   http://freightinthecity.com/2016/06/tfl-expands-retiming-deliveries-work-in-the-capital/#YrKjJaQKV1huxE8Y.99 (last accessed 18 July 2018).
4   http://www.rfidjournal.com/articles/view?7753 (last accessed May 2013).
5   http://www.independent.co.uk/news/business/news/tesco-accused-of-using-electron ic-armbands-to-monitor-its-staff-8493952.html (last accessed May 2013).

References

Allen J, Browne M and Woodburn A (2014) London Freight Data Report: 2014 Update, Report by Univeristy of Westminster for Transport for London, London.

Bose I and Yan S (2011) The green potential of RFID projects: A case-based analysis. *IT Professional* 13(1): 41–47.

Boyer KK, Frohlich MT and Hult GTM (2005) *Extending the Supply Chain: How Cutting-edge Companies Bridge the Critical Last Mile into Customers' Homes*: AMACOM/American Management Association.

Browne M and Leonardi J (2009) Différentes méthodes de quantification du CO_2 du transport de fret. *Journée INRETS Supply-chains, énergie et CO_2*, Paris.

Browne M, Rizet C, Leonardi J and Allen J (2008) Analysing energy use in supply chains: The case of fruits and vegetables and furniture. *Proceedings of the Logistics Research Network Conference*, 10–12 September, Liverpool, UK.

Cholette S and Venkat K (2009) The energy and carbon intensity of wine distribution: A study of logistical options for delivering wine to consumers. *Journal of Cleaner Production* 17(16): 1401–1413.

Coughlan AT, Anderson E, Stern LW and Ansary AI (2006) *Marketing Channels*. Englewood Cliffs, NJ: Prentice Hall.

Croxton KL (2003) The order fulfillment process. *The International Journal of Logistics Management* 14(1): 19–32.

Dao V, Langella I and Carbo J (2011) From green to sustainability: Information Technology and an integrated sustainability framework. *The Journal of Strategic Information Systems* 20(1): 63–79.

Delen D, Hardgrave BC and Sharda R (2007) RFID for better supply chain management through enhanced information visibility. *Production and Operations Management* 16(5): 613–624.

Dukovska-Popovska I, Lim MK, Steger-Jensen K and Hvolby H (2010) RFID technology to support environmentally sustainable supply chain management. *RFID-Technology and Applications (RFID-TA) 2010 IEEE International Conference*: 291–295.

Dutta A and Whang S (2007) Radiofrequency identification applications in private and public sector operations: Introduction to the special issue. *Production and Operations Management* 16(5): 523–524.

Dutta A, Lee HL and Whang S (2007) RFID and operations management: Technology, value, and incentives. *Production and Operations Management* 16(5): 646–655.

Edwards J and McKinnon A (2009) Comparing the environmental impact of online and conventional shopping: Auditing 'last mile' anomalies. *Retail Digest*, Fall: 10.

Edwards J, McKinnon A and Cullinane S (2011) Comparative carbon auditing of conventional and online retail supply chains: A review of methodological issues. *Supply Chain Management: An International Journal* 16(1): 57–63.

Fernie J, Sparks L and McKinnon AC (2010) Retail logistics in the UK: Past, present and future. *International Journal of Retail & Distribution Management* 38(11): 894–914.

Goodman RW (2005) Whatever you call it, just don't think of last-mile logistics. *Global Logistics and Supply Chain Strategies*, December. Available at: www.kn-portal.com/fileadmin/_public/documents/material/KNUCLRP_LastMile_Logistics.pdf (last accessed 25 October 2013).

Holweg M and Miemczyk J (2002) Logistics in the 'three-day car' age: Assessing the responsiveness of vehicle distribution logistics in the UK. *International Journal of Physical Distribution & Logistics Management* 32(10): 829–850.

Holweg M and Miemczyk J (2003) Delivering the 3-day car: The strategic implications for automotive logistics operations. *European Journal of Purchasing and Supply Management* 9: 63–71.

Huang H-P, Chen C-S and Chen T-Y (2006) Mobile diagnosis based on RFID for food safety. *Automation Science and Engineering, 2006. CASE '06. IEEE International Conference on*: 357–362: IEEE.

Hult GTM, Ketchen DJ and Nichols EL (2002) An examination of cultural competitiveness and order fulfillment cycle time within supply chains. *Academy of Management Journal* 45(3): 577–586.

Karakasa Y, Suwa H and Ohta T (2007) Evaluating effects of RFID introduction based on CO_2 reduction. *Proceedings of the 51st Annual Meeting of the ISSS*, 5–10 August, Tokyo.

Kelepouris T, Pramatari K and Doukidis G (2007) RFID-enabled traceability in the food supply chain. *Industrial Management & Data Systems* 107(2): 183–200.

Lee HL (2002) Aligning supply chain strategies with product uncertainties. *California Management Review* 44(3): 105–119.

Lee HL, Padmanabhan V and Whang S (1997) The bullwhip effect in supply chains. *Sloan Management Review* 38(3): 93–102.

Mallen B (1996) Selecting channels of distribution: a multi-stage process. *International Journal of Physical Distribution and Logistics Management* 26(5): 5–15.

Mather H (1988) *Competitive Manufacturing*. Englewood Cliffs, NJ: Prentice Hall.

Nemoto T, Browne M, Visser J and Castro J (2006) Intermodal transport and city logistics policies. *Recent Advances in City Logistics. The 4th International Conference on City Logistics*, 12–14 July, Langkawi, Malaysia.

O'Connor K (2010) Global city regions and the location of logistics activity. *Journal of Transport Geography* 18(3): 354–362.

Ricker FR and Kalakota R (1999) Order fulfillment: The hidden key to e-commerce success. *Supply Chain Management Review* 11(3): 60–70.

Rizet C, Cornelis E, Browne M and Léonardi J (2010) GHG emissions of supply chains from different retail systems in Europe. *Procedia-Social and Behavioral Sciences* 2(3): 6154–6164.

Shapiro BP, Rangan VK and Sviokla JJ (2001) Staple yourself to an order. *Harvard Business Review* 78(2).

Visich JK, Li S and Khumawala BM (2007) Enhancing product recovery value in closed-loop supply chains with RFID. *Journal of Managerial Issues* 19(3): 436–452.

Webster FE (1976) The role of the industrial distributor in marketing strategy. *Journal of Marketing* 40: 10–16.

Wolfinbarger M and Gilly M (2002) comQ: Dimensionalizing, measuring, and predicting quality of the e-tail experience. *Marketing Science Institute Report (02–100)*. Cambridge, MA.

Zeithaml VA, Parasuraman A and Malhotra A (2002) Service quality delivery through web sites: A critical review of extant knowledge. *Journal of the Academy of Marketing Science* 30(4): 362–375.

Part C
Policy, tools and implementation

CHAPTER 12

Supply chain mapping and evaluation

LEARNING OBJECTIVES

By the end of this chapter you should be able to:

● Define the links between sustainable supply strategy and policy, tools and implementation;

● Describe the rationale behind supply chain mapping;

● Evaluate the use of tools such as life-cycle assessment and carbon footprinting;

● Describe the challenges of introducing low carbon procurement;

● Analyse trends in sustainability policy and the implications for supply chains.

12.0 Introduction

This chapter introduces supply chain mapping and evaluation as key elements to starting the implementation process towards a sustainable supply chain: the overarching theme of Part C. While the development of strategy is an important first step towards sustainability, it is often only when firms attempt to put into practice what they have been talking about that the real challenges begin to emerge. It is important, therefore, to understand the links between supply strategy, external policy, enabling tools and implementation that allow the shift towards sustainability to take root (Figure 12.1). The first steps in implementing a sustainable supply chain involves more than considerations around organizational change, requiring an in-depth understanding of the types of impact the firm seeks to target as a priority. Figure 12.1 on the next page presents an overview of the major elements involved, which are addressed over the coming chapters.

The chapter starts by discussing the background and evaluative capability of tools such as supply chain mapping. It discusses the policies and practice which not only help firms in being more effective and resource-efficient, but also actively engages them in the broader vision of supply chain sustainability. This means considering the views of external policy drivers such as the World Wide Fund for Nature (WWF) and implementing practices internally which are in tune with long-term planetary concerns such as ecological depletion and climate change (see Note 12.1).

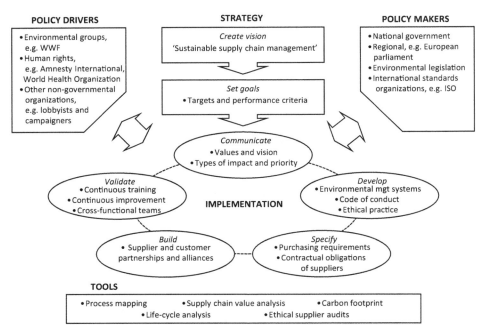

Figure 12.1 Framework linking sustainable supply strategy, policy, tools and implementation

Tools such as mapping can help firms achieve a deep level of understanding over processes, information and cross-organizational activities as a route towards gaining closer collaboration and integration with the supply chain. It is important to understand the differences between the variety of maps available to the supply chain investigator and their various applications, for example, tactical (i.e. high detail, internal orientation) and strategic (low detail, external orientation). Yet the visualization of supply chains using maps is becoming more complicated as firms pursue outsourcing strategies and delivery systems that are typically more global than in the past. As supply chains have become increasingly extended, new evaluative methods involving maps are needed to allow for carbon accounting and reducing the risk from potential breaches in corporate social responsibility. A criticism of mapping is that too often the technique is considered the realm of independent consultants, whereas with a little training, managers, staff and students are very capable of using the tools for themselves. Gardner and Cooper (2003: 37) argue that there need to be well-established processes in place for map building so that knowledge can be transferable and exchangeable between firms. Maps should provide a foundation for the strategic planning process and to 'facilitate evaluation of supply chain membership and structure'. There are many compelling reasons to create a map of the supply chain, such as the need to catalogue and distribute key information for survival in dynamic environments; to provide a communication tool that reaches across firms, functions and corporate units; to alert managers to possible constraints or problems in the system; to facilitate monitoring of the supply chain integration process; and crucially to provide the link between corporate (i.e. firm-level) and supply chain strategy to enable changes to be implemented.

Note 12.1

The Living Planet Report: 'business as usual' is not an option

The release of the 'Living Planet Report', a joint publication by the WWF and the Organisation for Economic Co-operation and Development (OECD) every two years, serves as a reminder of the urgency of developing greener and more sustainable economies. Using a series of measures which include habitat loss, over-exploitation of species, pollution and climate change collectively called the 'ecological footprint', it shows a doubling of our demands on the natural world since the 1960s and a fall of 30 per cent in the health of species that form the totality of our ecosystems. The report provides clear indicators that demonstrate the unprecedented drive for wealth and well-being over the past 40 years is putting unsustainable pressures on the planet. In the words of James Leape, Director General of WWF International:

> The implications are clear. Rich nations must find ways to live much more lightly on the Earth – to sharply reduce their footprint, including in particular their reliance on fossil fuels. The rapidly growing emerging economies must also find a new model for growth – one that allows them to improve the well-being of their citizens in ways the Earth can actually sustain.

Source: WWF, 2010 Living Planet Report

12.1 Representation of organizational processes, flows and systems

The use of analysis tools such as charts and maps that incorporate the concepts of process and flow to understand how organizations deliver goods and services has a strong following in management practice (Womack and Jones, 1996a; 1996b; Hines and Rich, 1997; Rother and Shook, 1998; Gardner and Cooper, 2003). One of the earliest examples is the use of simple flowcharts as a diagrammatic representation of manufacturing shop-floor operations, providing a step-by-step solution to problems in workstation or machine process sequencing. Developed by US industrial engineer Frank Gilbreth in the 1920s, individual process operations are represented by boxes, and the arrows connecting them represent flow of control. Flowcharts are used in designing and analysing a process or programme where data flows are not always depicted, but are implied by the order of operational steps or activities. Creating a flowchart aids troubleshooting and enables managers to visualize what is going on. It helps them to understand a process, find bottlenecks and flaws, and ultimately develop more effective ways of working.

Subsequent developments around 'flow process chart' methods in the 1940s meant the need for standardization of a range of symbols and a capability to reflect the increase in data processing and associated documentation leading to the use of charts in business improvement programmes in corporations such as Procter & Gamble and IBM. The spread of the use of computers in industry resulted in flowcharts being used to plan computer programs. The planning and coding method of US pioneers Goldstine and von Neumann in their 1947 'electronic computing instruments' is an early illustration of the connection between physical activity and information-based process flows. With process analysis tools capable of representing goods and information, their use in the following decades expanded into general business improvement and more specialist fields such as quality control (e.g. Ishikawa, 1985).

Recognition of the widening role of information technology beyond a common view in the 1960s of computers as back-office data processors, and the rise of Strategic Information Systems, meant ICT could provide greater organizational control leading to a need for more holistic and systemic representations of firm activity (Ariav and Ginzberg, 1985). Systems theory considers the firm in terms of an open or closed system whose sum of parts are considered as a whole in order to understand the firm's reaction to internal or external stimulus. The origins of systems theory stems from the examination of holistic organizational behaviour and structure, deriving its analysis from comparisons made with the interactions of organisms in nature (Von Bertalanffy, 1950). Developments in popular tools such as Soft Systems Methodology (Checkland, 1981) enabled management researchers to represent various information processing activities in the organization as linked variables on a map, drawn as self-reinforcing or balancing loops, similar in approach to the ideas around systems thinking and 'virtuous circles' in the learning organization by Senge (1990).

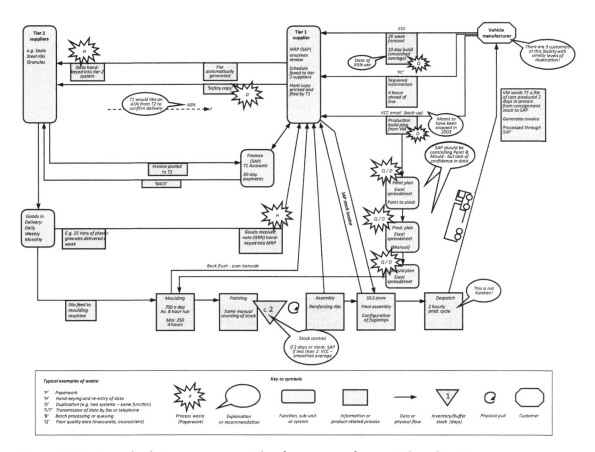

Figure 12.2 A supply chain process map: identifying areas of stress, risk and waste

As the global reach of information systems has increased with the rise of the Internet, the advantages of almost unlimited connectivity between customer, buyer and supplier is offset by the possibility for communication systems to resemble a spaghetti-like mess! There is a compelling need, therefore, to represent process flows in the context of their complex environments, as a juxtaposition of physical production, decision making and information shared between the individual, department and firm. One area of development is in business process modelling notation (BPMN), which includes features such as swim lanes, that enable the investigator to capture multiple and overlapping layers of organizational exchange (e.g. White, 2004). Here, process maps are drawn to reflect the unifying nature of information systems as they interact between multiple stakeholder groups showing not only whom or what it interfaces with, i.e. human or computer, but how the delivery process is supported in complex business settings. Fawcett and Magnan (2002: 351) argue that firms need to go further than using the rhetoric of collaboration, defining how they understand and approach the thorny issue of supply chain integration. The reality, however, is often that upstream relationships are 'handed off' to first-tier suppliers through a lack of supply chain knowledge and understanding of evaluative tools such as maps.

The scope of activity and scale over what the process chart, map or systems diagram tries to convey goes beyond the tactical boundaries set by individual firms. Mapping methodology today is capable of framing the creation of value as a strategic activity, using common notations which provide a connected understanding of the whole supply chain (Gardner and Cooper, 2003). Figure 12.2, for example, shows a supply chain map from the automotive industry which uses universally recognized symbols (i.e. boxes, rectangles, triangles, etc.) to indicate a process or system, connected by arrowed lines to indicate flow of goods or information. It spans upstream from the vehicle manufacturer to include tier 1 and 2 suppliers, illustrating physical process and information flow with comments included to suggest possible sources of bottlenecks in the system (Goldratt and Cox, 1984). Although some production data is omitted for clarity, pinpointing key areas or 'hotspots' using starred symbols to indicate where unnecessary activity or excess inventory can be eliminated enables business performance to be evaluated and improved. Any benefits achieved such as reduced lead time and cost can then be passed on to the customer in the form of added value. This elimination of wasteful activity has a knock-on benefit for the firm's environmental strategy, for example in the reduction of carbon dioxide emissions and other airborne or water-based pollutants. Process improvement must be seen as both part of a firm-level business process and as part of the 'bigger picture' regarding common, supply chain–wide practices on sustainability. This means reaching an agreement on specific targets with suppliers in key impact areas such as emissions, water use, remanufacturing and investment in renewable or so-called clean energy technology (e.g. wind, solar).

Next we examine established business mapping tools such as supply chain value analysis (SCVA) and, later, discuss how more environment-orientated tools such as life-cycle analysis and footprinting can be used in conjunction. Adopting established business process improvement tools for use in sustainability initiatives has the advantage of familiarity when it comes to persuading the 'outliers' in supply chains such as tier 2 and tier 3 suppliers of their efficacy. The wide range of tools available to choose from across the business improvement and environmental management spectrum means managers must be clear (and realistic) about what they are trying to achieve before they adopt them. Often, such tools are used as part of a wider corporate change initiative, where the firm selects a particular blend of business and environmental priorities to target specific supply chain outcomes (Melnyk *et al.*, 2010).

12.2 Supply chain value analysis

The concept of the value chain may already be familiar to readers of this book who are followers of Michael Porter (1980, 1985), whose work champions the search for competitiveness in the marketplace. Porter argues that competitive advantage cannot be understood by looking at firms as a whole but through understanding each discrete activity. These activities are categorized into primary (i.e. inbound logistics, operations, outbound logistics, marketing and sales) and support activities (i.e. infrastructure, human resource management, technology development and procurement). Each activity is then assessed in terms of contribution to the firm's relative cost position and as a basis for market differentiation. If the activity does not create a competitive advantage, then the clear implication is for the firm to consider outsourcing to a partner capable of creating a cost or value advantage.

Christopher (2005: 13) offers an extended view on Porter where 'the supply chain becomes the value chain'. As outsourcing has become increasingly prevalent, the value chain extends beyond the boundary of the firm, meaning supply chain management is critical to the business. Christopher cites the personal computer firm Dell as one of the first in the Internet era to appreciate the importance of achieving a truly integrated supply chain and understanding that it is how a product is sold, i.e. directly to the customer, with minimal waiting and a high rate of inventory turnover that constitutes a unique advantage over conventional businesses.

Having become familiar with the rise of lean thinking and the link between 'lean and green' in Chapter 8, this section discusses the application of associated lean tools such as SCVA used in industry for process improvement and change management programmes. Central to the philosophy of all lean tools are the concepts of the 'value stream' and 'value stream management' (Rother and Shook, 1988; Womack and Jones, 1996a; 1996b; Hines and Rich, 1997; Hines *et al.*, 2000). The value stream is the sum of all processes within and between firms required to deliver a product or service from extraction of raw materials to acceptance by the customer. Developing a value stream management approach using lean tools across the supply chain requires starting with an understanding of value and waste, and the value-adding (and non-value-adding) processes involved throughout. In lean thinking, value is understood to be defined by the customer, and not necessarily what the company thinks it wants to sell to the market.

Womack and Jones (1996b) argue there is a need to rethink value as starting from the perspective of the customer, and defining the whole product-service package in terms of target cost. Achieving target cost involves the logic of identifying and removing waste (Shingo, 1988; Bicheno, 1994). Using the language of Japanese manufacturing operations, waste or 'muda' can exist in many forms. The seven traditionally accepted wastes being overproduction, waiting transportation, inappropriate processing, unnecessary inventory, unnecessary motion and defects (Monden, 1983). Yet the focus on business improvement is shifting away from manufacturing, with new priorities emerging such as supporting the service economy, e.g. tourism, retail, health (Swank, 2003). As part of this evolution, lean is beginning to tackle issues with a sustainability focus, such as 'wasted energy, water [and] natural resources' (Bicheno and Holweg, 2009: 25).

Value streams typically cut across functions; hence choosing the appropriate tool to expose wasteful activities in areas such as communication, variation, inventory and workplace layout is as important as understanding the nature of the business in terms of its production and service orientation. Although there are a number of different SCVA tools designed to target specific types of waste in the organization (Hines and Rich, 1997), the most common starting point is the value stream map. The value stream map (VSM) – an improvement process also known as 'mapping' – is an extremely effective way of quickly getting to the causes of general process-related waste in the organization. The underlying ideas which support this mapping technique are the five stages in lean thinking developed by Womack and Jones (1994; 1996a; 1996b):

- Specify value (i.e. start with the customer).

- Identify the value stream (i.e. draw all related product/service processes and data flows).

- Flow (i.e. eliminate 'batch and queue' and other forms of waste).

- Pull (i.e. only provide something when the customer asks for it).

- Perfection (i.e. continuously improve the process).

While originally devised as an internal tool for use within the firm, VSM is often used today in supply chain settings where several organizations are included as part of an exercise to map product and information-based flows, similar to the process map in Figure 12.2. Process mapping is increasingly being used as a means of highlighting wasteful energy and resource use in the firm, as an indicator of where high levels of carbon dioxide and other greenhouse gases are suspected to reside across the supply chain (CAC, 2013). There is controversy, however, over adapting original lean tools to meet the aims of sustainability due to the perceived conflict in interests between value-based supply chain economics and the resultant impact on society and the natural environment. Some authors, such as Bicheno and Holweg (2009), argue that adapting lean tools is acceptable especially when able to support sustainable strategy by revealing previously undetected environmental waste using new perspectives which link activities between organizations.

Drawing a map is a good way to start developing one's understanding of the business, whatever type of change or improvements you have in mind. Value stream and general

Figure 12.3 Value stream mapping workshop facilitator at work

process mapping is usually conducted as a workshop and thus requires a facilitator. Attendees of the workshop should include a range of staff and managers who represent as many of the key functions in the organization as possible, e.g. purchasing, operations, finance. The facilitator ensures the group is comfortable with the chosen topic for analysis, such as the order fulfilment process for a product that is known to be troublesome. The facilitator then proceeds to record the current state process guided by workshop participants who have had to use it or have relevant knowledge. As a picture of the full process emerges, the participants are free to alter the positioning of the Post-It™ notes and whiteboard marker lines drawn under the guidance of the facilitator until the map represents an accurate, real-life portrayal of the current business process as is possible (Figure 12.3). A discussion is then held over where the major issues in terms of waste and delay occur in the system. This is usually expressed in terms of the number of stock units held, hours or days of delay/waiting time, staffing levels, and instances of IT system failure. The finished map is then redrawn electronically and distributed to all workshop attendees to reflect on how the current process can be improved. After a minimum period of several weeks, a second workshop is held where the same participants create a future state map (Rother and Shook, 1988), which represents the culmination of all of the recommendations for improvements in waste elimination raised during the first session. Once consensus is reached over the nature and causes of each problem, the facilitator then agrees an action plan with participants to engage them fully in the pathways toward implementation.

The description above in reality often covers a period spanning many months, particularly if there are spending decisions over new equipment to be made involving multiple departments. The facilitator can work with more than one firm, and can join the maps to create a more extended supply chain perspective for further analysis. Where specific problems or constraints are known to occur in the system, such as related to excess product variety, information-sharing issues or data quality (Towill, 1996; Lee et al., 1997), then more specific tools can be applied. Hines and Rich (1997) outline a number of variations of VSM tools found most useful in their work with the automotive, health and retail sectors. A selection of the most popular are briefly reviewed here:

- *Process activity mapping* has its origins in industrial engineering and is used to eliminate waste, inconsistencies and irrationalities from the workplace. Based on the study of flow of processes, a detailed recording of all the types of activity involved in the process under consideration is required. After calculating the distance moved, time taken and people involved, the final table (i.e. a list of activities in order of sequence) can then be used as a basis for further analysis and involvement of the workforce in seeking areas for improvement.

- *Production variety funnel* enables the analyst to understand how underlying complexity in the operation affects the supply chain. As the number of variants increases during the production and assembly process, this is reflected in the widening of the 'funnel' over a given timescale. Different profiles of funnel – for example 'T' or 'V' shaped – reflect the relationship between production process and the accumulation of product variety. The production variety funnel tool can sometimes be used for decisions over the delay or postponement of complexity, enabling product configuration to occur only when really necessary, i.e. 'closer' or further downstream towards the customer. It challenges managers to eliminate the costs associated with unnecessary complexity in the production process while maintaining an optimum level of product variety to satisfy customer choice.

- *Demand amplification mapping* is used to capture the effects of information delay, uncertainty and distortion across the supply chain which can lead to excessive inventory holding by suppliers as they attempt to mitigate the risk of a stock-out situation. In supply chains with poor information sharing capability and excess manufacturing capacity, small changes in demand from the customer can become increasingly exaggerated by the order patterns of successive firms upstream, resulting in many weeks or months of unnecessary stock being held usually at the point furthest from the market. This phenomenon is generally referred to as a 'bullwhip' inventory profile (Lee *et al.*, 1997) or the 'Forrester effect' and is based on the systems dynamics work of Forrester (1958). Demand amplification tools involve plotting actual retail sales data with supplier order data over time to highlight any major areas of fluctuation and mismatch. Ultimately, the sources of tension between firms that is the cause of poor communication and information sharing must be resolved before supply chain inventories can fall and follow a more appropriate level governed by customer demand.

12.3 Life-cycle analysis

Life-cycle thinking is the consideration of the potential environmental impacts that a product can have during its life cycle; from extraction and processing of raw materials, through manufacturing, distribution and use, to recovery or recycling and disposal of any remaining waste. Life-cycle assessment (LCA) is the process of quantitatively evaluating the environmental impacts of a product over its entire life period. Life-cycle thinking seeks to identify possible improvements to goods and services in the form of lower environmental impacts and reduced use of resources across all life-cycle stages. This begins with raw material extraction and conversion, then manufacture and distribution, through to use and/or consumption. It ends with reuse, recycling of materials, energy recovery and ultimate disposal.

Note 12.2

Wind turbines and washing machines

The importance of life-cycle thinking can be explained through the example of wind turbines. Here the use phase of the product's life produces very few impacts especially related to carbon dioxide (CO_2) emissions. Therefore it is important to view the other life-cycle stages such as manufacturing and the end of life. It is during manufacturing, in fact, where most of the impacts actually reside. In this case companies have established the idea of carbon payback, how long it takes for the renewable energy process to be in operation. This is often between six and nine months of operation, but actions can be taken to reduce this further. For example, the weight of steel turbine towers has been reduced over the last ten years by 50 per cent, reducing the energy used in production and transport.

Another interesting example of balancing different types of impact comes from the household goods sector, specifically washing machines. Life-cycle assessment was carried out on washing machines to demonstrate the difference between detergents that operate in lower temperatures and those that work at normal temperatures. There was suspicion that these low temperature detergents would be more damaging to the water environment through phosphate pollution while saving energy. Results showed that the net impact was improved with these detergents: a solution that also saved consumers money on their electricity bills.

The key aim of life-cycle thinking is to avoid burden shifting. This means minimizing impacts at one stage of the life cycle, or in a geographic region, or in a particular impact category (e.g. non-renewable energy, carbon dioxide, raw materials), while helping to avoid increases elsewhere, e.g. saving energy during the use phase of a product, while not increasing the amount of material needed to provide it. Taking a life-cycle perspective requires a policy developer, environmental manager or product designer to look beyond their own knowledge and in-house data. It requires cooperation up and down the supply chain. At the same time it also provides an opportunity to use the knowledge that has been gathered to gain significant economic advantages.

Traditionally, reducing environmental impacts focused on production processes, treatment of waste and effluent streams. While this remains important, these actions can also help to address issues such as reducing air and water pollution from specific operations. However, this does not necessarily reduce the negative environmental impacts related to the consumption of materials and resources. It also does not account for the shifting of burdens: solving one problem while creating another (see Note 12.2). Solutions therefore may not be optimal and may even be counter-productive, and reflects the emergent nature of the subject, and the relatively early stage thinking with associated life-cycle tools such as carbon footprinting. On balance, life-cycle thinking can help to identify opportunities and lead to decisions that help improve environmental performance, corporate image and economic benefits. This approach also demonstrates that an active responsibility for reducing environmental impacts is being taken by the firm.

Looking at the bigger picture with regard to LCA, businesses do not always consider their supply chains or the 'use' and 'end-of-life' processes associated with their products. Government actions often focus on a specific country or region, and not on the impacts or benefits that can occur in other regions or that are attributable to their own levels of consumption. In both cases, without consideration of the full life cycle of goods and services (i.e. supply/use/end of life), the environment suffers resulting in poorer financial performance and higher potential for reputation damage. There are a number of decision levels regarding life-cycle analysis which need to be addressed:

- *Micro-level decision support:* life-cycle-based decision support on a micro-level, i.e. typically for questions related to specific products. 'Micro-level decisions' are assumed to have limited and no structural consequences outside the decision context, i.e. they are supposed not to change available production capacity.

- *Meso/macro-level decision support:* life-cycle-based decision support at a strategic level (e.g. raw materials strategies, technology scenarios, policy options). 'Meso/macro-level decisions' are assumed to have structural consequences outside the decision context, i.e. they are supposed to change available production capacity.

- *Accounting:* purely descriptive documentation of the system's life cycle under analysis (e.g. a product, sector or country), without being interested in any potential additional consequences on other parts of the economy.

- *Life-cycle thinking:* provides a broader perspective. As well as considering the environmental impacts of the processes within our direct control, attention is also given to the raw materials used, supply chains, product use, the effects of disposal and the possibilities for reuse and recycling.

Choosing the appropriate LCA tool can be difficult, particularly with the 'multiple agendas' presented by the need to transition towards more sustainably aware modes of supply chain management. Note that in the descriptions of types of life-cycle tools below, we include carbon footprinting because it is both part of LCA as well as carbon management (described in the next section):

12.3.1 Streamlined life-cycle analysis

One example of a streamlined approach is called 'Ecodesign', which draws on a subset of so-called Key Environmental Performance Indicators (KEPIs). The KEPIs are identified through a more detailed ISO LCA and reflect the main considerations or 'hot spots' in the firm or supply chain. The advantages of such an approach is a simplified set of criteria, based on more robust LCAs and other information, can be used to develop eco-labels. However, care is needed when undertaking a streamlined LCA. Without some baseline knowledge about the product's life-cycle impact, the results may be misleading and might inadvertently lead to unintentionally shifting the burden to elsewhere in the enterprise or supply chain. Effort could be spent on life-cycle stages that do not have the greatest opportunity for environmental improvement. It is best, therefore, to use streamlined approaches only where solid experience from using ISO LCAs has already been gained.

12.3.2 Carbon footprinting (CP)

This involves data on carbon dioxide emissions collected throughout the entire life cycle at a consistent level of detail as in an ISO LCA, although not all emissions, resources consumed and impact categories are evaluated. This approach provides a focus on carbon as one of the principal gases whose build-up in the earth's lower atmosphere through anthropometric activity is causing a warming effect and climatic change. However, simply focusing on carbon presents the issue of burden shifting: solving one problem while creating another. This can have the effect of unfairly promoting products that do not necessarily have a better overall environmental performance, or environmental footprint.

12.3.3 Ecological footprinting

This life-cycle approach considers some of the impacts of human activities on the Earth's natural environment. The technique helps to compare the demand placed on ecosystems – the land and the sea that we use and the resources we extract from them – against the earth's capacity to meet this demand, such as through regeneration of resources and assimilation of waste. Results are presented in planet equivalents, that is, how many planets we would need if the same level of consumption of resources was replicated worldwide. This can build on ISO LCAs, but does not consider all impact categories.

12.3.4 Environmental input-output analysis

An economic input-output (I-O) analysis describes the financial inputs and outputs (transactions of goods and services) between given business sectors of the economy within a prescribed geographical area, region, country or continent. An environmental I-O analysis can help to estimate the impacts of one sector relative to another and highlight significant sectors in terms of their environmental impacts. When combined with environmental data for these sectors, an estimate of the environmental impact per unit value of a sector (for example, per euro) can be made. This is often called environmental I-O analysis, or I-O LCA. One of the difficulties reported is in economic valuation.

12.3.5 Material flow analysis

A material flow analysis (MFA) examines the movements of materials through, for example, an industry sector and its supply chain, or a given region. MFAs are used to identify key environmental issues related to the resource efficiency of systems and develop strategies to improve them. The approach links well to other supply chain mapping approaches, such as value stream mapping.

12.3.6 Life-cycle costing (LCC)

Similar to life-cycle assessment, life-cycle costing (sometimes called 'whole life costing') is an economic application based on life-cycle thinking. This technique takes into account all the costs across the lifetime of a product, including purchase, operation, maintenance and disposal. Similar approaches are also emerging to estimate social impacts and benefits associated with a product's life cycle. This information is valuable in understanding the total cost of an investment or ownership. For example, while upfront costs may be greater for an eco-model, the overall lifetime cost is lower due to cheaper running costs.

A key point about life-cycle assessment is that not only does it take into account the different life stage of a product, but it also considers the wide variety of impact types that can result from the processes at each stage. These impacts are summarized in Table 12.1.

Table 12.1 Summary of impact types

Category of impact	Description
Climate change	Carbon dioxide, methane and other greenhouse gases released into the environment allow sunlight to pass through the earth's atmosphere, but absorb the infrared rays that reflect off land and water. This inhibits their escape and therefore heats up the atmosphere.
Ozone depletion	The release of substances, such as CFCs, HCFCs, halons, methyl bromide, carbon tetrachloride and methyl chloroform, contribute to stratospheric ozone depletion and increased ultra violet radiation to the earth's surface.
Acidification	Emissions of chemicals such as sulphur dioxide, nitrogen oxides, ammonia and hydrochloric acid directly, or through conversion to other substances, lower the pH of soil and water bodies, affecting animal and plant life.
Eutrophication	The release of nutrients, mainly nitrogen and phosphorus, from sewage outlets and fertilized farmland, causes nutrient enrichment. This results in changed species composition in nutrient-poor habitats and in algal blooms in water bodies, causing a lack of oxygen and fish death.
Photochemical ozone creation	Ground-level ozone, which has impacts on animal and plant life, is produced by reactions of hydrocarbons and nitrogen oxides to light ('summer smog').
Human toxicity	Exposure to a chemical substance over a designated time period can cause adverse health effects to humans.
Ecotoxicity	Emissions of substances (residues, leachate or volatile gases) that disrupt the natural biochemistry, physiology, behaviour and interactions of the living organisms that make up ecosystems. A distinction is made between different ecosystems, such as freshwater and terrestrial.
Ionizing radiation	Impacts as a result of radioactive substances in the environment and/or other sources of radiation.
Land use	The use (occupation) and conversion (transformation) of land area by product-related activities such as agriculture, roads, housing, mining, etc.
Resource depletion	The consumption of non-renewable resources such as water and crude oil, limiting their availability for future generations and affecting the areas they are taken from.

12.4 Carbon management, footprinting and procurement

Concerns over the release of increasing quantities of carbon dioxide and other greenhouse gases into the atmosphere from anthropometric (i.e. man-made) activity and its effect on public health and climatic change are being raised with rising urgency. Although carbon dioxide is generated in nature by plants during the process of photosynthesis, it is the vast quantities generated by modern cities, industrial growth and the spread of transportation networks and the poisonous variants such as carbon monoxide and sulphur dioxide emitted from vehicle tailpipes and factory flues that has produced a wave of legislation seeking to limit emissions. Since 2010, over 200 legislative acts have been passed by EU member states and in the US, associated with managing the reduction of carbon through controlling emission levels. The UK is seeking to lead the way with its Climate Change Act (DECC, 2008) and one of the first low carbon initiatives 'Procuring for Carbon Reduction: 'P4CR', led by the National Health Service (HM Government, 2009), followed by a sustainable procurement strategy by the Ministry of Defence (MoD, 2010).

The themes of energy and CO_2 reduction are closely linked, with estimates of opportunities for savings per country through energy integration from public spending, i.e. including all sources of renewable energy generation, estimated at around 18–20 per cent by 2020. Yet convincing all stakeholders in the supply chain of the urgency and feasibility of emissions reduction is not proving to be straightforward. While many large corporations facing pressure from consumers and government are working together with NGOs to implement low carbon schemes, many suppliers are taking longer to come on board. In the Carbon Disclosure Project (CDP), for example, only a third of suppliers questioned in 2010 reported even having a carbon reduction target, and of those that do, the average annual reduction figure was only 3.5 per cent (AT Kearney, 2011). Although improvements in carbon emissions are being realized through efforts by multinational corporations such as Air France-KLM, Bloomberg and Dell, upstream supply chain partners are typically lagging behind in their contribution towards managing emissions. Many smaller firms find the range of sustainability terminology and scope of legislation confusing and worry that committing to such green engagement might cost them their business.

Research carried out into low carbon procurement (LCP) at the University of Exeter Business School shows the initial reactions of small-medium enterprises to participating in low carbon initiatives often turn from reluctance, i.e. 'we don't do sustainability here' (SME Managing Director), to increasing enthusiasm as they realize the 'win-win' opportunities which simultaneously reduce energy consumption while lowering business costs. Engaging with suppliers requires sensitive handling and strong leadership from their customers, with lead organizations setting targets for carbon and energy reduction but presenting them as part of a longer-term supply chain strategy. Support for firms should be offered in the form of practical training, including the use of carbon tools such as LCA, action learning and process mapping workshops (Clear About Carbon, 2013).

Procurement has become a powerful force in the efforts to reduce not only greenhouse gas emissions, but on all global sourcing ethical issues and environmental/ecological goals (Walker and Preuss, 2008; Bolton, 2008; Walker and Brammer, 2009). With European countries spending around 16 per cent of the EU's GDP each year on the purchase of goods and services – the UK government alone spends £220billion – spending on such a scale provides a strong lever in encouraging private industry to adopt proposed changes. Since the Rio de Janiero summit in 1992 which identified the direct role of procurement in influencing environmental protection, a wide range of initiatives on sustainable public procurement have emerged (UNDESA, 1992).

Implementing a low carbon approach requires a basic level of 'carbon literacy' from firms in understanding terms such as carbon management, footprinting and procurement. Carbon management (CM) is defined as 'the measurement and management of emissions of carbon dioxide and of the other five greenhouse gases covered by the Kyoto protocol'. Carbon footprinting (CF) is the process of measuring direct and indirect greenhouse gas emissions. LCP is somewhat different again, defined by Correia *et al.* (2013: 60) as:

> The process whereby organizations seek to procure goods, services, works and utilities with a reduced carbon footprint throughout their lifecycle and/or leading to the reduction of the overall organizational carbon footprint when considering its direct and indirect emissions.

The distinction between direct and indirect emissions is important because of their implications for firm ownership and boundaries of the firm. Direct emissions include the impact from goods and services that are owned and controlled by the organization and that lead to reductions in emissions through, for example, purchasing lower carbon emitting alternatives for in-house energy generation and consumption.

Indirect emissions include energy from third-party sources not owned by the organization that lead to reductions in emissions, e.g. through purchasing energy directly from non-carbon or lower carbon–emitting sources and/or energy-efficient goods and services that can equally lead to reductions in emissions across the supply chain. Indirect emissions also include upstream and downstream goods and services that are not owned by the organization, but which lead to reductions in emissions, e.g. purchasing products or services with a reduced overall life-cycle carbon footprint when compared to alternatives, including considerations from material extraction to product disposal.

In terms of where low carbon procurement fits within the scope of other initiatives, managers need to consider the hierarchical relationship between sustainable, green and LCP approaches (Correia *et al.*, 2013). The low carbon movement is an element of wider environmental concerns, which in turn are part of the wider sustainability agenda. Procurers will often have to deal with multiple trade-offs between LCP and other complex organizational or political priorities, where there are no clear solutions. For example: trying to meet the challenges of multiple competing agendas such as the 'food versus fuel' or 'renewable energy versus habitat loss' dilemma around production and consumption of bio-fuels. Another is the issue around the concept of food miles, where overseas purchases can be used in the argument for local economic protectionism but also have a negative impact on poverty eradication efforts in developing countries which are heavily dependent on food exports.

12.5 Supplier sustainability ratings tools

A further set of supply chain tools is related to mapping the supply base of companies in order to understand where the main risks lie. One of the key challenges in managing sustainability in the supply chain is that companies will typically deal with many suppliers potentially all over the globe. So far this chapter has dealt with tools that cover single supply chains (mapping tools) or the life cycle of specific products. However, companies are being asked to assess the impact and risks across their supply base, e.g. where there might be exploitation of labour. The resources to collate sustainability data from many suppliers and then assess where action needs to be taken can be very significant and single buying companies find this extremely challenging. At the same time companies may not have the know-how to assess the suppliers they have collected information from. A number of solution providers have started to offer new tools to help manage this issue – including the likes of Sedex and EcoVadis – and these can be broadly characterized as supplier ratings providers.

The new platforms set up by solution providers offer many advantages to both suppliers and buyers. However, there are now many hundreds of such tools available to companies to manage this issue. The Sustainable Purchasing Leadership Council (which comprises purchasing directors from companies such as Microsoft) recently assessed many of these platforms to provide some guidance to purchasing managers on what to look for and which tools might provide the best value. They came up with some key elements worth evaluating before choosing one or other tool (SPLC, 2018). These were as follows:

- Data relevance, and scope covering the main sustainability issues
- Availability of training for suppliers to provide data
- Verifying the data provided is trustworthy
- Converting data into a fair and simple score which can be acted on
- Benchmarking suppliers against other similar suppliers
- Linking to corrective actions and feedback

These types of tools are part of the trend in technology to provide better visibility in supply chains by reducing the costs of sharing data and creating shared formats to allow the tracking of progress and comparability as discussed in the innovation chapter. These tools also support companies in dealing with the burgeoning number of policies and standards that they need to comply with, an issue which is discussed in Chapter 13, which will also look at how companies approach the topic of supplier assessment and evaluation.

SUPPLIER RATINGS TOOL, ECOVADIS

CASE STUDY 12.1

EcoVadis is an SME based in Paris that provides sustainability ratings for suppliers, to be used by purchasing teams who face complexity in their supply base. The large number of standards and reporting formats means that suppliers face complexity and additional costs in responding to buyers' requests for information and reporting requirements.

The benefits for a purchasing department of centralizing this activity into a single service provider include providing reliable measures, leveraging suppliers and the use of a collaborative platform and scorecards that can be acted on. On the supplier side, the benefits include a reduction in administrative burden, the ability to benchmark within sector, targeted action planning and the opportunity to demonstrate good CSR performance. EcoVadis works with many global brands worldwide, such as L'Oréal, GSK, Nokia, Air France-KLM, Renault, Henkel, ING, Nestlé and Veolia.

The assessment process by EcoVadis comprises a number of steps. First, supplier companies register on the EcoVadis platform and complete an online questionnaire which is tailored to their company size, industry sector and geographic location. The following is an example of the survey and some of the initial fields to be completed.

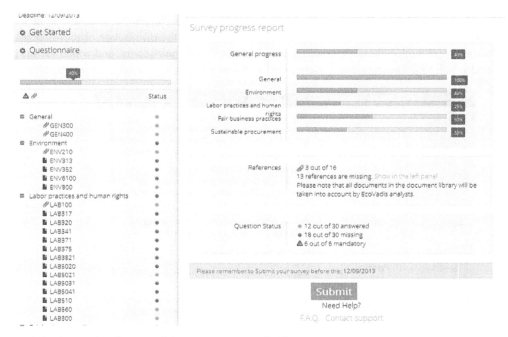

Figure 12.4 Example of some of the questionnaire fields

Next, documents are uploaded through the portal to provide evidence and answers to their response to the questionnaire. The documents that are collected are secured and guaranteed confidentiality. These might include policies, codes of practice, ISO certificates and REACH declarations (relating to registration, evaluation, authorization and restriction of chemicals).

A last step at this point is a check by EcoVadis on secondary sources of information to verify the self-report. This includes information and data from more than 2,500 sources including media, governments, trade unions, NGOs and other business networks. Other sources include Regulatory Datacorp (RDC) watch lists and politically exposed persons (PEPs) databases, China Labor Watch, WWF and Greenpeace. New sources emerge regularly and EcoVadis scans these to keep up to date.

This information is then verified by EcoVadis CSR experts who check the questionnaire answers and documents that were collected. In total 21 CSR-related criteria are used in the ratings system which are based on the Global Compact, ISO 26000, ILO and GRI. The themes are grouped into environment, social, ethics and supply chain issues.

Suppliers are then assessed according to formalized policies and any external endorsements. The actions are also analysed related to measures, coverage and certifications and labels. A last part of this evaluation examines the results of these actions (KPIs) and any awards or condemnations. This approach can be seen as broadly based on the plan–do–check–act cycle and is indeed seen as a cyclical evaluation with a continuous improvement vision.

The scoring scale that is then developed allows comparison between suppliers as well as helping focus action plans with suppliers. The scoring system is shown in Figure 12.5.

The purchasing organization can then view a dashboard (Figure 12.6) based on all their suppliers that are registered in the EcoVadis platform. This can show the distribution of scores across the supply base, where the suppliers are based globally, according to their scores, and which sectors are involved and which KPIs the company is doing well and less well on from a supplier perspective.

	CSR Performance	
85–100	*Outstanding*	• Structured proactive CSR approach • Policies and tangible actions on all topics • Comprehensive CSR reporting on actions and KPIs • Innovative practices and external recognition
65–84	*Advanced*	• Structured proactive CSR approach • Policies and tangible actions on major topics • Significant CSR reporting on actions and KPIs
45–64	*Confirmed*	• Structured proactive CSR approach • Policies and tangible actions on major topics • Basic CSR reporting on actions or KPIs
25–44	*Partial*	• No structured CSR approach • Few tangible actions on selected topics • Partial certification or possible products with eco-labels
0–24	*None*	• No engagements or tangible actions regarding CSR • Evidence in certain cases of misconduct (e.g. pollution, corruption)

Figure 12.5 Example of the scoring system

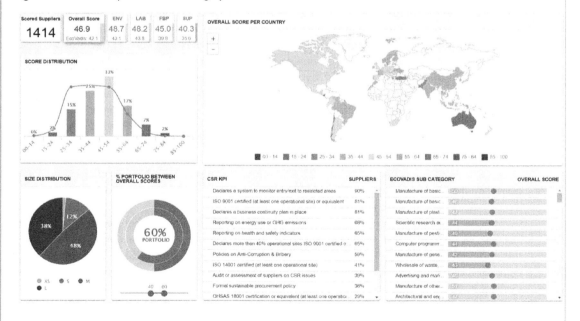

Figure 12.6 Dashboard showing various indicators for the purchasing organization

Suppliers can also obtain tailored reports based on their company size, geographic area and the industry sector within which they operate and in this sense can act as a comparison tool. The scorecard then looks as in Figure 12.7 for any given supplier.

Based on these elements the EcoVadis supplier ratings tool can be seen as an example of good practice as it covers many of the elements mentioned in the previous section.

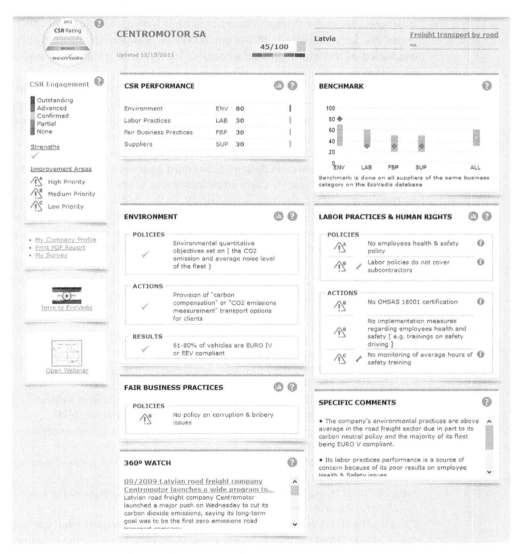

Figure 12.7 Example of a supplier scorecard

12.6 Conclusion

Moving from the formulation of supply strategy towards engagement and taking action on sustainability through implementation introduces a number of new challenges. Firstly, the aim of reducing the firm's impact on the planet cannot be added to existing performance targets in the form of a wish list. Considerable thought must be given to the types of impact the firm judges to be the most applicable to target given current policy indicators and the order of priority in which they will be tackled. It is possible that 'win-win' situations may occur through efficiency savings having the knock-on effect of reducing emissions, for example, but this is not always so. A supply chain–wide analysis must be conducted of the whole product or service life cycle for an in-depth understanding of overall impact.

Once the issues around environmental impact are understood in relation to the business as a whole, the appropriate tools must be selected. Some tools, such as value stream mapping, can be used to gauge not only efficiency and effectiveness, but also potential hotspots or areas in the firm or supply chain where resources are being wasted. Life-cycle analysis data can provide in-depth and accurate analysis of disposal options, as well as the environmental impact of different consumer options. Firms must understand the iterative and often shifting nature of sustainable supply chain implementation, where changes by policy drivers (and makers) may require a response in approach from the market. Purchasing is on the front line of coping with such changes, where buying products or services with a reduced carbon footprint when compared to alternatives requires extensive knowledge of the process from material extraction to product disposal. This means lead organizations must be better at connecting with all levels of their business, not just tier 1, and communicating the benefits of a coordinated supply chain implementation with all participants: buyers, suppliers, customers, governments and NGOs.

References

Ariav G and Ginzberg M (1985) DSS design: A systematic view of decision support. *Communications of the ACM* 28(10): 1045–1052.

AT Kearney (2011) Carbon disclosure project supply chain report. Report written by AT Kearney for the CDP. Available at: www.cdproject.net (last accessed 3 November 2013).

Bicheno J (1994) *The Quality 50: A Guide to Gurus, Tools, Wastes, Techniques and Systems*. Buckingham, UK: PICSIE Books.

Bicheno J and Holweg M (2009) *The Lean Toolbox: The Essential Guide to Lean Transportation*. 4th edn, Buckingham, UK: PICSIE Books.

Bolton P (2008) Protecting the environment through public procurement: The case of South Africa. *Natural Resources Forum* 32(1): 1–10.

Checkland PB (1981) *Systems Thinking, Systems Practice*. Chichester, UK: John Wiley & Sons Ltd.

Christopher M (2005) *Logistics and Supply Chain Management: Creating Value-Adding Networks*. 3rd edn, Harlow, UK: FT Prentice Hall.

Clear About Carbon (2013) Carbon matters: Explorations in low carbon procurement. Internal project report: University of Exeter Business School.

Correia F, Howard M, Pye A, Hawkins B and Lamming R (2013) Low carbon procurement: An emerging agenda. *Journal of Purchasing & Supply Management* 19: 58–64. Research Note.

DECC (2008) Climate Change Act. Department of Energy and Climate Change. Available at: www.decc.gov.uk.

Fawcett S and Magnan G (2002) The rhetoric and reality of supply chain integration. *International Journal of Physical Distribution & Logistics Management* 32(5): 339–361.

Forrester J (1958) Industrial dynamics: A major breakthrough for decision makers. *Harvard Business Review*, July–August: 37–66.

Gardner J and Cooper M (2003) Strategic supply chain mapping approaches. *Journal of Business Logistics* 24(2): 37–64.

Goldratt E and Cox J (1984) *The Goal: A Process of Ongoing Improvement.* Great Barrington, MA: North River Press.

Hines P and Rich N (1997) The seven value stream mapping tools. *International Journal of Operations & Production Management* 17(1): 46–64.

Hines P, Lamming R, Jones D, Cousins P and Rich N (2000) *Value Stream Management: Strategy and Excellence in the Supply Chain.* Harlow, UK: FT Prentice Hall.

HM Government (2009) The UK Low Carbon Industrial Strategy. London, HM Government. Department for Innovation, Business and Skills. Department for Energy and Climate Change.

Ishikawa K (1985) *What is Total Quality Control? The Japanese Way.* New Jersey: Prentice Hall.

Lee H, Padmanabhan V and Whang S (1997) The bullwhip effect in supply chains. *Sloan Management Review,* Spring: 93–102.

Melnyk S, Davis E, Spekman R and Sandor J (2010) Outcome-driven supply chains. *MIT Sloan Management Review*, Winter(special issue): 33–38.

MoD (2010) Sustainable procurement strategy, Ministry of Defence.

Monden Y (1983) *Toyota Production System – A Practical Approach to Production Management.* Atlanta, GA: Industrial Engineering and Management Press.

Porter ME (1980) *Competitive Strategy.* New York: The Free Press.

Porter ME (1985) *Competitive Advantage.* New York: The Free Press.

Rother M and Shook J (1988) *Learning to See: Value Stream Mapping to Create Value and Eliminate Muda.* Cambridge, MA: The Lean Enterprise Institute.

Senge P (1990) T*he Fifth Discipline: The Ar*t and *Practice of the Learning Organization.* New York: Doubleday.

Shingo S (1988) *Non-stock Production: The Shingo System for Continuous Improvement.* Cambridge, MA: Productivity Press.

SPLC (2018) SPLC insight: Supplier sustainability ratings 2018: Landscape and assessment framework. Available at: https://www.sustainablepurchasing.org/splc-insight-guide-to-supplier-sustainability-raters/ (last accessed 18 July 2018).

Swank CK (2003) The lean service machine. *Harvard Business Review*, October: 123–128.

Towill DR (1996) Industrial dynamics modelling of supply chains. *The International Journal of Physical Distribution & Logistics Management* 25(2).

UNDESA (1992) Agenda 21. Section I: Social and Economic Dimensions. Chapter 4: Changing Consumption Patterns. *UN Department of Economic and Social Affairs. Division for Sustainable Development.* Available at: http://www.un.org/esa (last accessed 3 November 2013).

Von Bertalanffy L (1950) The theory of open systems in physics and biology. *Science* 111: January, 23–29.

Walker H and Brammer S (2009) Sustainable procurement in the United Kingdom public sector. *Supply Chain Management: An International Journal* 14(2): 128–137.

Walker H and Preuss L (2008) Fostering sustainability through sourcing from small businesses: Public sector perspectives. *Journal of Cleaner Production* 16(15): 1600–1609.

White SA (2004) Introduction to BPMN. IBM Corporation. www.bptrends.com (last accessed 3 November 2013).

Womack JP and Jones DT (1994) From lean production to the lean enterprise. *Harvard Business Review* 72(2): 93–103.

Womack JP and Jones DT (1996a) Beyond Toyota: How to root out waste and pursue perfection. *Harvard Business Review*. Sept.–Oct.

Womack JP and Jones DT (1996b) *Lean Thinking: Banish Waste and Create Wealth in Your Corporation.* New York: Simon and Schuster.

Womack JP, Jones DT and Roos D (1990) *The Machine That Changed the World.* New York: Rawson Associates.

WWF (2010) *The Living Planet Report: Biodiversity, Biocapacity and Development.* Private report.

Useful websites

Carbon Disclosure Project www.cdproject.net (last accessed 3 November 2013)

Carbon Trust www.carbontrust.com (last accessed 3 November 2013)

Clear About Carbon www.clearaboutcarbon.com (last accessed 3 November 2013)

Department for Environment, Food and Rural Affairs www.defra.gov.uk (last accessed 3 November 2013)

World Wide Fund for Nature www.worldwildlifefund.org (last accessed 3 November 2013)

CHAPTER 13

Policy, standards and supplier assessment

LEARNING OBJECTIVES

By the end of this chapter you should be able to:

- Understand the role of standards and legislation in purchasing and supply chain practices;

- Review typical standards and legislation related to sustainable purchasing and supply chains;

- Classify the main types of codes of conduct and their uses and limitations;

- Understand the role of supplier assessment and audits in achieving compliance.

13.0 Introduction

What does Arnold Schwarzenegger have to do with sustainability in supply chains? Actually quite a lot, as he signed the California Supply Chain Transparency Act in 2010, which requires companies to disclose what they are doing to limit slavery and human trafficking in their direct supply chain. The purpose of this chapter is to provide an overview of key international standards, guidelines and legislation (collectively termed 'policy') affecting sustainability in global trade in general and impacting purchasing in particular. In line with the focus of this book, this overview examines those frameworks that are developed to support sustainability imperatives set by international organizations and institutions. In this sense policy can affect any of the three pillars of sustainability across environmental (waste, pollution), social (slavery, child labour) and economic (fair pricing, avoidance of corruption) spheres. This chapter does not aim to cover all policies exhaustively, but instead shows the types of policies and some examples of each. Thus this chapter provides insights into how purchasing and supply decisions may be affected by sustainability-related policy.

In general policy relating to sustainability tends to focus on environmental issues such as waste and pollution. Regulations provide a framework of rules within which companies can operate in accordance with the social norms accepted in a region or even globally through multilateral agreements. Typically these rules are seen as a set of constraints to companies, preventing *laissez-faire* free market forces from allowing business practices to harm the environment and society, and so are designed to cope with classical market failures.[1] For example, 'Globalization critics argue that international trade spurs a race to the bottom among national environmental standards' (Prakash and Potoski, 2006: 350). As such, suppliers selling into a market or buyers sourcing from a specific region need to be aware of these constraints in order to meet these legal minimums. Having regulation does not imply that all companies comply, though, and it also does not mean that companies meet all societal expectations. Hence, standards and guidelines (codes of practice) have also been developed to provide a framework within which companies can operate, where specific laws are absent (Preuss, 2009), but social norms still exist. In particular international standards (specifically those developed by ISO) provide further frameworks allowing companies to demonstrate how they deal with specific issues such as environmental management or socially sensitive behaviours and practices. In general these international standards are put in place to provide a minimum level of control (King *et al.*, 2005), so that companies on a global basis can show how they control these issues, providing a level playing field. Guidelines and codes of practice tend to be more flexible and more targeted towards specific sectors or practices, and are also a way of showing that companies meet certain (minimum) requirements.

Internationally recognized regulations, standards and guidelines are becoming more important in the domain of purchasing and supply chain management where we see a continued trend in internationalizing operations and a global spread of sourcing activities.

This chapter is organized as follows. First, international standards related to both environmental and social sustainability are discussed, as developed by the International Organization for Standardization (ISO). Second, international legislation related to sustainability and affecting supply chains is presented. This mainly focuses on European directives developed to minimize waste and pollution from chemical products. An additional part of this section also discusses some pertinent international agreements that affect international trade. The third part provides a description of sustainability-related codes of conduct and guidelines and shows how there are different types of codes. A fourth section outlines key issues in supplier assessment and auditing for sustainability. The case study at the end of the chapter looks at Valment, which with their global footprint needs to have processes in place to assess and monitor their supply base to ensure compliance across multiple businesses.

13.1 International standards focusing on sustainability

The first part of the chapter focuses on the ISO standards which have been used to provide a framework for managing many business activities. The ISO is the world's largest developer of international standards (existing as a network of national standards bodies, including BSI in the UK and AFNOR in France, for example). The organization provides a forum for the negotiation of global standards in order to address business and social problems. This forum includes firms, non-governmental organizations (NGOs) and governmental bodies which work to meet the requirements of business and the broader needs of society. ISO has a membership of 163 national standards bodies in all regions of the world, including industrialized, developing and in-transition economies. ISO has a portfolio of over 18,000 standards which provide business, government and society with practical tools for the three dimensions of sustainable development: economic, environmental and social. This section will start by discussing quality standards as these have been used in supplier selection processes for many years and this standard has been the basis for subsequent standards more focused on the environment and social issues.

13.1.1 Quality standards

One of the main standards developed by ISO and adopted by hundreds of thousands of organizations around the world is related to quality management. While this standard does not link directly to the issues of sustainability (except in the area of product safety perhaps), it has formed the basis of standards linking to environmental management (ISO14001) and guidance on managing social issues (ISO26000). The main elements of the main quality standard developed by ISO – ISO9000 quality management standard – are:

- Top management commitment
- Establish implementation team
- Start ISO9001 awareness programmes
- Provide training
- Conduct initial status survey
- Create a documented implementation plan
- Develop quality management system documentation
- Document control
- Implementation
- Internal quality audit
- Management review
- Pre-assessment audit
- Certification and registration
- Continual improvement

While these steps are specific to quality management systems, they have also formed the basis of the recently developed environmental and social standards. One of the advantages of adopting the ISO series of standards is that they require similar implementation which means they can be combined (i.e. combining document control and audit procedures across quality, environment, safety and social management systems). The ISO standards can also have different scopes depending on the requirements of the company. For example, with the ISO9000 series companies can chose to focus the system on just the assembly and testing of products (ISO9003), include production systems in the scope (ISO9002) or include all these plus product design, development, installation and services in the management system (ISO9001). The main countries in terms of volumes of certifications across the world include China, Italy, UK, Japan, Spain and the USA.

A number of studies have shown that there are benefits to ISO9000 related to improved quality awareness, better customer service, greater discipline, improved internal procedures and even increased organizational efficiency (Johansson *et al.*, 1993; Poksinska *et al.*, 2002). Some researchers have also shown that positive financial performance is often achieved from the first year of certification (Corbett *et al.*, 2005) and in terms of the costs and benefits certification is worthwhile investment (Lundmark and Westelius, 2006).

However, there have been some criticisms with some commentators stating that ISO9000 has turned into a pursuit of certificates rather than quality itself, that certification requires a 'mountain' of paperwork, the process is only for documentation and that it discourages free-thinking (Barnes, 1998). Furthermore, the implementation of ISO9001 in particular can be costly with estimated average costs of $245,200 per certification. Most of this cost relates to employees' time, training and the use of consultants (the actual registration cost being a rather smaller percentage). However, despite these potential downsides – which are more related to the method of deployment than the standard itself – ISO9000 certification has become a commonly accepted order qualifier for many buying organizations around the world.

13.1.2 Environmental standards

While it is important to have an awareness of quality management systems, this chapter is focused on sustainability-related standards. This sub-section reviews the two main environmental management system (EMS) standards ISO14001 and EMAS. An EMS is one of the tools that an organization can use to implement an environmental policy. It consists of 'a number of interrelated elements that function together to help a company manage, measure and improve the environmental aspects of its operations' (Welford, 1999).

ISO 14001 is the EMS specification developed by the ISO and is part of the ISO14000 series of environmental management documents. It was issued as both an International and American National Standard in September 1996. The Second Edition of ISO14001, ISO 14001:2004, was issued as an International Standard in November 2004. There is often confusion over the use of the term ISO14000 because many people say ISO14000 when they mean ISO14001. ISO14000 refers to the series of voluntary standards and guidelines for environmental management developed by subcommittees of ISO Technical Committee 207 (TC 207); ISO14001 is one of those standards. Ultimately, TC 207 may develop 15–20 environmental management documents in the ISO14000 series. This standard is seen as the most widely adopted environmental management system, although there are criticisms that it only provides a minimum level of process control (Prakash and Potoski, 2006).

The main steps to obtain ISO14001 are as follows:

1 Obtain commitment from top management.

2 Define responsibilities, appoint management representative(s), establish EMS steering committee, develop implementation plan, initial training on EMS.

3 Planning: identify environmental aspects, legal and other requirements; formulate environmental policy; establish environmental objectives and targets and programmes.

4 Implementation and operation: develop documentation and processes.

5 Checking: develop processes for monitoring and measurement and corrective and preventive action.

6 Develop and deliver presentation for awareness of the EMS.

7 Establish internal audit programme, including training; conduct initial internal audit to evaluate conformity to requirements of ISO14001, including evaluation of compliance.

8 Follow up internal audit with improvements to system.

9 Conduct initial management review of EMS.

10 Implement improvements from management review.

ISO14001 is designed to be adopted by any type of organization in any industrial sector. Although organizations seeking ISO14001 can self-declare, there are greater benefits with third-party certification notably in reinforcing the credibility of certifications with customers, regulatory agencies, and the community. Due to third-party certification, ISO14001 can be more costly than other voluntary codes such as Responsible Care (a US-based code for the chemicals industry). The certification costs can vary widely, depending on the size of the company, the type of its operation and the environmental system already in place. Estimates

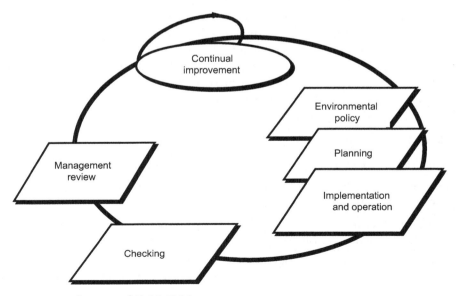

Figure 13.1 Elements of ISO14000

range from less than $50,000 for small firms to greater than $200,000 for larger firms (Watkins and Gutzwiller, 1999). These estimations involve the certification process only and do not take into account the cost of organizational changes that firms may have to carry out to attain the ISO14001 standard.

One important aspect of ISO14001 is the idea of continuous improvement (actually stated continual improvement in the standard).[2] This is based on the plan–do–check–act cycle that has been used in quality management systems for many years, again demonstrating the strong link to quality management systems.

Since 1996 ISO14001 has been developed further to include other standards related to the environmental management systems. These developments include further guidance on evaluating the company itself such as how to measure performance, but have also expanded to include product-related issues such as life-cycle assessment. Table 13.1 provides the main components available as part of the ISO14001 series standard.

From a purchasing and supply chain perspective, the life-cycle elements of ISO14000 are of particular interest as they can provide a standardized way of assessing the sustainability-related aspect of products and services bought by companies.

Research on ISO14001 is rather mixed in terms of showing the benefits. Some research shows no economic benefits, only awareness and reputation enhancement (Vastag and Melnyk, 2002), whereas other studies have shown better performance on environment actions, disclosure, supplier actions and targets in general (Welch et al., 2003). Other research has shown that economic benefits of environmental improvements are not realized by smaller suppliers (Nawrocka, 2008), which is not so surprising given the investment costs of such actions.

In 1993, the European Commission adopted the EMAS regulation, which established a voluntary system in which industrial sites could participate by implementing an EMS and pledge to achieve continual improvement in environmental performance (Kollman and Prakash, 2001). Although voluntary, EMAS was established by the European Commission, an executive body composed of members of the European Union countries, rather than from industry or NGOs. The standard requires not only third-party certification but also companies to issue a public statement with information on their environmental performance (Delmas, 2002). The reporting element of EMAS is particularly interesting for companies to track their suppliers' progress. Like ISO14001 this type of EMS can also be verified by a third-party audit company, which means the environmental report on performance is checked independently and publicly available.

Table 13.1 Main standards in the ISO14000 series

Organizational evaluation	Product evaluation
Environmental management systems ISO14001 and ISO14004	Environmental labelling ISO14021–1402X
Environmental auditing ISO14010–14012 and ISO14015	Life-cycle assessment ISO14040–14043
Environmental performance evaluation ISO14031	Guide for the inclusion of environmental aspects of product standards ISO Guide 64
Terms and definitions ISO14050	

Note 13.1

Tata Beverages and ISO14001

'We don't trumpet our standards – they're a business tool, not a marketing tool, there to drive performance. They help achieve consistency in our production processes, and drive the right behaviours', says Denise Graham, Technical Manager, Tata Global Beverages. This reinforces the view that, done right, standards can help drive the right processes and performance improvement and not just be a cost to the business. Tata Beverages has plants in the UK, India and Czech Republic, serving more than 250 million cups of tea and other beverages per day globally, including Tetley. The standard provides a framework on which to drive and formalize business practices and audit processes ensure they're on track and that their policies and procedures are robust. 'ISO14001 provides a framework for our continued attention to environmental issues – we've just reduced water consumption by 20%, for instance.' Alongside ISO14001 they also adopted ISO50001 which focuses on reducing energy consumption and related impacts. With this standard Tata Beverages have to show year-on-year improvements in energy use which both reduces the carbon footprint but also the cost of energy. The initial audit showed that 96 per cent of energy in their plant in the north of the UK was electricity. From this audit they focused investments on fitting intelligence software to compressors running on electricity, to help them work more efficiently, which saw the company make overall savings of £56,000 in the first year, and an additional £28,000 in the second. As a result of ISO standards, the team are qualified auditors who can now also carry out food quality and safety audits at their own suppliers, widening the impact and experience in general.

Source: BSI Case Study Tata Global Beverages

13.1.3 Social standards

This section discusses the main development related to social standards. While there have been a number of voluntary developments in the area of social sustainability in the past years (notably SA8000), the most recent and formalized effort is the guidance developed by ISO in the form of ISO26000. Table 13.2 on the next page is a summary of the key issues typically covered by social standards, and which form the basis for many voluntary codes, guidance notes and standards relating to social issues. As codes of conduct are covered in the next section, this section will deal only with the recent ISO formulation of social sustainability which will supersede the majority of previous guidance.

From 2005 to 2010, ISO conducted negotiations with its membership of national standards organizations as well as international agencies, governmental bodies, industry groups and nongovernmental organizations associated with codes of conduct in the domain of corporate social responsibility (CSR). The process of standard negotiation has been studied, showing the stakeholders involved included national bodies, e.g. BSI and AFNOR, but also WBCSD, GRI, ILO, UNEP and so on (Helms *et al.*, 2012).

Table 13.2 Main issues in social sustainability

Principles	Application to core subjects
Accountability	The organization is answerable to those affected by its decisions and activities.
Transparency	The organization should reasonably disclose policies, decisions, and activities, including known and likely impacts.
Ethical behaviour	Behaviour should be based on honesty, ethics and integrity
Respect for stakeholder interests	The organization should take into account the rights, claims and interests of all stakeholders.
Respect for rule of law	The organization must comply with all applicable laws and regulations.
Respect for international norms of behaviour	An organization respects international norms of behaviour while respecting the rule of law.
Respect for human rights	The organization respects and fosters the rights covered in the International Bill of Human Rights.

ISO negotiated a consensus on a global definition of CSR and to document what activities constitute appropriate CSR practices. ISO26000 is not a management system standard, however, unlike ISO14001. It is not intended or appropriate for certification purposes or regulatory or contractual use. Any offer to certify, or claims to be certified, to ISO26000 would be a misrepresentation of the intent and purpose and a misuse of the standard. As ISO26000 does not contain requirements as such, any such certification would not be a demonstration of conformity. According to ISO, social responsibility should be an integral part of core organizational strategy with assigned responsibilities and accountability at all appropriate levels of the organization. It should be reflected in decision making and considered in implementing activities.

Table 13.3 outlines the main elements of ISO26000, with the section reference linked to each section in the guidance.

As this ISO guidance is so new there is no evidence of how it will be taken up by companies and the effect it will have on social sustainability performance. However, it is very likely that it will form the basis of many companies' reporting structures and audit schemes. Ethical supplier audits will be treated in Section 13.4 where more details of how different elements of the ISO26000 and other codes of conduct can be assessed within supplying companies. In summary, the international standards for quality and environmental management have been taken up by many organizations around the world in order to help harmonize practices in these areas. This has been driven by global trade where finding and assessing suppliers becomes a huge challenge, and so these standards help reduce the impact of this challenge. Although very new, ISO26000 was expected to have similar adoption rates as the other standards such as ISO9001 and ISO14001 to help companies understand how their suppliers are managing social issues and to compare them on an international basis. However, some commentators suggest that as this is only a guidance document among many others, the impact may be limited (Moratis and Cochius, 2017).

Table 13.3 The main elements of ISO26000

Organizational governance 6.2	
Human rights 6.3	Issue 1 : Due diligence 6.3.3
	Issue 2 : Human rights risk situations 6.3.4
	Issue 3 : Avoidance of complicity 6.3.5
	Issue 4 : Resolving grievances 6.3.6
	Issue 5 : Discrimination and vulnerable groups 6.3.7
	Issue 6 : Civil and political rights 6.3.8
	Issue 7 : Economic, social and cultural rights 6.3.9
	Issue 8 : Fundamental principles and rights at work 6.3.10
Labour practices 6.4	Issue 1 : Employment and employment relationships 6.4.3
	Issue 2 : Conditions of work and social protection 6.4.4
	Issue 3 : Social dialogue 6.4.5
	Issue 4 : Health and safety at work 6.4.6
	Issue 5 : Human development and training in the workplace 6.4.7
The environment 6.5	Issue 1 : Prevention of pollution 6.5.3
	Issue 2 : Sustainable resource use 6.5.4
	Issue 3 : Climate change mitigation and adaptation 6.5.5
	Issue 4 : Protection of the environment, biodiversity and restoration of natural habitats 6.5.6
Fair operating practices 6.6	Issue 1 : Anti-corruption 6.6.3
	Issue 2 : Responsible political involvement 6.6.4
	Issue 3 : Fair competition 6.6.5
	Issue 4 : Promoting social responsibility in the value chain 6.6.6
	Issue 5 : Respect for property rights
Consumer issues 6.7	Issue 1 : Fair marketing, factual and unbiased information and fair contractual practices 6.7.3
	Issue 2 : Protecting consumers' health and safety 6.7.4
	Issue 3 : Sustainable consumption 6.7.5
	Issue 4 : Consumer service, support, and complaint and dispute resolution 6.7.6
	Issue 5 : Consumer data protection and privacy 6.7.7
	Issue 6 : Access to essential services 6.7.8
	Issue 7 : Education and awareness 6.7.9
Community involvement and development	Issue 1 : Community involvement 6.8.3
	Issue 2 : Education and culture 6.8.4
	Issue 3 : Employment creation and skills development 6.8.5
	Issue 4 : Technology development and access 6.8.6
	Issue 5 : Wealth and income creation 6.8.7
	Issue 6 : Health 6.8.8
	Issue 7 : Social investment

13.2 Policy focusing on sustainability

This section outlines some of the key legislation that affects buying decisions relating to sustainability. As social sustainability, labour practices and so on are treated by international guidelines (such as those developed by the ILO) and not subject to international law, they are not dealt with here. Despite this, a number of new policy developments do have significant supply chain relevance, notably on supply chain transparency and modern slavery issues. Environmental sustainability, due to its transboundary nature (see more on this in Chapter 14), is subject to numerous international, multilateral agreements. As a result of this, international trade flows and in particular importation into certain regions, is subject to laws and restrictions that exporters, importers and buyers need to be aware of.

This section does not describe all such policy, but instead highlights the types of legislation – with a number of examples – that constrain the free movement of goods in supply chains. The difficulty for businesses is that they need significant investment in skills, compliance personnel, consultancies and so on to assure compliance, with companies often complaining that 'the rules are too complex, they are unclear, they require unreasonable expenditures and they change too often' (Ruhl *et al.*, 2002: 25).

13.2.1 Supply chain transparency and modern slavery policy

In 2010, The California Supply Chain Transparency Act was one of the first examples of a supply chain responsibility law being enacted. Signed by Arnold Schwarzenegger, this piece of legislation requires companies with a turnover of $100 million or more to disclose how they plan to eradicate slavery and human trafficking from their direct supply chain. Related to this, the UK Modern Slavery Act of 2015 requires that companies also look into their supply chain to disclose the risks of modern slavery and trafficking. In particular a company is required to show its:

> due diligence processes in relation to slavery and human trafficking in its business and supply chains; (d) the parts of its business and supply chains where there is a risk of slavery and human trafficking taking place, and the steps it has taken to assess and manage that risk; (e) its effectiveness in ensuring that slavery and human trafficking is not taking place in its business or supply chains, measured against such performance indicators as it considers appropriate.[3]

The French law on Corporate Duty of Vigilance, signed into law in February 2017, is designed to require companies of a certain size in France to declare whether they have social sustainability risks such as health and safety violations, human rights and even environmental risks in their supply chains. These companies will have to prepare a due diligence plan for these risks and include provisions for mapping supply chain risks and provide evidence of evaluation and an alert system in the case of high risks. Companies could be liable for a €10million penalty if they cannot provide the required evidence. While the legislation is yet to be applied in law by French decree, this is the first step for any country to create a real supply chain liability policy. Other countries such as the Netherlands and Switzerland are following closely behind.

13.2.2 Restricting unsustainable supply inputs

Restrictions on hazardous substances (RoHS) and the restriction of the use of hazardous substances in electrical and electronic equipment (EEE)[4] is EU legislation restricting the use of hazardous substances in electrical and electronic equipment (RoHS Directive 2002/95/EC) and promoting the collection and recycling of such equipment (WEEE Directive 2002/96/EC) has been in force since February 2003. The legislation provides for the creation of collection schemes where consumers return their used e-waste free of charge. The objective of these schemes is to increase the recycling and/or re-use of such products. It also requires heavy metals such as lead, mercury, cadmium and hexavalent chromium and flame retardants such as polybrominated biphenyls (PBB) or polybrominated diphenyl ethers (PBDE) to be substituted by safer alternatives.

The aim of the RoHS was also to reduce administrative burdens and ensure coherency with newer policies and legislation covering, for example, chemicals and the new legislative framework for the marketing of products in the European Union. A revised RoHS Directive was published in the *Official Journal* on 1 July 2011. In the revision of the RoHS Directive on the restriction of hazardous substances in electrical and electronic equipment it continues to ban lead, mercury, cadmium, hexavalent chromium and so on but has now been extended to all electronic equipment, cables and spare parts.

Inadequately treated e-waste poses environmental and health risks. In December 2008, the European Commission therefore proposed to revise the directives on electrical and electronic equipment in order to tackle the increasing waste stream of these types of products. The aim is to increase the amount of e-waste that is appropriately treated and to reduce the volume that goes to landfill disposal.

A complementary regulation is the REACH Regulation (EC) No 1907/2006 that applies to substances in articles (products such as household goods). REACH stands for regulation on registration, evaluation, authorization and restriction of chemicals and entered into force on 1 June 2007. All substances manufactured or imported above 100 tonnes per year have to be registered.[5] Manufacturers and importers of chemicals must identify and manage risks linked to the substances they manufacture and market. For substances manufactured or imported in quantities of 1 tonne or more per year per company, manufacturers and importers need to demonstrate that they have appropriately done so by means of a registration dossier, which must be submitted to the European Chemicals Agency (ECHA). This can apply to many different types of products ranging from furniture, clothes, vehicles, books, toys and electronic equipment. This means that all buyers of products in Europe must obtain a complete chemical inventory of the products they buy within or from outside Europe. Eventually this regulation will be linked to substance restrictions as defined in the ROHS regulation and to further limitations on the types of substances that can be put on sale in Europe.

13.2.3 Producer responsibility (WEEE and ELV Directives)

Other regulations restricting supply chain operations in Europe in particular include those related to producer responsibility. These directives such as the Directive 2002/96/EC on waste electrical and electronic equipment[6] (but also the end-of-life vehicle – ELV – Directive) forces distributors and manufacturers of products in Europe to take responsibility for the

Table 13.4 Examples of international environmental agreements affecting supply chains

Name	Main focus	Supply chain implications
Montreal Protocol	Enforced from 1989 this international agreement was put in place to phase out ozone-depleting substance such as CFCs to protect the atmospheric ozone layer. Largely replaced by HFCs which are also greenhouse gases that have negative effects on global warming instead. However the protocol is hailed a success with complete ozone layer recovery by 2050	Companies had to ensure that they produced or sold no products that contained CFCs which required product redesign with the supply base
Stockholm Convention	Effective from 2004, aimed to restrict the use of persistent organic pollutants, POPs, which are used in electrical transformers, capacitors and in paint and lubricants. These can lead to the release of dioxins which are cancerous	Companies had to ensure their industrial processes phased out POPs and to ensure supplied products, such as industrial paints, did not contain POPs
Basel Convention	This treaty was enforced in 1992, with the aim to control transboundary movement of hazardous waste especially from developed to developing countries. The treaty ensures the restriction of toxic wastes and to help developing countries manage wastes	In order to avoid toxic colonialism, i.e. exporting hazardous wastes to developing countries, which could result from current recycling practices in Europe such as export of mobile phones and electronics
Rotterdam Convention	Restricts the imports of hazardous chemicals and pesticides and requires proper labelling and informing purchasers of any hazards	The onus is on exporters but this provides more information to buying companies on the products they source from overseas
Convention on Biological Diversity	From 1993, this aims to conserve biodiversity by ensuring ecosystems and biological resources are protected, especially if for commercial uses	Many supply chains rely on ecosystem resources such as freshwater, soil timber and wood fibre and as such this convention ensures the equitable sharing of these resources and by implication the restriction of supply in certain instances.
CITES	From 1975, the Convention on International Trade in Endangered Species of wild fauna and flora aimed to ensure species survival is not threatened, and controlled the trade of selected species (more than 34,000)	This is a particular challenge to supply chain traceability of certain 'wild' products such as python skins that are used in the luxury fashion sector, where only farmed materials should be used.

waste generated by the disposal of their products. This implies that companies both restrict certain hazardous substances in their products but also design their products so they can be recyclable. A further element of these laws makes manufacturers responsible for the free (to end users) take-back and recycling of these products. Again this implies that suppliers have to take part in design for recycling initiatives with car and electric equipment manufacturers in order to help their customers comply with these new laws.

13.3 Other policy agreements affecting trade

Over the last decades there have been a number of crucial multilateral agreements – between national governments – concerning the environment in particular. The reasoning for this is that environmental issues including pollution do not respect politically agreed boundaries and frontiers and therefore the control of impacts can only be done cooperatively between nation states through multilateral agreements. Therefore companies have to be constantly vigilant that they meet these requirements if applicable to the products they are either buying or distributing on a global basis. In general these policies have very little impact on global trade from an overall cost perspective (Harris *et al.*, 2002); however, there are implications for the knowledge levels of supply chain professionals who have to be aware of what is allowed and what is not. Due diligence is now an important part of the supply professional's remit, and compliance to regulation is one important element of this. There are particular challenges to supply chain traceability in this case (see Note 13.2). Table 13.4 outlines some of the key international multilateral agreements affecting global trade and proposes some of the supply chain implications.

Note 13.2
The global trade in python skins

Based on a new International Trade Centre report the problem of illegal trade in snake skins is getting worse. This trade in skins largely destined for luxury handbags is very significant with up to half a million exported each year. Snakes skins can be used legally if the snakes have been bred – farmed – in captivity for this purpose. However, the high value of these products leads to much illegal trade in snakes from the wild. As an example, a local Indonesian might capture a python and sell its skin for 30 dollars, but the final selling price in France or Italy can be 15,000 dollars. Often the authorities don't have the resources to check all potential cargoes, or even do not take this trade seriously. Therefore a much better system of traceability is needed. For the fashion houses the problem is that they cannot trust their sources of supply and guarantee to their customers that their handbag has not brought pythons closer to extinction.

Source: http://www.bbc.co.uk/news/science-environment-20509720 (last accessed 3 November 2013)

In summary, there are a burgeoning number of laws and regulations aimed at reducing environmental impacts of business activities, which employees involved in international trade need to be aware of. With the growing number of codes of practice and standards being put in place, compliance is the baseline from which to start, but even achieving this can be a huge challenge and it is no wonder companies often claim involuntary non-compliance due to the sheer complexity of these policies (Ruhl *et al.*, 2002). Even high-profile legal experts admit that 'slippage' in compliance is almost inevitable (Farber, 1999). Although there is a cost implication to non-compliance this is often low compared with the investment required to meet rules. However, the media does not care whether companies willingly break laws or do so 'by accident'; the impact on reputation is the same – you are either evil or incompetent!

13.4 Codes of conduct and sector standards

Alongside increasing sustainability-related policies, one of the most significant developments in recent years, particularly regarding self-regulation and corporate responsibility, is the development and adoption of codes of conduct (CoC). There are different types of CoC including specific company codes (Levi Strauss was one of the first), industry association codes, multi-stakeholder codes (comprising NGOs and private enterprises), model codes (not adopted directly but serving as guidance, e.g. by Amnesty International on labour practices) and intergovernmental codes such as those developed by the ILO or the UN Global Compact as well as some issue-specific codes or agreements (Fransen and Kolk, 2007). Some industries are particularly advanced in the development of codes with textiles, clothing and footwear sectors being the most represented in most studies. This section outlines these main types of codes of conduct and gives examples of each.

13.4.1 Company-specific codes

These types of codes were among the first to be developed in order to protect companies from exposures to social non-compliance in particular (risk of child labour in the supply chain). Typically these are used for trading relationships and define the terms on which suppliers are dealt with and the requirements (minimum) they must fulfil to engage with the buying company.

In 1991, Levi Strauss & Co. was one of the first companies to establish a code of conduct for dealing with supply chain issues. This was named the Global Sourcing and Operating Guidelines (GSOG).[7] The company claims the guidelines were developed to help improve the lives of workers manufacturing products, make responsible sourcing decisions and protect commercial interests. Originally, the guidelines were based on values and standards set by the United Nations, particularly the Universal Declaration of Human Rights and many of the International Labour Organization's (ILO) Core Conventions. Over time, Levi's have modified the GSOG based on the suggestions of NGOs and to reflect what they have learned through experience. These are viewed as a cornerstone of the sourcing strategy and of business relationships with hundreds of contractors worldwide.

The GSOG are made up of two components. The first, Country Assessment Guidelines, address large, external issues beyond the control of Levi Strauss & Co.'s individual business partners. These help assess the opportunities and risks of doing business in a particular country. The second part of the guidelines is the Business Partner Terms of Engagement (TOE). These deal with issues that are controllable by individual business partners and are an integral part of their business relationships. Levi's employees and their business partners understand that complying with the TOE is not less important than meeting quality standards or delivery times. Overall these actions are believed to help the company use supply chain practices to improve on corporate reputation (Preece *et al.*, 1995).

13.4.2 Professional and industry association codes

Associations which bring together companies in the same sector or individuals from a profession have been prevalent in the development of codes of practice in a number of areas. For example, in the supply management domain associations such as the ISM[8] in the USA and CIPS[9] in the UK have developed codes providing informal rules of ethical behaviour for their members. As sustainability often affects industrial sectors in different ways, associations at the sector level have also started to develop codes of practice in the sustainability area. Matten and Moon (2008) argue that industry associations are a key feature of the European corporate social responsibility approach giving these actions an 'explicit', rather than internally focused (implicit), nature.

One recent example is the ICTI CARE Process (ICP) which is a toy industry ethical manufacturing programme which aims to ensure 'safe and humane workplace environments for toy factory workers worldwide'. To achieve these goals, ICTI provide education, training and a single, fair, thorough and consistent monitoring programme for toy factories. The main focus is on China, Hong Kong and Macau, where approximately 80 per cent of the world's toys are manufactured.

One argument against these types of codes is that no single company benefits more than another in terms of reputational value, hence where is the competitive value of such approaches? It is clear from the above example that companies do not intend to compete on these issues, but instead enhance reputation at an industrial sector level (Biedermann, 2006).

13.4.3 Multi-stakeholder codes

This section deals with multi-stakeholder codes 'in which several ... groups, usually at least business and NGOs, but sometimes also government representatives, work together' (Fransen and Kolk, 2007). The word 'code' is used in a loose sense here because these initiatives are more than a list of requirements, but also an approach to dealing with sustainability issues. The global reporting initiative and the ethical trade initiative are dealt with because they are some of the most prevalent of these types of 'codes'. Some of these codes are also specific to issues of concern, so an example related to palm oil is also discussed here.

The Global Reporting Initiative (GRI) is a significant multi-stakeholder approach, focusing on standardizing reporting metrics, and has led to one of the world's most prevalent standards for sustainability reporting.[10] GRI seeks to make sustainability reporting by all organizations as routine as, and comparable to, financial reporting. A sustainability report is a company report that gives information about economic, environmental, social and governance performance. GRI Guidelines are widely used with more than 4,000 organizations from 60 countries using the guidelines to produce their sustainability reports. GRI Guidelines apply to corporate businesses, public agencies, smaller enterprises, NGOs, industry groups and others. Environmental transparency is one of the main areas of activity under the scope of the GRI. The standardized reporting guidelines concerning the environment are contained within the GRI Indicator Protocol Set. There are 30 environmental indicators ranging from

EN1 (materials used by weight) to EN30 (total environmental expenditures by type of investment). Similarly, there are standardized indicators for social, economic and governance issues. The benefit from a supply chain perspective is that there is a common method for measuring the selected indicators, so that monitoring performance from suppliers can be easier to compare and potentially to aggregate (if used as an input into life-cycle assessment).

The Ethical Trading Initiative (ETI) is an alliance of companies, trade unions and voluntary organizations working in partnership to improve the working conditions of people who make or grow goods.[11] Established in 1998 in the UK with the support of the Department for International Development (DFID), ETI has over 70 member companies with a combined turnover of over £107billion including John Lewis, ASDA, Tesco, Inditex and WH Smith.[12] Trade union members represent nearly 160 million workers around the world in every country where free trade unions can operate. NGO members range from large international development charities such as Oxfam and CAFOD, to specialized labour rights organizations such as Anti-Slavery International. Companies that join ETI must adopt the ETI Base Code in full (ETI). The ETI Base Code is derived from the standards of the ILO. They must also sign up to ETI's Principles of Implementation, which set out the approaches to ethical trade that the companies should follow. Member companies must also play an active part in ETI activities alongside their trade union and NGO counterparts, including in members' meetings, supply chain programmes and working groups. In 2010, ETI member companies' ethical trade activities covered over 9.8 million workers around the world and asked that their suppliers take over 133,000 separate actions to improve workers' conditions.

Other multi-stakeholder codes have focused on specific issues. One example is developed by the Roundtable on Sustainable Palm Oil with the WWF. This code has been developed in answer to many campaigns from NGOs about the impacts of palm oil production.[13] The main issues relate to deforestation – conversion of forest to plantation – which then has an impact on habitats for endangered species such as orangutans, particularly in areas such as Borneo and Sumatra. There are other significant impacts on the environment including soil erosion and pollution, and pollution of fresh water sources. In addition to the negative environmental consequences there are also social implications based on land use rights and ownership, and impacts on local community livelihoods. According to this code companies should:

1 Join the RSPO and be an active member.

2 Make a commitment to source 100 per cent RSPO-certified palm oil by 2015 at the very latest.

3 Be transparent about their use of palm oil.

4 Start using certified sustainable palm oil immediately.

5 Start investing in traceable supply chains of certified sustainable palm oil.

6 For retailers, go beyond 'own brand commitments'.

7 Raise awareness of the RSPO and certified sustainable palm oil globally.

Certified sustainable palm oil (CSPO), which is produced according to the standards established by the Roundtable on Sustainable Palm Oil (RSPO), provides assurance that valuable tropical forests have not been cleared and that environmental and social safeguards have been met during the oil's production.

13.4.4 Codes from international governmental organizations

Probably the best-known code in this category is the United Nations Global Compact, also known as Compact or UNGC. This is a United Nations initiative to encourage businesses worldwide to adopt sustainable and socially responsible policies, and to report on their implementation.[14] The Global Compact is a principle-based framework for businesses, stating ten principles in the areas of human rights, labour, the environment and anti-corruption. Under the Compact, companies are brought together with UN agencies, labour groups and civil society. The Global Compact is the world's largest corporate citizenship initiative with two objectives: 'Mainstream the ten principles in business activities around the world' and 'Catalyze actions in support of broader UN goals, such as the Millennium Development Goals (MDGs)'. The Compact was announced by the then UN Secretary-General Kofi Annan in an address to The World Economic Forum on 31 January 1999, and was officially launched at UN Headquarters in New York on 26 July 2000.

The Global Compact is not a regulatory instrument, but rather a forum for discussion and a network for communication including governments, companies and labour organizations, whose actions it seeks to influence, and civil society organizations, representing its stakeholders. Hence, there have been some criticisms of the Global Compact. The Compact contains no mechanisms to sanction member companies for non-compliance with the Compact's principles. A company's continued participation is not dependent on demonstrated

Table 13.5 Main principles of the Global Compact

Human rights	Principle 1: support and respect the protection of internationally proclaimed human rights
	Principle 2: make sure that they are not complicit in human rights abuses
	Principle 3: the freedom of association and the effective recognition of the right to collective bargaining
Labour standards	Principle 4: the elimination of all forms of forced and compulsory labour
	Principle 5: the effective abolition of child labour
	Principle 6: the elimination of discrimination in employment and occupation
Environment	Principle 7: support a precautionary approach to environmental challenges
	Principle 8: undertake initiatives to promote environmental responsibility
	Principle 9: encourage the development and diffusion of environmentally friendly technologies
Anti-corruption	Principle 10: Businesses should work against corruption in all its forms, including extortion and bribery

progress. Some sources have stated that the Global Compact has admitted companies with dubious humanitarian and environmental records in contrast with the principles demanded by the Compact.

13.4.5 Reflections on codes for sustainability

In summary, codes of conduct and other voluntary means to monitor and control what happens in supply chains are some of the most important developments in the field of sustainability in recent years. In particular, multi-stakeholder codes (or standards as stated by some authors) are seen to be put in place in response to a lack of formal government or inter-governmental-led policies, but should not be seen as a replacement of existing legal frameworks (Sobczak, 2003). As an overall observation on these 'codes', there is great variability in the constitution of these stakeholder groups and also the relative involvement of the stakeholders included (Fransen and Kolk, 2007). This means that these approaches also vary in their level of legitimacy (a concept returned to in the next chapter concerning stakeholder management). Furthermore, the sum of company-specific codes, sector-level guidelines, multi-stakeholder standards plus international standards and policies leads to a highly complex set of obligations for suppliers with repetition, redundancy and idiosyncrasies. How to focus on the most important, which elements take precedence, are questions that have not been resolved to date and although standards such as ISO26000 seek to simplify the situation they also risk further obfuscation.

13.5 Supplier assessment: monitoring and mentoring

Chapter 2 briefly outlined the need for evaluation of supplier performance as the final stage of the purchasing process. In addition to evaluation at the end of each purchasing exchange, purchasing and supply management practitioners generally regard it as essential to control and monitor supplier performance on an ongoing basis. Typically, buyers use supplier evaluation, or assessment, to identify areas where performance is below the expected performance level and issue penalties accordingly. If supplier performance continues to be below the expected level, companies can decide to fire the supplier and find another supplier. However, this is just one aspect of supplier assessment and in many ways an outdated mode of operation.

So, what is the wider rationale for supplier assessment? Proponents of the reliance on trust as a safeguard mechanism might argue that this form of control is unnecessary and damages trust between the two parties. However, trust should not be based purely on subjective feeling but on proven performance, otherwise trust is blind or naive. The concept of customer–supplier competence trust requires that the supplier demonstrate its competence and that the customer validate supplier performance. Therefore, supplier assessment does not conflict with relying on trust but is a prerequisite.

A sustainability perspective further emphasizes the need for supplier assessment. If a supplier does not comply with a company's sustainability standards and is exposed in the media the damage is significant and simply blaming the supplier will most likely cause a significant backlash. Consider British Petroleum's (BP) initial response to the oil spill in the Gulf of Mexico. BP's internal inquiry into the causes of the disastrous oil spill provoked immediate criticism from its contractors, as well as US politicians who said the British group was 'happy to slice up blame, as long as it gets the smallest piece' (*Financial Times*, 9 September 2010). BP accepted that its engineers should shoulder some of the blame but attempted to pass on the responsibility to its contractors, Transocean, the owner of the Deepwater Horizon drilling rig that exploded, and Halliburton, the company responsible for cementing the Macondo well. The lesson of this accident is that a company cannot simply blame its supplier when something goes wrong and will have to shoulder the responsibility. Consequently, companies must evaluate and monitor supplier practices and performance even if the company trusts the supplier.

13.5.1 Supplier assessment methods

Few companies these days do without structured supplier assessment schemes, even small and medium-sized enterprises (SMEs) have them: one survey of UK SMEs (Pressey *et al.*, 2009) showed that almost 50 per cent relied on some form of regular supplier assessment and only 16 per cent made no or very little use of supplier assessment. Basically, measuring performance is a form of evidence-based management (Pfeffer and Sutton, 2006). This is reflected in the well-known statement in performance management circles: 'What you measure is what you get' (Kaplan and Norton, 1992). Or, if you do not measure something you cannot manage it. This logic provides a strong argument in favour of extensive use of key performance indicators (KPIs), including supplier assessment, because if a company does not measure supplier performance, suppliers will not perform.

The potential tautology of that argument indicates a potential flipside of the argument: 'What gets measured is only what gets done'. To put it differently, by measuring selected aspects of performance those that are not measured will suffer as suppliers will not focus on those areas. Typically, performance assessment is biased towards cost reduction. As discussed in Chapter 3, KPIs should be aligned with purchasing strategy so if this is based around cost it makes strategic sense to focus on cost-focused KPIs. All too often cost is chosen as an important KPI because it is easy to measure and because it is assumed that cost is the major driver of performance. Therefore, supplier assessment criteria should reflect purchasing strategy, which in turn should reflect business and corporate strategy.

Performance measurement also has a motivating impact and it can even help to create a comfort zone of individual buyers. Almost 20 years ago research by Dumond (1994) showed that lack of performance measurement systems led buyers to inconsistency in their decisions and mediocre performance and affected not only decisions, but also what she called the 'comfort level' about the environment and the individual's performance. Individuals who were provided with no performance measures and no performance feedback were confused about their performance and lacked commitment to improve, perhaps because they actually believed they were doing well when there was nothing to be measured against (Dickinson *et al.*, 2010).

Continuing to use a supplier may be regarded as a reward in itself but much more can be done that is a relatively low level of investment for the buying company but of tremendous value to the supplier. In addition to moving suppliers towards a more strategic category, companies can do a range of things to reward suppliers for excellent performance. It is good practice, for example, to hold annual supplier award ceremonies where prizes are presented for different categories of performance such as best quality, most innovative or most improving supplier.

Japanese automotive companies, such as Toyota, are very good at motivating suppliers through award ceremonies. In March 2012, Continental Automotive's Chassis and Safety division received an excellence award at Toyota Motor Engineering and Manufacturing North America, Inc.'s (TEMA) Annual Supplier Business Meeting (ABM). This brought together approximately 900 delegates from across North America. On receiving the award, the chief executive officer (CEO) of Continental's NAFTA region, Samir Salman, stated: 'We are very proud to be recognized by Toyota for both technology development and quality performance … We strive every day to exceed our customers' expectations. To be recognized for excellence is certainly gratifying and appreciated.'[15]

Which criteria, then, are typically measured? Companies use a range of criteria, or measures. These often include measurable performance criteria such as quality, delivery, price, service and flexibility. In addition, aspects of internal processes within supplier companies can also be measured, including, for example, defects, schedule realization and cost (Prahinski and Benton, 2004). Rather than simply evaluating a series of outcome measures, many companies adopt process-based supplier evaluation methods, thus engaging more actively in understanding the supplier's process capabilities.

Figure 13.2 provides a supplier balanced scorecard of different ways to measure supplier performance. The outcome measures are those that result from the supplier performance. These are divided into strategic and financial value measures. The former focus on ways in which the supplier can contribute to critical value-adding activities of the company whereas the latter are measured in financial terms. The predictive, or process, measures are divided into operational and relationship quality measures: operational performance measures are all important but those that are critical are those that are aligned with overall business (and purchasing/supply strategy). In addition to those shown in Figure 13.2, it is also possible to

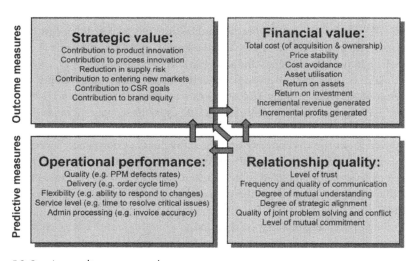

Figure 13.2 A supplier scorecard

Source: Hughes (2005).

think of underlying performance measures that would enable the supplier to perform on these dimensions. For example, in addition to measuring quality through 'parts per million' (PPM) defect rates, it is useful to evaluate if the supplier has quality management processes in place, such as TQM or ISO9000 processes. The fourth and final dimension, 'Relationship Quality', suggests a very different perspective as it focuses not on the performance of the supplier (or its products/services) but on the performance of the relationship between the two parties.

In essence this kind of scorecard can also include aspects of sustainability. While performance will be one indicator, having the right processes in place is also key. This means the emphasis relating to processes is not only on controlling costs and quality, but can be expanded to the management of environmental and social requirements or standards that are imposed by the buying company, or are already in place at the supplying company.

13.5.2 Supplier audits

While measuring performance and checking standards, legislation and codes of conduct are important to provide the rules of the game for suppliers, it is also clear that companies need to undertake their own due diligence. This often takes the form of supplier audits. IKEA is a good example of a company that has used audits extensively at suppliers with their Compliance and Monitoring Group to implement its code of conduct with a sustainability focus (Ivarsson and Alvstam, 2010). For example:

> An audit typically takes one or two days and is conducted using a checklist covering the approximately 90 issues of the code. During the audit, a number of randomly selected employees and management representatives are interviewed. Apart from conducting interviews, the auditors go through relevant documents, such as employment contracts and pay slips, and make observations of the working conditions around the factory. Issues that need to be improved are noted in an audit report.
>
> (Andersen and Skjoett-Larsen, 2009: 80).

While ISO standards such as ISO14001 provide a format and procedure for audits – as well as certification of auditors – to verify ISO standards, checking that companies meet voluntary codes can be far more challenging. As a response to this, one example is the Global Social Compliance Programme developed by the Consumer Goods Forum based in France. Their stated aim is:

> a business-driven programme for companies whose vision is to harmonize existing efforts in order to deliver a shared, global and sustainable approach for the continuous improvement of working and environmental conditions across categories and sectors in the global supply chain.[16]

The guidance according to the GSCP[17] includes:

- Select internal or external auditors that are competent and appropriately qualified/ trained and therefore able to undertake assessments professionally, responsibly and to the standards required by the organization.

- Provide clear guidance to the supplier on the purpose, scope and focus of an audit and how the outcomes of the audit are used, including corrective actions that can support continuous improvement in social performance.

- Provide guidance for suppliers on the required frequency of audits, as well as providing guidance on the required time-frame for completion of corrective actions and the arrangement of any follow-up audits.

- Provide guidance to auditors on the length of an audit, including reference to the number of workers on site. The audit length is expressed in terms of auditor days, i.e. a smaller site may require one auditor for one day whilst a large site may require two auditors for two days (four auditor days).

- Prioritize audits at suppliers and sites considered to be high risk on the basis of risk assessment, self-assessment or other sources of information.

Furthermore, GSCP suggests there are a number of audit tools and processes used by organizations to support their audit programmes (The Consumer Goods Forum, 2012):

- *Audit process*: best practice guidance regarding the minimum requirements for the audit process (before, during and after the audit)

- *Self-assessment questionnaire*: used to enable suppliers or sites to provide information about the employment site, how it manages social compliance issues and its performance against local law and labour standards

- *Pre-audit employment site profile*: a form or tool sent by an auditor in advance of an audit. This collects general information about the location, size, workforce profile and production processes of the employment site

- *Audit checks*: a form or tool providing auditors with the minimum requirements of the audit methodology

- *Alert notification*: used to communicate a 'critical' non-compliance to the organization (or other audit requestor) as soon as it is identified

- *Audit report guidance*: provides a structure and guidance on the content of an audit report

- *Supplementary audit information*: a form or tool to report information considered to be too sensitive for the audit report, i.e. concerns which cannot be substantiated through evidence and/or interviews; general management.

Supplier audits are essential to find out whether suppliers are meeting their obligations to codes of conduct and to verify that they meet the stipulations of standards and regulations. Without this, buying companies have to rely on self-reporting and potential risks of non-reported issues or inaccurate reporting of performance. Clearly auditing takes resources and it is not feasible to be constantly monitoring all suppliers, so companies try to find a compromise between the investment and the risks.

To date there is little research examining the effectiveness of supplier audits related to social sustainability (Morimoto *et al.*, 2005). Although some research suggest the effects can be positive (Gao and Zhang, 2006), other researchers highlight the issues of imposing values (Gray, 2006) and claims of cultural imperialism (Banerjee, 2003) or cultural relativism (Walker and Phillips, 2009). In this case there are challenges of imposing absolute cultural values such as zero tolerance of child labour and disengagement of suppliers who use or have used children in labour, compared with a more subtle approach to engaging with communities to provide alternatives to work through education and other community support actions (Winstanley *et al.*, 2002).

Valmet – tackling supply chain sustainability

Valmet is a world leader in technologies, automation and services for the global pulp, paper and energy industries. Its customer base is widely defined as industries that use bio-based raw materials. Headquartered in Espoo in Finland, Valmet employs around 12,000 people worldwide and turns over around €2.9billion (2016).

The roots of Valmet date back more than 200 years. Over the years the company has grown from a state-owned Finnish company with a diverse and changing product portfolio, which included trains, aeroplanes, clocks and weapons, to become a focused international player specializing in pulp, paper and energy. Its market positions range from first to third across its business divisions or 'business lines'. The company now operates globally with presence in North America, Europe, Middle East, Africa, Asia-Pacific and China. Valmet's primary production sites are located in Jyväskylä in Finland, Karlstad and Sundsvall in Sweden, and Xian and Shanghai in China.

Valmet has four business lines: services (40 per cent), automation (10 per cent), pulp and energy (28 per cent) and paper (22 per cent):

1. Services business line provides customers with mill improvements, roll and workshop services, spare parts, fabrics, and life-cycle services. Valmet serves over 2,000 pulp and paper mills globally. This means that annually more than half of the world's 3,800 pulp and paper mills buy services from Valmet.

2. Pulp and energy business line provides technologies and solutions for pulp and energy production as well as for biomass conversion. The pulp projects range from process equipment deliveries to complete pulp mills. Valmet's energy solutions include, e.g. biomass-based energy boilers. In addition, Valmet continuously develops new biomass conversion technologies.

3. Paper business line delivers complete board, tissue and paper production lines and machine rebuilds. Board, tissue and paper are used in a number of end products such as packaging, handkerchiefs, toilet paper and hand towels as well as printing and writing papers.

4. Automation business line delivers automation solutions ranging from single measurements to mill wide process automation systems. The main products are distributed control systems, quality control systems, analysers and measurements, vision systems, and performance and

CASE STUDY 13.1

service solutions. The main automation customer industries are the pulp and paper and other process industries, energy production, marine, and oil and gas.

Valmet's mission is 'to convert renewable resources into sustainable results'. Its supply chain perspective goes beyond the traditional focus on delivery, inventory and cost to place sustainability at the heart of its supply chain strategy. The company strives to develop transparency and traceability of its entire supply chain from sourcing of raw materials to recycling of products. The commitment to sustainability is even reflected in Valmet's corporate logo: a green, forward-pointing arrow with the word Valmet in steel grey. Launched in 2014, Valmet's 'Sustainability 360°' agenda identifies five core areas:

- Corporate citizenship: a trusted partner and respected corporate citizen

- Supply chain: develop sustainable supply chain practices

- Health, safety and environment: protect the safety of its people and partners and minimize its environmental impact

- Our people: a responsible employer and promote diversity

- Our solutions: develop and provide solutions that support sustainability. Valmet commits to reporting its sustainability performance according to global standards (Global Reporting Initiative – GRI) with third-party assurance. Moreover, Valmet is a member of the Dow Jones Sustainability Index, is included in the 2016 Climate A-List by CDP (formerly the Carbon Disclosure Project) and is a constituent of the Ethibel Sustainability Index (ESI) Excellence Europe since March 2017.

Valmet's sustainable supply chain

Valmet's global operations are supported by a global supply chain with procurement offices worldwide. Valmet's suppliers supply a wide range of metals-based products and components, electronics and services: annual spend in direct purchases is €1–2billion. Products and components comprise 72 per cent and purchased services 28 per cent of Valmet's total procurement spend.

Cost savings are a major key performance indicator with annual savings targets of at least 3 per cent in procurement and to implement a sustainable supply chain. However, the supply chain focus is moving from traditional cost reduction to new actions including design-to-cost projects to create new sources for savings, enhancing global category management, and improving supplier involvement through supplier relationship management.

Valmet sources from around 10,000 suppliers spread across over 50 countries, although over 50 per cent is still sourced from nearby Finland and Sweden. The company has seen an increase in sourcing from emerging markets which represents new challenges. The company believes that 75 per cent of purchases come from low sustainability risk countries but 25 per cent come from medium or high sustainability risk countries.

All suppliers must comply with Valmet's Sustainable Supply Chain Policy[18] which concerns business ethics, compliance, human rights and labour rights, occupational health and safety, environmental management and sustainability in products and services. The principles outlined in the policy provide

Table 13.6 Ten largest sourcing countries (million euros)

	2016	2015
Finland	758	770
Sweden	211	194
USA	130	143
China	114	132
Germany	75	78
Poland	65	30
Italy	40	29
Estonia	30	35
UK	29	20
Brazil	24	74

Source: Valmet Annual Review report 2016.

a baseline for suppliers and act as a basis for supplier evaluations, self-assessments and sustainability audits. Supplier risks are assessed on the basis of country of purchase and purchasing category. As of 2015–2016, key statistics from Valmet's sustainable supply chain efforts were:

- 100 per cent of suppliers assessed on sustainability risks

- 11,000 policies sent to suppliers globally

- 430 supplier self-assessments

- 91 supplier sustainability audits

- 700 corrective actions

- 450 Valmet procurement professionals have received sustainable supply chain training. Plans for 2016–2018 show detailed actions and targets for each sustainability focus area. Key targets are to develop sustainable procurement practices globally and to support selected key suppliers to meet the level of sustainability expected by Valmet. As of 2017, 100 per cent of new direct suppliers have gone through the supplier approval process and 50 supplier sustainability audits per year are being carried out. Supplier sustainability audits were conducted in, for example, Brazil, Mexico, China, India, the USA, Poland, Finland and Sweden.

Valmet's sustainability audit protocol was created in late 2015, and all audits done in 2016 used the new checklist. The protocol ensures the process is consistent and enables comparability between suppliers. Sustainability audit evaluations are based on non-compliance with Valmet's Sustainable Supply Chain Policy or local or international law. Where audits identify problems, Valmet follows up with a corrective action plan and monitors and verifies accordingly. If the supplier does not proceed

CASE STUDY 13.1

with corrective actions agreed together, Valmet is prepared to support the supplier in implementing the corrective action or, if necessary, Valmet reserves the right to terminate the contract with the supplier.

Reported non-compliance mostly relates to human and labour rights and health and safety problems. Audit challenges during 2016 related to follow-up action, where Valmet sometimes experienced long response times from audited suppliers to the agreed corrective actions. In 2016, Valmet developed tools and guidance related to the sustainability audit process and continued with internal training, and enhanced ways to operate for its global procurement organization.

Specific action plans aim to:

- Ensure globally aligned approval process for new suppliers;

- Increase the number of nominated Valmet sustainability auditors in selected areas;

- Develop templates and guidelines for sustainability audit practices;

- Continue with sustainability training for global procurement and integrate sustainability into procurement training programmes;

- Continue with a programme to ensure compliance with hazardous substances;

- Develop carbon footprint calculation;

- Establish a sustainability engagement programme for medium- and high-risk key suppliers with targets, KPIs and follow-up mechanisms

13.6 Conclusion

The most important point from this chapter is to understand the role of international policies and standards for purchasers and supply chain managers and how they are acted upon. These policies and standards allow a comparison between companies from different regions of the world in terms of their management systems and processes to control and monitor performance in the area of quality, the environment and to an extent social requirements (along the lines of the ILO, UN Bill of Human Rights and other equivalent guidelines). Where ISO-based standards or laws are either missing or do not provide sufficiently high levels of requirements, companies alone, in cooperation at a sector level, and in cooperation with other stakeholders, have developed their own standards, codes of practice and guidelines. The danger here is that if each company has its own standard, suppliers have to face multiple reporting requirements, multiple audits and different levels of pressure. This can lead to disillusionment and eventually a lack of commitment from suppliers.

One of the advantages of adopting internationally recognized standards and norms is that this helps address some of the challenges of global sourcing. With a vast array of potential suppliers globally, even having visibility of their level of basic compliance is problematic. Despite this, international standards are often a pre-qualifier for supplier selection, but they do not allow buying companies to differentiate further and at this point the more traditional selection criteria will come into play. For example, ISO14001 certification does not necessarily lead to superior environmental performance (King *et al.*, 2005). From this it is difficult to see companies using the requirements in these standards for competitive advantage, e.g. to go beyond compliance and meeting minimums in order to win new customers.

Verification of performance and compliance to policies and standards is also crucial to ensuring risks are minimized in supply chains. Yet truly verifying all parts of the supply chain is probably unattainable for any single organization, therefore standardizing and using external audit organizations along with standard reporting can be a solution to this problem, as mentioned in Chapter 12. Of course, this depends on the political will to drive standardization. It is important not to just stop at verifying and attaining compliance, but also to build capacity for performance improvement across all levels of sustainability. There are clear opportunities to go beyond compliance in the area of environmental performance (by reducing costs); however, improving the target level for ethical and social practices is far more challenging (Brandon-Jones, 2013) as the basic compliance achievement is still immature in many industries. Some of these issues of development and capability building are covered in the next chapter.

Notes

1 Externalities (pollution), incomplete information (chemical content), property rights (ownership of the ocean and forests), lack of competition (mineral, energy monopolistic, cartels, oligopolistic).

2 The difference between continuous and continual is subtle but means companies do not need to show uninterrupted improvement throughout a period, for example, only an improvement at the audit date compared to a reference date.

3 http://www.legislation.gov.uk/ukpga/2015/30/contents/enacted (last accessed 19 July 2018).

4 http://ec.europa.eu/environment/waste/rohs_eee/ (last accessed 11 April 2013).

5 http://ec.europa.eu/enterprise/sectors/chemicals/reach/index_en.htm (last accessed 11 April 2013).

6 http://ec.europa.eu/environment/waste/weee/pdf/final_rep_okopol.pdf (last accessed 3 November 2013).

7 http://www.levistrauss.com/library/levi-strauss-co-global-sourcing-and-operating-guidelines-0 (last accessed 3 November 2013).

8 http://www.ism.ws/SR/content.cfm?ItemNumber=4762 (last accessed 3 November 2013).

9 http://www.cips.org/Documents/About CIPS/CIPS Code of Ethics.pdf (last accessed 3 November 2013).

10 https://www.globalreporting.org/reporting/guidelines-online/G3Online/Pages/default.aspx (last accessed 3 November 2013).

11 http://www.ethicaltrade.org/about-eti (last accessed 3 November 2013).

12 http://www.ethicaltrade.org/about-eti/our-members (last accessed 3 November 2013).

13 http://www.rspo.org/en/history (last accessed 3 November 2013).

14 http://www.unglobalcompact.org/AboutTheGC/TheTenPrinciples/index.html (last accessed 3 November 2013).

15 https://www.prnewswire.com/news-releases/continental-receives-supplier-awards-from-toyota-144211075.html (last accessed 11 September 2018).

16 www.gscpnet.com (last accessed 3 November 2013).

17 http://www.gscpnet.com/working-plan/step-4-management-systems.html (last accessed 3 November 2013).

18 https://www.valmet.com/globalassets/about-us/procurement/valmets-sustainable-supply-chain-policy-eng.pdf (last accessed 19 July 2018).

References

Andersen M and Skjoett-Larsen T (2009) Corporate social responsibility in global supply chains. *Supply Chain Management: An International Journal* 14(2): 75–86.

Banerjee SB (2003) Who sustains whose development? Sustainable development and the reinvention of nature. *Organization Studies* 24(1): 143–180.

Barnes FC (1998) ISO 9000 myth and reality: A reasonable approach to ISO 9000. *SAM Advanced Management Journal* 63(2): 23–30.

Biedermann R (2006) From a weak letter of intent to prevalence: The toy industries' code of conduct. *Journal of Public Affairs* 6(3–4): 197–209.

Brandon-Jones E (2013) *Institutional and Capability Perspectives on Sustainability in Operations and Supply Management: A Dual Theoretic Analysis of the UK Fashion Sector*. Unpublished PhD Thesis, University of Bath, UK.

Corbett CJ, Montes-Sancho MJ and Kirsch DA (2005) The financial impact of ISO 9000 certification in the United States: An empirical analysis. *Management Science* 51(7): 1046–1059.

Delmas MA (2002) The diffusion of environmental management standards in Europe and in the United States: An institutional perspective. *Policy Sciences* 35(1): 91–119.

Dickinson G, Johnsen T and Harland C (2010) Evidence-based purchasing: Does evidence make any difference to purchasing decisions? In: *Proceedings of the 18th IPSERA Conference*, 16–19 May, Lappeeranta University, Finland.

Dumond EJ (1994) Making best use of performance measures and information. *International Journal of Operations and Production Management* 14(9): 16–31.

Ethical Trading Initiative (ETI) (2013) The ETI base code. Available at: www.ethicaltrade.org.

Farber DA (1999) Taking slippage seriously: Noncompliance and creative compliance in environmental law. *Harvard Environmental Law Review* 23: 297.

Fransen LW and Kolk A (2007) Global rule-setting for business: A critical analysis of multi-stakeholder standards. *Organization* 14(5): 667–684.

Gao SS and Zhang JJ (2006) Stakeholder engagement, social auditing and corporate sustainability. *Business Process Management Journal* 12(6): 722–740.

Gray R (2006) Social, environmental and sustainability reporting and organisational value creation?: Whose value? Whose creation? *Accounting, Auditing & Accountability Journal* 19(6): 793–819.

Harris MN, Konya L and Matyas L (2002) Modelling the impact of environmental regulations on bilateral trade flows: OECD, 1990–1996. *The World Economy* 25(3): 387–405.

Helms WS, Oliver C and Webb K (2012) Antecedents of settlement on a new institutional practice: Negotiation of the ISO 26000 standard on social responsibility. *Academy of Management Journal* 55(5): 1120–1145.

Hughes J (2005) Supplier metrics that matter. *CPO Agenda*, Autumn: 19–23.

Ivarsson I and Alvstam CG (2010) Supplier upgrading in the home-furnishing value chain: An empirical study of IKEA's sourcing in China and South East Asia. *World Development* 38(11): 1575–1587.

Johansson C, Lindgren M and Lissgard P (1993) Att lyckas med ISO 9000: En ingaende studie av 23 foretag (To succeed with ISO 9000: A thorough study of 23 companies). *Ord & Form AB*, Uppsala.

Johnstone N (1998) The implications of the Basel Convention for developing countries: The case of trade in non-ferrous metal-bearing waste. *Resources, Conservation and Recycling* 23(1): 1–28.

Kaplan RS and Norton DP (1992) The balanced scorecard – Measures that drive performance. *Harvard Business Review* 70(1): 71–80.

King AA, Lenox MJ and Terlaak A (2005) The strategic use of decentralized institutions: Exploring certification with the ISO 14001 management standard. *Academy of Management Journal* 48(6): 1091–1106.

Kollman K and Prakash A (2001) Green by choice: Cross-national variations in firms' responses to EMS-based environmental regimes. *World Politics* 53: 399–430.

Lundmark E and Westelius A (2006) Effects of quality management according to ISO 9000: A Swedish study of the transit to ISO 9000: 2000. *Total Quality Management* 17(8): 1021–1042.

Matten D and Moon J (2008) 'Implicit' and 'explicit' CSR: A conceptual framework for a comparative understanding of corporate social responsibility. *Academy of Management Review* 33(2): 404–424.

Moratis L and Cochius T (2017) *ISO 26000: The Business Guide to the New Standard on Social Responsibility.* London: Routledge.

Morimoto R, Ash J and Hope C (2005) Corporate social responsibility audit: From theory to practice. *Journal of Business Ethics* 62(4): 315–325.

Nawrocka D (2008) Inter-organizational use of EMSs in supply chain management: Some experiences from Poland and Sweden. *Corporate Social Responsibility and Environmental Management* 15(5): 260–269.

Pfeffer J and Sutton RI (2006) Evidence-based management. *Harvard Business Review* 84(1): 63–74.

Poksinska B, Dahlgaard JJ and Antoni M (2002) The state of ISO 9000 certification: A study of Swedish organizations. *The TQM Magazine* 14(5): 297–306.

Prahinski C and Benton WC (2004) Supplier evaluations: Communication strategies to improve supplier performance. *Journal of Operations Management* 22(1): 39–62.

Prakash A and Potoski M (2006) Racing to the bottom? Trade, environment, governance, and ISO 14001. *American Journal of Political Science* 50(2): 350–364.

Preece S, Fleisher C and Toccacelli J (1995) Building a reputation along the value chain at Levi Strauss. *Long Range Planning* 28(6): 88–98.

Pressey AD, Winklhofer HM and Tzokas NX (2009) Purchasing practices in small- to medium-sized enterprises: An examination of strategic purchasing adoption, supplier evaluation and supplier capabilities. *Journal of Purchasing and Supply Management* 15: 214–226.

Preuss L (2009) Ethical sourcing codes of large UK-based corporations: Prevalence, content, limitations. *Journal of Business Ethics* 88(4): 735–747.

Ruhl J, Salzman J, Song K-S and Yu H (2002) Environmental compliance: Another integrity crisis or too many rules. *Natural Resources and Environment* 17: 24–29.

Shinkuma T and Huong NTM (2009) The flow of E-waste material in the Asian region and a reconsideration of international trade policies on E-waste. *Environmental Impact Assessment Review* 29(1): 25–31.

Sobczak A (2003) Codes of conduct in subcontracting networks: A labour law perspective. *Journal of Business Ethics* 44(2–3): 225–234.

The Consumer Goods Forum (2012) *Global Social Compliance Programme: Reference Tool on Supply Chain Social Performance Management Systems.* Paris: The Consumer Goods Forum.

Vastag G and Melnyk SA (2002) Certifying environmental management systems by the ISO 14001 standards. *International Journal of Production Research* 40(18): 4743–4763.

Walker H and Phillips W (2009) Sustainable procurement: Emerging issues. *International Journal of Procurement Management* 2(1): 41–61.

Watkins RV and Gutzwiller EC (1999) Buying into ISO 14001. *Occupational Health & Safety* 68(2): 52–54.

Welch EW, Rana A and Mori Y (2003) The promises and pitfalls of ISO 14001 for competitiveness and sustainability. *Greener Management International* 44: 59–73.

Welford R (1999) *Corporate Environmental Management.* Hyderabad, India: Universities Press.

Winstanley D, Clark J and Leeson H (2002) Approaches to child labour in the supply chain. *Business Ethics: A European Review* 11(3): 210–223.

Useful links and organizations

Better Cotton Initiative www.bettercotton.org (last accessed 29 October 2013)

Business for Social Responsibility www.bsr.org (last accessed 29 October 2013)

Business Social Compliance Initiative (BSCI) www.bsci-intl.org (last accessed 29 October 2013)

Electronic Industry Citizenship Coalition (EICC)/GeSI www.eicc.info (last accessed 29 October 2013)

Ethical Trading Initiative (ETI) www.ethicaltrade.org (last accessed 29 October 2013)

Fair Factories Clearinghouse www.fairfactories.org (last accessed 29 October 2013)

Fair Labor Association www.fairlabor.org (last accessed 29 October 2013)

Fair Wear Foundation www.fairwear.org (last accessed 29 October 2013)

Global Reporting Initiative www.globalreporting.org/CurrentPriorities/SupplyChain/(last accessed 29 October 2013)

Global Social Compliance Programme (GSCP) www.gscpnet.com (last accessed 29 October 2013)

Initiative Clause Sociale (ICS) www.ics-asso.org (last accessed 29 October 2013)

ICTI CARE Foundation www.toy-icti.org (last accessed 29 October 2013)

IDH www.idhsustainabletrade.com/en/about-idh (last accessed 29 October 2013)

International Labour Organization (ILO): Declaration on Fundamental Principles and Rights at Work

ILO: Tripartite Declaration of Principles Concerning Multinational Enterprises and Social Policy

ISEAL Alliance www.isealalliance.org (last accessed 29 October 2013)

OECD: Guidelines for Multinational Enterprises www.oecd.org/dataoecd/43/29/48004323.pdf (last accessed 29 October 2013)

OECD: The Corporate Responsibility to Respect Human Rights in Supply Chains: Discussion Paper

Portal for Responsible Supply Chain Management www.csr-supplychain.org (last accessed 29 October 2013)

Rainforest Alliance www.rainforest-alliance.org (last accessed 29 October 2013)

Sedex www.sedex.org.uk (last accessed 29 October 2013)

Social Accountability Accreditation Services (SAAS) www.saasaccreditation.org (last accessed 29 October 2013)

Social Accountability International (SAI) www.sa-intl.org (last accessed 29 October 2013)

UNHR: Guiding Principles on Business and Human Rights

UNHR: The Corporate Responsibility to Respect Human Rights, an Interpretive Guide

United Nations Global Compact Supply Chain Portal http://supply-chain.unglobalcompact.org/ (last accessed 29 October 2013)

Worldwide Responsible Accredited Production (WRAP) www.wrapcompliance.org (last accessed 29 October 2013)

CHAPTER 14

Towards sustainable supply networks

LEARNING OBJECTIVES

By the end of this chapter you should be able to:

- Explore how supply chains fit in the context of broader sustainability debate including concepts such as natural capital, eco-efficiency and sustainable development goals;

- Link supply chain thinking to industrial ecology;

- Understand the theory on stakeholder engagement and partnership for sustainability, including base of the pyramid challenges;

- Understand the role of supplier development in sustainability;

- Identify the limits to defining sustainable supply networks.

14.0 Introduction

The purpose of this chapter is to discuss some of the key themes of sustainability as they relate to supply networks. For this chapter we adopt the term networks instead of chains because, as is shown later, the scope of activity is much wider than immediate links in a chain. The field of sustainability and sustainable development has continued to evolve since the original Rio summit in 1992 and the publication of the seminal Brundtland report issuing from this global event. United Nations summits and meetings have continued over the last 20 years, creating more precise definitions of sustainability in general and treating specific issues in detail (e.g. biodiversity and climate change). Therefore it is useful to critically discuss some of the latest thinking on sustainability and to reflect on how this evolution impacts on the management of supply networks.

In parallel, management practices have continued to evolve. Supply networks have become more complex and further constrained by institutional environments (as shown in Chapter 12). From this, certain practices have emerged as important for sustainability of supply in the economic, social and environmental sense. One example is industrial ecology whereby companies in a locality exchange waste by-products to create a self-sustaining localized supply chain (Seuring, 2004), showing evidence of a circular economy. A second significant development over the last 20 years is the role of stakeholder engagement in the supply chain activity where non-economic actors are involved in the business decision-making process (Park-Poaps and Rees, 2010), one reason we increasingly talk about networks rather than supply chains. Part of the reason for this practice is to increase the legitimacy of business decisions in the eyes of not just consumers but also non-governmental organizations (NGOs) who lobby governments and influence the public on issues related to sustainability (Mueller *et al.*, 2009).

This chapter first discusses the main principles of sustainability and how these might influence companies managing their supply network. Within this part concepts such as natural capital and eco-efficiency are discussed. The last part of this section returns to the broader concept of footprints and how economic activity is shown to impact ecosystems and society overall. This demonstrates that supply networks are an integral part of global sustainability actions, but the challenge is to understand how to make the link between global objectives and supply network actions. The second part looks at the example of industrial ecology, showing how supply networks can be part of an integral – almost self-sustaining – system. Here the industrial systems and the natural ecosystem are coupled and mutually dependent. The third section addresses how companies are moving from responding to stakeholder concerns to actively engaging in joint activities with stakeholders to improve performance economically, socially and environmentally. This partnership approach is seen as key to addressing these 'global' issues mentioned earlier. The following section addresses the difficulties in truly defining and identifying sustainable supply networks and that this is still in early development today. Before the end a section is included to cover the issues of supplier development and how this links to capability building in certain regions. Finally, the case study describes the actions of Finnish Metsä Group in attempting to create a sustainable wood supply chain and integrates many of the topics covered in this chapter.

14.1 Core principles of sustainability in supply networks

This section returns to the overall sustainability perspective of this book, in order to provide discussion of the core principles which are used to define sustainability in supply chains today. In summary, for a supply chain to demonstrate sustainability it is paramount that the environmental, social and economic elements are considered and shown to preserve the available resources for future generations. There are a number of concepts which help decide whether sustainability objectives are truly met. These include the comparison of the ecological footprint of human activities, comprising the preservation of natural capital (the natural resources on which economic systems depend) and also the balance between resources and their consumption, e.g. eco-efficiency. As mentioned in Chapter 12, the inclusion of social and economic imperatives is much less developed than environmental issues; however, more recent developments in the sustainability debate have attempted to improve the integration of the three elements. Notably the interpretation of the 'millennium goals' as planetary 'boundaries' and 'must haves' (Griggs *et al.*, 2013; Rockstrom *et al.*, 2009) shows the interdisciplinary work that still needs to be done to integrate sustainability at intergovernmental, national and company levels. At the level of the supply chain there is even less evidence that the three pillars of sustainability are equally treated, again with the social dimension being less integrated overall (Miemczyk *et al.*, 2012) and particularly that supply chain metrics are not well aligned with global targets for improving the level of sustainability (Whiteman *et al.*, 2013). The following section discusses some of these recent developments in the sustainability arena and how they might be applied in a supply chain context, starting with the concept of ecological footprint.

14.1.1 Ecological footprint

Today the most widespread ecological footprints are calculated at the national level and are the basis for stating that humanity is living beyond its means in ecological terms and are the origin of statements such as 'each year we are consuming one and a half earths'. Footprint analysis has taken a number of forms, however, from calculating the 'carbon' footprint (of a company or a product – see Chapter 11), to other related methods such as ecological rucksack[1] which is related to the weight of material input into a product (see Note 14.1). However, there is a growing recognition that beyond specific material inputs or carbon, the overall impact on ecosystems needs to be taken into account in order to understand the real footprint of a product, company or even country.

Note 14.1
The 1.7 kilogram microchip

As an example of the ecological footprint or rucksack of a product, the analysis done by Williams *et al.* (2002) shows that the material inputs for a 2g microchip reaches 1.7 kilograms or 850 times the weight of the product itself. For the typical 32MB DRAM chip the majority of this equivalent weight is from fossil fuels. Looking back into the production chain of the silicon wafers, the researchers found that the purification to chip quality uses 160x more energy than for other uses of silicon outside of semiconductors and therefore demonstrates how energy intensive this process really is.

Source: Williams *et al.* (2002)

Ecosystems can be thought of as dynamic and complex systems comprising plants, animals, micro-organisms and the non-living components which interact, are self-sustaining and include feedback mechanisms for self-regulation (Diaz, 2005). While this is an ecologist view of the natural environment, recent thinking has come to see ecosystems as not only intrinsically valuable but also providing valuable services to humanity. Hence the idea of ecosystem services has arisen to demonstrate how they provide supporting, provisioning, regulating and cultural services to humanity (UNEP, 2005). The link to supply chains is that these ecosystem services provide the necessary resources for the products we produce.

Table 14.1 The ecosystems services

Ecosystem services	Definition – Supply chain implications
Provisioning services	Goods obtained directly from ecosystems (e.g. food, medicine, timber, fibre and bioenergy). The raw materials used by companies to manufacture products.
Regulating services	Benefits obtained from the regulation of natural processes (e.g. water filtration, waste decomposition, climate regulation, crop pollination and regulation of some human diseases, CO_2 absorption). Maintaining a regular supply of the goods mentioned above.
Supporting services	Regulation of basic ecological functions and processes that are necessary for the provision of all other ecosystem services (e.g. nutrient cycling, photosynthesis and soil formation). Particularly important for maintaining the supply of high-quality biologically derived materials.
Cultural services	Contributing to the well-being of communities

A related idea to ecosystem services is how the concept of 'capital' can be applied to the natural environment (Russo, 2003). Natural capital can be defined as the raw materials and ecological cycles (water cycles, nitrogen cycle and so on) provided by the natural environment. Typically footprint analysis takes into account the stock of living ecological assets that yield goods and services on a continuous basis. Therefore the ecological part of natural capital is closely linked to ecosystem services. The reasonable assumption that natural capital or ecosystem services are limited links well to another supply chain concept: capacity. In this case bio-capacity is a way of understanding the limits to natural capital and its related services. Although these concepts may seem too global to concern businesses and their supply chains, some companies are already using these ideas to formulate their sustainability objectives, particularly in developing countries. For example, Dow Chemicals has developed a pilot site in Santa Vitria, Brazil, to undertake a comprehensive analysis of services that nature provides to Dow's operations and the community. Specifically this initiative aims to analyse the impacts and dependencies on ecosystem services in the region specifically related to crop production (sugar cane to polyethylene and biomass fuel), access to freshwater sources, forest habitat, sediment reduction (i.e. erosion control) and nutrient retention.[2] Furthermore, some companies are now actively engaged in understanding how to value natural capital economically in order to correct the fact that markets typically do not take into account these 'externalities', with at least $72trillion worth of ecosystem services currently given for free.[3] A significant consortium of global business have categorized the business reasons – many of which have significant supply chain implications – for valuing natural capital and ecosystem services (Simmons *et al.*, 2012). Although this is a viewpoint from a select few large companies, it does show that the concepts are now starting to enter mainstream business jargon. The following set of actions can be employed to positively impact natural capital and business operations (Simmons *et al.*, 2012).

Risk reduction:

- Avoid supply chain and operational disruptions caused by scarcities of natural resources.

- Reduce threats to business continuity and harm to facilities, workers and communities in places vulnerable to extreme weather, flooding, drought, fires, desertification or resource scarcity.

- Stay ahead of impending regulatory changes that could limit product or production choices.

- Avoid fines, suspensions, lawsuits or other liabilities due to over-exploitation or contamination of natural systems, and improve relationships with local communities and host governments.

- Avoid damage to corporate reputation and brand.

Cost reduction:

- Discover new ways to reduce expenses and increase margins, as reducing ecosystem impacts helps reveal opportunities to boost resource productivity and increase energy efficiency.

- Save money by reducing waste and recapturing valuable materials that otherwise could harm ecosystems.

- Avoid costly manmade 'grey infrastructure' expenses by opting instead for 'natural infrastructure' investments in restoration of healthy forests, wetlands, watersheds and coastal ecosystems – often the cheaper and more effective long-term solution.

- Explore natural solutions to cut costs on stormwater management, flood mitigation, air quality management, carbon sequestration, water purification and climate-related threats.

- Postpone or avoid cost increases due to rising resource scarcities by investing in sustainable sourcing practices.

Brand reputation improvement:

- Win trust and loyalty from growing ranks of customers who value sustainability leadership.

- Differentiate brand from competitors by communicating superior purchasing, operating or investment practices.

- Draw and retain top talent, as a growing number of employees value working for a company with a culture and values they share.

- Attract investors and lenders who increasingly factor companies' environmental performance and exposures into their decisions.

Improving revenue generation:

- Win sales by meeting customers' growing demands for products and services that do no harm to sensitive ecosystems.

- Create new revenue opportunities by innovating solutions that alleviate pressure on the environment or restore healthy ecosystems.

- Exploit opportunities to educate consumers about high-performance sustainable products to increase demand and create new market segments.

- Leverage emerging 'natural capital' markets such as water-quality trading, wetland banking and threatened species banking, and natural carbon sequestration.

The first major attempt to calculate the ecological footprint and bio-capacity of nations began in 1997 (Wackernagel *et al.*, 1997). Building on these assessments, in 2003 the Global Footprint Network initiated its National Footprint Accounts (NFA) programme. An NFA is an accounting framework which aims to quantify the annual supply and demand of key ecosystem services by means of two measures (Wackernagel *et al.*, 2002). The supply part of these accounts are based on bio-capacity calculations and the demand part related to ecological footprint analysis. The ecological footprint is usually measured in global hectares, where 1 gha represents a biologically productive hectare with world average productivity.[4]

National Footprint Accounts (NFAs) monitor resources for each individual country, making up the global ecological footprint. These accounts include crops and fish for human food and other uses, wood, and grass and feed crops for livestock. One limitation is that carbon emissions are currently the only waste product tracked, given the efforts to minimize and avoid certain waste streams. In 2008, the Earth's total biocapacity was 12.0 billion gha, or 1.8 gha per person, while humanity's ecological footprint was 18.2 billion gha, or 2.7 gha per person. This discrepancy means it would take 1.5 years for the earth to fully regenerate the renewable resources that people used in one year.

Humanity's annual demand on the natural world has exceeded what the earth can renew in a year since the 1970s. This 'ecological overshoot' has continued to grow over the years, reaching a 50 per cent deficit in 2008.

14.1.2 Eco-efficiency and Factor X improvement

Another concept used to guide decisions on sustainability in business is that of eco-efficiency. The World Business Council for Sustainable Development (WBCSD) is known to have first used the term eco-efficiency in the book *Changing Course* (Schmidheiny, 1992) which states that 'corporations that achieve ever more efficiency while preventing pollution through good housekeeping, materials substitution, cleaner technologies, and cleaner products and that strive for more efficient use and recovery of resources can be called "eco-efficient"'. The purpose of eco-efficiency is to maximize value creation while at the same time minimizing the use of resources and emissions of pollutants (Bidwell and Verfaillie, 2000). Measuring eco-efficiency is important in order to measure the decoupling of economic growth and environmental pressure. Eco-efficiency is in most cases expressed by the following ratio:

Eco-efficiency = Product or service value/Environmental influence

One advantage of using eco-efficiency indicators is that it solves the problem that 'traditional' environmental performance indicators might vary according to changes in production volume and therefore hide real changes in environmental performance. While eco-efficiency has gained some ground in the implementation of sustainability in companies, some proponents of this approach have suggested specific targets such as Factor 4 or Factor 10 improvements in efficiency of resource use (Reijnders, 1998). In a sense this concept links well to lean production as described in Chapter 8. Therefore one way to link supply chains to sustainability is to integrate the concepts of lean supply chains with eco-efficiency as in the end these both have the same goals.

14.1.3 Sustainable Development Goals (SDGs)

In order to understand the contribution of supply chain management to sustainability, the way sustainability is defined by governments and international agencies such as the UN is important. While the three pillars of sustainability is a useful first step, this is a rather simplistic view of the issues involved. One of the more recent developments in the definition of sustainability can be linked to the Millennium Declaration that was signed in 2000 by 189 countries in order to 'create an environment – at the national and global levels alike – which is conducive to development and the elimination of poverty'. The declaration was part of the development of a series of more specific goals for reaching sustainable development as it was originally defined (see Figure 14.1 for the recent goals) Many of the concepts already defined in this book have clear links to the goal of environmental sustainability (for example, closed-loop supply chains), but supply chain activities can also impact on other goals such as that of global partnership, reducing poverty, access to education and health issues, especially in developing regions or the so-called base of the pyramid (BOP). The BOP includes regions where the population survives on less than $2 per day and covers around 4 billion people globally. Despite the challenge, these goals provide an overarching sustainability framework that guides governmental action, and therefore will impact on the way that supply chains are organized. It can be a challenge to see how companies might integrate these goals into business strategy, so many of these targets are integrated into business-relevant aspirations, such as those listed in the UN Global Compact, as mentioned in Chapter 13. However, some companies, especially those with a multinational footprint, impact on developing regions through their sourcing activities, which are engaging directly with these SDGs, putting in place specific plans, including Metsä – described at the end of this chapter. For example, Paul Polman, Unilever's CEO has stated:

> There is no business case for enduring poverty. We have an opportunity to unlock trillions of dollars through new markets, investments and innovation. But to do so, we must challenge our current practices and address poverty, inequality and environmental challenges.[5]

In part, the intentions of the SDGs are enacted through Unilever's Responsible Sourcing Policy, with the aim of sourcing all agricultural products sustainably by 2020, including soy, sugar and palm oil.

Figure 14.1   The UN Sustainable Development Goals

Table 14.2 Going beyond the planetary boundaries

Earth's lives or planetary boundaries	Limit	Actual
ACID OCEANS – Global mean saturation state of aragonite in surface sea water	2.75	2.90
OZONE DEPLETION – Concentration of ozone (Dobson unit)	276	283
FRESH WATER Consumption of freshwater by humans (km^3 per year)	4000	2600
BIODIVERSITY Extinction rate (number of species per million species per year)	10	>100
NITROGEN AND PHOSPHORUS CYCLES – Amount of N2 removed from the atmosphere for human use (millions of tonnes per year) Quantity of P flowing into the oceans (millions of tonnes per year)	35	121
LAND USE Percentage of global land cover converted to cropland	15	11.7
CLIMATE CHANGE – (i) Atmospheric carbon dioxide concentration (parts per million by volume) 350 387 280 (ii) Change in radiative forcing (watts per metre squared)	350 1	385 1.5
AEROSOL LOADING – Overall particulate concentration in the atmosphere, on a regional basis	TBD	TBD
CHEMICAL POLLUTION – For example, amount emitted to, or concentration of persistent organic pollutants, plastics, endocrine disrupters, heavy metals and nuclear waste	TBD	TBD

Source: Based on Rockstrom *et al.* (2009).

14.1.4 Earth's 9 lives, planetary boundaries and 'must haves'

The idea of the nine planetary boundaries (Rockstrom *et al.*, 2009) or the earth's nine lives concept (Pearce, 2010) is based on the idea that there are a limited number of life-supporting mechanisms that need to be protected if mankind (and the economy) is to maintain the current level of quality of life. The nine lives or boundaries are shown in Table 14.2 and the overshoot in terms of going beyond what is viewed as sustainable is shown in grey.

Although these nine elements provide the basics for humanity's existence, recent work has estimated that we have already surpassed the threshold for three of these boundaries or life-support mechanisms, namely climate change, the nitrogen cycle and biodiversity loss. Again it is difficult to see how companies can directly impact these boundaries, but there can be no doubt individual firms and more importantly their supply chains directly affect the underpinning resources for each of these issues.

Recognizing that the planetary boundaries concept is limited to resources and ecosystem services, Griggs *et al.* (2013) move the debate on by defining 'planetary must haves', regrouping some of these boundaries and adding the limitations on materials use which has a clear link to supply chain management processes. They also show that these 'limits' need to be compared with the goals for development as outlined by the previously mentioned SDGs, and in synthesizing these objectives come to the following list of overall objectives, which can be thought of as the most complete set of defined objectives balancing environmental, social and economic imperatives at a global level.

- Thriving lives and livelihoods

- Sustainable food security

- Sustainable water security

- Universal clean energy

- Healthy and productive ecosystems

- Governance for sustainable societies

Although this section has focused on macro-level indicators, it is clear that companies are starting to integrate these indicators driven by various stakeholder activities (see Section 14.3). In fact this raises the issue of the disconnect between high-level targets and how they are measured, and the individual impacts of companies and their supply chains. Recent management research has recognized this gap in levels of analysis and action and encourages a dialogue on how companies and their supply chains play a role in keeping within the limits set at a societal level (Whiteman *et al.*, 2013). In some cases researchers have also attempted to link supply chain activities at the country level with country level sustainability performance, showing a link between them (Vachon and Mao, 2008). It can be argued that companies and their supply chains can only really demonstrate sustainability if they can link to these macro-objectives, but the work to translate these into deliverable aims and actions is still to be done and to date only a few large multinationals have started to examine how this can be done. One example of how 'macro-level' objectives can be translated into business actions is through public procurement (Chapter 3). Here national governmental objectives are integrated as policies for public buyers and due to the scale this can have a significant impact. Despite the difficulties of creating sustainable supply networks, there are some examples of how supply networks can be viewed as part of ecosystems and this is discussed next.

14.2 Industrial ecology and industrial symbiosis

This stream of sustainability-related practice is based on the coordination of local networks and has strong links to the previously discussed circular economy perspective, where 'waste of one process can be used as resource for another process'. A related concept is industrial symbiosis (IS) which is defined as exchange structures to progress to a more eco-efficient industrial system, by establishing a collaborative network of material and energy exchanges among different organizations. Three types of activity are associated with IS (Chertow, 2007):

- By-product exchanges (the sale of one company's by-products to be used as an input to a process by another);

- Utility sharing (the shared management and/or provision of a utility such as electricity, water, wastewater by a number of companies);

- Service sharing (the shared provision of ancillary services with explicit environmental benefits for a third party).

In reality the exchange of 'wastes' between independent firms in some sectors has been taking place for many centuries, as it makes good business sense. However, the naming of 'industrial ecosystems' is a relatively new development. The most renowned example is the town of Kalundborg, Denmark (Jacobsen, 2006). This industrial ecosystem involves an oil refinery, a gypsum factory, a pharmaceutical firm, a fish farm, a coal-fired electrical power station and the municipality of Kalundborg. Within Kalundborg steam and various raw materials such as sulphur, fly ash and sludge are exchanged. Participating companies gain economically from reduced costs for waste disposal, improved efficiencies of resource use and improved environmental performance. For example, gas captured from the oil refinery which had previously been flared off is sent to the electrical power station which typically saves the equivalent of 30,000 tonnes of coal a year. Figure 14.2 represents the industrial ecology system at Kalundborg.

Note 14.2
Industrial ecology at Guitang Group in Guangxi province in southern central China

The Guitang Group (GG) operates one of the largest sugar refineries in China. The GG first invested in developing its own collection of downstream companies to utilize nearly all by-products of sugar production. This strategy has generated new revenues and reduced environmental emissions and disposal costs, while simultaneously improving the quality of sugar. Internally, the GG's complex consists of interlinked production of sugar, alcohol, cement, compound fertilizer and paper and includes recycling and reuse. The company has developed and distributed two organic fertilizers to their farm suppliers of sugar cane. Both are made from alcohol residue, with one mixed with nitrogen, phosphorus and potassium, whereas the other includes white sludge and bottom/fly-ash derived from the GG's production processes. The company has shown that these fertilizers, compared with typical inorganic fertilizers, have increased the sugar cane yield by 12 to15 tonnes per hectare (to 81 tonnes/hectare),while slightly increasing the sugar content of the cane by 0.5 per cent, benefiting both the farmer and the company. Externally, the GG has established a strong customer base as a result of its product quality, has worked to maintain and expand its supply base through technological and economic incentives to farmers (and even to competitors), and has had to react to a strong government presence that affects its operations. There are significant challenges, though, especially with a volatile globalized sugar market. One significant danger for examples like this in developing countries is that the economics of the operation are sensitive to global trade, and as China opens more markets to international trade, the greater the risks that such mechanisms are no longer viable. However, this could drive further efficiencies and innovations in the process for the future.

Source: Zhu *et al.* (2007)

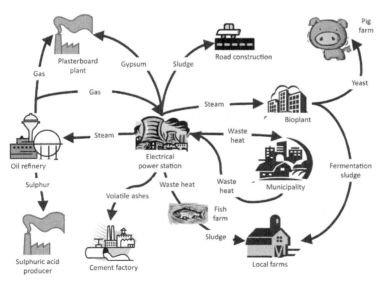

Figure 14.2   Industrial ecology at Kalundborg

Source: Created by the author.

14.3 Stakeholder engagement and working with NGOs in supply networks

In order to understand the broader role of the environment that surrounds firms, an important concept is that of stakeholders. As Freeman (1984) explains, 'given the turbulence that organizations are currently facing and the very nature of the external environment, as consisting of economic and socio-political forces, there is a need for conceptual schemata which analyse these forces in an integrative fashion'. Therefore stakeholder theory is enlightening to supply networks because by definition it involves inter-organizational relationships. A stakeholder is 'any group or individual who can affect or is affected by the achievement of the organisation objectives' (Freeman, 1984) or more recently 'the stakeholders in a firm are individuals and constituencies that contribute, either voluntarily or involuntarily, to its wealth-creating capacity and activities, and who are therefore its potential beneficiaries and/or risk bearers' (Post *et al.*, 2002). A depiction of a firm's stakeholders is shown below (Figure 14.3), which has been adapted to include the important link to NGOs.

Stakeholder management can be defined as 'the development and implementation of organizational policies and practices that take into account the goals and concerns of all relevant stakeholders' (Post *et al.*, 2002). From this perspective, especially relating to risk, customers have a stake in suppliers and suppliers in customers. It is important to point out here that using a stakeholder view demands a different perspective on supply chain management. While much of SCM is focused on immediate supply chain actors, the stakeholder view warrants a wider network-level approach, searching for, and engaging with, organizations outside of a company's typical supply chain relationships. As Starik and Rands (1995: 908) point out, stakeholder thinking implies multiple levels of engagement from

Figure 14.3 A firm's potential stakeholders

Source: Based on Post *et al.* (2002).

'individual, organizational, political-economic, socio-cultural and ecological environment levels'. Thus, returning to Figure 1.1 in the first chapter of this book, we can see that taking a stakeholder view implies that we see supply chain management as a network.

Stakeholder salience is an important element of stakeholder management or engagement. In other words, which stakeholders are important, and which ones should be engaged with? In order to provide a theoretical basis for answering this question, Mitchell *et al.* (1997) explain that power, legitimacy and urgency are key traits of stakeholders that should be considered and can help define salience. Power is clearly important especially where stakeholders can coerce companies to take actions, for example through policy (as shown in Chapter 12). Legitimacy, which underpins the normative view of stakeholder thinking, is defined as 'a generalized perception or assumption that actions of an entity are desirable, proper or appropriate within some socially constructed system of norms, value, beliefs and definitions' (Suchman, 1995). Companies often seek to engage with stakeholders to increase their legitimacy, often communicating their 'partnership' with certain NGOs with consumers. Urgency is used to move the theory from a static model to a dynamic one. Thus urgency is 'the degree to which stakeholder claims call for immediate attention' (Mitchell *et al.*, 1997), for example when there is an immediate threat to an ecosystem as is the case raised by the Palm Oil Roundtable. Mitchell *et al.* (1997) go on to argue that corporate social responsibility has two divisions. First, there is a moral focus on social responsibility, and second, there is an amoral focus on social responsiveness. They propose that their theoretical perspective integrates these two views by considering power, legitimacy and urgency traits of stakeholders.

Stakeholders are said to have varying influences from an ecological perspective ranging from indirect to direct influences depending on the type of stakeholder. For example, in their study, Madsen and Ulhoi (2001) demonstrate that while legislators and regulators are seen as having a direct influence on firms, others such as the media are more indirect influencers. Taking this idea further, research by Henriques and Sadorsky (1999) show a link between stakeholder types and levels of environmental response. While more proactive firms perceive all environmental stakeholders as important with the exception of the media, reactive firms only feel the media are important stakeholders. Other research has linked proactive strategies with deeper stakeholder relationships, showing that environmental leadership or proactivity is not linked to strong influence of regulatory stakeholders (Buysse and Verbeke, 2003).

Stakeholders have a number of influences on supply chains, including environmental and social responsibility of suppliers, helping local communities where supply chains are located, impacts through consumers (food safety), risk concerns from investors and requirements on measurable actions, to name a few (Tate *et al.*, 2010). The most obvious influence of stakeholders is that they hold companies responsible for the actions of their suppliers. Some notable research has shown that inattention to bad practices of suppliers can often bring unwanted attention of stakeholders and that proactive management of suppliers can help manage relationships with stakeholders wanting to highlight negative events. One well-known case study is of US universities' sourcing of sports apparel from sweatshops in Central America. Here student activists formed coalitions with the media to force the universities and businesses to change their practices. For example, the students demanded that the University of Notre Dame:

> Withdraw from FLA,[6] monitor with organizations that workers can trust, not corporations like Price Waterhouse Cooper, deny the three industry representatives on the anti-sweatshop task force a vote, as they have a conflict of interest, appoint student activists to

the task force, send task force members on a fact-finding delegation to Central America to ask workers how we should monitor and what our code of conduct should contain, include fair wages, women's rights, right to organize, and full disclosure [of factory location] in our code of conduct.

(Wright *et al.*, 2007: 71)

This case demonstrates the power stakeholders can exert, especially if coordinated, questioning the legitimacy of other stakeholders such as the FLA and the creation of urgency through media involvement.

Although stakeholders are seen as a source for coercive pressure to become more sustainable, they are increasingly seen as part of the solution, being a source of knowledge, influence and legitimacy. In this sense stakeholder engagement has moved towards a partnership model, away from just responding to bad press to attempting to integrate the moral responsibility elements of sustainability. This has been recognized by the United Nations, for example, which has attempted to stimulate these kinds of arrangements (see Note 14.3).

Note 14.3
Johannesburg partnerships and the cement industry

These partnerships are voluntary, non-negotiated, multi-stakeholder, international, collaborative projects for sustainable development. Partnership members are drawn from governments, international organizations, private corporations, and from civil society. Partnerships are referred to as Type II agreements to distinguish them from the politically negotiated agreements and commitments that were considered the first outcome of the summit.

(Hale and Mauzerall, 2004: 220)

One of the first examples of these types of partnerships was the Cement Sustainability Initiative (CSI) which is a global group of 24 major cement producers with operations in more than 100 countries who believe there is a strong business case for the pursuit of sustainable development. Collectively the companies account for around 30 per cent of the world's cement production and range in size from very large multinationals to smaller local producers. The CSI's Agenda for Action was published in 2002, following a two-year programme of scoping, research and stakeholder consultation looking at what sustainable development means for the cement industry. It sets out a five-year work programme to take the companies towards practical actions, focusing on the five main work areas outlined below:

- CO_2 and Climate Protection
- Responsible Use of Fuels and Raw Materials
- Employee Health and Safety
- Emissions Monitoring and Reduction
- Local Impacts on Land and Communities

Source: http://www.wbcsdcement.org/ (last accessed 4 November 2013)

An early example of partnerships for sustainability is related to product recycling. Roy and Whelan (1992) describe an advisory group made up of material producers, manufacturers, retailers, reclamation firms, local authorities, research organizations and government. This group provided information exchange, sharing of best practice and initiated 'collaborative ventures'. In general there is less research focusing on the stakeholder engagement and partnerships in the context of supply chains. Innovation and learning are also seen as an element of stakeholder engagement, for example in the case where local authorities in Sweden were involved in improving environmental practices of SMEs in a public service provider's supply network (von Malmborg, 2007). This highlights one particular challenge where SMEs may be required to adopt standards and practices but have neither the means nor the competencies to do so, and so stakeholders can be solicited to aid this capacity-building activity of suppliers. In a case study of Nestlé's Nespresso supply chain, Alvarez *et al.* (2010) find that the quality of the relationships are paramount, especially at the beginning of multi-stakeholder initiatives to improve the sustainability of products. Although the aims of these partnerships are clearly to improve performance, there are possible downsides. Smith (2008) discusses a range of supply chain stakeholder initiatives in the food sector, such as the Sustainable Agriculture Initiative platform, originally involving Unilever, Danone and Nestlé. This showed that while there are clear benefits to involvement, there are also costs and risks to this, as shown in Table 14.3.

Table 14.3 Benefits and costs of involvement in a multi-stakeholder supply chain approach

Stakeholder	Positive elements	Negative elements
Manufacturers and retailers in importing countries	More credibility and stability in supply	No value if consumers ambivalent 'Buy in' to standards from external parties
Social NGOs	Greater impact – more influence on pricing	Working with the enemy
Environmental NGOs	Best practices becomes the business standard	Standards watered down by other parties with different priorities
Responsible plantations and growers organizations	Levelling the playing field	Costs of implementation and documentation
Smallholder farmers	Improved participation and performance	Low influence, imposed by customers, costs to implement and document
Governments/public sector	Consistent adoption of standards and policy, viewed as more responsive to business	Local power reduced

Source: Adapted from Smith (2008).

Partnerships with NGOs are seen as a big opportunity for buying companies to work with distant parts of their supply chain or work on issues that are more in the competence area of specialist NGOs. One example is the World Wide Fund for Nature (WWF) which has worked with many multinationals, especially in the 'middle' of supply chains, to influence both upstream and downstream actors in these networks. For example, the WWF has worked closely with Sodexo on improving the sustainability of seafood sourcing, while at the same time Sodexo would work to convince their customers of the value of sustainably sourced seafood, for example in school and public office catering.

In summary, stakeholder engagement and partnerships for sustainability are now seen as a key element of managing sustainability in the context of supply chains. Not only can companies avoid bad press by working with NGOs, for example in developing countries, but this can also help in the development and spread of best practices across increasingly complex supply networks. This approach is starting to be integrated into company supplier development processes, which have traditionally focused on suppliers' operational performance improvement, i.e. cost, quality and delivery, but are increasingly expanded to address sustainability performance improvements. In the following section, we first provide a brief introduction to traditional supplier development programmes and their basis in supplier assessment, before considering how these link to supplier sustainability improvement.

14.4 Supplier development

In many ways the process of defining the performance measures and what you do with it is more important than the measures themselves. The process of defining supplier performance measures should be used to facilitate dialogue with suppliers. Even better, measures could be defined jointly with suppliers and used collaboratively (Hughes, 2005). Certainly, the data must be shared with suppliers so that suppliers actually know where they stand (Modi and Mabert, 2007; Prahinski and Benton, 2004). That way, the results of the assessment can be used to address problem areas and to improve rather than simply penalize suppliers when performance is below par.

Supplier assessment results should be used to determine areas for supplier performance improvement and many companies regard supplier evaluation as a critical part of, or even a prerequisite for, successful supplier development programmes. Using purchasing portfolio models to differentiate different types of suppliers (Kraljic, 1983; Bensaou, 1999), companies increasingly devote their efforts to developing and managing a small number of critical, or strategic, supplier relationships. These are typically well-established, mature relationships developed over a long period of time and often represent high supply value and risk (Kraljic, 1983; Gelderman and Van Weele, 2005).

The practice of supplier development is widely used across industries but it has its origins in the Japanese automotive industry as a natural extension of continuous improvement – or *kaizen*. Supplier development is concerned with improving the suppliers' capabilities. Being closely linked to lean production, two objectives are to:

- root out wasteful (non-value-adding) activities;
- achieve long-term improvement of suppliers' quality, cost and delivery performance.

Sako's (2004) work on the Japanese automotive industry showed how Honda, Nissan and especially Toyota pioneered supplier development. Toyota stated as early as 1939 that: 'Once nominated as Toyota suppliers, they should be treated as part of Toyota … Toyota shall carry out business with these suppliers without switching to others, and shall make every effort to raise the performance of these suppliers' (Toyota 1939 Purchasing Rules). The logic of supplier development at Toyota, as well as at other lean manufacturers, is that once lean manufacturing has been perfected internally, it needs to be cascaded into the supply chain. The Operations Management Consulting Division (OMCD) at Toyota cascades the Toyota Production System (i.e. lean production) to suppliers through lectures, seminars and training courses, individual assistance and *Jishuken* groups (joint problem-solving supplier groups). Some activities are focused on short-term improvement and problem solving whereas others focus on long-term capability enhancement. Many suppliers in turn have their own OMCD-like operations, cascading their learning further upstream.

Toyota's agreement with suppliers involved in supplier development stipulates that suppliers be allowed to keep the savings resulting from improvement activities. Given the constant cost pressure of Toyota on suppliers, Toyota will naturally benefit from this activity but it is an important part of motivating suppliers to commit to supplier development. As an added benefit, working with suppliers as part of supplier development gives Toyota in-depth insights into supplier cost breakdowns. This means that they gain cost transparency without having to resort to open-book negotiation, i.e. asking its suppliers to disclose its books – a practice that often leads to cheating (Lamming *et al.*, 2005).

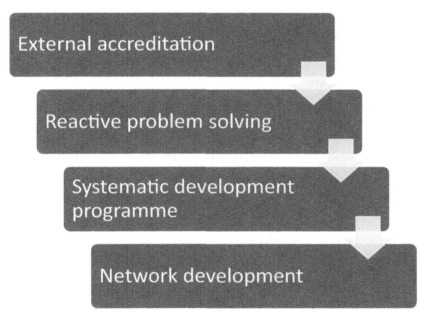

Figure 14.4 Four steps in supplier development

Source: Adapted from Hines *et al.* (2000).

Hines *et al.* (2000) suggest that supplier development programmes typically progress through four steps, beginning with efforts to accredit suppliers, followed by reactive problem solving with suppliers, developing into a more systematic supplier development programme and ultimately into a process of 'network development'. Where the third step focuses on knowledge flowing vertically from the focal company to its suppliers, the fourth step is characterized by mutual sharing of knowledge amongst buyers and suppliers both vertically and horizontally.

14.4.1 Supplier assessment and development activities focused on sustainability

Although supplier assessment and development activities are originally focused on measuring and improving operational performance, the same principles apply when companies seek to assess and improve the sustainability performance of their suppliers. A challenge clearly exists in converging operational and sustainability performance methods and initiatives.

The literature on sustainability identifies two approaches for implementing sustainability initiatives in supply chains: a monitoring/control approach and a mentoring approach (Vachon, 2007; Vachon and Klassen, 2006). The monitoring and control approach is akin to traditional supplier assessment and includes:

- Auditing factories – this can be done either by the company itself or through a third party, in order to evaluate that suppliers comply with the company's requirements and standards;

- Sending out questionnaires for the supplier to complete;

- Gathering information and reports on suppliers' environmental performance;

- Inspecting suppliers' materials for environmental performance;

- Stipulating that suppliers achieve environmental management system accreditation such as European Eco-Management and Audit Scheme (EMAS) and ISO14001.

The mentoring approach aims at enhancing the suppliers' sustainability capabilities (Ciliberti *et al.*, 2008) and is based on collaboration and close relationships between customers and suppliers (Vachon and Klassen, 2006). Similarly to traditional supplier development programmes, the mentoring approach focuses on:

- Educating and training supplier personnel (Min and Galle, 2001);

- Involving suppliers in product design to consider environmental requirements;

- Providing financial assistance for suppliers to improve the environmental performance of their processes, equipment and materials (Rao, 2002);

- Mutual problem solving, and knowledge and expertise sharing with suppliers.

The monitoring and control approach requires less time and fewer resources but it does not enable the company to verify suppliers' actual sustainability performance (Vachon and Klassen, 2006). In the worst case this approach may lead to 'green-washing' behaviour, i.e. the supplier will cover up the reality and paint a rosy – or rather a green – image. The mentoring approach is more likely to foster real improvement in supplier practices and performance (Seuring and Müller, 2008) but requires significant investment (Rao and Holt, 2005).

Recent trends in practices show that there is convergence between the supplier assessment and development processes, and working with stakeholders to help develop capabilities of suppliers especially in the area of sustainability. Gualandris *et al.* (2015) point to sustainable evaluation and verification processes that are selectively inclusive of different stakeholder groups to leverage their different capabilities. These might include NGOs or other specialists who are able to add to the understanding of a particular issue and might work with suppliers to help improve performance in a certain area (Gualandris and Klassen, 2018). This is particularly the case in developing regions where multinationals are sourcing raw materials, for example from agricultural producers, and working with these 'brokers' can help leverage local knowledge and access parts of the supply network which are challenging for Western/Northern companies (Saunders *et al.*, 2018).

14.4.2 Supplier development at the base of the pyramid

The management of supply chains at the base of the pyramid (BOP) has mainly focused on the social, infrastructure and development issues to an extent neglecting the environmental aspects of sustainability (Gold *et al.*, 2013). One key activity is capacity building, which the United Nationals Development Programme (UNDP) defines as a long-term continual process of development that involves all stakeholders; such as including ministries, local authorities, non-governmental organizations, professionals, community members, academics and other appropriate internal and external entities. While capacity building is not always aimed at business organizations, there is a focus on transferring knowledge to suppliers in order to improve their processes and practices. A key difference with supplier development is the inclusion of multiple stakeholders in the capacity-building process, where the transfer of knowledge can occur across multiple organizational boundaries. In the context of sustainable development, especially with regard to BOP communities, supplier development and capacity building can be seen as related activities. The key difference, however, is the need to include other local parties, such as financing institutions, in the improvement processes of local producers, in order to create an external environment that can support the supplier, achieve positive economic outcomes and reach sustainability goals. Recent developments in this area are now taking a wider view to supporting the BOP alongside the SDGs mentioned earlier. A clear example of this is the Sustainable Cocoa Initiative, which aims to support a broader development of local producer communities in countries such as Ghana and Cote d'Ivoire.

SUSTAINABLE FOREST SUPPLY CHAINS IN METSÄ GROUP

According to the WWF:

> forests are a vital resource for life on earth. They provide invaluable environmental, social and economic benefits to us all. Forests improve air and water quality, reduce soil erosion and act as a buffer against global warming. The forest industry also generates over US$168billion in global trade through wood products. Every business interacts with the forest industry on some level because of high levels of demand for timber and paper.[7]

However, there is no doubt that forests continue to be under threat, with the WWF estimating that the equivalent area of 36 football pitches is lost each minute, particularly in Amazon, Borneo and Sumatra, the Congo Basin, and the Russian Far East. This is due to both the non-renewable harvesting of wood (beyond the replacement rate) as well as significant illegal logging across the world.

As an example, according to WWF Russia, the 'Ussuri Taiga' forests of eastern Russia are under huge pressure from illegal logging in order to supply flooring and furniture factories in China, which then sell their products in the US and Europe. Not only is the loss of forest itself a problem, but this ecosystem is home to the endangered Amur tiger. Due to levels of criminal activity and low policing, the stocks of oak, ash, elm and linden trees are declining. This illegal logging accounts for twice as much Mongolian oak being cut than permitted by law. Although laws in the US preventing companies from using criminal suppliers have been strengthened in recent years, wider global action is needed to prevent these practices. For example, the Global Forest & Trade Network (GFTN)[8] engages companies throughout the supply chain and around the world to adopt responsible forest management and trade practices. GFTN works with hundreds of companies at all levels of the wood and paper supply chain in 34 countries. Yet despite these actions the risks persist and further actions are required. According to the latest WWF Living Forests report chapter on forest products, the following actions are required:

- Ensuring legality and sustainable forest management; more sustainable plantations; rationalized and inclusive landscape-scale forest zoning; responsible procurement practices

- Increased mill and recycling efficiencies; new low-footprint wood products

- Stronger social safeguards; effective enforcement of regulations

- Incentives to reduce the rate of forest conversion and destructive logging, such as public policy measures to reward forest stewardship that delivers carbon storage, biodiversity conservation or water regulation services

- Information on long-term ecological impacts of various forms of natural forest management and intensive plantations
- More repeat use of individual wood fibres; new consumption patterns that meet the needs of the poor while eliminating waste and over-consumption by the affluent. (This includes wood products as well as food and energy, as all commodities are competing for land and water.)

One company that is doing a great deal in the area of sustainable forestry is the Metsä Group. In 2016 the Metsä group purchased 88 per cent certified wood from forests in Finland, Sweden, Estonia and Russia (as well as some minor sourcing from Germany, Austria, Lithuania and France). In a recent review of their sustainability strategy they have aligned their target alongside the UN SDGs and aim to show progress in key SDGs related to the business, and having listened to stakeholders will renew the focus on social sustainability as well as a circular bio-economy.

Ensuring sustainable wood sourcing[9]

Metsä Group Purchasing is organized into 17 main categories, including pulp, energy, logistics, chemicals and pigments as well as indirect materials and services. Purchasing wood raw material is the responsibility of the Metsä Forest division. The majority of the purchases (99 per cent) are from Europe. The company has a policy to use local suppliers when feasible and 88 per cent of the purchases are from countries where they have their own manufacturing operations. Wood is the biggest spend category with more than 80 per cent coming from certified forests. Most of Metsä Group's wood supply is from Finland (nearly 75 per cent of the whole supply) with part coming from the neighbouring areas around the Baltic Sea. Wood imports from outside the EU are almost entirely from Russia (about 7 per cent of the whole supply).

One of the most important developments in the Metsä Group has been the creation of wood origin tracing systems in Russia, which as shown at the beginning of this case presents the greatest supply chain risk. The group collects wood origin information from the beginning of the wood supply operations in Russia and uses wood supplier and logging site audits to verify the wood origin and sustainability of the wood supply. The company uses digital maps to follow the origin of wood and to avoid wood originating from unacceptable sources where logging is prohibited, such as conservation areas. Metsä Group holds third-party verified Chain-of-Custody[10] certificates for the whole wood supply. This means the buyers of wood should be able to trust the stated source as the data is checked by a third-party audit specialist company. In most cases, the wood originates from family-owned forests, belonging to owner-members of Metsä Forest, about 125,000 Finnish forest owners. Metsä Group uses forest certification as a tool to ensure both the sustainability of the supply chain and forestry operations. While only 10 per cent of all the forests in the world have been certified, the target of Metsä Group is to sustain the amount of certified wood in their operations above 80 per cent. Metsä Group is actively promoting forest certification initiatives in the whole wood supply region. In 2016, 88 per cent of the wood supplied by Metsä Group was either PEFC or FSC® (Licence Code FSC-C014476) certified, or both.

Industrial symbiosis and closed-loop supply chains

Metsä Group can also be thought of as using an industrial symbiosis approach in some of its manufacturing units. A bio-power plant was launched in conjunction with Metsä Board's Kyro Mill, which replaced natural gas with renewable fuels, mainly bark, tree chips, crushed stumps and other wood residues. The plant produces electricity and heat for Kyro mill as well as for the neighbouring district of Hämeenkyrö; so using waste by-products to produce energy used by the plant and local community. By doing this the fossil-fuel CO_2 emissions from Kyro mill is reduced by nearly 100,000 tonnes per year. Also, the carbon footprints for folding boxboards and wallpaper base produced at Kyro mill is reduced by half. A second example is a bio-energy heating plant, which again uses wood by-products from production, completed in Lohja in conjunction with Metsä Wood's Kerto Mill. Metsä Wood and its partners started supplying steam to the mill and district heat to the local community.

While these are limited examples of industrial ecology, it does demonstrate how manufacturing plants can contribute to community energy needs (power and heat), while reducing waste.

Stakeholder actions

The parent group Metsalitto is a stakeholder-driven company because the cooperative is owned by more than 100,000 forest owners. At the same time the recognition that forests provide ecosystem services through carbon capture and biodiversity means that NGOs and other interest groups are regularly part of the dialogue about how to manage this natural resource. Metsä Group started to test Finland's new Forest Stewardship Council® (FSC®, Licence Code FSC-C014476) certification standard in part of its own forests in 2012. As part of this process, the company invited several interest groups who are active in certification in Finland to state their views about the project. These stakeholders included the local Reindeer Herders' Association, the Finnish Association for Nature Conservation, the Finnish Forest Centre and WWF Finland. In addition, Metsä Group also took part in a cooperation network under the METSO programme which was launched in 2011. This network aims to improve the nature management of the ecotones forest areas in order to enhance game species' and related forest habitat requirements. A further stakeholder project led by the Forestry Development Centre Tapio aims to develop landscape management practices, establish a network of example areas and produce up-to-date training material for forest owners and result in a landscape management guide for forest owners.

Regenerative actions

In 2012, the total amount of residuals and waste generated by Metsä Group's production units was 691,572 tonnes, mainly consisting of fibre sludge, ashes from energy production and lime ash from chemical pulp production. Of this only 81,435 tonnes was landfilled and 608,117 tonnes representing 88 per cent of the total waste amount was recycled. Metsä Forest will provide an ash fertilization service for forest owners from the beginning of 2013. Both lime mud and fibre sludge also have great potential in fertilization and soil improvement.

In conclusion, it is clear that Metsä Group is implementing most of the WWF recommendations stated earlier in the case study. Furthermore, the very concepts of ecological footprint and biocapacity are the basis for the overall business. Without available biocapacity the supply of wood is impossible and therefore actions are taken to ensure that the ecological footprint, specifically the elements of forest footprint, does not exceed the capacity. In addition, forests provide a valuable sink for carbon from the atmosphere, thus providing one of the key ecosystem services described earlier in this chapter relating to climate regulation. In fact forests provide all of the ecosystem services – provisioning of timber, regulation of climate, supporting through photosynthesis and cultural services for the communities that both own and live in forests. The challenge now is to transfer some of these best practices to those regions of the world where the danger of deforestation and habitat destruction is still ongoing. For this to happen there needs to be an incentive for local forest owners and logging companies to increase their costs to implement new practices. This needs to be driven by consumers who select certified wood, new supply chain practices and effective policing of protected forests, including through the work of industry groups such as the GFTN.

14.5 Conclusion

Moving towards sustainable supply networks means that companies need to be aware of their role in meeting macro-level objectives, even if this role is an indirect one. At one point or another, all supply chains are affected by the availability of natural capital, and like financial capital, growth is not possible unless this resource is managed in a sustainable manner. As shown at the beginning of this chapter, while the developed nations have the biggest footprint, the developing countries have the biocapacity. Therefore, it is inevitable that global supply chains will continue to put resources under pressure in developing regions, so that we can maintain and improve the standard of living on a global scale. In some industries such as in forestry and the chemicals sector this link is relatively clear due to the integrated nature of the network. However, in other sectors this performance is hidden in the context of a complex web of supply network relationships and so innovative means of integrating sustainability are needed, perhaps looking outside of the traditional scope of supply chains.

Industrial ecology offers a partial solution to these issues of natural capital scarcity, by re-circulating resources through industrial systems both in the developed and developing world. But there are limits to the extent materials and energy can be reused with current technological advances and this approach only focuses on achieving environmental sustainability. Stakeholder engagement is an essential tool for companies to integrate the wider sustainability debate into supply chain decisions. This does not need to be reactive only, though; the approach can also be used to help develop capabilities in the supply chain, especially where suppliers are an integral part of the social system where natural resources occur and are exploited (as shown in the Metsä case study). More and more companies are looking to partner with NGOs and specialists to help build the capability of the supply base to deliver sustainably sourced products in a way that preserves social justice and protects the local and global environment. This is seen as an essential part of how organizations achieve a balance between the fundamental business needs of value generation and the expectations of society which both consumes and produces the products and services generated by these supply chains.

Notes

1 The material input of a product (service) minus the weight of the product itself. The material input is defined as the life-cycle-wide total quantity (in kg) of natural material moved (physically displaced) by humans in order to generate a good. Source: EEA, 1999. Making sustainability accountable: Eco-efficiency, resource productivity and innovation. Topic report No 11/1999.

2 http://sustainabledevelopment.un.org/index.php?page=view&type=1006&menu=1348&nr= 699#deliverables; http://www.youtube.com/watch?v=QaohSaEy5lo&feature=youtu.be (both last accessed 4 November 2013).

3 http://www.corporateecoforum.com/valuingnaturalcapital/ (last accessed 4 November 2013).

4 A productivity weighted area used to report both the biocapacity of the earth, and the demand on biocapacity (the ecological footprint). The global hectare is normalized to the area-weighted average productivity of biologically productive land and water in a given year. Because different land types have different productivity, a global hectare of, for example, cropland, would occupy a smaller physical area than the much less biologically productive pasture land, as more pasture would be needed to provide the same biocapacity as one hectare of cropland. Because world bio-productivity varies slightly from year to year, the value of a gha may change slightly from year to year (Global Footprint Network, 2012).

5 https://www.unilever.com/sustainable-living/our-approach-to-reporting/un-global-goals-for-sustainable-development/ (last accessed 19 July 2018).
6 Fair Labor Association – because the students felt it ineffective.
7 http://worldwildlife.org/initiatives/transforming-business (last accessed May 2013).
8 http://worldwildlife.org/initiatives/global-forest-trade-network (last accessed 19 July 2018).
9 Metsä Group Sustainability Report 2017.
10 Chain of Custody: the path taken by raw materials, processed materials, finished products and co-/by-products from the forest to the consumer or (in the case of reclaimed/recycled materials or products containing them) from the reclamation site to the consumer, including each stage of processing, transformation, manufacturing, storage and transport where progress to the next stage of the supply chain involves a change of ownership (independent custodianship) of the materials or the products. https://ic.fsc.org/fsc-std-20-011-coc-evaluations.441-19.htm (last accessed 4 November 2013).

References

Alvarez G, Pilbeam C and Wilding R (2010) Nestlé Nespresso AAA sustainable quality program: An investigation into the governance dynamics in a multi-stakeholder supply chain network. *Supply Chain Management: An International Journal* 15(2): 165–182.

Bensaou M (1999) Portfolios of buyer–supplier relationships. *Sloan Management Review*, Summer: 35–44.

Bidwell R and Verfaillie HA (2000) Measuring eco-efficiency: A guide to reporting company performance. *World Business Council on Sustainable Development*, Geneva, Switzerland: 2–37.

Buysse K and Verbeke A (2003) Proactive environmental strategies: A stakeholder management perspective. *Strategic Management Journal* 24(5): 453–470.

Chertow MR (2007) 'Uncovering' industrial symbiosis. *Journal of Industrial Ecology* 11(1): 11–30.

Ciliberti F, Pontrandolfo P and Scozzi B (2008) Investigating corporate social responsibility in supply chains: A SME perspective. *Journal of Cleaner Production* 16: 1579–1588.

Diaz S (2005) Biodiversity regulation of ecosystem services. In: Hassan R, Scholes R and Ash N (eds) *Eco-systems and Human Well-being: Current State and Trends*. Washington, DC: Island Press, pp. 297–329.

Freeman RE (1984) *Strategic Management: A Stakeholder Approach*. Boston. MA: Pitman.

Gelderman CJ and Van Weele AJ (2005) Purchasing portfolio models: A critique and update. *The Journal of Supply Chain Management* 41(3): 19–28.

Gold S, Hahn R and Seuring S (2013) Sustainable supply chain management in 'Base of the Pyramid' food projects – a path to triple bottom line approaches for multinationals? *International Business Review* 22(5): 784–799.

Griggs D, Stafford-Smith M, Gaffney O, Rockstrom J, Ohman MC, Shyamsundar P, Steffen W, Glaser G, Kanie N and Noble I (2013) Policy: Sustainable development goals for people and planet. *Nature* 495(7441): 305–307.

Gualandris J and Klassen RD (2018) Delivering transformational change: Aligning supply chains and stakeholders in non-governmental organizations. *Journal of Supply Chain Management* 54(2): 34–48.

Gualandris J, Klassen RD, Vachon S and Kalchschmidt M (2015) Sustainable evaluation and verification in supply chains: Aligning and leveraging accountability to stakeholders. *Journal of Operations Management* 38: 1–13.

Hale TN and Mauzerall DL (2004) Thinking globally and acting locally: Can the Johannesburg partnerships coordinate action on sustainable development? *The Journal of Environment & Development* 13(3): 220–239.

Henriques I and Sadorsky P (1999) The relationship between environmental commitment and managerial perceptions of stakeholder importance. *Academy of Management Journal* 43(1): 87–99.

Hines P, Lamming R, Jones D, Cousins P and Rich N (2000) *Value Stream Management: Strategy and Excellence in the Supply Chain.* Harlow, UK: Financial Times/Prentice Hall.

Hughes J (2005) Supplier metrics that matter. *CPO Agenda*, Autumn: 19–23.

Jacobsen NB (2006) Industrial symbiosis in Kalundborg, Denmark: A quantitative assessment of economic and environmental aspects. *Journal of Industrial Ecology* 10(1–2): 239–255.

Kraljic P (1983) Purchasing must become supply management. *Harvard Business Review*, Sept.–Oct.: 109–117.

Lamming R, Caldwell N, Phillips W and Harrison D (2005) Sharing sensitive information in supply relationships: The flaws in one-way open-book negotiation and the need for transparency. *European Management Journal* 23(5): 554–563.

Madsen H and Ulhoi JP (2001) Integrating environmental and stakeholder management. *Business Strategy and the Environment* 10: 77–88.

Miemczyk J, Johnsen TE and Macquet M (2012) Sustainable purchasing and supply management: A structured literature review of definitions and measures at the dyad, chain and network levels. *Supply Chain Management: An International Journal* 17(5): 478–496.

Min H and Galle WP (2001) Green purchasing practices of US firms. *International Journal of Operations and Production Management* 21(9): 1222–1238.

Mitchell RK, Agle BR and Wood DJ (1997) Toward a theory of stakeholder identification and salience: Defining the principle of who and what really counts. *Academy of Management Review* 22(4): 853–887.

Modi SB and Mabert VA (2007) Supplier development: Improving supplier performance through knowledge transfer. *Journal of Operations Management* 25(1): 42–64.

Mueller M, dos Santos V and Seuring S (2009) The contribution of environmental and social standards towards ensuring legitimacy in supply chain governance. *Journal of Business Ethics* 89(4): 509–523.

Park-Poaps H and Rees K (2010) Stakeholder forces of socially responsible supply chain management orientation. *Journal of Business Ethics* 92(2): 305–322.

Pearce F (2010) Earth's nine lives. *New Scientist* 205(2749): 30–35.

Post JE, Preston LE and Sachs S (2002) Managing the extended enterprise: The new stakeholder view. *California Management Review* 45(1): 6–29.

Prahinski C and Benton WC (2004) Supplier evaluations: Communication strategies to improve supplier performance. *Journal of Operations Management* 22(1): 39–62.

Rao P (2002) Greening the supply chain: A new initiative in South East Asia. *International Journal of Operations and Production Management* 22(6): 632–655.

Rao P and Holt D (2005) Do green supply chains lead to competitiveness and economic performance? *International Journal of Operations and Production Management* 25(9): 898–916.

Reijnders L (1998) The Factor X debate: Setting targets for eco-efficiency. *Journal of Industrial Ecology* 2(1): 13–22.

Rockstrom J, Steffen W, Noone K, Persson A, Chapin FS, Lambin EF, Lenton TM, Scheffer M, Folke C, Schellnhuber HJ, Nykvist B, de Wit CA, Hughes T, van der Leeuw S, Rodhe H, Sorlin S, Snyder PK, Costanza R, Svedin U, Falkenmark M, Karlberg L, Corell RW, Fabry VJ, Hansen J, Walker B, Liverman D, Richardson K, Crutzen P and Foley JA (2009) A safe operating space for humanity. *Nature* 461(7263): 472–475.

Roy R and Whelan RC (1992) Successful recycling through value-chain collaboration. *Long Range Planning* 25(4): 62–71.

Russo MV (2003) The emergence of sustainable industries: Building on natural capital. *Strategic Management Journal* 24(4): 317–331.

Sako M (2004) Supplier development at Honda, Nissan and Toyota: Comparative case studies of organizational capability enhancement. *Industrial and Corporate Change* 13(2): 281–308.

Saunders LW, Tate WL, Zsidisin GA and Miemczyk J (2018) The influence of network exchange brokers on sustainable initiatives in organizational networks. *Journal of Business Ethics*, forthcoming.

Schmidheiny S (1992) *Changing Course: Executive Summary: A Global Business Perspective on Development and the Environment.* Cambridge, MA: MIT Press.

Seuring S (2004) Industrial ecology, life cycles, supply chains: Differences and interrelations. *Business Strategy and the Environment* 13(5): 306–319.

Seuring S and Müller M (2008) From a literature review to a conceptual framework for sustainable supply chain management. *Journal of Cleaner Production* 16: 1688–1710.

Simmons PJ, O'Meara A and Lapinski M (2012) The new business imperative: Valuing natural capital. Corporate Eco Forum and The Nature Conservancy.

Smith BG (2008) Developing sustainable food supply chains. *Philosophical Transactions of the Royal Society of London B: Biological Sciences* 363(1492): 849–861.

Starik M and Rands GP (1995) Weaving an integrated web: Multilevel and multisystem perspectives of ecologically sustainable organizations. *Academy of Management Review* 20(4): 908–935.

Suchman MC (1995) Managing legitimacy: Strategic and institutional approaches. *Academy of Management Review* 20(3): 571–610.

Tate WL, Ellram LM and Kirchoff JF (2010) Corporate social responsibility reports: A thematic analysis related to supply chain management. *Journal of Supply Chain Management* 46(1): 19–44.

UNEP (2005) Millennium ecosystem assessment synthesis report: Millennium Ecosystem Assessment.

Vachon S (2007) Green supply chain practices and the selection of environmental technologies. *International Journal of Production Research* 45(18–19): 4357–4379.

Vachon S and Klassen R (2006) Extending green practices across the supply chain – the impact of upstream and downstream integration. *International Journal of Operations and Production Management* 26(7): 795–821.

Vachon S and Mao Z (2008) Linking supply chain strength to sustainable development: A country-level analysis. *Journal of Cleaner Production* 16(15): 1552–1560.

von Malmborg F (2007) Stimulating learning and innovation in networks for regional sustainable development: The role of local authorities. *Journal of Cleaner Production* 15(17): 1730–1741.

Wackernagel M and Rees WE (1997) Perceptual and structural barriers to investing in natural capital: Economics from an ecological footprint perspective. *Ecological Economics* 20(1): 3–24.

Wackernagel M, Schulz NB, Deumling D, Linares AC, Jenkins M, Kapos V, Monfreda C, Loh J, Myers N, Norgaard R and Randers J (2002) Tracking the ecological overshoot of the human economy. *Proceedings of the National Academy of Sciences* 99(14): 9266–9271.

Whiteman G, Walker B and Perego P (2013) Planetary boundaries: Ecological foundations for corporate sustainability. *Journal of Management Studies* 50(2): 307–336.

Williams ED, Ayres RU and Heller M (2002) The 1.7 kilogram microchip: Energy and material use in the production of semiconductor devices. *Environmental Science and Technology,* 36(24): 5504–5510.

Wright CM, Smith ME and Wright BG (2007) Hidden costs associated with stakeholders in supply management. *The Academy of Management Perspectives* 21(3): 64–82.

Zhu Q, Lowe EA, Wei, Y and Barnes D (2007) Industrial symbiosis in China: A case study of the Guitang Group. *Journal of Industrial Ecology* 11(1): 31–42.

Useful website

http://www.cbd.int/development/doc/cbd-good-practice-guide-forestry-booklet-web-en.pdf (last accessed 4 November 2013).

CHAPTER 15
Conclusion

15.0 Introduction

This final chapter calls attention to the major conclusions and messages of the book for purchasing and supply chain management students and professionals. In particular, we highlight the different ways in which sustainability impacts purchasing and supply chain management practices. Following this brief summary of key points, we set out what we see as key sustainability challenges for purchasing and supply chain management. We conclude by reflecting on recent developments in higher education towards sustainable, or responsible, management in general and, more specifically, purchasing and supply chain management education.

15.1 Main messages for purchasing and supply chain management

The following points summarize the major messages and implications of this book for purchasing and supply chain management theory and practice, especially those that stem from the need to seize the sustainability challenge:

1 Purchasing (or procurement, sourcing) needs to be managed as a strategic business function. The perception of purchasing as a function that primarily aims to buy products at the lowest prices possible is long outdated.

2 Most modern companies have outsourced extensively so that they can focus on core competencies and compete on what they do best; this includes both production and service activities. Consequently the ability of companies to produce products or services that will not only satisfy but delight customers depends heavily on the performance of their suppliers. Without a highly competent and strategically orientated purchasing function the company is inhibited in its ability to capitalize on the specialized capabilities offered by its suppliers. This does not mean that purchasing is highly competent and strategic in all companies – but it *should* be.

3 The concept of sustainable development includes three dimensions: environment, social and economic development. These are interlinked and none should be excluded at the expense of others; if purchasing and supply chain management is to be sustainable it requires consideration of all three dimensions.

4 The sustainability trend provides an opportunity for purchasing to assume a strategic focus and to make a contribution to the creation of sustainable competitive advantage. Sustainability presents a risk to companies but also an opportunity. The danger is that managers simply enforce minimum standards (such as ISO), and do not seek revenue- and reputation-enhancing opportunities.

5 Companies have outsourced to low-cost countries for years, not least in search of cheap labour. This is no longer sustainable in its current form and the sustainability agenda is forcing companies to rethink their global sourcing strategies.

6 The concept of supply chain management assumes a linear industrial system where suppliers at different tiers are linked to, and highly dependent on, each other in satisfying end-customer needs and requirements. The chain metaphor was always over-simplistic and the need to create sustainable supply chains makes the chain metaphor completely obsolete. Sustainable supply chains are circular, closed-looped cradle-to-grave structures. Better understood as supply networks, they include actors that are not normally considered part of the supply chain; these include non-governmental organizations (NGOs) and other stakeholders that play critical roles, for example in monitoring and developing a sustainable supply base.

7 While there is now considerable evidence and some literature around the theme of organizations adopting more sustainable ways of operating and including this approach in their overall business strategy, a huge challenge remains in implementing new behaviour and practices by suppliers, particularly those furthest away from the customer.

8 Visibility and transparency are critical in supply chain management but are not limited to operational information such as demand, capacity and inventory. Traceability of product ingredients/materials and supplier processes is the real transparency challenge.

9 Products *and* services must be understood as an integrated package that has major implications when it comes to dealing with issues of extended life cycle, designing product recovery systems, emergent new operating models, and how organizations such as manufacturers will engage with suppliers and customers in future.

10 It is important to understand the linkages between strategy, implementation, external policy and enabling tools that allow sustainability to take root in the supply chain. Tools such as value chain mapping and life-cycle analysis help firms to be not only resource efficient, but actively engage with the broader vision of promoting sustainability.

15.2 Sustainability challenges for purchasing and supply chain management

Since we published the first edition of our book in 2014, we have realized that the field of sustainable purchasing and supply management has been developing at such a rate that a new edition of our book would soon be required. In the period between the first and second editions, the world has witnessed an increasing awareness of acute sustainability challenges, such as plastic pollution in our oceans and modern slavery. We have also witnessed a boom in circular economy thinking that was really only in the embryonic stage when we wrote the first edition. In addition, the global political climate has changed, threatening critical sustainability advances and the viability of global supply chains. These changes are coupled with advances in technology and the Industry 4.0 challenges that look set to transform the way supply chains operate.

The good news is that in our view academics (i.e. researchers and educators) and practitioners across industries continue to make great progress in developing sustainable purchasing and supply chain management practices. More and more companies have embraced sustainability, including those that were initially reluctant. For example, the fashion industry has made great strides in addressing some of the inherent problems it has faced. In academia, the latest research is pushing the idea of an ecologically dominant view that prioritizes ecology (or environment) first, social sustainability second and economic sustainability last. This implies that at least the environment and social sustainability cannot be sacrificed at the expense of pursuing a purely money-making agenda.

We are now convinced that the purchasing and supply management profession is becoming deeply engaged in leading the development towards more sustainable or 'responsible' sourcing practices. Likewise, supply chain management appears to be really embracing the sustainability challenge. In the first edition of our book we pointed to the risk that sustainability could be viewed as a special theme rather than permeating through all the ways in which business is conducted. We pointed to the fact that most supply chain management textbooks have a chapter towards the end dedicated to sustainability (or 'ethical issues') but is not integrated or viewed as a core supply chain management concern. We criticized the influential annual supply chain ranking by the leading research and consultant company Gartner, Inc. for not considering sustainability as part of their measures to determine the world's best supply chains. In fact, straight after the first edition of our book was published, Gartner launched a new ranking in which sustainability has now been included. Sustainable supply chain management is rapidly becoming mainstream.

We believe sustainability should become integrated into companies' fabric: all their processes, including purchasing and supply chain management, should take into account the need for sustainability. This was the key purchasing and supply chain management challenge we set out to address at the beginning of this book. We hope we have made current and future purchasing and supply chain managers really reflect on the ways in which they operate and help them to transform their supply business models.

15.3 The rise of sustainability in education

As we wrote in the Foreword, this book is intended as a core textbook for purchasing and supply chain management courses at universities and business schools. At a higher level our ambition is to inspire the development of future purchasing and supply chain management leaders.

This book integrates sustainability into each chapter and each aspect of purchasing and supply chain management. Our sincere hope is that the book will play its small part in not only educating, but also changing the mindsets of current and future purchasing and supply chain management professionals.

In fact, more and more programmes at universities and business schools seek to take sustainability into account or even try to use sustainability to differentiate their student offerings. For example, when we began writing this book, one of our institutions, the University of Exeter, had already launched its 'One-Planet MBA' supported by the WWF. The Politecnico di Milano also considers sustainability to be a critical ingredient in its management teaching, including its MBA programmes and specialized master's, and ESCP Europe Business School has dedicated specializations and master's programmes in sustainability. Further away from our home institutions, other schools have gone down similar routes, including major league players such as Stanford, Michigan (Ross), Cornell (Johnson), Erasmus (Rotterdam) and MIT (Sloan) to name a few.

Business school and programme rankings are emerging which focus specifically on sustainability, e.g. the 'Beyond Grey Pinstripes' and 'Corporate Knights' rankings. Education bodies and organizations have emerged that are dedicated to creating more responsible management education, including UN PRME (United Nations Principles for Responsible Management Education) and Net Impact.

In our view, there is little doubt that the trend towards further emphasis on sustainability in higher education is going to continue. We certainly hope so, because education bodies have a responsibility to ensure that the leaders of the future play their part in ensuring managers are able to challenge established thinking and to think and act differently for the benefit of business, society and our 'one' planet.

Index

Note: page references in *italics* indicate figures; **bold** indicates tables.